Case Studies

MW00754018

Boxes of Special Interest

Macroeconomics

The Addison-Wesley Series in Economics

MACROECONOMICS

Seventh
Edition

R O B E R T   J .   G O R D O N

Stanley G. Harris Professor in the Social Sciences
Northwestern University

with the assistance of J A M E S   A .   W I L C O X

Haas School of Business
University of California at Berkeley

 **ADDISON-WESLEY**

An imprint of Addison Wesley Longman, Inc.

READING, MASSACHUSETTS   MENLO PARK, CALIFORNIA   NEW YORK   HARLOW,
ENGLAND   DON MILLS, ONTARIO   SYDNEY   MEXICO CITY   MADRID   AMSTERDAM

Acquisitions Editor: *Denise Clinton*
Senior Project Manager: *Mary Clare McEwing*
Project Coordination: *Louis C. Bruno, Jr.*
Text and Cover Design: *Regina Hagen*
Original Cover Illustration: © 1997 *by Jane Sterrett*
Photo Researcher: *Billie Porter*
Marketing Manager: *D. Quinn Perkson*
Compositor: *Typo-Graphics, Inc.*
Printer and Binder: *World Color Book Services*
Cover Printer: *The Lehigh Press, Inc.*

For permission to use copyrighted material, grateful acknowledgment is made to the copyright holders in source notes throughout the text, which are hereby made part of their copyright page.

Photo credits: Chapter 2, page **34**: Netscape Communications Corp., photograph by Daly Yoo/Addison-Wesley. Netscape Communications Corporation has not authorized, sponsored, or endorsed, or approved this publication and is not responsible for its content. Netscape and the Netscape Communications Corporate Logos, are trademarks and trade names of Netscape Communications Corporation. All other product names and/or logos are trademarks of their respective owners. Chapter 4, page **100**: Robert Tolchin; page **117**: Cameramann International, Ltd. Chapter 7, page **208**: Cameramann International, Ltd.; page **209**: Cameramann International, Ltd.; page **214**: UPI/Corbis-Bettmann. Chapter 9, page **280**: Donna Coveney/MIT. Chapter 11, page **349**: Robert Gordon. Chapter 12, page **377**: *The Wizard of Oz,* copyright 1939, Loews, Inc. Anthony Suau/Gamma Liaison; page **369**: AP/Wide World Photos. Chapter 13, page **419**: Michael Marsland/Yale University Office of Public Affairs. Chapter 15, page **485**: Donna Coveney/MIT. Chapter 16, page **519**: Diego Goldberg/Sygma. Chapter 17, page **535**: UPI/Corbis-Bettmann; page **537**: Patricia Evans/University of Chicago. Chapter 18, page **583**: Reuters/Corbis-Bettmann.

Library of Congress Cataloging-in-Publication Data
Gordon, Robert J. (Robert James), 1940–
    Macroeconomics / Robert J. Gordon with the assistance of James A. Wilcox.—
7th ed.
        p.   cm.
    Includes bibliographical references and index.
    ISBN 0-321-01438-3
    1. Macroeconomics.   I. Wilcox, James Allen, 1952–   .   II. Title.
HB172.5.G67   1997
339—dc21   97-27357
                                                                          CIP

Reprinted with corrections, June 1998

2 3 4 5 6 7 8 9—RNT—01009998

with love, for Julie

Contents

Preface: To The Instructor

Students come to their intermediate macroeconomics course in the late 1990s in an understandable state of confusion. They hear media reports about the "Cinderella economy," which month after month displays the lowest unemployment rate since 1973 and the lowest inflation rate since the early 1960s. They and their families may be among those Americans who respond on surveys that they find jobs unusually easy to get. Some students may have parents who own or manage small businesses and who have found that, as a result of low unemployment, good workers are hard to find and hard to replace when they quit.

Despite this ebullient economic performance, students may also sense that all is not well in the Cinderella economy. A friend or family member may have been among the millions who lost their jobs in the 1990s. Students and their parents alike have experienced apparent stagnation in real wages and family incomes. Productivity growth in the 1990s has been slower than in the 1970s and 1980s, not to mention slower than in the "golden age" of rapid productivity and real wage growth prior to 1972. Further, as a result of the growing inequality of income, growth in the median wage fell short of growth in the mean wage, which was bolstered by disproportionate income gains of those in the top 10 percent of the income distribution.

Why has the unemployment and inflation performance of the American economy been so outstanding in the mid-1990s, yet was so poor in the 1970s and early 1980s? Why was an unemployment rate close to 5 percent accompanied by accelerating inflation during 1987-90 but by stable inflation in 1996-97? Should this performance be attributed to brilliant monetary policy, a set of lucky breaks, or both?

Unique Features of This Text

This macroeconomics textbook is unique in providing answers to questions like these in a linear and well-integrated treatment of the business cycle, unemployment, inflation, and economic growth. A number of distinctive features allow this text to deliver not just theories and concepts but also possible explanations to the central macroeconomic puzzles that are introduced in the first few pages of the book.

Early, Unified Development of Core Business Cycle Theory

The basic organizational principle of the text has been consistent in all its editions: Take the student directly from national income accounting (which develops the principles that income equals expenditure and leakages equal injections) without detours through the tried-and-true *IS-LM* model of income determination. After an introduction to macroeconomic issues and measurement, the closed- and open-economy versions of the *IS-LM* model are developed in Chapters 3-6, followed by Chapter 7 on the *AS-AD* model and Chapter 8 with the dynamic Phillips curve model *(SP-DG)*, which begins with an explicit graphical derivation of the short-run Phillips curve from the *AS-AD* diagram. This organizational principle can be likened to the "inverted pyramid" principle of journalism—put the most important topics first, and place the less essential topics last so that instructors facing time constraints can teach the book in order while covering all the most critical material. In contrast, virtually every other leading text takes numerous detours *between* the measurement chapter and the *IS-LM* model into topics that are either unrelated or inessential at that early point in the book, including the production function, growth theory, theories of frictional unemployment, classical theories of inflation, role of financial intermediaries, the money-creation multiplier, open-market operations, and the detailed theory of consumption and investment expenditures and the demand for money.

In response to numerous requests from users and reviewers, the development of the elementary model of income determination and the initial development of the *IS-LM* model uses a running numerical example, which maintains the same basic parameter values throughout and varies those parameters to illustrate the workings of the multiplier and of monetary and fiscal policy. Then, in order to avoid unnecessary details, in Chapter 5 the numerical example is dropped in favor of a qualitative analysis of strong and weak effects of monetary and fiscal policy.

New Perspectives on Inflation, Unemployment, Growth, and Productivity

This is the first macroeconomics text that not only *describes* the Cinderella confluence of low unemployment and inflation in the 1990s but actually *explains* it in terms of the theory developed in the text. The benign behavior of inflation, which allowed monetary policymakers to tolerate unusually low unemployment rates without raising interest rates, is attributed to a specific set of beneficial supply shocks that are explained within the same theoretical model as the adverse supply shocks of the 1970s. The author, whose research has been at the forefront of empirical investigations of the U. S. inflation-unemployment relation for more than two decades, shows that economic performance throughout the postwar period can be explained by a single consistent model, once the natural rate of unemployment is allowed to vary over time.[1]

Macroeconomics is concerned not just with business cycles, but also with economic growth. Even as the U.S. economy succeeded in achieving an unusually favorable combination of low unemployment and low inflation in the mid-1990s, concern continued about abysmally slow growth in productivity and the stagnation of real wages. This text provides a new perspective on the interrelations among growth theory, the productivity growth slowdown, and real wage stagnation.

The novel treatment of these issues in Chapters 9-11 links both the traditional and new theories of economic growth to productivity and real wage

---

[1]For background and supplementary reading, see Robert J. Gordon, "The Time-Varying NAIRU and its Implications for Economic Policy," *Journal of Economic Perspectives,* vol. 11 (February 1997), pp. 11-32.

growth, long-run aspects of fiscal policy, and to measurement errors—a field in which the author is an internationally recognized expert. A new chapter (Chapter 10) explores the sources of America's malaise—the slow growth in productivity and real wages—and develops a simple theoretical demonstration that there is no simple cause-and-effect from slow productivity growth to slow real wage growth. Productivity and the real wage are like chicken and egg; they are both endogenous variables with feedback going each way between them. Unique among macro texts, this chapter shows that increasing income inequality matters for macro performance, since it causes the median real wage to grow more slowly than the mean real wage and thus is relevant for understanding the behavior of real wage growth for the median American household.

Internationalization of Macroeconomics

For several editions, this text has been a leader in setting American economic problems in an international context. This leadership continues in the seventh edition, with the treatment of macro theory integrating international macro throughout. Unlike many other approaches, net exports are introduced at the very beginning, rather than "tacked on" later. Net exports and the foreign sector appear in the circular-flow treatment of national income accounting (Chapter 2) and in the expenditure function of the Keynesian cross model and multiplier (Chapter 3); net exports are also included among the variables that can shift the *IS* curve in the *IS-LM* model (Chapters 4-5). A new open-economy Chapter 6 directly after the development of the *IS-LM* model introduces the balance of payments, determination of the exchange rate, exchange rate systems, links between exchange rates, interest rates, and net exports, capital mobility, and the Mundell-Flemming version of the *IS-LM* analysis.

In addition, International Perspective boxes compare U.S. macro performance and problems with those of other leading industrial nations. These vignettes compare the performance of the U.S. economy with that of Europe and Japan along many dimensions, including unemployment, inflation, monetary and fiscal policy, saving, investment, productivity growth, real wage growth, and changes in inequality.

Case Studies

The seventh edition continues to emphasize substantive case studies. These case studies are numbered text sections (not boxes) that appear in the middle of chapters adjacent to the relevant theoretical sections. The case studies continually remind the student that the theory helps explain real-world episodes. As in previous editions, many of the case studies use consistent data series developed in the author's research on the natural unemployment rate, natural real GDP, and the natural employment deficit. This research has recently been updated to allow the natural rate of unemployment to vary through time, and this edition incorporates new series on natural real GDP and the GDP gap that are consistent with the time-varying natural rate of unemployment.

Modern Treatment of Stabilization Policy

The debate between rules and activism, now treated in Chapter 14, is becoming obsolete. More relevant is the question of whether rules or activism can be implemented. The new treatment shows that there is "slippage," taking the form of money supply shocks, commodity demand shocks, money demand shocks, and supply shocks, which intervene between the policy instruments directly controlled by the Fed and the ultimate goals of policy such as inflation and unemployment. Policymakers face a tradeoff between loose control or no control over the goal variables—they can follow rules for a policy instrument, or they can attempt to establish a rule for a goal variable that may be infeasible and require unstable behavior by the policy instruments. The treatment of monetary policy contrasts the challenges faced by the Federal Reserve in the United States, where beneficial supply shocks have eased its task of achieving low unemployment and low inflation, with the quite different environment of central banks in Europe, which have allowed unemployment rates to rise as a consequence of policies adopted to prepare for European Monetary Union.

Unity from Beginning to End

As before, the book opens with six central macro concepts and six associated puzzles concerning their behavior. Unlike most books that "just stop," this edition (like the last) has a final wrap-up chapter, which goes back to the six puzzles and asks, "What have we learned?", "What do we know?", and "What are the remaining macro mysteries?" This last question is examined in a section exploring unsettled issues that continue to be the subject of lively debate as we move toward the twenty-first century.

Changes in the Seventh Edition

The traditional core of macroeconomics—the study of income determination, the causes of business cycles, and the potential for stabilization policy—is less controversial today than at any time in the past twenty-five years. The new-classical revolution has come and gone,[2] and a new consensus has emerged for the macroeconomics of the late 1990s. The American economy is resolutely Keynesian, characterized by sticky prices and markets that do not clear promptly. The economy's operation is described with a surprising degree of accuracy and insight by the *IS-LM* model, together with a dynamic Phillips curve that incorporates both supply and demand shocks.

As discussed previously, a consistent strength of the approach in this text has been its early development of the *IS-LM* model and the dynamic Phillips curve. In this edition the *IS* and *LM* curves cross on page 114. The seventh edition accentuates this strength and reflects the de-emphasis on

---

[2]Robert Lucas has recently admitted that "monetary shocks just aren't that important. That's the view I've been driven to. There's no question, that's a retreat in my view," (John Cassidy, "The Decline of Economics," *The New Yorker,* December 2, 1996, p. 55.)

macroeconomic controversy by condensing the treatment of new-classical and new-Keynesian macroeconomics from two chapters to one and moving it to a new unit at the back of the book (Chapter 17). This allows the treatment of the dynamic Phillips curve (Chapter 8) to follow directly after the development of the static aggregate demand-supply model (Chapter 7).

The unit on growth, real wage stagnation, and long-run fiscal policy is moved earlier to Chapters 9-11. The growth theory chapter (Chapter 9) features an added section called "Puzzles that Solow's Theory Cannot Explain" to motivate the new endogenous growth theory. It also contains a new case study on "The Economic Miracle of the Four Tigers," which broadens the discussion beyond the old and new growth theories to incorporate government policy, property rights, income equality, and other aspects of the East Asian miracle.

The most important advance in the treatment of growth is Chapter 10, "Explanations of Slow Growth in Productivity and Real Wages," which is almost entirely new. It goes far beyond the treatment of these topics in previous editions, and indeed in any other text, by examining reverse feedback from low real wages to low productivity, discrepancies between data on productivity and the real wage, and the radical implications of the recent report of the CPI Advisory Commission implying that growth in both productivity and real wages has been substantially understated.

The treatment of international macroeconomics is unified in a new Chapter 6, which integrates and further develops material on the balance of payments, exchange rates, and open-economy macroeconomic adjustment that was formerly split between the last part of Chapter 5 and the first part of Chapter 14. The chapter on stabilization policy (Chapter 14) now contrasts the traditional analysis of rules vs. discretion in a closed-economy setting with the quite different orientation of policymakers in open economies, such as the European countries preparing for European monetary union. A set of 21 International Perspectives boxes, many of them new, and international case studies are provided on such topics as "Why Higher Income Raises the Trade Deficit," "How Japan Uses Fiscal Policy," "Did Disinflation in Europe Differ from that in the United States?", "The Economic Miracle of the Four Tigers," "Is the U. S. Productivity Slowdown Unique?", "The Indexed Bond Has Arrived," "Where in the World Is All the U. S. Currency?", and "A Single European Currency as a Monetary Policy Rule." Almost every box is illustrated with a graph that vividly illustrates how the nations compare.

The treatment of measurement in Chapter 2 includes a new box explaining the calculation of the new official "chain-weighted" measures of real GDP and the GDP deflator. Chapter 2 also incorporates a unified treatment of the measurement of unemployment previously split between here and later in the book. New material on sources of bias in the Consumer Price Index, developed in part by the author as a member of the recent Boskin Commission, is included both in Chapter 2 and, in the context of real wage growth, in Chapter 10.

Pedagogy

The seventh edition retains the main pedagogical features of the previous editions to aid student understanding. Color is used consistently in diagrams, with red lines identifying demand curves and black lines identifying supply curves. Key terms are introduced in bold type, defined in the margin, and listed at the end of each chapter. The glossary at the end of the book provides an alphabetical list of all these definitions with cross-references to the sections where terms are introduced. Each chapter is broken up with at least three self-test questions so that students can immediately determine whether they understand what they have read. Each chapter ends with a summary, list of key terms, a revised set of questions and problems, and answers to the self-test questions. Finally, a revised set of data appendixes is provided, covering annual data for the U. S. back to 1875, quarterly data back to 1947, and annual data since 1960 for other leading nations.

Other pedagogical features, carried over from the previous edition, include:

1. *Notation.* As in the previous edition, Y is used for real GDP, X for nominal GDP, NX for net exports, and z for the influence of supply shocks on the rate of inflation.

2. *Learning About Diagrams Boxes.* Each of these boxes covers on a single page every aspect of the key schedules, including *IS, LM, AS, AD,* and *SP,* including why they slope as they do, what makes them rotate and shift, and what is true on and off the curves.

3. *Diagrams* have been completely replotted, using modern computer technology to ensure accuracy, and take into account the 1996 and 1997 revisions in the National Income and Product Accounts. Theoretical diagrams have been redrawn, incorporate a new consistency in the use of color, and in many cases have new explanatory boxes to explain the meaning of shifts and new equilibrium points.

Ancillary Material

The Study Guide has been completely and thoroughly updated to reflect the new and reorganized content of the seventh edition. Andrew Foshee of McNeese State University prepared the revision. The study guide segments each chapter of the main text into a series of main questions, with each question covering a specified topic. Students are asked to fill in blanks (from one word or numerical value to a short essay), circle correct answers, draw graphs, or use current data.

The Instructor's Manual with Transparency Masters has been thoroughly revised for the seventh edition. The Instructor's Manual portion, revised by Jim Eaton of Bridgewater College, provides chapter outlines, chapter overviews, a discussion of changes in the seventh edition from the sixth edition, answers to end-of-chapter questions and problems, and additional questions that instructors may wish to use for homework assignments, classroom discussion, or essay examination questions.

The transparency masters are enlarged versions of figures from the text. They may be used to create transparency acetates suitable for overhead projection in the classroom.

The Test Bank, revised by Andrew Foshee of McNeese State University, combines previous Test Banks 1 and 2 for a total of over 2,000 multiple-choice questions.

The Computerized Test Bank is available for both Windows and Macintosh, and contains all questions from the print version. The testing software (TestGen-EQ with Quizmaster) is fully networkable. The interface enables instructors to easily view, edit, and add questions; transfer questions to tests; and print tests in a variety of fonts and forms. Search-and-sort features let the instructor quickly locate questions and arrange them in a preferred order. Quiz Master-EQ automatically grades the exams, stores results on disk, and allows the instructor to view or print a variety of reports.

The PowerPoint Presentation CD-ROM contains the full set of figures from the book with chapter outlines. Add your own lecture notes to customize the presentation to fit your class. Transparency masters can be created by printing from the presentation, and these can be used to make overhead transparencies or student handouts from customized, individual slides.

A Web site has been developed for this book. It contains links to relevant sites on the Internet for gathering data and doing research in macroeconomics, plus other interesting features. Visit the site at http://hepg.awl.com/gordon/macro.

A set of videos, selected from the MacNeil/Lehrer Business Reports New Hour and featuring correspondent Paul Solman, complements the text.

Acknowledgments

I remain grateful to all those who were thanked in the preface of the first six editions. Space limitations prevent me from repeating all of these acknowledgments.

Above all, I am grateful to Jim Wilcox, of the Haas School of Business at the University of California at Berkeley, who has joined the project as co-author of Chapters 13-16 in this edition. Jim's extensive experience in teaching finance and monetary economics, as well as macroeconomics, brings a fresh eye and new insight to the many issues, new and old, that are treated in these chapters.

I am also grateful to Jim Eaton of Bridgewater College for his many contributions to the seventh edition. Jim checked every page of manuscript as it was being copy-edited, revised and rewrote end-of-chapter questions and problems, checked answers to self-tests, and scrutinized every piece of page proof for any errors, large or small. He has also revised the Instructor's Manual. Thanks go also to Andrew Foshee for revising the Test Bank and the Study Guide.

The development of the seventh edition was greatly aided by a substantial number of reviews of the previous edition by both users and non-users alike. Several reviewers of this edition made valuable suggestions during the writing process. The reviewers of this edition were John P. Burkett, University of Rhode Island; Oscar Brookins, Northeastern University; Richard Cebula, Georgia Institute of Technology; Abdur Chowdhury, Marquette University; M. O. Clement, Dartmouth College; Steven Cobb, Xavier University; Donald Dutkowsky, Syracuse University; Jim Eaton, Bridgewater College; Dave Findlay, Colby College; John Graham, Rutgers University; Philip J. McLewin, Ramapo College; W. Douglas McMillin, Louisiana State University; Jerry Miner, Syracuse University; Farrokh Nourzad, Marquette University; Richard Rosenberg, University of Wisconsin, Parkside; Alden Shiers, California Polytechnic State University; Allan Stone, Southwest Missouri State University; Nora Underwood, University of California, Davis; and John Veitch, University of San Francisco.

The book contains a great deal of data, some of it originally created for this book, both in the text and data appendixes. Tomonori Ishikawa developed all the data, tables, and graphs, as well as the Data Appendixes. All data were provided electronically to ST Associates, who rendered new versions of every piece of art in the book.

Thanks go to the staff at Addison Wesley Longman and their predecessors at HarperCollins. Bruce Kaplan and Lisa Pinto at HarperCollins conceived the process of reviewing the previous edition and contributed a set of priorities for the current revision. Denise Clinton at Addison Wesley Longman picked up the ball when the former HarperCollins college division was acquired by AWL and coordinated the final set of changes in concept and organization.

No words are sufficient to thank the Project Manager, Mary Clare McEwing, who brought the many pieces of this project together, including every chapter, review, and loose end. Never in my experience of textbook authorship has the inevitable nagging (almost entirely by e-mail with only one phone call over a twelve-month interval) been carried out with such consideration, style, and humor.

Thanks go to Meredith Nightingale, who was the first art editor in many editions to develop a consistent plan about how color could be used to support substance and pedagogy. Many elements of the graphs, including the use of color to designate equilibrium points but not points in graphs which represent a menu of possibilities, are attributable to her care and attention to detail. Thanks also to Lou Bruno and Billie Porter, who efficiently managed the final stages of handling proof and other prepublication details.

Finally, thanks go to my wife Julie for putting up with the overwhelming litter of manuscript and proofs that often spilled off desks and tables onto the floor of two different houses, since we moved between them in the midst of the project. As always, her unfailing encouragement and welcome diversions made the book possible.

Robert J. Gordon
Evanston, IL
September, 1997

Preface: To the Student

Macroeconomics is one of the most important topics for college students, because the health of the economy will have an influence on your whole life. The overall level of employment and unemployment will determine the ease with which you find a job after college and with which you will be able to change jobs or obtain promotions in the future. The inflation rate will influence the interest rate you receive on your savings and pay when you borrow money, and also the extent to which the purchasing power of your savings will be eroded by higher prices.

This macroeconomics text will equip you with the principles you need to make sense out of the conflicting and contradictory discussions of economic conditions and policies in newspapers and news magazines. You will be better able to appraise the performance of the President and Congress, and to predict the impact of their policy actions on your family and business.

Who Should Read This Book?

Most college students taking this course will have taken a course in economic principles. But this book has been written to be read by *all* students, even those who have not previously enrolled in an economics course. How is this possible? In Chapters 1-3 we review material covered in every principles course. By the end of Chapter 3, all students will have learned the concepts essential to understanding the new material to be developed.

This book has been carefully designed to look and read like a principles text. The entire presentation is graphic, with simple ninth-grade algebra used only in the review of elementary ideas. Examples are used frequently. Most chapters have at least one "case study" that gives you a breather from the analysis and shows how the ideas of the chapter can be applied to real-world episodes. "International Perspective" boxes show you how U.S. economic performance compares with that in other nations, such as Germany and Japan. To help with vocabulary problems, new words are set off in boldface type and defined both in the margins and in the Glossary in the back of the book. Many end-of-chapter questions provide numerical examples for you to solve, in order to cement your understanding of the theory. Finally, end-of-chapter appendixes for Chapters 5 and 8 provide optional algebraic treatments of the theory, available for assignment by instructors or for those students who want to do independent work that will deepen their command of the material.

A unique feature of this textbook is the set of "Self-Test" questions. These questions, which appear three or four times in each chapter, test your understanding of the main point of the preceding section. Write down your answers on a sheet of paper and compare them with those provided at the end of each chapter. You will quickly see whether you have understood what you have been reading, or whether you need to review the material again.

How to Read This Book

Each chapter begins with an introduction linking it to previous chapters, and ends with a summary. When you begin a chapter, first read the introduction to make sure you understand how the chapter differs from the previous ones. Then plan to read each chapter twice. On the first reading, use the Self-Test questions and answers to check whether you understand what you have been reading. Then, after completing your first reading of the chapter, study the Summary and try to answer the end-of-chapter questions, marking those points you do not understand. Finally, go back for a second reading, paying attention to the discussion of issues you may not have grasped fully at first.

Always try to write out answers to the questions and problems. Those who have purchased the accompanying *Study Guide* find that the path to greater comprehension has been laid out for you in detail.

If you should get lost in the course of reading the text, remember that there are built-in study aids to help, in addition to the Self-Test questions. If you don't understand a particular section, turn to the Summary at the end of the chapter. If you forget the meaning of a word, turn to the Glossary. (The Glossary will also help you tackle any outside readings assigned by your instructor.) A Guide to Symbols on the back inside covers of the book will help you with the alphabetical symbols that are used in equations or in diagrams as labels.

Optional Material

Footnotes and chapter appendixes have been provided as a place to put more difficult or less important material. Your instructor will decide whether an appendix is to be assigned, but even if not assigned, tackle it on your own when you have mastered the ideas in the chapter. Footnotes contain qualifications, bibliographical references (valuable if you ever need to write a term paper on these topics), and cross-references to related material and diagrams in the book.

Finally, notice that tables in the appendix contain historical data starting with 1875 and updated to mid-1997. These figures can help you determine what was going on in periods not covered by the case studies or can be used in outside assignments and term papers. Don't forget possible applications in history, political science, and sociology courses.

The World Wide Web has made it much easier for you to locate recent data to update the graphs and tables in this book. For information on using the Web to find data, turn to pages 34-35.

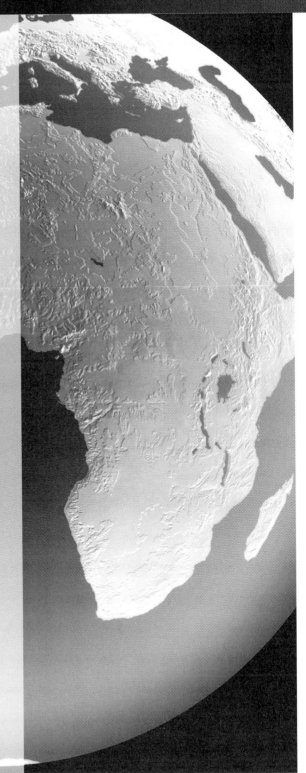

PART ONE

Introduction and

Measurement

CHAPTER 1

What Is Macroeconomics?

Business will be better or worse.
—Calvin Coolidge, 1928

1-1 How Macroeconomics Affects Our Everyday Lives

Macroeconomics is the study of the major economic totals, or aggregates.

Macroeconomics is concerned with the big economic issues that determine your own economic well-being, as well as that of your family and everyone you know. Each of these issues involves the overall economic performance of the nation, rather than that of particular individuals.

For instance, do citizens find it easy or difficult to find jobs? On average, are prices rising rapidly, slowly, or not at all? How much total income is the nation producing, and how rapidly is total income growing year after year? Is the interest rate charged to borrow money high or low? Is the government spending more than it collects in tax revenue? Is the nation as a whole accumulating assets in other countries or is it becoming more indebted to them?

Each of these six questions involves a central macroeconomic concept introduced in this chapter. The basic task of macroeconomics is to study the behavior of each of the six concepts, why each matters to individuals, and what the government can do (if anything) to improve macroeconomic performance. Of course, there are many additional concepts in macroeconomics beyond the six selected here as the most central. But for now it helps to start slowly by focusing just on the six, so let us take each one in turn and see how it affects everyday life.

The **unemployment rate** is the number of jobless individuals who are actively looking for work (or are on temporary lay-off) divided by the total of those employed and unemployed.

1. The **unemployment rate.** The higher the overall unemployment rate, the harder it is for each individual who wants a job to find work. College seniors who want permanent jobs after graduation are likely to have more job offers if the national unemployment rate is low, as in 1996–97, than high, as in 1991–92. All adults fear a high unemployment rate, which raises the chances that they will be laid off, be unable to pay their bills, have their cars repossessed, lose their health insurance, or even lose their homes through mortgage foreclosures. In "bad times," when the unemployment rate is high, crime, mental illness, and suicide also increase. It is no wonder that many people consider unemployment to be the single most important macroeconomic issue. And this is nothing new. Robert Burton, an English clergyman, wrote in 1621 that "employment is so essential to human happiness that indolence is justly considered the mother of misery."

The **inflation rate** is the percentage rate of increase in the economy's average level of prices.

2. The **inflation rate.** A high inflation rate means that prices, on average, are rising rapidly, while a low inflation rate means that prices, on average, are rising slowly. An inflation rate of zero means that prices remain essentially the same, month after month. In inflationary periods, retired people,

or those about to retire, lose the most, since their hard-earned savings buy less and less as prices go up. Even college students may lose as the rising prices of room, board, and textbooks erode their savings accounts from past summer and after-school jobs. While a high inflation rate harms those who have saved in the past, it helps those who have borrowed. It is this capricious aspect of inflation, taking from some and giving to others, that makes people dislike inflation. People want their lives to be predictable, but inflation throws a monkey wrench into individual decision making, creating pervasive *uncertainty.*

Productivity is the average output produced per employee or per hour.

3. **Productivity** growth. "Productivity" is the average output per hour of work that a nation produces in total goods and services; it was about $33 per worker-hour in the United States in 1997. The higher a nation's average productivity, the more goods and services there are to go around. The faster average productivity grows, the easier it is for each member of society to improve his or her standard of living. If productivity were to grow at 3 percent from 1997 to the year 2017, U.S. productivity would rise from $33 per worker-hour to $61 per worker-hour. When multiplied by all the hours worked by all the employees in the country, this extra $28 per worker-hour would make it possible for the nation to have more houses, cars, hospitals, roads, schools, and airplane trips, without the need for cutting spending elsewhere. But if the growth rate of productivity were zero instead of 3 percent, U.S. productivity would remain at $33 in the year 2017. To have more houses and cars, we would have to sacrifice by building fewer hospitals and schools. Such an economy, with no productivity growth, has been called the "zero-sum society," because any extra good or service enjoyed by one person requires that something be taken away from someone else. Clearly the achievement of rapid productivity growth and the avoidance of a zero-sum society is a crucially important issue.

The **interest rate** is the percentage rate that is paid by borrowers to lenders.

4. The **interest rate.** When interest rates increase, as they did in the United States in 1994–95, borrowing becomes expensive. The biggest losers are those who would like to become homeowners, since high interest rates boost the monthly payments on mortgages enough to make homeownership unaffordable for many people. College students and recent college graduates find that monthly payments on the new car of their dreams become too high, and they are forced to buy a smaller car, a used car, or perhaps no car at all. *Changes* in interest rates, whether up or down, disrupt financial planning for everyone and create windfall gains and losses for savers, investors, and borrowers.

The **government budget deficit** is the excess of government expenditures (on goods, services, and transfer payments) over the government's tax revenues.

5. The **government budget deficit.** When the government spends more money than it takes in as tax revenue, it runs a deficit. People benefit from a budget deficit at the time it occurs, since they gain from the higher level of government spending (or lower taxes) than would occur if the budget were balanced. This is not a free lunch, however, because eventually someone must pay the bill. Today's deficit will be paid, directly or indirectly, by citizens in the future, including college students now reading this book. Citizens will eventually pay the bill for today's government deficit through lower government spending than would have occurred otherwise, through higher taxes, or through lower income.

The **foreign trade deficit** is the excess of the nation's imports of goods and services over its exports of goods and services.

6. The **foreign trade deficit.** During the 1980s and 1990s, Americans purchased far more goods and services from foreign nations than they sold

as exports. To pay for all these imports, Americans sold many assets to foreigners, including most of the hotels in Honolulu and the Burger King hamburger chain, and the United States ran up a debt to foreigners of hundreds of billions of dollars. The net result is that tomorrow's citizens will be poorer because they will have to pay a fraction of their future income as interest payments to foreigners.

These and other macroeconomic concepts appear in the newspaper every day and influence our dealings with other nations. Year after year, American imports of Japanese autos, Chinese textiles, and other products are largely responsible for multibillion dollar U.S. trade deficits. This has contributed to hostile anti-Japanese speeches by politicians and anti-Japanese editorials in newspapers.

Macroeconomic concepts also play a big role in politics. Incumbent political parties benefit when unemployment and inflation are relatively low, as in the landslide victories of Lyndon Johnson in 1964, Richard Nixon in 1972, George Bush in 1988, and Bill Clinton in 1996. Incumbent presidents who fail to gain reelection often are the victims of a sour economy, as in the cases of Herbert Hoover in 1932 and Jimmy Carter in 1980. The recession of 1990–91 and the weak recovery of 1992 helped Bill Clinton defeat George Bush in the presidential election of 1992.

1-2 Defining Macroeconomics

How Macroeconomics Differs from Microeconomics

An **aggregate** is the total amount of an economic magnitude for the economy as a whole.

Most topics in economics can be placed in one of two categories: macroeconomics and microeconomics. *Macro* comes from a Greek word meaning large; *micro* comes from a Greek word meaning small. Put another way, macroeconomics deals with the totals, or **aggregates,** of the economy, and microeconomics deals with the parts. Among these crucial economic aggregates are the six central concepts introduced in the last section. Related aggregates that play a prominent role in macroeconomics are total wealth, money, income, and business investment.

Microeconomics is devoted to the relationships among the different *parts* of the economy. For example, in macro we study fluctuations in the national income of all U.S. citizens, while in micro we try to explain the wage or salary of one type of worker in relation to another. For example, why is a professor's salary more than that of a secretary but less than that of a university president?

Economic Theory: A Process of Simplification

Economic theory derives its understanding of the economy through a process of simplification. Ignoring the detailed differences among the millions of individuals, firms, and products in the economy, theory throws a spotlight on just a few key relations. There is no conflict between macroeconomics and microeconomics. Instead, they spotlight different relationships. Microeconomics examines the behavior of individual households and firms by making the simplifying assumption that aggregates like national income and the unemployment rate remain constant. In contrast, macroeconomics examines the behavior of aggregates like national income and the unemployment rate while ignoring differences among individual households.

It is this process of simplification that makes the study of economics so exciting. By learning a few basic macroeconomic relations, you can quickly learn how to sift out the hundreds of irrelevant details in the news in order to focus on the few key items that foretell where the economy is going. You also can begin to understand which national and personal economic goals can be attained, and which are "pie in the sky."

1-3   Business Cycles, Inflation, and "Natural Real GDP"

Recurring Business Cycles

Business cycles consist of expansions occurring at about the same time in many economic activities, followed by similarly general recessions and recoveries that merge into the expansion phase of the next cycle.

The **peak** is the highest point reached by real output in each business cycle.

The **trough** is the lowest point reached by real output in each business cycle.

The **recession** is the interval in the business cycle between the peak and the trough.

The **expansion** is the period in the business cycle between the trough and the peak.

Throughout history the economy has experienced **business cycles,** alternating periods of good times and bad times. The worst "bad time" ever experienced by the U.S. economy was the Great Depression of 1929–33, when real output declined by 30 percent in one continuous and catastrophic downward movement.

The hallmark of business cycles is their pervasive character, which affects many different types of economic activity at the same time. Business cycles are recurrent but not periodic. This means that they occur again and again but not always at regular intervals, nor are they the same length. Business cycles in the past have ranged in length from one to twelve years.

Figure 1-1 illustrates two successive business cycles in real output. The high point in real output in each cycle is called the business-cycle **peak.** The low point is called the **trough.** The period between peak and trough is called a **recession.** After the recession comes the **expansion,** which continues until the following peak.[1]

Although a simplification, Figure 1-1 contains two realistic elements that have been common to most real-world business cycles. First, the expansions last longer than the recessions. Second, the two business cycles illustrated in the figure differ in length. Since World War II, business-cycle expansions have been as short as one year (July 1980 to July 1981) and as long as nine years (February 1961 to December 1969).[2]

Why Too Much or Too Little Real Output Is Undesirable

Although business cycles have recurred for centuries, they are not desirable. Much of the subject of macroeconomics is concerned with the feasibility of

---

[1] A comprehensive source for the chronology of and data on historical business cycles, as well as research papers by distinguished economists, is Robert J. Gordon, ed., *The American Business Cycle: Continuity and Change* (University of Chicago Press, 1986).

[2] The first part of the expansion is sometimes called the recovery. The recovery begins when the economy reaches the trough and continues until the level of real GDP exceeds its value at the previous peak.

Figure 1-1
Basic Business Cycle Concepts
The real output line exhibits a typical succession of business cycles. The highest point reached by real output in each cycle is called the *peak* and the lowest point the *trough*. The *recession* is the period between peak and trough; the *expansion* the period between the trough and the next peak.

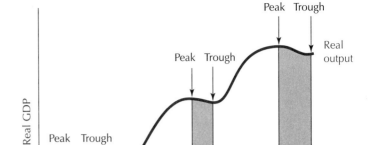

A SUCCESSION OF CYCLES

government attempts to "dampen" business cycles—that is, to make the growth of real output smoother and the up-and-down fluctuations less severe. But we cannot tell just by looking at Figure 1-1 what a government's goal should be. Should a nation's government aim at maintaining real output at the peak, the trough, or somewhere in between?

Since more real output provides more goods and services for the average citizen, a first answer would seem to be that a nation's government should attempt to keep real output at its peak level all the time. This is wrong. Why? Unfortunately, maximum production tends to make inflation worse. When business firms are producing "flat out," they find it easy to raise prices. Thus too much real output is inflationary and must be avoided if the overall inflation rate is to be kept from accelerating.

Too little real output is also undesirable. Low levels of real output mean layoffs, unemployment, and a lower standard of living. For instance, real output was too low in 1991 and 1992; millions lost their jobs, and millions more feared for their jobs. Such harmful effects are only partly balanced by the tendency of the inflation rate to slow down in such a situation.

Real GDP: Actual and Natural

Gross domestic product is the value of all currently produced goods and services sold on the market during a particular time interval.

In almost every economy in the world, the official measure of the economy's total output is called **gross domestic product,** abbreviated GDP. The amount of an economy's total production that we previously called real output will henceforth be called real GDP. As you will learn in Chapter 2, real GDP includes all currently produced goods and services sold on the market within a given time period and excludes certain types of economic activity. As you

real output = real GDP

---

[3] The economic expansion of the 1980s began in the trough quarter November 1982, and ended in July 1990, lasting 92 months, or 7 2/3 years. The most recent recession began in the peak month, July 1990, and continued for eight months until the trough was reached in March 1991.

will also learn, the adjective "real" means that our measure of output reflects the quantity produced corrected for any changes in prices.

Actual real GDP is the amount an economy actually produces at any given time. Sometimes too much production of real GDP causes inflation to get worse, but too little real GDP wastes resources and deprives people of jobs. In between is some desirable compromise level that keeps the inflation rate constant. This intermediate level of real GDP has been called "natural," a situation in which there is no tendency for inflation to accelerate or decelerate.

Figure 1-2 illustrates the relationship between actual real GDP, natural real GDP, and the rate of inflation. In the upper frame the red line is actual real GDP, exhibiting the same business cycles as in Figure 1-1. In the lower frame is shown the inflation rate. The thin dashed vertical lines connect the two frames. The first dashed vertical line marks time period t_0. Notice in the bottom frame that the inflation rate is constant at t_0.

By definition, **natural real GDP** is equal to actual real GDP when the inflation rate is constant. Thus, in the upper frame, at t_0 the red actual real GDP line is crossed by the black natural real GDP line. To the right of t_0, actual real

Actual real GDP is the value of total output corrected for any changes in prices.

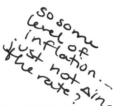
[handwritten margin note:] So some level of inflation. just not ↗ the rate? rising

Natural real GDP designates the level of real GDP at which the inflation rate is constant, with no tendency to accelerate or decelerate.

Figure 1-2
The Relation Between Actual and Natural Real GDP and the Inflation Rate

In the upper frame the solid black line shows the steady growth of natural real GDP—the amount the economy can produce at a constant inflation rate. The red line shows the path of actual real GDP, which is the same as in Figure 1-1. In the gray region in the top frame, actual real GDP is below natural real GDP, so the inflation rate, shown in the bottom frame, slows down. In the region designated by the red area, actual real GDP is above natural real GDP, so in the bottom frame inflation speeds up.

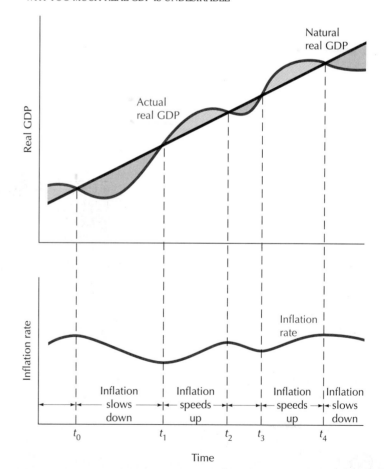

GDP falls below natural real GDP, and we see in the bottom frame that inflation slows down. This continues until time period t_1, when actual real GDP recovers until once again it is equal to natural real GDP. Here the inflation rate stops falling and is constant for a moment before it begins to rise.

This cycle repeats again and again. *Only when actual real GDP is equal to natural real GDP is the inflation rate constant.* For this reason, natural real GDP is a compromise level to be singled out for special attention. During a period of low actual real GDP, designated by the gray area, the inflation rate slows down. During a period of high actual real GDP, designated by the red area, the inflation rate accelerates. Sometimes the condition of excessive actual real GDP is called "an overheated economy," a designation that you can link to the red area on the diagram.

Unemployment: Actual and Natural

When actual real GDP is low, many people lose their jobs, and the unemployment rate is high, as shown in Figure 1-3. The top frame duplicates Figure 1-2

Figure 1-3
The Behavior over Time of Actual and Natural Real GDP and the Actual and Natural Rates of Unemployment

When actual real GDP falls below natural real GDP, designated by the gray shaded areas in the top frame, the actual unemployment rate rises above the natural rate of unemployment, as indicated in the bottom frame. The red areas designate the opposite situation. When we compare the gray-shaded areas of Figures 1-2 and 1-3, we see that the time intervals when unemployment is high (1-3), also represent time intervals when inflation is slowing down (1-2). Similarly, the red shaded areas represent time intervals when inflation is speeding up and unemployment is low.

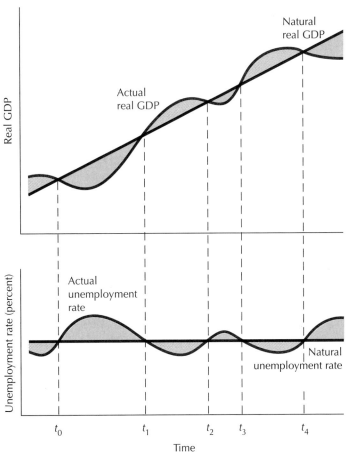

UNEMPLOYMENT CYCLES ARE
THE MIRROR IMAGE OF REAL GDP CYCLES

exactly, comparing actual real GDP with natural real GDP. The red line in the bottom frame is the actual percentage unemployment rate, the first of the six central concepts of macroeconomics. The unemployment rate is defined as the number of jobless individuals who are actively looking for work (or are on temporary layoff), divided by the total of those employed and unemployed. The thin vertical dashed lines connecting the upper frame and lower frame show that whenever actual and natural real GDP are equal in the top frame, the actual unemployment rate is equal to the **natural rate of unemployment** in the bottom frame.

The **natural rate of unemployment** designates the level of unemployment at which the inflation rate is constant, with no tendency to accelerate or decelerate.

$\uparrow$ inflation = $\downarrow$ unemp. $\notin$
        $\uparrow$ GDP

The definition of the natural rate of unemployment corresponds exactly to natural real GDP, describing a situation in which there is no tendency for the inflation rate to change. When the actual unemployment rate is high, actual real GDP is low (shown by gray shading in both frames), and the inflation rate slows down. In periods when actual real GDP is high and the economy prospers, the actual unemployment rate is low (shown by red shading in both frames) and the inflation rate speeds up. Notice that in Figures 1-2 and 1-3 the peak of the business cycle occurs when actual real GDP is high, and the trough occurs when actual real GDP is low. But this is not always the case. The short 1980–81 business-cycle expansion was incomplete, and at the peak in August 1981, actual real GDP was still below natural real GDP.

The natural rate of unemployment in the bottom frame of Figure 1-3 is illustrated as a horizontal line just for convenience. In the real world the natural rate of unemployment is not necessarily constant. Possible causes of changes in the natural rate of unemployment are a matter of debate and are discussed in Chapter 9 and 12. There we will see that the natural unemployment rate is neither optimal nor immutable, and it can be reduced by policies that help the economy function better.

Figures 1-2 and 1-3 summarize a basic dilemma faced by government policymakers who are attempting to achieve a low unemployment rate and a low inflation rate at the same time. If the inflation rate is high, lowering it requires a decline in actual real GDP and an increase in the actual unemployment rate. If, on the contrary, the policymaker attempts to provide jobs for everyone and keep the actual unemployment rate low, then the inflation rate will speed up. The United States made the transition from roughly a 9 percent inflation rate in 1981 to a 3 percent inflation rate in 1986 only at the cost of very high unemployment during much of the intervening five years. The low unemployment rate in 1988–89 caused an increase in the inflation rate, and the decreased inflation of 1991–94 was achieved only at the cost of a higher unemployment rate during 1991–93.

SELF-TEST

> There is a natural level of output, defined in the previous section. There is a natural rate of unemployment, defined in this section. Is there a *natural rate of inflation?*

Real GDP and the Six Macro Concepts

The total amount that the economy produces, actual real GDP, is closely related to several of the six central macroeconomic concepts introduced earlier in this chapter. First, as we see in Figure 1-3, the *difference* between actual and natural real GDP moves inversely with the *difference* between the actual and natural unemployment rates. When actual real GDP is high, unemployment is low, and vice versa.

The second link is with inflation, since inflation tends to speed up when actual real GDP is higher than natural real GDP (as in Figure 1-2). The third link is with productivity, which is defined as actual real GDP per employee or per hour; data on actual real GDP are required to calculate the level or growth rate of productivity.

Each of these links with the central macroeconomic concepts requires that actual real GDP be compared with *something else* in order to be meaningful (it must be compared to natural real GDP to provide a link with unemployment and inflation, or it must be divided by the number of employees or hours to compute productivity). Actual real GDP by itself, without any such comparison, is not meaningful, which is why it is not included on the list of the six major macro concepts.

1-4   CASE STUDY: A Century of Business Cycles

This section examines U.S. macroeconomic history since the late nineteenth century. You will see that unemployment, as bad as it was in the early 1980s and early 1990s, did not reach the extreme crisis levels of the 1930s.

Real GDP

Figure 1-4 is arranged just like Figure 1-3. But whereas Figure 1-3 shows hypothetical relationships, Figure 1-4 shows the actual historical record. In the top frame the solid black line is natural real GDP, an estimate of the amount the economy could have produced each year without causing acceleration or deceleration of inflation.

The red line in the top frame plots actual real GDP, the total production of goods and services each year measured in the constant prices of 1992. Can you pick out those years when actual and natural real GDP are roughly equal? Some of these years were 1900, 1910, 1924, 1964, 1972, 1979, 1987, 1990, and 1994.

In years marked by gray shading, actual real GDP fell below natural real GDP. A maximum deficiency occurred in 1933, when actual real GDP was only 64 percent of natural GDP; about 36 percent of natural real GDP was thus "wasted," that is, not produced. Before 1929 and since 1950 these intervals of substantial output deficiency have been much less serious than in the Great Depression but nevertheless have added up to billions in lost output.

In some years actual real GDP exceeded natural real GDP, shown by the shaded red areas. This occurred mainly in wartime, particularly during World War I (1917–18), World War II (1942–45), the Korean War (1951–53), and the first half of the U.S. involvement in the Vietnam War (1965–69).

Unemployment

In the bottom frame of Figure 1-4 the red line plots the actual unemployment rate. By far the most extreme episode was the Great Depression, when the

AN HISTORICAL REPORT CARD ON REAL GDP AND UNEMPLOYMENT

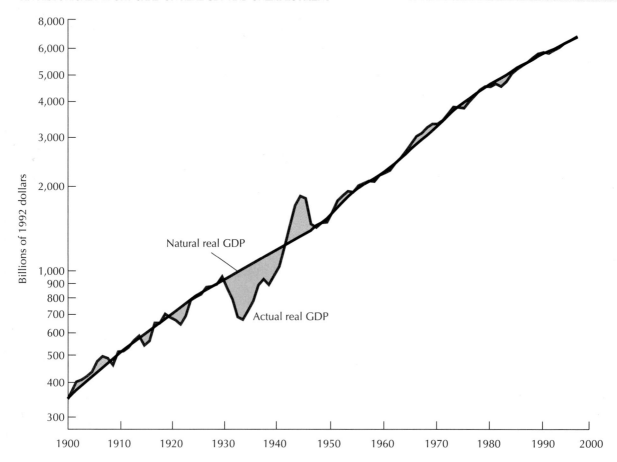

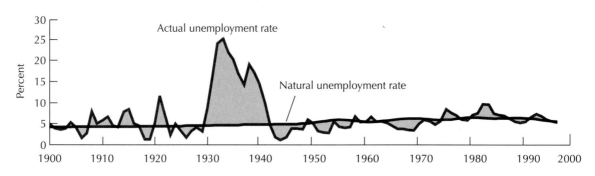

***Figure 1-4*   Actual and Natural GDP and Unemployment, 1900–96**

An historical report card for two important economic magnitudes. In the top frame the black line indicates natural real GDP. The red line shows actual real GDP, which was well below natural real GDP during the Great Depression of the 1930s and well above it during World War II. In the bottom frame the black line indicates the natural rate of unemployment, and the red line indicates the actual unemployment rate. Actual unemployment was much higher during the Great Depression of the 1930s than at any other time during the century. Notice how periods of high actual unemployment like the 1930s, designated by gray areas in the bottom frame, occur simultaneously with periods of low actual real GDP in the top frame. Red areas indicate times when the economy was "overheated," with high actual real GDP and low unemployment.

actual unemployment rate remained above 10 percent for ten straight years, 1931–1940. It is not surprising that the Depression left a profound mark on economic theory, government policy, and political alignments; the masses of unemployed of the 1930s had no welfare programs or unemployment insurance to ease their misery.

The black line in the bottom frame of Figure 1-4 displays the natural rate of unemployment, the minimum attainable level of unemployment that is compatible with avoiding an acceleration of inflation. The natural unemployment rate sets a lower limit on the level of actual unemployment that can be attained without accelerating inflation. The red shaded areas mark years when actual unemployment fell below the natural rate, as in 1917–19 and 1966–69. The gray shaded areas mark years when unemployment exceeded the natural rate.

Notice now the relationship between the top and bottom frames of Figure 1-4. The gray areas in both frames designate periods of low production, low real GDP, and high unemployment, such as the Great Depression of the 1930s and the "Great Recessions" of 1975 and 1981–82. The red areas in both frames designate periods of high production and high actual real GDP, and low unemployment, such as World War II and other wartime periods.

1-5 Macroeconomics in the Short Run and Long Run

Macroeconomic theories and debates can be divided into two main groups: (1) those that concern the short-run stability of the economy, and (2) those that concern its long-run growth rate. The terms *business cycles* and **economic growth** are frequently used to label these two main groups of topics.

Economic growth is the topic area of macroeconomics that studies the causes of sustained growth in natural real GDP.

The Short Run: Business Cycles

The main short-run concern of macroeconomics is to close the "gap" between actual and natural unemployment and real GDP. This means that they try to find ways of dampening the business cycle so that the economy's actual unemployment and real GDP stay as close to the natural level as possible.

Figure 1-5 contrasts two imaginary economies: "Volatilia" in the left frame and "Stabilia" in the right frame. Here, unlike in Figures 1-3 and 1-4, we omit the frame on unemployment, since we have already seen that the ups and downs of the unemployment gap regularly mimic the downs and ups of the real GDP gap. The two frames of Figure 1-5 have exactly the same vertical axis; real GDP and the black "natural real GDP" lines in both frames are *absolutely identical.* The two economies differ only in the size of their business cycles, shown by the size of their **real GDP gap,** which is simply the difference between actual and natural real GDP.

The **real GDP gap,** sometimes called the *output gap,* is the difference between actual and natural real GDP.

In the left frame Volatilia is a macroeconomic hell, with severe business cycles and large gaps between actual and natural real GDP. In the right frame Stabilia is macroeconomic heaven, with mild business cycles and small gaps between actual and natural real GDP. All macroeconomists prefer the economy depicted by the right-hand frame to that depicted by the left-hand frame. But the debate between macro schools of thought starts in earnest when we

ECONOMIC FAILURE AND SUCCESS

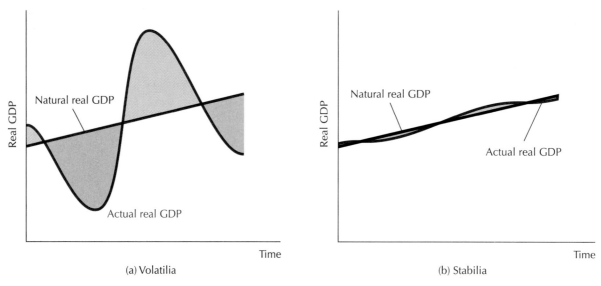

Figure 1-5   **Business Cycles in Volatilia and Stabilia**
The left frame shows the huge business cycles in a hypothetical nation called Volatilia. Short-run macroeconomics tries to dampen business cycles so that the path of actual real GDP is as close as possible to natural real GDP, as shown in the right frame for a nation called Stabilia.

ask how to achieve the economy of the right-hand frame. Active do-something policies? Do-nothing, hands-off policies? There are economists who support each of these alternatives, and more besides. But everyone agrees that Stabilia is a more successful economy than Volatilia.

Gap-closing is a worthy goal for policymakers, but it is not their only goal. Even with mild business cycles and stable inflation, macroeconomic problems may remain. The first problem is that maintaining the economy close to the natural level of real GDP, as in Stabilia, does not guarantee zero inflation. It only prevents inflation from getting worse. But what if inflation is already running at 10 percent per year? Many people would consider that rate of inflation excessive, and policymakers would face the dilemma of slowing inflation without creating high unemployment.

The Long Run: Economic Growth

The second problem is that gap-closing does not guarantee rapid economic growth. For a society to achieve an increasing standard of living, total output per person must grow, and such economic growth is the long-run concern of macroeconomists. Look at Figure 1-6, which contrasts two economies. Each has mild business cycles, like Stabilia in Figure 1-5. But in Figure 1-6 the left frame presents a country called "Stag-Nation," which experiences very slow growth in real GDP. In contrast, the right-hand frame depicts "Speed-Nation," a country with very fast growth in real GDP. If we assume that population growth in each country is the same, then growth in output per person is faster in Speed-Nation. In Speed-Nation everyone can purchase more consumer

ECONOMIC FAILURE AND SUCCESS IN ANOTHER DIMENSION

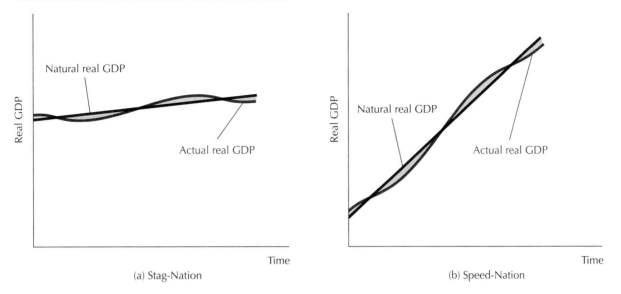

Figure 1-6 **Economic Growth in Stag-Nation and Speed-Nation**
In both frames the business cycle has been tamed, but in the left frame there is almost no economic growth, while economic growth in the right frame is rapid. For Speed-Nation there can be more of everything, while Stag-Nation in the left frame is a "zero-sum society," in which an increase in one type of economic activity requires that another economic activity be cut back.

goods, and there is plenty of output left over to provide better schools, parks, hospitals, and other public services. In Stag-Nation people must constantly face debates, since more money for schools or parks requires that people sacrifice consumer goods.

How do we achieve faster economic growth in output per person? In Chapters 9–11 we study the sources of economic growth and the role of government policy in helping to determine the growth in America's future standard of living.

SELF-TEST

Indicate whether each item in the following list is more closely related to short-run (business cycle) macro or to long-run (economic growth) macro: (1) the Federal Reserve reduces interest rates in a recession in an attempt to reduce the unemployment rate; (2) the federal government introduces national standards for high-school students in an attempt to raise math and science test scores; (3) consumers cut back spending because news of layoffs makes them fear for their jobs; (4) the federal government gives states and localities more money to repair roads, bridges, and schools.

1-6 The Six Macroeconomic Puzzles

Now we are ready to take a closer look at the period since 1960. Corresponding to each of the six key macroeconomic aggregates—the unemployment rate, inflation rate, productivity growth, interest rate, government budget deficit, and foreign trade deficit—is a puzzle concerning the recent behavior of the economy. A basic task of this book is to develop the tools that will help us solve these puzzles.

Puzzle 1: Why Has the Unemployment Rate Been So High and So Variable?

We have seen that the unemployment rate is the mirror image of real GDP, rising when real GDP falls and vice versa. As shown in Figures 1-4 and 1-7, a graph of the unemployment rate looks like a roller coaster, moving up and down every few years. The unemployment rate is just one of many macroeconomic aggregates exhibiting cyclical movements. We focus on unemployment in the first puzzle because of its obvious importance to the great majority of people, who want to be able to find jobs easily.

Puzzle 1 has two parts. The first is why the unemployment rate is so volatile—that is, why it moves up and down so much. Why can't the economy be managed so as to keep the unemployment rate at a stable level? This question can be stated even more directly: Why can't business cycles be prevented?

The second part of the puzzle is why there was a tendency in the 1970s and early 1980s for the peaks in each unemployment cycle to become higher and higher. The business-cycle recession of 1969–70 brought unemployment to a peak rate of 6.1 percent; in the worst month of the 1973–75 recession the unemployment rate soared to 9.1 percent; and in the recession of 1981–82, the unemployment rate rose to an even higher 10.8 percent. Even in 1989, a good year by recent standards, unemployment was higher than the *average* achieved in 1962–74. The recession of 1990–91 and the subsequent expansion were the first in a long time to break this trend toward ever-higher unemployment.

Figure 1-7
The U.S. Unemployment Rate, 1960–96

This graph shows data for the U.S. unemployment rate for each quarter between 1960 and 1996. Notice how unemployment was higher in the second half of the period than in the first, and its lowest level of 1996 was well above the lower levels reached in the 1960s. *Note:* Gray vertical bands designate recessions.

THE FIRST PUZZLE

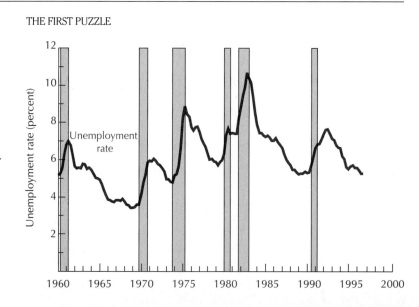

Puzzle 2: Why Has the Inflation Rate at Times Been So High and So Variable?

The behavior of the inflation rate since 1960 is shown in Figure 1-8. The inflation rate was much higher between 1973 and 1982 than before or after. Inflation soared to a peak rate of almost 10 percent in early 1981. The high rates of inflation reached in 1974–75 and 1979–81 indirectly caused the high rates of unemployment shown in the previous figure for the years 1974–76 and 1980–82. The reason is that policymakers in Washington believed that the primary economic problem was inflation, which called for restrictive economic policies designed to depress real GDP and raise the unemployment rate. In short, policymakers deliberately created recessions and caused an upsurge of unemployment in those years.

The second aspect of the inflation puzzle is why the inflation rate was so variable, particularly between 1973 and 1984. Because inflation affects people directly and also indirectly causes unemployment through the reaction of policymakers in Washington, a central task of this book is to explain what causes inflation and how to cure it. Is it possible to maintain a low rate of inflation? Can inflation be kept at a low and stable rate, as in 1993–94, without wild swings, such as those that occurred during 1973–84?

Puzzle 3: Why Has Productivity Grown So Slowly?

Productivity is defined as real GDP divided by the total number of hours spent on the job by the nation's workers. The rate of productivity growth determines how rapidly the well-being of the average citizen increases. Will today's college students belong to the first generation in U.S. history that fails to exceed the living standards of its parents? The answer will depend in part on whether productivity growth remains as slow as it has since 1973, or whether it picks up speed.

Figure 1-8

The U.S. Inflation Rate, 1960–96

This graph shows data for the U.S. rate of inflation for the four quarters ending in each quarter between 1960 and 1996. Notice how inflation was much higher and more variable between 1973 and 1981 than before or after. The acceleration of inflation in 1987–89 is clearly visible, as is the deceleration of 1990–94. *Note:* Gray vertical bands designate recessions.

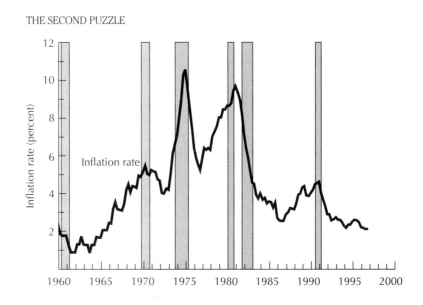

THE SECOND PUZZLE

Figure 1-9 shows the percentage rate of productivity growth on an annual basis since 1948. The line zigzags, but it reveals a disturbing downward trend, averaging 1.0 percent per year since 1973, compared to the 2.8 percent average rate achieved during 1948–73.

The slowdown in productivity growth is one of the most mysterious puzzles in macroeconomics. The U.S. economy no longer increases its annual average output per worker as quickly as it used to. Nor does it match the increases in productivity still being achieved by such countries as Japan, Germany, and France. Because the productivity puzzle continues over several successive business cycles, it is part of long-run macroeconomics and its treatment is postponed until Chapter 10.

Puzzle 4: Why Have Real Interest Rates Been So High?

Despite the serious problems of unemployment and inflation in the 1970s and 1980s, the numbers recorded in Figures 1-7 and 1-8 did not set historical records. Unemployment was worse in the Great Depression of the 1930s. Inflation was worse in several previous episodes, particularly during the Civil War and World War I and immediately after World War II. But the behavior of interest rates in the early 1980s was novel, with no historical precedent in the past century.

After being below 5 percent in the early 1960s and below 10 percent in 1979, the **nominal interest rate** (depicted as the black upper line in Figure 1-10) surged up, reaching 16 percent in 1981. Then in 1982 the interest rate dropped, and by early 1986 it was again back down to 9 percent. However, even in 1996 the rate was higher than at any point in the 1960s.

The **nominal interest rate** is the market interest rate actually charged by financial institutions and earned by lenders.

A high interest rate is a boon to those who have substantial savings. But it is a disaster for many business firms, large and small, that have to borrow money regularly. The high interest rate in the 1980s also contributed to a mas-

---

Figure 1-9
Labor Productivity Growth, 1948–96

The zigzag line shows data for the annual percentage change in output per hour (productivity) in the U.S. between 1948 and 1996. The average growth rate of productivity between 1973 and 1996 was only 1.0 percent per year, much less than the 2.8 percent average rate between 1948 and 1973.

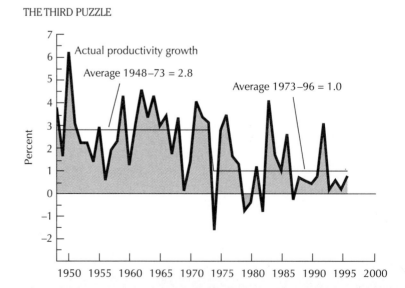

THE THIRD PUZZLE

Figure 1-10
**The Nominal and Real Corporate
Bond Rate, 1960–96**
The upper black line shows the actual
interest rate on corporate bonds,
which reached an unprecedented
level during 1981. The lower red line
shows the real interest rate and is
equal to the top line minus the rate of
inflation from Figure 1-8. Notice that
investors earned a negative real rate
of interest in 1974, and that the real
rate of interest was higher after 1980
than before 1980.

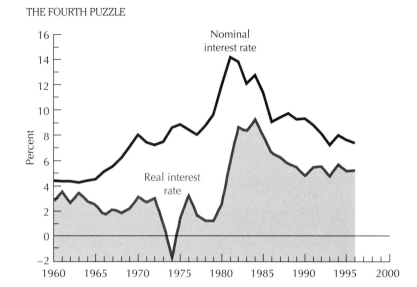

THE FOURTH PUZZLE

sive federal government budget deficit, since the federal government had to
make interest payments on its outstanding debt. The effect on business firms
contributed to the record business bankruptcy rate.

Notice the similarity between the inflation rate in Figure 1-8 and the interest rate in Figure 1-10. Both rates were low in the early 1960s and rose sharply
in the 1970s. So it might appear that inflation contributed to higher interest
rates. The lower red line in Figure 1-10 is the **real interest rate,** which is simply the nominal interest rate, plotted as the upper line in Figure 1-10, minus
the rate of inflation (from Figure 1-8). Even with adjustment for inflation, the
real interest rate is highly variable and also reached an unprecedented level
in the 1980s. The real interest rate in 1996 was higher than that reached during any year in the 1960s or 1970s.

The puzzle of the high real interest rate is one of the first that we tackle
in the book. Chapters 3 and 4 develop a simple model that helps explain the
movements of both interest rates and real GDP. The distinction between the
nominal and real interest rate is explored further in Chapter 12, where we
inquire into the effects of inflation on savers and borrowers.

> The **real interest rate** is
> the nominal interest rate
> minus the inflation rate.

Puzzle 5: Why Has the Government Budget Deficit Persisted?

The government budget deficit (Figure 1-11) is closely related to three of our
other puzzles. When the government spends more than it takes in, it must
borrow from households and business firms, who then have less remaining
for consumption and investment spending. A government deficit may therefore cut private investment; this may lead to slower growth in capital per
worker and hence lower productivity growth (Puzzle 3). A government deficit
may also account in part for higher interest rates (Puzzle 4), since when
borrowing funds to pay its bills, the government may have to pay a higher
interest rate. Finally, a government deficit can lead to a trade deficit
(Puzzle 6).

Figure 1-11

The U.S. Budget Surplus as a Percent of GDP, 1960–96

This graph shows the total U.S. government budget surplus, including the budgets of all state and local governments, as well as the federal government. What is unusual about the 1980s and 1990s is that the budget deficit remained so large, year after year, without any periods of budget surplus.

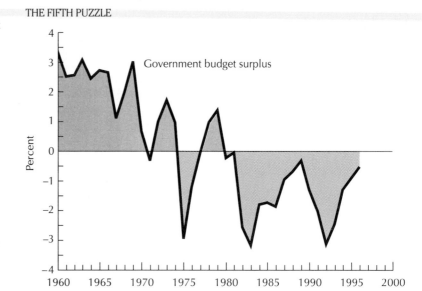

THE FIFTH PUZZLE

As shown in Figure 1-11, the government's budget has been in deficit (shown by red shading) in most years since 1980. What is unusual about the 1980s and 1990s is the *persistence* of the deficit, continuing year after year instead of going away promptly as in previous episodes. When the government runs a deficit, it adds to the national debt. The federal government's outstanding debt held by private investors more than quadrupled between 1980 and 1996, from $700 to $3800 billion.

These ongoing government deficits have created an ongoing debate among politicians and economists. Politicians argue about the underlying cause of the deficits—was it higher expenditures or lower taxes? Economists argue about whether the deficits are harmful or not. But few economists deny that the deficits have allowed Americans to consume more than they produce, and that at some point in the future Americans will have to tighten their belts and consume less than they produce.

Puzzle 6: Why Has the United States' Trade Dropped into Persistent Deficit?

How can a nation buy more imports from foreigners than it sells to them in the form of exports? Just as a government deficit requires the issuance of debt, so a trade deficit requires that the nation go into debt to foreigners. This debt can consist of pieces of paper, as when a Japanese investor holds a U.S. government bond. Or it can consist of foreign ownership of American factories, office buildings, and hotels. The United States has financed its foreign trade deficit in both ways, through sales of securities to foreigners and through foreign purchases of U.S. assets.

The collapse of the U.S. trade balance in the 1980s was even more sudden and dramatic than that of the government budget, as shown in Figure 1-12.

Figure 1-12
The U.S. Foreign Trade Surplus as a Percent of GDP, 1960–96

Shown is the U.S. trade surplus, defined as exports of goods and services minus imports of goods and services. After running a persistent trade surplus before 1970, the United States ran a persistent trade deficit in every year starting in 1976. In comparing the government budget surplus in Figures 1-11 and 1-12, notice a difference: the trade deficit improved temporarily in 1990–92, whereas the budget deficit got worse, while the reverse happened in 1994–96.

THE SIXTH PUZZLE

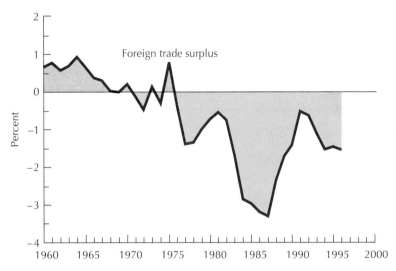

Between 1983 and 1987 the trade balance plunged into a large deficit. Each year's deficit required that more and more U.S. assets be sold to foreigners. By the late 1980s the United States was by far the world's largest debtor nation. After a brief recovery during 1991–92, the trade deficit grew again, and the United States fell even further in debt to other nations.

The implications of the trade deficit are not happy ones for today's college students. The only way to cure the trade deficit is through further declines in the **foreign exchange rate** of the U.S. dollar. This means that anything produced abroad is likely to become gradually more expensive as compared to goods produced at home, including German beer, Japanese cameras, and summer vacations to Europe. It is not far-fetched to predict that summer trips to Europe, enjoyed by millions of young Americans in the past, may become a thing of the past if the trade deficit continues and causes the foreign exchange rate of the U.S. dollar to decline.

The **foreign exchange rate** is the amount of another nation's money that residents of a country can obtain in exchange for a unit of their own money.

Conclusion Regarding the Six Puzzles

The six puzzles focus mainly on problems faced by the American economy. The task of macroeconomics is to study these problems and, if possible, find solutions. Yet we should not form the impression that macroeconomics is a subject entirely about failure. Modern economies have scored many successes as well. The 50 years since World War II represent the longest period of sustained real economic growth in human history. We learned many lessons from the Great Depression of the 1930s, and no such depression has happened again. As recently as 1997 the American economy registered a robust rate of growth in real GDP, with the lowest inflation rate in 35 years. As we study macroeconomics, we will learn much from episodes of both failure and success.

1-7 Taming Business Cycles: Stabilization Policy

Macroeconomic analysts have two tasks: to analyze the causes of changes in important aggregates and to predict the consequences of alternative policy changes. In policy discussions the group of aggregates that society cares most about—inflation, unemployment, and the long-term growth rate of productivity—are called goals, or **target variables.** When the target variables deviate from desired values, alternative **policy instruments** can be used in an attempt to achieve needed changes. Instruments fall into three broad categories: **monetary policies,** which include control of the money supply and interest rates; **fiscal policies,** which include changes in government expenditures and tax rates; and a third, miscellaneous group, which includes wage and price controls and employment policy.

Target variables are aggregates whose values society cares about.

Policy instruments are elements that government policymakers can manipulate directly to influence target variables.

Monetary policy tries to influence target variables by changing the money supply or interest rate or both.

Fiscal policy tries to influence target variables by manipulating government expenditures and tax rates.

How are target variables and policy instruments related to the six central macroeconomic concepts introduced at the beginning of this chapter? The first three concepts—the unemployment rate, inflation rate, and productivity growth—are the key target variables of economic policy, the goals society cares most about. The next two concepts are policy instruments. The interest rate is the policy instrument for monetary policy. Since people also care about interest rates, the effectiveness of monetary policy in dealing with the three target variables can sometimes be inhibited if the actions needed to achieve change would require interest rates to be too high or too volatile. The fifth concept, the government budget deficit, is also a policy instrument. The sixth concept, the foreign trade deficit, can *constrain* the policymakers from achieving their target variables with their available policy instruments. For instance, to avoid a large trade deficit and the indebtedness to foreigners that it implies, policymakers may have to sacrifice a low unemployment rate or stable prices.

The Role of Stabilization Policy

A stabilization policy is any policy that seeks to influence the level of aggregate demand.

Macroeconomic analysis begins with a simple message: Either type of **stabilization policy,** monetary or fiscal, can be used to offset undesired changes in private spending. The effects of monetary and fiscal policy on the price level and on real GDP are the main subjects of Parts Two and Three of this book. Fiscal policy can raise output and employment by increased government spending that creates jobs through government hiring. Or fiscal policy can stimulate private spending by cutting tax rates, thus inducing a higher level of private purchases, production, and employment. A monetary policy stimulus to output and employment takes the form of a reduction in interest rates and may, in turn, boost stock prices and make lending institutions more willing to grant credit.

There are many problems in applying stabilization policy. It may not be possible to control aggregate demand instantly and precisely. A policy stimulus intended to fight current unemployment might boost aggregate demand only after a long and uncertain delay, by which time the stimulus might not be needed. The impact of different policy changes may also be highly uncertain. These and other limitations of policy "fine-tuning" or "activism" are central themes in the consideration of monetary and fiscal policy in Part Five.

Relation Between Theory and Policy

This book uses economic theory to examine the causes of changes in real GDP, unemployment, and the price level. Instead of just describing a collection of unrelated economic facts, theory isolates the important economic variables that help explain inflation and unemployment. Theory also creates useful generalizations to describe the relationships among groups of variables, such as consumption and income or money and interest rates. We can then look at the facts to test whether the generalizations of theory have predictive power.

Positive economics is the scientific attempt to describe and explain the behavior of the economy.

Normative economics involves recommendations for changes in economic policy to achieve an optimal or desirable state of affairs.

Economists use theory for two quite separate purposes: for **positive economics,** which *explains* the behavior of important variables, and for **normative economics,** which *recommend* changes in economic policy. Economists have developed theories that explain most of the changes observed in the unemployment rate or the rate of inflation and why interest rates are now higher than they were 30 years ago. Most disagreements among economists no longer focus on different explanations of these major phenomena; rather they center on the proper conduct of economic policy, a normative issue.

Most policy disagreements stem from the incompatibility of worthy economic goals. Most people would like the price level to be stable and the unemployment rate to be close to zero. But this state of nirvana cannot be achieved instantly, if ever. Macroeconomics, like economics in general, is the science of *choice* in the face of limitations for each of the possible alternatives. Choices emphasized in this book include whether to reduce the inflation rate at the cost of higher unemployment during a transition period that may last five years or longer and whether to boost investment and economic growth at the cost of higher federal tax rates.

SELF-TEST

Is it the task of stabilization policy to set the unemployment rate to zero? Why or why not? Is it the task of stabilization policy to set the inflation rate to zero? Why or why not? What are the two big problems in applying stabilization policy to control aggregate demand?

1-8 The "Internationalization" of Macroeconomics

More than ever before, macroeconomics is an international subject. The days are gone when the effects of U.S. stabilization policy could be analyzed in isolation, without consideration for their repercussions abroad. This old view of the United States as a **closed economy** described reality in the first decade or so after World War II. In the 1940s and 1950s, trade accounted for only about 5 percent of the U.S. economy, exchange rates were fixed, and financial flows to and from other nations were restricted.

A **closed economy** has no trade in goods, services, or financial assets with any other nation.

An **open economy** exports goods and services to other nations, imports from them, and has financial flows to and from foreign nations.

The United States has increasingly become an **open economy.** Imports now exceed 12 percent of U.S. GDP. The exchange rate of the dollar has been flexible since 1973 and has fluctuated far more widely than anyone had predicted prior to that time. International financial flows are massive and often instantaneous, with computers sending messages to buy or sell stocks and bonds at the speed of light among the major financial centers of Tokyo, London, New York, and Chicago.

INTERNATIONAL PERSPECTIVE

How Does U.S. Economic Performance Rank?

One result of the internationalization of macroeconomics is an increased attention to the comparative economic performance of the United States. The figure shows how the United States compares with Japan and the major European nations in its unemployment, inflation, and productivity growth rates (the first three of our "big six" macroeconomic concepts). The data are presented as a set of bar graphs, with the unemployment performance displayed in the top frame, inflation in the middle frame, and productivity growth in the bottom frame. Three bars are grouped together in each frame for each region, showing performance during the years 1960–73, 1973–79, and 1979–95.

Above all, one startling fact stands out. The economic performance of Japan is superior to both the United States and Europe in most periods. Japan had a lower unemployment rate in all three periods and a much lower inflation rate in the most recent period. Japanese productivity growth was faster than that in the United States in all three periods, although slower than in Europe in the most recent period. Compared to Europe, the United States did better on unemployment and inflation in the most recent period. The clear failing of the U.S. performance is in its productivity growth; in 1979–95, productivity growth in the United States was less than half that in Europe. In short, the United States has done better at providing jobs, but Europe has done better at boosting average real income per job.

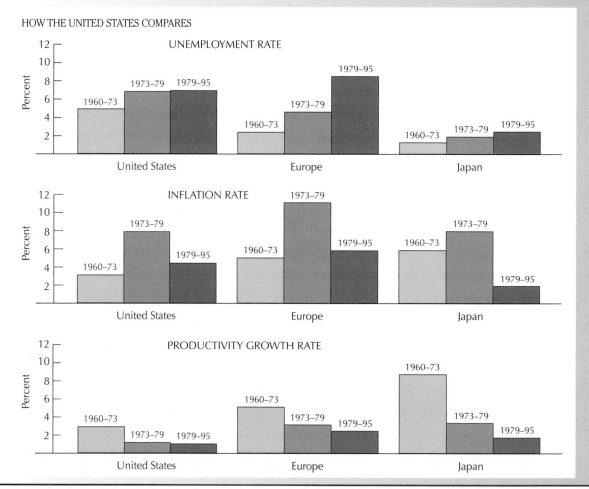

HOW THE UNITED STATES COMPARES

As the economy has become internationalized, so has macroeconomic analysis. This textbook reflects this trend by including the foreign trade balance and its deterioration as one of the six major macroeconomic concepts and puzzles. We find the influence of international flows of goods, services, and finance affecting many topics. No longer can we assume that a large government budget deficit automatically depresses or crowds out private investment spending. Instead, the economy may get the capital it needs to finance both private investment and the government deficit from abroad through foreign purchases of U.S. stocks, bonds, factories, and hotels. The availability of foreign capital has this good side but also a bad side. By financing the government budget deficit through capital flows from abroad, Americans have run up a massive foreign debt, which will require a sacrifice by future generations to pay the interest bill.

Just as budget deficits are financed differently in an open economy, the operation of the Federal Reserve Board's monetary policy is also affected by an open economy. If the Fed pushes down interest rates to stimulate the economy, that could push down the exchange rate of the dollar and worsen inflation. We can no longer analyze U.S. inflation without considering the effects of foreign trade. Here also there is a good and bad side. Reliance on foreign trade was bad when higher prices of imported oil jolted inflation upward in the 1970s, but good when falling oil prices facilitated the disinflation of the 1980s. It is good when the availability of cheap foreign goods helps keep the lid on prices of products made inside the United States, but bad when U.S. workers find their employers unable to afford pay increases. And it is bad when the falling dollar boosts the prices of imports as well as domestic goods competing with imports.

Along with a new analysis of fiscal and monetary policy and of the determinants of inflation, internationalization brings new concerns about American efficiency and competitiveness. Why was the trade deficit still above 1 percent of GDP in 1996? Were Americans "hooked" on foreign goods because they were superior in actual or perceived quality or because some products (like VCRs) were not made by U.S. manufacturers?

Throughout this book, we will take an international perspective, evaluating U.S. economic performance not only on its own merits but also in comparison with the economic performance of other leading industrial nations such as Japan, Germany, and the United Kingdom.

SUMMARY

1. The six central macroeconomic concepts are those that most affect everyday lives. They include the unemployment rate, inflation rate, productivity growth, interest rate, government budget deficit, and foreign trade deficit.

2. Macroeconomics differs from microeconomics by focusing on aggregates that are summed up over all the economic activities in the economy. Theory in macroeconomics is a process of simplification that identifies the most important economic relationships.

3. Gross domestic product (GDP) is a measure of the overall size of the economy. While it does not affect everyday life directly, the behavior of GDP helps us to understand the behavior of the six central macroeconomic concepts that do influence everyday life.

4. Neither too much nor too little real GDP is desirable. The best compromise level is called natural real GDP and is consistent with a constant inflation rate. When the economy is operating at its natural level of real GDP, it is also by definition operating at its natural rate of unemployment.

5. In this century, U.S. inflation has fluctuated widely but was worse during wars and between 1965 and 1991. Periods of high unemployment have coincided with those of low real GDP. The Great Depression clearly scored worst on both counts.

6. Macroeconomics studies both short-run business cycles and the sources of long-run economic growth.

7. Each of the six central macroeconomic concepts has exhibited puzzling behavior since the early 1970s. The unemployment rate, inflation rate, interest rate, and both budget and foreign trade deficits have all been unusually high and variable, while productivity growth has slowed down.

8. Of the six central macroeconomic aggregates, three (unemployment rate, inflation rate, and productiv-ity growth) are the main targets of stabilization policy. Stabilization policy may not be effective in improving well-being if both unemployment and inflation are too high, and stabilization policy may operate with a long delay or have effects that are highly uncertain.

9. Macroeconomics is now an international subject. International repercussions influence the way fiscal and monetary policy work and how the inflation process operates. The foreign trade deficit raises new concerns about U.S. competitiveness.

CONCEPTS

macroeconomics
unemployment rate
inflation rate
productivity
interest rate
government budget deficit
foreign trade deficit
aggregate
business cycles
peak
trough
recession
expansion
gross domestic product
actual real GDP
natural real GDP

natural rate of unemployment
economic growth
real GDP gap
nominal interest rate
real interest rate
foreign exchange rate
target variables
policy instruments
monetary policy
fiscal policy
stabilization policy
positive economics
normative economics
closed economy
open economy

QUESTIONS

1. Using the quarterly data in Table A-2 (Appendix A), attempt to identify the recession phases of the basic business cycle depicted in Figure 1-1 for the period 1947–96. (Assume that a recession must be two or more consecutive quarters of decline in real GDP.)

2. How are the natural real GDP and the natural real unemployment rates related to the rate of inflation?

3. Between January and December 1994, U.S. unemployment fell from 6.7 percent to 5.4 percent of the labor force. The Federal Reserve, the nation's monetary-policy-making authority, took active measures beginning in February 1994 to raise short-term interest rates. What might have motivated policymakers to raise interest rates and what were they hoping to accomplish?

4. What are the main concerns of short-run and long-run macroeconomics?

5. The inflation performance of the U.S. economy in the 1980s was, in part, attributable to the fact that America's trade balance dropped into persistent deficit. Explain.

6. Some individuals benefit from inflation while others suffer. Is the same true with respect to the rising foreign trade deficit and an overvalued dollar on the foreign exchange market? Who gains? Who loses?

7. Which of the following statements are the subject of positive economics? Which are the subject of normative economics?
   (a) A decrease in the interest rate causes an increase in GDP.
   (b) The foreign trade deficit should be decreased.
   (c) The United States should increase its economic growth rate.
   (d) The growth rate in Japan is higher than in the United States because the Japanese save a larger percentage of their income.
   (e) The current natural rate of unemployment is too high.

8. Why might two economists share a common economic theory but disagree on policy recommendations?

9. Is the foreign trade deficit a target variable? Why or why not?

10. Is real GDP a target variable? Why or why not?

11. How does the performance of the U.S. economy compare and contrast with Japan and Europe since 1960?

SELF-TEST ANSWERS

p. 10 There is no such thing as a natural rate of inflation. At the natural rate of unemployment, when the economy is producing the natural level of real GDP, we know only that the inflation rate is constant, *but not what that inflation rate will be*. This depends on the history of inflation, and on how long and how far unemployment has differed from the natural rate of unemployment. (Notice in the bottom frame of Figure 1-2 that there are no numbers for the inflation rate on the vertical axis.)

p. 15 (1) short-run, (2) long-run, (3) short-run, (4) both (the money can create jobs during a recession but also will stimulate long-run productivity growth).

p. 23 Stabilization policy cannot set the unemployment rate to zero or any other rate below the natural rate of unemployment without causing accelerating inflation. Stabilization policy can set the inflation rate to zero only at the cost of a recession and a substantial cost in terms of lost output. The two big problems are lags and uncertainty. A policy change may affect aggregate demand only after a long and uncertain delay, and the impact of different policy changes may also be highly uncertain.

The Measurement of Income, Prices, and Unemployment

It has been said that figures rule the world; maybe. I am quite sure that it is figures which show us whether it is being ruled well or badly.
—*Johann Wolfgang Goethe, 1830*

Our first task is to develop a simple theoretical model to explain real output (gross domestic product, or GDP) and the price level. Before we can turn to theory in Chapter 3, however, we must stop in Chapter 2 for a few definitions. What are GDP and the price level? How are they measured? What goods and services are included in or excluded from GDP? How are private saving, private investment, the government deficit, and the foreign trade deficit related to one another? How are the inflation rate and unemployment rate measured?

2-1 Why We Care About Income

In Chapter 1 we identified two key links between real GDP and the six central concepts of macroeconomics. First, in Figure 1-4 we noted that movements in the unemployment rate (the first central concept) are closely related to the parallel movements of the gap between actual and natural real GDP. Thus the key to understanding changes in unemployment is the change in <u>actual real</u> GDP, which is the same thing as <u>total real *product*</u> and <u>total real *income*</u>.

+tl. real income = +tl. real prod̶u̶c̶t̶ = ̶t̶o̶t̶a̶l̶ ̶p̶r̶o̶d̶ actual real GDP

Second, the level and growth rate of our standard of living are measured by productivity (the third central concept), defined as the ratio of output to the number of hours worked. Output is the same as real GDP. Thus any discussion of U.S. productivity performance in comparison with the country's history or with other nations requires an understanding of the data on real GDP.

This chapter begins by asking what is included in GDP and why. We then learn about the different sectors of the economy and the expenditures that those sectors make to purchase portions of the total GDP and how that GDP is divided up into different types of income. We see that understanding changes in the price level requires an understanding of the distinction between nominal and real GDP, and we learn how the price level and rate of inflation are measured. Finally, we learn how the unemployment rate is measured and how the unemployment rate is related to real GDP.

2-2 The Circular Flow of Income and Expenditure

Let us begin with a very simple economy, consisting of households and business firms. We will assume that households spend their entire income, saving nothing, and that there is no government.[1] Figure 2-1 depicts the operation of our simple economy, with households represented by the box on the left and business firms by the box on the right. There are two kinds of transactions between the households and the firms.

First, the firms sell goods and services (product)—for instance, bread and shoes—to the households represented in Figure 2-1 by the lower dashed line, labeled product. The bread and shoes are not a gift, but are paid for by a flow of money *(C)*, say $1,000,000 per year, represented by the solid line, labeled **consumption expenditures.**

Consumption expenditures are purchases of goods and services by households for their own use.

Second, households must work to earn the income to pay for the consumption goods. They work for the firms, selling their skills as represented by the upper dashed line, labeled labor services. Household members are willing to work only if they receive a flow of money, usually called wages, from the firms for each hour of work. Wages are the main component of income *(Y)*, shown by the upper solid line.

Since households are assumed to consume all of their income, and since firms are assumed to pay out all of their sales in the form of income to households, it follows that income *(Y)* and consumption expenditures *(C)* are equal. For the same reason, the labor services provided in return for income are equal to the goods and services (product) sold by the firms to households in return for the money flow of consumption expenditures:

$$\text{income } (Y) = \text{labor services}$$
$$= \text{consumption expenditures } (C) \tag{2.1}$$
$$= \text{product}$$

Figure 2-1
The Circular Flow of Income and Consumption Expenditures

Circular flow of income and expenditure in a simple imaginary economy in which households consume their entire income. There are no taxes, no government spending, no saving, no investment, and no foreign sector.

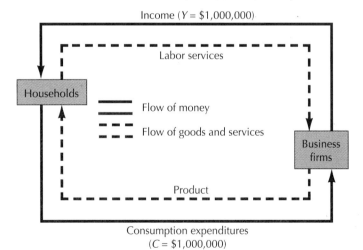

A SIMPLE IMAGINARY ECONOMY

---

[1]Because households do no saving, there is no capital or wealth, and all household income is in the form of wages for labor services.

SELF-TEST

Imagine that a student purchases a haircut, priced at $10, with a $10 bill. Describe in words how the student's haircut will be included in each of the four flows of Figure 2-1.

A **flow magnitude** is an economic magnitude that moves from one economic unit to another at a specified rate per unit of time.

Each of the four elements in equation (2.1) is a **flow magnitude**—any money payment or physical good or service that flows from one economic unit to another. A flow of expenditure, just like a flow of water through a pipe, can be measured only if we first specify the length of time over which the flow is measured. Thus U.S. GDP (= income = expenditure = factor services) in 1996 was more than $7500 billion *per year.* Most flow magnitudes in the United States are measured at annual rates. If the flow of GDP in a quarter-year is $1875 billion, this amounts to $7500 billion at an annual rate.

$$GDP = income = expenditure = factor \ svcs$$

A **stock** is an economic magnitude in the possession of a given economic unit at a particular point in time.

A flow is distinguished from a **stock,** which is the economic magnitude of a single unit at a particular moment of time. A stock of money or savings accounts or business equipment or government debt can be measured by adding up its value at a given point in time—for instance, midnight on December 31, 1997. Measuring a stock is like taking a flash snapshot. It requires specifying a particular date, not a time interval.

2-3 What Transactions Should Be Included in Income and Expenditure?

National Income and Product Accounts is the official U.S. government economic accounting system that keeps track of GDP and its subcomponents.

The **National Income and Product Accounts** (also called NIPA, or national accounts, for short) is the official U.S. government accounting of all the millions of flows of income and expenditure in the United States. The basic ideas and methods used in the NIPA were originally developed in the 1930s by economists working at the National Bureau of Economic Research, including Simon Kuznets (one of the first winners of the Nobel Prize in economics). During World War II, the U.S. Department of Commerce took over the task of computing the NIPA, and it has gradually refined and updated the procedures.[2] Historical data for GDP and other macro concepts are listed in Appendix A for the United States and in Appendix B for other major nations. A guide to government data sources is provided in the box on pp. 34–35.

Defining GDP

Final product includes all currently produced goods and services that are sold through the market but are not resold.

In our free-market economy, the fact that a good or service is sold is usually a sign that it satisfies certain human wants and needs; otherwise people would not be willing to pay a price for it. So by including in the GDP only things that are sold through the market for a price, we can be fairly sure that most of the components of GDP do contribute to human satisfaction. There are three major requirements in the rule for including items in the total **final product,** or GDP:

---

[2]A general introduction is provided in Allan H. Young and Helen Stone Tice, "An Introduction to National Income Accounting," *Survey of Current Business,* March 1985. Suggested additional readings are provided in *Survey of Current Business,* January 1997, pp. D71–72 and inside back cover. The most recent data and information are available on the BEA Web site at http://bea.doc.gov.

> *Final product consists of all currently produced goods and services that are sold through the market but not resold during the current time period.*

1. **Currently produced.** The first part of the rule—*to be included in final product, a good must be currently produced*—obviously excludes sales of any used items such as houses and cars, since they are not currently produced. It also excludes any transaction in which money is transferred without any accompanying good or service in return. Among the **transfer payments** excluded from national income in the United States are gifts from one person to another and "gifts" from the government to persons, such as Social Security and unemployment and welfare benefits. Also excluded are capital gains accruing to persons as the prices of their assets increase.

Transfer payments are those made for which no goods or services are produced in return.

2. **Sold on the market.** The second part of the rule—*goods included in the final product must be sold on the market and are valued at market prices*—means that we measure the value of final product by the market prices that people are willing to pay for goods and services. We assume that a Cadillac gives 10,000 times as much satisfaction as a package of razor blades for the simple reason that it costs about 10,000 times as much. Excluded from GDP by this criterion is the value of personal time spent engaged in activities that are not sold on the market (time spent commuting, baking a cake, and so on). Also excluded is any allowance for the costs of air pollution, water pollution, acid rain, or other by-products of the production process for which no explicit charge is made. — externalities

3. **But not resold.** The third part of the rule—*to be included in final product, a good must not be resold in the current time period*—further limits the acceptability of items. The many different goods and services produced in the economy are used in two different ways. Some goods, like wheat, are mainly used as ingredients in the making of other goods, in this case, bread. Any good resold by its purchaser, rather than used as is, goes by the name **intermediate good.**

A **final good** is part of final product, whereas an **intermediate good** is resold by its purchaser either in its present form or in an altered form.

The opposite of an intermediate good is a **final good,** one that is not resold. Bread sold at the grocery is a final good, used by consumers, as are shoes, clothes, haircuts, and everything else the consumer buys directly. Only final goods are included in final product; intermediate goods are not.

Why Intermediate Goods Are Excluded from GDP

Why can't we just add up all transactions in the economy and call that total GDP? Why must we take the trouble to exclude intermediate goods? The answer is simple: many sales transactions amount to much more than the income created by the seller. To include all of these transactions in GDP would double-count materials created at an early stage of production and resold in later stages.

Look at Figure 2-2, which shows how the $1.00 that a consumer spends for a loaf of bread is divided among the four firms that produce the bread. The bars on the left side of the diagram show the receipts of each of the firms involved in making and selling the bread, and those on the right side show the income of the firms' workers, managers, and stockholders *after* the purchase

FINAL PRODUCT EQUALS TOTAL INCOME CREATED

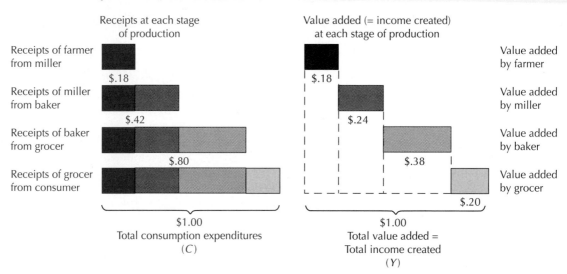

Figure 2-2   **The Contribution of One Loaf of Bread to Consumption Expenditures and Income Created**

The bar graph on the left shows the amount that each firm—farmer, miller, baker, and grocer—receives in the process of producing one loaf of bread. These total receipts are used for two purposes. First, part of the receipts of each firm are used to pay for the intermediate goods purchased from the firm listed directly above (for instance, the miller pays $.18 to the farmer for the wheat). Second, what is left over, shown on the right side of the diagram, is the income created or value added (such as wages, salaries, profits; $.24 in the case of the miller).

Value added is the value of the labor and capital services that take place at a particular stage of the production process.

of the intermediate goods. By excluding from final product all goods that are resold (the intermediate goods) and including only the final $1.00 purchase by the consumer who actually uses the bread, we automatically guarantee that final product ($C = \$1.00$) equals total income created or **value added** ($Y = \$1.00$).

The $1.00 paid by the consumer for the bread is an ingredient in the lower loop of consumption expenditures *(C)* in Figure 2-1. The $1.00 of income created is part of the upper loop of income *(Y)* in Figure 2-1. Now we can see why, by definition, the two loops are equal in size.

2-4 Components of Expenditure

Types of Investment

Private investment is the portion of final product that adds to the nation's stock of income-yielding physical assets or that replaces old, worn-out physical assets.

The goods and services produced by business firms, which are not resold as intermediate goods to other firms or consumers during the current period, qualify by our rule as final product. But the business firm does not consume them. Final goods that business firms keep for themselves are called **private investment** or private capital formation. These goods add to the nation's stock of income-yielding assets. Private investment consists of *inventory investment* and *fixed investment*.

Inventory investment includes all changes in the stock of raw materials, parts, and finished goods held by business.

1. **Inventory investment.** Bread purchased by the grocer but not resold to consumers in the current period stays on the shelves, raising the level of the grocer's inventories. Since all the bread that is produced is included in GDP, we must define expenditure so as to include the bread, whether it is sold to consumers and is part of consumption, or whether it remains unsold on the shelf. *By including the change in inventories as part of expenditure, we guarantee that GDP (that is, total product) by definition equals total expenditure.*

SELF-TEST

Imagine that a grocer has 10 loaves of bread at the close of business on December 31, 1996. Valued at the wholesale baker's price of $.80, the value of the grocer's inventory is $8.00. At the close of business on March 31, 1997, the grocer has 15 loaves or $12.00 of bread on the shelves. What is the implication of these numbers for the contribution of the grocer's inventories to GDP in the first quarter of 1997?

Fixed investment includes all final goods purchased by business that are not intended for resale.

2. **Fixed investment.** Fixed investment includes all final goods purchased by business, other than additions to inventory. The main types of fixed investment are <u>structures</u> (factories, office buildings, shopping centers, apartments, houses) and equipment (cash registers, computers, trucks). Newly produced houses and condominiums sold to individuals are also counted as fixed investment—a household is treated in the national accounts as a business firm that owns the house as an asset and rents the house to itself.[3]

Relation of Investment and Saving

Figure 2-1 described a simple imaginary economy in which households consumed their total income. Figure 2-3 introduces investment into that economy. Total expenditures on final product are the same as before, but now they are divided into consumption expenditures by households (C) and business purchases of investment goods (I). Households spend part of their income on purchases of consumption goods and save the rest.

Personal saving is that part of personal income that is neither consumed nor paid out in taxes.

The portion of household income that is not consumed is called **personal saving.** What happens to income that is saved? The funds are channeled to business firms in two basic ways:

1. Households buy bonds and stocks issued by the firms, and the firms then use the money to buy investment goods.

2. Households leave the unused income (savings) in banks and other financial institutions. The banks then lend the money to the firms, which use it to buy investment goods.

---

[3]An individual who owns a house is treated as a split personality in the national accounts: as a business firm *and* as a consuming household. My left side is a businessperson who owns my house and receives imaginary rent payments from my right side, the consumer who lives in my house. The NIPA identifies these imaginary rent payments as "imputed rent on owner-occupied dwellings," which makes rent payments the most important exception to the rule that a good must be sold on the market to be counted in GDP. See Table 2-1, line E.2a.

WHERE TO FIND THE NUMBERS: *A Guide to the Data*

The first place to look for macroeconomic data is the appendixes in the back of this textbook. There you will find annual data covering more than a century (from 1870 on) and quarterly data since 1947 on major macroeconomic concepts. Also included are several important annual data series for Japan, Canada, and the major European nations for the period since 1960.

Time Passes and Revisions Occur: How to Cope

The appendixes are unlikely to satisfy all of your data needs for any of three reasons: (1) you may want to find a data series that does not appear in the appendixes; (2) you may need data for quarters and years not included in the appendixes (which are current through mid-1997); and (3) some of the data in the appendixes may have been revised. Whether you are curious about more recent developments or need to complete a class assignment, you need to know where to look.

You are unlikely to find what you need at the newsstand or college bookstore; instead head to the library. There you can find the following sources of economic data (ask the reference librarian for assistance).

Economic Report of the President (ERP). Published annually in early February, the back half of this paperback book is a wonderful treasure chest of current and comprehensive data. Every number presented is current, to within a few days of publication, and data revisions are incorporated in all the data series presented. The book packs a huge amount of information into a small space, with about 100 full-page tables, each with about 10 columns of data for different series, most covering the entire postwar era.

Economic Indicators. A slim monthly supplement to the *ERP,* this is the place to look for the latest values of many series during the months between the publication dates of the *ERP.*

Survey of Current Business. This monthly publication contains the latest NIPA data and periodic articles on such specific data as metropolitan area income and international balance of payments statistics.

The "Big Three" Agency Publications

Often an economist needs data at a more detailed level than is available in the general sources listed above—for instance, data on the unemployment rate for blacks aged 20–24, or productivity in the electric utility industry, or how much U.S. consumers spend on funerals. For these and many other series, turn to one of the data periodicals published by the specialized government agencies that actually produce the data. The three most important of these agencies are the Bureau of Economic Analysis (BEA, a branch of the Commerce Department), the Bureau of Labor Statistics (BLS, a branch of the Labor Department), and the Federal Reserve Board (usually called by its nickname, the Fed).

National Income Data

All the data on GDP, and related income and product series, are produced by the BEA in an organized system of tables called the National Income and Product Accounts (NIPA). These extend back to 1929 for annual data and to 1947 for quarterly data and are published for the most recent quarters in the white pages of the *Survey of Current Business.* Each year, fig-

(continued)

ures for the last three years are revised and are published in the July issue of the *Survey*.

Immediate access to the latest NIPA data is available through the World Wide Web (http://www.stat-usa.gov/BEN/Services/ebbhome.html) and through telnet (ebb.stat-usa.gov). The subscription rates for the World Wide Web location are $24.95 for three months, or $100 per year; the rate for telnet is $45 per year. Access is free for libraries that have government document sections. Information about the EBB is available at (202) 482-1986.

Other statistical agencies also have Web sites. The BLS site is http://stats.bls.gov. Recent data from the BEA, BLS, and the Federal Reserve can be found on http://www.stat-usa.gov.

Labor Market, Price, and Wage Data

While the BEA mainly reprocesses data originally produced by other agencies, the BLS is a primary producer of data on employment, unemployment, consumer and producer prices, and wage rates. The BLS runs large surveys, contacting thousands of families each month to learn about their employment and unemployment experience and contacting thousands of retail outlets to track price changes. While the BLS data series at the most aggregated level are published in the general data sources listed above,

users needing more detailed figures consult the BLS monthly publications *Monthly Labor Review, Employment and Earnings,* and *Producer Prices and Price Indexes.*

Financial Market Data

The Federal Reserve compiles data on interest rates, the money supply, and other figures describing the banking and financial system. Its major publication is the monthly *Federal Reserve Bulletin.* One of the regional Feds, the Federal Reserve Bank of St. Louis, publishes several monthly and quarterly publications containing data on financial and general economic variables. Numerous economists obtain their numbers, where possible, from the St. Louis Fed publications because these are available by mail without charge.

Overall, the federal government's many statistics-gathering activities cost the taxpayer $1.8 billion per year. And the list above does not even include the grandfather of all statistics agencies, the Bureau of the Census, which conducts the decennial Census of Population and, every five years, economic censuses of business establishments. The Census data form the raw material for much of the BEA's work in creating the national accounts, not to mention much research by economists on both macro and micro topics.

Figure 2-3
Introduction of Saving and Investment to the Circular Flow Diagram

Our simple imaginary economy (Figure 2-1) when households save 20 percent of their income. Business firms' investment accounts for 20 percent of total expenditure. Again, we are assuming that there are no taxes, no government spending, and no foreign sector.

SAVINGS LEAKS OUT OF THE SPENDING STREAM BUT REAPPEARS AS INVESTMENT

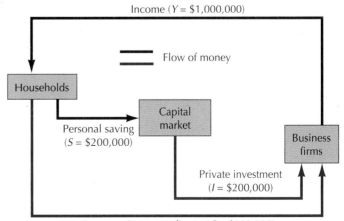

In either case, business firms obtain funds to purchase investment goods. The box labeled "capital market" in Figure 2-3 symbolizes the transfer of personal saving to business firms for the purpose of investment.

In other words, saving is a "leakage" from the income used for consumption expenditures. This leakage from the spending stream must be balanced by an "injection" of nonconsumption spending in the form of private investment.

Net Exports

Exports are goods produced within one country and shipped to another.

Imports are goods consumed within one country but produced in another country.

Net exports and **net foreign investment** are both equal to exports minus imports.

Exports are expenditures for goods and services produced in the United States and sent to other countries. Such expenditure creates income in the United States but is not part of the consumption or investment spending of U.S. residents. **Imports** are expenditures by U.S. residents for goods and services produced elsewhere and thus do *not* create domestic income. For instance, an American-made Chevrolet exported to Canada is part of U.S. production and income but is Canadian consumption. A German-made Mercedes imported to the United States is part of German production and income but is U.S. consumption. If income created from exports is greater than income spent on imported goods, the net effect is a higher level of domestic production and income. Thus the difference between exports and imports, **net exports,** is a component of final product and GDP.

SELF-TEST

> Chapter 1 introduced "foreign trade deficit" as one of the six major macroeconomic concepts. How is the foreign trade deficit related to net exports?

Another name for net exports is **net foreign investment,** which can be given the same economic interpretation as domestic investment. Why? Both domestic and foreign investment are components of domestic production and income creation. Domestic investment creates domestic capital assets; net foreign investment creates U.S. claims on foreigners that yield us future flows of income. An American export to Japan is paid for with Japanese yen, which can be deposited in a Japanese bank account or used to buy part of a Japanese factory.[4] The opposite occurs as well. When the United States imports more than it exports, as it has in every year since 1981, net foreign investment is negative. U.S. payments for imports provide dollars that Japanese investors use to buy American factories, hotels, and other assets.

Gross national product (GNP) is goods and services produced by labor and capital supplied by U.S. residents, whether the actual production takes place within the borders of the United States or in a foreign country.

GNP vs. GDP

Until 1991 the main aggregate in the national income accounts was **gross national product (GNP),** not gross domestic product (GDP). The two terms

---

[4]There is an additional alternative. American exporters may not want a Japanese asset but may want payment in U.S. dollars. They can obtain dollars from a U.S. bank in trade for yen. The increased holdings of yen and other currencies in U.S. banks count as a foreign capital asset, or can be used to pay off U.S. debts, reducing U.S. liabilities to foreigners.

differ only in their geographical coverage. GDP covers goods and services produced within the borders of the United States, whereas GNP covers goods and services produced by labor and capital supplied by U.S. residents, whether the actual production takes place within the borders of the United States or in a foreign country. To convert GDP into GNP, we must add in elements, such as the income of American residents earned abroad and dividends that McDonald's receives from sales of its hamburgers in London and Tokyo, and then subtract income that we pay to foreigners, like profits earned by Honda on its auto plant in Ohio.

Since the additions are slightly smaller than the subtractions, GNP is a bit smaller than GDP. For example, GNP was 0.1 percent smaller than GDP in 1996. In recent years GNP has grown slightly more slowly than GDP, since negative net foreign investment means that foreign income from American production has been growing faster than American income earned on foreign production.

The Government Sector

Up to this point we have been examining an economy consisting only of private households and business firms. Now we consider the government, which collects taxes from the private sector and makes two kinds of expenditures. Government purchases of goods and services (tanks, fighter planes, schoolbooks) generate production and create income. The government can also make payments directly to households. Social Security, unemployment compensation, and welfare benefits are examples of these transfer payments, given the name *transfer* because they are "gifts" from the government to the recipient without any obligation for the recipient to provide any services in return. As you learned in Section 2-3, transfer payments are not included in GDP.

Figure 2-4 adds the government (federal, state, and local) to our imaginary economy of Figures 2-1 and 2-3. A flow of tax revenue *(R)* passes from the households to the government.[5] The government buys goods and services *(G)*. In addition the government sends transfer payments *(F)*, such as welfare payments, to households, leaving a deficit that must be financed. To do this, the government sells bonds to private households through the capital market, just as business firms sell bonds and stock to households to finance their investment projects.

Also shown in Figure 2-4, in the bottom right corner, is the foreign sector. Imports are already included in consumption and investment spending, so imports are shown as a leakage by the black arrow pointing down toward the foreign sector box. Exports are spending on domestic production, as shown by the red arrow going from the foreign sector to the business firms. To keep the diagram simple, exports equal imports.[6]

---

[5]In the real world both households and business firms pay taxes. Here we keep things simple by limiting tax payments to personal income taxes.

[6]If imports exceed exports, there is a flow equal to the difference going from the foreign sector box to the capital market box. This is the inflow of foreign capital available to finance private investment or the government deficit.

Figure 2-4

Introduction of Taxation, Government Spending, and the Foreign Sector to the Circular Flow Diagram

Our simple imaginary economy with the addition of a government collecting $100,000 in tax revenue, paying households $100,000 in transfer payments, and purchasing $100,000 of goods and services. Its total expenditures ($200,000) exceed its tax revenues ($100,000), leaving a $100,000 deficit that is financed by selling government bonds to the households.

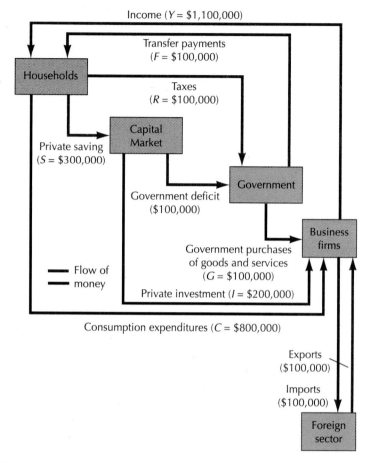

THE GOVERNMENT SURPLUS OR DEFICIT BALANCES
THE REQUIREMENTS OF THE CAPITAL MARKET
AND THE GOVERNMENT SECTOR

The Circular Flow in Equations

The circular flow depicted in Figure 2-4 helps us visualize the main components of the national income accounts. The relations among these components can also be summarized in some simple equations, which help us to see how the government finances a budget deficit.

Total income created (Y) is equal to total expenditure on final product (E), the sum of all the spending arrows pointing toward the Business Firms box in Figure 2-4.[7]

$$Y \equiv E$$

There are four types of expenditure on final product: consumption expenditures (C); private domestic investment (I); government purchases of goods and services (G); and net exports (NX).

---

[7]A three-bar equality sign ($\equiv$) is an "identity" and means that the relationship is true by definition.

expenditures $$E \equiv C + I + G + NX \tag{2.1}$$

The total <u>personal income</u> that households receive consists of the income created from production (Y) and transfer payments from the government (F). This total $(Y + F)$ is available for the purchase of consumption goods (C), saving (S), and the payment of taxes (R):

$$Y + F \equiv C + S + R$$

An equivalent expression is obtained if we subtract F from both sides:

$$Y \equiv C + S + R - F \tag{2.2}$$

Transfer payments (F) can be treated as negative taxes. Thus there is no reason to distinguish tax revenues from transfers. Instead, we define net tax revenue (T) as taxes (R) minus transfers (F), converting equation (2.2) into the simpler expression:

$$Y \equiv C + S + T \tag{2.3}$$

net taxes
taxes – tnsfr payts

Leakages, Injections, and the Government Budget Deficit

Since $Y \equiv E$, the right side of equation (2.3) is equal to the right side of equation (2.1), and we obtain:

$$
\begin{array}{rl}
C + S + T \equiv & C + I + G + NX \\
-C & -C \\
\hline
S + T \equiv & I + G + NX
\end{array}
\quad \text{(subtracting } C \text{ from both sides)} \tag{2.4}
$$

The bottom line of (2.4) can be translated to a general rule:

> *Since income is equal to expenditure, the portion of income not consumed (saving plus net taxes) must be equal to the nonconsumption portion of expenditure on final product (investment plus government spending plus net exports).*

Leakages describe the portion of total income that flows to taxes or saving rather than into purchases of consumer goods.

In other words, **leakages** out of the income available for consumption goods $(S + T)$ must be exactly balanced by **injections** of nonconsumption spending $(I + G + NX)$.

This rule helps explain how the economy finances the **government budget deficit.** Rearranging equation (2.4), we have:

3 ways to finance it

$$G - T \equiv S - (I + NX) \tag{2.5}$$

govt budget deficit

Injections is a term for nonconsumption expenditures.

On the left side of this important definition is the government budget deficit. Shown on the right side, and available to finance the government budget deficit, is the excess of private saving (S) over total investment, both domestic (I) and foreign (NX). The definition indicates that there are only three ways for an economy to finance a government budget deficit. First, private saving can go up. Second, domestic private investment can go down— later we will call this the crowding-out effect of government deficits. Third, foreign investment can go down, and if foreign investment drops far enough and becomes negative, we call it foreign borrowing.

The government budget deficit is the excess of government spending on goods and services over net tax revenue.

how would these finance them?

After 1979 the United States ran persistent, year-after-year government budget deficits, but it did not finance them through higher saving. During most of the 1980s it financed them through foreign borrowing (the same thing as a trade deficit, designated by a negative value of *NX* in equation [2.5]). The box on pp. 44–45 compares U.S. budget deficits and their financing to those in Japan and Europe.

how would that really finance a gov't deficit?

2-5 A Summary of Types of Spending

Table 2-1 summarizes the NIPA treatment of expenditures. In section A of the table total expenditure on final goods and services (GDP) is split into four basic components: private consumption, private investment, government spending, and net exports. Private consumption and investment exclude purchases of intermediate goods, which are listed separately on line C.

The treatment of government spending is different. All government purchases of goods and services, whether intermediate or final, and whether consumption or investment, are included in the GDP and are on line A.3.

Which items are excluded from GDP, and why? These items are shown at the bottom of Table 2-1, in sections B through E. Recall that GDP includes *currently produced* goods and services, thus ruling out items that do not represent current production. These include government interest and transfer payments (line B), because the recipient does not have to provide a good or service in return. Also excluded on line D are purchases of used assets (houses, cars), since they do not involve current production (except for sales commissions).

Intermediate goods on line C are excluded, as we learned previously, to avoid double-counting. Finally, the goods and services included in GDP must be *sold on the market*. This rules out a number of nonmarket activities listed in section E. The single largest excluded item is the value of leisure time—that is, the value people place on the time spent in all activities other than work. We know that people value their leisure time because many could obtain additional part-time jobs but willingly give up the extra wages to avoid working extra hours. An additional nonmarket item excluded is the value people receive from their consumer durables (in contrast to the value of housing services, which are included as explained in footnote 3 of this chapter). Costs of air and water pollution (illness, dirty clothes) are excluded, because they are not charged for on the market. Illegal activities are excluded, even though there is a market for illegal drugs and other activities, because of obvious difficulties in obtaining data.

2-6 How Much Income Flows from Business Firms to Households?

Income, Leakages, and the Circular Flow

An important lesson of circular flow diagrams like Figure 2-4 (see p. 38) is that the expenditures on GDP (consumption, investment, government spending, and net exports) create income, and this income is available to be spent on another round of expenditure. Households receive only part of the GDP

Table 2-1   **Items Included in and Excluded from GDP**

Type of expenditure	Included in GDP?	1996 spending, $ billions	Examples
A. Final goods and services (GDP)	Yes	7580.4	
1. Consumption	Yes	5152.3	
a. Durable goods	Yes	632.2	Autos, TV sets
b. Nondurable goods	Yes	1545.1	Food, clothes, shoes
c. Services	Yes	2974.7	Haircuts, airline trips
2. Private investment (*I*)	Yes	1119.8	
a. Change in business inventories	Yes	19.3	Raw materials, unsold goods
b. Producers' durable equipment	Yes	584.1	Computers, tractors
c. Structures	Yes	516.4	
i. Nonresidential	Yes	213.7	Factories, office buildings, shopping centers
ii. Residential	Yes	302.7	Houses, condominiums
3. Government purchases of goods and services (*G*)	Yes	1407.9	
a. Consumption	Yes	1174.8	Fire fighters, police officers, city parks, street cleaners
b. Investment	Yes	233.1	Airports, university dormitories, hospitals
4. Net exports (exports minus imports, *NX*)	Yes	−99.6	*Exports:* tractors, computers *Imports:* coffee, bananas, wine
B. Government interest and transfer payments	No	1080.1	Social security, welfare, unemployment benefits
C. Private intermediate goods	No	—	Wheat, iron ore
D. Private purchases of used assets	No	—	Purchases of used houses, used cars
E. Nonmarket activities			
1. Value of leisure time	No	—	Watching television, playing tennis
2. Services from existing durables			
a. Housing	Yes	—	Estimated value of services from housing stock, included above on line A.1.c.
b. Other durables	No	—	Value of use of auto, dishwasher
3. Cost of pollution	No	—	Costs of smog, water pollution
4. Illegal activities	No	—	Earnings from theft, drugs, illegal betting

Source: Bureau of Economic Analysis Web site, http://bea.doc.gov, February 1997.

generated by business firms; the rest leaks out of the circular flow in the form of tax revenue for government and saving that provides funds to the capital market. Recall from equation (2.4) that total leakages (taxes and saving) must by definition equal total nonconsumption spending, also called *injections*.

Table 2-2 provides a concise summary of the steps by which income travels from business firms to households. Down the left-hand side are the various concepts of total income; these differ depending on which tax and saving leakages are included. The three remaining columns identify the major types of saving and tax leakages, as well as transfer payments (which work like taxes in reverse).

Table 2-2   **Households Get What Remains After All the Leakages**

Concept	Leakage into saving	Leakage into taxes	Transfers from government
1. Gross domestic product (7576.1)			
2. Less:	→ Depreciation (consumption of fixed capital, 858.3)		
3. Equals: Net domestic product (6717.8)			
4. Less:		→ Indirect business taxes (600.4)	
5. Equals: Domestic income (6117.4)			
6. Less:	→ Undistributed profits (162.6)	→ Social Security and corporate taxes (922.7)	
7. Plus:			Transfer payments and interest (1420.2)
8. Equals: Personal income (6452.3)			
9. Less:		→ Personal income taxes (863.8)	
10. Equals: Personal disposable income (5588.5) Divided among:			
11. Personal consumption expenditure (5151.4)	→ Personal saving (274.4)		
12. Interest payments (162.7)			

Note: 1996 amounts in $ billions are shown in parentheses. Several minor items are included with larger items.

Source: Survey of Current Business, April 1997.

Line 1 starts with GDP, the total amount of income created by domestic production. The first leakage, on line 2, is for **depreciation,** sometimes called consumption of fixed capital, which is the amount that business firms must set aside to replace structures and equipment that wear out or become obsolete (like old jet aircraft that still work but use too much fuel or make too much noise). Since depreciation deductions are not counted as corporate profits, such deductions do not count as income. What remains after depreciation deductions appears on line 3, and is called **net domestic product (NDP).** This represents how much we produce each year after setting aside enough to replace worn-out and obsolete capital.

*The terms **gross** and **net** in economics usually refer to the inclusion or exclusion of depreciation. Thus the difference between "gross investment" and "net investment," or between "gross saving" and "net saving," is exactly the same type of distinction as that between GDP and NDP.*

Next, line 4 in Table 2-2 deducts indirect business taxes, which include state and local sales and property taxes. These tax payments are not available as income to households or business firms. Only what is left over, called **domestic income** (line 5), is available to provide net income to the domestic factors of production (labor and capital) that produce current output.

By far the most important portion of domestic income is compensation paid to employees (which includes wages, salaries, and fringe benefits). Next in order of importance are net interest income, proprietors' income (from small businesses like farms and shops), corporate profits, and rental income.

From Domestic Income to Personal Income

Not all of domestic income is paid out to households as personal income, and personal income also includes some receipts by households that are not counted in GDP or domestic income. Lines 6 and 7 in Table 2-2 explain these differences. First, part of domestic income is kept by corporations in the form of undistributed profits—that is, the part of corporate profits that are not paid as dividends to stockholders or corporate taxes to the government. Undistributed profits are a type of saving leakage, providing funding for the capital market to finance investment spending.

Next, large amounts flow to the government in the form of corporate and Social Security tax payments, then back from the government to households in the form of transfer payments like Social Security and unemployment benefits. Government funds also are paid out for interest on the national debt. Adjusting domestic income for government deductions and additions yields **personal income,** the sum of income payments to households (line 8). Personal income represents the current flow of purchasing power to households coming from *both* the productive activities of business firms *and* transfers from the government sector.

All personal income is not available to households to spend, first because they must pay personal income taxes to the government (line 9). What remains is one of the most important concepts in national income accounting, **personal disposable income** (line 10). This is available for households to use in the three ways shown at the bottom of Table 2-2: consumption expenditure, personal interest payments, and personal saving (lines 11 and 12).

Depreciation (consumption of fixed capital) represents the part of the capital stock used up due to obsolescence and physical wear.

Net domestic product is equal to GDP minus depreciation.

In economics **gross** refers to the inclusion of depreciation; **net** refers to the exclusion of depreciation.

Domestic income is the earnings of domestic factors of production, computed as net domestic product, minus indirect business taxes, which are taxes levied on business sales.

Personal income is the income received by households from all sources, including earnings and transfer payments.

Personal disposable income is personal income minus personal income tax payments.

INTERNATIONAL PERSPECTIVE

Saving,

Investment, and

Government

Deficits Around

the World

We have seen that the government budget deficit in the United States has been persistent since 1979 (this was the fifth of our macro concepts and puzzles in Chapter 1). How has the government financed this deficit? Do other major industrial countries run similar deficits, and how do they finance theirs?

The figure covers the period since 1980. It shows the workings of equation (2.5), which states that the government budget deficit equals private saving minus total investment (domestic and foreign). For the United States, in the top frame, saving (*S,* the black line) has exceeded total investment (*I* + *NX,* the red line) in every year, and the shaded red area between the two lines represents the government budget deficit. In the bottom frame, the European Community was also consistent in running even larger budget deficits throughout this period. Japan went from large deficits to a government budget surplus between 1986 and 1991, followed by deficits during 1992–95.

How were budget deficits financed? In the United States saving (*S*) declined slowly and thus did not help finance the budget deficits at all. Instead, total investment declined. Domestic investment (*I*) and foreign investment (*NX*), while not shown separately in the figure, are listed separately in the table for three periods: 1978–80, before the large budget deficits began; and two more recent periods, 1986–88 and 1994–95.

In the second and third intervals, we see that both private saving and domestic investment declined by the same amount, for reasons not directly related to the budget deficits, so the job of financing the budget deficits was accomplished by foreign borrowing.

For Japan each period is different. In the first, a large budget deficit was financed by an excess of private saving over domestic investment. In the second period the budget was almost balanced, so excess private saving was sent abroad as foreign investment. Finally, in the third period the excess of private saving over private investment was so large that it was sufficient to finance both a large government deficit and substantial foreign investment.

In Europe, the story is simpler. In all three periods there were large government deficits and a small positive amount of foreign investment, both financed by a large excess of private saving over private investment.

The figure and tables reveal several similarities and differences among the three regions. In all three, private saving and private domestic investment declined from one period to the next. Investment in Europe declined from 22.1 percent in the first period to 11.6 percent in the third—a bigger decline than in the United States or in Japan. Finally, the U.S. continues to have the lowest rate of private saving but no longer falls behind Europe in the share of GDP devoted to domestic private investment.

How the Government Budget Deficit Was Financed in the United States, Japan, and Europe, Selected Intervals (all figures are percents of GDP)

		G − T =	S − (I + NX)
U.S.	1978–80	0.6 =	20.7 − (20.3 − 0.2)
	1986–88	3.8 =	16.7 − (16.1 − 3.2)
	1994–95	2.7 =	15.6 − (15.0 − 2.1)
Japan	1978–80	4.9 =	36.5 − (31.7 − 0.1)
	1986–88	−0.4 =	32.6 − (29.4 + 3.5)
	1994–95	2.7 =	31.1 − (25.9 + 2.5)
EC	1978–80	4.2 =	26.6 − (22.1 + 0.3)
	1986–88	3.9 =	20.5 − (16.0 + 0.6)
	1994–95	5.5 =	17.6 − (11.6 + 0.5)

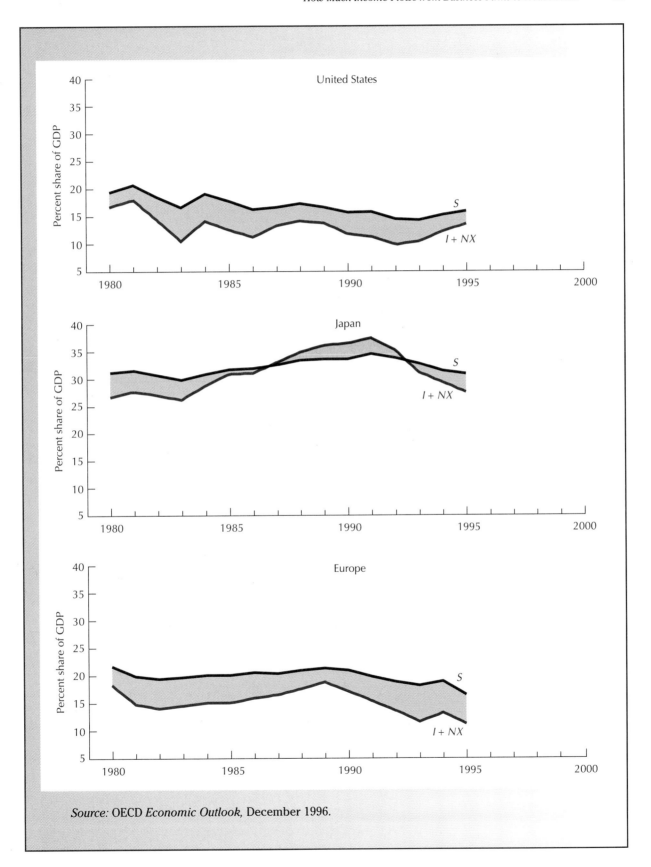

Source: OECD *Economic Outlook,* December 1996.

The total saving and tax leakages (with transfers treated as a negative tax) are symbolized as $S + T$ in equation (2.4) on p. 39, which shows that, by definition, they must be equal to nonconsumption spending (injections), symbolized by $I + G + NX$.

2-7   Nominal GDP, Real GDP, and the GDP Deflator

Thus far all the terms and relationships of national income accounting apply to a particular time period (a quarter or a year) and are measured at the prices actually paid by households and firms. Any economic magnitude measured at the prices actually paid is described by the adjective **nominal.** For instance, **nominal GDP** is the total amount of current product valued at the prices actually paid on the market.

Nominal is an adjective that modifies any economic magnitude measured in current prices.

Nominal GDP is the value of gross domestic product in current (actual) prices.

Real and Nominal Magnitudes

Nominal amounts are not very useful for economic analysis because they can increase either when people buy more physical goods and services—more cars, steaks, and haircuts—or when prices rise. An increase in my nominal spending on consumption goods from $20,000 in 1996 to $25,000 in 1997 might indicate that I became able to buy more items, or it could simply mean that I had to pay more in 1997 for the same items purchased in 1996.

Are we better off if we spend more money? Or have price increases chewed up all our higher spending, leaving us no better off than before? Changes in nominal magnitudes cannot answer these questions; they hide more than they reveal. So economists concentrate on changes in real magnitudes, which eliminate the influence of year-to-year changes in prices and reflect true changes in the number, size, and quality of items purchased.

Real GDP and Real Output

Nominal GDP suffers the defects of any nominal magnitude, since its increases could reflect increases either in real production or in prices. To focus on changes in production and eliminate the influence of changing prices, we need a measure of real gross domestic product, or real GDP. Like any real magnitude, real GDP is expressed in the prices of an arbitrarily chosen base year. The official measures of GDP in the United States currently use 1992 as the base year. Real GDP for every year, whether 1929 or 1997, is measured by taking the production of that particular year expressed at the constant prices of 1992.

For instance, 1997 real GDP measured in 1992 prices represents the amount that the actual 1997 production of goods and services would have cost if each item *had been sold at its 1992 price.* Similarly, 1929 real GDP measured in 1992 prices represents the amount that the actual 1929 production of goods and services would have cost if each item had been sold at its 1992 price.

Since prices usually increase each year, nominal GDP is higher than real GDP for years after 1992. Similarly, nominal GDP is lower than real GDP for years before 1992. You can see this regular pattern in Figure 2-5, which displays nominal and real GDP for each year since 1900. Only in 1992 are nominal and real GDP the same.

NOMINAL GDP ALWAYS GROWS FASTER THAN REAL GDP WHEN PRICES RISE

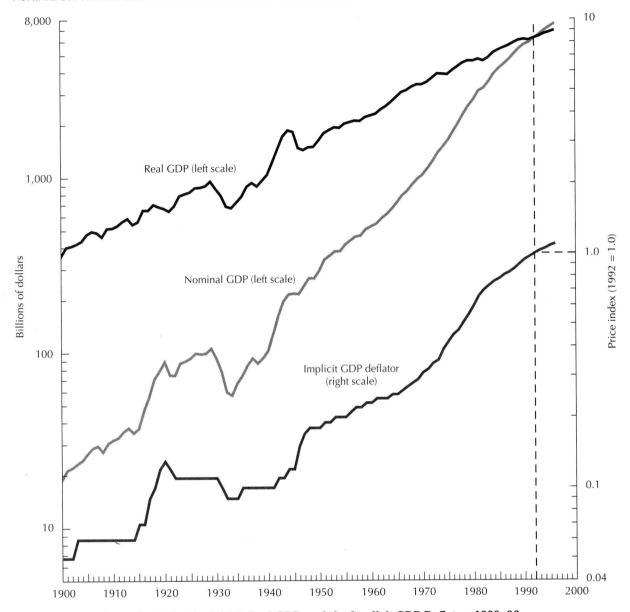

Figure 2-5   **Nominal GDP, Real GDP, and the Implicit GDP Deflator, 1900–96**
Notice how the nominal GDP line lies below the real GDP line before 1992 but lies above the real GDP line after 1992. This reflects the fact that before 1992 the current prices used to measure nominal GDP were lower than the 1992 prices used to measure real GDP. After 1992, the current prices used to measure nominal GDP were higher than the 1992 prices used to measure real GDP. Notice how the nominal GDP line crosses the real GDP line in 1992, the same year that the GDP deflator attains the value of 1.00.

Later on we will consider other real magnitudes, such as real consumption and the real money supply. An alternative label for real magnitudes is constant-dollar; in contrast, nominal magnitudes are usually called current-dollar. In other words:

Current vs constant dollar
aka nominal vs real

	Alternative labels for magnitudes		
Items measured in prices of a single year	Constant-dollar	or	Real
Items measured in actual prices paid in each separate year	Current-dollar	or	Nominal

SELF-TEST

Without looking at Figure 2-5, you should now be able to answer the following: Is the implicit GDP deflator greater or less than 1.00 in every year before 1992? In every year after 1992? In what year is the implicit GDP deflator equal to exactly 1.000?

2-8 How Nominal GDP Is Split Between Inflation and Changes in Real GDP

For most problems in economic analysis, we are interested in comparing measurements of income and expenditures for different time periods. Hence we must measure these magnitudes in *real terms*—that is, in terms adjusted for the effects of price changes. How do the national income accountants take the recorded nominal income and expenditure of two separate years in which prices were different (say, 1987 and 1997) and compute real GDP adjusted for all effects of price changes?

Real GDP cannot be observed directly. No one can see, feel, or touch it. There's an old saying that "you can't add apples and oranges." Real GDP carries that saying to its limit, since real GDP consists not just of apples and oranges, but also computers, electricity, haircuts, restaurant meals, and thousands of other goods and services that can't be added directly. The only way to combine the different products is to place a value on each component of GDP, and that requires using the prices of the goods and services produced. However, since prices are constantly changing, our measure of real GDP and its changes will depend on which time period we choose to take the prices for this essential valuation of the components of GDP.[8]

How We Calculate Changes in Real GDP

Table 2-3 shows how the change in real GDP between year 1 and year 2 differs, depending on the prices that are used. Lines 1 and 2 show the hypothetical prices and quantities of oranges and apples used in this imaginary two-good economy. Notice that the price of oranges doubles between year 1 and year 2, while the price of apples goes up only 25 percent (from $0.20 to $0.25). As a result, the consumption of oranges drops in year 2 while the consumption of apples doubles. As you will see, the change in measured real GDP between years 1 and 2 depends on the importance we assign to the big decline in orange consumption and the big increase in apple consumption.

---

[8]The explanation in this section and portions of the numerical example are adapted from "Note on Calculating Output and Price Indexes," *Survey of Current Business*, July 1995, pp. 32–33.

Table 2-3   **Calculation of Fixed-Weight and Chain-Weighted Real GDP and GDP Deflators in an Imaginary Economy Producing Only Oranges and Apples**

	Year 1	Year 2
1. Prices		
a. Oranges	$0.10	$0.20
b. Apples	0.20	0.25
2. Quantities		
a. Oranges	30	20
b. Apples	10	20
3. Current-dollar expenditures		
a. Oranges (1.a times 2.a)	$3.00	$4.00
b. Apples (1.b times 2.b)	2.00	5.00
c. Total: Nominal GDP	5.00	9.00
4. Constant-dollar expenditures each year		
a. At fixed year 1 prices	$5.00	$6.00
b. At fixed year 2 prices	8.50	9.00
5. Expenditures each year		
a. At fixed year 1 quantities	$5.00	$8.50
b. At fixed year 2 quantities	6.00	9.00
6. Real GDP (index, year 1 = 1.00)		
a. At fixed year 1 prices	1.00	1.20
b. At fixed year 2 prices	1.00	1.06
c. Chain-weighted (geometric mean, 5.a and 5.b)	1.00	1.13
7. GDP Deflator (index, year 1 = 1.00)		
a. At fixed year 1 quantities	1.00	1.70
b. At fixed year 2 quantities	1.00	1.50
c. Chain-weighted (geometric mean, 6.a and 6.b)	1.00	1.60
8. Additional indexes, year 1 = 1.00		
a. Nominal GDP (3.c)	1.00	1.80
b. Implicit GDP deflator (8.a/6.c)	1.00	1.59

Sources, by line, for Table 2-3:
   4.a. Year 1 same as 3c. Year 2 ($.10 \times 20 + .20 \times 20 = 6.00$)
   4.b. Year 2 same as 3c. Year 1 ($.20 \times 30 + .25 \times 10 = 8.50$)
   5.a. Year 1 same as 3c. Year 2 ($.20 \times 30 + .25 \times 10 = 8.50$)
   5.b. Year 2 same as 3c. Year 1 ($.10 \times 20 + .20 \times 20 = 6.00$)
   6.a. Year 2 divided by year 1 from line 4a, $6.00/5.00 = 1.20$
   6.b. Year 2 divided by year 1 from line 4b, $9.00/8.50 = 1.06$
   6.c. Year 2 is geometric mean of year 2 from the two lines above, $\sqrt{1.20 \times 1.06}$
   7.a. Year 2 from line 5a, $8.50/5.00 = 1.70$
   7.b. Year 2 from line 5b, $9.00/6.00 = 1.50$
   7.c. Year 2 is geometric mean of year 2 from the two lines above, $\sqrt{1.70 \times 1.50}$

One approach, which was used until recently to calculate real GDP in the United States, was to hold the value of all products fixed over all years at the prices of a single year. The actual dollars spent on oranges, apples, and total fruit are shown on line 3 of the table. The expenditures, measured in fixed year 1 prices, are shown on line 4.a. This yields an increase in real GDP in year 2 (measured in the constant prices of year 1), of 20 percent, since the ratio of year 2 expenditures to year 1 expenditures ($6.00/$5.00) is 1.20. This gives us line 6.a, showing that real GDP, using year 1 prices, increases from 1.00 in year 1 to 1.20 in year 2.

But we get a different answer if we measure constant-dollar expenditures in each year using fixed year 2 prices. As shown on line 4.b, expenditures in year 2 increase from $8.50 to $9.00. This yields an increase in real GDP in year 2 (measured in the constant prices of year 2), of 6 percent, since the ratio of year 2 expenditures to year 1 expenditures ($9.00/$8.50) is 1.059. Why does this second method give us a lower estimate of the increase in real GDP? This occurs because year 2 prices are relatively lower for apples compared to oranges, and using year 2 prices places a lower importance on the big jump in apple consumption.

This example shows a general tendency—that choosing the prices of a later year tends to give us a lower increase in real GDP, since the later year places a lower valuation on the quantities that have increased most rapidly. This is particularly important in recent years in actual calculations of real GDP, since the prices of some goods, such as personal computers, TV sets, and telephone equipment, have been declining rapidly in contrast to continuous increases in the prices of many other goods and services.

The New "Chain-Weighted" Calculation of Real GDP

Which is the correct measure of the increase in real GDP in this example? Is 20 percent correct or is 6 percent? The startling fact is that *there is no single answer to this question,* because the prices of each year are equally valid as alternative ways to value the quantities actually produced. A reasonable compromise is to average the two answers together. To do this, economists have long known that the best type of average is a geometric average, which is obtained by multiplying the two answers together and then taking the square root, that is: $\sqrt{1.20 \times 1.06} = 1.13.$[9]

Chain-weighted real GDP is calculated by valuing changes in quantities by the average of prices charged at the beginning and end of the period of change.

The United States now calculates real GDP using this technique of geometric averaging across hundreds of different types of products. The outcome is called **chain-weighted real GDP,** because the weights move forward from year to year. For instance, the percentage change in real GDP between 1995 and 1996 uses a geometric average of 1995 and 1996 price weights. Then the percentage change in real GDP between 1996 and 1997 shifts to a geometric average of 1996 and 1997 price weights. The resulting percentage changes are chained together into an index of real GDP, moving forward and backward from the base year of 1992. For instance, if the percentage change in real GDP for 1992–93, 1993–94, 1994–95, 1995–96 are, respectively, 4, 2, 3, and 4 percent, the index numbers of real GDP for the five years 1992–96 on a 1992 base will be

1992	1.00
1993	1.04
1994	1.061
1995	1.093
1996	1.136

---

[9]Take a scientific calculator and check the answer for yourself. Multiplying 1.20 by 1.06 and then taking the square root yields an answer of 1.128. An alternative method to arrive at exactly the same answer is to take the natural logarithm of 1.20 and 1.06, which are .1823 and .0583, respectively, add them together (.2406), divide by 2 (.1203), and then take the antilogarithm (e^x) of the answer, yielding 1.128.

The dollar amount of real GDP in 1996 would be the 1992 level of GDP (both nominal and real are the same in 1992) of $6244.4 billion times 1.136, or $7096 billion.

The orange-apple example suggests that measures of real GDP can be quite misleading when prices of a year that does not reflect current expenditure patterns are chosen to value changes in quantities. This was a serious problem in the official U.S. measures of real GDP published prior to 1996. Under the old system, the prices of a single year (1987) were applied not just to the subsequent year (1988) but to *all* years between 1929 and the most recent date. Obviously, using 1987 prices to value changes in quantities between 1929 and 1930 placed very different values on different goods and services than would be the case were the actual prices paid in the years 1929 and 1930 used. Under the new system, the depth of the 1974–75 recession is measured using the prices of 1974 and 1975, not the less relevant prices of 1987. Similarly, fluctuations of real GDP up and down in different episodes are measured using the prices that actually were in effect during those episodes, not the prices of a year like 1987 a decade or two later.

The Implicit Deflator and the Chain-Weighted Deflator

The **implicit GDP deflator** is the economy's aggregate price index and is defined as the ratio of nominal GDP to chain-weighted real GDP.

The method illustrated in line 6.c of Table 2-3 yields the chain-weighted measure of real GDP. There are two different GDP deflators. One, the **implicit GDP deflator,** is simply the ratio of nominal GDP to chain-weighted real GDP.

The implicit deflator tells us the ratio of prices actually charged in any single year (say, 1959) to the prices charged in the base year 1992. For instance, the implicit GDP deflator in 1959 was 0.229, the ratio of actual nominal GDP ($507.2 billion) to spending for the same year measured in 1992 prices was ($2212.3 billion):

$$\frac{\text{implicit GDP}}{\text{deflator for 1959}} = 0.29 = \frac{507.2 \text{ billion}}{2212.3 \text{ billion}} = \frac{\text{nominal GDP}}{\text{real GDP}}$$

In words, this equation states that the implicit GDP deflator in 1959 was 0.229 because 1959 nominal GDP was 22.9 percent of the value of the 1959 real GDP. This percentage in turn reflects the fact that the average level of prices in 1959 was less than one-quarter the level of the base year 1992.

The second type of GDP deflator is calculated directly from the prices and quantities of the goods and services in the economy. Returning to the example of oranges and apples in Table 2-3, we can calculate in line 5.a and 5.b the expenditures in each year using *actual prices* of each year but the *fixed quantities* of either year. Line 5.a shows that expenditures using actual prices but fixed year 1 quantities, increase from $5.00 in year 1 to $8.50 in year 2, an increase of 70 percent. Accordingly, this method yields a price index in year 2 of 1.70, when year 1 is used as a base of 1.00; these indexes are shown separately on line 7.a. Likewise, using year 2 quantities gives us a price index in year 2 of 1.50 (line 7.b).

The **chain-weighted GDP deflator** is calculated by weighting price changes by the average of quantities sold at the beginning and end of the period of change.

Once again, neither answer is correct. The best approximation is to take a geometric average; this results in a price index of 1.60, as shown in line 7.c. This is the method used to construct the **chain-weighted GDP deflator.** Normally, the implicit and chain-weighted deflators give very close to the

DO GOVERNMENT PRICE INDEXES OVERSTATE INFLATION?

In addition to the implicit and chain-weighted GDP deflator (and deflators for all the subcategories of GDP, such as consumption and investment), the government publishes several other price indices. By far the most important is the Consumer Price Index (CPI). The CPI, along with the Producer Price Index, is compiled and published by the Bureau of Labor Statistics.

Differences and Similarities Between the CPI and the Deflators

The CPI, which is published monthly, is based on the prices of several thousand products. Prices paid by consumers are recorded by hundreds of price collectors, who visit thousands of stores and service establishments each month. The thousands of price changes recorded are sorted into 207 groups, the changes for each group are averaged, and then the 207 groups, in turn, are combined into the all-items CPI.

Unlike the GDP deflator, the CPI does not use the chain-weighted method of calculation. Instead, it measures the change in price of a fixed market basket based on actual consumer expenditures in a previous period. From 1986 to 1997, the expenditure weights in the CPI were based on expenditures in 1982–84, so that by 1997 the weights were 14 years out of date. Starting in January 1998, the weights will be based on expenditures in 1993–95.

The GDP deflator and the deflator for consumer expenditures (the PCE deflator) have several similarities to and differences from the CPI. The basic similarity is that the actual price series for most of the GDP product groups (e.g., TV sets or apples) are obtained directly from the CPI, so any flaws in the CPI affect the deflators as well. The main difference is that the deflators are based on up-to-date chain weights, reflecting very recent expenditures, instead of the weights in the CPI, which, at times, have been more than a decade out of date. The second significant difference is that for selected goods and services, most notably personal computers and medical care, the deflators use different price data than the CPI, and most experts regard the data used by the deflators as more accurate. As a result of these differences, the CPI and PCE deflators can give quite different estimates of consumer inflation. In the 12 months ending in December 1996, the CPI rose 3.3 percent while the PCE deflator rose by 2.5 percent, about three-quarters as much.

Sources of Upward Bias in the CPI and in the Deflators

While the two differences indicate that the PCE deflator is a better measure of consumer price inflation than the CPI, the similarity (the PCE deflator uses most of the same basic price data as the CPI) indicates that several flaws in the CPI price data affect the GDP and PCE deflators as well. What are these flaws?

1. **Substitution bias.** When the price of oranges rises relative to apples, as in Table 2-3, the CPI does not allow for changes in consumer expenditure patterns, e.g., rising purchases of apples relative to oranges. Thus the CPI (which would calculate the price index based on year 1 quantities, as in line 7.a) systematically overstates the inflation rate. The deflators use the chain-weighted system correctly for the major categories in the CPI, but the deflators use CPI price averages for narrower groupings of commodities, and thus do not reflect consumer substitution away from goods (like oranges in our example) with rising relative prices. Hence, both the deflators and the CPI overstate inflation by failing to take account of substitution, although the CPI overstates inflation by a greater amount (by failing to use chain weights or geometric averages in either narrow or broad categories).

2. **Outlet bias.** New types of discount stores, such as Wal-Mart, Home Depot, and Best Buy, have gained an increased share of the retail market by offering lower prices than competitors. Consider an example in which a consumer previously bought toothpaste at $2.39 a tube at a small drug store and switches to buying the same toothpaste for $1.59 at Wal-Mart. The CPI does not treat this as a price decline, since the CPI does not count price differences between one outlet and another. This flaw in the CPI affects the deflators as well.

3. **Quality change and new product bias.** Many products continuously improve—TV sets offer

better pictures and sound, computers offer faster speeds and greater memory, many products use less energy and require less frequent repairs than previously. But neither the CPI nor the deflators have adequate methods to take improvements in product quality into account, and as a result inflation is overstated. Similarly, many new products undergo rapid declines in price in the first few years after their introduction, as do, for example, VCRs in the 1980s and cellular phones in the 1990s. Yet new goods are typically introduced into the CPI many years after they have undergone most of these rapid declines in price. This late introduction of new goods adds to the overstatement of inflation in the CPI and the deflators. Finally, the value of inventions—for instance, the ability to watch movies at home with a VCR and thus avoid the cost of baby sitters and the admission price of going to a movie theater—are not taken into account in the CPI.

In 1996 a commission of experts established by the U.S. Senate determined that the CPI overstates inflation by 1.1 percent per year. Since most of the sources of bias described above also apply to the deflators, the PCE deflator probably overstates inflation by about 0.8 percent per year. This overstatement of inflation has two very important consequences. First, many measures of American economic performance are too pessimistic. According to the commission, true inflation is slower than in the government statistics and true growth in real GDP (as well as in productivity and real wages) is faster than in the government statistics. Second, numerous government benefits (such as Social Security payments) increase each year by the rate of inflation as measured by the CPI. If the CPI overstates inflation, then these benefit payments rise too rapidly, thus contributing to the government deficit. The commission estimated that if the overstatement of inflation by the CPI were corrected, after 12 years the national debt would be more than *$1 trillion* lower than if the correction were not made.

Some of the flaws in the government price indexes are relatively easy to fix, but others are much harder to achieve. As this book went to press, government statisticians were making plans to improve the price indexes, and Congress and the administration were trying to determine how to cope with the impact of incorrect price measurement on the government deficit and national debt.

same answer. For instance, in our example the implicit deflator in year 2 is 1.593 (line 8.b), while the chain-weighted deflator is 1.60 (line 7.c). In recent years the implicit deflator in the United States has been rising slightly more slowly than the chain-weighted deflator—for example, the implicit deflator rose at a rate of 1.4 percent in the fourth quarter of 1996 compared to 1.8 percent for the chain-weighted deflator.

2-9 Measuring Unemployment

The unemployment rate is the first of the central macro concepts introduced in Chapter 1. Families dread the financial and emotional disruption caused by layoffs, so news of an increase in the unemployment rate creates public concern and plummeting popularity ratings for incumbent politicians. Because of widespread public awareness, the unemployment rate is generally considered the most important of the central macro concepts (although slow growth in productivity may have a greater impact on the lives of more people in the long run). In this section we learn how the unemployment rate is measured.

The Unemployment Survey

Many people wonder how the government determines facts such as "the teenage unemployment rate in November 1996 was 17.0 percent," because they themselves have never spoken to a government agent about their own experiences of employment, unemployment, and time in school. It would be too costly to contact everyone in the country every month; the government attempts to reach each household to collect information only once each decade when it takes the decennial Census of Population. However, it would not be enough to collect information just once every ten years, because then policymakers would have no guidance for conducting current policy.

As a compromise, each month 1500 Census Bureau workers interview about 60,000 households, or about 1 in every 1400 households in the country. Each month one-fourth of the households in the sample are replaced, so that no family is interviewed more than four months in a row. The laws of statistics imply that an average from a survey of a sample of households of this size comes very close to the true figure that would be revealed by a costly complete census.

Questions asked in the survey.   The interviewer first asks each separate household member, "What were you doing most of last week—working, keeping house, going to school, or something else?" Anyone who has done any work at all for pay during the past week, whether part-time (even one hour per week), full-time, or temporary work, is counted as employed.

For those who say they did no work, the next question is "Did you have a job from which you were temporarily absent or on layoff last week?" If the person is awaiting recall from a layoff or has obtained a new job but is waiting for it to begin, he or she is counted as unemployed.

If the person has neither worked nor been absent from a job, the next question is, "Have you been looking for work in the last four weeks? and if so, What have you been doing in the last four weeks to find work?" A person who has not been ill and has searched for a job by applying to an employer, registering with an employment agency, checking with friends, or other specified job-search activities is counted as unemployed. The remaining people who are neither employed nor unemployed, mainly homemakers who do not seek paid work, students, disabled people, and retired people, fall in the category of "not in the labor force."

The **unemployed** are those without jobs who are either on temporary layoff or have taken specific actions to look for work.

The **total labor force** is the total of the civilian employed, the armed forces, and the unemployed.

Definitions based on the interview.   Despite the intricacy of questions asked by the interviewer, the concept is simple: People with jobs are employed; people who do not have jobs and are looking for jobs are **unemployed;** people who meet neither labor-market test are not in the labor force. The **total labor force** is the total of the civilian employed, the armed forces, and the unemployed. Thus the entire population aged 16 and over falls into one of four categories:

1.   Total labor force
     a. Civilian employed
     b. Armed forces
     c. Unemployed

2. Not in the labor force

The **unemployment rate** is the ratio of the number unemployed to the number in the labor force, expressed as a percentage.

The actual **unemployment rate** is defined as the ratio:

$$U = \frac{\text{number of unemployed}}{\text{civilian employed} + \text{unemployed}}$$

Example: In January 1997 the BLS reported an unemployment rate of 5.4 percent. This was calculated as the ratio:

$$U = \frac{\text{number of unemployed}}{\text{civilian employed} + \text{unemployed}} = \frac{7,268,000}{128,580,000 + 7,268,000}$$

or

$$U = 5.4 \text{ percent}$$

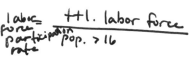

The labor force participation rate is the ratio of the total labor force (civilian employed, armed forces, and the unemployed) to the population aged 16 or over. Those who do not participate in the labor force include those above age 15 who are in school, retired individuals, people who do not work because they are raising children or otherwise choose to stay at home, and those who cannot work because they are ill, disabled, or have given up on finding jobs. In 1996 this rate was 66.6 percent.

Flaws in the definition.   The government's unemployment measure sounds relatively straightforward, but unfortunately it disguises almost as much as it reveals:

1. *The unemployment rate by itself is not a measure of the social distress caused by the loss of a job.* Each person who lacks a job and is looking for one is counted as "1.0 unemployed people," whether the person is the head of a household responsible for feeding numerous dependents or a 16-year-old looking only for a 10-hour-per-week part-time job to provide pocket money. Only a minority of the unemployed can be described as workers who have lost one job and are looking for another.

2. *The government's unemployment concept misses some of the people hurt by a recession.* Some suffer a cut in hours, being forced by their employers to shift from full-time to part-time work. Still counted as employed, these "involuntary part-time" workers never enter the unemployment statistics.

3. *A person lacking a job must have performed particular specified actions to look for a job during the past four weeks.* What about people who have looked and looked and have given up, convinced that no job is available? They are not counted as unemployed at all. They simply disappear from the labor force, entering the category of "not in the labor force." Those out of the labor force who would like to work but have given up on the job search are sometimes called "discouraged workers" or the "disguised unemployed."

Do the flaws matter?   Since the official concept of the unemployment rate omits those who are involuntarily working part time when they would prefer full-time employment, and also omits the discouraged workers, it is generally agreed that the official concept understates the total amount of unemployment. Yet this does not turn out to be very important, since a broader measure of unemployment, which includes the effect of involuntary part-time work as well as the discouraged workers, exhibits cyclical fluctuations similar to those of the official concept of the unemployment rate. Recessions and expansions occur at the same time. The primary impediment to achieving low unemployment, which is the tendency of the economy to generate accelerating inflation when the unemployment rate becomes too low, is completely independent of the particular unemployment measure that is used.

2-10   CASE STUDY: Unemployment and the Output Ratio

We have now concluded our discussion of the measurement of nominal and real GDP, the price level, and the unemployment rate, and can begin to learn how these central macroeconomic variables are determined. However, our focus in the next few chapters will be on the determination of real GDP, and we shall have little to say about the determination of unemployment. Why? Because fluctuations in unemployment are the mirror image of fluctuations in real GDP or, more precisely, the ratio of real GDP (Y) to natural real GDP (Y^N). Once we establish that a particular event, say an increase in government military spending, tends to increase the output ratio (Y/Y^N), we know that the same event tends to decrease the unemployment rate.

The close relationship between the unemployment rate and the output ratio is illustrated in Figure 2-6. There we notice the cluster of prosperous years, 1965–69, in the lower right corner, with values of Y/Y^N well above 100 percent and unusually low unemployment rates. The contrasting situation in the upper left corner occurred in the recession years 1975 and 1982, when massive layoffs caused high unemployment. The negative slope of the black line going through the points in Figure 2-6 just reflects common sense. When sales slump, workers are laid off and the jobless rate rises. But when sales boom and the output ratio is high, some of the jobless are hired and the unemployment rate goes down.

The close negative connection between the unemployment rate (U) and the output ratio was first pointed out in the early 1960s by the late ArthurM. Okun, who was chairman of the Council of Economic Advisers in the Johnson administration. Because this theory has held up so well, the relationship is known as **Okun's law.** U tends to follow the major movements in the output ratio; in addition, the percentage-point change in the unemployment rate tends to be roughly 0.5 times the percentage change in the output ratio, in the opposite direction. For instance, the downward-sloping Okun's law line is drawn so that an output ratio of 100 percent corresponds to an average actual unemployment rate of 6.2 percent. A drop in the output ratio by 5 percentage points, from 100 to 95, would correspond to an increase in the unemployment rate of 2.5 percentage points, as indicated by the Okun's law line going through 8.7 percent unemployment on the vertical axis and 95 percent on the horizontal axis.

Consider, for instance, the following examples in which a change in the output ratio was accompanied by a change in the unemployment rate in the opposite direction of roughly 50 percent:

Okun's law is a regular negative relationship between the output ratio (Y/Y^N) and the gap between the actual unemployment rate and the average rate of unemployment.

A HIGH OUTPUT RATIO GOES WITH LOW UNEMPLOYMENT, AND VICE VERSA

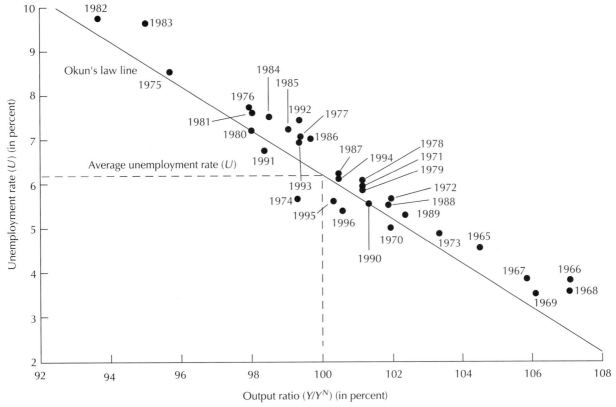

Figure 2-6 **The U.S. Ratio of Actual to Natural Real GDP *(Y/Y^N)* and the Unemployment Rate, 1965–96**

This diagram illustrates that unemployment *(U)* moves inversely with the output ratio *(Y/Y^N).* In prosperous years, such as 1966–69, the observations are in the lower right corner, with a high output ratio and low unemployment. The opposite extreme occurred in 1982, with the observation plotted at the upper left corner. A recession occurred, the output ratio fell, and workers were laid off. The black line expresses the relationship between U and Y/Y^N, sometimes called Okun's law. (*Source:* U.S. Bureau of Labor Statistics.)

Years	U	ΔU	$100(Y/Y^N)$	$100\,\Delta(Y/Y^N)$	$\Delta U/\Delta(Y/Y^N)$
1973	4.85	—	103.3	—	—
1975	8.50	3.65	95.7	−7.7	−47.4
1979	5.85	−2.65	101.2	5.5	−48.0
1982	9.70	3.85	93.7	−7.5	−51.2
1989	5.28	−4.42	102.4	8.7	−50.8
1991	6.72	1.45	98.4	−4.0	−36.5
1996	5.38	−1.35	100.6	2.2	−61.8

The Okun's law relationship shown as the negatively sloped black line in Figure 2-6 can also be written as an equation:

General Linear Form: $$U = \overline{U} - h[100(Y/Y^N) - 100]$$

Numerical Example: $$U = 6.2 - 0.5[100(Y/Y^N) - 100]$$

(2.6)

The general form states that the actual unemployment rate *(U)* equals the average rate of unemployment *($\overline{U}$)* minus the slope coefficient *(h)*, times the difference between the output ratio and 100 percent. (The "100" in front of the Y/Y^N term is necessary to convert the output ratio into a percent.)[10]

SELF-TEST   Use the numerical example in equation (2.6) to compute the unemployment rate for sample output ratios of 95 and 105.

SUMMARY

1. This chapter is concerned with the definition and measurement of national income—what is included and excluded, and why, as well as with the measurement of real GDP, inflation, and the unemployment rate.

2. A flow magnitude is any money payment, physical good, or service that flows from one economic unit to another per unit of time. A flow is distinguished from a stock, which is an economic magnitude in the possession of an individual or firm at a moment of time.

3. Final product (GDP) consists of all currently produced goods and services sold through the market but not resold during the current time period. By counting intermediate goods only once, and by including only final purchases, we avoid double-counting and ensure that the value of final product and total income created (value added) are equal.

4. Leakages out of income available for consumption spending are, by definition, exactly balanced by injections of nonconsumption spending. This equality of leakages and injections is guaranteed by the accounting methods used.

5. In the same way, by definition, total income (consumption plus leakages) equals total expenditure (consumption plus injections). Injections of nonconsumption spending fall into three categories—private domestic investment (on business equipment and structures, residential housing, and inventory accumulation); foreign investment or net exports; and government spending on goods and services. The definitions require private sav-

ing to exceed private investment (domestic and foreign) by the amount of the government deficit.

6. GNP includes all income received by U.S. residents, whereas GDP includes only economic production within the borders of the United States.

7. Net domestic product (NDP) is obtained by deducting depreciation from GDP. Deduction of indirect business taxes from NDP yields domestic income, the sum of all net incomes earned by domestic factors of production in producing current output. If we deduct corporate undistributed profits, corporate income taxes, and Social Security taxes, and add in transfer payments, we arrive at personal income, the sum of all income payments to individuals. Personal disposable income is simply personal income after the deduction of personal income taxes.

8. Chain-weighted GDP is calculated by valuing changes in quantities by the average of prices charged at the beginning and end of the period of the change.

9. The chain-weighted GDP deflator is calculated by weighting price changes by the average of quantities sold between the beginning and end of the period of the change.

10. The implicit GDP deflator is defined as nominal GDP in actual current prices divided by chain-weighted real GDP.

11. Those aged 16 and over are counted as unemployed if they are temporarily laid off or want a job, and take specified actions to find a job. The unemployment

---

[10]Equation (2.6) is a simplified version of Okun's law that corresponds exactly to the negatively sloped black line in Figure 2-6. A more precise version relates the gap between the actual and natural unemployment rates $(U - U^N)$ to the output ratio:

$$U - U^N = -0.5[100(Y/Y^N) - 100]$$

This is the same as equation (2.6) in the text but replaces U by U^N. This version is more precise, because in reality U^N is not equal to the average unemployment rate *(U)*, but instead varies over time (data showing the quarter-to-quarter movements in U^N are provided in Appendix A).

rate is the number of unemployed expressed as a percent of the total number of persons employed and unemployed.

12. The gap between the actual and natural unemployment rates tends to move in the opposite direction from the output ratio, and by about half as much.

CONCEPTS

consumption expenditures
flow magnitude
stock
National Income and Product Accounts
final product
transfer payments
final good
intermediate good
value added
private investment
inventory investment
fixed investment
personal saving
exports
imports
net exports
net foreign investment
gross national product (GNP)
leakages

injections
government budget deficit
depreciation (consumption of fixed capital)
net domestic product
gross
net
domestic income
personal income
personal disposable income
nominal
nominal GDP
chain-weighted real GDP
implicit GDP deflator
chain-weighted GDP deflator
unemployed
total labor force
unemployment rate
Okun's law

QUESTIONS AND PROBLEMS

Questions

1. Explain the difference between a stock magnitude and a flow magnitude. Label each of the following as either a stock or a flow:
   (a) depreciation
   (b) saving
   (c) wealth
   (d) government debt
   (e) government deficit
   (f) foreign trade deficit
   (g) savings
   (h) money supply
   (i) labor force
   (j) labor services
   (k) net exports
   (l) net taxes

2. Decide whether each of the following transactions is included in GDP. If the transaction is included, determine which component of final spending it represents. If the transaction is excluded from GDP, explain why.
   (a) You buy a new copy of this textbook from your college bookstore.

   (b) You buy a used copy of this textbook from a friend.
   (c) Your college bookstore buys 300 new copies of this textbook from the publisher.
   (d) The publisher buys two tons of paper on which to print this textbook.
   (e) The publisher buys a new printing press for printing textbooks.
   (f) You thoroughly outline each chapter of this book to help yourself learn macroeconomics.
   (g) The publisher prints 500 copies of the book, which are not sold this year.
   (h) A professor in Canada adopts this textbook, which is produced in the United States, and Canadian students buy 100 copies of it.
   (i) A public school district buys new textbooks for a high school economics class.
   (j) A private high school buys new textbooks for an economics class.

3. What are the major drawbacks in using GDP as a measure of social welfare?

4. Assume that the GDP of the United States is eight

times as large as the GDP of China. Can you conclude, based on this information, that the average individual in the United States is eight times as well-off as the average individual in China? Why or why not?

5. The term "underground economy" encompasses economic activity that people do not report because it is illegal or because they hope to avoid paying taxes. Though the size of the underground economy is unknown, it may be a sizable fraction of the nation's GDP. How does the underground economy affect the accuracy of official measures of GDP, unemployment, and productivity, and complicate the tasks of policymakers?

6. One way to calculate the production taking place within a country would be to sum all value added during the production process. Yet the U.S. Bureau of Economic Analysis does not do this. Why not? What technique is used to calculate production taking place in the United States? Do we get the same answer as the value-added approach? Why or why not?

7. If all other things remain equal in the current period (GDP, *G*, *T*, *S*, *C*, etc.), what do you predict will happen to the level of domestic investment if the exchange rate between the dollar and the yen appreciates? Explain how it is possible for consumption *(C)* to remain constant in this situation. What do you predict will happen to GDP in the next period?

8. Saving and taxes are called leakages. From what do they leak? Where do they go? Imports are also a leakage. From what do they leak? Where do they go?

9. What are the sources of money flows in the capital market? How are these funds used?

10. Explain why the *change* in inventories and not the *level* of inventories is included in the calculation of GDP.

11. In the national income and product accounts, personal income can be calculated by subtracting from national income any income earned but not received and adding back in any income received but not earned. Explain.

12. Four hundred tires are produced by a tire manufacturer and sold for $75 each to General Motors in December 1995. In February 1996, General Motors puts the tires on 100 newly produced cars and sells each car for $30,000. What is the contribution made to GDP in 1995 and 1996, by the transaction described? (Assume all other components of the cars are produced in 1996.)

13. Starting from the situation depicted in Figure 2-3, assume that business firms produce an additional $500,000 worth of goods, of which only $450,000 are bought during the current year. What are the new values for the following categories?
    (a) income
    (b) consumption expenditure
    (c) personal saving
    (d) investment

14. Before 1983 the government often had a budget deficit, but the economy as a whole experienced a foreign trade surplus. After 1983 both the government budget and foreign trade account were running deficits. What does this imply about the relationship that existed between private saving and private domestic investment in the periods before and after 1983?

15. If you learn that nominal GDP for 1995 is greater than nominal GDP for 1994, what do you know about changes in the level of output during this period? changes in prices during this period? Would your answer change if it were real GDP that had increased in 1995?

16. How do chain-weighted real GDP and the chain-weighted GDP deflator differ from the calculations that government statisticians formerly used to measure aggregate output and inflation? Why were the chain-weighted measures adopted?

17. A panel of experts concluded that the Consumer Price Index significantly overstates inflation. Why might this be true, and why are flaws in the measure of inflation a political issue as well as an economic one?

Problems

1. Use the following data to answer the questions below (all figures are in billions of dollars):

Item	Amount
Government purchases of goods and services	$ 815.3
Exports	370.0
Receipts of factor income from the rest of the world	145.0
Depreciation (consumption of fixed capital)	438.5
Net fixed investment	200.1
Corporate income taxes	90.1
Consumption expenditures	2582.1
Indirect business taxes	338.6
Imports	446.9
Payments of factor income to the rest of the world	140.0
Inventory change	30.0

Social Security contributions	300.3
Undistributed corporate profits (retained earnings)	75.0
Government transfer and interest payments	546.7
Personal interest payments	87.4
Personal taxes	492.7

(a) What is gross domestic product?
(b) What is gross national product?
(c) What is net domestic product?
(d) What is domestic income?
(e) What is personal income? (*Hint:* Personal interest payments are part of the category "transfer payments and interest" in Table 2-2.)
(f) What is disposable personal income?
(g) What is personal saving?

2. Assume that gross private domestic investment is $800 billion and the government (state, local, and federal combined) is currently running a $400 billion deficit. If households and businesses are saving $1000 billion, what is the value of net exports? Use equation (2.5) to explain your answer.

3. Assume that a country produces only two services, bowling games and miniature golf games. Information regarding output and prices for two years is given below:

	Year 1	Year 2
Bowling games		
Output	90	60
Price	$2.00	$4.00
Miniature golf games		
Output	30	60
Price	$4.00	$6.00

(a) Fill in the following table based on the above data:

	Year 1	Year 2
Nominal GDP	_____	_____
Real GDP in year 1 prices	_____	_____
Real GDP in year 2 prices	_____	_____

(b) Using the technique of "chain-weighting," calculate the percentage change in real GDP between year 1 and year 2.
(c) Letting year 1 = 1.0, calculate the chain-weighted GDP deflator for year 2.

4. If nominal GDP is $6000 and chain-weighted real GDP is $4500, what is the value of the implicit GDP deflator?

5. If the implicit GDP deflator in year 1 is 1.20 and in year 2 it is 1.26, what was the rate of inflation in year 2?

6. This problem uses Okun's law, as presented in equation (2.6), to estimate values for U and Y/Y^N. Assume $\overline{U} = 5$ percent and $h = 0.3$.
(a) If $Y^N = 100$, what is U when $Y = 96$? When $Y = 102$? When $Y = 106$?
(b) Now assume that $Y^N = 120$. What must Y be to have a U of 8.0 percent? 3.5 percent? 5.75 percent?
(c) If the current U is 6.5 percent, by how much will Y have to increase to lower U to 5.9 percent?

7. In 1991, civilian employment was 116,877,000, and unemployment was 8,426,000. What was the unemployment rate?

8. Using your answer to Problem 7 and the Okun's Law relationship in equation (2.6), estimate the output ratio (Y/Y^N) in 1991. Given that 1991 real GDP (in 1992 chained dollars) was $6079 billion, calculate the natural real GDP (Y^N) for 1991 and find how much real GDP was "lost" that year because unemployment exceeded its average rate.

SELF-TEST ANSWERS

p. 30 The payment of the $10 bill to the barber is a flow of money shown by the solid red line labeled consumption expenditure. The provision of the haircut by the barber for the student is shown by the dashed red line labeled product. The barber's income of $10 is shown by the solid black line labeled income and the barber's provision of labor services to perform the haircut is shown by the dashed black line labeled labor services.

p. 33 Included in GDP for the first quarter of 1997 is the change in the value of the grocer's inventories between December 31, 1996 and March 31, 1997. This is $12.00 minus $8.00, or $4.00. If the level of inventories had fallen, instead of rising as in the example, inventory investment would have been negative.

p. 36 The foreign trade deficit and net exports are the same concept, but with the sign reversed. For instance, if exports are 90 and imports are 100, we say that there is a foreign trade deficit of 10, and that net exports are −10.

p. 48 Less than 1.0 in every year before 1992; greater than 1.0 in every year after 1992, equal to 1.0 in 1992.

p. 58 With an output ratio of 95 percent the actual unemployment rate is 8.7 percent, and with an output ratio of 105 it is 3.7 percent.

PART TWO

Income,

Interest Rates,

Policy,

and the

Global Economy

CHAPTER 3

The Simple Keynesian Theory of Income Determination

An honest man is one who knows that he can't consume more than he has produced.
—Ayn Rand, 1966

Macroeconomics is about both the long run and short run. Long-run macroeconomics concerns the sources of growth in a nation's productivity and standard of living. Why has the United States for the past century been the world's most productive economy with the highest standard of living for the average citizen? Why more recently has productivity been growing slowly, with other nations catching up? Answers to these critical questions may determine whether today's college students will achieve a higher standard of living than their parents. We address these questions in Part Four, Chapters 9–11.

Short-run macroeconomics is more often in the news: It concerns the causes of and cures for business cycles, those recurring alternating periods of prosperity, characterized by high output and low unemployment, followed by recessions, when output falls and unemployment rises. This chapter begins a two-part unit, spanning Chapters 3–8, that develops a theory of business cycles and the potential role of monetary and fiscal policy in dampening the amplitude of cycles. Our first interest is in fluctuations in real GDP and interest rates; subsequently we link these fluctuations to the government budget deficit, the foreign trade deficit, price movements, and inflation.

3-1 Business Cycles, Unemployment, and Income Determination

Early in this book you learned that fluctuations in unemployment are the mirror image of fluctuations in output, or, more precisely, in the difference (gap) between actual and natural real GDP. When that gap rises into positive territory as the economy expands, the unemployment rate falls; when that gap becomes negative as the economy slides into a recession, the unemployment rate rises. *Thus the key to understanding the causes of fluctuations in unemployment is to develop a theory of fluctuations in real output or GDP.*

What We Explain and What We Take as Given

Any theoretical model in economics, starting with the simple microeconomic model of supply and demand in the elementary economics course, sets limits on what it tries to explain. The simple supply-demand model attempts to explain only the price and quantity for a particular product, holding constant a host of other factors, including the prices of other products, consumer

Endogenous variables are those explained by an economic theory.

Exogenous variables are those that are relevant but whose behavior the theory does not attempt to explain; their values are taken as given.

income, the number of demanders and suppliers, consumer tastes, the weather, and technology. In any model, no matter how simple, the limited number of variables to be explained are called **endogenous variables.** The large number of variables that are taken as given and are not explained are called **exogenous variables.**

In macroeconomic theory we begin with a short list of endogenous variables and treat most as exogenous. Gradually we move some from the exogenous list to the endogenous list as our theory becomes more realistic. Table 3-1 shows the major variables that we analyze and their status as endogenous or exogenous.

This list excludes some variables that are treated as exogenous throughout, especially the money supply, the level of government spending, and tax rates. Although not included in the list, other exogenous elements, sometimes called *demand shocks,* are some of the basic causes of business cycles; they include the effects of wars and other political crises, and unpredictable changes in spending on consumption, investment spending, and net exports. Finally, other exogenous variables, *supply shocks,* include major changes in the price of oil or other raw materials.

Leaving aside these excluded exogenous variables, we see from Table 3-1 that our theory develops one element at a time, successively moving variables from the exogenous to the endogenous category. We begin in the next section with a simple theory that explains consumption and real output, treating investment (and government spending, taxes, and net exports) as exogenous.

3-2 Planned Expenditure

Total Expenditure, Planned and Unplanned

Our study of national income accounting in Chapter 2 identified four types of expenditure on GDP. By definition total expenditure on GDP *(E)* is equal to

Table 3-1   Endogenous and Exogenous Variables in the Theory of Business Cycles

	Endogenous	*Exogenous*
Chapter 3	Real output Consumption	Investment Interest rate Price level
Chapter 4	Real output Consumption Investment Interest rate	Price level
Chapter 7	Real output Consumption Investment Interest rate Price level	

the sum of these four components: consumption *(C)*, investment *(I)*, government spending on goods and services *(G)*, and net exports *(NX)*.

$$E = C + I + G + NX \tag{3.1}$$

[handwritten: only thing that can differ from what is planned]

The starting point of our theory is that expenditure is not always what is desired or planned. A key simplification is that only investment can differ from what is planned; *consumption, government spending, and net exports are always equal to the planned amount.*

Because only investment differs from the planned amount, we divide up total investment spending into two parts, planned (I_p) and unplanned (I_u). In practice, unplanned investment takes the form of changes in inventory investment. When business firms produce more than people want to buy, some of the goods they produce pile up on the shelves, and unplanned investment is positive. The reverse occurs when firms produce less than people want to buy. Business firms do not like unplanned investment, and whenever it happens they adjust production to get rid of the unwanted inventories or produce more product to meet demand.

The total amount of spending that people want to do includes only the planned portion, called planned expenditure (E_p). This includes planned investment (I_p), plus the other types of spending, the total of which is always equal to the planned amount:

$$E_p = C + I_p + G + NX \tag{3.2}$$

[handwritten: planned expenditure]

The Consumption Function

At the beginning, we treat only consumption spending *(C)* as endogenous, or explained by the theory, and treat the other three types of planned spending as exogenous. An obvious way to explain consumption is that people spend more when their incomes go up and vice versa. The income that matters for consumption decisions is income after taxes, defined in the last chapter as disposable personal income. Ignoring all types of taxes and saving in Table 2-2 except personal taxes *(T)* and personal saving, we find that disposable income can be written as total real income *(Y)* minus personal taxes paid, or $Y - T$.[1] *[handwritten: personal taxes pd. = real disposable income (Y); real income]*

How do households divide their disposable income between consumption and saving? Let us imagine that households always spend $250 billion on consumption spending at every level of income, an amount we shall call **autonomous** consumption. *Autonomous* consumption is completely independent of income. If autonomous consumption were the only form of consumption, then consumption expenditures *(C)* would simply be:

$$C = 250 \tag{3.3}$$

An **autonomous** magnitude is independent of the level of income.

---

[1]The notation *T* in this chapter continues, as in Chapter 2, to mean "total taxes minus transfer payments." The only difference is that here we simplify by excluding several of the leakages of Chapter 2 (see Table 2-2), namely two tax leakages (indirect business taxes and corporate taxes) and two saving leakages (depreciation and undistributed corporate profits). Thus *Y* continues to mean real GDP, *T* includes only personal taxes minus personal transfers, and $Y - T$ is personal disposable income.

But we know that people tend to consume more as their disposable income increases. The amount by which consumption expenditures increase for each extra dollar of disposable income is a fraction called the **marginal propensity to consume.** For instance, we shall assume in our example that households consume 75 cents more for each extra dollar of disposable income they receive. This component of consumption is called **induced consumption.** If induced consumption were the only form of consumption, then consumption expenditures *(C)* would simply be the marginal propensity to consume (0.75) times disposable income *(Y − T)*:

The **marginal propensity to consume** is the dollar change in consumption expenditures per dollar change in disposable income.

Induced consumption is the portion of consumption spending that responds to changes in income.

$$C = 0.75\ (Y - T) \qquad (3.4)$$

→ disposable income

Both equations (3.3) and (3.4) are unrealistic. It is more realistic to combine them, allowing consumption to consist of both an autonomous component and an induced component. In our numerical example, the autonomous component is 250 and the induced component is 0.75 *(Y − T)*. This combined relationship is called the *consumption function* and shows the amount of total consumption spending for each level of disposable income:

Numerical Example   *induced component*

$$\text{Consumption function} = C = 250 + 0.75\ (Y - T) \qquad (3.5)$$

autonomous component

A more general way of writing the consumption function, which does not require us to specify particular numbers, uses letters of the alphabet as symbols for autonomous consumption *(a)*, the marginal propensity to consume *(c)*, and induced consumption [*c (Y − T)*]:

General Linear Form   *a + cons.*

$$C = a + c(Y - T) \qquad (3.6)$$

mpc

Either way of writing the consumption function states that total consumption is the sum of autonomous and induced consumption.

The consumption function can also be shown graphically, as in Figure 3-1. The thick red line shows on the vertical axis the amount of consumption for alternative values of disposable income (measured along the horizontal axis). When disposable income is zero, total consumption consists just of the autonomous component ($250 billion). For each extra $1000 billion of disposable income, as we move to the right on the graph, the red consumption function line rises by $750 billion, since its slope (the marginal propensity to consume) is 0.75. For instance, at point *D* disposable income is $4000 billion and total consumption is $3250 billion (consisting of $3000 billion of induced consumption and $250 billion of autonomous consumption).

Induced Saving and the Marginal Propensity to Save

The simplest way to show the amount of saving is to use a graph like Figure 3-1. The thick black line shows the amount of disposable income in both a horizontal and a vertical direction. Since the thick red line shows the consumption function, the distance between the two lines indicates the total amount of saving. To the right of point *F*, total saving is positive because disposable income exceeds consumption; this is indicated by the red shading. To the left of point *F*, total saving is negative because consumption exceeds disposable income; this is indicated by the gray shading. How can

Figure 3-1
A Simple Hypothesis Regarding Consumption Behavior

The red line passing through *F* and *D* illustrates the consumption function. It shows that consumption is 75 percent of disposable income plus an autonomous component of $250 billion that is spent regardless of the level of disposable income. The red shaded area shows the amount of positive saving that occurs when income exceeds consumption; the gray area shows the amount of negative saving (dissaving) that occurs when consumption exceeds income.

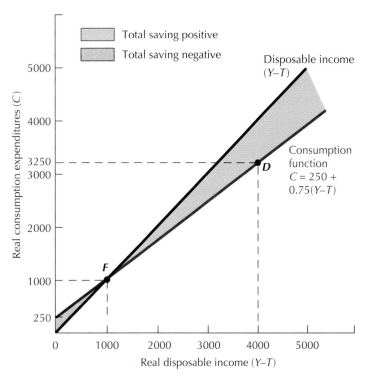

HOW DISPOSABLE INCOME IS DIVIDED BETWEEN CONSUMPTION AND SAVING

saving be negative? Individuals can consume more than they earn, at least for a while, by withdrawing funds from a savings account, by selling stocks and bonds, or by borrowing. Negative saving is quite typical for many students who borrow to finance their education.

Figure 3-2 illustrates the relationship between induced saving, autonomous consumption, and total saving. The top frame duplicates Figure 3-1 but emphasizes the division of disposable income between induced consumption $[0.75(Y - T)]$ and induced saving $[0.25(Y - T)]$. The bottom frame subtracts induced consumption from the top frame and isolates the relationship between autonomous consumption and induced saving. As in Figure 3-1, the red and gray shaded areas show the amount of total saving.

The shaded vertical distance between the black and red lines represents saving *(S)*, that is, the difference between disposable income and consumption:

General Linear Form   Numerical Example

$$S = Y - T - C = Y - T - a - c(Y - T) \qquad S = Y - T - C = Y - T - 250 - 0.75(Y - T)$$

$$= -a + (1 - c)(Y - T) \qquad\qquad = -250 + 0.25(Y - T) \qquad (3.7)$$

This <u>*saving function*</u> starts with the definition of saving as personal disposable income minus consumption; then it substitutes the consumption function from equation (3.6). The last line simplifies the saving function, which now

Figure 3-2
The Relation Between Induced Consumption, Induced Saving, and the Consumption Function

The upper frame duplicates Figure 3-1. The thin black line shows the dividing line between induced saving and induced consumption. Starting at zero disposable income, each dollar of disposable income is divided between 75 cents of induced consumption and 25 cents of induced saving. The lower frame subtracts induced consumption from the upper frame. It shows the relation between induced saving and autonomous consumption. Total saving in both parts of the diagram is shown by the red and gray shading and equals induced saving minus autonomous consumption.

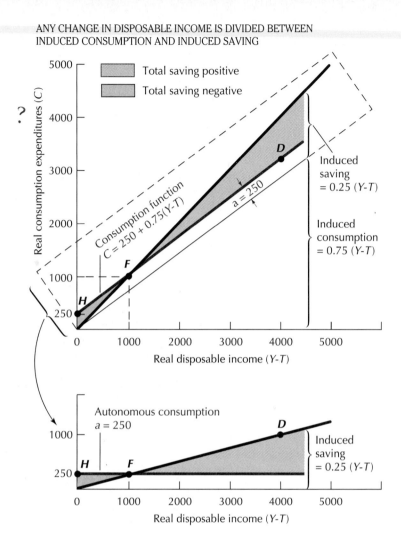

ANY CHANGE IN DISPOSABLE INCOME IS DIVIDED BETWEEN INDUCED CONSUMPTION AND INDUCED SAVING

Marginal propensity to save is the change in personal saving induced by a $1 change in personal disposable income.

states that personal saving equals minus the amount of autonomous consumption $(-a)$ plus the **marginal propensity to save** $(1 - c)$ times disposable income $(Y - T)$.

Notice the three points in both frames of Figure 3-2 marked with letters corresponding to different levels of disposable income. At H, disposable income is zero, so consumption is a, or 250, and saving from equation (3.7) is $-a$, or -250. At F, disposable income and consumption are equal, so saving is zero. At D, consumption of 3250 is less than disposable income of 4000, so saving is a positive 750.

SELF-TEST

> Can you derive a general expression showing how the level of consumption and disposable income at point F depend on autonomous consumption (a) and the marginal propensity to consume (c)? If disposable income is 2500 rather than 4000, the economy in Figure 3-2 will be at a point between points F and D. Calculate the values of consumption (C) and saving (S) when disposable income is 2500.

When disposable income falls very low, as it did during the Great Depression, households take money out of their savings accounts or borrow in order to buy the basic necessities of life.[2] Saving is negative (dissaving) because consumers must draw on their savings accounts and other assets in order to purchase the consumption goods that their disposable income alone can no longer purchase.

How can this happen, you may ask, when many people have no jobs? Indeed, people who have exhausted their savings accounts and cannot borrow are incapable of consuming more than their income. But even in the Great Depression many households still held jobs and still had funds in their savings accounts that could be drawn down to allow consumption spending to exceed income. After all, when the Depression began, people held financial assets equal to at least one year's GDP, and this provided ample opportunity for some people to draw on their savings accounts, bonds, and stocks in those perilous times.

Figure 3-3, arranged exactly like Figure 3-1, shows the actual values of disposable income, consumption, and saving in the United States during the years 1929–94. Three major conclusions can be drawn from the evidence. First, both consumption and saving have increased as disposable income has grown during the years since World War II. Second, in the worst years of the Great Depression, households consumed more than their incomes, so that saving was negative in 1932 and 1933 (about −3.9 percent of disposable income in 1933). Third, these usual peacetime relationships were interrupted during World War II (1942–45), when consumer goods were unavailable or rationed. In that period households were forced to consume much less and save much more than is normal in peacetime, fully 25 percent of disposable income in 1944. After the war, consumers rushed out to spend their accumulated savings, helping to maintain prosperity in spite of the drastic drop in government spending that occurred in 1945–46.

3-4 The Economy In and Out of Equilibrium

As already indicated, the only component of planned spending that we are now trying to explain is consumption. The other components—planned investment *(I_p)*, government spending *(G)*, and net exports *(NX)*—are assumed to be fixed, or unchanging, in our calculations. Total planned expenditure is written simply by substituting the general form of the consumption function (3.6) into the definition of planned expenditure (3.2):

$$E_p = a + c(Y - T) + I_p + G + NX \qquad (3.8)$$

---

[2]Be careful to distinguish between "savings" (with a terminal "s"), which is the stock of assets that households have in savings accounts or under the mattress, from "saving" (without a terminal "s"), which is the *flow* per unit of time that leaks out of disposable income and is unavailable for purchases of consumption goods. It is the flow of *saving* that is designated by the symbol *S*.

Figure 3-3
Consumption, Saving, and Disposable Income, 1929–96

Notice that in 1933 U.S. saving was negative. In 1996 saving was positive and amounted to 4.3 percent of disposable income. The remainder was split between 92.9 percent for consumption and 2.8 percent for interest payments. Saving was unusually high during World War II because consumer goods were rationed. (*Source:* National Income and Product Accounts.)

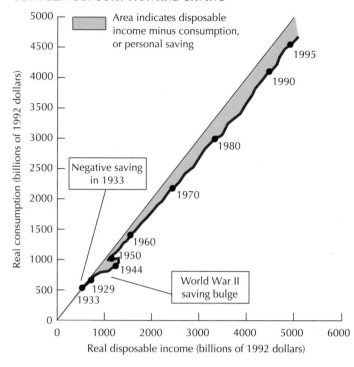

HOW ACTUAL U.S. DISPOSABLE INCOME HAS BEEN SPLIT BETWEEN CONSUMPTION AND SAVING

In words, this states that planned expenditure equals autonomous consumption, plus the part of consumption that depends on disposable income (induced consumption), plus the fixed values of planned investment, government spending, and net exports.

A **parameter** is a value taken as given or known within a particular analysis.

The word **parameter** means something that is taken as given, including not only exogenous variables but also fixed elements of a function. In the case of the consumption function, there are two such fixed elements (a and c), and we will take both as given. In addition, the three components of planned expenditure other than consumption (I_p, G, and NX) can be considered as both exogenous variables and parameters.

For our numerical example, we will continue to assume that autonomous consumption (a) is 250 and that the marginal propensity to consume (c) is 0.75. We will temporarily set tax revenues (T) and government spending (G) at zero, and assume that planned investment (I_p) is 600 and net exports (NX) are -100. Thus, the numerical example corresponding to equation (3.8) is:

Numerical Example

$$E_p = 250 + 0.75(Y - 0) + 600 + 0 - 100 \qquad (3.9)$$

Autonomous Planned Spending

It helps to simplify the subsequent analysis if we take all the elements of (3.8) that do not depend on total income (Y) and call them *autonomous planned spending (A_p)*:

General Linear Form

means autonomous (independent of income levels)

$$A_p = a - c\overline{T} + I_p + G + NX \qquad (3.10)$$

In words, this states that autonomous planned spending consists of all the components of spending that do not depend on income, and these are, in order, autonomous consumption (a), the effect of taxes in reducing consumption $(-c\overline{T})$, planned investment (I_p), government spending (G), and net exports (NX). Note that there is now a "bar" written on top of the T in the tax term; this reminds us that we must assume that tax revenues are autonomous and do not depend on income. This means that for now we cannot consider taxes like the federal income tax that do depend on income; our treatment of income taxes comes later in this chapter.

As our numerical example, we use the numbers given in equation (3.9) above. These imply that autonomous planned spending is equal to a total of 750:

Numerical Example

$$A_p = 250 - 0.75\,(0) + 600 + 0 - 100 = 750 \qquad (3.11)$$

Overall, we have learned that total planned expenditure (E_p) has two parts, autonomous planned spending (A_p) and induced consumption (cY).

General Linear Form	Numerical Example	
$E_p = A_p + cY$	$E_p = 750 + 0.75Y$	(3.12)

Figure 3-4 provides a graph of equation (3.12). The top frame copies the consumption function from Figure 3-1 and adds the planned expenditure line. Recall that the consumption function is autonomous consumption (250) plus induced consumption. Planned expenditure is autonomous planned spending (750) plus induced consumption. Thus, the planned expenditure line lies above the consumption function by 500, not just along the vertical axis but everywhere in the graph. In our numerical example, this extra 500 of spending consists of planned investment $(I_p = 600)$ plus net exports $(NX = -100)$.

Because equation (3.12) relates total planned expenditure to total income (Y) rather than to disposable income $(Y - T)$, the variable on the horizontal axis of Figure 3-4 is total income (Y). The 45-degree line now represents all points where income equals planned expenditure $(Y = E_p)$.

The bottom frame of Figure 3-4 shows the autonomous components of spending, with induced consumption excluded. The lower line, autonomous consumption, lies at a vertical distance of 250 and is copied from the bottom frame of Figure 3-2. The upper line, autonomous planned spending, lies at a vertical distance of 750.

When Is the Economy in Equilibrium?

A basic lesson of Chapter 2 was that *actual* expenditure (E) and total income (Y) are always equal by definition. But there is no reason for income (Y) always to equal *planned* expenditure (E_p). Only when the economy is in **equilibrium** is income equal to planned expenditure. Only then do households, business firms, the government, and the foreign sector want to spend exactly the amount of income that is being generated by the current level of production.

Equilibrium is a state in which there exists no pressure for change.

$\therefore E_p = Y$

Figure 3-4
Autonomous Planned Spending and the Level of Total Planned Expenditure

The lower red line repeats the red consumption function from Figure 3-1. When we add $500 billion of autonomous non-consumption spending, we obtain total planned expenditure, as illustrated by the upper red line.

HOW THE INTRODUCTION OF INVESTMENT AFFECTS TOTAL PLANNED EXPENDITURE

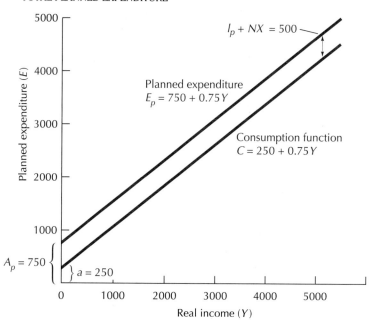

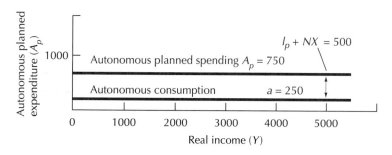

Equilibrium is *a situation in which there is no pressure for change.* When the economy is *out of equilibrium,* production and income are out of line with planned expenditure, and business firms will be forced to raise or lower production. When the economy is *in equilibrium,* production and income equal planned expenditure, and on the average, business firms are happy to continue the current level of production.

This idea is illustrated in Figure 3-5. The thick black line in the top frame has a slope of 45 degrees; everywhere along it the level of income plotted on the horizontal axis is equal to the level of expenditure plotted on the vertical axis. Hence the black line is labeled $E = Y$. The red line is the total level of planned expenditures (E_p) and is copied directly from Figure 3-4. Only where the black and red lines cross at point B is income equal to planned expenditure, with no pressure for change. Households and business firms want to spend $3000 billion when income is $3000 billion. And this amount of income is created by the $3000 billion of production of the goods and services that households and business firms want to buy.

Figure 3-5
How Equilibrium Income Is Determined

The economy is in equilibrium in the top frame at point *B*, where the red planned expenditure (E_p) line crosses the 45-degree income line. At any other level of income, the economy is out of equilibrium, causing pressure on business firms to increase or reduce production and income. For instance, at point *H*, E_p falls $250 billion short of production, so $250 billion of output piles up on the shelves unsold $(I_u = 250)$. In the lower frame equilibrium occurs at point *B*, where induced saving (sY) equals autonomous planned spending (A_p).

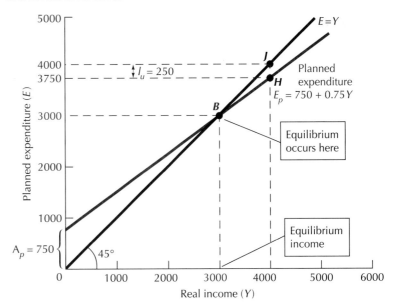

THE ECONOMY IS IN EQUILIBRIUM ONLY WHERE THE RED AND BLACK LINES CROSS

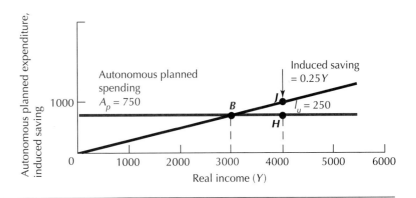

What Happens Out of Equilibrium?

The economy is out of equilibrium at all points other than *B* along the 45-degree income line (labeled $E = Y$). For instance, at point *J*, income is $4000 billion. How much do households and business firms want to spend? The two components of planned expenditure are:

$$\begin{array}{rl} \text{autonomous planned spending } (A_p) = & 750 \\ \underline{\text{induced consumption } (0.75Y) =} & \underline{3000} \\ \text{planned expenditure } (E_p) = & 3750 \end{array}$$

Thus at an income level of $4000 billion, planned expenditure (E_p) is only $3750 billion (point *H* on the E_p line), leaving business firms with $250 billion of merchandise that nobody wants to purchase.

The $250 billion of unsold production is counted as inventory investment in the official national income accounts. But businesses do not desire this

why not $\cancel{just}$ cut prices too?

Unintended inventory investment is the amount business firms are forced to accumulate when planned expenditure is less than income.

If you cut income wouldn't that result in even less spending... shift the whole line?

· oh! if you cut my income, I'll also spend less... hence, closer to B

inventory buildup (if they did, they would have included it in their planned investment, I_p). To bring inventories back to the original desired level, businesses react to the situation at J by cutting production and income, which moves the economy left toward point B. In the diagram, the distance between points J and H, amounting to $250 billion, is labeled I_u, which stands for **unintended inventory investment.**

The distance JH measures the excess of income over planned expenditure—that is, the positive value of I_u. Production and income will be cut until this discrepancy disappears and the unwanted inventory buildup ceases $(I_u = 0)$. This occurs only when the economy arrives at B. Only at B are businesses producing exactly the amount that is demanded.

Example: In early 1995, consumer purchases of automobiles declined, and industry found itself producing more cars than consumers wanted to buy. The Chrysler Corporation had accumulated inventories equivalent to more than 100 days of sales for several of its models. Since Chrysler neither planned nor desired this inventory accumulation, the company reacted by cutting production, which caused a drop in Chrysler's contribution to national income and national product.

SELF-TEST

What happens in the top frame of Figure 3-5 when income is only $2000 billion? Describe the forces that move the economy back to equilibrium at B.

At point J, as in every situation, income and actual expenditure are equal by definition:

$$\text{income } (Y) \equiv \text{expenditure } (E)$$

$$\equiv \text{planned expenditure } (E_p) + \qquad (3.13)$$

$$\text{unintended inventory investment } (I_u)$$

By contrast, the economy is in equilibrium only when unintended inventory accumulation or decumulation is equal to zero $(I_u = 0)$ (see Table 3-2).

Table 3-2   Comparison of the Economy's "Always True" and Equilibrium Situations

	Always true by definition	*True only in equilibrium*
1. What concept of expenditure is equal to income?	Actual expenditure including unintended inventory accumulation	Planned expenditure
2. Amount of unintended inventory investment (I_u)	Can be any amount, positive or negative	Must be zero
3. Which equation is valid, (3.13) or (3.14)?	(3.13) $Y = E = E_p + I_u$	(3.14) $Y = E_p$
4. How does equilibrium differ from other points in the top frame of Figure 3-5?	Any point on 45-degree income line (example: point J)	Only at point where E_p line crosses 45-degree income line
5. Numerical example in Figure 3-5 of nonequilibrium and equilibrium situations.	At point J, $$Y(4000) = E(4000)$$ $$= E_p(3750) + I_u(250)$$	At point B, $$Y(3000) = E_p(3000)$$

Equation (3.13) can be rewritten to describe the economy's equilibrium situation:

$$Y = E_p$$

(3.14)

economy's eq. situation

Autonomous Planned Spending Equals Induced Saving

The lower frame of Figure 3-5 illustrates the determination of equilibrium income in an equivalent but slightly different way. It subtracts induced consumption from both income and planned expenditure. The red horizontal line is total autonomous planned spending (A_p) of $750 billion.

Take the definition of equilibrium in equation (3.14) and subtract induced consumption (cY) from both sides of that equation:

$$Y - cY = E_p - cY$$

We can replace $E_p - cY$ on the right-hand side by its equivalent, autonomous planned spending, A_p, which is simply total planned expenditure (E_p) minus induced consumption (cY).

$$(1 - c)Y = A_p$$

(3.15)

Because the marginal propensity to save equals 1.0 minus the marginal propensity to consume $(s = 1 - c)$, we can rewrite (3.15) as

General Linear Form	Numerical Example	
$sY = A_p$	$0.25Y = 750$	(3.16)

Induced saving is the portion of saving that responds to changes in income.

Thus, equilibrium can occur only if **induced saving** (sY) equals autonomous planned spending (A_p). The black sloped induced saving line in the lower frame of Figure 3-5 rises by $0.25 per $1.00 of income and crosses the red A_p line at point B, which is at an income level of $3000 billion and lies directly beneath the top frame's point B. The economy is in equilibrium at B in the top frame because production (Y) equals planned spending (E_p). When this occurs, point B in the lower frame shows that the induced leakage into saving (sY) just balances autonomous planned spending (A_p) injected back into the spending stream.

The equilibrium level of income in this simple model is always equal to autonomous planned spending (A_p) divided by the marginal propensity to save (s), as we can see when both sides of (3.16) are divided by s:

General Linear Form	Numerical Example	
$Y = \dfrac{A_p}{s}$ *eq. level of income*	$Y = \dfrac{750}{0.25} = 3000$	(3.17)

Equilibrium income adjusts to generate enough induced saving to balance autonomous planned spending. In our numerical example, $3000 billion of income is required to generate the $750 billion of induced saving needed to balance $750 billion of autonomous planned spending.

General Method for Determining Equilibrium Income

The lower frame of Figure 3-5 and equation (3.17) both illustrate the two-step method used throughout the chapter for determining equilibrium income. To represent this in a graph, first draw a horizontal line at a height equal to autonomous planned spending (A_p). Then plot a line through the origin with a slope equal to the marginal propensity to save (s). The point where the horizontal A_p line crosses the sloped sY line indicates the equilibrium level of income. At any other point, for instance, J, sY does not balance A_p, indicating a discrepancy between E_p and Y and hence an unplanned increase or decrease in inventories.

Income equilibrium can be determined using the same technique with the symbols in equation (3.17). The numerator A_p corresponds to the horizontal A_p line in the figure. The denominator is the fraction of income that leaks out of the spending stream into saving (s), corresponding to the slope of the induced saving line in the figure.

3-5   The Multiplier Effect

The conclusion of Section 3-4, that equilibrium income equals $3000 billion, is absolutely dependent on the assumption that autonomous planned spending (A_p) equals $750 billion. A change in autonomous planned spending will cause a change in equilibrium income. To illustrate the consequences of a change in A_p, we shall assume that business people become more optimistic, raising their guess as to the likely profitability of new investment projects. They increase their investment spending by $250 billion, boosting A_p from $750 billion to $1000 billion. In each situation where a change is described, a numbered subscript is used to distinguish the original from the new situation. Thus A_{p0} denotes the original level of A_p ($750 billion), and A_{p1} denotes the new level ($1000 billion).

Calculating the Multiplier

Economic theorists typically examine the effects of a change in one parameter on the assumption that all other things are constant. In equation (3.17) where the only "other thing" besides A_p determining income is s, we assume that s is constant. We use (3.17) to calculate the equilibrium level of income in the new and old situations:

	General Linear Form	Numerical Example
Take new situation	$Y_1 = \dfrac{A_{p1}}{s}$	$Y_1 = \dfrac{1000}{0.25} = 4000$
Subtract old situation	$Y_0 = \dfrac{A_{p0}}{s}$	$Y_0 = \dfrac{750}{0.25} = 3000$
Equals change in income	$\Delta Y = \dfrac{\Delta A_p}{s}$	$\Delta Y = \dfrac{250}{0.25} = 1000$ (3.18)

The top line of the table calculates the new level of income when A_{p1} is at the new value of 1000. The second line calculates the original level of income when A_{p0} is at the old value of 750. The change in income, abbreviated ΔY, is simply the first line minus the second. The **multiplier** (k) is defined as the ratio of the change in income (ΔY) to the change in planned autonomous spending (ΔA_p) that causes it:

The **multiplier** is the ratio of the change in output to the change in autonomous planned spending that causes it. It is also 1.0 divided by the marginal leakage rate (the fraction of an extra dollar of income that is not spent on consumption).

General Linear Form

Numerical Example

$$\text{multiplier } (k) = \frac{\Delta Y}{\Delta A_p} = \frac{1}{s} \qquad \frac{\Delta Y}{\Delta A_p} = \frac{1}{0.25} = 4.0 \qquad (3.19)$$

In Figure 3.6 we can see why the multiplier (k) is $1/s$, or 4.0. Figure 3-6 reproduces from Figure 3-5 the original situation, with A_p at its original value of $750 billion.

The $250 billion increase in A_p causes the A_p line to shift upward by $250 billion and to intersect the fixed induced saving line at point J. Because only 25 percent of extra income is saved, income must rise by $1000 billion to generate the required $250 billion increase in induced saving. In terms of the line segments:

$$\text{multiplier } (k) = \frac{\Delta Y}{\Delta A_p} = \frac{RJ}{RB} = \frac{1}{s} \text{ (since } s = \frac{RB}{RJ}\text{)}$$

Example of the Multiplier Effect in Action

How does the magic of the multiplier work? One answer is given by Figure 3-6, which is based on the idea that the economy can be in equilibrium only when induced saving (sY) is equal to autonomous planned spending (A_p). If A_p rises, sY must rise by exactly the same amount, and this can happen only if income (Y) rises by $1/s$ times the increase in A_p.

A real-life example provides another answer. An example of an increase in planned investment is the decision by United Airlines in 1991 to purchase $4 billion of Boeing 777 aircraft. Initially the $4 billion of new investment spending would raise income by the $4 billion earned by Boeing workers in

Figure 3-6
The Change in Equilibrium Income Caused by a $250 Billion Increase in Autonomous Planned Spending

Increasing autonomous planned spending (A_p) by $250 billion raises the horizontal red A_p line by $250 billion, moving the equilibrium position from B to J. Thus, a change in A_p has a multiplier effect, raising income by $1000 billion.

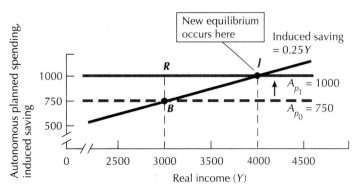

HOW HIGHER AUTONOMOUS PLANNED SPENDING RAISES INCOME

Seattle, where the aircraft plant is located. But, using our example of a marginal propensity to consume *(c)* of 0.75, the Boeing workers would soon spend 0.75 of the $4 billion, or $3 billion, on goods and services at Seattle stores. The stores would have to reorder $3 billion of additional goods, causing production to rise at plants all over the country that supply the goods to the stores in Seattle. Workers at these supplying plants also have a marginal propensity to consume of 0.75, adding another $2.25 billion of income. So far, in the first three rounds of spending income has gone up by $4.0 plus $3.0 plus $2.25 billion, or $9.25 billion. But the process continues, as induced consumption is increased in each successive round of spending. Eventually, the total increase in income will be four times the initial increase in planned investment, or $16 billion (= $4 billion times 1/.25), just as in Figure 3-6.[3]

3-6   Recessions and Fiscal Policy

Is a multiplier expansion or contraction of output following a change in autonomous planned spending desirable or not?

Assume that the desired level of real GDP is $4000 billion. In Figure 3-6 a level of autonomous planned spending *(A_p)* of $1000 billion would be perfect, for it would bring about an equilibrium level of actual real GDP of $4000 billion at point *J*, the desired level. On the other hand, a decline in A_p by $250 billion would cut equilibrium income to $3000 billion at *B* and would open up a gap of $1000 billion between actual and the desired level of real GDP.

What might cause actual real GDP to decline below the desired level? A drop in planned investment, a major component of A_p, can be and has been a major cause of actual real-world recessions and depressions. In the Great Depression, for instance, fixed investment dropped by 74 percent, and this contributed to the 29 percent decline in actual real GDP between 1929 and 1933.

---

[3]It is possible to use an algebraic trick to prove that the sum of ΔA_p plus the induced consumption at each round of spending is exactly equal to the multiplier $\dfrac{1}{1-c}$ times ΔA_p. The first round round of consumption is $c\Delta A_p$. The second is c times the first, $c(c\Delta A_p)$, or $c^2 A_p$. Thus the total ΔY is the series:

$$\Delta Y = \Delta A_p + c\Delta A_p + c^2\Delta A_p + \cdots + c^n\Delta A_p \tag{a}$$

Factor out the common element ΔA_p on the right-hand side of equation (a):

$$\Delta Y = \Delta A_p(1.0 + c + c^2 + \cdots + c^n) \tag{b}$$

Multiply both sides of equation (b) by $-c$:

$$-c\Delta Y = \Delta A_p(-c - c^2 - \cdots - c^n - c^{n+1}) \tag{c}$$

The difference between lines (b) and (c) is

$$(1-c)\Delta Y = \Delta A_p(1.0 - c^{n+1}) \tag{d}$$

Since c^{n+1} is almost zero (because c is a fraction and $n+1$ is large), we can ignore it. Dividing both sides of equation (d) by $(1-c)$, we obtain the familiar

$$\Delta Y = \frac{\Delta A_p}{1-c}$$

Government Spending and Taxation

The government can adjust its expenditures on goods and services as well as its tax revenues in an attempt to offset fluctuations in real GDP caused by movements in autonomous consumption, in planned investment, and in net exports. Our definition of autonomous planned spending (A_p) in equation (3.10) already includes government spending (G) and the effect of autonomous taxes (T) on consumption. For convenience we repeat equation (3.10):

General Linear Form

$$A_p = a - c\overline{T} + I_p + G + NX \qquad (3.10)$$

SELF-TEST Why is I_p written with a p subscript, but the other components of autonomous planned spending—a, $-c\overline{T}$, G, and NX—are not?

Equation (3.10) states that autonomous planned spending equals the sum of five components. It also implies that the *change* in autonomous planned spending equals the sum of the *change* in each of the same five components. We can state this idea as an equation if we insert the "change in" symbol, Δ, in front of each element in equation (3.10). The only remaining element without a Δ symbol is the marginal propensity to consume (c), which we are assuming to be fixed throughout this discussion:

$$\Delta A_p = \Delta a - c\Delta \overline{T} + \Delta I_p + \Delta G + \Delta NX \qquad (3.20)$$

In sum, the five causes of changes in A_p are:

1. A $1 change in autonomous consumption (a) changes A_p by $1 in the same direction.

2. A $1 change in autonomous tax revenue $(\overline{T})$ changes A_p by c (the marginal propensity to consume) times $1 in the opposite direction. For example, a $100 billion increase in $\overline{T}$ would reduce A_p by $75 billion if c were 0.75. Households pay for the other $25 billion in higher tax revenue by reducing their saving.

3. A $1 change in planned investment (I_p) changes A_p by $1 in the same direction.

4. A $1 change in government spending (G) changes A_p by $1 in the same direction.

5. A $1 change in net exports (NX) changes A_p by $1 in the same direction.

Once the change in A_p has been calculated from this list, our basic multiplier expression from (3.18) determines the resulting change in equilibrium income:

$$\Delta Y = \frac{\Delta A_p}{s} \qquad (3.18)$$

SELF-TEST Notice that there is no Δ in front of the s in equation (3.18). Why?

Fiscal Expansion

To provide an example of a situation in which higher government spending can expand real income, let us assume that initially the level of autonomous planned spending (A_p) is 750. This means that the level of real income will be 3000, as shown at point B in the top frame of Figure 3-7. This is unsatisfactory, because natural real GDP is at the higher level of $4000 billion. Thus point B represents a situation in which actual real GDP and real income are $1000 billion too low, and in which many members of the labor force are jobless. How can government fiscal policy correct this situation through its control over the level of government expenditure?

It is clear from our basic income-determination formula (3.18) that the required $1000 billion increase in real income and real GDP can be achieved by any action that raises autonomous planned spending (A_p) by $250 billion. Two possibilities are ① a $250 billion increase in G (government spending on goods and services) and ② a $333 billion reduction in autonomous tax revenue.[4]

The $250 billion change in government spending $(\Delta G = 250)$ in Figure 3-7 has exactly the same effect on income as any other $250 billion increase in A_p. The economy reaches a new equilibrium at point J, just as it did in Figure 3-6. The multiplier (k) for ΔG is also the same. As before, we calculate the multiplier by taking the change in income (ΔY) and dividing it by the factor that is changing $(\Delta G$ in this case):

General Linear Form   Numerical Example

$$k = \frac{\Delta Y}{\Delta G} = \frac{\Delta Y}{\Delta A_p} = \frac{1}{s} \qquad\qquad k = \frac{\Delta Y}{\Delta A_p} = \frac{1}{0.25} = 4.0 \qquad (3.21)$$

In the top frame of Figure 3-7 the government manages to push total income up from $3000 billion at point B to $4000 billion at point J by making $250 billion of purchases.

The Government Budget Deficit and Its Financing

Any change in government expenditure or tax revenue has consequences for the government's budget. The government budget surplus has already been defined in Section 2-6 as tax revenue minus government expenditure $(T - G)$. The government budget deficit is simply a negative value of the surplus. In the example illustrated in Figure 3-7, the government starts with a balanced budget, having no expenditures and no tax revenues:

$$\text{government budget deficit at } B = G - T = \$0$$

---

[4]Why $333 billion? Because according to equation (3.20), a reduction in taxes raises A_p by c times the reduction, where c is the marginal propensity to consume. If $c = 0.75$, as in our numerical example, then

$$\Delta A_p = -c\,\Delta \overline{T} = -0.75(-333) = 250$$

Recall that transfer payments (welfare, Social Security, and unemployment benefits) are equivalent to negative taxes, so that a $333 billion reduction in taxes has the same impact on A_p as a $333 billion *increase* in transfer payments.

Figure 3-7
Effect on Income of a $250 Billion Increase in Government Spending Followed by a $250 Billion Increase in Autonomous Tax Revenue

The top frame is identical to Figure 3-6. It shows that a $250 billion increase in government spending moves the economy from B to J, having the same multiplier impact on equilibrium income as a $250 billion increase in A_p caused by alterations in private spending decisions. In the lower frame the $250 billion tax increase reduced A_p by only $187.5 billion, since the remaining $62.5 billion of tax revenue is paid for by lower saving. The economy moves from point J down to point K.

GOVERNMENT SPENDING AND TAXES ALSO HAVE MULTIPLIER EFFECTS

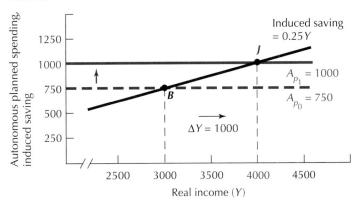

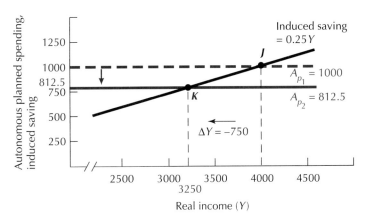

Then, the government begins spending $250 billion, moving the economy from B to J. Since its tax revenues remain at zero, the government's purchases cause a government budget deficit of $250 billion:

government budget deficit at $J = G - T = \$250$ billion

How is this budget deficit financed? Recall from Chapter 2 (see Figure 2-5) that government deficit equals the difference between private saving and investment minus net exports.

$$G - T \equiv S - I - NX$$

Similarly, the change in the left side of the equation must balance the change in the right side:

$$\Delta G - \Delta T = \Delta S - \Delta I - \Delta NX \tag{3.22}$$

The movement in the top frame of Figure 3-7 from point B to point J assumes that autonomous consumption, investment, and net exports are fixed ($\Delta a = \Delta I = \Delta NX = 0$) and that tax revenue remains at zero ($\Delta T = 0$). Thus the only elements of (3.22) that are changing are ΔS and ΔG:

$$\Delta S - \Delta I - \Delta NX \equiv \Delta G - \Delta T$$

$$s\Delta Y - 0 - 0 \equiv 250 - 0$$

$$0.25(1000) \equiv 250$$

The $1000 billion increase in output induces $250 billion of extra saving. Each extra dollar of saving is available for households to purchase the $250 billion of government bonds that the government must sell when it runs its $250 billion budget deficit.

3-7 Effects of Tax Changes Multiplier

Effect of Autonomous Taxes

The government may prefer not to run a budget deficit. If equilibrium were at point J in Figure 3-7, with $G = \$250$ billion, what would happen if autonomous tax revenues $(\overline{T})$ were raised from zero to $250 billion $(\Delta\overline{T} = 250)$? Once again we assume everything else remains the same (*ceteris paribus*), so we can use our basic two-step method to calculate the change in income. First, the change in A_p in equation (3.20) is:

$$\Delta A_p = \Delta a - c\Delta\overline{T} + \Delta I_p + \Delta G + \Delta NX$$
$$= 0 - c\Delta\overline{T} + 0 + 0 + 0 \tag{3.20}$$
$$= -0.75(250)$$
$$= -187.5$$

A $250 billion increase in autonomous tax revenues $(\Delta\overline{T} = 250)$ reduces autonomous planned spending by only $187.5 billion because households "pay" the remaining $62.5 billion of higher taxation by saving less than they otherwise would.

The lower frame of Figure 3-7 illustrates the effect of a tax increase on income. Autonomous spending drops by $187.5 billion, from $1000 billion to $812.5 billion, and equilibrium income drops from $4000 billion to $3250 billion (point K).

What multiplier expression corresponds to the change from J to K? The only component of autonomous spending that is changing is tax revenue. Thus we can take our general expression used to calculate income change (3.18) and substitute for ΔA_p the expression $-c\Delta\overline{T}$ that indicates the response of A_p to the tax change:

<table>
<tr><td align="center">General Linear Form</td><td align="center">Numerical Example</td><td></td></tr>
<tr><td align="center">$\Delta Y = \dfrac{\Delta A_p}{s} = \dfrac{-c\Delta\overline{T}}{s}$</td><td align="center">$\Delta Y = \dfrac{-(0.75)250}{0.25} = -750$</td><td align="center">(3.23)</td></tr>
</table>

The multiplier for an increase in taxes is the income change in equation (3.23) divided by $\Delta\overline{T}$.

<table>
<tr><td align="center">General Linear Form</td><td align="center">Numerical Example</td><td></td></tr>
<tr><td align="center">$\dfrac{\Delta Y}{\Delta\overline{T}} = \dfrac{\Delta A_p}{s\Delta\overline{T}} = \dfrac{-c\Delta\overline{T}}{s\Delta\overline{T}} = \dfrac{-c}{s}$</td><td align="center">$\dfrac{\Delta Y}{\Delta\overline{T}} = \dfrac{-0.75}{0.25} = -3.0$</td><td align="center">(3.24)</td></tr>
</table>

SELF-TEST   What is the multiplier for a balanced budget fiscal policy operation that raises both government spending and autonomous taxes by $250 billion?

Effect of Income Taxes

When the government raises some of its tax revenue (T) with an income tax in addition to the autonomous tax $(\bar{T})$, its total tax revenue is:

$$T = \bar{T} + \bar{t}Y \tag{3.25}$$

The first component, as before, is the autonomous tax. The second component is income tax revenue, the tax rate $(\bar{t})$ times income (Y). Disposable income $(Y - T)$ is total income minus tax revenue:

$$Y_D = Y - T = Y - \bar{T} - \bar{t}Y = (1 - \bar{t})Y - \bar{T} \tag{3.26}$$

Leakages from the spending stream. Following any change in total income (Y), disposable income changes by only a fraction $(1 - \bar{t})$ as much. For instance, if the tax rate $(\bar{t})$ is 0.2, then disposable income changes by 80 percent of the change in total income. Any change in total income (ΔY) is now divided into induced consumption, induced saving, and induced income tax revenue. The fraction of ΔY going into consumption is the marginal propensity to consume disposable income (c) times the fraction of income going into disposable income $(1 - \bar{t})$. Thus the change in total income is divided up as shown in the following table.

Fraction going to:	General Linear Form	Numerical Example
1. Induced consumption	$c(1 - \bar{t})$	$0.75(1 - 0.2) = 0.6$
2. Induced saving	$s(1 - \bar{t})$	$0.25(1 - 0.2) = 0.2$
3. Induced tax revenue	$\bar{t}$	0.2
Total	$(c + s)(1 - \bar{t}) + \bar{t}$ $= 1 - \bar{t} + \bar{t} = 1.0$	1.0

As in (3.14), the economy is in equilibrium when income equals planned expenditures:

$$Y = E_p \tag{3.14}$$

As before, we can subtract induced consumption from both sides of the equilibrium condition. According to the table above, income (Y) minus induced consumption is the total of induced saving plus induced tax revenue. Planned expenditure (E_p) minus induced consumption is autonomous planned spending (A_p). Thus the equilibrium condition is

induced saving + induced tax revenue

$$= \text{autonomous planned spending } (A_p) \tag{3.27}$$

From the table just given, (3.27) can be written in symbols as:

$$[s(1 - \bar{t}) + \bar{t}]Y = A_p \tag{3.28}$$

The term in brackets on the left-hand side is the fraction of a change in income that does not go into induced consumption—that is, the sum of the fraction going to induced saving $s(1 - \bar{t})$ and the fraction going to the government as income tax revenue $(\bar{t})$. The sum of these two fractions within

The **marginal leakage rate** is the fraction of income that is taxed or saved rather than being spent on consumption.

the brackets is called the **marginal leakage rate**. The equilibrium value for Y can be calculated when we divide both sides of (3.28) by the term in brackets:

General Linear Form

Numerical Example

$$Y = \frac{A_p}{s(1 - \bar{t}) + \bar{t}} \qquad Y = \frac{1000}{0.25(0.8) + 0.2} = \frac{1000}{0.4} = 2500 \qquad (3.29)$$

The numerical example shows that if autonomous planned spending (A_p) is $1000 billion, income will be only $2500 billion, rather than $4000 billion. Why? A greater fraction of each dollar of income now leaks out of the spending stream—0.4 in this numerical example—than occurred due to the saving rate of 0.25 by itself. This allows the injection of autonomous planned spending $(A_p = 1000)$ to be balanced by leakages out of the spending stream at a lower level of income.

Income Taxes and the Multiplier

The change in income (ΔY) is simply the change in autonomous planned spending (ΔA_p) divided by the marginal leakage rate:

$$\Delta Y = \frac{\Delta A_p}{s(1 - \bar{t}) + \bar{t}} \qquad (3.30)$$

The multiplier $(\Delta Y/ \Delta A_p)$ is simply 1.0 divided by the marginal leakage rate. The multiplier was $1/s$ when there was no income tax. Now, with an income tax:

$$\text{multiplier} = \frac{1}{\text{marginal leakage rate}} = \frac{1}{s(1 - \bar{t}) + \bar{t}} \qquad (3.31)$$

Earlier in the chapter, when the income tax rate was zero, the numerical example of the multiplier was 4. Now that we have introduced an income tax rate of 0.2, the marginal leakage rate is 0.4 [see equation (3.29)] and the multiplier is 1/0.4 of 2.5. Thus, raising the income tax rate reduces the multiplier and vice versa. This gives the government a new tool for stabilizing income. When the government wants to stimulate the economy and raise income, it can raise income in (3.29) and the multiplier in (3.31) by cutting income tax rates. This actually occurred in 1985. And, when the government wants to restrain the economy, it can raise income tax rates, as occurred in 1993.

The Government Budget Deficit

The government budget deficit is defined as before; it equals government expenditure minus tax revenue, $G - T$. Substituting the definition in (3.25) which expresses tax revenue (T) as the sum of autonomous and induced tax revenue, we can write the government deficit as:

Automatic stabilization is the effect of income taxes in lowering the multiplier effect of changes in autonomous planned spending

$$\text{government budget deficit} = G - T = G - \bar{T} - \bar{t}Y \qquad (3.32)$$

Thus the government budget deficit automatically shrinks when the level of income expands. This consequence of the income tax is sometimes called **automatic stabilization.** This name reflects the automatic rise and fall of

INTERNATIONAL PERSPECTIVE

Why Higher Income Raises the Trade Deficit

As you have learned in this chapter, part of each extra dollar of income is spent on consumption, while the remaining part leaks out of the spending stream into saving, taxes, and net exports. The higher the fraction that leaks out (the marginal leakage rate), the lower is the multiplier.

One of the most important sources of leakage from the spending stream is foreign trade. When income increases, imports also increase, causing net exports to decline. The figure shows that change in real income is the single most important source of changes in net exports. In countries that had large increases in real income over the period shown (e.g., Germany and Austria), net exports declined significantly. The opposite is also true: in countries that had large decreases in real income (most notably Finland), net exports increased significantly.

The dots for the various countries do not all lie perfectly on the straight line, since there are other causes of changes in net exports (as you will learn in Chapter 6). In the case of the United States, for instance, net exports increased significantly, despite a substantial increase in real income, because the foreign exchange rate of the dollar had declined over the previous few years, causing U.S. exports to increase rapidly and imports to increase more slowly than would otherwise have been the case.

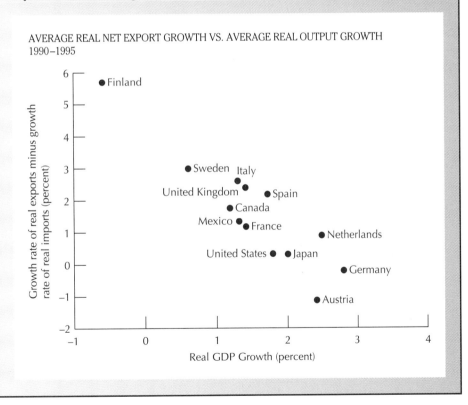

AVERAGE REAL NET EXPORT GROWTH VS. AVERAGE REAL OUTPUT GROWTH 1990–1995

income tax revenues as income rises and falls. When income rises, income tax revenues rise and siphon off some of the income before households have a chance to spend it. Similarly, when income falls, income tax revenues fall and help minimize the drop in disposable income. This is why the presence of an income tax makes the multiplier smaller.

Does the government budget deficit grow or shrink in an economic expansion? In a recession?

3-8 International Trade, Net Exports, and the Multiplier

The theory of income determination in equation (3.29) states that equilibrium income equals autonomous planned spending (A_p) divided by the marginal leakage rate. When the United States trades with nations abroad, U.S. producers sell part of domestic output as exports. Households and business firms purchase imports from abroad, so part of U.S. expenditure does not generate U.S. production.

How do exports and imports affect the determination of income? We learned in Chapter 2 that the difference between exports and imports is called net exports and is part of GDP. When exports increase, net exports increase. When imports increase, net exports decrease. Designating net exports by NX, we can write the relationship between net exports and income (Y) as:

$$NX = \overline{NX} - nxY \qquad (3.33)$$

Net exports contains an autonomous component $(\overline{NX})$, reflecting the fact that the level of exports depends mainly on income in foreign countries (which is exogenous, not explained by our theory) rather than on domestic income (Y). Net exports also contains an induced component $(-nxY)$, reflecting the fact that imports rise if domestic income (Y) rises, thus reducing net exports.

Because we now have a new component of autonomous expenditure, the autonomous component of net exports $(\overline{NX})$, we can rewrite our definition of A_p as the following in place of equation (3.10):

$$A_p = a - c\overline{T} + I_p + G + \overline{NX} \qquad (3.34)$$

Because imports depend on income (Y), the induced component of net exports $(-nxY)$ has exactly the same effect on equilibrium income and the multiplier as does the income tax. Imports represent a leakage from the spending stream, a portion of a change in income that is not part of the disposable income of U.S. citizens and thus not available for consumption. The fraction of a change in income that is spent on net exports (nx) is part of the economy's marginal leakage rate.

Types of leakages	*Marginal leakage rate*
Saving only	s
Saving and income tax	$s(1 - \bar{t}) + \bar{t}$
Saving, income tax, and imports	$s(1 - \bar{t}) + \bar{t} + nx$

When we combine (3.29), (3.34), and the table, equilibrium income becomes:

$$Y = \frac{A_p}{\text{marginal leakage rate}} = \frac{a - c\overline{T} + I_p + G + \overline{NX}}{s(1 - \bar{t}) + \bar{t} + nx} \qquad (3.35)$$

SELF-TEST

> In Belgium both exports and imports are a much higher fraction of income than in the United States. Which country has the higher multiplier for changes in government spending, Belgium or the United States?

This completes our analysis of the simple Keynesian model of income determination. As explained at the beginning of the chapter, we have maintained two crucial assumptions—that both the interest rate and the price level are fixed. We now turn in Chapter 4 to a more realistic model that builds on what you have learned but allows the interest rate to vary and to influence the level of autonomous planned spending. We retain the assumption of a fixed price level throughout Chapters 4 and 5 before allowing the price level to be flexible, starting in Chapters 6 and 7.

SUMMARY

1. This chapter presents a simple theory for determining real income. Important simplifying assumptions include the constancy of the interest rate and the price level.

2. Disposable income is divided between consumption and saving. Throughout the chapter consumption is assumed to be a fixed autonomous amount, $250 billion in the numerical example, plus 0.75 of disposable income. Saving is the remaining 0.25 of disposable income minus the $250 billion of autonomous consumption.

3. During the 1929–95 period, U.S. consumption was a roughly constant fraction of disposable income. Exceptions were during the worst year of the Great Depression, when consumption exceeded income, and during World War II, when rationing prevented households from obtaining the goods they desired and forced them to save an abnormal fraction of their income.

4. Output and income (Y) are equal by definition to total expenditures (E), which in turn can be divided up between planned expenditure (E_p) and unintended inventory accumulation (I_u). We convert this definition into a theory by assuming that business firms adjust production whenever I_u is not zero. The economy is in equilibrium, with no pressure for production to change, only when there is no unintended inventory accumulation or decumulation $(I_u = 0)$.

5. Autonomous planned spending (A_p) equals total planned expenditure minus induced consumption. The five components of autonomous planned expenditure are autonomous consumption (a), planned investment (I_p), government spending (G), net exports (NX), and the effect on consumption of autonomous tax revenue $(-cT)$.

6. Any change in autonomous planned spending (ΔA_p) has a multiplier effect: an increase raises income and induced consumption over and above the initial boost in A_p. Income must increase until enough extra saving has been induced $(s\Delta Y)$ to balance the injection of extra autonomous planned spending (ΔA_p). For this reason, the multiplier, the ratio of the change in income to the change in autonomous planned spending $(\Delta Y/\Delta A_p)$, is the inverse of the marginal propensity to save $(1/s)$.

7. The same multiplier is valid for a change in any component in A_p. Thus, if private spending components of A_p are weak, the government can raise its spending (G) or cut taxes (T) to maintain stability in A_p and thus in real output.

8. The multiplier is the inverse of the marginal propensity to save only if there is no income tax and no foreign trade. More generally, the multiplier is the inverse of the marginal leakage rate, which consists of the fraction of GDP that leaks out of the spending stream into saving, income tax revenue, and imports.

9. Reductions in the income tax rate raise income and the multiplier, while increases in the income tax rate reduce income and the multiplier.

CONCEPTS

endogenous variables
exogenous variables
autonomous magnitudes

marginal propensity to consume
induced consumption
marginal propensity to save

parameter
equilibrium
unintended inventory investment
induced saving

multiplier
marginal leakage rate
automatic stabilization

QUESTIONS AND PROBLEMS

Questions

1. Explain the distinction between exogenous variables and endogenous variables. Explain the distinction, if any, between a parameter and an exogenous variable. For the most complete model used in this chapter, which of the following variables are endogenous? Which are exogenous?
   (a) autonomous taxes
   (b) marginal leakage rate
   (c) consumption
   (d) marginal propensity to consume
   (e) exports
   (f) net exports
   (g) GDP
   (h) price level
   (i) interest rate
   (j) tax rate
   (k) investment
   (l) tax revenue
   (m) disposable income
   (n) saving
   (o) foreign trade surplus (deficit)
   (p) government budget surplus (deficit)

2. Given a consumption function of the form $C = a + c(Y - T)$ and $T = \overline{T} + \overline{t}Y$, write the formula for the expanded consumption function. Write the formula for the expanded saving function that is implied by the stated consumption function.

3. Why do we distinguish between autonomous consumption and induced consumption?

4. Does the existence of positive inventory change imply that the economy is out of equilibrium? Why or why not?

5. What moves the economy toward equilibrium when unintended inventory investment is either positive or negative rather than zero?

6. Assume that there is an increase in autonomous investment of $100 billion. Under which circumstance will the ultimate impact on the level of equilibrium GDP be greater: (a) with a relatively high marginal propensity to consume, or (b) a relatively low marginal propensity to consume? Explain.

7. How would your answer in question 6 change if the alternatives read: (a) with a relatively high marginal leakage rate, or (b) with a relatively low marginal leakage rate? Explain.

8. Is it more desirable for an economy to have a large multiplier or a small multiplier?

9. What is the effect on the multiplier of including induced taxes in the model of income determination presented in this chapter?

10. Explain why government action that increases the deficit is expansionary fiscal policy. What about action which decreases the surplus?

11. Why are imports considered to be a leakage in the economy? How are imports included in the model presented in this chapter?

Problems

1. Consider an economy in which all taxes are autonomous and the following values of autonomous consumption, planned investment, government expenditure, taxes, and the marginal propensity to consume are given:

   $a = 400$ $I_p = 450$ $G = 300$ $\overline{T} = 400$ $c = .75$

   (a) What is the level of consumption when the level of income (Y) equals $4200?
   (b) What is the level of saving when the level of income (Y) equals $4200?
   (c) What is the level of planned investment when

   the level of income (Y) equals $4200? What is the level of actual investment? What is the level of unintended inventory investment?
   (d) Show that injections equal leakages when income (Y) equals $4200.
   (e) Is the economy in equilibrium when income $(Y) = $4200? If not, what is the equilibrium level of income for the economy described in this question?

2. $C = a + c(Y - T)$
   $T = \overline{T} + \overline{t}Y$
   $NX = \overline{NX} - nxY$

where:

$a = 300$	$I_p = 400$	$\overline{T} = 200$	$\overline{NX} = 400$
$c = 0.5$	$t = 0.3$	$nx = 0.1$	$G = 500$

(a) Determine the equilibrium levels of GDP, consumption, saving, and taxes.

(b) What is the value of the marginal propensity to save? What is the value of the marginal leakage rate? Why are these two magnitudes not equal?

(c) At the equilibrium level of GDP, is there a surplus or deficit in the government budget? How much?

(d) What is the balance of trade in the foreign sector at the equilibrium level of income?

(e) What is the new equilibrium level of GDP if government spending increases by $30 billion?

(f) Given the relationship that $S - I - NX = G - T$, show how the $30 billion increase in government spending in part (e) is financed.

3. Given a consumption function in the form $C = a + c(Y - T)$ and $T = \overline{T} + tY$, and given the following values,

$$a = 300 \quad c = 0.8 \quad \overline{T} = 100 \quad t = 0.25$$

(a) What is the level of tax revenue when $Y = \$5000$ billion?

(b) What is the level of disposable income $(Y - T)$ when $Y = \$5000$ billion?

(c) What is the level of consumption when $Y = \$5000$ billion?

(d) Assuming that saving and taxes are the only leakages in this economy, what is the value of the marginal leakage rate?

(e) Assuming that the only other source of spending in the economy is government spending, what must the value of G be in order to generate an equilibrium value of $Y = \$5000$?

(f) What is the value of the government budget surplus or deficit in this example?

4. Assume that in addition to strictly autonomous investment and government spending, the economy has the following behavioral equations for consumption (C), net tax revenue (T) and net exports (NX):

$$C = a + c(Y - T)$$
$$T = \overline{T} + tY$$
$$NX = \overline{NX} - nxY$$

where:

$a = 170$	$I_p = 600$	$\overline{T} = 800$	$X = N800$
$c = .9$	$t = .25$	$nx = 0.175$	$G = 1650$

(a) What is the value of autonomous planned expenditure?

(b) What is the value of the marginal leakage rate?

(c) What is the equilibrium value of income (Y)?

(d) What is the size of the government surplus or deficit? The foreign trade surplus or deficit?

(e) At equilibrium, how is the level of investment being financed? (*Hint:* Show that leakages equal injections in this situation.)

5. Assume that the marginal propensity to consume equals 0.6 for every consumer in the economy. You have just been paid $20,000 to produce a research report for the Commerce Department. How will this action by the government affect your spending plans? What would be the total effect on the economy of this action? (Assume that $t = 0$ and $nx = 0$.) What would be the total effect if $t = 0.2$ and $nx = 0.08$?

6. Assume that the marginal propensity to consume equals 0.6 for every consumer in the economy. You have just received a tax cut of $20,000. How will this action by the government affect your spending plans? What would be the total effect on the economy of this action? (Assume that $t = 0$ and $nx = 0$). What would be the total effect if $t = 0.2$ and $nx = 0.08$? Are your answers the same for problems 5 and 6? Why or why not?

SELF-TEST ANSWERS

p. 70 At point F consumption and disposable income are equal. Thus consumption, $a + c(Y - T)$, equals disposable income, or $Y - T$. Setting these two equal, we can subtract $c(Y - T)$ from $Y - T$ to obtain $a = (1 - c)(Y - T)$. Dividing by $1 - c$, we obtain the answer that disposable income $(Y - T)$ is equal to $a/(1 - c)$ and so is consumption. Thus at point F consumption equals 250/0.25, or 1000, while saving equals zero. When disposable income is 2500, consumption $C = 250 + 0.75(2500) = 2125$. Saving $= Y - T - C = 2500 - 2125 = 375$.

p. 76 When income is only 2000, planned expenditure is equal to autonomous spending $(600 + 250 - 100)$ plus induced consumption $(0.75 \text{ times } 2000 = 1500)$, for a total of 2250. Thus planned expenditure exceeds income, forcing firms to reduce their inventories in order to meet demand. Unintended inventory investment is -250, and firms raise production in order to provide goods to meet planned expenditures; this increase in production moves the economy toward the equilibrium income level of 3000.

p. 81 We write planned investment as I_p with a p subscript, to reflect our assumption that *consumers and the government are always able to realize their plans,* so that there is no such thing as autonomous unplanned consumption, autonomous tax revenues, or government spending. Only business firms are forced to make unplanned expenditures, as occurs when investment *(I)* is not equal to what they plan *(I_p)*, but also includes unplanned inventory *(I_u)*.

p. 81 The absence of a Δ in front of the s in equation (3.18) reflects the fact that we are interested in the effects of a change in autonomous spending, *while holding constant the marginal propensity to consume (c) and to save ($s = 1 - c$).* To keep the formula simple, it assumes there is no change in s.[5]

p. 85 The balanced budget multiplier is the multiplier for a change in government spending ($1/s$) from equation (3.21) plus the multiplier for a change in autonomous taxes ($-c/s$) from equation (3.24). Adding ($1/s$) and ($-c/s$), we obtain $(1 - c)/s = 1$. Thus, the balanced budget multiplier is unity whenever there is no income tax or leakage from spending into imports. See if you can work out the value of the balanced budget multiplier for the more general case based on equation (3.35).

p. 88 Because government tax revenues grow in an economic expansion, the government budget deficit shrinks in an expansion and grows in a recession.

p. 89 Because Belgium has a much higher nx in equation (3.35), it will have a lower multiplier for any change in autonomous spending, including a change in government spending.

---

[5]Using the calculus formula for the change in a ratio, the change in income when both A_p and s are allowed to change is:

$$\Delta Y = \Delta A_p/s - A_p \Delta s/\Delta s^2$$

Equation (3.18) in the text simply sets Δs equal to zero in this expression.

The IS-LM Model

*It may be laid down as a maxim, that wherever a great deal can
be made by the use of money, a great deal will commonly
be given for the use of it.*
—Adam Smith, 1776

4-1 Introduction

The basic theme of the last chapter was that income and real GDP change by
a *multiple* of any change in autonomous planned spending. But changes in
autonomous planned spending (ΔA_p) were assumed to be already known;
that is, they were *exogenous* and were not explained. In this chapter we
accept everything in Chapter 3 as valid. But we go further and relate the level
of autonomous planned spending to the level of the interest rate.

If autonomous planned spending depends partly on the interest rate,
what determines the interest rate? First we will explore the connection
between the interest rate and the supply of money. Then we will see how the
government uses its control over the money supply to influence the interest
rate, and thus the equilibrium level of income. We will learn that both the
level of income and the level of the interest rate can be affected by monetary
and fiscal policy, working separately or in combination.

*PUZZLE 4: WHY HAVE
REAL INTEREST RATES
BEEN SO HIGH?*

This chapter adds to our understanding of the process of income determination, and begins our investigation of the key questions at the heart of
recent economic debates:

1. Why have real interest rates been so high? This is Puzzle 4 identified at
   the beginning of the book. Why, for instance, was the real interest rate as
   high as 6.8 percent in the 1980s and 5.2 percent in the 1990s, when in the
   1960s and 1970s its average was a much lower 3.3 percent?[1]

2. What have been the effects of unprecedented federal budget deficits in
   the years since 1981? Once we allow for an increase in the interest rate,
   does an expansion in government spending or a tax cut (a fiscal policy
   stimulus) have the full multiplier effect of Chapter 3?

3. If an increase in the interest rate reduces the size of the multiplier, which
   components of spending are affected? Will planned private domestic
   investment be crowded out, or will the main effect of the fiscal stimulus
   be to reduce net exports and net foreign investment?

4. If a stimulus to the economy is needed when actual real GDP is below natural real GDP, should that stimulus be provided by monetary policy or by
   fiscal policy?

In this chapter, as in Chapter 3, we will assume that the price level is fixed.
All changes in real income and real GDP are accompanied by the same change

---

[1]These figures refer to the real interest rate plotted in Figure 1-10 on p. 19.

in nominal income and nominal GDP. All effects of spending on inflation and of inflation on the interest rate are postponed for treatment later.

4-2   Interest Rates and Rates of Return

The central focus of this chapter is on the interest rate. While in the real world there are many different interest rates, here we simplify by assuming that there is only a single interest rate. Savers receive this rate as a return on their savings accounts and holdings of bonds. And both business firms and consumers pay this interest rate when they borrow from financial institutions.

Functions of Interest Rates

Interest rates help the economy allocate saving among alternative uses. For savers, the interest rate is a reward for abstaining from consumption and waiting to consume at some future time. The higher the interest rate, the greater the incentive to save. For borrowers, the interest rate is the cost of borrowing funds to invest or buy consumption goods. At a higher interest rate, people will borrow fewer funds and purchase fewer goods. Thus if the desire to borrow exceeds the willingness to save sufficient funds, the interest rate tends to rise.

Business borrowers decide how much to invest by comparing the interest rate charged on borrowed funds with the earnings of investment projects. The projects—for example, structures like office buildings and durable goods like airplanes and computers—would not be undertaken unless the investor expected earnings to remain after paying expenses like wages and rent. These earnings provide the funds needed to pay the interest charged for borrowed funds. Clearly, any increase in the interest rate will reduce the likelihood that earnings will be large enough to cover interest payments, and as a result investment is likely to fall. The same reasoning applies to consumer borrowing. Consumers compare the interest payments on a loan with the desirability of having a good like a house or car sooner rather than later. Higher interest rates will cause some consumers to wait rather than buy now, and autonomous consumption will fall.

Interest rates are central to the role of monetary policy. Since the government, through the Federal Reserve Board (the Fed), can influence the interest rate, it can affect the cost of borrowed funds to private borrowers.

Types of Interest Rates

Banks offer a variety of interest rates on checking and savings accounts. Some types of accounts allow customers to earn interest instantly; others require customers to leave funds on deposit for a year or more. The phrase "short-term interest rate" refers to interest that is paid on funds deposited for three months or less; "long-term interest rate" refers to interest on funds deposited for a year or more.

In addition to short-term interest rates on bank deposits, there are short-term interest rates that apply to funds borrowed by the government (the

Treasury bill rate), by businesses (the commercial paper rate), and by banks (the federal funds rate). Similarly, in addition to long-term rates on bank deposits, there are long-term interest rates that apply to funds borrowed by the government (the Treasury bond rate), by businesses (the corporate bond rate), and by households (the mortgage rate). The business sections of most local newspapers and the *Wall Street Journal* publish the daily values of these rates.

The hallmark of a good theory is its ability to spotlight important relationships and to ignore unnecessary details. For most purposes, the differences between alternative interest rates fall into that category of detail, in contrast to the important overall *average* level of interest rates. Thus "the" interest rate discussed in this chapter can be regarded as an average of all the different interest rates listed in the previous paragraph.

4-3 The Relation of Autonomous Planned Spending to the Interest Rate

We begin by asking why planned investment (a component of autonomous planned spending) depends on the interest rate. Business firms attempt to profit by borrowing funds to buy investment goods—office buildings, shopping centers, factories, machine tools, computers, airplanes. Obviously, firms can stay in business only if the earnings of investment goods are at least enough to pay the interest on the borrowed funds (or to attract enough investors to warrant a new issue of stock).

Example of an Airline's Investment Decision

The **rate of return** on an investment project is its annual earnings divided by its total cost.

American Airlines calculates that it can earn $10 million per year from one additional Boeing 757 jet airliner after paying all expenses for employee salaries, fuel, food, and airplane maintenance—that is, all expenses besides interest payments on the borrowed funds. If the 757 costs $50 million, that level of earnings represents a 20 percent **rate of return** ($10,000,000/ $50,000,000), defined as annual earnings divided by the cost of the airplane. If American must pay 10 percent interest to obtain the funds for the airplane, the 20 percent rate of return is more than sufficient to pay the interest expense.

In the top frame of Figure 4-1, point *A* shows that the 20 percent rate of return on the first 757 exceeds the 10 percent interest rate on borrowed funds. The steplike red line in the top frame of Figure 4-1 shows the rate of return on the first through fifth planes. The gray area between point *A* and the 10 percent interest rate represents the annual profit rate made on the first plane. Point *B* for the second plane also indicates a profit. Point *C* shows that purchase of a third extra 757 earns only a 10 percent rate of return, or $5 million (10 percent of $50 million) in extra earnings after payment of all noninterest expenses.

Why do the second and third planes earn less than the first? The first plane is operated on the most profitable routes; the second and third must fly on routes that are less likely to yield full passenger loads. A fourth plane (at point *D*) would have an even lower rate of return, insufficient to pay the interest cost of borrowed funds. How many planes will be purchased? The third

Figure 4-1
The Payoff to Investment for an Airline and the Economy

The red ceplike line in the top frame shows the rate of return to American Airlines for purchases of additional 757s. If the interest rate is 10 percent, a profit is made by purchasing the first two planes, and the company breaks even by buying the third plane. Purchase of a fourth or fifth plane would be a mistake, because the planes would not generate enough additional profit to pay for the cost of borrowing the money to buy them. The bottom frame shows the same phenomenon for the economy as a whole.

AN INCREASE IN PLANNED PRIVATE SPENDING REDUCES THE RATE OF RETURN

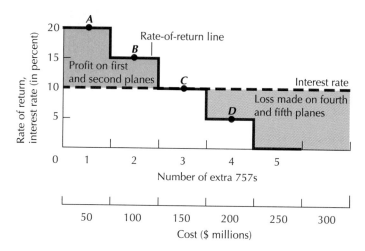

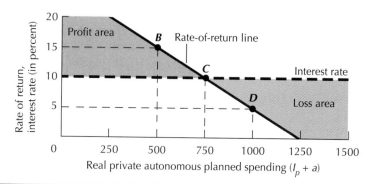

can pay its interest expense and will be purchased, but the fourth will not. If the interest cost of borrowed funds were to rise above 10 percent but remain below 15 percent, American would purchase two planes instead of three. If the interest rate were to fall to 5 percent or below, then American would purchase four planes.

The Interest Rate and the Rate-of-Return Line

The interest rate not only influences the level of business investment but also affects the level of household consumption. For instance, households deciding whether to purchase a dishwasher or a second automobile will consider the size of the monthly payment, which depends on the interest rate. In the bottom frame of Figure 4-1 the rate-of-return line shows that the return on planned investment and autonomous consumption spending ($I_p + a$) declines as the level of spending increases. As for American Airlines, each successive investment good purchased by business firms is less profitable than the last. Similarly, each successive consumption good purchased by households provides fewer services than the last (for instance, a family's second car is less important and useful than its first car).

The rates of return for three alternative quantities of $I_p + a$ are plotted along the rate-of-return line in the bottom frame of Figure 4-1. They are

Point	$I_p + a$	Rate of return	Interest rate	Profit
B	500	15	10	5
C	750	10	10	0
D	1000	5	10	−5

The gray area shows that if the interest rate is 10 percent, a profit will be made on the first $750 billion of $I_p + a$. However, the rate of return of further spending is below the interest rate and creates the losses indicated by the red shaded area.

Thus, determination of the level of $I_p + a$ is a two-step process. First we plot the rate-of-return line representing firms' and consumers' expectations of the benefit of additional purchases. Second, we find the level of $I_p + a$ at the point where the rate-of-return line crosses the interest rate level.

When the interest rate is 10 percent, as in Figure 4-1, autonomous planned spending $(I_p + a)$ will be $750 billion at point C, as long as the level of business and consumer optimism remains constant. A decrease in the interest rate will increase purchases $(I_p + a)$; for instance, a decrease from 10 percent to 5 percent moves autonomous planned spending from $750 billion at C to $1000 billion at D.

Business and Consumer Optimism

Can purchases ever change when the interest rate is held constant at 10 percent? Certainly—an increase in business and consumer optimism about the expected payoff of additional purchases can shift the entire rate-of-return line to the right, as indicated by the red "new rate-of-return line" in Figure 4-2. This shifts to the right (to point F) the intersection of the rate-of-return line with the fixed horizontal interest rate line.

Summarizing, we can show the amount of $I_p + a$ spending that would occur at different interest rates and different levels of confidence.

Figure 4-2
Effect on Autonomous Planned Spending of an Increase in Business and Consumer Confidence

The dashed red "original rate-of-return line" is an exact copy of the solid red "rate-of-return line" in Figure 4-1. If the level of business and consumer confidence were to increase, the spending schedule would shift rightward to the solid red "new rate-of-return line." If the interest rate were to stay constant at 10 percent, then autonomous planned spending (A_p) would increase from $750 billion at point C to $1000 billion at point F.

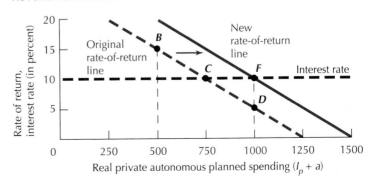

HIGHER BUSINESS AND CONSUMER CONFIDENCE RAISES AUTONOMOUS SPENDING

Figure 4-3
Relation of the Various Components of Autonomous Planned Spending to the Interest Rate

The vertical black line shows that three components of autonomous planned spending do not depend on the interest rate. These are government spending *(G)*, the effect of autonomous taxes *(−cT̄)*, and net exports *(NX)*. The sloped line shows that autonomous consumption *(a)* and planned investment *(I_p)* depend inversely on the interest rate. Hence, the total demand for autonomous planned spending, as shown by the "*A_p* demand schedule," also depends inversely on the interest rate.

BOTH CONSUMPTION AND INVESTMENT BY BUSINESS FIRMS RESPOND TO THE INTEREST RATE

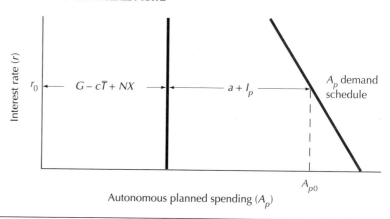

	Demand for $I_p + a$	
Interest rate	*Original rate-of-return line (pessimistic expectations)*	*New higher rate-of-return line (optimistic expectations)*
15	500 (at *B*)	750
10	750 (at *C*)	1000 (at *F*)
5	1000 (at *D*)	1250

The left-hand column (pessimistic expectations) is plotted as the "original rate-of-return line" (red dashes) in Figure 4-2. The right-hand column (optimistic expectations) is plotted as the solid red "new rate-of-return line."

The Demand for Autonomous Planned Spending

You learned earlier that there are five components of autonomous planned spending (A_p): planned investment, autonomous consumption, government spending, the effect of taxes on consumption, and net exports. We have already seen that planned investment and autonomous consumption both depend on the interest rate; both types of spending are stimulated by a lower interest rate.

In Figure 4-3 we plot the relationship of the components of autonomous planned spending on the horizontal axis to the interest rate on the vertical axis. The negative relationship between the interest rate and both planned investment and autonomous consumption $(I_p + a)$ is copied from Figure 4-2. The other three components of autonomous spending do not depend on the interest rate.[2] Accordingly, the total amount of government spending, the effect of taxes on consumption, and net exports $(G − cT̄ + NX)$ are plotted as the black vertical line in Figure 4-3, since a vertical line indicates that the

---

[2] Chapter 6 identifies an indirect link between the interest rate and net exports, working through the foreign exchange rate. But the direct link is minor and can be ignored here.

variable being described does not depend on the variable plotted along the vertical axis.

Total autonomous planned spending also consists of autonomous consumption (a) and planned investment (I_p), both of which depend negatively on the interest rate, so *the amount of these two components added to the first three depends on the interest rate.* The lower the interest rate, the larger a and the larger I_p. The total of all five components is shown by the line on the right labeled "A_p demand schedule." This schedule shows that the total of all autonomous planned spending depends on the interest rate, because two of its components ($a + I_p$) depend on the interest rate.

Shifts in the A_p Demand Schedule

As before, government spending, taxes, and net exports are given exogenous amounts. A change in any of these will shift the A_p demand schedule. As you previously learned, a shift of business expectations toward optimism and confidence will boost planned investment regardless of the interest rate, so such attitudes will also shift the A_p demand schedule. Finally, an improvement in consumer confidence will raise autonomous consumer spending and shift the schedule in the same way.

In summary, five different events can shift the A_p demand schedule to the right (the opposite events will shift the A_p demand schedule to the left):

1. An increase in government spending (ΔG), caused for instance by an outbreak of war or a need to boost spending on education or highway repair.

2. A cut in taxes, which boosts consumption ($-c\,\overline{\Delta T}$), perhaps as the result of campaign promises by politicians.

3. An increase in net exports, such as American firms beginning to sell more toys to Japan through the new Toys R Us stores in Tokyo.

4. A change in business expectations toward more optimism as rising airline traffic causes airline executives to raise their estimates of the profitability of purchasing new planes.

5. An improvement in consumer confidence as newspaper stories about plant closings and layoffs become less frequent.

SELF-TEST   How will the A_p demand schedule shift to the left, right, or not at all in response to the following events: (1) a reduction in auto imports from Japan as the quality of American-built cars improves, (2) the stimulus to housing given by lower mortgage interest rates, and (3) higher taxes levied by the government in an attempt to reduce the budget deficit?

4-4 The *IS* Curve

You have now learned that total autonomous planned spending (A_p) depends on the interest rate. And in Chapter 3 you learned that the total level of real GDP and real income depend on the total level of autonomous planned spending. Now, if we put these two relationships together, we conclude that total

HOW INTEREST RATES AFFECT HOUSE SALES

Textbooks traditionally emphasize the effect of changes in the interest rate on investment by business firms. But changes in interest rates also have a profound effect on the ability of ordinary people to purchase homes and consumer durable goods like automobiles. This means that changes in interest rates affect not only business investment in nonresidential structures and equipment, but also investment in residential structures and consumer durable expenditures.

Most people who buy homes must obtain a mortgage loan from a financial institution. In judging an

individual's ability to qualify for a mortgage, the loan officer compares income with the annual mortgage payment (including interest and principal). One common rule of thumb is that the mortgage payment should be no more than 25 percent of income. When interest rates go up, the mortgage payment increases, so that some people who formerly qualified for mortgages no longer qualify. These people are thus prevented from buying homes, and the demand for housing decreases. This phenomenon is an additional reason for the negative relationship between planned autonomous spending and the interest rate, developed in Section 4-3.

As an example of how higher mortgage rates influence people's ability to buy homes, the following table explores how the required annual mortgage payment doubled between 1978 and 1982, far exceeding the growth in median family income. As a result, median family income fell as a percentage of qualifying income (four times the mortgage payment) from 82.6 percent in 1978 to 55.0 percent in 1982. By 1985 interest rates had fallen sufficiently to reverse this process, bring the percentage back to 67.2 in 1985, with a further improvement to 80.5 percent in 1991 and 98.1 percent in 1994.

The annual number of houses constructed (housing starts) dropped in line with the sharp decline in the ability of people to afford mortgage payments, from 2.0 million in 1978 to 1.1 million in 1982, and then recovered to 1.7 million in 1985 and 1.5 million in 1988. Then housing starts collapsed to 1.0 million in 1991, breaking the relationship. Housing starts recovered to 1.5 million in 1994, still below the record 1978 number, even though family income in 1994 was much higher in relation to qualifying income than had been true in 1978.

	Single-family median home price	*Mortgage interest rate*	*Annual mortgage payment*	*Qualifying income—four times mortgage payment*	*Median family income*	*(5) As percentage of (4)*
	(1)	(2)	(3)	(4)	(5)	(6)
1978	$ 55,700	9.58%	$ 5,336	$21,344	$17,640	82.6%
1982	69,300	15.38	10,658	42,632	23,433	55.0
1985	84,300	12.24	10,319	41,276	27,735	67.2
1988	112,500	10.49	11,801	47,204	32,172	68.2
1991	120,000	9.30	11,160	44,640	35,939	80.5
1994	120,000	7.47	9,711	38,844	38,105	98.1

Note: All data in the table are from the Census Bureau, except for the mortgage interest rate, which is from the National Association of Realtors. Housing starts are from the Economic Report of the President.

real GDP and real income must depend on the interest rate. In this section we derive a graphical schedule that shows the different possible combinations of the interest rate and real income that are compatible with equilibrium, given the state of business and consumer confidence, the marginal propensity to save, and the level of government spending, taxes, and net exports. This schedule is the **IS curve.**

The **IS curve** is the schedule that identifies the combinations of income and the interest rate at which the commodity market is in equilibrium; everywhere along the IS curve, the demand for commodities equals the supply.

How to Derive the *IS* Curve

The lower left-hand corner of Figure 4-4 shows the first ingredient in the derivation of the *IS* curve. The "A_p demand schedule" shows the demand for autonomous planned spending at different levels of the interest rate and is copied from the "original rate-of-return line" in Figure 4-2. Notice that at a 10 percent interest rate (point *C*), A_p will be $750 billion, just the same as *(at point C)* in Figure 4-2. To simplify the discussion, initially we assume that there are no government spending, tax revenue, or net exports, so total autonomous spending consists simply of the two components, $I_p + a$, both of which depend negatively on the interest rate.[3]

What will be the equilibrium level of real income if A_p equals $750 billion? We answer this question, just as in Chapter 3, by plotting the level of A_p in the upper right-hand corner of Figure 4-4 as the horizontal red line (with a height of $750 billion). Where the $A_p = 750$ line crosses the upward-sloping Induced saving line at point *C*, equilibrium real income is $3000 billion. In the lower right-hand side of Figure 4-4 is plotted the equilibrium level of real income of $3000 billion against the assumed 10 percent level of the interest rate.

The figure also shows other possibilities; for instance, at point *B* in the lower right-hand frame the assumed 15 percent interest rate is plotted against the $2000 billion level of real income that is compatible with it. Point *B* in the other frames shows the determination of autonomous spending and induced saving.

SELF-TEST

What interest rate is compatible with a $4000 billion level of equilibrium real income? At what point does this equilibrium occur in the lower right-hand frame of Figure 4-4?

Because A_p depends on the interest rate, equilibrium income does also. The *IS* curve in Figure 4-4 plots the values of equilibrium real income when the marginal propensity to save is 0.25 and the multiplier is 4.0, as in the preceding chapter. Notice that points *B*, *C*, and *D* along the *IS* curve are all plotted at a horizontal distance exactly 4.0 times the value of the A_p line in the lower left-hand frame.

---

[3] The equation of the A_p demand schedule in the lower left quadrant of Figure 4-4 is:

$$1250 - 50r$$

Thus, when the interest rate is at 10 percent in the vertical direction, the level of autonomous planned spending along the A_p demand schedule is $1250 - (50 \times 10) = 750$.

WHY EQUIBLIBRIUM REAL INCOME DEPENDS ON THE INTEREST RATE

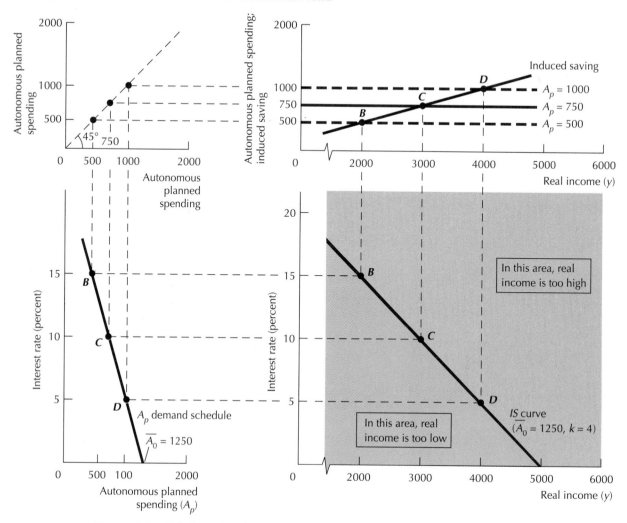

Figure 4-4   **Relation of the IS Curve to the Demand for Autonomous Spending and the Amount of Induced Saving**

In the lower left frame the "A_p demand schedule" is copied from the dashed red line in Figure 4-2. It shows that the demand for autonomous planned spending depends on the interest rate. For instance, at a 10 percent interest rate the level of A_p is $750 billion at point C. Following the thin dashed black line up from point C and over to the upper right frame, we see that the economy is in equilibrium at point C, where both A_p and induced savings are equal. This equilibrium level of income is $3000 billion and is plotted directly below in the lower right-hand frame, opposite the 10 percent interest rate that we assumed at the beginning.

What the *IS* Curve Shows

 The *IS* curve shows all the different combinations of the interest rate (*r*) and income *(Y)* at which the economy's market for commodities (goods and services) is in equilibrium, which occurs only when income equals planned expenditures. At any point off the *IS* curve the economy is out of equilibrium.

know this for the test!! (handwritten)

LEARNING ABOUT DIAGRAMS: THE *IS* CURVE

Since the *IS* curve is so important and useful, we pause here to study it more closely. (A full algebraic treatment of the *IS-LM* model is given in the appendix to Chapter 5.)

Diagram Ingredients and Reasons for Slope

The vertical axis is the interest rate and the horizontal axis is the level of income.

The *IS* curve takes information from two other graphs, the A_p demand schedule and the equilibrium between induced saving and autonomous planned spending. Because A_p depends on the interest rate, and because equilibrium income is a multiple (k) of A_p, equilibrium income becomes a negative function of the interest rate.

The horizontal position (equilibrium income) along the *IS* curve is equal to the horizontal position along the A_p demand schedule times the multiplier k.

The *IS* curve slopes down because income is a multiple of A_p, and A_p depends negatively on the interest rate. The *IS* curve becomes flatter, the more responsive is A_p to the interest rate, and the larger the multiplier. The *IS* curve becomes steeper, the less responsive is A_p to the interest rate, and the smaller the multiplier.

What Shifts and Rotates the *IS* Curve?

The *IS* curve is equal to the interest-dependent level of A_p times the multiplier (k). Anything that shifts the A_p demand schedule will shift the *IS* curve in the same direction. Five factors will shift the *IS* curve to the right: an increase in business or consumer confidence, an increase in government spending or net exports, and a decrease in taxes (or increase in transfers). Opposite changes will shift the *IS* curve to the left.

Figure 4-5 illustrates the effect of a rightward shift in the A_p demand schedule. The result is a rightward shift in the *IS* curve by an amount equal to the A_p shift times the multiplier.

The multiplier (k) transforms the A_p demand schedule into the *IS* curve. An increase in the multiplier (due, for instance, to a smaller marginal propensity to save) rotates or twists the *IS* curve outward around its intercept on the vertical interest rate axis. Thus the higher the multiplier, the flatter the *IS* curve.

Anything that makes investment or consumption demand less sensitive to the interest rate (for instance, a tendency for firms to pay for investment goods with internal funds rather than borrowed funds) rotates or twists the *IS* curve upward around its intercept on the horizontal income axis. Thus the less sensitive the response of autonomous spending to the interest rate, the steeper the *IS* curve.

What Is True of Points That Are Off the *IS* Curve?

The entire area to the left of each *IS* curve is characterized by too low a level of production and income for the economy to be in equilibrium. There is undesired inventory decumulation (negative unplanned investment, I_u).

The entire area to the right of each *IS* curve is characterized by too high a level of production and income for the economy to be in equilibrium. There is undesired inventory accumulation (positive unplanned investment, I_u).

At any point off the *IS* curve there is pressure for business firms to adjust production until the economy returns to the *IS* curve.

It will be convenient to have a label for the horizontal position of the A_p line, since this in turn will affect the horizontal position of the *IS* curve.[4] *Let*

---

[4] We call the *IS* schedule a "curve," even though we have drawn it as a straight line, because in the real world the relationship might be a curve. Also the term *IS* curve has been familiar to generations of economists since its invention by the late Sir John Hicks in a classic article, "Mr. Keynes and the Classics: A Suggested Interpretation," *Econometrica*, vol. 5 (April 1937), pp. 147–159.

HOW INCREASED CONFIDENCE SHIFTS THE *IS* CURVE

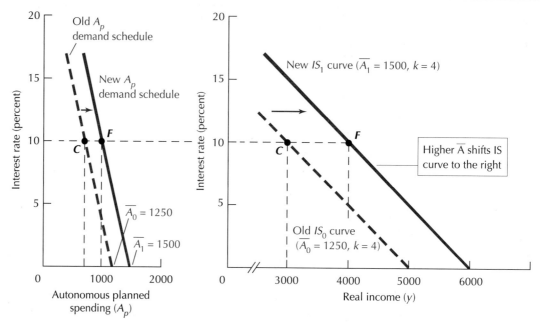

Figure 4-5   **Effect on the IS Curve of a Rightward Shift in the Demand for Autonomous Planned Spending**

The "old" A_p demand schedule and *IS* curve are copied from Figure 4-4. Now we assume that an increase in the level of business and consumer confidence shifts the $\overline{A}$ line \$250 billion to the right, just as occurred in Figure 4-2. The *IS* curve shifts to the right by four times as much. Notice that the horizontal intercept of the new *IS* curve at 6000 is four times the horizontal intercept of the $\overline{A}$ line—that is, $\overline{A} = 1500$.

---

us define $\overline{A}$ *as the value of autonomous planned spending that would take place at an interest rate of zero.* In Figure 4-4 the A_p line intersects the horizontal axis at \$1250 billion, so our label for this A_p line will be $\overline{A}_0 = 1250$. The *IS* curve always lies at a horizontal distance 4.0 times the A_p line, because the multiplier (k) is 4.0. Notice in Figure 4-4 that the *IS* curve intersects the horizontal axis at \$5000 billion, exactly 4.0 times the level of $\overline{A}_0 = 1250$.

What Shifts the *IS* Curve?

Figure 4-4 demonstrates that the horizontal intercept of the *IS* curve is always equal to the multiplier (k) times $\overline{A}$, the amount of autonomous planned spending that would occur at a zero interest rate. Anything that changes $\overline{A}$ will shift the *IS* curve. Anything that changes the multiplier (k) will rotate the *IS* curve.

Both the A_p demand schedule and the *IS* curve will shift to the right if businesses and consumers become more optimistic and desire to spend more at any given interest rate.

In Figure 4-5 the left-hand frame shows two A_p lines. Along the left-hand "old A_p demand schedule" confidence is relatively low, but the "new A_p demand schedule" reflects a higher level of confidence and lies everywhere exactly $250 billion farther to the right. Since the multiplier is 4.0 the "new *IS* curve" lies $1000 billion to the right, so that at an interest rate of 10 percent, equilibrium real income is $4000 billion at point *F*.

Once again, it is convenient to label each *IS* curve by the amount of autonomous planned spending that would occur at an interest rate of zero— that is, $\overline{A}_0 = 1250$ along the "old A_p demand schedule" and $\overline{A}_1 = 1500$ along the "new A_p demand schedule."

The rightward shift in Figure 4-5 of $250 billion in the A_p line and of $1000 billion in the *IS* curve can be caused by any event that raises by $250 billion the amount of autonomous spending desired at a given interest rate. These events include an increase in business or consumer confidence, an increase in government spending, a reduction in autonomous taxes, or an increase in autonomous net exports.

The Missing Relation

The *IS* curve is like a menu, providing us with innumerable combinations of interest rates and income that are consistent with equilibrium in the commodity market. But which item on the menu should we choose? There is not enough information here to make a choice. We need to find another relationship to link income and the interest rate in order to tie down the economy's position along the *IS* curve. In the familiar language of elementary algebra, we have two unknowns but only one equation. In the next sections we supply the missing equation and arrive at a complete theory of how income and the interest rate are determined.[5]

4-5   Why People Use Money

The second relationship between real income and the interest rate (in addition to the *IS* curve) occurs in the "money market," a general expression for the financial sector of the economy. In reality, the financial sector consists of many assets in addition to money, including short-term debt of corporations and the government, as well as bonds, stocks, and mutual funds of various types. In this chapter we will limit our attention to the segment of the financial sector generally referred to as "money."

The money supply con-
sists of currency and
transactions accounts,
including checking
accounts at banks and
thrift institutions.

The **money supply** (M^s) consists of two parts: currency and checking accounts at banks and thrift institutions. At this stage in the book the money supply may be considered to be a policy instrument that the Federal Reserve Board (the Fed) can set exactly at any desired value, just as we have been assuming that the government can precisely set the level of its fiscal policy instruments—that is, its purchases of goods and services and tax revenues. Later, in Chapter 13, we will learn how the Fed achieves its control over the money supply in actual practice.

---

[5] Despite its name, the *IS* curve has no unique connection with investment *(I)* or saving *(S)*. It shifts whenever there is a shift in the A_p demand schedule, which can be caused by a change in government spending, in taxes or transfers, or in net exports, as well as by changes in business and consumer confidence.

The theory developed in this chapter establishes a link between the money supply, income, and interest rates. In order to understand the hypothesis underlying the demand for money, we begin by examining the three traditional functions of money—its roles as a medium of exchange, a store of value, and a unit of account.

A Medium of Exchange

A **medium of exchange** is used for buying and selling goods and services and is a universal alternative to the barter system.

The most important function that differentiates money from other assets is its role as a **medium of exchange.** Money is one of the most important inventions in human history because it has allowed society to rise above the cumbersome method of exchange known as the barter system. With barter, one good or service is exchanged directly for another. If, as a professor, I want a leaky faucet fixed, I must find a plumber who wants to learn about economics. It might take weeks or months to find such a plumber, since the matching of services requires a "double coincidence of wants."

A barter society remains primitive because people have to spend so much time arranging exchanges that they have little time remaining to produce efficiently. As a result, to avoid arranging exchanges they must become self-sufficient (I would have to fix my own leaking faucet), thus failing to take advantage of the essential role of specialization in the development of an advanced economic system. Money eliminates the need for barter and the double coincidence of wants.

Which types of assets serve as a medium of exchange? Thirty years ago almost all exchanges in the United States involved coins, currency, or checking accounts that paid no interest. Gradually other methods of exchange have developed, including interest-bearing checking accounts, savings accounts, and money market mutual funds against which checks can be written. The requirements for an asset to qualify as a medium of exchange include ready acceptability, protection from counterfeiting, and divisibility (ability to use for small transactions).

A Store of Value

A **store of value** is a method of storing purchasing power when receipts and expenditures are not perfectly synchronized.

People do not always spend the entirety of their income the instant they receive it. Some receipts may be spent a day or two later, but others may be saved for a substantial period of time. People need some way of storing the purchasing power of their receipts until a later time. Any asset that performs this function is called a **store of value.** There are many financial instruments that serve as a store of value but not as a medium of exchange, including passbook savings accounts that do not provide check-writing services, as well as bonds and stocks. Money can be used both as a medium of exchange and as a store of value.

A Unit of Account

A **unit of account** is a way of recording receipts, expenditures, assets, and liabilities.

Money is also used for accounting purposes. How much your employer will pay you in wages, how much you owe the bank, how much a firm has earned, and how much a bond is worth are all recorded in some **unit of account.** This unit is called dollars in the United States, pounds sterling in the United Kingdom, deutsche marks in Germany, and so on. The dollars entered on accounting records do not physically exist, in the sense that no coin or piece of currency corresponding to each one exists in a particular location. Some dollars that serve as bookkeeping entries can also serve as a medium of exchange without any piece of paper actually changing hands, as in wire transfers between bank accounts.

4-6 Income, the Interest Rate, and the Demand for Money

The hypothesis that links the money supply, income, and the interest rate states that *the amount of money that people demand in real terms depends both on income and on the interest rate.* Why do households give up interest earnings to hold money balances that pay no interest? The main reason is that at least *some* holding of money is necessary to facilitate transactions, due to the role of money as a medium of exchange.

Income and the Demand for Money

Funds held in the form of stocks or bonds pay interest but cannot be used for transactions. People have to carry currency in their pockets or have money in their bank accounts to back up a check before they can buy anything. (Even if they use credit cards, they need money in their bank accounts to keep up with their credit card bills.) Because rich people make more purchases, they generally need a larger amount of currency and larger bank deposits. Thus the demand for **real money balances** increases when everyone becomes richer—that is, when the total of real income increases.

Real money balances equal the total money supply divided by the price level.

Changes in real income alter the demand for money in real terms—that is, adjusted for changes in the price level. Let us assume that the demand for real money balances *(M/P)* equals half of real income *(Y):*

$$\left(\frac{M}{P}\right)^d = 0.5Y$$

The superscript *d* means "the demand for."

If real income *(Y)* is \$4000 billion, the demand for real money balances $(M/P)^d$ will be \$2000 billion, as shown in Figure 4-6 by the vertical line *(L′)* drawn at \$2000 billion. The line is vertical because we are assuming initially that the demand for real balances $(M/P)^d$ does not depend on the interest rate *(r)*.

The Interest Rate and the Demand for Money

The *L′* line is unrealistic, however, because individuals will not hold as much money at a 10 percent interest rate as at a zero interest rate. Why? Because the interest rate plotted on the vertical axis is paid on *assets other than money,* such as bonds and savings certificates. The higher the reward *(r)* for holding interest-earning financial assets (that are not money), the less money will be held.

Figure 4-6
The Demand for Money, the Interest Rate, and Real Income

The vertical line L' is drawn on the unrealistic assumption that the demand for real balances is equal to half of real income ($4000 billion in this case), but does not depend on the interest rate. The L_0 curve maintains income at $4000, but it allows the demand for real balances to decrease by $500 billion for each 5 percent increase in the interest rate. The gray area shows the amount shifted into other assets, an amount that grows as the interest rate rises, leaving a smaller and smaller amount to be held as money.

[handwritten] Δ in y or real output shifts Mₒ line

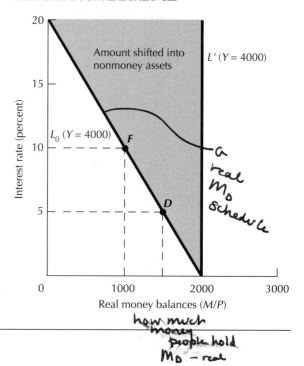

HOW INCOME AND THE INTEREST RATE DETERMINE THE DEMAND FOR REAL BALANCES

Amount shifted into nonmoney assets

$L'(Y = 4000)$

$L_0(Y = 4000)$

F

[handwritten] G
real Mₒ schedule

D

Interest rate (percent)

Real money balances (M/P)

[handwritten] how much money people hold Mₒ — real

If the interest rate (r) paid on nonmoney assets were less than the interest paid on money, there would be no point in holding them. Individuals would hold all of their financial assets in the form of money to take advantage of its convenience. But if the interest rate on them were higher than the interest paid on money, individuals would cut down on their average money holding in order to earn the higher interest available on alternative assets. They would consider these higher interest earnings sufficient compensation for the nuisance of periodically converting these assets into money.

In Figure 4-6 the downward slope of the L_0 line through points F and D indicates that when real income is $4000 billion and the interest rate is zero, the demand for real balances is $2000 billion. But when the interest rate rises from zero to 5 percent, people suffer inconvenience to cut down their money holdings from $2000 billion to $1500 billion (point D). When the interest rate is 10 percent, only $1000 billion of money is demanded (point F). The new L_0 line can be summarized as showing that the real demand for money $(M/P)^d$ is half of income minus $100 billion times the interest rate:

$$\left(\frac{M}{P}\right)^d = 0.5Y - 100r$$

A change in the interest rate moves the economy up and down its real money demand schedule, whereas a change in real output (Y) shifts that schedule to the left or right, as shown in Figure 4-7.

SELF-TEST   What are the two determinants of the real demand for money? What is the effect of each determinant on the real demand for money? Does a change in either determinant shift the *IS* curve?

Figure 4-7
**Effect on the Money Demand Schedule
of a Decline in Real Income from $4000
to $3000 Billion**

The L_0 line is copied from Figure 4-6 and
shows the demand for real balances at
different rates of interest, assuming that
real income is $4000 billion. A $1000 billion drop in the level of income to $3000
billion causes the demand for real balances to drop by half as much, or $500
billion, at each interest rate level. For
instance, at an interest rate of 10 percent
the demand for real balances falls from
$1000 billion at point F to $500 billion at
point C.

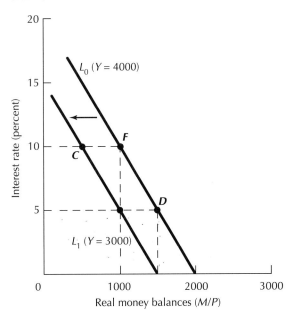

A DROP IN THE LEVEL OF INCOME SHIFTS
THE MONEY DEMAND SCHEDULE TO THE LEFT

4-7   The *LM* Curve

Thus far we have learned that the supply of money (M^s) is controlled by the
Fed, and that the real quantity of money demanded by households $(M/P)^d$
depends on both income and the interest rate. Now we can tie these two relationships together by assuming that the money market is always *in equilibrium* (a situation where there is no pressure for change), with the real supply
of money equal to the real demand for money. This equilibrium condition for
the money market allows us to derive a relationship called the *LM curve,* just
as we previously derived an equilibrium condition for the commodity market
called the *IS curve.* To achieve equilibrium in the money market, the real supply of money (M^s/P) must equal the demand for real money $(M/P)^d$:

$$\frac{M^s}{P} = \left(\frac{M}{P}\right)^d = 0.5Y - 100r \tag{4.1}$$

If the amount of money supplied by the government is $1000 billion and the
price index (P) is set at a constant value of 1.0, then M^s/P equals $1000 billion.
To simplify the analysis, we assume that the supply of money does not
depend on the interest rate, so M^s/P is drawn in the left frame of Figure 4-8 as
a vertical line at a level of $1000 billion for every interest rate. The two money
demand schedules, L_0 and L_1, are copied from Figure 4-7.

How to Derive the *LM* Curve

The sloped money demand line L_0, drawn for an income of $4000 billion,
crosses the M^s/P line at point F, where the interest rate is 10 percent.

A FIXED MONEY SUPPLY IS CONSISTENT WITH MANY DIFFERENT LEVELS OF INCOME

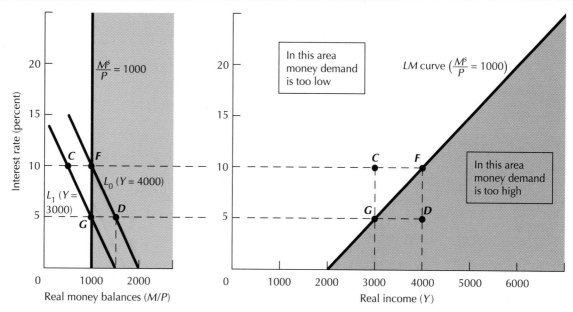

Figure 4-8   Derivation of the LM Curve

In the left frame the L_0 and L_1 schedules are copied from the previous figure. The vertical M^s/P line shows the available supply of money provided by the government. The money market is in equilibrium where the supply line (M^s/P) crosses the demand line $(L_0$ or $L_1)$. When income is $4000 billion, equilibrium occurs at point F, plotted again in the right frame. When income is $3000 billion, equilibrium occurs where L_0 crosses M^s/P at point G, also plotted in the right frame. The LM curve or schedule shows all combinations of Y and r consistent with equilibrium in the money market.

The demand for money at F is $1000 billion, and the supply of money is also $1000 billion. Because the two are equal, the money market is in equilibrium when $Y = 4000$ (assumed in drawing the L_0 line) and $r = 10$ percent. This equilibrium combination of values is plotted at point F in the right frame of Figure 4-8.[6]

If income is $3000 billion instead of $4000 billion, the demand for money is shown by schedule L_1 passing through points C and G in the left frame of Figure 4-8. Now the demand for real money balances can be equal to the fixed real supply of money only at point G, where the interest rate is 5 percent. Thus $Y = 3000$ and $r = 5$ is another combination consistent with equilibrium in the money market, and this is plotted at point G in the right frame of Figure 4-8.[7]

---

[6] Thus, in equation (4.1)

$$1000 = 0.5(4000) - 100(10)$$
$$= 2000 - 1000$$
$$= 1000$$

[7] Thus, in equation (4.1)

$$1000 = 0.5(3000) - 100(5)$$
$$= 1500 - 500$$
$$= 1000$$

What the *LM* Curve Shows

The *LM* curve is the schedule that identifies the combinations of income and the interest rate at which the money market is in equilibrium; on the LM curve the demand for money equals the supply of money.

The line connecting points G and F in the right-hand frame of Figure 4-7 is called the **LM curve.** The *LM* curve represents all combinations of income (Y) and interest rate (r) where the money market is in equilibrium—that is, where the real supply of money equals the real demand for money.

At any point off the *LM* curve, say point D, the money market is not in equilibrium. The problem at D and all other points in the red shaded area is that the demand for real money exceeds the available supply. At point C and all other points in the white area there is an excess supply of money that exceeds the demand.

How does the economy adjust to guarantee that the given supply of money created by the government is exactly equal to the demand when the money market is out of equilibrium, as at point D? One possible adjustment, a reduction in the price level, will be considered later. In this chapter we assume the price index (P) to be equal to 1.0. Without changing prices, the economy might achieve money market equilibrium from point D by increasing the interest rate from 5 to 10 percent. This would move it to point F, cutting the demand for money. Or, instead, income might fall from \$4000 billion to \$3000 billion while the interest rate remains fixed. This would cause a movement to point G and would also cut the demand for money. Or some other combination might occur, with a partial drop in income and a partial increase in the interest rate.

SELF-TEST

By how much does the demand for money change when the economy moves from point D to point F in Figure 4-8? From point D to point G? If you are stumped, you need to review the money demand equation (4.1) and footnotes 6 and 7, which show how to use it in specific examples.

What Makes the *LM* Curve Shift?

The position of the *LM* curve is determined by the size of the money supply, and any change in the money supply will cause the *LM* curve to shift its position. What happens when the Fed decides to alter M^s, the nominal money supply? If the price level (P) is fixed, this will alter the real money supply (M^s/P). In Figure 4-9, for instance, a \$500 billion increase in the money supply from \$1000 to \$1500 billion shifts the *LM* curve from the left-hand dashed line (LM_0) to the right-hand solid line (LM_1). Since each dollar of extra available money makes possible 2.0 extra dollars of income, the *LM* curve shifts horizontally by \$1000 billion.

Another way to interpret the effect of a higher money supply is also shown in Figure 4-9. How does the economy adjust if real income remains fixed at $Y = 4000$? In the left frame of Figure 4-9, the demand-for-money line, labeled $L_0(Y = 4000)$, shows the amount by which the demand for money increases as the interest rate declines, holding the level of income fixed at $Y = 4000$. If the money supply is at its original value of 1000, the money market is in equilibrium at point F, with an interest rate of 10 percent. When the money supply increases from 1000 to 1500, the left frame shows that the interest rate must decline from 10 percent at point F to 5 percent at point D in order to maintain equilibrium in the money market by boosting the demand for money by the same amount as the money supply has risen—that is, from 1000 to 1500.

HOW A HIGHER REAL MONEY SUPPLY CAN REDUCE THE INTEREST RATE

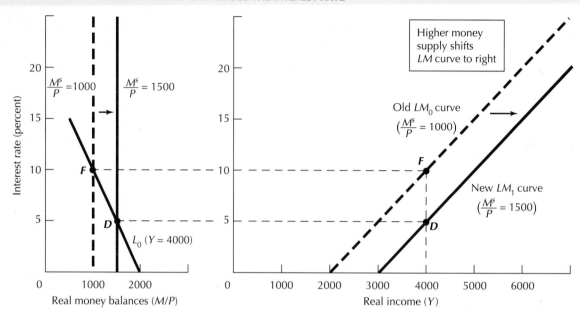

<figure>*Figure 4-9*   **The Effect on the LM Curve of an Increase in the Real Money Supply from $1000 Billion to $1500 Billion**

The dashed LM_0 line in the figure is identical to *LM* in Figure 4-8. When the money supply is increased, the money available to support output increases and the *LM* curve shifts rightward by 2.0 dollars per dollar of extra money to the new LM_1 line.</figure>

In the right frame of Figure 4-9, points *F* and *D* are plotted at the same horizontal position, since the level of income is assumed to be 4000. When the money supply is at the original level of 1000, the economy operates along the original LM_0 curve at point *F.* When the money supply increases to the new value of 1500, the *LM* curve shifts rightward to its new position LM_1 at point *D.*

Which outcome will occur following an increase in the money supply? Will income increase while the interest rate remains constant? Or will the interest rate decline (as from point *F* to point *D*) while income remains constant? *Once again, we cannot determine the value of two unknowns with only one relation—that is, the LM curve.* We must use both relations, the *IS* curve and the *LM* curve, to determine the two unknown variables—income and the interest rate. The next section joins together the *IS* and *LM* curves to determine the level of both unknown variables.

4-8   The *IS* Curve Meets the *LM* Curve

Equilibrium in the commodity market occurs only at points on the *IS* curve. Figure 4-10 copies the IS_0 schedule from Figure 4-5 drawn for a value of $\overline{A} = 1250$. At any point off the IS_0, curve, for instance *G* and *F,* the commodity market is out of equilibrium. *C, D,* and E_0 all represent different combinations of income and the interest rate that are compatible with commodity-market

LEARNING ABOUT DIAGRAMS: THE *LM* CURVE

The *LM* curve is as important and useful as the *IS* curve. This box explains the slope of the curve and what makes it shift and rotate its position.

Diagram Ingredients and Reasons for Slope

The vertical axis is the interest rate and the horizontal axis is the level of income (same as the *IS* curve).

The *LM* curve shows the different combinations of the interest rate and income consistent with setting the demand for money equal to a *fixed* supply of money. Since the demand for money is fixed everywhere along the *LM* curve, but income increases as we move to the right, something must happen to offset the higher demand for money that results from higher income. That something is the higher interest rate, which induces people to shift some assets into nonmonetary assets, freeing up more of the fixed available money to be used for the higher level of transactions.

Along any given *LM* curve the level of real money balances (M^s/P) is fixed, but real income (Y) varies. The ratio of real income to real balances is called the *velocity* of money (V):

$$\text{velocity } (V) = \frac{Y}{M^s/P} = \frac{PY}{M^s}$$

The right-hand expression states that velocity is also equal to nominal income (PY) divided by the nominal money supply (M^s). The higher the interest rate, the higher is velocity. Why? If r increases, people wish to hold less money. But the money supply is fixed. To maintain equilibrium in the money market, there *must be an increase in income* to induce households to hold the fixed existing quantity of money. Anything that can cause the economy to move up and down along a fixed *LM* curve achieves a change of velocity by altering Y while M^s/P is fixed.

What Shifts and Rotates the *LM* Curve?

The *LM* curve is drawn for a fixed real supply of money (M^s/P). A higher nominal supply of money (M^s) will shift the *LM* curve to the right, as in Figure 4-9, and a lower nominal supply of money will shift the *LM* curve to the left. An increase in the price level (P) will shift the *LM* curve to the left, and vice versa.

Anything that makes the demand for money less sensitive to the interest rate makes both the money demand schedule, $L(Y)$, and the *LM* curve steeper (rotating it upward around its horizontal intercept). Anything that makes the demand for money less responsive to changes in income will make the *LM* curve flatter and also shift it outward.

What Is True of Points That Are Off the *LM* Curve?

The entire area to the left of the *LM* curve has an excess supply of money because income is lower than that needed to create a sufficient demand for money to match the supply.

The entire area to the right of the *LM* curve has an excess demand for money because income is higher than required to match the demand for money to the fixed supply.

At any point off the *LM* curve there is pressure for interest rates to change. For instance, when there is an excess demand for money, people try to obtain money by selling bonds and other financial assets, and this pushes up the interest rates on bonds and other financial assets.

equilibrium. At which equilibrium point will the economy come to rest? The single IS_0 schedule does not provide enough information to determine *both* income and the interest rate. *Two* schedules are needed to pin down the equilibrium values of *two* unknown variables.

The *LM* curve provides the necessary additional information, showing all combinations of income and the interest rate at which the money market is in equilibrium for a given real money supply—in this case, $1000 billion.

Figure 4-10
The IS and LM Schedules Cross at Last

The IS_0 schedule is copied from Figure 4-5; the LM_0 schedule is copied from Figure 4-8. Only at the red point, E_0, is the economy in "general" equilibrium, with the conditions for equilibrium attained in both the commodity market (along IS) and the money market (along LM). At points U, V, G, and F the commodity market is out of equilibrium. At points U, V, C, and D the money market is out of equilibrium.

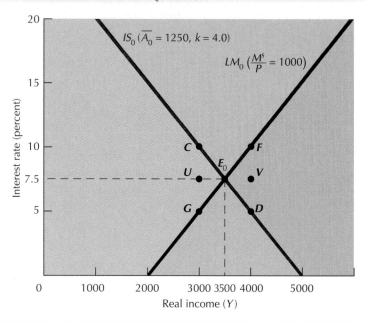

THE ECONOMY'S "GENERAL" EQUILIBRIUM

Figure 4-10 copies the LM_0 schedule from Figure 4-9 drawn for a value of $M^s/P = 1000$. At any point off the LM_0 curve, for instance, points C and D, the money market is out of equilibrium. At D income is too high and the real demand for money exceeds the real supply. At C income is too low and the real demand for money is below the real supply. Equilibrium in the money market occurs only at points such as G, F, and E_0, each representing combinations of income and the interest rate at which the real demand for money is equal to a real money supply of $1000 billion.

General equilibrium is a situation of simultaneous equilibrium in all the markets of the economy.

How does the economy arrive at its **general equilibrium** at point E_0 if it starts out at the wrong place, such as at points U or V? If the commodity market is out of equilibrium and involuntary inventory decumulation or accumulation occurs, firms will step up or cut production, pushing the economy in the direction needed to reach E_0. If the money market is out of equilibrium, there will be pressure to adjust interest rates, since people will have to sell stocks and bonds if they cannot otherwise satisfy their demand for money. Either way the economy arrives at E_0.

4-9 Monetary Policy in Action

The *IS-LM* model uses two relations (or schedules) to determine the two endogenous variables, real income and the interest rate. The exogenous variables, which the model does not explain, are the level of business and consumer optimism, the single instrument of monetary policy (the money supply), the two instruments of fiscal policy (government spending and tax revenues), and net exports. Whenever there is a change in one of the exogenous variables, the result will be a change in either or both of the two endogenous variables, real income and the interest rate. In this section we will see that a decision by the Fed to change the money supply will normally lead to a change in both real income and the interest rate.

What level of real GDP does the Fed desire? We shall assume that the desired level of income, "natural real GDP," is $4000 billion. In Figure 4-10 the equilibrium level of real income (GDP) at point E_0 is only $3500 billion. Thus, there is a $500 "gap" between actual and natural real GDP that needs to be filled. What should the Fed do?

To raise GDP by the required $500 billion, the Fed must increase the money supply. This action is called an **expansionary monetary policy.** Conversely, if natural real GDP is lower than actual real GDP, the Fed can decrease the money supply. This is an example of a **contractionary monetary policy.**

> An **expansionary monetary policy** is one that has the effect of lowering interest rates and raising GDP.
>
> A **contractionary monetary policy** is one that has the effect of lowering GDP and raising interest rates.

Normal Effects of an Increase in the Money Supply

Will an increase in the money supply increase real income, reduce the interest rate, or both? If the *IS* and *LM* curves have the "normal" shapes displayed in Figure 4-10, the answer is "both." As we shall see in the next chapter, there are extreme cases in which the *IS* and/or the *LM* curves are vertical or horizontal, and the entire impact of a change in the money supply may fall just on real income or just on the interest rate. But here, where the *IS* curve has its normal negative slope and the *LM* curve has its normal positive slope, monetary policy changes both real income *and* the interest rate.

Figure 4-11 repeats the LM_0 curve of Figure 4-10, drawn on the assumption that the real money supply is $1000 billion. Also repeated is the IS_0 curve of Figure 4-10, which assumes that $\overline{A} = 1250$ and $k = 4.0$. The economy's general equilibrium, the point where both the money and commodity markets are in equilibrium, occurs at point E_0.

Figure 4-11
The Effect of a $500 Billion Increase in the Money Supply with a Normal LM Curve

We repeat the $500 billion increase in the money supply that was shown in Figure 4-9. In order to maintain equilibrium in both the commodity and money markets here, two effects occur: equilibrium income rises and the interest rate declines, as indicated by the movement from E_0 to E_1.

A HIGHER MONEY SUPPLY BOOSTS INCOME AND CUTS THE INTEREST RATE

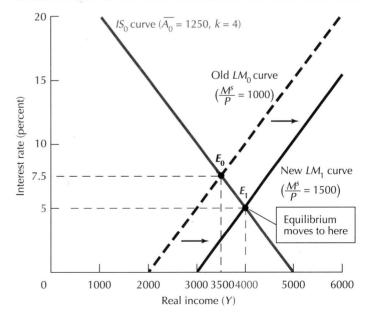

Assume that the Fed now raises the nominal money supply from $1000 billion to $1500 billion. As long as the price level stays fixed at 1.0, the real money supply increases by the same amount. The *LM* curve shifts to the right by $1000 billion. Now, at the new, higher real money supply of $1500 billion, there is an "excess supply of money" of $500 billion. How can the economy generate the $500 billion increase in the real demand for money needed to balance the new higher supply?

Finding themselves with more money than they need, individuals transfer some money into savings accounts and use some to buy stocks, bonds, and commodities. This raises the prices of bonds and stocks and reduces the interest rate. The initial decline in interest rates is sometimes called the "liquidity effect" of a monetary expansion. The lower interest rate raises the desired level of autonomous consumption and investment spending, requiring an increase in production. This is the "income effect" of a monetary expansion. Only at point E_1, with an income level of $4000 billion and interest rate of 5 percent, are both the money and commodity markets in equilibrium. Compared to the starting point E_0, the increase in the real money supply has caused both an increase in real income and a reduction in the interest rate, due to the combined impact of the liquidity and income effects.

Monetary policy works exactly the same in reverse. If the desired level of real income was not $4000 billion but rather $3500 billion, the Fed could move the economy leftward from point E_1 in Figure 4-11 to point E_0, simply by reducing the real money supply from $1500 billion to $1000 billion. As a result, the LM_1 curve would shift leftwards to LM_0, and income would decline from $4000 billion to $3500 billion.

4-10 How Fiscal Expansion Can "Crowd Out" Investment

In the last section we examined the effects on real income and the interest rate of changes in monetary policy by shifting the *LM* curve along a fixed *IS* curve. Now we shall do the reverse and shift the *IS* curve along a fixed *LM* curve. The original *IS* curve is copied from Figure 4-10 and is labeled in Figure 4-12 as the "old IS_0 curve"; it is drawn on the assumption that the amount of autonomous planned spending that would occur at a zero interest rate ($\overline{A}$) is equal to $1250 billion.

Expansionary Fiscal Policy Shifts the *IS* Curve

Since autonomous planned spending includes government spending, an expansionary fiscal policy taking the form of a $250 billion increase in government purchases raises $\overline{A}$ by the same amount and shifts the *IS* curve to the right. The new *IS* curve is labeled "new IS_1 curve" in Figure 4-12; the $250 billion increase in government spending has boosted $\overline{A}$ from $1250 to $1500 billion. Note that the horizontal distance between the old and new *IS* curves is not $250 billion but $1000 billion, since the horizontal position of *IS* is $\overline{A}$ times the multiplier, still assumed to be 4.0.

Figure 4-12 demonstrates that the effect of an expansionary fiscal policy on real income is not indicated by our original Chapter 3 multiplier ($k = 4.0$)

Figure 4-12
The Effect on Real Income and the Interest Rate of a $250 Billion Increase in Government Spending

Along the original IS_0 curve the autonomous spending desired at a zero interest rate $(\overline{A})$ is 1250 and the economy's equilibrium occurs at point E_0. A $250 billion increase in government spending boosts $\overline{A}$ from 1250 to 1500, and shifts the IS curve rightward to IS_1. The economy's equilibrium slides up the LM curve from point E_0 to E_5. In contrast to Chapter 3's multiplier of 4.0, now the government spending multiplier is only 2.0. But, since income increases from E_0 to E_5, crowding out is partial, not complete.

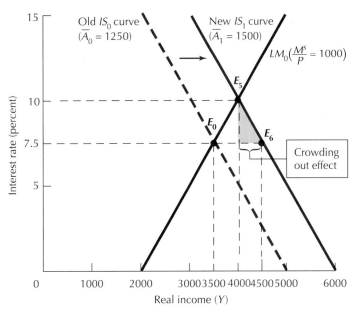

THE CROWDING OUT EFFECT CUTS THE FISCAL MULTIPLIER

once the money market is taken into consideration. The full fiscal multiplier of $k = 4.0$ would move the economy horizontally from the initial equilibrium position at E_0 to point E_6, where income is $1000 billion higher. At E_6, however, the money market is not in equilibrium, because E_6 is off the LM_0 curve. Income is higher than at E_0, raising the demand for money, but the real supply of money remains unchanged at the original assumed value $M^s/P = 1000$. There is an excess demand for money.

To cut the demand for money back to the level of the fixed supply, the interest rate must rise. But an increase in the interest rate makes point E_6 untenable by reducing planned consumption and investment expenditures. *Only at point E_5 are both the commodity and money markets in equilibrium.* Real income does not increase by the full $1000 billion, but only by half as much, $500 billion.

The higher interest rate accounts for the fact that the fiscal policy multiplier is 2.0, rather than 4.0, when the requirement for money market equilibrium is taken into account. The increase in the interest rate from 7.5 to 10 percent cuts private autonomous planned consumption and investment spending by $125 billion, fully half of the $250 billion increase in government spending. Thus, fully half of the original multiplier of 4.0 is "crowded out."

Comparison of equilibrium positions E_0 and E_5

	Initial E_0	New E_5
Interest rate (r)	7.5	10.0
Private autonomous spending	875	750
$\quad(I_p + a = 1250 - 50r)$		
Government spending (G)	0	250
Total autonomous spending	875	1000
$\quad(A_p = I_p + a + G)$		
Income ($Y = 4.0A_p$)	3500	4000

INTERNATIONAL PERSPECTIVE

How Japan

Uses Fiscal

Policy

One idea for reducing the amplitude of business cycles is for the government to run a "countercyclical" fiscal policy, reducing government expenditures when the economy is strong and raising government expenditures when the economy is weak. The big problem in carrying out this idea is administrative —how can funds be allocated rapidly and fairly? If the government takes a long time to develop plans for specific government spending projects, then the weakness in the economy may have disappeared and the fiscal policy stimulus may no longer be needed.

Several decades ago the Japanese developed a system of countercyclical public works expenditures that avoids time lags in starting new projects, as well as the dislocation and inefficiency caused when projects are cancelled. The Japanese technique is simple— increase or decrease the speed with which a given project is completed. For instance, the 115-mile Tokyo Coastal Bay Expressway was under construction for two decades. The Japanese central government decided each year how much money should be allocated to

it, depending on the stabilization needs of the economy. No one knew exactly when the expressway would be completed, since that depended on the state of the economy.

In recent years the Japanese economy has been weak, and with interest rates already very low, monetary policy has limited scope to provide the necessary stimulus. Thus fiscal policy receives substantial emphasis as the government attempts to stimulate the economy. In September 1995 the government announced a program of fiscal expansion that was primarily in the form of increases in government expenditure. The total size of the package was equivalent to 1.7 percent of Japan's GDP, and all of the extra spending was scheduled to occur by the end of 1996. Of this amount more than half was designated for construction and relief of victims of the 1995 Kobe earthquake. Other spending programs included purchases of land to prop up sagging land prices, subsidies to small firms and home buyers, and a modest allocation for improvement of Japanese telecommunication networks.

The Crowding Out Effect

The **crowding out effect** describes the effect of an increase in government spending or a reduction of tax rates in reducing the amount of one or more other components of private expenditures.

Some economists and journalists use the phrase **crowding out effect** to compare points such as E_6 and E_5 in Figure 4-12. The $500 billion difference in real income between points E_6 and E_5 results from the investment and consumption spending crowded out by the higher interest rate. Point E_6, used in calculating the size of the crowding out effect, is a purely hypothetical position that the economy cannot and does not reach. Actually, far from being crowded out, total private spending is higher in the new equilibrium situation at E_5 than at the original situation at E_0—real income has increased by $500 billion, of which only $250 billion represents higher government purchases, leaving the remaining $250 billion for extra private expenditures. The composition of private spending changes, however, as a result of the higher interest rate. Induced consumption spending increases, but autonomous private spending decreases. Expenditures are divided up as follows in the two situations:

	At E_0	*At E_5*
Government purchases	0	250
Autonomous private spending ($I_p + a$)	875	750
Induced consumption	2625	3000
Total real expenditures	3500	4000

Can Crowding Out Be Avoided?

The fundamental cause of crowding out is an increase in the interest rate that is required whenever income rises and the supply of money is fixed while the demand for money responds positively to an increase in income. To offset the increase in the demand for money caused by higher income, it is necessary for the interest rate to rise by enough to offset the effects of higher income on the demand for money.

The simplest way to avoid crowding out would be for the Fed to increase the money supply, thus allowing the *LM* curve to shift rightward by the same amount as the *IS* curve. Another possible exception to crowding out would be if the demand for money did not depend on income. Other hypothetical situations in which crowding out would be avoided are when the *IS* curve is vertical (i.e., the interest responsiveness of spending is zero) or when the *LM* curve is horizontal (i.e., the interest responsiveness of the demand for money is infinite).

In the next chapter we will begin by examining some of these situations, in which monetary policy and fiscal policy are unusually strong or weak, then study interactions among monetary and fiscal policy, and finally learn about effects of fiscal deficits on trade, investment, and growth.

SUMMARY

1. Interest rates allocate the supply of funds available from savers to alternative borrowers. Not only do private households and firms borrow in order to buy consumption and investment goods, but the government also borrows to finance its budget deficit.

2. Private autonomous planned spending (A_p) depends partly on the interest rate. The higher the interest rate, the lower is A_p.

3. Private autonomous planned spending (A_p) also depends on the optimism or pessimism of investors and consumers about the future. An increase in optimism tends to raise A_p for any given level of the interest rate.

4. The *IS* curve indicates all the combinations of the interest rate and real income at which the economy's commodity market is in equilibrium. At any point off the *IS* curve the commodity market is out of equilibrium.

5. The main functions of money are its use as a medium of exchange, a store of value, and a unit of account.

6. The real quantity of money that people demand depends both on real income and on the interest rate. Equilibrium in the money market requires that the real supply of money equal the demand for real money balances.

7. The *LM* curve represents all the combinations of real income and of the interest rate where the money market is in equilibrium.

8. An increase in the money supply raises real income and reduces the interest rate when the *IS* curve has its normal negative slope and the *LM* curve has its normal positive slope.

9. A fiscal expansion raises real income and the interest rate, causing crowding out if the money supply is held constant and both the *IS* and *LM* curves have their normal slopes.

CONCEPTS

rate of return
IS curve
money supply
medium of exchange
store of value
unit of account

real money balances
LM curve
general equilibrium
expansionary monetary policy
contractionary monetary policy
crowding out effect

QUESTIONS AND PROBLEMS

Questions

1. Which among the exogenous variables listed in Question 1 at the end of Chapter 3 have become endogenous in the complete *IS-LM* model of this chapter? Is this true as well for autonomous consumption expenditure? Velocity? Have any other endogenous variables been introduced in this chapter? Exogenous variables?

2. In early 1989 many economic forecasters predicted that a major recession would occur in late 1989 or early 1990. How might these forecasts have affected the actual performance of the economy?

3. Describe the automatic adjustment that will take place in the economy when the current position of the economy is off the *IS* curve.

4. Describe the automatic adjustment that will take place in the economy when the current position of the economy is off the *LM* curve.

5. Why is the distinction between autonomous expenditure and induced expenditure crucial to an understanding of the crowding out effect?

6. Under what circumstances could government spending (federal, state, and local) be crowded out? Do you think this is likely to be the case?

7. What happens to the velocity of money when the economy moves along a given *LM* curve? Why does velocity behave this way?

8. Describe the situation in the commodity market and the money market at point *V* in Figure 4-10. What will happen to the economy if the current position is at point *V*?

9. During the 1980s the size of the federal government debt became so large that servicing the interest payments became a significant portion of total federal expenditure. In response, many representatives and senators felt that the federal deficit needed to be reduced. If government spending (*G*) became negatively sensitive to changes in the interest rate, what effect would this have on the slope of the *IS* curve? If autonomous taxes (T_0) become positively sensitive to changes in the interest rate, what effect would this have on the slope of the *IS* curve?

10. A change in which of the following would cause the *IS* curve to shift? To rotate? To both shift and rotate? Which do not affect the position or slope of the *IS* curve?
    (a) autonomous planned expenditure (A_p)
    (b) marginal tax rate (t_0)
    (c) marginal propensity to save (s)

(d) share of imports in GDP (nx_0)
(e) interest rate (r)
(f) marginal leakage rate
(g) multiplier (k)
(h) interest sensitivity of the A_p demand schedule
(i) business and consumer confidence
11. Suppose Congress raises autonomous taxes to help reduce the budget deficit. How will this tax hike

affect real income? The interest rate? Consumption? Planned investment?
12. Evaluate the following argument using the *IS-LM* model: When consumer and business confidence are high and the economy is booming, the interest rate is high. Therefore, during a recession the Fed could promote a higher level of income if it used monetary policy to raise the interest rate.

ESSAY TYPE ?

Problems

1. Let the structure of the commodity market be represented by the following equations: $C = a + 0.75(Y - T)$, $a = 50 - 10r$, $T = 200 + 0.2Y$, $I_p = 300 - 30r$, and $G = 400$.
   (a) What is the value of the multiplier (k)?
   (b) What is the equation of the autonomous planned expenditure function? (*Hint:* Just substitute the equations given above for a, T, and I_p and the value given above for G into the general formula for A_p: $A_p = a - cT_0 + I_p + G + NX$. In this problem $NX = 0$.)
   (c) What is the equation of the IS curve? (*Hint:* The general equation for the IS curve is $Y = kA_p$.)
   (d) What is the slope of the IS curve $(\Delta r/\Delta Y)$?
   (e) If government spending increased by 50, at what value on the horizontal axis would the new IS curve intersect it? What would happen to the slope of the IS curve?

2. The equation of the LM curve is given by the following formula: $Y = [(M^s/P) + fr]/h$, where M^s/P is the real money supply, h is the response of money demand to a $1 change in income at a fixed interest rate, and f is the response of money demand to a one percentage point change in the interest rate. Assume the following values for the exogenous variable M^s/P and parameters h and f in the LM curve: $M^s/P = 300$, $h = 0.4$, and $f = 50$.
   (a) What is the horizontal intercept of the LM curve?
   (b) What is the slope $(\Delta r/\Delta Y)$ of the LM curve?
   (c) What is the equation of the LM curve?
   (d) If the Fed increased the money supply by 100, at what value on the horizontal axis would the LM curve intersect it? What happens to the slope of the LM curve?

3. Using the information contained in problems 1 and 2 above, what is equilibrium real income (Y) and the interest rate (r)
   (a) in the initial situation (i.e., $G = 400$, $M^s/P = 300$)?
   (b) if G increases to 450? What is the amount of autonomous spending that is crowded out in this situation? What happens to velocity?
   (c) if M^s/P increases to 400?

(d) if both G and M^s/P increase (i.e., $G = 450$ and $M^s/P = 400$)?
4. Assume that the economy is initially in equilibrium at a level of real output (Y) of $5000 and an interest rate (r) of 5 percent. If as a result of an increase in government spending of $500, the economy moves to a new equilibrium at $Y = \$5750$ and $r = 6.5$ percent (and given that $k = 3$), how much Y would be crowded out due to the increase in the interest rate? How much autonomous spending would be crowded out? What is the value of the coefficient for interest-rate responsiveness of the IS curve? Of the A_p demand schedule?
5. Assume that the following equations summarize the structure of the economy: $C = a + 0.8Y$, $(M/P)^d = 0.2Y - 20r$, $a = 160 - 10r$, $M^s/P = 160$, and $I_p = 240 - 10r$. Answer the following questions:
   (a) What is the equation of the IS curve?
   (b) What is the equation of the LM curve?
   (c) What is the equilibrium real output?
   (d) What is the equilibrium interest rate?
   (e) What is the level of consumption at equilibrium?
   (f) What is the level of investment at equilibrium?
   (g) Assume that $r = 4$ and $Y = 1200$. Is there an excess demand for money or excess supply of money in this situation? How much? Is there unplanned inventory change? If so, what is its value?
   (h) Assume that $r = 4$ and $Y = 1600$. Is there excess demand for money or excess supply of money in this situation? How much? Is there unplanned inventory change? If so, what is the value of the unplanned inventory change?

SELF-TEST ANSWERS

p. 99 (1) A reduction of imports raises net exports and shifts the A_p schedule to the right. (2) A change in interest rates moves the economy *along* the schedule but does not shift it. (3) Higher taxes reduce consumption and thus shift the A_p schedule to the left.

p. 101 An interest rate of 5 percent is compatible with a $4000 billion level of equilibrium real income. This occurs at point *D* on the *IS* curve in the lower right-hand frame of Figure 4-4.

p. 108 The level of income *(Y)* and of the interest rate on assets other than money *(r)* are the two determinants of the real demand for money, $(M/P)^d$. An increase in *Y* raises the real demand for money, and an increase in the interest rate reduces the real demand for money. Neither determinant shifts the *IS* curve, because the axes of the *IS* curve diagram are these very determinants, *Y* and *r*.

p. 111 In going from *D* to *F,* the interest rate rises from 5 to 10 percent, and the demand for money decreases by the interest responsiveness (100) times the change in the interest rate (5)—that is, by 500. In going from *D* to *G,* the level of real income falls from 4000 to 3000. The demand for money decreases by the income responsiveness (0.5) times the change in real income (1000)—that is, by 500.

CHAPTER 5
Monetary Policy, Fiscal Policy, and the Government Budget

Any jackass can draw up a balanced budget on paper.
—Lane Kirkland, 1980

5-1 Introduction

We have now learned how to use the *IS-LM* model to determine the value of both real income (GDP) and the interest rate. We have also learned that there is a desirable level of real GDP, which we call "natural real GDP." When the economy is operating with actual real GDP equal to natural real GDP, there is no need for monetary or fiscal policy actions to boost or restrain the level of actual real GDP.[1]

But sometimes actual real GDP may not be at the desired level. In this case, monetary and/or fiscal policy actions may be necessary to boost real GDP if it is too low, or reduce real GDP if it is too high. At the end of the previous chapter we examined the normal effects of an expansionary monetary policy, where an increase in the money supply raises real GDP while simultaneously reducing the interest rate. We also examined the normal effects of an expansionary fiscal policy, where an increase in government spending raises real GDP while simultaneously raising the interest rate. Both monetary and fiscal policy can have the opposite effects when a contractionary policy is desired. A reduction in the money supply normally reduces real GDP while raising the interest rate. And a reduction in government spending normally reduces real GDP while reducing the interest rate.

In the first topic of this chapter we will see that other effects of monetary and fiscal policy are possible. There are conditions, at least in theory, under which expansionary or contractionary monetary or fiscal policy have no effects at all on real GDP, making any attempt to stabilize the economy with monetary or fiscal policy an exercise in futility. We will also see what happens when, instead of being used separately, monetary and fiscal policy are used *together*. When monetary and fiscal policy actions are coordinated, it is possible for an increase or decrease in real GDP to occur without any change in the interest rate. It is also possible for monetary and fiscal policy to be used together to raise or reduce the interest rate without causing any change in real GDP.

Next, the chapter takes a closer look at fiscal policy. We study the government budget deficit and find that not only do changes in the deficit influence the economy but that changes in the economy can also influence the size of the deficit. We learn that there is an alternative deficit concept, which

---

[1]*Review:* "Natural" real GDP and the "natural" rate of unemployment are defined in Section 1-3.

eliminates this influence of the economy on the deficit and provides a useful measure of the influence of fiscal policy.

The chapter concludes by examining the effects of the government budget deficit not just on the economy today but in the future. Persistent fiscal deficits, such as those run by the U.S. federal government since 1981, tend not only to raise the interest rate and crowd out private investment (as we learned in Chapter 4), but also to reduce the rate of growth of income per person, thus eroding the standard of living of the average citizen in future years. Persistent deficits can also lead to borrowing from foreign citizens, companies, and governments, creating a burden of interest payments that future citizens must meet.

5-2   Strong and Weak Effects of Monetary Policy

The *IS-LM* model that we have developed shows how real income (or GDP) and the interest rate are determined. The exogenous variables, which the model does not explain, are the level of business and consumer confidence, the single instrument of monetary policy (the money supply), the three instruments of fiscal policy (government spending, autonomous taxes, and the income tax rate), and the autonomous component of net exports. The model also does not explain the price level, which is assumed to be fixed.

Previously, in Figure 4-11 on p. 115, we examined the "normal" effects of an increase or decrease in the money supply. With the assumed *IS* curve and the *LM* curve labeled LM_0 (which assumes a real money supply of $1000 billion), the economy's equilibrium occurred at a real income of $3500 billion and was labeled E_0. We repeat the same assumed equilibrium point E_0 in Figure 5-1. The diagram differs from those in Chapters 3 and 4, however, by dropping specific numbers from the vertical and horizontal axes. Now that we have learned how the *IS-LM* model works, we can simplify our analysis by labeling each point with alphabetical symbols rather than specific numbers. For instance, in Figure 5-1 the equilibrium level of income along the initial LM_0 curve is labeled Y' and the equilibrium interest rate is labeled r'.

Now we will ask, as in Chapter 4, how much will real income increase if the Fed raises the money supply enough to shift the *LM* curve from the old *LM* curve to the new *LM* curve? We do not need to calculate the exact numerical value of the change in income and the interest rate, since we will be interested in answers to two simple questions. First, following an increase in the real money supply, does real income increase by a lot, a little, or not at all? Second, does the interest rate decline by a lot, a little, or not at all?

Strong Effects of Monetary Expansion

The answer to these questions depends on the slopes of both the *IS* and *LM* curves. With the normal slopes shown in the top frame of Figure 5-1 the economy moves from point E_0 to point E_1. The higher money supply boosts income from Y' to Y_1 and lowers the interest rate from r' to r_1. The economy's

Figure 5-1
The Effect of an Increase in the Money Supply with a Normal *LM* Curve and a Vertical *LM* Curve

The top frame shows the normal effect of an increase in the real money supply, which is to raise real income and to reduce the interest rate. In the bottom frame the *LM* curve is vertical, and the same increase in the real money supply leads to a greater drop in the interest rate and a greater increase in real income.

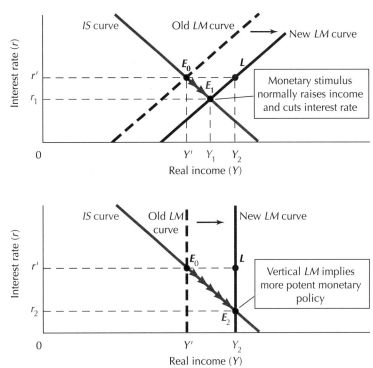

WHY A VERTICAL *LM* CURVE MAKES MONETARY POLICY MORE POTENT

equilibrium rises from E_0 to E_1, just as in Figure 4-11. Higher income and lower interest rates suffice to boost the demand for money by the amount needed in order to match the assumed higher supply of money that the Fed has created.

What would it take for the impact of the same increase in the money supply to differ from this normal case? In one variant, monetary expansion has an unusually strong effect on income. This occurs when the *LM* curve is steep (due to a low interest responsiveness of the demand for money). Shown in the bottom frame of Figure 5-1 is the same starting place at E_0, and exactly the same *IS* curve as in the top frame. But now the old and new *LM* curves are vertical, indicating the extreme case of a zero interest responsiveness of the demand for money. The same increase in the money supply as in the top frame moves the *LM* curve to "new *LM*" (note that the horizontal shift in the *LM* curve in both the top and bottom frame is the distance marked from E_0 to *L*). As a result, the economy moves from point E_0 to point E_2. Income increases twice as much in the lower frame as in the upper frame, while the interest rate falls twice as much.

Why does monetary policy exert a greater stimulus in the bottom frame? In both frames the money supply increases by the same amount, and so does money demand. But in the bottom frame the demand for money is totally insensitive to a reduction in the interest rate, so *all the work of boosting money demand must be achieved by higher income.* Since the lower interest rate offers no help in boosting money demand, income must rise further than in the top frame. And, to maintain commodity-market equilibrium along the fixed *IS* curve, a greater drop in the interest rate is needed to achieve the required boost in income.

SELF-TEST
> If the demand for money is independent of the interest rate, is the *LM* curve vertical or horizontal? Does an increase in the money supply have strong or weak effects when the *LM* curve is steeper than normal? When it is flatter than normal?

Weak Effects of Monetary Policy

The Fed boosts the money supply when it believes that income is too low. For instance, the Fed may believe that the income level Y' in Figure 5-1 is too low and that the desirable level of income is Y_1. The rightward shift in the *LM* curve shown in the top frame of Figure 5-1 is just right, taking the economy from Y' to Y_1, but the same rightward shift in the bottom frame takes the economy too far to the right, to Y_2, because in this particular case the effects of monetary policy are so strong.

But in some circumstances the Fed may have the opposite problem. Here the effects of monetary policy are so weak that the policy cannot boost real income sufficiently to reach Y_1. This section reviews two such cases. First, changes in the interest rate may have only weak effects on autonomous planned spending (A_p). Second, money demand might be extremely sensitive to changes in the interest rate.

Steep *IS* Curve.   The first case is shown in the top frame of Figure 5-2. The zero interest responsiveness of A_p implies that the *IS* curve is vertical. This situation occurs when business firms are so pessimistic about the future that they do not boost investment spending in response to lower interest rates. As a result, a lower interest rate does not raise equilibrium income. Income is "stuck" at point Y' in response to the same rightward shift in the *LM* curve that occurs in the top frame of Figure 5-1. The only effect of the higher money supply in the top frame of Figure 5-2 is a lower interest rate as the economy moves from point E_0 down vertically to point E_3. Since real income is stuck at Y', all the work of boosting money demand now must be achieved by a lower interest rate. *will they respond? since skeptical?*

Flat *LM* Curve.   The second case of weak monetary policy occurs when the demand for money is extremely responsive to the interest rate, which makes the *LM* curve very flat, as shown in the bottom frame of Figure 5-2. Once again, the money supply goes up by the same amount as before, and the *LM* curve shifts horizontally by the distance shown between E_0 and point L. But now, because the *LM* curve is so flat, the economy's equilibrium position hardly moves at all, from E_0 to E_4. Before the interest rate falls enough to stimulate an increase in autonomous planned spending, it is already low enough to boost money demand and falls no further. In the extreme case of a horizontal *LM* curve, the Fed loses control over both output

Figure 5-2
Effect of the Same Increase in the Real Money Supply with a Zero Interest Responsiveness of Spending and with a High Interest Responsiveness of the Demand for Money

In the top frame the higher money supply does not stimulate expenditures because expenditures are assumed to be independent of the interest rate—that is, the *IS* curve is vertical. In the bottom frame the *LM* curve is so flat that the same increase in the money supply (as in the top frame of this figure and in both frames of Figure 5-1) hardly reduces the interest rate at all, and so real income hardly increases at all.

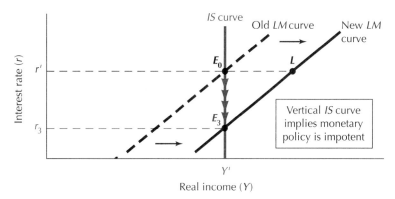

TWO EXAMPLES OF IMPOTENT MONETARY POLICY

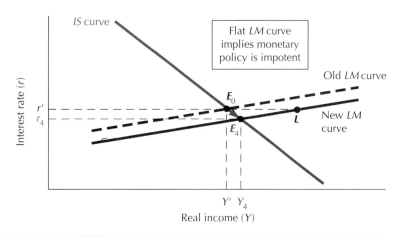

and the interest rate, which remain unchanged in response to a higher money supply.[2]

5-3   Strong and Weak Effects of Fiscal Policy

The effect of a fiscal policy stimulus on real income depends on the slopes of the *IS* and *LM* curves. Fiscal policy is strong when the demand for money is highly interest-responsive, as illustrated in the top frame of Figure 5-3. With this extreme case of a horizontal *LM* curve, the multiplier becomes just the

---

[2]Normally an increase in the money supply reduces the interest rate because people try to get rid of the excess money by purchasing bonds and other financial assets, thus raising the price of bonds and other financial assets and reducing the interest rate. In an extreme (and hypothetical) case called the "liquidity trap," people are convinced that the prices of bonds and other financial assets are unusually high and are likely to fall, so they hold onto the extra money and refuse to buy any financial assets. As a result the Fed loses control of the interest rate and the *LM* curve becomes a horizontal line that no longer shifts its position in response to a higher money supply.

Figure 5-3
Effect of a Fiscal Stimulus When Money Demand Has an Infinite and a Zero Interest Responsiveness

In the top frame, an infinite interest responsiveness means that the interest rate is fixed, and no crowding out can occur. In contrast, the same fiscal stimulus has no effect on income when the interest responsiveness is zero (bottom frame), because then a higher interest rate releases no extra money to support higher income, and the income level is completely determined by the size of the real money supply. Since the fiscal stimulus causes no growth at all in income from E_0 to E_7, crowding out is complete.

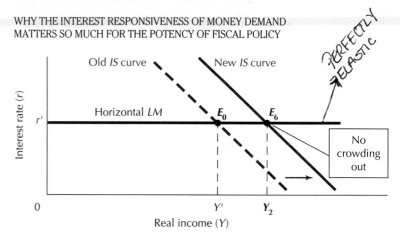

WHY THE INTEREST RESPONSIVENESS OF MONEY DEMAND MATTERS SO MUCH FOR THE POTENCY OF FISCAL POLICY

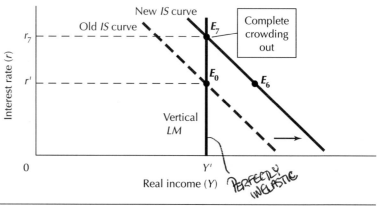

simple multiplier *(k)* of Chapter 3. There is no crowding out effect, since the interest rate remains constant.

The opposite situation occurs when the interest responsiveness of money demand is zero, which makes the *LM* curve vertical. An increase in government spending shifts the *IS* curve to the right in the bottom frame of Figure 5-3, exactly as in the top frame, but real income cannot increase without throwing the money market out of equilibrium. Why? An increase in real income would raise the demand for money above the fixed money supply. Because of the zero interest responsiveness of money demand, no increase in the interest rate can bring money demand back down into balance with the fixed money supply. In this case the only effect of a fiscal stimulus is to raise the interest rate. The crowding out effect is complete, with the higher interest rate cutting autonomous *private* spending by exactly the amount by which government spending increases, leaving total autonomous spending unchanged.

Which diagram is the most accurate depiction of the effects of expansionary fiscal policy with a fixed real money supply: the "normal" case depicted in Figure 4-12 or the extreme cases show in Figure 5-3? Numerous historical episodes suggest that the original analysis of Figure 4-12 is accurate—the crowding out effect is partial rather than complete or nonexistent. Furthermore, statistical evidence shows that the interest responsiveness of the demand for money is neither zero nor infinity. For this reason we should regard Figure 4-12 as giving a reliable example of the effects of expansionary fiscal policy, while Figure 5-3 depicts two artificial and extreme cases, rather than realistic possibilities.

Summary of Crowding Out

The fundamental cause of crowding out is an increase in the interest rate caused by a fiscal policy stimulus. Crowding out can be avoided only if there is no upward pressure on the interest rate when the *IS* curve shifts rightward; with a fixed money supply this requires a horizontal *LM* curve as in the top frame of Figure 5-3. In this frame, there is zero crowding out.

Crowding out can be either partial or complete. If there is any increase in real income in response to the fiscal policy stimulus, crowding out is partial. This is shown in Figure 4-12, where the economy's equilibrium level of income increases from point E_0 to E_5. If there is no increase in income at all in response to the fiscal policy stimulus, then crowding out is complete. This occurs in the bottom frame of Figure 5-3, where there is absolutely no increase in income at the new point E_7, as compared with the initial point E_0.

SELF-TEST

> Is crowding out zero, partial, or complete in the following cases? (1) Zero interest responsiveness of autonomous planned spending, (2) zero interest responsiveness of the demand for money, (3) infinite interest responsiveness of the demand for money.

5-4   CASE STUDY: **How Large Are Actual Multipliers?**

The previous analysis suggested extreme conditions under which the theoretical multipliers for monetary and fiscal policy could be zero—that is, either monetary policy could have no effect on real output or an increase in government spending could have no effect on real output. Are these extreme cases realistic?

An **econometric model** is a group of equations, each one representing a different relation in the economy, in which the parameters are estimated by the statistical study of past historical episodes.

Economists answer these questions by building an **econometric model** of the economy. Each macroeconomic relationship, such as the response of consumption spending to changes in income and the response of investment to changes in the interest rate, is estimated by statistical methods based on historical data for an actual economy like that of the United States. Then, once values of the key economic responses (e.g., the marginal propensity to consume) are determined, the model can be subjected to experiments to determine its behavior.

The top frame of Figure 5-4 shows two versions of the government spending multiplier, with time in years measured along the horizontal axis and the multiplier itself, expressed as the dollar response of real GDP divided by the dollar change in government spending, measured along the vertical axis. The multiplier shown as the black line unrealistically assumes that the interest rate remains unchanged and is equivalent to point E_6 in Figure 5-3. The multiplier shown as the red line in the top frame of Figure 5-4 assumes that the money supply remains unchanged. The difference between the two lines shows the crowding out effect that occurs as the fiscal expansion raises the interest rate, which occurs along the red line but not along the black line.

GOVERNMENT SPENDING MULTIPLIER

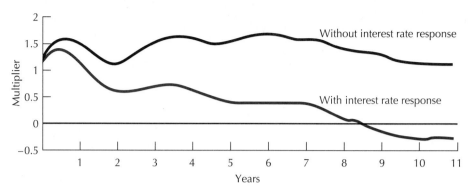

MONEY MULTIPLIER

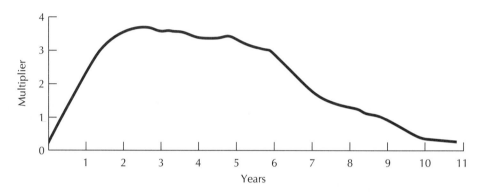

Figure 5-4   **Actual Fiscal and Monetary Multipliers**

This graph shows multipliers for monetary and fiscal policy over ten years, following a policy change, with time plotted on the horizontal axis. The vertical axis plots the ratio of the change in real GDP to the change in government spending (top frame) or to the money supply (bottom frame). The two lines in the top frame show the response of GDP to an increase in government spending. The red line shows the actual multiplier, which holds the money supply constant and peaks after two quarters at a 1.4 dollar increase in real GDP in response to a 1.0 dollar increase in government spending. After three quarters this multiplier fades away, reaching zero after eight years. The black line in the top frame shows the hypothetical multiplier on the alternative assumption that the interest rate remains fixed; it does not fade away. The bottom frame shows the multiplier for an increase in the money supply, which fades away after about ten years. *Source:* Allen Sinai, "Financial and Real Business Cycles," *Eastern Economic Journal,* vol. 18, no. 1 (Winter 1992), pp. 1–54, Figures 5 and 17. Used by permission.

What actually happens in the economy to make the fiscal policy multiplier fade away over time along the red line?

● The higher interest rate reduces consumer spending on items that are typically financed by borrowing, particularly cars and residential houses and condominiums.

● The higher interest rate tends to raise the foreign exchange rate of the dollar (as we learn in the next chapter), cutting exports by making them more expensive for foreigners to buy, and raising imports by making them cheaper for Americans to buy.

- The higher interest rate forces consumers to make higher interest payments on previously accumulated debt. With more of their household budgets dedicated to making interest payments on debt they had incurred to buy goods and housing in the past, consumers are forced to cut back their purchases on new goods and services.
- Higher interest rates also increase the burden of interest payments for business firms, reducing the funds they have available for investment expenditures.
- Higher interest rates tend to depress the stock market, making consumers feel less wealthy, which tends to reduce consumption, and making it harder for business firms to finance new investment projects.

The bottom frame of Figure 5-4 shows the multiplier for a monetary stimulus, measured as the dollar change in real GDP per dollar change in the money supply. Notice that the peak in the red line occurs later in the bottom frame than the top frame; an important characteristic of real-world monetary policy is its *long lag time*—that is, the delay between the initial change in the money supply and the subsequent response of real GDP.

Why does the multiplier for monetary policy fade away, as shown in the bottom frame? Initially the impact of a higher money supply is to reduce the interest rate. Then real GDP begins to grow over the subsequent two years. Since the demand for money responds positively to this increase in income, the interest rate begins to rise back toward its initial level. As this increase in the interest rate occurs, it generates exactly the same kind of negative impacts on spending as occur in the case of a fiscal stimulus. Eventually, these negative impacts on real GDP cancel out the initial positive impacts of a monetary stimulus.

One reason both the fiscal and monetary multipliers eventually fade away is that eventually a fiscal or monetary stimulus causes an increase in the price level, which tends to reduce the real money supply and further increase the interest rate. This is an important aspect of real-world behavior that has not yet been taken into account in our theoretical *IS-LM* model. We return in Chapter 7 to an analysis of the effects of stimulative or restrictive policy action on the price level.

5-5   The Fiscal-Monetary Policy Mix

So far we have used the *IS-LM* model to examine, first, the effects of a monetary expansion and, second, the separate effects of a fiscal expansion. Yet the two types of policy do not always work in isolation. The Fed's monetary policy, formed on the "west side" of Washington, may strengthen or dampen the fiscal policy formed on the "east side" of Washington.[3]

---

[3]Monetary policy is formulated in the Federal Reserve building, about ten blocks west of the Washington Monument. Fiscal policy is formulated not just in the White House (near the Washington Monument) but in the Capitol and nearby Senate and House office buildings, which are about 15 blocks east of the Washington Monument.

A FISCAL STIMULUS MAY HAVE A BIG IMPACT ON INCOME OR NONE AT ALL

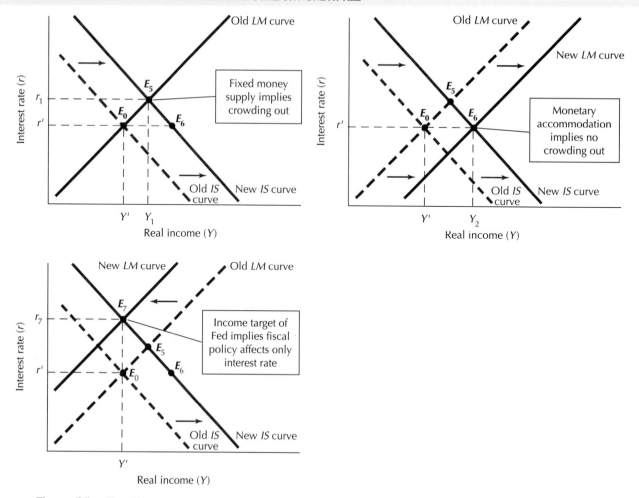

Figure 5-5   **The Effect on Real Income of a Fiscal Stimulus with Three Alternative Monetary Policies**
In the top left frame the real money supply is held constant and the stimulus of fiscal policy on real income is partly crowded out (as in Figure 4-12). In the top right frame the Fed maintains a fixed interest rate, which eliminates the crowding out effect (as in the top frame of Figure 5-3). In the bottom left frame the Fed attempts to maintain a constant level of real income by shifting *LM* to the left whenever *IS* shifts to the right, implying complete crowding out; in this case fiscal policy influences only the interest rate, not real income.

The Fiscal Multiplier Depends on the Monetary Response

How does the response of income to a fiscal policy stimulus (the fiscal multiplier) depend on the Fed? The basic idea is simple: The more the Fed *expands* the money supply, the larger is the fiscal multiplier; the more the Fed *contracts* the money, the smaller the fiscal multiplier. If the Fed contracts the money supply enough, the fiscal multiplier could even be negative.

Three cases are shown in Figure 5-5. In the upper left frame we repeat the standard case from Figure 4-12. When the Fed holds the money supply constant, the *LM* curve remains at its original position. A fiscal stimulus consisting of either an increase in government spending or a tax cut shifts the *IS* curve rightward to the "new *IS* curve."[4] Because the money supply is fixed, the higher demand for money created by rising income forces interest rates higher, crowding out some investment and consumption spending. The economy goes from point E_0 to E_5.

In the upper right frame is a second possibility. If the Fed's goal is to keep the interest rate fixed, the money supply must be allowed to change passively whenever there is a shift in the *IS* curve (due not only to fiscal policy but also to changes in consumer and business confidence and to changes in net exports). If the Fed allows the money supply to change by the amount needed to keep the interest rate constant at r', it must shift the *LM* curve rightward. The result of the fiscal stimulus is now the same as the Chapter 3 multiplier *(k)*, which ignored the money market and the impact of interest rate changes. The economy goes from E_0 to E_6, the same as the new equilibrium position in the top frame of Figure 5-3. When trying to stabilize the interest rate and allowing the money supply to respond passively to any change in the *IS* curve, the Fed is said to "accommodate" fiscal policy. In effect, the east side of Washington has taken control of the west side.

The third possibility is that the Fed does not care about the money supply or the interest rate, but rather attempts to stabilize real income. If the Fed wants to maintain income at Y', for instance, it can respond to the fiscal stimulus *by moving the* LM *curve in the opposite direction from the movement in the* IS *curve.* Thus, if government spending is increased, the Fed must reduce the money supply. If the Fed calculates the exact value of the money supply needed to hold income constant after a fiscal stimulus, the situation is illustrated by the bottom left frame of Figure 5-5. The economy moves from E_0 to E_7 (the same position shown in the bottom frame of Figure 5-3). When the Fed behaves this way, fiscal policy no longer has any control over the level of income and affects only the interest rate. The effect of fiscal policy is to raise the interest rate from r' to r_7.

The Monetary–Fiscal Mix

The bottom left frame of Figure 5-5 illustrates an important point about monetary and fiscal policy. Once the government has decided on the desirable level of income, say Y', it can achieve that level of income with many different interest rates, of which r' and r_7 are only two examples.[5] We can assume that points E_0 and E_7 share not only the same level of output, but also the same level of employment and unemployment. What are the differences?

Point E_7 offsets the fiscal policy stimulus, assumed to be a higher level of government spending, by reducing the money supply (shown by the leftward

---

[4]*Review:* The rightward shift in *IS* in response to an increase in government spending is the Chapter 4 multiplier *(k)* times the increase, that is, $k\Delta G$. The rightward shift for a cut in autonomous tax revenues is $-kc\Delta \overline{T}$.

[5]Defining what income level is desirable is a separate issue. To simplify Figure 5-5, we assume here that income level Y' is desirable. Earlier, the discussion of Figures 5-1 and 5-2 assumed that Y_1 was the desirable level of output. The point of Figure 5-5—that the fiscal policy multiplier depends on the response of the Fed—remains valid whatever the desirable level of output. We return in Chapters 7 and 8 to the question of which output level is desirable, based on the concept of the natural level of output, first introduced in Chapter 1.

movement to the "new LM curve"). In contrast, point E_0 has a higher real money supply (shown by the fact that the LM curve is farther to the right) but a tighter fiscal policy (shown by the fact that the IS curve is farther to the left). The higher interest rate at E_7 crowds out planned investment and autonomous consumption below that at point E_0, in order to "make room" for a higher level of government spending.

The two points E_0 and E_7 are said to differ in the mix of monetary and fiscal policy. Point E_0 has a **policy mix** of "easy money, tight fiscal," while point E_7 has the opposite policy mix of "tight money, easy fiscal." Which mix should society prefer? At E_0, investment is higher; thus the economy is building for the future, and its future level of productivity growth will be higher. At E_7, government spending is higher than at E_0, and investment is lower. Should society prefer the faster output growth of point E_0 or the higher level of public services of point E_7?

This is a central question of macroeconomics to which we return in Chapters 9–11. Its solution depends on whether the government spending consists largely of government consumption (national defense, police, and fire protection) or government investment (highways and school buildings). If the extra government spending at point E_7 consists of government consumption, then the choice between points E_7 and E_0 depends on society's taste for present consumption goods and services (at E_7) versus future consumption, since a high investment strategy at E_0 yields higher consumption only in the future. If the extra government spending at E_7 consists of government investment, then the choice depends on whether there is a higher payoff for society from government investment (of which there is more at E_7) as compared with private investment (of which there is more at E_0). The same criteria are relevant if the fiscal stimulus takes the form of a tax cut that can stimulate either private investment or consumption, depending on the types of taxes that are cut.

> The **policy mix** refers to the combination of monetary and fiscal policy in effect in a given situation. A mix of tight monetary and easy fiscal policy leads to high interest rates, while a mix of easy monetary and tight fiscal policy leads to low interest rates.

5-6 The Pervasive Effects of the Government Budget Deficit

Each year the government sets its budget. If revenue exceeds expenditures, there is a government budget surplus. If expenditures exceed revenues, there is a government budget deficit. In the United States since the early 1980s the government has run a budget deficit in every year. In this section we introduce the pervasive effects of a *persistent government budget deficit.* The basic cause of the persistent deficits, as we shall see in detail in Chapter 11, is that federal government transfer payments have gradually increased as a share of GDP, while federal tax revenue has remained roughly constant as a share of GDP.

Crowding Out of Net Exports

Thus far our analysis of the *IS-LM* model has emphasized that a fiscal expansion, taking the form of an increase in government spending or a reduction in tax rates, is likely to crowd out domestic private investment. But, in addition, a fiscal expansion may crowd out net exports. We can review equation (2.5) in Chapter 2 (here renumbered as equation 5.1) to see why one or the other type of crowding out, or both together, must occur:

$$G - T = S - (I + NX) \qquad (5.1)$$

On the left-hand side of this definition is the government budget deficit $(G - T)$. On the right-hand side, and available to finance the government budget deficit, is the excess of private saving (S) over total investment, both domestic (I) and foreign (NX). Recall from Chapter 2 that net exports and foreign investment are the same thing. The definition indicates that there are only three ways to finance a government deficit. First, private saving can go up. Second, domestic private investment can go down; this is the crowding out effect that we have examined in the context of our *IS-LM* model. Third, foreign investment can go down, and if it drops far enough and becomes negative, we call it foreign borrowing.

For most of the period of persistent federal budget deficits since 1981, the U.S. government financed them through foreign borrowing. Stated another way, in most years since 1981 the United States ran both a government budget deficit and a foreign trade deficit (more precisely, a current-account deficit) at the same time. Since these two deficits are interrelated through equation (5.1), they are often called the *twin deficits*. But as we shall see, the twin deficits are not always twins, since it is possible in equation (2.5) for a government deficit to be balanced by a decline in private investment (I) relative to saving (S), with the current-account deficit (NX) equal to zero.

Impact on Future Generations

Persistent government budget deficits have another implication as well. As we shall see, a deficit raises the public (or national) debt. Future generations, including current college students reading this book, will be obliged to pay higher taxes than otherwise would be necessary so the government can pay interest on its debt. Some of that interest will be paid to other domestic citizens who own the debt, but some will be paid to foreign citizens, as a result of U.S. foreign borrowing. Further, the crowding out of domestic private investment by the government budget deficit means that future citizens will have a smaller stock of capital (machines, commercial and industrial buildings, and residential houses and condominiums) than otherwise would occur.

Clearly, a persistent budget deficit has pervasive consequences on domestic investment, foreign investment or borrowing, and the wealth of citizens in the future. This is ample motivation to study closely in the remainder of this chapter the causes and effects of the budget deficit.

5-7   CASE STUDY: The U.S. Government Budget Deficit in Historical Perspective

The government budget deficit is defined as government expenditure minus government revenue. Throughout history the largest deficits have been incurred as a result of wars, when government expenditures increased more than government tax revenues. Governments choose not to pay the full cost of wars through taxation for fear that heavy taxes will demoralize citizens when their utmost efforts are needed for war production.

The top frame of Figure 5-6 plots U.S. government real expenditures (including transfer payments) and revenues, both as a percentage of natural real GDP, for this century. The difference between expenditures and revenues

A CENTURY OF DEFICITS

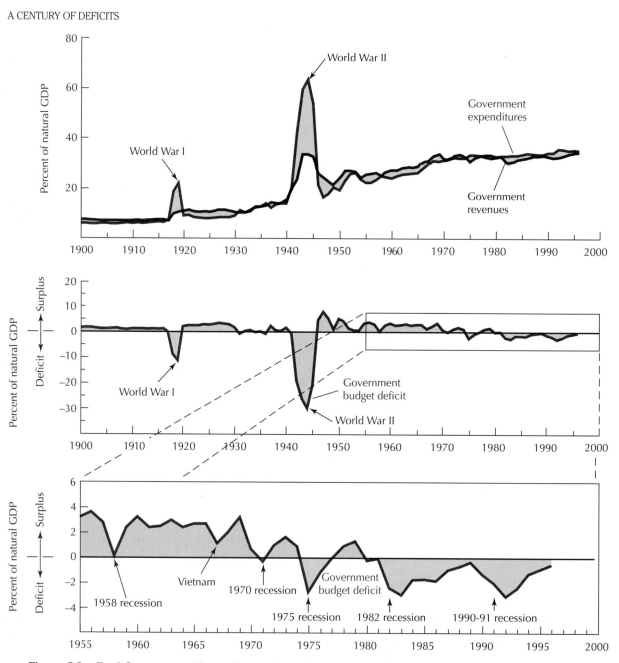

Figure 5-6   **Real Government Expenditures, Real Government Revenues, and the Real Government Budget Deficit, 1900–96**

The top frame compares real government expenditures and revenues as a share of natural GDP, and shows the dramatic effects of wars and also the gradual increase in the expenditure share in the 1970s and 1980s. The middle frame shows the government budget deficit for the century, and the bottom frame is a blowup of the deficit experience of the 1955–96 period, calling attention to the unusual post-1982 deficits that involve neither war nor recession.

is shaded: red shading indicates a government budget deficit and gray shading indicates a government budget surplus. Included is not just the federal government budget, but also the budgets of the state and local governments.

Wars and the Increasing Size of Government

Four facts stand out in the top frame of Figure 5-6. First, government expenditures exhibit a marked spike in war years, with World War II having a much greater impact than World War I. Second, tax revenues also exhibit a spike in wartime, but a smaller spike than expenditures, so deficits increase in wartime. Third, the size of government has increased in the years since World War II, as compared with the years before 1930, with real expenditures averaging about 30 percent of natural real GDP and edging up to about 35 percent in the 1990s. Fourth, expenditures increased more than revenues after 1980, leading to a persistent budget deficit.

The middle frame shows the government budget deficit and surplus. The areas in red and gray shading in the middle frame are identical to the corresponding areas in the top frame. Here the tendency of wars to create deficits is even more evident. The deficits since 1980 pale in comparison with the gigantic deficit of World War II. To compare more clearly the deficits that have occurred since 1980, the period 1955–96 is magnified in the bottom frame. Here we see a relatively small deficit in 1971, the result of 1970 recession. Substantially larger deficits occurred in 1975–76 and 1982–96.

The Effect of Recessions

During a recession government revenues decline and transfer payments increase. Notice in the bottom frame how deficits occurred during the recessions of 1970, 1975, 1982, and 1990–91 and in the recession of 1958 the surplus dropped sharply almost creating a deficit.

If government deficits had frequently been associated with recessions in the past, why did the deficits of the 1980s and 1990s create so much controversy? The answer is visible in the bottom frame of Figure 5-6. Each previous recession deficit episode has a sharp V shape, and the government budget deficit quickly dropped to zero as the economy recovered after the recession. But 1982–96 was different. As the economy recovered after the 1982 recession, the *government budget deficit did not disappear but remained relatively large.* The large budget deficits after 1982 occurred in peacetime, not in wartime, and in a situation of economic recovery and expansion rather than recession (except for the mild recession of 1990–91).

5-8   Structural and Cyclical Budget Deficits

In this section we distinguish between two types of change in the government budget deficit. The first type, called **cyclical deficit,** occurs *automatically* as a result of the business cycle. Recessions cause government revenues to shrink and the cyclical deficit to grow; this condition is followed by recoveries and expansions that cause government revenues to grow and the cyclical deficit

The **cyclical deficit** is the amount by which the actual government budget deficit exceeds the **structural deficit,** which in turn is defined as what the deficit *would be* if the economy were operating at natural real GDP.

to shrink. The second type is called **structural deficit;** this is the deficit that remains after the effect of the business cycle is separated out. The structural deficit is calculated by assuming that current levels of government spending and tax rates remain in effect, but that the economy is operating at natural real GDP rather than the actual observed level of real GDP.

Automatic Stabilization

Recall from Chapters 2 and 3 that the symbol T stands for "net" tax revenues, that is, total tax revenues minus government transfer payments. If net tax revenues (T) rise when income is high and fall when income is low, we can express net tax revenue as equal to the average net tax rate (t) times real income (Y):

$$T = tY \qquad (5.2)$$

This implies that the government budget can be written as

$$\text{budget surplus} = T - G = tY - G \qquad (5.3)$$

The government budget deficit is simply a negative value of the surplus, as defined in (5.3). The purpose of writing the government budget surplus or deficit in this way is to distinguish two main sources of change in the surplus or deficit: (1) **automatic stabilization** through changes in Y, and (2) **discretionary fiscal policy** through changes in G and t.

Automatic stabilization occurs because government tax revenues depend on income, causing the economy to be stabilized by the leakage of tax revenues from the spending stream when income rises or falls.

When real GDP increases in an economic expansion, the government surplus automatically rises as more net tax revenues are generated (that is, gross tax revenues rise and transfer payments such as unemployment benefits fall). The higher surplus (or lower deficit) helps to stabilize the economy, since the extra net tax revenues that are generated by rising incomes leak out of the spending stream and help restrain the boom. Similarly, tax revenues drop and transfers rise in a recession, cutting the leakages out of the spending stream and helping dampen the recession.

Discretionary fiscal policy alters tax rates and/or government expenditures in a deliberate attempt to influence real output and the unemployment rate.

The automatic stabilization effect of real income or GDP (Y) on the government surplus or deficit is illustrated in Figure 5-7. The horizontal axis is real income and the vertical axis is the government budget surplus and deficit. In the gray area above the zero level on the vertical axis, the government runs a surplus, with tax revenues exceeding expenditures. In the red area below zero, the government runs a deficit, with expenditures exceeding tax revenues. Along the horizontal line separating the gray and red areas, the government budget is balanced, with expenditures exactly equal to tax revenues.

The **budget line** shows the government budget surplus or deficit at different levels of real income.

The red upward-sloping BB_0 schedule is the **budget line,** which illustrates the automatic stabilization relationship between the government budget and real income when other determinants of the budget in equation (5.3) are constant, that is, at the assumed values G_0 and t_0. The budget line BB_0 has a slope equal to the tax rate t_0. In Figure 5-7 the budget line BB_0 is drawn so that the government runs a balanced budget at point A, when real income is equal to natural real GDP (Y^N). If the economy were to fall from Y^N to Y_0, the economy would move from point A to point B, where the government is running a deficit because its tax revenues have fallen by $t_0 \, \Delta Y$.

Figure 5-7
The Relation Between the Government Budget Surplus or Deficit and Real Income

In the gray area the government budget is in surplus, while in the red area the government budget is in deficit. The budget line BB_0 shows all the levels of the government budget surplus or deficit that are compatible with a given level of government expenditures (G_0) and tax rates (t_0). The BB line slopes upward to the right, because as we move rightward from B to A, the higher real income (Y) raises tax revenues $(t_0 Y)$, thus increasing the surplus or reducing the deficit by the amount $t \Delta Y$.

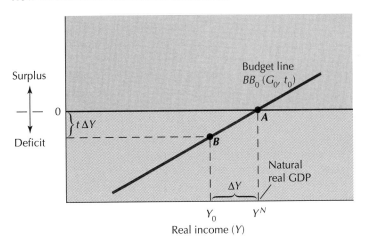

HOW THE ECONOMY INFLUENCES THE BUDGET

Discretionary Fiscal Policy

The second source of change in the government budget deficit comes from alterations in government spending *(G)* and in the tax rate *(t)*. It is evident from equation (5.3) that a decline in government spending *(G)* reduces the budget deficit, while a decrease in the tax rate *(t)* raises the deficit. How do such discretionary changes affect the budget line? Figure 5-8 copies the budget line BB_0 from Figure 5-7. The initial budget line BB_0 is drawn on the assumption that government spending is G_0. An increase in government spending from G_0 to G_1 shifts the red budget line downward for any given level of real income, since at a given level of income the government spends more and has a higher deficit at G_1 compared with the original spending level G_0. The new budget line is shown in the position BB_1.

Find point *C* along the new budget line BB_1. This shows that at the new higher level of government spending (G_1), the budget would have a large deficit at a real income level of Y_0. There are three ways to reduce the deficit. One way, shown by a movement from *C* to *D*, would be to increase real income to Y^N. The second way, shown by a movement from *C* to *B*, would be to reduce government spending. A third way, not shown separately, would be to increase the tax rate (t_0), which would also shift the budget line upward.[6] Changes in the actual budget deficit provide no indications of specific discretionary fiscal policy actions (that is, changes in government spending and the tax rate), since the actual budget deficit can also change as real income increases or decreases with no change in tax rates or government expenditures, as from *C* to *D* or *B* to *A*.

---

[6]An increase in the tax rate *rotates* the budget line about its fixed vertical intercept, shifting it upward while making it steeper. A reduction in the tax rate rotates the budget line down, making it flatter.

The Natural Employment Surplus or Deficit

Since the actual budget surplus or deficit cannot identify discretionary fiscal policy changes, how can we summarize the effect of fiscal policy on the economy? In Figure 5-8 the more expansionary budget line BB_1 has a *lower* vertical position than the original budget line BB_0. Thus its expansionary effect can be summarized by describing the vertical position of the budget line at some standard agreed-upon level of real income, for instance, when real income is equal to natural real GDP (Y^N).

The budget surplus or deficit at the natural level of real GDP is called the natural employment surplus or the **natural employment deficit (NED).** It is defined as the government budget deficit that *would occur if* actual real GDP (Y) were equal to natural real GDP (Y^N). If we substitute natural real GDP (Y^N) for actual real GDP in equation (5.3), we can define the natural employment surplus as:

$$\text{natural employment surplus} = tY^N - G \qquad (5.4)$$

The natural employment deficit is simply a negative value of the surplus in (5.4) and changes when there is a change in government spending (G), the tax rate (t), or natural real GDP (Y^N) itself.

In Figure 5-8 there is a different natural employment deficit for each of the two budget lines shown. For the original budget line BB_0, the natural employment deficit is abbreviated NED_0. The value of NED_0 is zero, since along BB_0 the government budget is in balance at Y^N. For the new budget line BB_1, the natural employment deficit is NED_1 and is shown by the distance AD, since along BB_1 the government deficit is the amount AD when the economy is operating at Y^N.

We can now review the major budget concepts with the help of Figure 5-8. The actual budget deficit is shown by the economy's actual position along the appropriate BB line in the figure, for instance at points like B or C. The natural employment deficit is the deficit along each budget line measured at the natural level of real GDP. *Structural deficit* is another name for the nat-

The **natural employment deficit** is government expenditures minus a hypothetical figure for government revenue, calculated by applying current tax rates to natural real GDP rather than actual real GDP.

Figure 5-8
Effect on the Budget Line of an Increase in Government Expenditures

The upper budget line BB_0 is copied from Figure 5-7 and assumes a value for government spending of G_0. The lower budget line BB_1 assumes that the level of government spending has increased to G_1, thus reducing the government budget surplus or increasing the government budget deficit at every level of real income.

DOES THE BUDGET INFLUENCE THE ECONOMY, OR DOES THE ECONOMY INFLUENCE THE BUDGET?

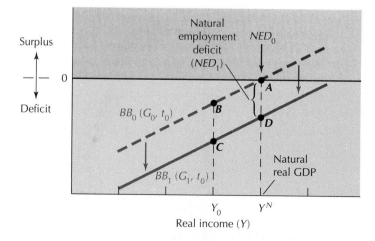

ural employment deficit. The structural deficit changes whenever there is a change in government expenditures or tax rates. The cyclical deficit is the difference between the actual deficit and the natural employment deficit, the vertical distance between A and B along budget line BB_0, and the vertical distance between D and C along budget line BB_1. Automatic stabilization is represented by the slope of the budget line, since higher tax revenues and lower transfer payments cause a greater amount of real income to leak out of the spending stream whenever real income expands.

SELF-TEST

How would the following be shown in Figure 5-8? More spending for highway repair? An increase in the Social Security tax rate? An increase in Social Security benefits? A recession that increases the unemployment rate from 5 to 10 percent? What effect would each of these have on the natural employment deficit?

The Actual and Natural Employment Deficits: Historical Behavior

How have actual and natural employment deficits differed over the last thirty years? The red line in Figure 5-9 is copied from the bottom frame of Figure 5-6 and displays the actual government budget outcome. The new element in Figure 5-9 is the natural employment surplus or deficit, shown by the black line.

The black line isolates the structural component of the budget deficit. The distance between the red and black lines represents the cyclical

THE REAGAN-BUSH NATURAL EMPLOYMENT DEFICIT TOPPED VIETNAM'S

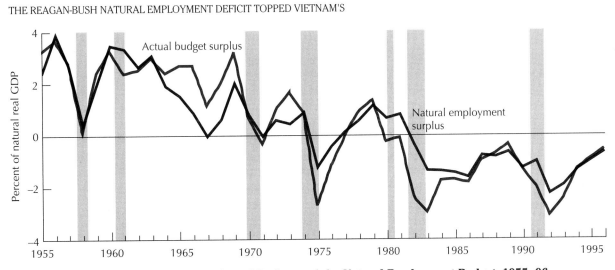

Figure 5-9 **A Comparison of the Actual Budget and the Natural Employment Budget, 1955–96**
The black "natural employment surplus or deficit" line lies above the red "actual surplus or deficit" line in years when the economy is weak and lies below when the economy is strong. The two main periods exhibiting a natural employment deficit were 1975–76, when taxes were cut to stimulate the economy, and 1983–96, due to the combination of increased expenditures (as a share of GDP) with roughly constant tax revenues.

component of the deficit. When the red line is underneath the black line, as in 1958, 1975–77, 1980–85, and 1991–93, the economy is weak, with actual real GDP falling below natural real GDP. When the red line is above the black line, the economy is prosperous, with actual real GDP greater than natural real GDP. Primary examples of periods with a high level of actual real GDP are 1955, 1964–69, 1972–73, and 1988–89.

The black natural employment deficit line highlights two periods when there was a large structural budget deficit. The first occurred in 1975–76, when taxes were cut during the recession to stimulate the economy. A second and even greater structural deficit occurred after 1982. The structural deficit peaked in 1992 at about 2 percent of GDP. The rapid increase in the deficit during 1982–84 was due to the combined effects of the Reagan-era income tax cuts and increases in defense spending. The reduction after 1992 primarily reflects a slowdown in the growth of spending, particularly for defense, together with the revenue-raising features of the 1993 tax reform act.

5-9   National Saving and the Consequences of Budget Deficits

We have now learned that there is a distinction between the actual budget deficit and the natural or structural budget deficit that corrects for the impact of the business cycle on government revenues and expenditures. The persistent structural budget deficit since 1982 is unprecedented; before 1981 structural deficits tended to occur mainly as the result of wars. In this section we study the impact of the budget deficit on the nation's total saving, which determines its ability to finance total investment.

Fiscal Policy and National Saving

National saving is the sum of private saving (by both households and business firms) and government saving. In turn, government saving is the government budget surplus; a government budget deficit subtracts from national saving.

In order to invest, a nation must save. Its total saving is called **national saving** and consists of private saving (S) plus government saving, which is the same thing as a government budget surplus $(T - G)$. A government budget deficit reduces national saving. In turn, national saving is the amount available to finance domestic investment (I) and net foreign investment, which is the same as net exports (NX). The relation between national saving and the two types of investment is summarized in the following equation, which is a simple rearrangement of equation (5.1) on p. 135:

$$S + (T - G) = I + NX \qquad (5.5)$$

In words, this equation states that national saving $(S + T - G)$ on the left-hand side must equal the sum of domestic and foreign investment $(I + NX)$ on the right-hand side.

We can illustrate the impact of the government budget on national saving and on investment with a simple example. Let us say that private saving is equal to 8 percent of real GDP, and then let us consider three different hypothetical levels of the government budget: a surplus of +4 percent of GDP, a balanced budget (a surplus of zero), and finally a deficit of −4 percent of GDP.

	Private saving	Government budget	Available for I + NX
A	8	4	12
B	8	0	8
C	8	−4	4

This example shows, in a striking way, the enormous difference that the government budget makes in the ability of an economy to finance investment. With a government budget surplus of 4 percent of GDP, the economy on line A can finance domestic plus foreign investment equal to 12 percent of GDP. But with a government budget deficit equal to −4 percent of GDP, the economy on line C can finance domestic plus foreign investment equal to only 4 percent of GDP, just one-third as much. With so little investment, economy C can invest far less in new factories and machines and is likely to experience a much lower productivity growth rate than that of economy A.

Figure 5-10 displays the main components of equation (5.5) for the period 1960 to 1995. All data are expressed as a percentage of GDP, and a horizontal line is drawn at zero. The distance between the horizontal line and the black line at the bottom of the graph is the government budget deficit plotted as a negative number *(T − G)*, the same as the red line in Figure 5-9. The red line plots national saving *(S + T − G)*, so that the shaded distance between the

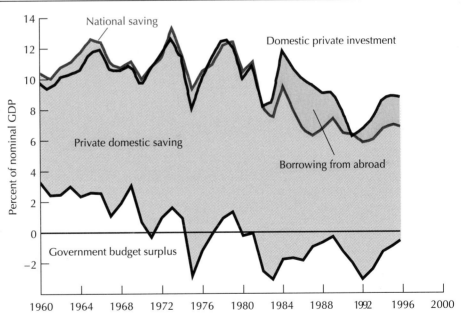

Figure 5-10   **Components of Net Saving and Investment, 1960–96**

The bottom black line is the government budget deficit and is the same as the red line in Figure 5-9. The red line is national saving, and the red-shaded area between those lines is domestic private saving. The thin black line represents domestic private investment and the gray-shaded area represents foreign borrowing. Thus the chart shows how in the 1980s and 1990s domestic private investment was partly financed by national saving and partly by foreign borrowing. Before 1980 both private and national saving were higher. The light red area shows foreign investment, and the graph shows how in the pre-1980 period the uses of national saving were divided between domestic private investment and foreign investment.

INTERNATIONAL PERSPECTIVE

Budget Deficits and National Saving Around the World

The sharp decline in U.S. national saving since 1980 has been due to a combination of lower public saving (i.e., larger government deficits) and lower private saving. This information is shown in the top two lines of the accompanying table, which shows net national saving, public saving, and private saving divided into household and net business saving.

The United States is not alone in experiencing a decline in national saving since 1980 as compared with the two decades between 1960 and 1979. Every other nation experienced such a decline, but with a difference. *Except for the United Kingdom, the other nations had much higher national saving rates, both in 1960–79 and in the 1980s.* Japan's national saving rate for 1980–95 was more than four times that of the United States, and the national saving rates in Germany and Italy were more than twice as high.

Why did national saving rates decline? Except for Canada, all countries experienced the same phenomenon as in the United States, with lower public saving and lower private saving. In every country but Japan public saving declined. Canada, France, and the United Kingdom went from surplus to deficit, Germany ran a smaller surplus, and Italy ran a larger deficit. In every country but Canada, total private saving declined, and in all of these but Germany, household saving declined. Every country but Germany and Italy experienced a decline in business saving.

The table suggests that much of the reason for a higher national saving rate in other countries compared to the United States is their higher household saving rates, with Japan and Italy at the extreme of having high household saving rates. Later in the book we will look more closely at the reasons why household saving tends to be higher in some countries than in the United States. Among the reasons for high household saving in Japan have been a higher relative price of housing, which requires more saving for down payments; a less generous Social Security system that requires more saving for retirement; and less use of consumer credit. In addition, in the past the Japanese tax system exempted a portion of interest income from taxation to encourage saving.

National Saving in the Seven Major Industrial Countries, 1960–1992*

Countries	Periods	Net National Saving	Public	Net Private Total	Households	Business
United States	1960–79	9.9	−0.2	10.1	6.8	3.3
	1980–95	4.6	−3.9	8.2	6.2	2.0
Canada	1960–79	12.2	2.0	10.2	5.0	5.2
	1980–95	7.5	−3.7	11.8	9.1	2.7
Japan	1960–79	25.4	5.8	19.6	14.2	5.4
	1980–95	20.8	6.1	16.5	12.8	3.7
France	1960–79	18.1	3.6	14.5	11.5	3.0
	1980–95	8.6	−0.5	10.2	8.0	2.2
Germany	1960–79	17.5	5.0	12.5	8.6	1.2
	1980–95	10.9	1.3	10.6	9.2	1.4
Italy	1960–79	18.0	−1.6	19.6	18.4	1.2
	1980–95	9.9	−7.7	18.0	15.8	2.1
United Kingdom	1960–79	9.6	2.1	7.5	4.3	3.2
	1980–95	4.6	−0.9	6.7	4.9	1.8

*Expressed as a percentage of national income.
Source: OECD.

red line and the black line represents private domestic saving *(S)*. The gray-shaded area represents foreign borrowing *(−NX)*, so that the sum of national saving and foreign borrowing represents the total funds available to finance domestic private investment. If we move *NX* from the right side of equation (5.5) to the left side, the total funds available for domestic private investment can be written:

$$S + T - G - NX = I \qquad\qquad (5.6)$$

In words, this equation says that national saving *(S + T − G)*, plus foreign borrowing *(−NX)*, equals domestic private investment *(I)*.

Figure 5-10 dramatizes the shrinkage in U.S. national saving since the early 1980s. The concept plotted is *net* national saving, where (as we learned in Chapter 2) the adjective *net* means to exclude depreciation. Prior to 1980 net national saving did decline in recession periods, particularly in 1974–76; however, in many years national saving reached 8 to 10 percent of GDP. In contrast, since 1982 net national saving has never exceeded 5 percent. In terms of our example in the previous section, the United States shifted from being like economy B in the example, with a government budget that was roughly balanced over the years 1960–79, to being roughly like economy C, with a large budget deficit. It was the shift to a persistent government budget deficit, together with a decline in private saving, that caused U.S. net national saving to fall by half between 1960–79 and 1980–96.

Solutions to the National Saving Squeeze

To the extent that domestic private investment is the source of future economic growth, then the reduction in national saving depicted in Figure 5-10 is bad news for future generations of U.S. citizens, including today's college students. The only way that domestic private investment can exceed national saving is through foreign borrowing. But foreigners do not send investment funds to the United States as a "gift." Instead, they expect to receive interest and dividends on their investment. To the extent that the after-tax return on domestic private investment is just sufficient to pay interest and dividends to foreigners, domestic residents do not benefit from this investment (except to the extent that the government collects sales, Social Security, and corporate profits taxes from the foreign firms that make the investment).

Since foreign borrowing is no solution, what other options remain to increase national saving in order to stimulate domestic investment and long-run economic growth? The two obvious solutions are (1) to increase private saving, and (2) to reduce the government budget deficit.

Raise the Private Saving Rate. Many economists believe that the low U.S. household saving rate is unsustainable. To them, Americans are behaving irrationally, living beyond their means. They believe that as households realize how much debt they are in, they will reduce their spending and raise their saving. But these economists neglect an important fact. The U.S. household saving rate is low because households have enjoyed rapid appreciation of real estate and financial assets for the past two decades. Between 1975 and 1980 house prices doubled or tripled in many parts of the country, and there was a further surge in housing prices in some areas in the mid-1980s and in other areas in the mid-1990s. And, from its low point in 1982, the stock market has enjoyed a seemingly endless boom. The Dow Jones Industrial Average in August 1982 was just 750, as compared to a value of 8000 in October 1997, a more than tenfold increase. So, despite a decade of low saving, the ratio of household net worth (i.e., assets minus liabilities) to GDP climbed from a multiple of 4.5 in the early 1980s to 5.0 in mid-1997. We will return in Chapter 15 to a further analysis of household consumption and saving behavior.

Reduce the Deficit.   In 1997 Congress and the Administration reached an agreement to reduce the federal budget deficit to zero by the year 2002. If successful, this effort would boost national saving by the amount that the budget is currently in deficit, about 1 percent of GDP in 1997. Why did it take so many years for an agreement to be reached? The basic reason that the budget is in deficit, as we saw in Figure 5-6, is that federal government expenditures have been creeping up over the past few decades (expressed as a percentage of GDP) while federal government revenues have been roughly stable. Only by boosting tax rates or cutting expenditures can the deficit be reduced toward zero.

However, the main component of federal expenditures that has been increasing as a share of GDP has been transfer payments, not government spending on goods and services. And efforts to control the rapid spending growth of popular "entitlement" programs such as Social Security, Medicare, and Medicaid meet stiff political resistance whenever they are proposed. Despite the 1997 agreement to balance the budget by the year 2002, soon after that entitlement expenses are predicted to grow further throwing the government budget back into deficit. We will return in Chapter 11 to the debate regarding fiscal deficits and their long-run consequences.

5-10   Conclusion: The Role of Monetary and Fiscal Policy

In the 1990s the economic problems of the United States are perceived to be quite different from those of the other major industrialized nations, including Japan and the nations of western Europe. Japan has been in an economic slump since 1990–91, with very little growth in output or employment since then. In western Europe unemployment is much higher than it was twenty years ago, particularly for young people, and in some nations half of the unemployed are out of work for a year or more. The economic situation in the United States seems rosy in contrast, with an unemployment rate in 1997 of about 5.0 percent, no higher than in 1972, and with an inflation rate as low as in any year since the early 1960s.

What, then, do American policymakers have to worry about? At the end of Chapter 1 (p. 24) we were first introduced to the poor performance of the United States in achieving rapid growth in productivity—that is, output per worker-hour. The growth of U.S. productivity has been occurring at less than half the rate achieved by major European nations like France. This has led policymakers to look for macroeconomic policy changes that might boost the rate of American productivity growth.

Fiscal Policy and the Real Interest Rate

If the *IS* and *LM* curves have their normal slopes, and are neither vertical nor horizontal, the *IS-LM* model treats either monetary or fiscal policy as equally well suited to the task of controlling GDP. Yet economists have gradually come to agree that monetary policy is better suited than fiscal policy for controlling GDP, because the Federal Reserve can make decisions promptly. In contrast, fiscal policy decisions in the United States tend to be made slowly.

We learned in the bottom frame of Figure 5-5 that a given level of real GDP could be achieved with a large number of different levels of the interest rate, depending on the mix of monetary and fiscal policy that is used. If monetary policy focuses on stabilizing real GDP at the desired level of output—that is, at natural real GDP—then fiscal policy, by default, becomes responsible for the level of real interest rates. Stated another way, monetary policy has a *short-run orientation* toward the elimination of business cycles and fixing the level of real GDP as close as possible to that of natural real GDP. In contrast, fiscal policy has a *long-run orientation* toward the level of real interest rates, which in turn have a major influence on the long-run growth rates of productivity and income per person.

Real interest rates link the present and the future. They help determine how much of today's output will be invested rather than consumed, and thus available to produce more goods and services in the future. If monetary policy is given the task of controlling GDP in the short run, then fiscal policy becomes a major determinant of real interest rates and indirectly of the economy's rate of long-term economic growth. A successful economy does not consume all of its current production; it saves some fraction of that income in order to increase the nation's stock of productive wealth—not only structures and equipment, but also knowledge and education. Investment in new machines is the main channel by which advances in technology are incorporated into the productive process. Thus, a country with low saving and investment may stagnate technologically while other countries steadily introduce more modern and efficient methods of production.

Not only does fiscal policy have a major impact on the nation's rate of long-run economic growth, but it also has an impact on international aspects of macroeconomics, including the foreign exchange rate, the foreign trade deficit, and capital flows between the United States and other nations. We can see in equation (5.1) on p. 135 that a government budget deficit must be balanced either by a shortfall of domestic investment below domestic saving, by foreign borrowing, or by both. In this sense the persistent U.S. government budget deficit is a prime suspect in explaining the persistent U.S. deficit in foreign trade and its growing dependence on borrowing from foreigners, with the consequence of growing foreign indebtedness. We turn to these issues in the next chapter.

SUMMARY

1. The normal effect of an increase in the money supply is to raise real income and reduce the interest rate.

2. Monetary policy has a relatively strong effect on real income when the interest responsiveness of the demand for money is relatively low (steep *LM* curve). Monetary policy is weak when the interest responsiveness of the demand for money is very

high (flat *LM* curve), or when the interest responsiveness of autonomous planned spending is very low (steep *IS* curve).

3. The normal effect of a fiscal policy stimulus, consisting either of an increase in government spending or a reduction in tax rates, is to raise both real income and the interest rate. The fiscal multiplier is lower than the Chapter 3 multiplier *(k)*, due to partial crowding out of planned investment and autonomous consumption.

4. A fiscal stimulus has a relatively strong effect on real income when the interest responsiveness of the demand for money is relatively high (flat *LM* curve) or the interest responsiveness of autonomous spending is relatively low (steep *IS* curve). A fiscal stimulus has a relatively weak effect with the opposite pattern of interest responsiveness (steep *LM* curve or flat *IS* curve).

5. The effect of a fiscal stimulus on income (fiscal multiplier) is greatest, and there is no crowding out effect, if the Fed is attempting to stabilize interest rates, since this requires that the money supply passively accommodate the fiscal stimulus (the *LM* curve must move to the right by exactly the same distance as the *IS* curve).

6. An intermediate fiscal multiplier, with partial crowding out, occurs when the Fed maintains a constant real money supply.

7. The fiscal multiplier is zero when the Fed stabilizes real income, moving the *LM* curve in the opposite direction from the *IS* curve.

8. By varying the monetary–fiscal mix, government policymakers can maintain a given level of real income with many different interest rates. An "easy money, tight fiscal" mix yields a low interest rate and stimulates private investment. A "tight money, easy fiscal" mix yields a higher interest rate, less private investment, and some combination of additional government consumption, government investment, or private consumption, depending on the particular fiscal policy chosen.

9. The government has run a budget deficit for most of this century, most commonly because of wars and recessions.

10. The natural employment deficit (NED), or structural deficit, is distinguishable from the actual budget deficit. The latter changes through discretionary fiscal policy actions or because of business-cycle movements in real income. Since NED is defined for real income (as the natural level of real GDP), only discretionary fiscal policy changes or growth in natural real GDP can cause NED to move.

11. National saving in the United States fell after 1982, due to both persistent budget deficits and lower private saving. Low national saving limits the ability of an economy to invest for the future.

CONCEPTS

econometric model
policy mix
cyclical deficit
structural deficit
automatic stabilization

discretionary fiscal policy
budget line
natural employment deficit (NED)
national saving

QUESTIONS AND PROBLEMS

Questions

1. The effectiveness of fiscal policy may be limited if the demand for money is insensitive to the interest rate. The effectiveness of monetary policy may be limited if autonomous planned spending is insensitive to the interest rate. Explain.

2. If the LM curve is vertical, can there be any crowding out? If the IS curve is vertical, can there be any crowding out? Considering the slopes of both the IS and LM curves, under what circumstances is the crowding out effect the largest?

3. Assume that the Federal Reserve Board has decided

to maintain the interest rate at the current level. If Congress passes a $50 billion decrease in personal income taxes, what action, if any, would the Fed have to take? What would be the effect of Congress's actions on real output? What would be the effect of the Fed's actions on real output?

4. Assume that the Federal Reserve Board has decided to maintain the level of real GDP at the current level. If Congress passes a $50 billion decrease in personal income taxes, what action, if any, would the Fed have to take? Describe the effect of the actions of

Congress and the Fed on: (a) the interest rate, (b) the composition of output, and (c) the future growth rate of the GDP.

5. "If the Fed seeks to fix the interest rate, fiscal policymakers gain indirect control of the money supply." Explain.

6. You have heard that the actual government deficit for the current year is going to be $30 billion greater than in the past year. Based on this projection, what conclusions can you make regarding the government's fiscal policy?

7. Explain the distinction among the following concepts:
   (a) cyclical deficit
   (b) structural deficit
   (c) natural employment deficit
   (d) actual deficit

8. Respond to the following statements which might be made about an economy where government budget deficit has increased during a recession.
   (a) The increase in the budget deficit indicates that policymakers have implemented expansionary fiscal policies to bring the economy out of recession.
   (b) The increase in the budget deficit indicates that fiscal policymakers have been irresponsible. They should enact restrictive policies, such as tax hikes or spending cuts, to reduce the deficit.

9. During the 1983–85 period, the behavior of the government budget deficit was quite different from that of other recent postrecession periods. Explain in what way the budget deficit differed and why this difference occurred.

10. Explain why you would expect the actual government deficit to be larger than the natural employment deficit when the economy is weak.

Problems

1. Assume that the following equations summarize the structure of an economy:

$$C = a + 0.75(Y - T) \qquad G = 1000$$

$$a = 800 - 10r \qquad (M/P)^d = 0.4Y - 100r$$

$$T = 400 + 0.2Y \qquad M^s/P = 1000$$

$$I_p = 900 - 30r$$

   (a) What is the equation of the *IS* curve?
   (b) What is the equation of the *LM* curve?
   (c) What is the equilibrium interest rate and real output?
   (d) If G increases to 1280, what is the equilibrium interest rate and real output?
   (e) If G remains at 1000 but M^s/P increases to 1350, what is the equilibrium interest rate and real output?

2. Suppose the demand for money balances in the economy described in problem 1 changes to $(M/P)^d = 0.25Y - 25r$. All other parameters and exogenous variables have the values given in problem 1.
   (a) Find the equation for the *LM* curve and verify that the equilibrium interest rate and real output have the same values as you found for problem 1(c).
   (b) Compared to the money demand equation given in problem 1, has money demand become more or less responsive to the interest rate? Is the *LM* curve steeper or flatter as a result? How does this change in the interest responsiveness of money demand alter the amount by which real output will increase following an expansionary change in fiscal or monetary policy?
   (c) If G increases to 1280, what is the equilibrium interest rate and real output? Compare these results with your answer for problem 1(d). How and why do the results differ? Is your prediction in (b) confirmed?
   (d) If G remains at 1000, but M^s/P increases to 1350, what is the equilibrium interest rate and real output? Compare these results with your answer for problem 1(e). How and why do the results differ? Is your prediction in (b) confirmed?

3. Suppose that autonomous consumption and planned investment for the economy described in problem 1 change. Now they are $a = 1000 - 25r$, and $I_p = 1300 - 75r$. All other parameters and exogenous variables have the values given in problem 1.
   (a) Find the equation for the *IS* curve and verify that the equilibrium interest rate and real output have the same values as you found for problem 1(c).
   (b) Compared to problem 1, have autonomous consumption and planned investment become more or less responsive to the interest rate? Is the *IS* curve steeper or flatter as a result? How does this change in the interest responsiveness of autonomous spending alter the amount by which real output will increase following an expansionary change in fiscal or monetary policy?
   (c) If G increases to 1280, what is the equilibrium interest rate and real output? Compare these

results with your answer for problem 1(d). How and why do the results differ? Is your prediction in (b) confirmed?

(d) If *G* remains at 1000, but M^s/P increases to 1350, what is the equilibrium interest rate and real output? Compare these results with your answer for problem 1(e). How and why do the results differ? Is your prediction in (b) confirmed?

4. Refer again to the economy described in problem 1. Suppose now that there is a different mix of fiscal and monetary policies: government spending is 840 and the money supply is 1400.

(a) What is the equilibrium interest rate and real output in the economy? Compare these values to your answer for problem 1(c). What difference do you see? Why does this difference occur?

(b) How do the values of consumption, planned investment spending, and the government budget surplus under the mix of tighter fiscal and easier monetary policy in this problem differ from their values under the easier fiscal and tighter monetary policy mix of problem 1? Why do these differences occur? What is their implication for national saving and long-run economic growth?

5. Assume $Y^N = 3000$, $t = 0.15$, and $G = 500$.

(a) What is the level of the natural employment deficit (NED)?

(b) If *G* increases to 650, what happens to NED?

(c) Assume that *G* has the original value (500) and that there is a decrease in *t*, so that now $t = 0.10$. What is the new value of NED?

SELF-TEST ANSWERS

p. 126   If the demand for money is independent of the interest rate (the variable on the vertical axis), then the *LM* curve is vertical. An increase in the money supply has strong effects when the *LM* curve is steeper than normal, as occurs in the bottom frame of Figure 5-1. An increase in the money supply has weak effects when the *LM* curve is flatter than normal, as occurs in the bottom frame of Figure 5-2.

p. 129   (1) Zero crowding out, because the increase in the interest rate caused by a fiscal policy expansion does not have any effect in reducing planned invest-

ment or autonomous consumption; (2) complete crowding out, the case shown in the bottom frame of Figure 5-3; (3) zero crowding out, the case shown in the top frame of Figure 5-3.

p. 141   More spending for highway repair shifts budget line *BB* down (raises the natural employment deficit, NED). An increase in the Social Security tax rate moves *BB* up (reduces NED), an increase in Social Security benefits moves *BB* down (raises NED), while a recession moves the economy leftward down a fixed *BB* schedule (no change in NED).

APPENDIX TO CHAPTER 5

The Elementary Algebra of the *IS-LM* Model

When you see an *IS* curve crossing an *LM* curve, as in Chapters 4 and 5, you know that the equilibrium level of income *(Y)* and the interest rate *(r)* occur at the point of crossing, as at point E_0 in Figure 5-1. But how can the equilibrium level of income and the interest rate be calculated numerically without going to the trouble of making careful drawings of the *IS* and *LM* curves? Wherever you see two lines crossing to determine the values of two variables such as *Y* and *r*, exactly the same solution can be obtained by solving together the two equations describing the two lines.

In Section 3-8 we found that equilibrium income is equal to autonomous planned spending (A_p) divided by the marginal leakage rate (MLR), so that the autonomous spending multiplier *(k)* is equal to the

inverse of the marginal leakage rate *(k* = 1/MLR). Combining this with the definition of the marginal leakage rate as the fraction that leaks out of income into saving $[s(1 - t_0)]$, tax revenues (t_0), and imports (nx_0) we can write the multiplier as:

$$\text{multiplier} = k = \frac{1}{\text{marginal leakage rate}} \qquad (1)$$

$$= \frac{1}{s(1 - t_0) + t_0 + nx_0}$$

Choosing as examples $s = 0.25$, $t_0 = 0.2$, and $nx_0 = 0.1$, we have

$$k = \frac{1}{0.25(1 - 0.2) + 0.2 + 0.1} = \frac{1}{0.5} = 2.0$$

Once we have determined the multiplier from equation (1) above, we can write real income simply as:

General Linear Form

$$Y = kA_p \qquad (2)$$

Numerical Example

$$Y = 2.0A_p$$

In Section 4-3 the assumption was introduced that autonomous planned spending (A_p) declines when there is an increase in the interest rate (r). If the amount of A_p at a zero interest rate is written as A_0, then the value of A_p can be written:

General Linear Form

$$A_p = A_0 - br \qquad (3)$$

Numerical Example

$$A_p = A_0 - 100r$$

Here b is the interest responsiveness of A_p; in our example there is a $100 billion of decline in A_p per one percentage point increase in the interest rate. Substituting (2) into (1), we obtain the equation for the *IS* schedule:

General Linear Form

$$Y = k(A_0 - br) \qquad (4)$$

Numerical Example

$$Y = 2.0(A_0 - 100r)$$

Thus if A_0 is 2500 and $r = 0$, the IS_0 curve intersects the horizontal axis at 5000.

The *LM* curve shows all combinations of income (Y) and the interest rate (r) where the real money supply (M^s/P) equals the real demand for money $(M/P)^d$, which in turn depends on Y and r. This situation of equilibrium in the money market was previously written as equation (4.2) in the text:

General Linear Form

$$\left(\frac{M^s}{P}\right) = \left(\frac{M}{P}\right)^d = hY - fr \qquad (5)$$

Numerical Example

$$\left(\frac{M^s}{p}\right) = 1.0Y - 200r$$

In this example, where h is the responsiveness of real money demand to higher real income, 1.0 here, and f is the interest responsiveness of real money demand, there is a $200 billion decline in real money demand per one percentage point increase in the interest rate. Adding fr (or $200r$) to both sides of (5), and then dividing by h (or 1.0), we obtain the equation for the *LM* schedule when M^s/P is 2000:

General Linear Form

$$Y = \frac{\dfrac{M^s}{P} + fr}{h} \qquad (6)$$

Numerical Example

$$Y = \frac{2000 + 200r}{1.0}$$

We are assured that the commodity market is in equilibrium whenever Y is related to r by equation (4) and that the money market is in equilibrium whenever Y is related to r by equation (6). To make sure that both markets are in equilibrium, both equations must be satisfied at once.

Equations (4) and (6) together constitute an **economic model.** Finding the value of two unknown variables in economics is very much like baking a cake. One starts with a list of ingredients, the **parameters** (or knowns) of the model: A_0, M^s/P, b, f, h, and k. Then one stirs the ingredients together using the recipe instructions, in this case equations (4) and (6). The outcome is the value of the unknown variables, Y and r. The main rule in economic cake-baking is that the number of equations (the recipe instructions) must be equal to the number of unknowns to be determined. In this example there are two equations and two unknowns (Y and r). There is no limit on the parameters, the number of ingredients known in advance. Here we have six parameters, but we could have seven, ten, or any number.

To convert the two equations of the model into one equation specifying the value of unknown Y in terms of the six known parameters, we simply substitute (6) into (4). To do this, we rearrange (6) to place the interest rate on the left side of the equation, and then we substitute the resulting expression for r in (4). First, rearrange (6) to move r to the left side[1]:

$$r = \frac{hY - \dfrac{M^s}{P}}{f} \qquad (6a)$$

---

[1] First multiply both sides of (6) by h:

$$hY = \frac{M^s}{P} + fr$$

then subtract M^s/P from both sides:

$$hY - \frac{M^s}{P} = fr$$

Now divide both sides by f:

$$\frac{hY - \dfrac{M^s}{P}}{f} = r$$

Equation (6a) is then obtained by reversing the two sides of this equation.

Second, substitute the right side of (6a) for r in (4):

$$Y = k(A_0 - br) = k\left[A_0 - \frac{bhY}{f} + \frac{b}{f}\left(\frac{M^s}{P}\right)\right] \quad (7)$$

Now (7) can be solved for Y by adding $kbhY/f$ to both sides and dividing both sides by k:

$$Y\left(\frac{1}{k} + \frac{bh}{f}\right) = A_0 + \frac{b}{f}\left(\frac{M^s}{P}\right)$$

Finally, both sides are divided by the left term in parentheses:

$$Y = \frac{A_0 + \frac{b}{f}\left(\frac{M^s}{P}\right)}{\frac{1}{k} + \frac{bh}{f}} \quad (8)$$

Equation (8) is our master general equilibrium income equation and combines all the information in the *IS* and *LM* curves together; when (8) is satisfied, both the commodity market and money market are in equilibrium. It can be used in any situation to calculate the level of real income by simply substituting into (8) the particular values of the six known right-hand parameters in order to calculate unknown income.[2]

Because we are interested primarily in the effect on income of a change in A_0 or M^s/P, we can simplify (8):

$$Y = k_1 A_0 + k_2\left(\frac{M^s}{P}\right) \quad (9)$$

All we have done in converting (8) into (9) is to give new names, k_1 and k_2, to the multiplier effects of A_0 and M^s/P on income. The definitions and numerical values of k_1 and k_2 are:

General Linear Form

$$k_1 = \frac{1}{\frac{1}{k} + \frac{bh}{f}} \quad (10)$$

$$k_2 = \frac{b/f}{\frac{1}{k} + \frac{bh}{f}} = \left(\frac{b}{f}\right)k_1 \quad (11)$$

Numerical Example

$$k_1 = \frac{1}{\frac{1}{2.0} + \frac{100(1.0)}{200}} = 1.0$$

$$k_2 = \frac{100(1.0)}{200} = 0.5$$

Using the numerical values in (10) and (11), the simplified equation (9) can be used to calculate the value of real income:

$$\begin{aligned} Y &= k_1 A_0 + k_2\left(\frac{M^s}{P}\right) \\ &= 1.0(2500) + 0.5(2000) \quad (12) \\ &= 3500 \end{aligned}$$

This is an example of how the value of income, denoted Y' in Figure 5-1, can be calculated for a specific numerical example. With this equation it is extremely easy to calculate the new value of Y when there is a change in A_0 caused by government fiscal policy or by a change in business and consumer confidence, and when there is a change in M^s/P caused by a change in the nominal money supply. Remember, however, that the definitions of k_1 and k_2 in (10) and (11) do depend on particular assumptions about the value of parameters $b, f, h,$ and k.

The main point of Sections 5-2 and 5-3 is that changes in fiscal and monetary policy may have either strong or weak effects on income, depending on the answers to these questions.

1. How does the effect of a change in A_0 on income, the multiplier k_1, depend on the values of b and f (the interest responsiveness of the demand for commodities and money)?

2. How does the effect of a change in M^s on income, the multiplier k_2, depend on the values of b and f?

You should work through these sections to see if you can derive each of the diagrammatic results by substituting the appropriate definition of k_1 and k_2 into the simplified general equilibrium equation (9).

Example: The top frame of Figure 5-1 shows the effects of raising the money supply. In our example let us raise M^s/P from 2000 to 3000. We know, using (10), that the value of k_1 is 1.0. Using (11), the value of k_2 is 0.5. Thus using equation (9), income in the new situation at point E_1 in the top frame of Figure 5-1 is

$$\begin{aligned} Y &= k_1 A_0 + k_2\left(\frac{M^s}{P}\right) \\ &= 1.0(2500) + 0.5(3000) \\ &= 4000 \end{aligned}$$

Using equation (6a), we learn that the interest rate in the new situation is

---

[2] A parameter is taken as given or known within a given exercise. Parameters include not just the small letters denoting the multiplier *(k)*, and the interest and income responsiveness of planned expenditures and money demand *(b, h,* and *f)*, but also autonomous planned expenditures at a zero interest rate (A_0) and the real money supply (M^s/P). Most exercises involve examining the effects of a change in a single parameter, as in A_0 or in M^s/P.

$$r = \frac{[(1.0)(4000) - 3000]}{200} = 5.0$$

In the bottom frame, $f = 0$, and so

$$k_1 = \frac{1}{\dfrac{1}{k} + \dfrac{bh}{f}} = \frac{1}{\dfrac{1}{2} + \dfrac{100(1.0)}{0}} = 0$$

$$k_2 = \frac{b}{\dfrac{f}{k} + bh} = \frac{100}{0(0.5) + 100(1.0)} = 1.0$$

Thus in the bottom frame of Figure 5-1, the new equilibrium situation at point E_2 is as follows when the real money supply rises from 3500 along the old *LM* line to 4500 along the new *LM* line:

$$Y = k_1 A_0 + k_2\left(\frac{M^s}{P}\right) = 0(2500) + 1.0(4500) = 4500$$

We cannot solve for the interest rate using (6a), since the denominator *(f)* is zero. Instead, we can use equation (4) to solve for the interest rate along the *IS* curve. When (4) is solved for the interest rate, we obtain the general expression:

$$r = \frac{A_0 - Y/k}{b} = \frac{2500 - 4500/2}{100} = \frac{250}{100} = 2.5$$

This lower interest rate is depicted by point E_2 in the lower frame of Figure 5-1.

International Trade, Exchange Rates, and Macroeconomic Policy

Trade is the mother of money.
—*Thomas Draxe, 1605*

6-1 Introduction

An **open economy** sells exports to other nations, buys imports, and experiences capital flows consisting of purchases and sales of foreign assets by domestic residents and purchases and sales of domestic assets by foreign residents.

This chapter introduces the central concepts of **open economy** macroeconomic analysis, the study of economies engaged in trading goods and services with other nations and experiencing inflows and outflows of capital from and to other nations.

We have already learned that foreign trade contributes to overall economic activity. GDP includes not just consumption, investment, and government spending, but also net exports, which is the difference between exports and imports. When exports rise relative to imports, GDP increases. When exports decline relative to imports, GDP declines.

In addition, we have already learned that movements of capital between one country and another can be an important source of finance for the government budget deficit. As shown in equation (5.1) on p. 135, when the government runs a budget deficit, only three methods of financing are available—domestic saving by private firms and households must rise, domestic investment must fall, or the nation must borrow from foreigners. Hence foreign borrowing can become a major source of finance for a government budget deficit.

Goods, services, and capital flow among nations; problems arise when inflows do not balance outflows. How is such an imbalance to be corrected? The most straightforward way is to maintain a flexible exchange rate, which corrects an imbalance in the flow of goods and services by changing the prices paid by foreigners for a nation's exports and by that nation's citizens for its imports from abroad.

This chapter begins with the main components of the balance of payments, which records the main elements of a nation's foreign transactions, including its exports, imports, and capital flows. We learn how a persistent surplus in a nation's foreign trade tends to be balanced by outflows of capital. This causes a buildup of net international assets, such as U.S.-owned plants making Ford automobiles and Heinz catsup in foreign countries. The opposite can occur as well, since a persistent deficit in a nation's foreign trade causes a decline in net international assets and ultimately a buildup of net international indebtedness. Over the past decade assets in the United States owned by foreigners, such as Japanese-owned hotels in Hawaii and the Mercedes automobile plant in Alabama, have outweighed American investments abroad, leading to a large increase in American international indebtedness.

The foreign exchange rate of the dollar responds to imbalances in flows of exports, imports, and capital movements. We shall study the determinants of the foreign exchange rate and its interrelationship with monetary policy and interest rates. Later in the chapter we shall apply Chapter 4's *IS-LM* model to the analysis of the open economy. We shall learn that the effects of monetary and fiscal policy differ greatly, depending on whether the foreign exchange rate is fixed or flexible, and we shall learn why a persistent fiscal deficit in the United States since the early 1980s has been accompanied in most years by a persistent trade deficit.

6-2   Foreign Trade, the Balance of Payments, and International Indebtedness

The foreign trade deficit is part of the official data on the international transactions of the United States. Like any nation, the United States has a balance of payments that records these transactions. The **balance of payments** is divided in two main parts.

The first part is the **current account**, which records the types of flows that matter for current income and output (discussed in Chapter 2). The main components of the current account are exports and imports of goods and services, receipts and payments of investment income, and transfer payments. Just as purchases and sales of assets are excluded from GDP, so too are they excluded from the current account.

The second part of the balance of payments is the **capital account**, which records purchases and sales of foreign assets by U.S. residents and purchases and sales of American assets by foreign residents.

Any category of the balance of payments can generate a *credit* or a *debit*. To keep these terms straight, think of flows of money. Any international transaction that creates a payment of money to a U.S. resident is a credit. Included are exports of goods and services, investment income on U.S. assets held in foreign countries, transfers to U.S. residents, and purchases of U.S. assets by foreigners. Debits are the opposite of credits and result from payments of money to foreigners by U.S. residents. Debits are created by imports of goods and services, investment income paid on foreign holdings of assets within the United States, transfer payments by U.S. residents to foreigners, and purchases of foreign assets by U.S. residents.

The Balance of Payments: Surplus or Deficit?

When total credits are greater than total debits, the United States is said to run a balance of payments surplus. When this occurs, we receive more foreign money from the credits than the sum of dollars we pay out for the debits. The opposite situation, when we pay out more dollars for the debits, is called a balance of payments deficit. The overall balance of payments surplus or deficit is the sum of the balance for the current account and the capital account.

$$\text{Current account balance} + \text{capital account balance} = \tag{6.1}$$
$$\text{balance of payments outcome}$$

The **balance of payments** is the record of a nation's international transactions, and includes both credits (which arise from sales of exports and sales of assets) and debits (which arise from purchases of imports and purchases of assets).

The **current account** is the part of the balance of payments that includes exports, imports, investment income, and transfer payments to and from foreigners.

The **capital account** is the part of the balance of payments that records capital flows, which consist of purchases and sales of foreign assets by domestic residents, and purchases and sales of domestic assets by foreign residents.

Since the early 1980s, the United States has run a persistent current account deficit, because it has consistently run a deficit on its trade in goods and services and a deficit on its transfer payments as well. In the same time period, the United States has also run a persistent capital account surplus that has partly offset the current account deficit. When a nation runs a capital account surplus, households, firms, and the government *are engaged in net borrowing from foreigners* (borrowing from foreign central banks is counted not in the capital account but in the overall balance of payments surplus or deficit).

The U.S. balance of payments outcome for four different years (1970, 1980, 1990, and 1996) is presented in Table 6-1. In both 1970 and 1980 the current account was in surplus, but the capital account was in deficit by a greater amount, so the overall balance was negative. In 1990 and 1996 the situation was reversed. The current account registered a large deficit, which was partly but not entirely offset by a surplus in the capital account. As a result, the balance of payments was negative in 1990 and 1996, just as it was in 1970 and in 1980.

How is the balance of payments related to the foreign trade concepts introduced earlier, namely net exports (*NX*) and the foreign trade deficit (*–NX*)? Net exports are the same as the balance of trade in goods and services, shown on line 1a of Table 6-1.[1] The additional items on lines 1b and 1c make the current account deficit differ somewhat from the foreign trade deficit. The items on lines 2 and 3 show how the current account deficit was financed, mainly by a massive inflow of capital from foreigners. Part of this inflow came from the private sector of foreign countries—that is, foreign households and business firms—and is counted as the capital account surplus on line 2. The remaining inflow involved foreign central banks and is counted on line 3 as the financing that allowed the United States to run a balance of payments deficit.

Table 6-1   **The U.S. Balance of Payments, Selected Years**

	1970	*1980*	*1990*	*1996*
1. Current account	2.3	2.3	−94.6	−165.1
a. Trade in goods and services	2.3	−19.4	−80.3	−114.2
b. Net investment income	6.2	30.1	20.9	−8.4
c. Transfer payments	−6.2	−8.3	−35.2	−42.5
2. Capital account	−7.6	−27.1	58.5	49.0
3. Balance of payments (row 1 + row 2)	−5.3	−24.8	−36.1	−116.1

All figures are in billions of current dollars.
Method: Balance on current account given in source. Balance of payments is the sum of the following, with the sign of the sum reversed: (1) the increase in foreign official assets, net; plus (2) allocations of special drawing rights; minus (3) the increase in U.S. official reserve assets. Capital account is the residual.
Source 1970–90:   *Economic Report of the President, 1997,* Table B-101;
          1996:   *Survey of Current Business,* April 1997, Table A, p. 18.

---

[1]The late 1991 revision of the national accounts that introduced the shift from GNP to GDP as the nation's basic estimate of total output also involved a change in the definition of net exports to exclude investment income from or to the rest of the world.

As shown by equation (6.1) above, if the current account deficit and capital account surplus sum exactly to zero, then the balance of payments is also zero—that is, there is neither a deficit nor a surplus. But this was not the situation in any of the years shown in Table 6-1. For instance, in 1996 the current account deficit was much larger than the capital account surplus, so the overall balance of payments ran a large deficit. How was this financed? The United States borrowed funds from foreign central banks, and this allowed it to run a current account deficit larger than its capital account surplus.[2]

SELF-TEST

How much is the United States borrowing from (or lending to) foreign central banks in the following three situations? (1) Current account deficit of 100 and capital account surplus of 70; (2) current account surplus of 100 and capital account deficit of 70; (3) current account surplus of 70 and capital account deficit of 100.

Foreign Borrowing and International Indebtedness

A current account deficit must be financed either by net borrowing from foreign firms, households, and governments (counted as a capital account surplus), or from foreign central banks (counted as a balance of payments deficit). Either way, a country experiencing a current account deficit *automatically* must increase its indebtedness to foreigners in the private sector, to foreign governments, or to foreign central banks. Similarly, a current account surplus implies a reduction in foreign indebtedness or an increase in a country's net investment surplus. This relationship can be expressed in the following simple equation:

$$\text{Change in net international investment position} = \text{current account balance} \qquad (6.2)$$

Figure 6-1 illustrates the workings of equation (6.2) for the United States during the period since 1973. The top frame displays the U.S. current account, showing its shift into large deficits during 1981–87 and 1991–96, and the temporary shrinking of the deficit between 1987 and 1991.[3] The bottom frame displays the U.S. **net international investment position**. It shows a shift in the U.S. net investment position from surplus to indebtedness.

A nation's **net international investment position** is the difference between all foreign assets owned by a nation's citizens and domestic assets owned by foreign citizens.

How does this shift affect U.S. residents? Foreign assets owned by U.S. residents generate income for U.S. residents in the form of interest and dividend payments. Similarly, U.S. assets held by foreign residents generate interest and dividend income that the United States must send abroad. Each year that the net international investment position deteriorates, the net foreign investment income of U.S. residents (interest and dividends received minus those

---

[2]Technically, what in Table 6-1 is called the balance of payments is the official settlements balance. This is the difference between U.S. additions to its holdings of international reserves and additions by foreign central banks to their holdings of dollar reserves. When foreign central banks increase their holdings of dollar reserves by adding to their bank accounts in New York, the United States is engaging in foreign borrowing, just as if a foreign company like Toyota increased the size of its bank account in New York.

[3]The sharp drop in the current account deficit in 1991 was temporary, partly due to substantial transfer payments from foreign governments to the U.S. government to pay for the Gulf War (Operation Desert Storm).

00:00:07

A CURRENT ACCOUNT DEFICIT ERODES THE NET INVESTMENT POSITION

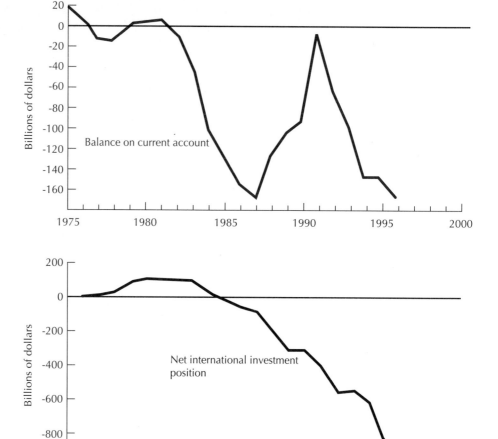

Figure 6-1   **The U.S. Current Account Balance and Its Net International Investment Position, 1975–96**

The top frame shows the persistent U.S. deficit on current account after 1982. The bottom frame shows that the net investment position fell in each year after 1982 except for 1990 and 1993. Overall, the net investment position fell by more than $1 trillion, from a peak of over +$100 billion in 1979 to nearly −$950 billion in 1996.

paid) must go down. In 1981 the United States earned 1.1 percent of GDP from its holdings of foreign assets, but by 1996, this was down to −0.1 percent of GDP, implying that the deterioration of the net international investment position over the intervening 15 years had cost U.S. residents a flow of income equal to 1.2 percent of GDP (or about $90 billion in 1997 prices) each year.

The Net International Investment Position and the Growth in the Standard of Living

The decline in the net foreign investment income of U.S. residents is entirely separate from the productivity slowdown that will be examined in Chapter 10.

Both phenomena reduce feasible growth in the standard of living of people of the United States. If the U.S. current account had been balanced over the 1981–96 period, instead of being in persistent deficit, the total income of U.S. citizens would have been roughly 1.2 percent higher each year. Stated another way, since U.S. productivity growth is proceeding at roughly 1 percent per year, the current account deficits of the 1981–94 period *had the effect of wiping out more than one year's growth in productivity.* If this deterioration continues at the same rate, in another ten years income equal to another 1 percent of GDP (one year's growth) will be lost.

6-3   Exchange Rates

Nations trade goods and services within their own borders using a particular currency. Within the United States, of course, the U.S. dollar is used for transactions. Canada uses the Canadian dollar, the United Kingdom uses the pound, Japan uses the yen, Germany uses the deutsche mark, France uses the French franc, and so on for all the other countries of the world. When an American wants to purchase a Japanese car, he or she wants to pay in dollars but the Japanese producer wants to be paid in yen.

How Exchange Rates Are Quoted

The **foreign exchange rate** is the amount of one nation's money that can be obtained in exchange for a unit of another nation's money.

To make the above transaction possible, there must be a price of yen in terms of dollars, and a price of dollars in terms of yen. This price is called the **foreign exchange rate.** The foreign exchange rate of the dollar is quoted separately for every currency in the world, and these quotes are reported every day in many newspapers, as shown in Table 6-2.

To take an example, look at the bottom of the first column at the line labeled Japan (Yen). The foreign exchange rate of the yen is shown two ways, first as dollars per yen and second as yen per dollar. The first listing shows that the price of one yen is $0.007927, or less than one cent. This price declined slightly from the previous day (in this case from Thursday to Friday). The next listing shows that 1.00 is worth 126.15 yen. These quotations are exactly equivalent—$0.007927 per yen is the same as 126.15 yen per dollar, since 1/126.15 = 0.007927.

It is conventional to express the foreign exchange rate of the dollar as units of foreign currency per dollar, i.e., 126.15 yen per dollar, rather than the other way around. However, there is one exception. The foreign exchange rate of the dollar with the British pound is always quoted as dollars per pound. In Table 6-2, on the line labeled Britain (Pound), we see listed an exchange rate of $1.6280 per pound. Why is Britain treated differently? This reflects the influence of history; until World War I it was Britain rather than the United States that was the center of the world monetary system.

Changes in Exchange Rates

In the typical example shown in Table 6-2, most exchange rates changed from the prior day. For instance, under Germany (Mark) we see that marks per

An **appreciation** is an increase in the value of one nation's currency relative to another nation's currency. When the dollar can buy more units of a foreign currency, say the German mark, the dollar is said to appreciate relative to that foreign currency.

dollar increased from 1.7199 on Thursday to 1.7205 on Friday. Any such increase in the value of the dollar, measured as the number of units of foreign currency that one dollar can buy, is called an **appreciation.** The opposite can occur as well. Under Switzerland (Franc), we see that Swiss francs per dollar declined from 1.4685 to 1.4610. Any such decline in the value of the dollar, measured as the number of units of foreign currency that one dollar can buy, is called a **depreciation.**

6-4   The Market for Foreign Exchange

When a U.S. tourist steps into a taxi at the Frankfurt airport, the driver will expect to be paid in German currency, not U.S. dollars. To obtain the needed German currency, the tourist must first stop at the airport bank and buy deutsche marks in exchange for U.S. dollars. Banks that have too much or too

Table 6-2   **Daily Quotations of Foreign Exchange Rates**

CURRENCY TRADING

Friday, April 11, 1997

EXCHANGE RATES

The New York foreign exchange selling rates below apply to trading among banks in amounts of $1 million and more, as quoted at 4 p.m. Eastern time by Dow Jones and other sources. Retail transactions provide fewer units of foreign currency per dollar.

Country	U.S. $ equiv. Fri	U.S. $ equiv. Thu	Currency per U.S. $ Fri	Currency per U.S. $ Thu
Argentina (Peso)	1.0012	1.0012	.9988	.9988
Australia (Dollar)	.7856	.7860	1.2729	1.2723
Austria (Schilling)	.08255	.08262	12.114	12.103
Bahrain (Dinar)	2.6525	2.6525	.3770	.3770
Belgium (Franc)	.02817	.02817	35.504	35.504
Brazil (Real)	.9398	.9445	1.0640	1.0588
Britain (Pound)	1.6280	1.6230	.6143	.6161
1-month forward	1.6274	1.6224	.6145	.6164
3-months forward	1.6258	1.6206	.6151	.6170
6-months forward	1.6236	1.6183	.6159	.6179
Canada (Dollar)	.7153	.7175	1.3981	1.3938
1-month forward	.7166	.7189	1.3954	1.3910
3-months forward	.7192	.7214	1.3904	1.3862
6-months forward	.7225	.7246	1.3841	1.3800
Chile (Peso)	.002387	.002389	418.95	418.55
China (Renminbi)	.1201	.1201	8.3269	8.3265
Colombia (Peso)	.0009428	.0009409	1060.71	1062.78
Czech. Rep. (Koruna)	....	....	....	....
Commercial rate	.03357	.03376	29.790	29.621
Denmark (Krone)	.1525	.1526	6.5555	6.5525
Ecuador (Sucre)	....	....	....	....
Floating rate	.0002618	.0002618	3820.00	3820.00
Finland (Markka)	.1941	.1950	5.1512	5.1289
France (Franc)	.1727	.1730	5.7890	5.7805
1-month forward	.1731	.1733	5.7775	5.7692
3-months forward	.1738	.1741	5.7528	5.7443
6-months forward	.1750	.1753	5.7129	5.7058
Germany (Mark)	.5812	.5814	1.7205	1.7199
1-month forward	.5824	.5826	1.7170	1.7164
3-months forward	.5850	.5851	1.7095	1.7091
6-months forward	.5891	.5892	1.6975	1.6973
Greece (Drachma)	.003694	.003699	270.74	270.36
Hong Kong (Dollar)	.1290	.1290	7.7490	7.7490
Hungary (Forint)	.005548	.005560	180.26	179.84
India (Rupee)	.02790	.02790	35.838	35.840
Indonesia (Rupiah)	.0004157	.0004156	2405.70	2406.00
Ireland (Punt)	1.5494	1.5477	.6454	.6461
Israel (Shekel)	.2944	.2946	3.3962	3.3947
Italy (Lira)	.0005894	.0005893	1696.75	1697.00
Japan (Yen)	.007927	.007946	126.15	125.85
1-month forward	.007961	.007980	125.61	125.31

Country	U.S. $ equiv. Fri	U.S. $ equiv. Thu	Currency per U.S. $ Fri	Currency per U.S. $ Thu
3-months forward	.008033	.008052	124.49	124.19
6-months forward	.008146	.008165	122.76	122.48
Jordan (Dinar)	1.4094	1.4094	.7095	.7095
Kuwait (Dinar)	3.2862	3.2862	.3043	.3043
Lebanon (Pound)	.0006474	.0006474	1544.75	1544.75
Malaysia (Ringgit)	.3991	.3991	2.5055	2.5057
Malta (Lira)	2.6008	2.5974	.3845	.3850
Mexico (Peso)	....	....	....	....
Floating rate	.1264	.1265	7.9110	7.9070
Netherland (Guilder)	.5169	.5170	1.9345	1.9342
New Zealand (Dollar)	.6935	.6930	1.4420	1.4430
Norway (Krone)	.1435	.1435	6.9708	6.9703
Pakistan (Rupee)	.02520	.02520	39.680	39.680
Peru (new Sol)	.3781	.3773	2.6447	2.6507
Philippines (Peso)	.03793	.03793	26.363	26.362
Poland (Zloty)	.3205	.3215	3.1205	3.1100
Portugal (Escudo)	.005811	.005808	172.10	172.18
Russia (Ruble) (a)	.0001744	.0001745	5734.00	5729.50
Saudi Arabia (Riyal)	.2666	.2666	3.7505	3.7505
Singapore (Dollar)	.6943	.6952	1.4403	1.4385
Slovak Rep. (Koruna)	.03080	.03080	32.473	32.473
South Africa (Rand)	.2247	.2244	4.4510	4.4555
South Korea (Won)	.001120	.001120	893.00	892.70
Spain (Peseta)	.006893	.006884	145.08	145.26
Sweden (Krona)	.1301	.1298	7.6853	7.7055
Switzerland (Franc)	.6845	.6810	1.4610	1.4685
1-month forward	.6866	.6831	1.4564	1.4639
3-months forward	.6911	.6875	1.4469	1.4545
6-months forward	.6984	.6946	1.4319	1.4396
Taiwan (Dollar)	.03627	.03627	27.572	27.570
Thailand (Baht)	.03834	.03835	26.085	26.079
Turkey (Lira)	.00000763	.00000765	131045.00	130705.00
United Arab (Dirham)	.2723	.2723.	3.6725	3.6720
Uruguay (New Peso)	....	....	....	....
Financial	.1092	.1101	9.1550	9.0850
Venezuela (Bolivar)	.002092	.002093	478.00	477.82
— — —				
SDR	1.3676	1.3693	.7312	.7303
ECU	1.1353	1.1340	....	....

Special Drawing Rights (SDR) are based on exchange rates for the U.S., German, British, French, and Japanese currencies. Source: International Monetary Fund.

European Currency Unit (ECU) is based on a basket of community currencies.

a-fixing, Moscow Interbank Currency Exchange.

The Wall Street Journal daily foreign exchange data for 1996 and 1997 may be purchased through the Readers' Reference Service (413) 592-3600.

Reprinted by permission of *The Wall Street Journal*, April 14, 1997, ©1997 Dow Jones & Company, Inc. All rights reserved worldwide.

A **depreciation** is a decline in the value of one nation's currency relative to another nation's currency. When the dollar can buy fewer units of a foreign currency, say the British pound, the dollar is said to depreciate relative to that foreign currency.

little of given types of foreign money can trade for what they need on the foreign exchange market. Unlike the New York Stock Exchange or the Chicago Board of Trade, where the trading takes place in a single location, the foreign exchange market consists of hundreds of dealers who sit at desks in banks, mainly in New York and London, but also in other financial centers like Frankfurt and Tokyo, and conduct trades by phone.

The results of the trading in foreign exchange are illustrated for four foreign nations in Figure 6-2. Each section of the figure illustrates the exchange rate, expressed as units of foreign currency per U.S. dollar. The data plotted are quarterly, so they do not show additional day-to-day and month-to-month movements. As is obvious from each section of the figure, major changes occurred during the years plotted. The exchange rates of the dollar against these four currencies have truly been flexible, rising and falling—often substantially—during each quarter.

The factors that determine the foreign exchange rate and influence its fluctuations can be summarized on a demand–supply diagram like those used in elementary economics to analyze many problems of price determination. In Figure 6-3 the vertical axis measures the price of the dollar expressed in deutsche marks. The horizontal axis shows the number of dollars that would be demanded or supplied at different prices.

Why People Hold Dollars and Marks

Currencies such as the U.S. dollar and the deutsche mark are held by foreigners who find dollars or marks more convenient or safer than their own currencies. For instance, sellers of goods or services may be willing to accept payment in dollars or marks, but not in the Finnish markka or the Malaysian ringgit. Thus, a change in the preference by holders of money for a currency such as the dollar will shift the demand curve for dollars and influence the dollar's exchange rate.

All currencies have a demand that is created by a country's exports and a supply generated by a country's imports. For instance, purchases of U.S. exports automatically create a demand for the dollar. So, too, do funds paid by foreigners who invest in U.S. factories, who repay previous loans, who send to the United States dividends and interest payments on U.S. overseas investments, and who are attracted to put money into U.S. savings accounts and government securities. Thus the demand curve for dollars D_0 in Figure 6-3 is labeled with two of the items that create the demand (U.S. exports, capital inflows). In the same way, the supply curve of dollars S_0 depends on the magnitude of the items that generate payments by U.S. citizens to foreigners—mainly U.S. imports and capital outflows.

What explains the slopes of the demand and supply curves as drawn in Figure 6-3? The demand curve D_0 will be vertical only if the price elasticity of German demand for U.S. imports is zero, that is, completely insensitive to changes in price. If the price elasticity of demand is negative, then the demand curve will be negatively sloped, as shown. For instance, consider a U.S. machine costing \$10,000, which would require Germans to pay 20,000 deutsche marks (DM) if the exchange rate were DM 2 per dollar (as at point A in the figure). If the exchange rate were to drop to DM 1.50 per dollar (as at point E_0), the cost of the same machine would drop to DM 15,000. If the German demand for such machines were to increase from 10 machines to 11

SINCE 1970 THE DOLLAR HAS ZIGZAGED UP AND DOWN AGAINST OTHER CURRENCIES

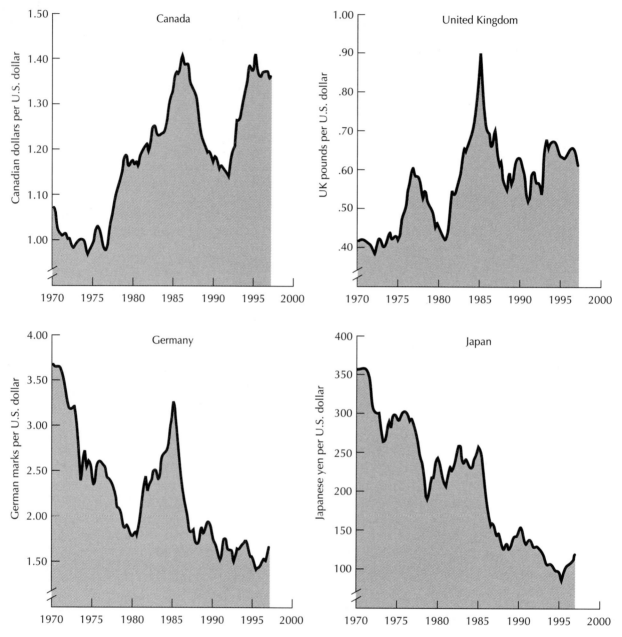

Figure 6-2 **Foreign Exchange Rates of the Dollar Against Four Major Currencies, Quarterly, 1970–97**

Each foreign exchange rate is expressed as units of foreign currency per dollar. Note that each rate displays quarter-to-quarter fluctuations together with a trend that lasts several years or more. Against the Canadian dollar, the U.S. dollar experienced a major appreciation between 1976 and 1986, followed by a depreciation until 1992, and another appreciation between 1992 and 1995. Against the British pound, the U.S. dollar has displayed erratic behavior, with major appreciations in 1975–76 and 1980–85. Against the German mark, the U.S. dollar has displayed a long-run tendency toward depreciation, interrupted by a temporary appreciation in 1980–85. Against the Japanese yen, the dollar has displayed a long-run tendency over the entire period to depreciate, especially between 1985 and 1995. .

Figure 6-3
Determination of the Price in deutsche Marks of the Dollar

The demand curve D_0 slopes downward and to the right, reflecting the increased demand for dollars induced by depreciation (a lowering in the dollar's price). The supply curve S_0 is assumed to slope upward, although this does not always occur (see text). The equilibrium price of the dollar in the diagram is assumed to be DM 1.50, at the crossing point of the D_0 and S_0 curves.

THE EXCHANGE RATE OF THE DOLLAR DEPENDS ON THE LAW OF SUPPLY AND DEMAND

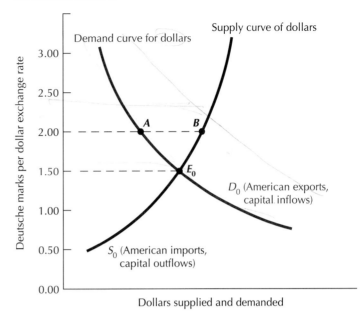

in response to the lower price, the German demand for dollars would increase from \$100,000 to \$110,000 (since the price in dollars is still unchanged, \$10,000). In short, a depreciation in the dollar along the demand curve from A to E_0 boosts the demand for dollars (plotted on the horizontal axis) and accounts for the negative slope of the demand curve.

The analysis for the supply curve S_0 is different. Here the supply curve will be vertical if the price elasticity of the U.S. demand for German imports is -1.0. Only in this situation are U.S. expenditures on imports in dollars independent of the exchange rate.[4] Only if the price elasticity is greater than unity (in absolute value) will the supply curve slope positively, as drawn in Figure 6-3.

SELF-TEST

> For each of the following events, state whether there is a shift in the supply or demand curve for dollars in Figure 6-3, and whether the curve shifts to the left or right: (1) an increase in the desire of German households to buy videotapes of old Hollywood movies; (2) popularity of Japanese luxury cars reduces U.S. purchases of Mercedes-Benz automobiles; (3) American

---

[4]The price elasticity of demand, a concept used in almost every elementary economics course, is defined as

$$elasticity = \frac{percentage\ change\ of\ quantity}{percentage\ change\ of\ price}$$

When the elasticity is -1.0, the percentage change of quantity is equal to and opposite in sign from the percentage change of price, so that revenue (= price × quantity) does not change. A depreciation of the dollar causes a given percentage increase in the price of German cars imported into the United States, provided the German price in DM does not change. If the number of cars purchased drops by the same percent, then total dollar expenditures do not change, and the supply curve is vertical.

Airlines discontinues a flight from Frankfurt to Miami that attracts mainly German passengers; (4) U.S. citizens start producing imitation German beer, which displaces imports of the real thing.

Determination of the Foreign Exchange Rate

The foreign exchange rate is determined where the demand curve D_0 crosses the supply curve S_0 in Figure 6-3. As the curves are drawn, the equilibrium exchange rate is DM 1.50 per dollar at point E_0, exactly the rate reached in July 1992. At a higher exchange rate, say DM 2.00 per dollar, the supply of dollars exceeds demand by the distance AB. The supply of dollars created by U.S. imports and by capital outflows exceeds the demand for dollars created by U.S. exports and capital inflows. In order to induce foreigners to accept their currency, U.S. citizens will have to accept a lower exchange rate, DM 1.50 per dollar.

If the U.S. government wants to maintain the higher exchange rate of DM 2.00 per dollar, it can do so only by intervention in the exchange market. It must buy up the excess supply of dollars from the foreigners who have received payments in dollars from U.S. purchases of imports. How does the government pay for these dollars obtained from foreigners? This is the purpose of international reserves. If the government does not intervene, or if it runs out of international reserves so that it cannot intervene, the foreigners holding excess dollars will sell them on the foreign exchange market, driving the price down to DM 1.50 per dollar.

6-5   Nominal and Real Exchange Rates in the Long Run

Nominal and Real Exchange Rates

For most issues in macroeconomics, we adjust variables for the effects of inflation. Real GDP is a more meaningful gauge of economic activity than nominal GDP. The level of saving and investment are related to the real interest rate, not to the nominal interest rate. Similarly, we shall see below that it is the **real exchange rate** that determines net exports, not the nominal exchange rate.

The **real exchange rate** is equal to the average nominal foreign exchange rate between a country and its trading partners, with an adjustment for the difference in inflation rates between that country and its trading partners.

The real exchange rate is equal to the nominal foreign exchange rate adjusted for changes in the price level between two countries. The definition can be written as a formula, where we express the real exchange rate (e) as equal to the nominal exchange rate (e'), times the ratio of the domestic price level (P) to the foreign price level (P^f):

$$e = e' \times P/P^f \qquad (6.3)$$

Real exchange rate = nominal exchange rate × ratio of domestic price level to foreign price level

To understand this relationship, let us assume that in 1997 the nominal and real exchange rates of the peso are both 8 per dollar, and the price level in both countries is 100:

$$8.0 \text{ pesos/\$} = 8.0 \text{ pesos/\$} \times (100/100)$$

Real exchange rate = nominal exchange rate × ratio of domestic
price level to foreign price level

Then, in 1998, the Mexican economy experiences a rapid inflation, causing the Mexican price level to double from 100 to 200, while the U.S. price level remains fixed at 100. If the nominal exchange rate were to remain at 8.0 pesos per dollar, the real exchange rate would fall by half:

$$4.0 \text{ pesos/\$} = 8.0 \text{ pesos/\$} \times (100/200)$$

Real exchange rate = nominal exchange rate × ratio of domestic
price level to foreign price level

In such a case we would say that the dollar has experienced a *real depreciation* against the peso, since one dollar buys only half as many pesos when adjusted for differences in national price levels. The opposite would be true as well; the Mexican peso would have experienced a *real appreciation*.

Normally, countries that experience unusually high inflation, as in this example, find that their nominal exchange rate depreciates while their real exchange rate remains roughly unchanged. For the real exchange rate to remain unchanged in this example, the nominal exchange rate of the peso would have to jump from 8.00 to 16.00 pesos per dollar (this is a nominal appreciation of the dollar and a nominal depreciation of the peso):

$$8.0 = 16.00 \times 100/200$$

Real exchange rate = nominal exchange rate × ratio of domestic
price level to foreign price level

This final example is quite realistic. Usually countries with unusually rapid inflation, as has been experienced by Mexico, Argentina, Brazil, and other Latin American countries at various times over the past several decades, witness a nominal depreciation of their currency without any major change in the real exchange rate. (We return to the causes and consequences of rapid inflation in Chapter 12.)

We care about the real exchange rate, not the nominal exchange rate, because it is a major determinant of net exports. When the real exchange rate appreciates (i.e., there is a real appreciation), imports become cheap for domestic residents to purchase, while exports become expensive for foreigners to purchase. The result is a squeeze on domestic profits and layoffs of domestic workers. In the opposite situation, when the real exchange rate depreciates, domestic profits improve and companies are eager to hire workers. As we shall see, fluctuations in the real exchange rate are the key to understanding major fluctuations in the U.S. current account balance plotted in Figure 6-1.

SELF-TEST

> Assume that the price level in 1997 in both the United States and Germany is 100, and that both the real and the nominal exchange rates of the mark are 1.7 marks per dollar. Now imagine that in 1998 the U.S. price level has increased from 100 to 110, while the German price level remains fixed at 100, and the nominal exchange rate changes to 1.5 marks per dollar. What is the real exchange rate of the dollar in 1998? Has the dollar experienced a real appreciation or depreciation?

INTERNATIONAL PERSPECTIVE

Big Mac

Meets PPP

If PPP worked perfectly, goods would cost the same in all countries after conversion into a common currency. An interesting test of PPP has been constructed by the *Economist* magazine, which for several years has collected data on the prices of Big Mac hamburgers in the United States and numerous foreign countries. In the month covered by the table, the Big Mac cost an average of $2.42 in four American cities. According to PPP, the cost in other countries should be $2.42 times the exchange rate of the other currency per dollar. Since the exchange rate of the Swedish kroner was 7.72, a Big Mac in Sweden should have cost 18.7 kroners. However, the actual cost in Sweden was 26 kroners, not 18.7. Stated another way, if the relative prices of Big Macs in Sweden and the United States were representative of all goods, a dollar has the purchasing power of 10.74 kroner (Big Mac Swedish price of 26 kroner divided by U.S. price of $2.42), not the mere 7.72 kroner available on the foreign exchange market. The foreign exchange market appears to undervalue the dollar by 39 percent (10.74–7.72)/7.72.

As shown in the right-hand column of the table, the dollar is undervalued against the currencies of most advanced countries, such as France, Germany, and Sweden (although not against such advanced countries as Australia, Canada, Japan, and New Zealand). It is overvalued mainly against the currencies of less developed nations, including China, Hong Kong, Hungary, Malaysia, Mexico, Russia, and others.

The table supports the instant impression of American tourists visiting western Europe—everyday goods cost much more than at home. Why? One explanation is that other countries make goods that the United States wants to import (creating a large supply of dollars) but are inefficient in producing "nontraded goods" like distribution and retailing services. Also, other countries often levy higher taxes on purchased goods and services. An implication of high prices abroad (at current exchange rates) is that measures of output per person are overstated by market exchange rates. Exchange rates based on PPP, such as those used to calculate the table on p. 275, are a much better guide to the relative well-being of Americans and residents of foreign nations.

The Theory of Purchasing Power Parity

The purchasing power parity (PPP) theory holds that the prices of identical goods should be the same in all countries, differing only by the cost of transport and any import duties.

The most important determinant of exchange rates is the fact that in open economies the prices of traded goods should be the same everywhere after adjustment for customs duties and the cost of transportation. This is called the **purchasing power parity (PPP) theory** of the exchange rate.

This theory implies that the real exchange rate (e) should be constant. We can set the real exchange rate at a constant value of unity in equation (6.3) above:

The Hamburger Standard

	Big Mac prices		Implied PPP* of the dollar	Actual $ exchange rate 4/7/97	Dollar under(−)/over(+) valuation, %[†]
	In local currency	In dollars			
United States‡	**$2.42**	**2.42**	—	—	—
Argentina	Peso2.50	2.50	1.03	1.00	− 3
Australia	A$2.50	1.94	1.03	1.29	+20
Austria	Sch34.00	2.82	14.0	12.0	−17
Belgium	BFr109	3.09	45.0	35.3	−28
Brazil	Real2.97	2.81	1.23	1.06	−16
Britain	£1.81	2.95	1.34††	1.63††	−22
Canada	C$2.88	2.07	1.19	1.39	+14
Chile	Peso1,200	2.88	496	417	−19
China	Yuan9.70	1.16	4.01	8.33	+52
Czech Republic	CKr53.0	1.81	21.9	29.2	+25
Denmark	DKr25.75	3.95	10.6	6.52	−63
France	FFr17.5	3.04	7.23	5.76	−26
Germany	DM4.90	2.86	2.02	1.71	−18
Hong Kong	HK$9.90	1.28	4.09	7.75	+47
Hungary	Forint271	1.52	112	178	+37
Israel	Shekel11.5	3.40	4.75	3.38	−40
Italy	Lire4,600	2.73	1,901	1,683	−13
Japan	¥294	2.34	121	126	+ 3
Malaysia	M$3.87	1.55	1.60	2.50	+36
Mexico	Peso14.9	1.89	6.16	7.90	+22
Netherlands	F15.45	2.83	2.25	1.92	−17
New Zealand	NZ$3.25	2.24	1.34	1.45	+ 7
Poland	Zloty4.30	1.39	1.78	3.10	+43
Russia	Rouble11,000	1.92	4,545	5,739	+21
Singapore	S$3.00	2.08	1.24	1.44	+14
South Africa	Rand7.80	1.76	3.22	4.43	+27
South Korea	Won2,300	2.57	950	894	− 6
Spain	Pta375	2.60	155	144	− 7
Sweden	SKr26.0	3.37	10.7	7.72	−39
Switzerland	SFr5.90	4.02	2.44	1.47	−66
Taiwan	NT$68.0	2.47	28.1	27.6	− 2
Thailand	Baht46.7	1.79	19.3	26.1	+26

*Purchasing power parity; local price divided by price in the United States.   †Against dollar   ‡Average of New York, Chicago, San Francisco, and Atlanta   ‡‡Dollars per pound   *Source: Economist*, April 12, 1997, p. 71
©1997 The Economist Newspaper Group, Inc. Reprinted with permission. Further reproduction prohibited.

$$1 = e' \times P/P^f \tag{6.4}$$

Fixed real exchange rate = nominal exchange rate × ratio of domestic price level to foreign price level

By swapping the left-hand and right-hand sides of equation (6.4), and solving for e', we emerge with the PPP theory of exchange rates:

$$e' = \frac{P^f}{P} \tag{6.5}$$

This states that if the foreign price level (P^f) increases faster than the domestic price level (P), there is an increase in P^f/P and the nominal exchange rate appreciates.

PPP and Inflation Differentials

Another way of writing equation (6.5) is to express the exchange rate and the two prices in terms of rates of growth.[5]

$$\Delta e'/e' = p^f - p \qquad (6.6)$$

*Growth rate of nominal exchange rate = growth rate of foreign price
level − growth rate of domestic price level*

The **inflation differential** is foreign inflation minus domestic inflation; the PPP theory of exchange rates predicts that when this differential is positive the domestic country's nominal exchange rate appreciates and when this differential is negative the nominal exchange rate depreciates.

Here the term $\Delta e'/e'$ is positive when there is an appreciation of a currency (as when the dollar appreciated from 1.4 to 1.7 DM in 1996–97). The same term is negative when there is a depreciation of a currency. The term $p^f - p$ is the **inflation differential** between foreign and domestic inflation. When this differential is positive, the PPP theory of exchange rates expressed in equation (6.6) states that $\Delta e'/e'$ is positive and the exchange rate of the domestic currency appreciates.

The PPP theory contains an essential kernel of truth: Nations that allow their domestic inflation rate (p) to exceed the world rate will experience a depreciation of their exchange rate, and vice versa. But there are numerous exceptions to the relationship, because the demand for and supply of foreign currency depend on factors other than the simple ratio of domestic and foreign aggregate price indexes.

Why PPP Breaks Down

The International Perspective box in this section shows that the PPP equation relating the change in the exchange rate to the inflation differential does not work well for most industrialized nations. There are numerous reasons why PPP breaks down. They all have a single fact in common—for any given inflation differential between two nations, there are numerous factors that can cause major appreciations and depreciations in the exchange rate without altering the inflation differential. Some of these factors are:

A nation may invent new products that other countries want to import, such as the Internet software perfected by U.S. firms in the 1990s. Such inventions may cause the dollar to appreciate without any change in the inflation differential.

A nation may discover new deposits of raw materials that it can sell to other nations, thus raising the demand for its currency. For instance, in the late 1970s the British began producing oil from the North Sea, causing the exchange rate of the pound to appreciate.

---

[5]The growth rate of a ratio such as P^f/P is equal to the growth rate of the numerator (P^f) minus the growth rate of the denominator (P).

The exchange rate depends not just on exports and imports but on the demand for a currency by foreigners. Customers from all over the world send funds to Switzerland and other countries for deposit in banks and other financial institutions, often to avoid taxes or to hide the proceeds from criminal activity. The higher demand for the Swiss franc and other such currencies causes them to appreciate.

The theory of PPP is based on the comparison of the exchange rate with an economywide price index in two countries, but that price index may include types of economic activity that are not traded (e.g., building construction and retail services). There is no mechanism that forces prices of nontraded goods and services to be the same across countries.

For any given inflation differential, government policy can cause a currency to depreciate when the government makes large foreign transfers. Governments can also interfere with free trade by subsidizing exports or taxing imports. Finally, a government may cause its currency to appreciate by running a tight-money and easy-fiscal policy, as did the United States in 1980–85.

As we shall see later in Figure 6-5, the U.S. real exchange rate has not remained constant, as assumed in the PPP equation (6.4), which suggests that PPP is not a good description of U.S. exchange rate behavior.

6-6   Exchange Rate Systems

A balance of payments deficit like the one experienced by the United States in 1996 means that more dollars are flowing abroad as a result of the current account deficit than are coming back in the form of capital inflows from foreign private investors. As a result, there is a net outflow of dollars. Two basic systems have been developed to handle a surplus or deficit in the balance of payments, like the deficit that the United States ran in 1996 (Table 6-1, line 3). The difference between these systems lies in whether the foreign exchange rate of the dollar is allowed, month after month, year after year, to change freely (say, from 2.0 marks per dollar this month to 1.7 marks per dollar next month) or is held fixed (at, say, 2.0 marks per dollar).

Flexible vs. Fixed Exchange Rates

In a **flexible exchange rate system** the foreign exchange rate is free to change every day.

Flexible Exchange Rate System.   Under a "pure" version of the **flexible exchange rate system**, an outflow of dollars would act just like an excess supply of any commodity—the price would go down until an equilibrium price is established. The balance of payments deficit would be eliminated by a decline in the foreign exchange rate of the dollar sufficient to raise exports and cut imports, as occurred in the United States following the huge 1985–87 decline in the value of the dollar. In addition, for reasons explained later, a decline in the exchange rate tends to stimulate larger private capital inflows. Although the exchange rates have varied widely since 1973, the current system of flexible exchange rates still is not a pure one. If it were, the United

States could not run a balance of payments deficit as it did in 1996, as shown in Table 6-1. Instead, today's system is a mixture of flexible and fixed exchange rates.

Fixed Exchange Rate System.   During the post World War II era prior to 1973, most major countries maintained **fixed exchange rate systems**. Under this system, central banks agreed in advance to finance any surplus or deficit in the balance of payments. To do this, central banks maintained **foreign exchange reserves**, mainly in gold and dollars. The banks stood ready to buy or sell dollars as needed to maintain the foreign exchange rate of their currencies.

Workings of the Fixed Exchange Rate System

In the 1950s and 1960s the German central bank (Bundesbank) maintained a rate of 4.0 marks per dollar. If an excess supply of dollars entered Germany (due, for instance, to higher U.S. imports of Volkswagens) and threatened to put downward pressure on the rate to, say, 3.5 marks per dollar, the Bundesbank could intervene by purchasing the excess dollars and adding them to its foreign exchange reserves. Similarly, if an excess demand for dollars (due, for instance, to exports of Boeing jet planes to Lufthansa, the German airline) put upward pressure on the rate to, say, 4.5 marks per dollar, the Bundesbank could intervene by selling dollars from its reserves, thus satisfying the excess demand for dollars.

Clearly, there is a flaw in this system. What if a country were to keep increasing its imports, paying for them by drawing down its reserves? Eventually it would run out of reserves, like a family whose bank balance has fallen to zero. Under the fixed exchange rate system, such an event would cause a crisis, and the country would be forced to reduce, or **devalue**, its exchange rate. An example occurred in 1967, when Britain was forced to devalue its currency, the pound sterling, thus making it less valuable in relation to the dollar. By doing so, Britain intended to make British exports less expensive and more attractive to foreign purchasers, thus increasing the demand for the pound sterling. An example in the opposite direction occurred in 1969 when Germany's reserves of dollars were growing rapidly, and it decided to **revalue** the mark (i.e., increase the value of the mark) by 5 percent.

The Breakdown of the Bretton Woods System

The fixed exchange rate system used before 1971 was designed at an international conference held in 1944 in Bretton Woods, New Hampshire. The system, known as the Bretton Woods system, had two main features. First, fixed exchange rates were maintained, with only occasional changes like the British devaluation of 1967. Second, not only gold but dollars could be used as reserves, thus introducing a special advantage for the United States compared to other countries like Britain. If the British imported too much, other countries would demand payment in gold or dollars, and the British would soon run out of reserves and be forced to devalue. But if the United States imported too much, as in the late 1960s, it could always pay in the form other countries wanted, dollars, by endlessly printing more dollars.

In a **fixed exchange rate system**, the foreign exchange rate is fixed for long periods of time.

Foreign exchange reserves are government holdings of foreign money used under a fixed exchange rate system to respond to changes in the foreign demand for and supply of a particular nation's money. Such reserves are also used for intervention under a flexible exchange rate system.

Under the fixed exchange rate system a nation **devalues**, or reduces the value of its money in terms of foreign money, when it runs out of foreign exchange reserves. A nation **revalues**, or raises the value of its money, when its foreign exchange reserves become so excessive that they cause domestic inflation.

The United States' special advantage proved to be the undoing of the Bretton Woods system. In the late 1960s the economic expansion, caused partly by the Vietnam War, led to ever-accelerating inflation and persistent trade deficits (illustrated later in the chapter in Figure 6-6). The supply of dollars greatly exceeded the demand. As a result, only massive purchases of dollars by other countries, particularly Germany and Japan, could maintain the fixed exchange rate of the dollar. Germany became alarmed at its inflated money supply, which ballooned as the direct consequence of huge German holdings of dollars, and at the resulting upsurge of German inflation.[6] Speculators made the safe bet that the fixed exchange rate of the dollar could not be maintained, and added to the excess supply of dollars by selling them to the governments of Germany and Japan. Finally, governments of the major nations abandoned the attempt to support the dollar's value, and on March 19, 1973 adopted the current flexible exchange rate system.

Characteristics of the Flexible Exchange Rate System

Under the old, fixed exchange rate system, changes in the exchange rate were very infrequent. The word *devaluation* was used for a decline in the value of a country's currency and the word *revaluation* was used for an increase in the value of a country's currency. In today's flexible exchange rate system, different terms are used, as we learned above. A depreciation of the foreign exchange rate occurs when a country's currency decreases in value in terms of other currencies. An appreciation in the foreign exchange rate occurs when a country's currency increases in value in terms of other currencies.

SELF-TEST

> As a college student planning a trip to Europe this summer, do you hope for an appreciation or a depreciation of the dollar? Looking ahead to the next page at the plot of the exchange rate in Figure 6-4, would you have preferred to travel to Europe in 1985 or 1995? If a German student had the same choice, when would he or she have preferred to travel to the United States?

Intervention occurs under the flexible exchange rate system when domestic or foreign central banks buy or sell a nation's money in order to prevent unwanted variations in the foreign exchange rate.

The current system is not a pure flexible exchange rate system because the Fed and foreign central banks do not allow the dollar to fluctuate with complete freedom. If they did, the United States would not have run a balance of payments deficit, as it did in 1996 (see Table 6-1). The system is not pure because central banks have practiced **intervention** to keep the dollar from falling farther than it did after 1985. Foreign central banks "propped up" the value of the dollar by buying massive amounts of it, thus artificially inflating the demand for dollars and keeping the dollar's foreign exchange rate higher than it otherwise would have been. In the period 1986–96, foreign central banks increased their dollar reserves by fully $566 billion as a result of their intervention.

Other terms are used to describe flexible exchange rate systems. A "clean" system is one that is pure, without any intervention by central banks.

---

[6]German exporters would bring excess dollars to the central bank, which would pay for them by issuing marks and then holding the dollars as assets of the Bundesbank. The German money supply, consisting of marks, rose steadily as the dollars flowed into the vaults of the Bundesbank.

Figure 6-4

Nominal Effective Exchange Rate of the Dollar, 1970–96

The dollar depreciated substantially in the early 1970s, when the flexible exchange rate system began, and again in 1977–79, as U.S. inflation accelerated relative to that in Germany and Japan. The most dramatic movements came in the 1980s, when a 60 percent increase between late 1980 and early 1985 was followed by an equal decline in an even shorter time. From 1990 to 1996 the dollar retained roughly the same value it had in 1980.

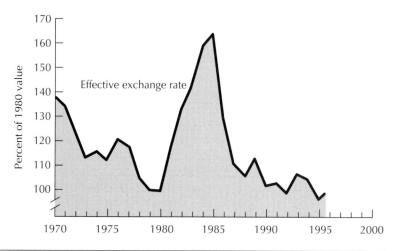

THE DOLLAR IN THE 1980s WAS LIKE A MOUNTAIN CLIMBER CROSSING THE ROCKIES

A "dirty," or "managed," flexible exchange rate system is one with frequent intervention by central banks. Why is the current system so dirty? Central banks in Europe and Japan fear a further collapse of the dollar, which would make American exports more competitive and reduce the American demand for imports. Such circumstances would create layoffs and factory closings in foreign countries, something that many European countries want to avoid in view of the already high unemployment rate that Europe has been experiencing in the 1980s and 1990s.

6-7   CASE STUDY: The Exchange Rate of the Dollar Since 1970

Since the flexible exchange rate system began in 1973, the dollar has experienced substantial volatility, particularly during the 1980s. Figure 6-4 shows the changes in the exchange rate of the dollar since 1970. Displayed is the effective exchange rate of the dollar, which weights the dollar's exchange rate against an average of the deutsche mark, British pound, Japanese yen, and other currencies, with each country weighted in proportion to its importance in American foreign trade. The base year for the effective exchange rate is 1980, so any period (like 1985) with an exchange rate greater than 100 indicates that the dollar was stronger than in 1980. Any period with an exchange rate less than 100 (like 1995) indicates that the dollar was weaker than in 1980.

Before 1971, when the fixed exchange rate system was in operation, the effective exchange rate of the dollar was quite stable. The transition to the flexible exchange rate system between 1971 and 1973 involved a substantial depreciation of the dollar, as shown in Figure 6-4, and by 1980 the dollar was lower than it had ever been before.

From 1980 to 1988 international economics was dominated by the effect of the enormous appreciation of the dollar, which peaked in February 1985, and was followed by a depreciation of equal magnitude. By 1988 the dollar was back roughly to its 1980 level, but in the meantime many American businesses had been decimated by the effects of the strong dollar and the resulting flood of cheap imports. The strong dollar caused millions of jobs to be lost. An important theme of this chapter is the role that fiscal and monetary policy played in causing the dollar to soar and collapse in the 1980s, and the effect of the dollar's sharp appreciation and subsequent depreciation on net exports and the current account deficit.

Since 1990 the dollar has fluctuated within a relatively narrow range. The effective exchange rate shown in Figure 6-4 weights together some currencies (like the yen and deutsche mark) against which the dollar has depreciated, with other currencies (like the Mexican peso and Italian lire) against which the dollar has appreciated. On average, weighting the depreciation and appreciation together, the dollar has not changed much in value over the 1990–96 period.

Has the real exchange rate behaved differently than the nominal effective exchange rate shown in Figure 6-4? As shown in Figure 6-5, between 1970 and 1973 the real exchange rate depreciated somewhat more rapidly than did the nominal exchange rate, indicating that during this interval the U.S. price level increased less than the foreign price level. Otherwise, the real exchange rate has mimicked virtually every movement of the nominal exchange rate since 1973, indicating that the U.S. and foreign price levels have increased at about the same rate.

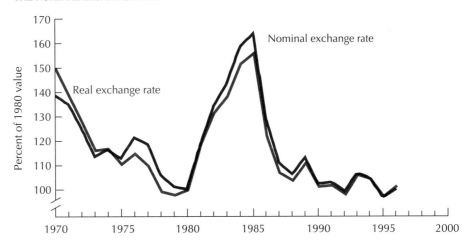

AFTER 1973 THE REAL EXCHANGE RATE MIMICKED THE NOMINAL EXCHANGE RATE

Figure 6-5 **Nominal and Real Effective Exchange Rates of the Dollar, 1970–96**

Except for a minor difference in the early 1970s, the real and nominal exchange rates for the United States followed essentially the same path. This means that the inflation differential between the United States and other nations was very small compared to the highly variable ups and downs of the nominal exchange rate. This implies that the real exchange rate should have mimicked the movements of the nominal exchange rate, which it did. By far the most dramatic movement of both the nominal and real exchange rates was the sharp appreciation of 1980–85 and the equally sharp depreciation of 1985–87.

6-8 Determinants of Net Exports

Now we are ready to fit the foreign exchange rate into the *IS-LM* model of income determination developed in Chapters 3–5. The analysis proceeds in two steps. First, we allow net exports, previously assumed to be exogenous, to depend both on income and on the exchange rate.[7] Second, we allow the exchange rate to depend on the interest rate. The combined effect of these two steps is to introduce an additional channel by which interest rates affect total expenditures.

The Foreign Trade Surplus and Deficit

Net exports *(NX)*, as we learned in Chapter 2, is an aggregate that equals exports minus imports, and it is a component of total expenditure in GDP, along with consumption *(C)*, investment *(I)*, and government spending *(G)*:

$$E = C + I + G + NX \tag{6.7}$$

A $100 billion increase in net exports provides just as much of a stimulus to income and employment as a $100 billion increase in consumption, investment, or government spending. A $100 billion decrease in net exports can offset much of the stimulus to expenditures provided by expansionary monetary and fiscal policy.

The **foreign trade surplus** is the same as net exports; the **foreign trade deficit** is net exports with the sign reversed.

A **foreign trade surplus** is an excess of exports over imports, that is, a positive quantity of net exports. A foreign trade deficit is an excess of imports over exports, that is, a negative quantity of net exports. The fluctuations in net exports are illustrated in Figure 6-6, which plots data on real exports, real imports, and real net exports from 1960 to 1996. Exports and imports have both risen in real terms, but not at an even pace.

There has been an excess of imports over exports (a trade deficit) during most years plotted in Figure 6-6 since 1960. The bottom frame of Figure 6-6 shows more clearly the size of the trade deficit. This widened during the 1960s, when the Bretton Woods system of fixed exchange rates was on the road to collapse. There was briefly a trade surplus for a single year in 1974, and then for three consecutive years in 1979–81. The trade deficit reached its highest level in 1986, one year after the peak value of the real exchange rate of the dollar (Figure 6-5), recovered nearly to a surplus in 1990–91, and then returned to a deficit of roughly $100 billion in the years 1993–96.

Net Exports and the Foreign Exchange Rate

Clearly the fluctuations of net exports (as illustrated in Figure 6-6) play an important role in the fluctuations of total real expenditures. Determining the ups and downs of net exports are real income and the foreign exchange rate.

Effect of Real Income.   We can indicate the dependence of net exports *(NX)* on income as

---

[7]In Section 3-8 and in the appendix to Chapter 5, we allowed net exports to depend on income.

UNPRECEDENTED TRADE DEFICITS IN THE 1980s AND 1990s

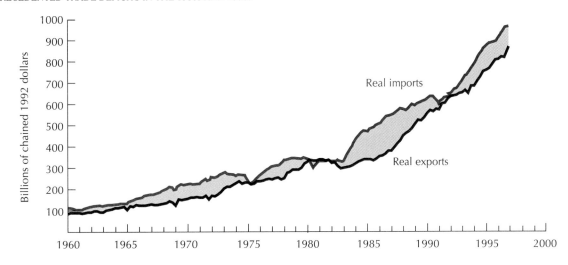

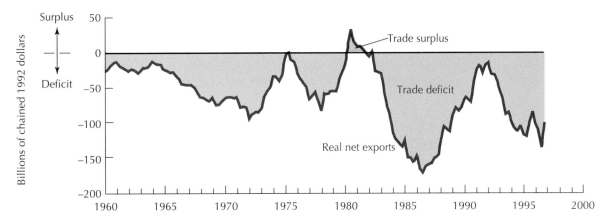

Figure 6-6   **U.S. Real Exports, Real Imports, and Real Net Exports, 1960–96**
The top frame shows real exports and imports, and the bottom frame shows real net exports. In each frame a trade surplus is indicated by gray shading and a trade deficit by red shading. After a period of positive net exports in 1979–81, the 1980s were characterized by a "V-shaped" trade deficit that worsened until early 1987, then steadily improved. But the improvement was temporary and was followed by another sharp deterioration in the 1990s.

$$NX = NX_0 - nxY \tag{6.8}$$

Here, NX_0 is the autonomous component of net exports (determined mainly by foreign income), nx is the fraction of a change in income that is spent on imports, and Y is real income.[8] If we ignored changes in the foreign exchange rate, (6.8) would adequately explain net exports. For the given level of foreign income that determines the autonomous component (NX_0), net exports

---

[8]This equation is identical to equation (3.33) in Chapter 3, p. 88.

would be low in economic expansions when income is high, causing a large volume of imports, and net exports would be high in recessions when income is low, causing a small volume of imports.

Effect of the Foreign Exchange Rate.   When the exchange rate appreciates against foreign currencies, U.S. exports become more expensive in terms of foreign currencies, so exports tend to decline. Also, the lower dollar prices of imports attract American customers, and the quantity of goods imported into the United States rises. With exports down and imports up, the appreciation of the foreign exchange rate causes a drop in net exports. This is just what happened in the United States in the 1980s. The appreciation of the dollar was shown in Figures 6-4 and 6-5, and the collapse of net exports is shown in Figure 6-7. In Figure 6-7 these two phenomena are brought together. The red net export line is copied from Figure 6-6. The red net export line is copied from Figure 6-6. The black foreign exchange rate line plots the real exchange rate of the dollar from Figure 6-5. The striking fact that stands out in Figure 6-7 is the strong negative relationship between net exports and the real exchange rate. When the real exchange rate was low in the late 1970s, U.S. net exports rose, peaking in 1980. The rise in the real exchange rate between 1980 and 1985 was accompanied by a continuous decline in net exports. The 1985–88 depreciation of the dollar led to a sharp jump in net exports after 1987.

To reflect this negative relationship, we amend equation (6.8) above to allow net exports *(NX)* to depend not just on income but also on the real exchange rate *(e)*, which is expressed as a percentage of a base year (for instance, 1980 = 100):

General Linear Form	Numerical Example	
$NX = NX_0 - nxY - ue$	$NX = 600 - .1Y - 2e$	(6.9)

This equation states in words that net exports are equal to autonomous net exports *(NX$_0$)*, minus a parameter *(nx)*, times real income *(Y)*, minus another parameter *(u)*, times the real exchange rate *(e)*. For any given level of income, an appreciation of the real exchange rate (as happened in the United States between 1980 and 1985) reduces net exports. For instance, if the economy is operating with actual real income at the natural real GDP level of $4000 billion, and the real exchange rate is 100, then net exports are zero $[= 600 - (0.1 \times 4000) - 2 \times 100)]$. An appreciation in the real exchange rate from 100 to 150 would reduce net exports in this example to −$100 billion $[= 600 - (0.1 \times 4000) - (2 \times 150)]$.

There is one puzzle evident in Figure 6-7 regarding the relation between net exports and the real exchange rate. Between 1992 and 1996 net exports declined substantially, by more than half as much as between 1980 and 1985. Yet, unlike 1980–85, there was no major appreciation of the dollar. In fact, there was little change in the dollar over the entire period 1988–96, at least in relation to the major changes that had occurred previously. Why then did net exports decline so much? The major reason is that the United States enjoyed an economic expansion during 1992–96 and had a significant increase in real income *(Y)*, which in equation (6.9) reduces net exports. At the same time, some foreign countries, particularly Japan and several of the major European countries, had real income levels that expanded very slowly, if at all. In Japan there was virtually no increase in real GDP between 1991 and 1996. Weak foreign economies pull down net exports in equation (6.6) by reducing the autonomous net export term *(NX$_0$)*.

A MIRROR IMAGE

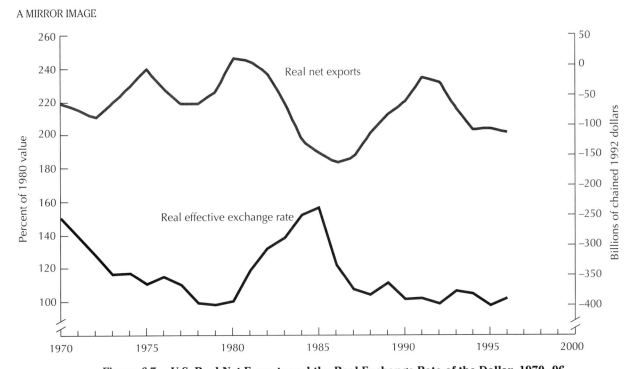

Figure 6-7   **U.S. Real Net Exports and the Real Exchange Rate of the Dollar, 1970–96**
The real net export line is copied from Figure 6-6. The real effective exchange rate line shows that the dollar depreciated in the 1970s, appreciated from 1980 to 1985, and then depreciated again after 1985. During the 1980s the two lines display a striking mirror-image relationship, indicating that an appreciating dollar tends to reduce net exports, and vice versa. During 1992–96 there was a decline in real net exports without an appreciation of the dollar, as discussed in the text.

6-9 The Real Exchange Rate and Interest Rate

The foreign exchange rate is set in the foreign exchange market. It is not a single room like the floor of the New York Stock Exchange, but consists of bank employees all over the world buying and selling different currencies by telephone and on-line computer networks. When the demand for a currency like the dollar rises relative to the supply of dollars, these bank employees (foreign exchange traders) bid up the value of the dollar, causing it to appreciate. When the demand for dollars falls, its value falls, or depreciates.

The Demand for Dollars and the "Fundamentals"

The demand for dollars stems from two sources, the desire to buy American products and the desire to buy securities denominated in dollars (like U.S. government bonds and the bonds issued by U.S. corporations). Changes in the worldwide desire to buy American products tend to occur gradually. Among the factors, sometimes called fundamentals, that might create such changes are the invention of new American products, like personal computers. A fundamental factor that could *reduce* the desire to hold dollars might be the development of new products in other countries, like Japanese VCRs or camcorders. Higher expected inflation in the United States than in other countries would also reduce the desire to hold dollars.

Because the fundamental factors tend to change slowly, they cannot account for much of the highly volatile movements evident in Figure 6-7 in the dollar's real exchange rate. Instead, these sharp up and down movements can be attributed to the second main source of the demand for dollars, the desire by foreigners to buy securities denominated in dollars. When U.S. securities become more attractive, the demand for dollars increases and the foreign exchange traders bid up the dollar's value. Similarly, when foreign securities become more attractive to Americans, U.S. residents supply extra dollars to the foreign exchange traders to obtain the foreign currencies they need to buy foreign securities and the dollar's value goes down.

The relative attractiveness of U.S. and foreign securities depends on the **interest rate differential**, defined as the average U.S. interest rate minus the average foreign interest rate. When the U.S. interest rate increases and the foreign interest rate remains unchanged, the interest rate differential increases. Foreigners find U.S. securities attractive; they demand additional dollars to buy them, and the foreign exchange rate of the dollar is bid up by the foreign exchange traders.

> The **interest rate differential** is the average U.S. interest rate minus the average foreign interest rate.

The Real Exchange Rate and the Monetary–Fiscal Policy Mix

The connection between the U.S. interest rate and the real exchange rate of the dollar establishes a link between U.S. fiscal policy and the value of the dollar. When the Fed holds the real money supply constant, as in the top left frame of Figure 5-5 on p. 132, a fiscal policy stimulus (for instance, an increase in government spending) raises both real income and the interest rate. Foreigners attempt to buy U.S. securities, and the dollar appreciates.

Another factor causing an appreciation of the dollar would be a restrictive monetary policy that shifts the *LM* curve leftward as the Fed reduces the real money supply. A particularly sharp appreciation of the dollar would be likely to accompany a shift in the policy mix from tight fiscal and easy money, as at point E_0 in the lower left frame of Figure 5-5, to easy fiscal and tight money, as at point E_7 in the same figure.

This section has suggested that an increase in the U.S. interest rate should cause an appreciation of the dollar, and a decrease in the U.S. interest rate should cause a depreciation of the dollar. The close positive relationship between the U.S. interest rate and the value of the dollar is demonstrated in Figure 6-8, which plots the two together for the period since 1970. The real interest rate is copied from Figure 1-10, where the puzzle of high interest rates was first introduced. The real exchange rate of the dollar is copied from Figure 6-7. The periods in the 1970s of the lowest real interest rates coincided with periods when the dollar was low. The period of high interest rates after 1980 was accompanied by an appreciation of the dollar. The 1984 peak in the real interest rate came shortly before the 1985 peak in the real exchange rate. The decline in the real interest rate during 1984–89 coincided with the decline in the real exchange rate from 1985 to 1989. Since 1990, both the real exchange rate and the real interest rate have fluctuated without any major trend. Overall, changes in the real interest rate cannot predict every wiggle in the dollar, but they capture the most important changes.

PUZZLE 4: WHY HAVE REAL INTEREST RATES BEEN SO HIGH?
PUZZLE 6: WHY HAS THE UNITED STATES' TRADE DROPPED INTO PERSISTENT DEFICIT?

Figure 6-8
The U.S. Real Corporate Bond Rate and the Real Exchange Rate of the Dollar, 1970–96

The real exchange rate is copied from Figure 6-7. The real corporate bond rate is copied from Figure 1-10. A positive relationship between the two lines is evident, with movements in the interest rate appearing to occur prior to movements in the exchange rate.

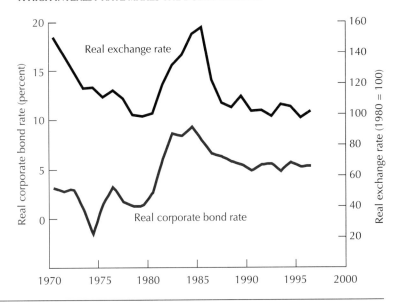

A HIGH INTEREST RATE MAKES THE DOLLAR STRONG

SELF-TEST Assuming that they pay cash for their summer vacation trips to Europe, would college students prefer a policy mix of tight monetary and easy fiscal, or easy monetary and tight fiscal, when they plan to go to Europe?

Interest Rates and Capital Mobility

The mechanism by which interest rates affect the exchange rate involves flows of capital between countries. As we have seen, a component of the balance of payments is the capital account, which registers purchases and sales of foreign assets by U.S. residents, as well as purchases and sales of U.S. assets by foreign residents. Will foreigners want to buy more American assets, putting the capital account into surplus (a capital inflow), or will Americans want to buy more foreign assets, putting the capital account into deficit (a capital outflow)? People are free to make this choice, because capital is freely mobile; that is, people can choose freely between domestic and foreign stocks, bonds, and other assets to find the highest available return in their own currency.

Perfect capital mobility occurs when investors regard foreign financial assets as a perfect substitute for domestic assets, and when investors respond instantaneously to an interest rate differential between domestic and foreign assets by moving sufficient assets to eliminate that differential.

An extreme case that is useful for economic analysis is called **perfect capital mobility**. This occurs when a resident of one country can purchase any desired assets in another country immediately, in unlimited amounts, with very low commissions and fees. The crucial implication of perfect capital mobility is that interest rates in one country are tightly linked to interest rates in other countries. Why? An American investor faced with a choice of a return of 6.0 percent at home and 6.6 percent in Germany would immediately choose to buy financial assets in Germany. This reduction in the supply of funds in the United States would raise the U.S. interest rate, and the increase in the demand for German securities would reduce the German interest rate. Interest rates in the two countries would converge at the same level, say 6.3 percent.

The implication of perfect capital mobility is profound. *Any event in one country that tends to change its interest rate (r) relative to the interest rate in foreign countries (r^f) will generate huge capital movements that will soon eliminate the interest rate differential ($r - r^f$).* As an example, a monetary expansion that reduces the domestic interest rate will generate a huge capital outflow that will bring the interest rate back to its original level. A fiscal expansion that raises the domestic interest rate will generate a huge capital inflow that will bring the interest rate back to its original level. This link between a fiscal expansion and capital inflows provides the crucial link between the U.S. twin deficits of the 1980s; the fiscal expansion of the early 1980s boosted U.S. interest rates and made it more attractive for foreigners to buy American assets. This relationship linked the fiscal deficit to the strong dollar of the mid-1980s and the resulting current account deficit. Hence the expression the *twin deficits*.

The Two Adjustment Mechanisms: Fixed and Flexible Rates

Perfect capital mobility implies that domestic monetary and fiscal policy do not affect the domestic interest rate. With fixed exchange rates a stimulative monetary policy will not reduce the domestic interest rate, but will instead cause the country to lose international reserves as the capital account in the balance of payments is thrown into deficit. In a pure flexible exchange rate system (in which there are no international reserves) the monetary policy stimulus generates an excess supply of dollars, and the exchange rate of the dollar drops until supply and demand are once again in balance.

In short, perfect capital mobility implies that both monetary and fiscal policy lose control over the interest rate. With fixed exchange rates, a monetary stimulus causes a loss of reserves and a fiscal stimulus causes an increase in reserves. With flexible exchange rates, a monetary stimulus causes a depreciation of the exchange rate and a fiscal stimulus causes an appreciation of the exchange rate. The reverse events occur with a monetary policy contraction or a fiscal policy contraction.

Is Perfect Capital Mobility Relevant for the United States?

A **small open economy** with perfect capital mobility has no power to set its domestic interest rate at a level that differs from foreign interest rates.

A **large open economy** can influence its domestic interest rate. A high domestic interest rate generates a steady stream of capital inflows that are not great enough to eliminate an interest rate differential between the domestic and foreign interest rate; a low domestic interest rate generates a steady stream of capital outflows.

As an analytical tool, perfect capital mobility is most relevant for a **small open economy**, too small to influence the world level of interest rates (r^f). In such an economy, because of perfect capital mobility, the small domestic capital market is swamped by capital inflows whenever there is even a minor increase in the domestic interest rate above the world interest rate (and capital outflows for even a minor decrease in the domestic interest rate). The United States is too large to be considered a small open economy, and even under perfect capital mobility its own domestic capital market is too large for capital movements to bring its domestic interest rate into perfect equality with the foreign interest rate. We examine the case of the **large open economy** in Section 6-11, after first studying how monetary and fiscal policy work in a small open economy with perfect capital mobility.

6-10 The *IS-LM* Model in a Small Open Economy

The assumption of perfect capital mobility introduces a new element into the *IS-LM* model of income determination. This is the assumption that the differential between domestic and foreign interest rates $(r - r^f)$ must remain at zero. Any small change in the domestic interest rate caused by shifts in monetary and fiscal policy (or in shifts in the *IS* curve due to different levels of consumer and business optimism) will generate capital flows that will quickly bring the domestic interest rate into line with the unchanged foreign interest rate.

The *BP* Schedule

Because perfect capital mobility implies that the interest rate differential must remain at zero, the balance of payments can be in equilibrium only at a single domestic interest rate (r) equal to the foreign interest rate (r^f). Any higher interest rate will lead to unlimited capital inflows, causing a huge balance of payments surplus. Any lower interest rate will lead to unlimited capital outflows, causing a huge balance of payments deficit. The balance of payments is in equilibrium, equal to zero, only along the horizontal line *BP* in Figure 6-9, drawn at the position where the domestic and foreign interest rates are equal $(r' = r^f)$.

Anywhere along the horizontal *BP* line the overall balance of payments is in equilibrium (equal to zero) and both the capital and current account balances are zero as well. Why? With a zero interest rate differential $(r - r^f = 0)$, capital flows are zero, implying that the capital account is zero. But to make the overall balance of payments equal to zero, the current account balance must be zero as well. In such an economy, along the horizontal *BP* line, Table 6-1 on p. 156 would show a 0 on lines 1, 2, and 3.

The Analysis with Fixed Exchange Rates

Now we will examine the effects of a monetary and then a fiscal expansion in a small open economy with fixed exchange rates. Throughout, we will assume that the price level is fixed. These results remain valid, even if the price level is allowed to change, as long as changes in the price level occur more slowly than the speed at which capital flows in and out of the small open economy.

Monetary Expansion. Initially, the monetary expansion depicted in Figure 6-9 raises the nominal money supply. Since the price level is fixed, the real money supply also increases, and this shifts the *LM* curve rightward from schedule LM_0 to LM_1. The *IS* curve is assumed to be unchanged. We previously found that such an expansion would move the economy from point E_0 to point E_1. But now the reduction of the interest rate to r_0, which is below the initial level r', generates huge capital outflows and losses of international reserves. To prevent this movement, the central bank must boost the interest rate back up to the initial level by reversing the monetary stimulus. The LM_1 curve shifts back to LM_0, and the economy returns to E_0. Because international capital flows move so quickly, all this would happen so fast that the economy would never actually get to point E_1. In short, with fixed exchange rates the

Figure 6-9
Effect of an Increase in the Money Supply with Fixed Exchange Rates

The increase in the real money supply initially shifts the *LM* curve rightward, from LM_0 to LM_1. However, the decline in the interest rate at point E_1 causes capital outflows and a loss of foreign exchange reserves. This reaction reduces the money supply, which continues until the *LM* curve shifts back to LM_0 and the economy moves back to point E_0.

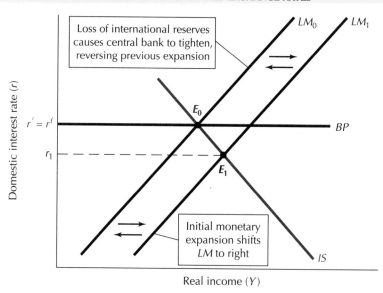

MONETARY POLICY IS IMPOTENT UNDER FIXED EXCHANGE RATES

Loss of international reserves causes central bank to tighten, reversing previous expansion

Initial monetary expansion shifts *LM* to right

central bank is impotent in a small open economy. It can neither reduce the interest rate nor expand output. It cannot carry out a contractionary policy either, since it would be swamped with capital inflows that would force it to carry out an offsetting policy expansion.

Fiscal Expansion.   With fixed exchange rates, the only way domestic policymakers can alter the level of real income is to use fiscal policy, as is shown in Figure 6-10. Here the initial situation is the same, point E_0. A fiscal expansion that shifts IS_0 rightward to IS_1 tends to move the economy to point E_5. But the increase in the interest rate attracts capital inflows, swamping the central bank with reserves. Under a fixed exchange rate system, the bank must respond by allowing the money supply to rise until the interest rate returns to its initial level. The money supply must be increased enough to shift LM_0 to LM_1. Instead of going to E_5 as would occur in a closed economy without capital inflows, the economy moves to point E_6.

Clearly, capital mobility with fixed exchange rates makes fiscal policy very effective. Point E_6 is exactly the same outcome that we reached with fiscal expansion in Chapter 5 under two situations, the first of which was a horizontal *LM* curve (top frame of Figure 5-3 on p. 128) and the second of which was accommodating monetary policy (top right frame of Figure 5-5 on p. 132). *Perfect capital mobility with fixed exchange rates forces monetary policy to be accommodative; in effect, fiscal policy gains control of monetary policy.*

The Analysis with Flexible Exchange Rates

In the previous section we learned that a fixed exchange rate system makes monetary policy impotent and fiscal policy very effective in changing the level of real income. In this section we learn that the opposite is true with flex-

Figure 6-10
Effect of a Fiscal Policy Stimulus with Fixed Exchange Rates

An increase in government spending or a reduction in tax rates shifts the *IS* curve rightward to position IS_1. The economy initially moves toward point E_5, but the higher interest rate creates a capital inflow and an increase in foreign exchange reserves, which in turn raises the money supply and shifts the *LM* curve rightward to LM_1. The economy winds up at point E_6.

FISCAL POLICY GAINS CONTROL OVER MONETARY POLICY UNDER FIXED EXCHANGE RATES

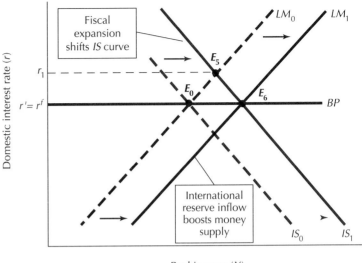

ible exchange rates. Monetary policy becomes extremely effective, whereas fiscal policy becomes ineffective.

When exchange rates are flexible, the central bank does nothing to prevent an exchange rate appreciation or depreciation. Thus any event that reduces the domestic interest rate will cause a capital outflow, raising the supply of domestic currency on the foreign exchange market and causing the exchange rate to depreciate. In an *IS-LM* diagram like Figure 6-11, the exchange rate depreciates whenever the economy moves below the *BP* line and appreciates whenever the economy moves above the *BP* line.

The new ingredient in the *IS-LM* model implied by flexible exchange rates was introduced in equation (6.9). An exchange rate appreciation reduces net exports and hence shifts the *IS* curve to the left (since net exports are a component of autonomous planned spending, and any change in autonomous planned spending shifts the *IS* curve). Similarly, an exchange rate depreciation raises net exports and shifts the *IS* curve to the right.

Monetary Expansion. In Figure 6-11, as before, a monetary expansion shifts LM_0 rightward to LM_1. Capital outflows lead to a depreciation of the exchange rate. In equation (6.9) this depreciation boosts net exports at any given level of income. The higher level of net exports shifts the initial IS_0 schedule to the new position IS_1. Once the economy arrives at E_6, the exchange rate stops depreciating and the economy is in full equilibrium; the balance of payments is in equilibrium along the *BP* line, and the economy is also on its current *IS* and *LM* schedules. The level of real income has increased because a depreciated exchange rate has boosted net exports for any given level of income, shifting *IS* to the right.

However, as also shown in equation (6.9), higher income boosts imports. As a result, when the economy arrives at its new equilibrium point E_6, the boost to net exports from the depreciated exchange rate is offset exactly by

Figure 6-11
Effect of a Monetary and Fiscal Policy Stimulus with Flexible Exchange Rates

An increase in the real money supply shifts the *LM* curve rightward to LM_1. The reduction in interest rates at point E_1 causes the exchange rate to depreciate, which in turn boosts net exports and shifts the *IS* curve rightward to IS_1. The economy winds up at point E_6. Starting again from E_0, a fiscal policy stimulus shifts the *IS* curve rightward to position IS_1. The economy initially moves toward point E_5, but the higher interest rate causes the exchange rate to appreciate, which in turn cuts net exports and shifts the *IS* curve back to IS_0. This movement cancels out the impact of the fiscal stimulus on both real income and the interest rate.

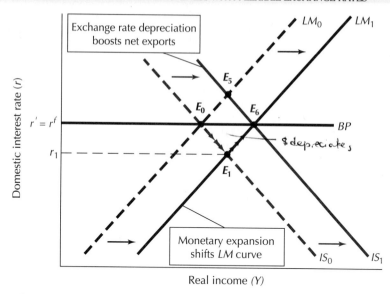

MONETARY POLICY GAINS EFFECTIVENESS WITH FLEXIBLE EXCHANGE RATES

Exchange rate depreciation boosts net exports

Monetary expansion shifts *LM* curve

Domestic interest rate (r)

$r' = r^f$

r_1

E_0 E_5 E_6 E_1

BP

\$ depreciates

LM_0 LM_1 IS_0 IS_1

Real income (Y)

the reduction in net exports caused by higher income. The current account is in balance and, because the domestic interest rate is equal to the foreign interest rate, the capital account is also in balance, thus balancing the overall balance of payments as required along the *BP* schedule.

Fiscal Expansion. The effects of a fiscal expansion in the form of higher government spending can also be shown in Figure 6-11. The normal effect of a fiscal expansion is to shift *IS* rightward and boost the domestic interest rate to a point like E_5. But now, with flexible exchange rates, fiscal expansion causes the exchange rate to appreciate. Domestic exports are made less competitive, and domestic residents start buying more imported goods. Net exports fall, and this continues until the *IS* curve shifts back to the left to its initial position, returning the economy to the original point E_0. In this example the *LM* curve does not shift. *Domestic crowding out is replaced by international crowding out, and international crowding out is complete.* The domestic interest rate and income are the same as they were initially at E_0; thus, so are domestic investment and saving. The increase in the fiscal deficit caused by the higher level of government spending is exactly offset by the decline in net exports, and the higher fiscal deficit is totally financed by foreign borrowing. *The twin deficits are identical,* and the cause of the foreign trade deficit is the fiscal deficit. To summarize these different cases:

With fixed exchange rates, fiscal policy is highly effective and the central bank is forced to accommodate fiscal policy actions. Monetary policy is impotent, since any increase in the money supply immediately flows abroad and fails to stimulate the domestic economy.

With flexible exchange rates, monetary policy is highly effective. The Fed can control the money supply and can stimulate the economy by causing the exchange rate to depreciate. This action boosts net exports until income has grown so much that (due to income-induced growth in imports) net exports return to their original level. With flexible exchange rates, fiscal policy is impotent and international crowding out is complete.

6-11 Capital Mobility and Exchange Rates in a Large Open Economy

In the last section we examined the effects of monetary and fiscal policy in a small open economy, one that has no control at all over its own interest rate. In such an economy, perfect capital mobility causes the domestic interest rate to equal the foreign interest rate.

How a Large Open Economy Differs from a Small Open Economy

In contrast to a small open economy, a large open economy like the United States has substantial control over its domestic interest rate. Its large size relative to the rest of the world means that capital flows are not sufficiently powerful to push its domestic interest rate into exact equality with the world interest rate. Capital mobility is imperfect. When the domestic interest rate rises above the foreign interest rate by a fixed amount, say 0.5 percent, only a limited inflow of foreign capital will occur, not enough to eliminate the interest rate differential.

In the previous section we examined the effects of monetary and fiscal policy in a small open economy, using the *BP* curves. How does this analysis differ in a large open economy? The main difference involves the *BP* curve, as shown in Figure 6-12. Recall that at every point along the *BP* curve the balance of payments is in equilibrium, so any current account surplus is offset by a capital account deficit, or vice versa.

For a small open economy, the *BP* curve is a horizontal line. In contrast, in a large open economy there can be a continuing capital inflow if the domestic interest rate is high enough and a continuing capital outflow if the domestic interest rate is low enough. As a result, the distinguishing characteristic of a large open economy is that the capital account is in surplus when the domestic interest rate is high and in deficit when the domestic interest rate is low. To achieve an overall balance of payments of zero, any surplus in the capital account must be offset by a deficit of exactly the same amount in the current account; this requires a high level of real income at a point like *C* in Figure 6-12, so that imports (which depend on income) are large and the current account is in deficit. The opposite occurs at a point like *A;* the deficit in the capital account is offset by a current account surplus, caused by low income that in turn reduces imports.

In short, the *BP* line slopes up for a large open economy, because capital inflows *depend positively on the interest rate*. At a high interest rate, capital inflows are large; at a low interest rate, capital outflows are large. The behavior of the U.S. economy in 1989–91 provides an example of a leftward movement along the *BP* curve for an open economy, from a point like *C* to a point like *B*. As the economy weakened, slower growth of imports reduced the current account deficit to nearly zero, while lower interest rates created an offsetting decline in the capital account surplus to nearly zero. Then in 1992–96,

Figure 6-12

The *BP* Line in a Small and Large Open Economy

The *BP* line shows the different combinations of the domestic interest rate and real income that are consistent with balance of payments equilibrium, that is, a zero total balance of the current account plus the capital account. The *BP* line, as in Figure 6-9 through 6-11, is horizontal for a small open economy that cannot control its own interest rate. The *BP* line is positively sloped for a large open economy. At a point like *A*, the interest rate is low, the capital account is in deficit, and the current account is in surplus due to low imports. At a point like *C*, the interest rate is high, the capital account is in surplus, and the current account is in deficit due to high imports.

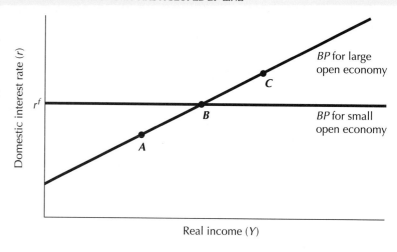

A LARGE OPEN ECONOMY HAS A SLOPED *BP* LINE

this was reversed. The economy returned from *B* to *C* as real income increased. The current account deficit increased, as did the capital account surplus.

Monetary and Fiscal Policy with Fixed and Flexible Exchange Rates

Once we adopt the positively sloped *BP* curve for a large open economy, the previous analysis of monetary and fiscal policy remains valid with only minor adjustments.

We previously concluded that with fixed exchange rates monetary policy was impotent, regardless of the slope of the *BP* curve. Thus monetary policy is equally impotent in both a small and a large open economy. Fiscal policy is effective, but somewhat less so than in a small open economy, since the effects of a fiscal policy stimulus are divided between an increase in real income and in the domestic interest rate, instead of being entirely directed toward an increase in real income.

With flexible exchange rates, fiscal policy is impotent in a large open economy, just as in a small open economy. The prompt collapse of net exports following the 1981 shift to fiscal deficits provides a perfect example of the impotence of fiscal policy in a large open economy. Monetary policy is highly effective with flexible exchange rates, as in a small open economy. However, since higher income is accompanied by higher interest rates (due to the upward sloping *BP* curve), there is some crowding out of domestic expenditure, and this must be offset by a larger stimulus to net exports than in a small open economy, requiring an even larger exchange rate depreciation.

To summarize these contrasting cases:

With fixed exchange rates, fiscal policy is highly effective, but a fiscal stimulus does not increase real income as much in a large open economy as in a small open economy. Monetary policy is impotent in both a large and a small open economy.

With flexible exchange rates, monetary policy boosts income even more in a large open economy than in a small open economy. With flexible exchange rates, fiscal policy is impotent in both a large and a small open economy. International crowding out is complete.

6-12 Conclusion: How Should Policymakers React to Exchange Rate Movements?

We have learned in this chapter that there are interactions among monetary and fiscal policy, the current account balance, and the foreign exchange rate. Expansionary fiscal policy in the early 1980s bears much of the responsibility for the appreciation of the dollar and the deterioration of the current account balance. Expansionary monetary policy in 1985–86 initiated the depreciation of the dollar and the subsequent recovery of the current account balance.

Should policymakers respond to movements in the exchange rate or in the current account balance? If a policy objective is to maintain a fixed exchange rate, then it is necessary for monetary policy to tighten by raising interest rates in response to any depreciation in the exchange rate. The central issue in European macroeconomics today is the political desire to have a common currency, that is, fixed exchange rates among European nations. This requires that central banks abandon concern with domestic policy objectives and orient monetary policy toward stabilization of the exchange rate.

Few observers feel that there is any need for the United States to maintain fixed exchange rates against other nations. Since 1789 the United States has achieved the goal that Europe currently covets—a fixed exchange rate among the 50 states that the United States comprises. A Vermont dollar has had a fixed exchange rate with a South Carolina dollar for more than 200 years, fostering internal economic and political stability, and it is understandable that Europe strives to emulate this achievement.

If the effective exchange rate of the U.S. dollar depreciates, is there any reason for the Federal Reserve to raise interest rates? Most economists feel that the goals of monetary policy should be limited to achieving low inflation within the domestic economy, and that it is neither practical nor important for the Fed to aim at a particular exchange rate or target for the current account balance. We shall return in future chapters to the objectives of the Fed, and the interrelations between domestic and international economic policy.

SUMMARY

1. The balance of payments consists of the current account (the balance of exports, imports, net investment income, and transfers) and the capital account (which registers purchases and sales of foreign assets by U.S. residents and of U.S. assets by foreigners). For most of the past four decades, the United States has run a current account deficit, which has been only partly offset by a capital account surplus, thus resulting in persistent balance of payments deficit.

2. A current account deficit must be financed by borrowing from foreigners. Borrowing from foreign households, firms, and governments is classified as a capital account surplus, while borrowing from foreign central banks is treated as a balance of payments deficit. A current account deficit thus increases net indebtedness to foreigners.

3. In a flexible exchange rate system, the foreign exchange rate is free to move every day. An increase in the amount of foreign currency that can be bought per unit of domestic currency is called an appreciation, and a decrease is called a depreciation.

4. In the absence of government intervention, the foreign exchange rate tends to appreciate when there is increased demand for a currency due to higher exports or capital inflows. The exchange rate tends to depreciate when there is an increased supply of a currency due to higher imports or capital outflows.

5. The real exchange rate remains constant if changes in the nominal exchange rate are exactly offset by the differential between domestic and foreign inflation. The purchasing power parity theory of long-run exchange rate determination predicts that the real exchange rate will remain constant.

6. The real exchange rate can change for many reasons not taken into account by the PPP theory. These include differences between nations in the rate of tech-nological change, their comparative rates of discovery of natural resources, and the balance of flows of capital and government transfer payments between them.

7. The Bretton Woods system of fixed exchange rates lasted from World War II until 1973. Since then, there has been an "impure" flexible exchange rate system, under which central banks practice intervention to prevent undesired movements in exchange rates.

8. Net exports, the difference between exports and imports, depend both on income and on the real exchange rate. In turn, the real exchange rate depends on the real interest rate. An increase in the real interest rate causes an appreciation of the real exchange rate, as foreign investors find domestic securities more attractive and bid up the exchange rate in order to buy them.

9. In a small open economy with fixed exchange rates, fiscal policy is highly effective and monetary policy is completely impotent. With flexible exchange rates the policy roles are reversed, since monetary policy is highly effective and fiscal policy is impotent.

10. In a large open economy with fixed exchange rates, monetary policy is impotent, but fiscal policy is effective (although less so than in a small open economy). With flexible exchange rates monetary policy is highly effective (even more so than in a small open economy), but fiscal policy is impotent.

CONCEPTS

open economy
balance of payments
current account
capital account
net international investment position
foreign exchange rate
appreciation
depreciation
real exchange rate
purchasing power parity (PPP) theory
inflation differential
flexible exchange rate system

fixed exchange rate system
foreign exchange reserves
devalue
revalue
intervention
foreign trade surplus
foreign trade deficit
interest rate differential
perfect capital mobility
small open economy
large open economy

QUESTIONS AND PROBLEMS

Questions

1. Explain the difference between a credit and a debit in the balance of payments.
2. Distinguish between the current account and the capital account in the balance of payments.
3. How is a current account deficit in the balance of payments financed? How does the shift in the U.S. net investment position from surplus to indebtedness affect U.S. residents?
4. There are two main ways to adjust to an imbalance between international receipts and expenditures. What are these two ways? How do they work?
5. Consider the foreign exchange market between the

U.S. dollar and the deutsche mark. What determines the supply and demand for U.S. dollars in this foreign exchange market? What is the connection between the German demand for U.S. dollars and the German supply of deutsche marks?

6. Under what conditions is the demand for foreign exchange negatively sloped?

7. Under what conditions is the supply of foreign exchange positively sloped? Negatively sloped?

8. Explain why Figure 6-4 is evidence against the theory of purchasing power parity. Does this inconsistency between theory and evidence have any policy implications? Explain.

9. What is a "dirty" flexible exchange rate system, and what incentives exist to transform a "clean" system into a "dirty" one?

10. What is the relationship between a country's foreign exchange rate and its net exports? Why?

11. What is the relationship between a country's interest rate and its foreign exchange rate? Why?

12. Explain the connection between the federal government budget deficit in the early 1980s and the accompanying twin foreign trade deficits.

13. What is the *BP* schedule? Why is the *BP* line horizontal for a small open economy but positively sloped for a large open one?

14. "Perfect capital mobility with fixed exchange rates forces monetary policy to be accommodative; in effect, fiscal policy gains control of monetary policy." Explain.

15. In a pure, flexible exchange rate system, monetary policy becomes extremely effective, whereas fiscal policy becomes ineffective. Explain.

Problems

1. Suppose the German demand for a U.S. machine is given by the following equation:

$$q = 200,000/p$$

Here q is the quantity of U.S. machines bought by the Germans and p is the price, in deutsche marks (DM), of the U.S. machine.

(a) If the exchange rate is 2 DM per dollar and the dollar price of the machine is $10,000, what is the DM price of the machine?

(b) According to the demand function given above, how many machines would the Germans buy?

(c) If the dollar price of the machine remained unchanged but the exchange rate fell to 1 DM per dollar, what would the DM price of the machine now be?

(d) Now how many machines would the Germans buy?

(e) At the exchange rate of 2 DM per dollar, what is the quantity demanded of dollars by the Germans?

(f) At the exchange rate of 1 DM per dollar, what is the quantity demanded of dollars by the Germans?

(g) If this machine were the only U.S. export to Germany, draw the German demand curve for dollars. Put dollars demanded on the horizontal axis and the DM/$ exchange rate on the vertical axis.

(h) At the exchange rate of 2 DM per dollar (or $0.50/DM), what is the quantity supplied of deutsche marks by the Germans?

(i) At the exchange rate of 1 DM per dollar (or $1/DM), what is the quantity supplied of deutsche marks by the Germans?

(j) If this machine were the only U.S. export to Germany, draw the German supply curve of deutsche marks. Put DM supplied on the horizontal axis and the $/DM exchange rate on the vertical axis. (Note the inversion of the exchange rate. Although there are exceptions, it is customary to express a country's exchange rate as the number of units of foreign currency that exchange for one unit of the domestic currency.)

2. Suppose we define the real exchange rate as follows:

$$e = e'(P/P^f)$$

Here the terms are as defined in the text.

(a) Provide a hypothetical numerical example in which you convert a nominal exchange rate to a real exchange rate.

(b) Explain, in terms of your example, why the definition makes sense.

(c) Express the above equation in terms of natural logarithms. Recall that $\ln(ab) = \ln a + \ln b$ and that $\ln(ab) = \ln a - \ln b$.

(d) Take the differential of your resulting logarithmic equation. Recall that $d\ln(a) = da/a$.

(e) Interpret your result.

3. The purchasing power parity theory (PPP), as expressed in equation (6.5) of the text, is repeated here:

$$e' = P^f/P$$

(a) Express this equation in terms of natural logarithms.

(b) Take the differential of your resulting logarithmic equation.

(c) Interpret your result.

(d) Using the results in Problem 2(d) and 3(b), prove the assertion that if PPP holds, then the real exchange rate would be a constant (i.e., $de/e = 0$).

4. Answer these questions for the small open economy whose structure is given by the following equations:

$C = a + 0.75\ (Y - T)$ $G = 400$
$a = 50 - 10r$ $M^s/P = 300$
$T = 200 + 0.2Y$ $h = 0.4$
$I_p = 300 - 30r$ $f = 50$
$NX = 400 - 0.1Y - 5e$

(a) We begin with the small economy and the world economy having the same interest rate, $r = r^f$. Let $e = 50$.
  (1) What is the equation for NX?
  (2) Given this NX, what is the equation for A_p?
  (3) What is the marginal leakage rate?
  (4) What is the equation for the IS curve?
  (5) What is the equation for the LM curve?
  (6) What is the equilibrium interest rate, r?
  (7) What is the equilibrium real output, Y?

(b) We now allow the small economy's interest rate to diverge temporarily from the world economy's interest rate. Now suppose that $G = 450$, while $e = 50$.
  (1) Given this G, what is the equation for A_p?
  (2) What is the equation for the IS curve?
  (3) What is the equilibrium interest rate, r?
  (4) What is the equilibrium real output, Y?

(c) Find the foreign exchange rate at which the small economy's interest rate again equals the world economy's interest rate. (Hint: Recall that the horizontal intercept of the IS curve is kA_0. Then the shift in IS represents an intercept change of $k\Delta A_0$. Find the ΔNX_0 that would offset this shift. Then find the Δe that would produce this change in NX_0.)

(d) Discuss the adjustment mechanism that brought the small open economy's interest rate equal to the world interest rate after the change in government spending.

(e) Was there crowding out or crowding in? If so, what component of total expenditure was crowded out or in? How much was crowded out or in?

SELF-TEST ANSWERS

p. **157** (1) balance of payments deficit of 30, which requires borrowing 30 from foreign central banks; (2) balance of payments surplus of 30, which requires lending 30; (3) same as (1).

p. **163** (1) Shifts the demand curve for dollars to the right. (2) No effect on the supply curve of dollars (people from the United States shift some of the supply of dollars from Germany to Japan). (3) Shifts the demand curve for dollars to the left. (4) Shifts the supply curve of dollars to the left.

p. **165** The real exchange rate in 1998 is $1.5 \times (110/100) = 1.65$ marks per dollar. Since the real exchange rate was 1.7 marks per dollar in 1997, the dollar has experienced a real depreciation.

p. **171** A college student going to Europe (like anyone buying foreign goods or services) hopes for an appreciation of the dollar. Other things remaining the same, you would have preferred traveling to Europe in 1985 when the dollar's foreign exchange value was approximately 60 percent higher than it was in 1995. For the German student, the situation is the opposite. He or she would prefer to travel to the U.S. when the dollar is weaker (and thus the mark relatively stronger) as was the case in 1995.

p. **179** College students going to Europe prefer a strong dollar. This means that they prefer high interest rates, which requires a mix of easy fiscal policy and tight monetary policy.

PART THREE

Aggregate Demand,

Aggregate Supply,

and Inflation

Aggregate Demand, Aggregate Supply, and the Self-Correcting Economy

The price of commodities in the market is formed by means of a certain struggle which takes place between the buyers and the sellers.
—Henry Thornton, 1802

Until now we have assumed that the level of prices is fixed. We have shown how real income (or GDP) and the interest rate are shifted about by changes in "exogenous disturbances." Some of these disturbances originate in the private sector, including changes in business and consumer confidence and in foreign trade (that is, in the autonomous component of net exports). Others originate in the government sector, sometimes because government policy-makers are trying to stabilize the economy through changes in government spending, tax rates, or the money supply, and sometimes because wars or other political events cause sharp changes in government spending.

7-1 The Role of Aggregate Demand and Supply

Now it is time to add the price level to the list of endogenous variables, like real income and the real interest rate, that our economic theory can explain. Recall that the price level is measured by an aggregate price index like the GDP deflator. When the prices of most goods are rising, the aggregate deflator *(P)* increases, and we have inflation. When the prices of most goods are falling, *P* decreases, and we have deflation. During a period of aggregate price stability, the prices of some goods increase and some decrease, but the average of all prices *(P)* stays approximately the same.

The purpose of this chapter is to show how exogenous disturbances originating either in the private sector or in the government can cause *simultaneous* changes in real income and the price level. We begin by showing that the *IS-LM* model developed in Chapter 4 implies a negatively sloped schedule, the **aggregate demand curve,** relating real income to the price level. When we hold constant the nominal money supply and autonomous planned spending, should the price level become higher for some reason, real income tends to decrease.

But the aggregate demand curve is just one relationship between real income and the price level and is inadequate to determine both variables, just as the *IS* curve by itself cannot determine real income and the interest rate without the help of a second schedule, the *LM* curve. Similarly, in this chapter we need a second schedule, the **short-run aggregate supply curve,** in order to determine real income and the price level. Both variables are determined at the point where the aggregate demand and supply curves intersect.

This chapter begins by deriving the aggregate demand and supply curves and explaining their positions and the factors that underlie their slopes. Subsequently, we use both curves to examine the differing views of various

The **aggregate demand curve** shows different combinations of the price level and real output at which the money and commodity markets are both in equilibrium.

The **short-run aggregate supply curve** shows the amount of output that business firms are willing to produce at different price levels.

groups of economists regarding the causes of business cycles and the effectiveness of stabilization policy.

7-2   Flexible Prices and the *AD* Curve

In this section we develop a new tool, the aggregate demand *(AD)* curve, which summarizes the effect of changing prices on the level of real income. It is derived directly from the *IS-LM* model developed in Chapter 4.

Effect of Changing Prices on the *LM* Curve

We already know that the *LM* curve shifts its position whenever there is a change in the real money supply. Until now every *LM* shift has resulted from a change in the nominal money supply, while the price level has been held at a constant level. The price level has been treated as a parameter, or a known variable, allowing us to concentrate on the determination of the two unknowns, real income *(Y)* and the interest rate *(r)*.

However, the *LM* curve can shift in exactly the same way when a change in the real money supply M^s/P is caused by a change in the price level P, while the nominal money supply M^s remains fixed at a single value, say M_0^s. The top frame of Figure 7-1 illustrates three *LM* curves drawn for three values of P and M_0^s/P, each assuming the same nominal money supply, M_0^s. Initially the economy is at point E_0, where the *IS* curve crosses the LM_0 curve, drawn for the initial assumed price level P_0. The economy is in equilibrium with income level Y_0 and interest rate r_0. So far, everything is the same as in Chapter 4, except that we have relabeled the horizontal axis "real GDP," which is the same as both real income and real output.

Now we consider something new, a change in the price level. If the price level were lower than P_0, say P_1, the real money supply would be larger (M_0^s/P_1). To maintain equilibrium in the money market, the interest rate would have to fall to r_1. This change would boost planned expenditures and cause real GDP to grow to the larger amount Y_1, so that the economy's equilibrium position would move from E_0 to point H. The reverse is true as well. A higher price level, say P_2, would reduce the real money supply and cause real GDP to shrink to the lower level Y_2, and the economy's equilibrium position would move to point J.

The bottom frame of Figure 7-1 presents the relationship between equilibrium real GDP *(Y)* and the assumed price level. The horizontal axis (real GDP) is the same as that in the top frame, but the vertical axis plots the price level. Points J, E_0, and H in the bottom frame plot the three different assumed price levels and the corresponding level of real GDP from the top frame. In this particular case, price level P_2 is twice as high as P_0, and P_0 is twice as high as P_1.

In the bottom frame, the aggregate demand curve (AD_0) connecting points J, E_0, and H shows all the possible combinations of P and Y consistent with the assumed level of the *nominal* money supply (M_0^s) and also with the assumed IS_0 curve.[1] If the price level is higher, then real spending and real

RVW s[be able to explain how dem. curve is derived ... w/Δ in both nom. ms & Price level.

---

[1]*Review:* Recall that the position of the *IS* curve depends on the levels of consumer confidence, business confidence, government spending, tax rates, the autonomous component of net taxes (taxes minus transfers), and the autonomous component of net exports.

Figure 7-1
Effect on Real Income of Different Values of the Price Level

In the top frame three different *LM* curves are drawn for three different hypothetical values of the price level. Corresponding to the three levels of the price level are three positions of equilibrium, *J*, E_0, and *H*. These three points are drawn again in the lower frame with the same horizontal axis (real income), but the price level for the vertical axis. A drop in the price index from point *J* to E_0, and then to *H*, raises the *real* money supply and stimulates real output along the aggregate demand curve AD_0.

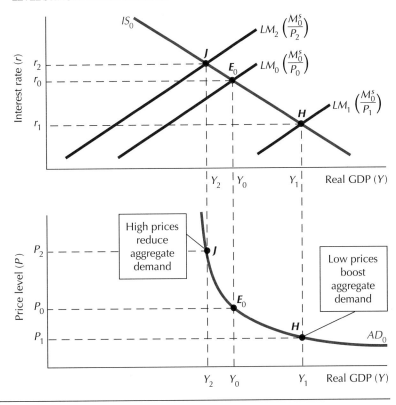

THE AGGREGATE DEMAND CURVE SHOWS THAT A DECLINE IN THE PRICE LEVEL STIMULATES REAL OUTPUT

GDP are low, and vice versa. Because the level of real GDP along the *AD* curve is always at a point where the *IS* and *LM* curves cross in the upper frame, *everywhere along the AD curve both the commodity and money markets are in equilibrium.*

Why is the *AD* curve a curved line instead of a straight line? The shape results from the fact that a given percentage decline in the price level boosts the real money supply by an even greater percentage, the lower is the price level, hence raising real GDP by more at a low price level than at a high price level. For instance, let us assume that the nominal money supply is 1000. Reducing the price level from 2 to 1.5 will raise the real money supply from 500 to 667, an increase of 33 percent. Reducing the price level from 1.5 to 1.0 will raise the real money supply from 667 to 1000, an increase of 50 percent. Reducing the price level from 1.0 to 0.5 will raise the real money supply from 1000 to 2000, an increase of 100 percent.

7-3 Shifting the Aggregate Demand Curve with Monetary and Fiscal Policy

Effects of a Change in the Nominal Money Supply

The *AD* curve is fixed in position by the assumed value of the nominal money supply and the assumed position of the *IS* curve, which in turn depend on consumer and business confidence, fiscal policy, and net exports. A change in any of these assumed conditions will shift the position of the AD curve and thus change the amount of spending and real GDP at any given price level.

To understand the factors that shift the AD curve, we begin with a doubling of the nominal money supply, from M_0^s to M_1^s. The economy starts out at point E_0, the same as in Figure 7-1. In the top frame of Figure 7-2 this doubling shifts the LM curve rightward to the new position LM_1. Since the price level has not changed, in the bottom frame the economy remains at the same vertical position as at point E_0 but moves horizontally to point H', which lies directly below point H' in the upper frame. The economy's real GDP is exactly the same at point H and H'. But, since we drew the initial AD_0 curve on the assumption that price level P_1 is half of P_0, it follows that the price level at H' is double its value at H in the bottom frame. Similarly, every point along the new, higher AD_1 curve is twice as high as along the original AD_0 curve. *The general rule is that an increase in the nominal money supply by a given percentage shifts the* AD *curve vertically by the same percentage.*[2] Why? The price level must shift upwards by the same percent as the nominal money supply in order to leave the real money supply unchanged, and the LM curve remains fixed as long as the real money supply is unchanged.

Figure 7-2
The Effect on the *AD* Curve of a Doubling of the Nominal Money Supply

In the top frame a doubling of the nominal money supply from M_0^s to M_1^s moves the LM curve rightward from LM_0 to LM_1 and moves the economy's general equilibrium (where IS crosses LM) from point E_0 to point H'. In the lower frame we remain at a vertical distance of P_0, since nothing has happened to the price level. The higher money supply raises real income and causes the economy's equilibrium position in the bottom frame to be at point H' rather than at point E_0. Notice that the new AD_1 curve running through point H' lies everywhere twice as high as the old AD_0 curve.

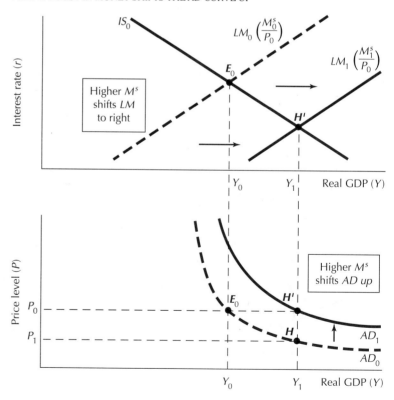

HOW A BOOST IN MONEY SHIFTS THE *AD* CURVE UP

---

[2]As a technical matter, the proportional vertical movement in the AD schedule requires that all forms of real wealth double when the nominal money supply doubles.

LEARNING ABOUT DIAGRAMS: *THE* AD *CURVE*

The aggregate demand *(AD)* curve, as drawn in the bottom frames of Figures 7-1 to 7-3, summarizes everything we have already learned about the *IS* and *LM* curves, and adds a single new ingredient, the ability of the price level to move higher or lower instead of remaining fixed (as in Chapters 3–5).

Diagram Elements and Reasons for Slope

The vertical axis is the price level and the horizontal axis is the level of real GDP (the horizontal axis is the same as that for both the *IS* and *LM* curves; recall that real GDP is the same as real income and real output).

The *AD* curve shows all the possible crossing points of a single *IS* commodity-market equilibrium curve with the various *LM* money-market equilibrium curves drawn for each possible price level. Everywhere along the *AD* curve *both* the commodity *(IS)* and money *(LM)* markets are in equilibrium (as shown in Figure 7-1).

The *AD* curve slopes downward because a lower price level *(P)* raises the real money supply, thereby lowering the interest rate and stimulating planned expenditures. This stimulus requires an increase in actual real GDP *(Y)* to keep the commodity market in equilibrium. The steeper the *IS* curve, the steeper the *AD* curve.

What Shifts the AD Curve?

The *AD* curve is drawn for a fixed nominal supply of money *(M^s)* and a fixed set of determinants of the *IS* curve (business and consumer confidence, government spending, tax rates, autonomous net taxes, and the autonomous component of net exports).

A given percentage increase in the nominal money supply will shift the *AD* curve *vertically* upward by a similar percentage. Why? The price level must shift upward by the same percent as the nominal money supply in order to leave the real money supply unchanged, and a fixed real money supply means a fixed *LM* curve.

Anything that shifts the *IS* curve also creates a parallel *horizontal* shift in the *AD* curve in the same direction. The *amount* of the horizontal shift of the *AD* curve is usually less than that of the *IS* curve, because of the crowding out effect.[a] The factors that can shift the *IS* curve, and hence the *AD* curve, include changes in business or consumer confidence, government spending, tax rates, autonomous net taxes, or the autonomous component of net exports.

What Is True of Points That Are Off the AD Curve?

The entire area to the right of the *AD* curve has an excess supply of commodities; too much is being produced relative to the demand for goods and services at that price level.

The entire area to the left of the *AD* curve has an excess demand for commodities; too little is being produced relative to the demand for goods and services at that price level.

At any point off the *AD* curve, there is pressure for change. For instance, at a point with excess production to the right of the *AD* curve, there is unplanned inventory accumulation, which places downward pressure on production. There is also downward pressure on prices as firms attempt to boost sales with lower prices.[b]

---

[a]For details, see equation (10) in the Appendix to Chapter 5. For any given change in, say, government spending, the *IS* curve shifts in the same direction by the multiplier k, while the *AD* curve shifts in the same direction by the multiplier k_1, defined in equation (10).

[b]The equation of the *AD* curve is the income equation (9) in the Appendix to Chapter 5.

$$Y = k_1 A_0 + k_2 \frac{M^s}{P}$$

Try to determine whether a steeper *LM* curve would make the *AD* curve steeper or flatter.

Effects of a Change in Autonomous Spending

In the last section, the *IS* curve remained fixed at its original position but an increase in the nominal money supply shifted the *LM* and *AD* curves. Now we reverse what is fixed and what changes. We hold fixed the nominal money supply but allow a drop in planned spending to shift the *IS* curve to the left. This change might occur because of a decline in consumer or business confidence, a decline in government spending, an increase in tax rates, an increase in autonomous net taxes, or a drop in the autonomous component of net exports.

When the *IS* curve shifts leftward in the top frame of Figure 7-3, the economy's equilibrium position shifts southwest from point E_0 to point F, at the crossing point of the new *IS* curve and the unchanged *LM* curve, drawn for the unchanged nominal money supply (M_0^s) and a given price level (P_0). In the bottom frame if the price level remains at P_0, the economy shifts from point E_0 to point F. Real GDP falls from Y_0 to Y_3. The drop in planned spending creates a leftward shift in the *AD* curve.

Figure 7-3
The Effect on the *AD* Curve of a Decline in Planned Autonomous Spending

Any event that reduces planned autonomous spending by shifting the *IS* curve leftward also creates a parallel leftward shift in the *AD* curve. Such events could include a drop in business or consumer confidence, a cut in government spending, an increase in tax rates, an increase in autonomous net taxes, or a reduction in the autonomous component of net exports. If the price level remains stable at P_0, the economy shifts leftward to point F and real income drops to Y_3. Another possibility is that the price level could drop to P_3, moving the economy down to point G and allowing real income to remain at the original Y_0. A drop in the price level to P_3 would increase the real money supply and shift the *LM* curve to the right in the top frame.

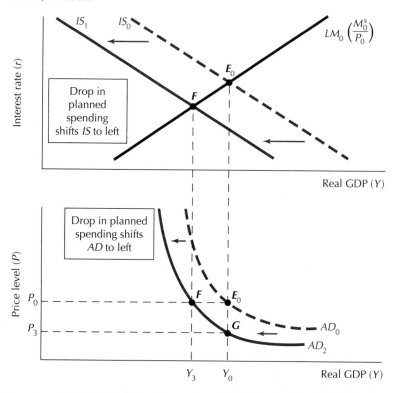

DOES A DECLINE IN PLANNED SPENDING CUT REAL INCOME, THE PRICE LEVEL, OR BOTH?

Comparing the bottom frames of Figures 7-2 and 7-3, we note that the shifts in the *AD* curve are different. A change in the nominal money supply, as in Figure 7-2, shifts the *AD* curve up or down *vertically.* However, a change in autonomous spending in Figure 7-3 shifts the *AD* curve to the left or right *horizontally.* The decline in real GDP in the bottom frame that results from a given leftward shift in the *IS* curve is exactly the same, no matter whether the initial price level is low or high.

Will the reduction in planned spending reduce real income and leave the price level unchanged? If so, the economy will move from point E_0 to point F, and real income will fall from Y_0 to Y_3. Or, will the reduction in planned spending reduce the price level and leave real income unchanged? If so, the economy will move from point E_0 to point G, and the price level will fall from P_0 to P_3. Which outcome will occur? Figure 7-3 cannot tell us, because the *AD* curve by itself does not contain enough information to pin down both the price level and real income. To ascertain where the economy will come to rest along the numerous possible positions along the *AD* curve, we must find another schedule to intersect the *AD* curve. We now turn to the possible shapes of this additional schedule, called the "short-run aggregate supply curve," and to its derivation.

7-4   Alternative Shapes of the Short-Run Aggregate Supply Curve

The short-run aggregate supply schedule shows how much business firms are willing to produce at different hypothetical price levels. Such a schedule of business firms' behavior can have several possible shapes. Depending on the shape, the implications of a shift in the aggregate demand curve (whether caused by an increase in the money supply or in autonomous spending) are quite different. In Figure 7-4 we show a rightward shift in the aggregate demand curve from AD_0 to AD_1.

Figure 7-4
Effect of a Rightward Shift in the *AD* Curve with Three Alternative Short-Run Aggregate Supply Curves

The horizontal supply curve at the price level P_0 reflects the "fixed price" assumption of Chapters 3–5. An increase in aggregate demand that shifts the AD_0 curve to AD_1 will move the economy from its initial position E_0 to new position E_1. In contrast, if the supply curve is vertical, higher aggregate demand pushes the economy from point E_0 to E_3. An intermediate possibility is that both output and prices rise *in the short run* to a point such as E_2, and that *in the long run* the *boost* in real GDP gradually disappears until we arrive at E_3.

THE REACTION OF REAL GDP AND THE PRICE LEVEL TO HIGHER AGGREGATE DEMAND DEPENDS ON THE SHAPE OF THE AGGREGATE SUPPLY CURVE

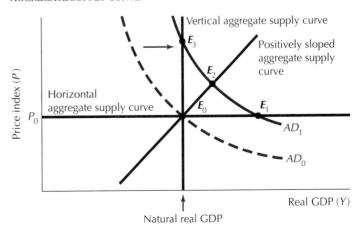

How will the increase in aggregate demand be divided between a higher level of real GDP and a higher price level? Three hypothetical answers, corresponding to three hypothetical aggregate supply curves, are shown in Figure 7-4. In Chapter 4 we assumed that the price level always remains fixed; thus we assumed that the economy moved from its initial position E_0 directly rightward to a higher level of real GDP at point E_1 along the horizontal aggregate supply curve. A second possibility is that real GDP is always fixed at the level of natural real GDP. If so, the same increase in aggregate demand would have no effect at all on real GDP. Instead, business firms would simply raise the price level from P_0 to a higher price level at point E_3 along the vertical aggregate supply curve in Figure 7-4, leaving their level of production (Y) unchanged. As we shall see, natural real GDP is the only output level consistent with equilibrium in the labor market.

A third possibility is shown by the line labeled "positively sloped aggregate supply curve." If this curve were valid, then the rightward shift in aggregate demand would cause business firms to raise *both* their prices and their level of production, moving the economy to a point like E_2. As we shall see, a point like E_2 is likely to be achieved only temporarily. In succeeding periods the positively sloped aggregate supply curve is likely to shift its position, so that eventually the economy winds up at a point like E_3, with real GDP back where it started but with a higher price level.

Comparative statics is a technique of economic analysis in which a comparison is made between two equilibrium positions but ignoring the behavior of the economy—either the length of time required or the route followed during the transition between the initial and final positions.

This analysis shares with previous chapters the approach of **comparative statics.** Our basic diagram measures the level, not the rate of change, of real output and the price level. Our analysis is just like a show of photographic slides. We show one slide in the form of a single static equilibrium position, we turn out the lights, and, when the lights come back on, the economy has moved to a new static equilibrium position, such as point E_2 in Figure 7-4. Our comparative static slide-show method of analysis cannot tell us anything about economic dynamics. How long does it take output and the price level to change? What is the rate of price change (the inflation rate) per year or per month? We will examine the dynamic relationship between the rate of inflation and real GDP in the next chapter.

7-5   The Aggregate Supply Curve When the Nominal Wage Rate Is Constant

In this section we show how an upward-sloping short-run aggregate supply curve, like that going through point E_2 in Figure 7-4, can be derived from the behavior of firms in the labor market. In our derivation the behavior of workers plays no role. We simply assume that the nominal wage rate is fixed at a particular value. Subsequently we will examine the factors that cause the nominal wage rate to change, and the effects of such a change on the position of the short-run aggregate supply curve.

The Short-Run Aggregate Supply Curve

We begin in the lower left-hand frame of Figure 7-5, which plots the real wage (W/P) on the vertical axis and the level of employment (N) on the horizontal axis. Since the real wage is the price that firms pay to hire workers, the downward-sloping labor demand curve (N_0^d) simply states that a decrease in the

A HIGHER PRICE LEVEL INDUCES BUSINESS FIRMS TO SUPPLY MORE REAL GDP

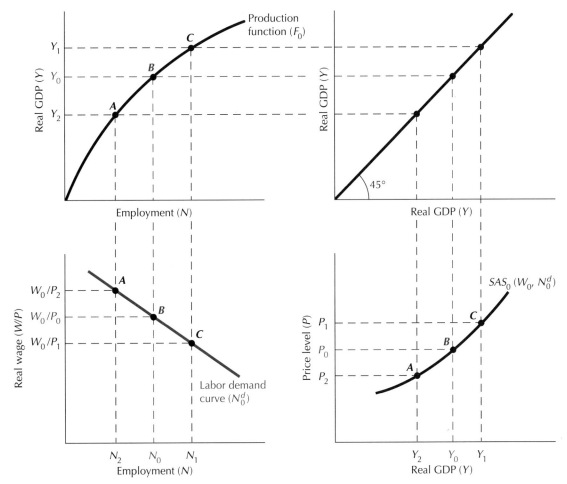

Figure 7-5   **The Labor Demand Curve, the Production Function, and the Short-Run Aggregate Supply Curve**

The lower left-hand frame displays the labor demand curve, which shows that a decline in the real wage induces firms to hire additional workers. The upper left-hand frame displays the production function, showing how much real GDP can be produced by differing numbers of workers. The lower right-hand frame shows that a higher price level (by reducing the real wage and inducing firms to hire additional workers) raises real GDP.

real wage will induce firms to hire more workers, and vice versa. Any given labor demand curve holds constant other factors of production that work together with labor, e.g., land, capital, materials, and energy. The vertical position of the labor demand curve represents the marginal product of labor; the labor demand curve slopes downward because the marginal product of labor declines as additional workers are hired to work with a fixed quantity of land, capital, materials, and energy.[3]

---

[3]The decline in the marginal product as one factor of production is added while the quantity of other factors remains fixed is called the "law of diminishing returns."

Firms hire workers up to the point that the real wage equals their marginal product. For instance, at point B in the lower left-hand frame of Figure 7-5, a real wage of W_0/P_0 induces firms to hire N_0 workers. To hire workers beyond that point, say to hire N_1 workers at point C, would mean hiring workers having a marginal product of labor less than the assumed real wage of W_0/P_0, causing firms to lose money on those extra workers.

The vertical position of the labor demand curve depends on everything that determines the marginal product of labor, including other factors of production (e.g., land, capital, materials, and energy) as well as the level of technology used by the firm. An increase in the quantity of any factor of production or in the level of technology will shift the labor demand curve upward, and vice versa.

The production function and the aggregate supply curve.   Now we can examine the relationship between employment and real GDP at different price levels. For instance, point B in the lower left frame shows that N_0 workers will be hired if the price level is P_0 and real wage is W_0/P_0. Looking directly above point B to the top left frame of Figure 7-5, we see a corresponding point B on the production function that shows the amount of real GDP (Y_0) that can be produced by N_0 workers. Then, following the dashed line to the right and down, we come to a third point B in the lower right frame. This shows that the price level P_0 induces firms to produce Y_0, as long as the wage rate is W_0. Similarly, we can trace around the diagram and find the amount of output that will be produced if the price level is higher, as at P_1, and lower, as at P_2.

The line connecting points A, B, and C in the lower right frame is the short-run aggregate supply curve, labeled with the symbol SAS. It slopes upward because a higher price level reduces the real wage and induces firms to hire more workers, which in turn raises real GDP. Notice that all three points—A, B, and C—share exactly the same nominal wage rate (W_0). For this reason, the SAS curve is labeled with the wage rate assumed in drawing it, W_0. Only the price level differs among the three points. Because a change in the price level also changes the real wage, it changes employment and real GDP. However, because the SAS curve is only valid over a short period before the nominal wage rate changes, it is called the *short-run* aggregate supply curve.

know how to derive it & why, slopes upward & what the effect of a p↑ or↓ is on GDP, emp, wage, etc.

SELF-TEST

> Which of the following causes a movement *along* the short-run aggregate supply *(SAS)* curve, and which causes a shift in the curve? If the curve shifts, does it shift up or down? (1) A union concession that reduces the wage rate to help a firm survive foreign competition. (2) A discovery of a giant oil field in Missouri that reduces the price of oil. (3) An increase in the money supply.

7-6   How the Wage Rate Is Set

So far we have seen that the aggregate supply curve slopes upward for any *given* nominal wage rate. But surely the wage rate will not stay at the same level forever. If the wage rate increases, the SAS curve will shift up, and its intersection point with the economy's aggregate demand curve *(AD)* will shift as well.

LEARNING ABOUT DIAGRAMS: *THE* SAS *CURVE*

The short-run aggregate supply curve, abbreviated *SAS*, depicts the amount of output that business firms are willing to produce at different alternative price levels.

Diagram Elements and Reasons for Slope

The *SAS* curve is plotted with the same vertical and horizontal axes as the *AD* curve; the aggregate price level is on the vertical axis and real GDP (same as real income) is on the horizontal axis. Examples are shown in the lower right quadrant of Figures 7-5 and 7-6.

The *SAS* curve slopes up because, with a fixed nominal wage rate, a higher price level makes it profitable for business firms to increase output. Since increasing output requires adding more workers, each of whom is less productive than the last, the real wage must decline for firms to be willing to produce more output, and hence the price level must increase.

The greater the decline in worker productivity as additional workers are added, the steeper is the *SAS* curve.

What Shifts the SAS Curve?

The *SAS* curve is drawn for a fixed nominal wage rate and a fixed set of determinants of the labor demand curve (symbolized by the production function showing how much each additional worker can produce).

A given percentage change in the nominal wage rate will shift the *SAS* curve upward by the same per-

centage. When the nominal wage rate and the price level (drawn on the vertical axis) increase by the same percentage, the real wage is fixed, employment and output are fixed, and we remain at the same horizontal position in the diagram.

Anything that shifts the production function will also shift the *SAS* curve. Larger inputs of capital, materials, or energy will shift the production function up and the *SAS* curve to the right, allowing more output to be produced at a given price level (because workers have become more productive). The reverse is also true; an event like a sharp increase in oil prices can reduce nonlabor inputs like energy, shifting the *SAS* curve to the left.

What Is True of Points That Are Off the SAS Curve?

Since the *SAS* curve shows the different combinations of output and the price level consistent with profit maximization by business firms, any point off the *SAS* curve would not be chosen by these firms.

A point to the right of the *SAS* curve indicates that firms are producing too much, hiring workers whose marginal product is below their real wage. Firms could boost profits by reducing output.

A point to the left of the *SAS* curve indicates that firms are producing too little, since additional workers could be hired who produce more than their real wage. Firms could boost profits by raising output.

Thus the determinants of the actual wage rate paid have a crucial effect on the nature of the economy's response to a change in aggregate demand.

The Equilibrium Real Wage Rate

Distinguishing the nominal and real wage rates. We first encountered the distinction between nominal and real variables in Chapter 2, where we introduced nominal and real GDP. The nominal wage rate is simply the actual wage rate paid. This is assumed to be a fixed amount in the derivation of supply curve SAS_0 of Figure 7-5. The real wage rate (W/P) is the nominal wage rate (W) divided by an aggregate price index such as the GDP deflator.

In Figure 7-6 we can see in operation the distinction between the nominal and real wage rates. As long as the labor demand curve is at the fixed position N_0^d, an increase in employment from N_0 to N_1 requires a decrease in the real wage rate from W_0/P_0 to W_0/P_1. If the nominal wage rate W_0 remains fixed, then this required decline in the real wage rate *must* be accomplished by an increase in the price level. When P increases and W remains fixed, the increase in labor employed, and hence in real output, causes the aggregate supply curve to slope up in the lower right frame of Figure 7-6.

A HIGHER NOMINAL WAGE RATE SHIFTS THE *SAS* CURVE UP

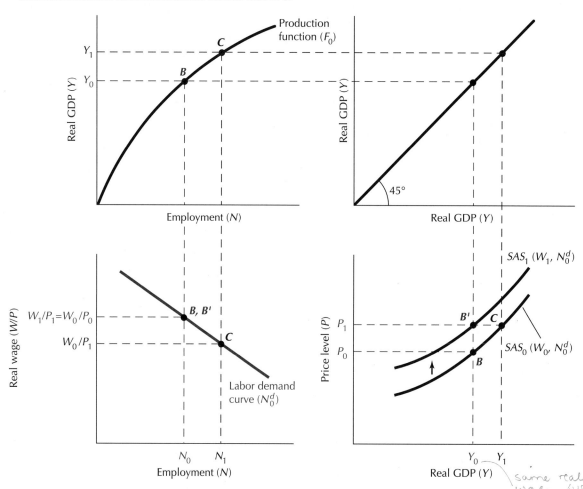

Figure 7-6   **The Short-Run Aggregate Supply Curve for Two Different Values of the Wage Rate, W_0 and W_1**

The labor demand curve, production function, and aggregate supply curve SAS_0 are identical to those drawn in Figure 7-5. So also are points B and C, the quantities N_0 and Y_0, and the price levels P_0 and P_1. The new ingredient here is a higher wage rate W_1, which shifts the aggregate supply curve up from SAS_0 to SAS_1. The higher wage rate shifts the *SAS* curve because at a given price level, workers are more costly, and so firms hire fewer workers and produce less output. Points B and B' in the lower left-hand frame are identical, because we assume that the percentage difference between W_1 and W_0 is the same as between P_1 and P_0. Thus point B' lies directly above point B in the lower right-hand frame.

But the nominal wage rate is unlikely to stay fixed forever. If it shifts up to W_1, then the aggregate supply curve will shift up from SAS_0 to SAS_1. In Figure 7-6 we assume that W_1 exceeds W_0 by the same percentage as P_1 exceeds P_0, so

$$\frac{W_1}{P_1} = \frac{W_0}{P_0}$$

Thus the real wage rate W_1/P_1 at point B' along the new SAS_1 line is exactly the same as the real wage rate W_0/P_0 at point B. Hence, the level of employment and real GDP (N_0 and Y_0) must be identical at points B and B'. Indeed we see in the lower left frame of Figure 7-6 that points B and B' coincide.

Determinants of the equilibrium real wage rate.   In Chapter 3 we defined equilibrium as a situation in which there is no pressure for change. The key insight into understanding aggregate supply behavior is the concept of the **equilibrium real wage rate,** which is determined by the intersection of labor demand and supply curves. In Figure 7-7 we have copied our previous labor demand curve (N_0^d), which shows the marginal product of additional labor input.

The supply of labor is also assumed to depend on the real wage, and in Figure 7-7 labor supply is represented by a labor supply curve that slopes upward. This indicates that a higher real wage rate would induce a higher quantity of labor supplied. For instance, a higher real wage rate might induce homemakers to take outside jobs by increasing their willingness to put up with the inconvenience of commuting and arranging day care for their children. A higher real wage rate might also make people more willing to moonlight, sacrificing leisure and sleep to take second jobs.

The position of the labor supply curve can shift if anything occurs that makes people more or less willing to take jobs at a given real wage rate. For instance, an increase in the working-age population, due to immigration or a high birth rate, will tend to shift the labor supply curve to the right. Factors that make jobs less attractive—for instance, the availability of generous

> The **equilibrium real wage rate** is the real wage rate for the point at which the labor supply and demand curves intersect, so there is no pressure for change.

Figure 7-7
Determination of the Equilibrium Real Wage Rate

Here the labor demand curve (N_0^d) is the same as in Figures 7-5 and 7-6. But now we add a labor supply curve (N_0^s). This slopes upward, indicating that more people will be willing to take jobs at a higher real wage rate. Whenever an event pushes the economy away from point B, there is pressure for the real wage rate to change, as shown by the arrows.

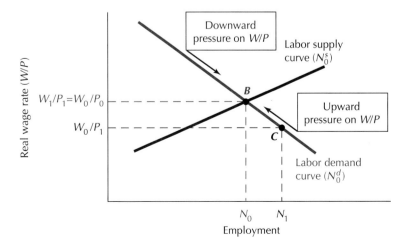

ANYWHERE AWAY FROM POINT B THERE IS PRESSURE FOR CHANGE

unemployment or welfare benefits for those not working—will tend to shift the labor supply curve to the left.

The equilibrium real wage rate is simply the real wage rate located where the labor demand curve crosses the labor supply curve. Such an intersection occurs at point B in Figure 7-7, with an equilibrium level of employment (N_0) and an equilibrium real wage (W_0/P_0). The diagram poses a dilemma for firms, however. If firms are to raise employment from N_0 to N_1, the real wage rate must be reduced, as shown at point C. But point C does not lie on the labor supply curve.

Employers need to find some factor that will make workers willing to provide more work than shown by their labor supply curve. Otherwise, we would never observe changes in employment, nor changes in real GDP, over the business cycle.

Pressure for change at point *C*.   At the equilibrium real wage rate, point B in Figure 7-7, by definition there is no pressure for W or N to change. But at point C, a real wage below equilibrium, *there is pressure for the real wage rate to rise.* This is the essence of our simple theory of how the nominal wage rate is set. We start at point B, with the economy in equilibrium. Then an increase in aggregate demand pushes up the price level, say from P_0 to P_1. The real wage falls, and the economy moves from B to C in Figure 7-7. Because the real wage has dropped below its equilibrium value, there is upward pressure for change. Workers demand real wage increases. As soon as the real wage increases are granted, the nominal wage rate rises from W_0 to W_1, and the real wage returns to its initial value, $W_1/P_1 = W_0/P_0$.

7-7   Fiscal and Monetary Expansion in the Short and Long Run

In Chapters 4 and 5 we examined the effect of a fiscal stimulus, assuming that the price level was fixed, and we found that the fiscal stimulus normally raised real output. Now we learn that the fiscal stimulus causes both output and the price level to increase in the short run.

In Figure 7-8, we begin in equilibrium at point B, with an actual price level equal to P_0. This is exactly the same as point B in Figures 7-5 and 7-6.

Initial Short-Run Effect of a Fiscal Expansion

Now a fiscal stimulus is introduced, in the form of an increase in government purchases that shifts the aggregate demand curve rightward from AD_0 to AD_1. Where do we find the new equilibrium levels of output and the price index? If the price level were to remain constant, we would move straight to the right from point B to point L. But the price level cannot remain fixed, because firms will insist on an increase in the price level in order to reduce the real wage and induce an increase in employment sufficient to raise the level of real GDP. In short, point L is off the short-run supply curve SAS_0 and is not a point at which firms will be willing to produce.

Be able to explain this & why pt.s like L are not stable

Figure 7-8
Effects on the Price Level and Real Income of an Increase in Planned Autonomous Spending from A_0 to A_1

Higher planned autonomous spending shifts the economy's equilibrium position from the initial point B to point C, where both the price level and the real output have increased. Point C is not a sustainable position, however, because the real wage rate has fallen below the equilibrium real wage rate. Only at point E_3 does the actual real wage rate return to its initial equilibrium value.

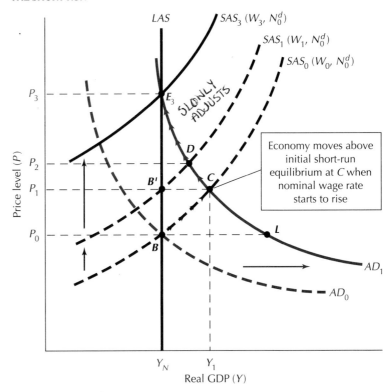

A FISCAL EXPANSION RAISES BOTH THE PRICE LEVEL AND REAL GDP IN THE SHORT RUN

Point C is at the intersection of the new AD_1 schedule and the SAS_0 schedule. The increase in government purchases has simultaneously raised the price level to P_1 and increased output to Y_1. This shift has occurred because higher aggregate demand has raised prices, stimulating business firms to produce more, at least as long as the wage rate fails to adjust.

Note that output has not increased by the full Chapter 4 multiplier based on a fixed price level, the horizontal distance between B and L. Instead, point C lies northwest of the constant price point L, because the higher price level at C reduces the real money supply and hence the demand for commodities. The situation illustrated in Figure 7-8 at point C would result from any stimulative factor that raises aggregate demand—not only an increase in government purchases, but also cuts in tax rates, or increases in transfer payments, business and consumer confidence, net exports, or the money supply. As long as the SAS curve slopes upward to the right, any of these changes will shift the AD curve rightward and simultaneously raise both output and prices to point C.

The Rising Nominal Wage Rate and the Arrival at Long-Run Equilibrium

Point C is not the end of the adjustment of the economy to the higher level of government purchases, however, because business firms are satisfied but

INTERNATIONAL PERSPECTIVE

How Do Labor Markets Differ in the United States and Japan?

THE UNITED STATES

The text and Figure 7-8 show that the slow adjustment of the nominal wage rate, often called "wage rigidity," is a crucial ingredient in explaining how business cycles in output can occur. The uniquely American system of three-year overlapping staggered contracts makes nominal wage rates more rigid and aggravates fluctuations in output and employment. This system can be traced to the 1948 contract between the United Auto Workers and General Motors, which established the first multiyear contract. It was the high cost of negotiation, as perceived by managers besieged in 1946–48 with annual strikes or threats of strikes, that led to the 1948 General Motors contract. The GM president had the idea of buying labor peace through a long-term contract, "bribing" the union with the first cost-of-living

protection. Since 1953 there have been eleven 3-year contracts in the auto industry. And statistical data show that U.S. wages and prices have been less flexible since 1950 than in the decades before 1950.

In explaining why the United States developed three-year contracts but the Japanese did not, differences in the perceived importance of industrial conflict played a major role. The United States had unionized in a hurry after the 1935 Wagner Act provided legal protection to unions. The first large-scale industrial conflicts in the late 1930s were widely publicized. Partly because unionization took the form of large industrial unions in key industries, especially coal, steel, and automobiles, there was a widespread perception that strikes were costly.

JAPAN

There are three features that are unique to Japanese labor markets—the lifetime employment system, the system of simultaneous one-year wage contracts, and large semiannual bonus payments based, at least partly, on the idea of profit-sharing.

The Japanese labor market is characterized by very low unemployment rates (averaging around 2 percent and in the recent economic slump rising

workers are not. The price level has risen from P_0 at point B to P_1 at point C. But for business firms to continue producing at point C would require a drop in the real wage rate, just as in Figure 7-7.

Each SAS curve assumes that the nominal wage rate is fixed at a particular value, which is W_0 for the supply curve SAS_0. Once workers learn that the actual price level has risen, they will discover to their dismay that the real wage rate has fallen. To achieve a return of their real wage to the original level, at the next round of wage bargaining workers will insist on an increase in the nominal wage rate to W_1. Just as in Figure 7-6, the new aggregate supply schedule SAS_1 shows the consequences of an increase in the nominal wage rate from W_0 to W_1.

Clearly the economy moves to point D, with a higher price level P_2. But now at point D once again workers are upset. The real wage rate is W_1/P_2,

only to 3.5 percent), relatively stable employment, and relatively flexible wages. Fostering these desirable features is the system of lifetime employment, in which workers and firms 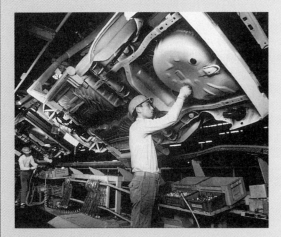 develop long-term attachments that last until retirement at the relatively early age of 55. Workers rarely quit to take jobs at rival firms, and firms reciprocate by rarely resorting to layoffs. The lifetime employment system is not universal; it is mainly concentrated in large firms and does not apply to women or employees of the numerous subcontractors and other satellite firms that act as a buffer during economic downturns.

The most important aspect of lifetime employment is the role of seniority rather than ability in determining payment; all 50-year-old workers are paid more than all 40-year-old workers, and pay differences among 50-year-old workers are minor. This payment sys-

tem tends to foster a feeling of equality, in contrast to the class distinctions that are more evident in many American and European firms. Pay differences between top executives and blue-collar workers are much smaller in Japan (and some European countries like Sweden) than in the United States.

Greater equality, in turn, reduces the potential for conflict between workers and firms, thus lowering costs of negotiation and causing both sides to be less concerned about the possibility of strikes. With less fear of strikes, both sides are more willing to enter into one-year wage contracts, in contrast to the U.S. three-year contracts that are designed, in part, to reduce the strike frequency.

In conclusion, economics provides some insight into labor market institutions by suggesting that contract forms may reflect a weighing of benefits and costs. For instance, three-year contracts achieve the benefit of reducing strikes at the cost of allowing a less frequent reaction by wage rates to macroeconomic events. But economics must be supplemented by sociology and history to provide a more complete understanding of why contract forms and duration differ across countries.

lower than the equilibrium real wage rate. Again they insist on an increase in the nominal wage rate. Eventually the economy must move up the AD_1 line to point E_3. Why? Because only at the initial level of real GDP (Y_0) and employment (N_0) is the real wage rate at its equilibrium value (W_0/P_0). Any time the economy is operating in the area to the right of Y_0, there is upward pressure on the nominal wage rate, and *SAS* will shift up.

The Long-Run Aggregate Supply Curve

The **long-run aggregate supply curve** is a vertical line drawn at the natural level of real GDP; it shows that equilibrium in the labor market can be achieved at many different price levels but only a single level of output.

The vertical line rising above the original real GDP level (Y_0) is called the **long-run aggregate supply curve (LAS).** Only at this one level of output, also called natural real GDP (Y^N), is the labor market in equilibrium at the original real wage (W_0/P_0). This is the only level of output where there is no pressure for change in the real wage, since this is the only level of output (and employment) where business firms are willing to produce and where workers are content with the real wage rate. This point of equilibrium in the labor market is where the labor supply and demand curves cross (in Figure 7-7).

> *Thus, only at the natural level of real GDP* (Y^N) *is the actual real wage rate equal to the equilibrium real wage rate. The vertical* LAS *line shows all the possible combinations of the price level* (P) *and natural real GDP* (Y^N).

does this correspond w/ IS/LM eq. too?

Short-Run and Long-Run Equilibrium

Short-run equilibrium occurs at the point where the aggregate demand curve crosses the short-run aggregate supply curve.

The economy is in **short-run equilibrium** when two conditions are satisfied. First, the level of output produced must be enough to balance the demand for commodities without any involuntary accumulation or decumulation of inventory. This first condition is satisfied at any point along the appropriate *AD* curve. Second, the price level *P* must be sufficient to make firms both able and willing to produce the level of output specified along the *AD* curve. This can happen only along a short-run supply curve *(SAS)* specified for a particular nominal wage rate (W_0).

Long-run equilibrium is a situation in which labor input is the amount voluntarily supplied and demanded at the equilibrium real wage rate.

The economy is in **long-run equilibrium** only when all the conditions for a short-run equilibrium are satisfied, and, in addition, the real wage rate is at its equilibrium value. In Figure 7-8, long-run equilibrium occurs only where all three schedules—*AD, SAS,* and *LAS*—intersect. The reason why the economy does not move immediately to its new long-run equilibrium following an *AD* shift is that adjustment takes time and there are time lags in the response of wages and prices.

SELF-TEST

> If the economy is to remain in long-run equilibrium, what must happen to the price level, the wage level, and the level of real GDP when the following events occur? (1) An increase in government-financed highway construction. (2) An increase in Japanese GDP that boosts U.S. net exports. (3) An increase in the U.S. money supply.

Interpretations of the Business Cycle

The preceding theory of price and output adjustment contains several troubling elements that have perplexed students and teachers for decades. First, it does not identify the factors that make workers willing to provide more or less employment than indicated along their labor supply curve. Second, the

A **countercyclical variable** moves over the business cycle in the opposite direction from real GDP.

theory requires a **countercyclical** movement of the real wage; that is, a movement in the real wage in the opposite direction from the movement in real GDP. But numerous statistical studies have failed to find the required countercyclical fluctuations in the real wage rate, thus raising a basic question about the validity of the theory. Finally, the theory does not recognize that labor markets behave quite differently in different countries, as the International Perspective box illustrates for the cases of Japan and the United States.

These concerns raise several questions about the sources of business cycles. Is it rational for workers to agree to work more in a business cycle expansion in order for output to increase? Will output increase if workers *know* that the source of the increase in aggregate demand is a deliberate attempt by the government to stimulate demand by conducting expansionary monetary or fiscal policy? Is a monetary or fiscal expansion of which workers and firms are aware effective in raising output, or is such expansion ineffective, leaving no trace of an effect on output but rather just causing the price level in Figure 7-8 to jump? Macroeconomics offers several schools of thought on these issues, and we now turn to some of the conflicting views.

7-8 Classical Macroeconomics: The Quantity Theory of Money and the Self-Correcting Economy

The classical economists who predated Keynes's *General Theory,* including Adam Smith, David Ricardo, John Stuart Mill, Alfred Marshall, and Arthur C. Pigou, believed that the economy possessed powerful **self-correcting forces** that guaranteed full employment and prevented actual real GDP *(Y)* from falling below natural real GDP (Y^N) for more than a short time. These forces consisted of flexible wages and prices, which would adjust rapidly to absorb the impact of shifts in aggregate demand. Because the classical economists did not believe that business cycles in real output or in unemployment were problems, they saw no need for the government to engage in stabilization policy.

The economy's **self-correcting forces** refer to the role of flexible prices in stabilizing real GDP under some conditions.

The Quantity Equation and the Quantity Theory of Money

The most important macroeconomic model developed by classical economists is the famous "quantity equation," relating the nominal money supply (M^s) and velocity *(V)* to the price level *(P)* and real GDP *(Y).*

$$M^s V = PY \qquad (7.1)$$

The quantity equation is true by definition, simply because velocity is *defined* as $V = PY/M^s$.

To convert the quantity equation into a theory, classical economists assumed that any change in M^s or *V* on the left-hand side of the equation would be balanced by a proportional change in *P* on the right-hand side of the equation, with no change in real GDP *(Y).* Primary emphasis in this theory, called the **quantity theory of money,** was placed on the idea that changes in the money supply (M^s) cause proportional changes in the price level *P.* Why did the theory focus on M^s rather than *V*? Velocity *(V)* was regarded as being relatively stable and primarily determined by changes in payment methods (for instance, cash vs. checks) that gradually evolved over time. Over shorter periods of two to five years, business cycles were attributed mainly to changes in the money supply.

The **quantity theory of money** holds that actual output tends to grow steadily, while velocity is determined by payment practices such as the use of cash vs. checks; as a result a change in the money supply mainly affects the price level and has little or no effect on velocity or output.

Any theory can be analyzed in terms of the quantity equation (7.1). For instance, the *IS-LM* model of Chapter 4 examines the effect of a change in government spending, which causes a shift in the *IS* curve but not in the *LM* curve, reflecting the assumption that changes in government spending do not change the money supply. Since both M^s and P are fixed, higher government spending raises V on the left-hand side of equation (7.1) and raises Y on the right-hand side. In this sense, the analysis of shifts in planned spending in the fixed-price *IS-LM* model is the opposite of the quantity theory, linking changes of V to changes in Y, unlike the quantity theory that links changes in M^s to changes in P.

Self-Correction in the Aggregate Demand-Supply Model

The approach of the old classicists, whose analytical model primarily relied on the quantity theory of money, can be translated into the aggregate demand and supply model developed in this chapter. Figure 7-9 has the same elements as Figure 7-8 but lacks a short-run aggregate supply *(SAS)* curve.

The classical economists assumed that the economy would not operate away from the long-run aggregate supply curve *(LAS)*. For instance, if a decline in demand caused the *AD* curve to shift leftward from AD_0 to AD_1 in Figure 7-9, the classical economists would predict that the economy would move from the initial point E_0 to the new point E_1 with only a brief interval (shown by the curved arrow on the left) during which actual real GDP would decline below natural real GDP. The price level would fall from its initial level at P_0 to the new level P_1.

The classical economists took the same view of the economy's behavior in response to an increase in aggregate demand. With Y above Y^N, firms would raise nominal wage rates and prices. Wage and price increases would continue until production fell back to the Y^N level.

Because the downward and upward movement of the economy from E_0 to E_1 and back again would not involve any significant movement of real GDP (Y) away from natural real GDP (Y^N), *no business cycle in real GDP would occur.* Yet there would be a business cycle in the price level, from P_0 down to P_1 and

---

Figure 7-9
Effect of a Decline in Planned Spending When the Price Level Is Perfectly Flexible

The classical economists assumed that the price level would decline whenever a drop in aggregate demand occurred. Starting from point E_0, a drop in planned spending would shift the *AD* curve from AD_0 to AD_1 and move the economy straight down to point E_1. The level of real GDP remains at Y^N, because the lower price level raises the level of real balances (M_0^s/P) by exactly enough to offset the decline in planned spending. A shift back to AD_0 would raise the price level and return the economy to the original position E_0.

A BUSINESS CYCLE IN PRICES, NOT IN REAL GDP OR UNEMPLOYMENT

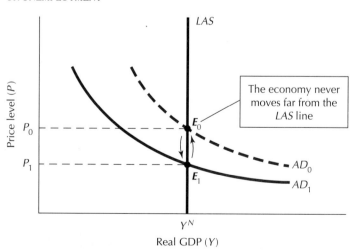

back to P_0, and it was this movement in the price level that the classical economists attempted to explain in their early theories of the business cycle. However, classical economists did not view price movements as sufficiently undesirable to warrant the intervention of government stabilization policy.

Classical View of Unemployment and Output Fluctuations

We have seen that classical economists did not believe that real GDP could remain for more than a short period below natural real GDP (Y^N). How, then, did they explain the unemployment that occurs in real-world modern economies when people are laid off and production is cut back? Jobless individuals were sometimes written off as irresponsible, having an insufficient desire to work. Any normal person would be compelled by hunger to seek work, some classical economists thought. And most believed that if there were not enough jobs to go around, competition among workers would reduce the real wage rate until an equilibrium was obtained in the labor market.

Although some journalists and a few isolated economists (including Karl Marx and Friedrich Engels) began to suggest that unemployment was an inevitable by-product of the newly emerging industrial society of England in the mid-nineteenth century, most classical economists dismissed unemployment as a transitory, self-correcting condition of only minor social importance. In fact, the term *unemployment* did not exist until the early twentieth century.

Ironically, some governments outside the United States developed unemployment insurance before classical economists were willing to recognize the existence of prolonged unemployment. The world's first unemployment insurance system was introduced in the United Kingdom by Winston Churchill in 1911; only afterward, in 1913, was the first important book by a classical economist (Arthur C. Pigou) written on the subject of unemployment.[4] The book attributed such unemployment as existed to the failure of wages to adjust fast enough to maintain equilibrium in the labor market. Suggested cures for unemployment involved remedies for wage stickiness rather than any suggestion that there was a role for the government to intervene and stimulate aggregate demand through expansionary monetary or fiscal policy.

7-9   The Keynesian Revolution: The Failure of Self-Correction

The Great Depression began with the stock market crash in late 1929 and by 1932 real GDP had declined by one-third and unemployment had spiraled

---

[4]This was Arthur C. Pigou's *Unemployment.* The description of the views of the classical economists in this section is taken from the much more detailed and fully documented treatment in John A. Garraty, *Unemployment in History: Economic Thought and Public Policy* (New York: Harper & Row, 1978), pp. 70–145.

John Maynard Keynes

(1883–1946) His The General Theory of Employment, Interest, and Money *(1936) is one of the most influential works in economics in the twentieth century.*

Monetary impotence is the failure of real GDP to respond to an increase in the real money supply.

Rigid wages refers to the failure of the nominal wage rate to adjust by the amount needed to maintain equilibrium in the labor market.

upward beyond 20 percent. Classical economists were caught flat-footed, without any explanation for the severe and prolonged unemployment beyond the claim that for some reason real wages were too high. Economics had lost its intellectual moorings, and it was time for a new diagnosis. In this atmosphere, it was perhaps not surprising that the 1936 publication of Keynes's *The General Theory of Employment, Interest, and Money* was eagerly awaited. Its publication transformed macroeconomics, and only one year later John R. Hicks published an article in which he set out the *IS-LM* model of Chapter 4 as an interpretation of what Keynes had written.

Monetary Impotence and the Failure of Self-Correction in Extreme Cases

We can use the aggregate demand and supply curves to illustrate Keynes's analysis of the high unemployment that bedeviled the world's economy in the 1930s. For Keynes, the economic problem could be divided into two categories, one concerning demand and one concerning supply. The demand problem was the possibility of **monetary impotence,** while the supply problem was that of **rigid wages.**

Unresponsive expenditures: The vertical *IS* curve. As we learned in Section 5-2, increases in the real money supply *(M^s/P)* can have either strong or weak effects, depending on the shapes of the *IS* and *LM* curves. One case of monetary impotence occurs when the *IS* curve is vertical. Any change in the nominal money supply shifts the *LM* curve up and down along the vertical and unchanging *IS* curve, leaving real GDP unaffected. Just as important, any decline in the price level *(P)* that raises the real money supply *(M^s/P)* leaves real GDP unaffected.

We examined a vertical *IS* curve in Figure 5-2; now, in Figure 7-10, we observe its implications for the aggregate demand curve. If *IS* is vertical at an income level like *Y′* , then a decline in *P* has no power to raise real GDP above

---

Figure 7-10
The Lack of Effect of a Drop in the Price Level When There Is a Failure of Self-Correction

The conditions of a failure of self-correction are either (1) a vertical *IS* curve that lies to the left of Y^N, or (2) a normal *IS* curve that intersects a horizontal *LM* curve to the left of Y^N. With a failure of self-correction, the aggregate demand schedule is a vertical line like *AD′*, in contrast to the normally sloped AD_0 curve. Because of a failure of self-correction, the higher real money supply is unable to stimulate the economy; thus, a decline in the price level just moves the economy down from *F* to *F′* to *F″*.

A VERTICAL *AD* LINE IMPLIES A FAILURE OF SELF-CORRECTION

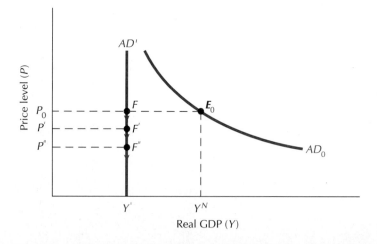

Y', so the aggregate demand curve is the vertical line AD' in Figure 7-10. Shown for contrast in Figure 7-10 is a normally sloped AD_0 curve, copied from Figure 7-8.

The liquidity trap: A horizontal *LM* curve.   The same problem of a vertical AD' curve that fails to intersect the *LAS* line may occur even with a normally sloped *IS* curve, if there is a horizontal *LM* curve and *if the* IS *curve intersects this horizontal* LM *curve to the left of* Y^N (a nearly horizontal *LM* curve was illustrated in the bottom frame of Figure 5-2). In this case an increase in M^s/P does not shift the *LM* curve down. Real GDP is stuck at, for example, point Y', where the horizontal *LM* curve crosses the normally sloped *IS* curve. Again, the aggregate demand curve is vertical, as in Figure 7-10.

Monetary impotence and a failure of self-correction arise when there is a vertical *IS* or horizontal *LM* curve.[5] In either case, the classical cure-all of deflation cannot remedy a cyclical recession or depression. In Figure 7-10, the price level can fall continuously, from P_0 to P' to P'', yet real GDP remains stuck at Y'. The economy just moves downward vertically from point F to F' to F'', without any rightward motion.

Fiscal Policy and the Real Balance Effect

The crucial problem that makes the AD' curve in Figure 7-10 lie to the left of natural real GDP (Y^N) is low business and consumer confidence. How can confidence be revived? All problems disappear if planned spending can be raised far enough to make the *IS* curve intersect *LM* at or to the right of Y^N. For this reason Keynes believed that fiscal policy, which can shift the *IS* curve, is the obvious antidepression tool to use.

In theory, however, government action may not be necessary. A. C. Pigou originally pointed out that the Keynesian dilemma illustrated by the vertical AD' curve in Figure 7-10 may not be a dilemma at all. Why? The demand for commodities may depend directly on the level of real money balances (M^s/P). This would make the *IS* curve shift rightward whenever P falls, thus raising M^s/P and *guaranteeing a negative slope for the* AD *curve*. The **Pigou effect** or **real balance effect** occurs when an increase in M^s/P influences the demand for commodities *directly*, without requiring a reduction in interest rates. With the real balance effect, the *AD* curve is *always* negatively sloped, like AD_0, and a price deflation can achieve any desired real GDP level if prices fall far enough. The *AD* curve *cannot be vertical* in the presence of a real balance effect.

Why is the real balance effect so powerful when the price level is flexible? Imagine yourself owning only a \$10 bill. You would not be able to consider

> The **Pigou** or **real balance effect** is the direct stimulus to aggregate demand caused by an increase in the real money supply and does not require a decline in the interest rate.

---

[5]A more precise definition of the conditions necessary for monetary impotence and a failure of self-correction is as follows: there must be (1) no effect of a change in M^s/P on the *IS* curve, and (2) the interest rate along the *IS* curve, where actual real GDP equals natural real GDP (Y^N) and which we can call r^N, lies below the minimum attainable interest rate along the *LM* curve, which we can call r_{min}. When the *LM* curve is not horizontal, r_{min} is zero, and condition 2 is satisfied whenever r^N is negative or whenever *IS* is vertical and lies left of Y^N (as in the top frame of Figure 5-2). When there is a liquidity trap, the *LM* curve is horizontal at the level of r_{min} and condition 2 is satisfied even with a normally sloped *IS* curve, as long as r^N is less than r_{min}.

purchasing a $70,000 Mercedes. But there is some price level at which your money would have more impressive buying power. If the price index were to decline from 1.0 to 0.0001, the price of the Mercedes would fall from $70,000 to $7.00, and your $10 would be more than ample to buy the Mercedes, leaving $3.00 in change! Although the numbers in this illustration are extreme, they forcefully illustrate the logic of the real balance effect. A fixed nominal amount of money buys more when the price level falls, so that individuals are bound to find some portion of their previous money balances excessive and to spend more on real commodities.

When the price level is perfectly flexible and the real balance effect is in operation, no monetary or fiscal policy is necessary. The Federal Reserve governors and the President's Council of Economic Advisers can "go fishing," confident that the *AD* curve crosses the *LAS* curve, as in Figure 7-8.

We have now identified two stimulative effects of price deflation:

The **Keynes effect** is the stimulus to aggregate demand caused by a decline in the interest rate.

1. The **Keynes effect** is the stimulus to aggregate demand (both consumption and investment) due to a decline in the interest rate, which in turn is brought about by an increase in the nominal money supply (M^s) or decrease in the price level (P), both of which increase the real money supply (M^s/P). It is the Keynes effect that can be thwarted by a vertical *AD* curve as in Figure 7-10.

2. The Pigou (or real balance) effect is the direct stimulus to consumption spending that occurs when a price deflation causes an increase in the real money supply; this stimulus does not require a reduction in the interest rate. The Pigou effect guarantees that the *AD* curve cannot be vertical.

Destabilizing effects of falling prices.   Unfortunately, the stimulative effects of price deflation are not always favorable, even when the Pigou or real balance effect is in operation. There are two major unfavorable effects of deflation.

The **expectations effect** is the decline in aggregate demand caused by the postponement of purchases when consumers expect prices to decline in the future.

1. The **expectations effect.** When people expect prices to continue to fall, they tend to postpone purchases as much as possible to take advantage of lower prices in the future. This decline in the demand for commodities may be strong enough to offset the stimulus of the Pigou effect.

The **redistribution effect** is the decline in aggregate demand caused by the effect of falling prices in redistributing income from high-spending debtors to low-spending savers.

2. The **redistribution effect** may be more important than the expectations effect. An unexpected deflation causes a redistribution of income from debtors to creditors. Why? Debt repayments are usually fixed in dollar value so that a uniform deflation in all prices, which was not expected when the debts were incurred, causes an increase in the real value of mortgage and installment repayments from debtors to creditors (banks and, ultimately, savers).[6] This redistribution reduces aggregate demand, since creditors tend to spend only a relatively small share of their added income, while debtors have nothing to fall back on and are forced to reduce their consumption to meet their higher real interest payments.

---

[6]A relatively advanced discussion of the consequences of these effects on the economy's self-correcting mechanism is contained in James Tobin, "Keynesian Models of Recession and Depression," *American Economic Review* (May 1975), pp. 195–202. See also Axel Leijonhufvud, *On Keynesian Economics and the Economics of Keynes* (New York: Oxford University Press, 1968), pp. 315–31.

During the Great Depression deflation of 1929–33, for instance, the GDP price deflator declined by 24 percent. Yet the interest income of creditors hardly fell at all, from \$4.7 to \$4.1 billion (current dollars). Farmers were hit worst by falling prices—their current-dollar income fell by two-thirds, from \$6.2 to \$2.6 billion—and many lost their farms through foreclosures as a result of this heavy debt burden. Although many factors were at work in the collapse of real autonomous spending during the Great Depression, it appears that the negative expectations and redistribution effects of the 1929–33 deflation may have dominated the stimulative Keynes and Pigou effects.

The expectations and redistribution effects are not just ancient fossils relevant only to the 1930s. In the early and mid-1980s, falling prices of farm products, farmland, and oil reduced the income of farmers, oil producers, and employees of farms and oil companies. Many of these people were severely hurt by falling prices, especially because in the 1970s some (especially farmers) had incurred a heavy burden of debt to buy high-priced farmland.

SELF-TEST   Not only do falling prices and a depressed economy affect aggregate demand, but so do rising prices and prosperity. Explain whether the Pigou (real balance) effect stabilizes or destabilizes the economy when aggregate demand is high. How does this effect occur? Similarly, explain whether the expectations and redistribution effects stabilize or destabilize the economy when prices are rising, and describe how these effects occur.

Nominal Wage Rigidity

Keynes attacked the classical economists on two fronts. As we have seen, his first line of attack was the possibility of a vertical AD' line that fails to intersect the LAS line, creating monetary impotence and a failure of self-correction. His second line of attack was simply that deflation would not occur in the necessary amount because of rigid nominal wages. And if little or no deflation occurred, *the debate about the relative potency of the Keynes, Pigou, expectations, and distribution effects would become irrelevant.*

Figure 7-11 shows the effects of rigid nominal wages. In the right-hand frame the two aggregate demand curves, AD_0 and AD_1, are copied from Figure 7-9. They have the normal negative slopes. AD_1 lies to the left of AD_0 because consumer and business pessimism lowers the assumed amount of planned spending. The short-run aggregate supply curve SAS_0 is fixed in position by the fixed nominal wage rate (W_0). Starting at point E_0, the leftward shift in aggregate demand moves the economy to point A, where the new AD_1 curve intersects the aggregate supply curve SAS_0.

Keynes pointed out that the economy would remain stuck at point A even with the normally sloped aggregate demand curve AD_1. Why? If the nominal wage is completely rigid and never changes from the value W_0, then the supply curve is fixed as well at the position SAS_0. The price level would not fall below P_2. Hence the economy would not move from point A to point E_1, as required in the analysis of the classical economists.

Failure to attain equilibrium in the labor market.   Keynes's assumption of a rigid *nominal* wage differs from the description of the economy's adjustment toward long-run equilibrium in Sections 7-6 and 7-7, which assumed that

UNEMPLOYMENT IN THE ORIGINAL KEYNESIAN MODEL

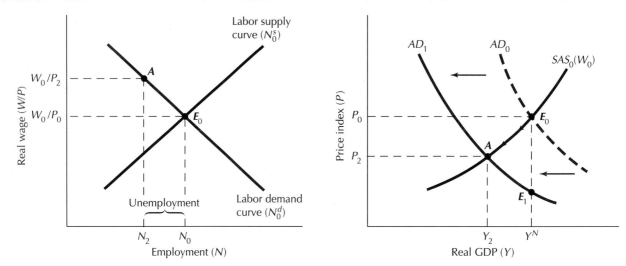

Figure 7-11   **Effect of a Decline in Planned Spending When the Nominal Rate Is Fixed at W_0**

The short-run aggregate supply curve SAS_0 in the right frame is fixed in position by the assumption of a rigid nominal wage rate, W_0. The decline in planned spending shifts the aggregate demand curve in the right frame leftward from AD_0 to AD_1, and the economy moves southwest from point E_0 to point A. In the left frame the reduction in the price level raises the real wage from the original W_0/P_0 to the new W_0/P_2, and the economy moves from point E_0 to point A. Unemployment is represented by the distance between N_2 and N_0.

---

there is an equilibrium *real* wage rate that equates demand and supply in the labor market.

Keynes's assumption of nominal wage rigidity fails to explain how or why the wage remains rigid. Its only virtue is that it provides an explanation of **persistent unemployment,** as at point A in the left frame of Figure 7-11, without requiring any special shape for the aggregate demand curve. But the arbitrariness of the assumption raises four important questions that will concern us in the next section as well as in Chapter 17.

Persistent unemployment is a situation in which a high level of unemployment can last for many years, as in the United States from 1929 to 1941 and from 1980 to 1985.

1. Is the nominal wage rigidity assumption realistic? Did the aggregate supply curve in the Great Depression remain at a fixed position like SAS_0, or did it steadily shift downward and bring the economy to long-run equilibrium, as the classical economists would have predicted? This question is the subject of the case study in the next section.

2. Is it possible to devise a convincing theory of business cycles without relying on either a vertical AD curve or rigid nominal wages? The Keynesian rigid nominal wage "story" raises a basic puzzle: Why do markets "fail to clear"? That is, why does the economy not operate continuously at the intersection of the labor supply and demand curves? Several prominent economists, particularly Milton Friedman, Robert Lucas, and Edward Prescott, have attempted to revive classical economics in a way that is consistent with observed business cycles yet allows for **market-clearing,** in contrast to the Keynesian tradition of **non–market-clearing.** We turn to these models in Chapter 17.

A **market-clearing model** or theory holds that the economy is always in equilibrium at the intersection of the supply and demand curves, particularly in the labor market.

A **non–market-clearing model** holds that the economy can be pushed off its supply and demand curves in the labor market and sometimes in other markets.

3. How do labor unions and current practices of wage negotiation relate to the Keynesian assumption of wage rigidity? Do they justify his assumption of non–market-clearing and support his explanation of persistent unemployment? This question is addressed in Chapter 17.

4. In a recession the real wage in the left-hand frame of Figure 7-11 rises from point E_0 to point A when real GDP declines from Y^N to Y_2. Does an adequate theory of the business cycle require such a *countercyclical* movement in the real wage? This issue has troubled many analysts in light of the limited or nonexistent countercyclical movements in the real wage evident in historical data, and is also addressed in Chapter 17.

7-10   CASE STUDY: What Caused the Great Depression?

This case study investigates several important aspects of the Great Depression years of 1929 to 1941. Three topics are given primary emphasis. First, why was aggregate demand so low? Is there evidence to support monetary impotence or a failure of self-correction? Second, did the economy's aggregate supply curve shift downward to provide self-correction, or did it remain stationary as it does in the right-hand frame of Figure 7-11 when the nominal wage is rigid? Third, was the nominal wage rigid, and did real wages fluctuate countercyclically?

Table 7-1 exhibits several important features of the period between 1929 and 1941. This twelve-year period is distinguished most by the unemployment figures shown in column 7, especially by the extraordinarily high level reached by the unemployment rate (25.2 percent in 1933), and the long

---

Table 7-1   **Money, Output, Unemployment, Prices, and Wages in the Great Depression, 1929–41**

Year	Money Supply ($ billions)	Real Money Supply	Real GDP	Real Fixed Investment	Output Ratio (Y/Y^N) (percent)	GDP Deflator (1929 = 100)	Unemployment Rate (percent)	Long-Term Interest Rate	Average Hourly Earnings (dollars)	Average Real Hourly Earnings (1929 dollars)
		($ billions, 1929 prices)								
	(1)	(2)	(3)	(4)	(5)	(6)	(7)	(8)	(9)	(10)
1929	26.0	26.0	103.1	14.9	107.1	100.0	3.2	3.6	.563	.563
1930	25.2	26.0	94.0	11.3	94.7	96.8	8.9	3.3	.560	.578
1931	23.5	26.5	86.7	7.9	84.5	88.0	16.3	3.3	.532	.600
1932	20.6	26.3	75.2	4.5	71.4	77.6	24.1	3.7	.485	.618
1933	19.4	25.3	73.7	3.9	68.2	76.0	25.2	3.3	.457	.596
1934	21.4	25.6	79.4	4.9	71.7	82.4	22.0	3.1	.512	.614
1935	25.3	29.5	85.5	6.3	75.6	84.8	20.3	2.8	.524	.612
1936	28.8	33.6	97.6	8.4	84.2	84.8	17.0	2.7	.534	.623
1937	30.2	33.7	101.8	9.7	86.3	89.6	14.3	2.7	.566	.632
1938	29.8	33.9	97.7	7.9	80.4	87.2	19.1	2.6	.576	.657
1939	33.4	38.4	105.5	9.5	84.6	86.4	17.2	2.4	.583	.670
1940	38.8	43.7	113.7	11.2	89.0	88.0	14.6	2.2	.597	.674
1941	45.4	48.2	134.3	12.8	102.3	93.6	9.9	2.0	.655	.694

Sources: See Appendix A. The interest rate is series B-72 in *Long-Term Economic Growth* (U.S. Department of Commerce, 1970); Average hourly earnings are from Martin N. Baily, "The Labor Market in the 1930s," in James Tobin, ed., *Macroeconomics, Prices, and Quantities* (Brookings Institution, 1983), Table 1, p. 23.

duration of high unemployment (ten straight years from 1931–40 with unemployment above 10 percent). An obvious puzzle is why the economy was so weak, especially between 1934 and 1939. In 1939 *the real money supply* (column 2) *was 48 percent higher than in 1929.* Yet in 1939 real GDP (column 3) *was only 2.3 percent higher than in 1929.* In 1939 the unemployment rate was still 17.2 percent.

Explanations of Weak Aggregate Demand

The Keynesian interpretation that the *IS* curve shifted far to the left is supported in Table 7-1 by column 4, which shows the collapse of real fixed investment from $14.9 billion in 1929 prices in 1929 to $3.9 billion in 1933, *a decline of 74 percent.* Also shown is the incomplete recovery of real fixed investment, with a value in 1939 that was 36 percent below the 1929 level. The failure of investment to recover fully to the 1929 level, despite a 48 percent increase in the real money supply since 1929, is consistent with either a vertical *IS* curve or a horizontal *LM* curve. Which diagnosis is more realistic?

For the *IS* curve to be vertical, a decline in the interest rate must fail to stimulate autonomous planned spending, which chiefly consists of fixed investment. As shown in Table 7-1, the interest rate declined substantially from 1934 to 1941 and yet real fixed investment in 1939, 1940, and even 1941 was far below its 1929 level.

For the *LM* curve to be horizontal, an increase in the real money supply must fail to reduce the interest rate. Yet the long-term interest rate fell fairly steadily from 3.7 percent in 1932 to 2.0 percent in 1941. Thus the observations between 1934 and 1941 seem consistent with the hypothesis that the demand for money depends inversely on the interest rate. There is no sign that the interest rate hit a minimum level at any time during the latter half of the Great Depression decade.

Monetary versus nonmonetary factors.   In recent years there has been a lively debate regarding the relative role of monetary and nonmonetary factors in causing the Great Depression, particularly the collapse of nominal and real GDP between 1929 and 1933. In an extensive statistical study of the data with James A. Wilcox, I have concluded that both monetary and nonmonetary factors were important, but at different times.[7] For instance, in the first two years of the contraction (1929–31) the decline in the nominal money supply (column 1) was much too small to account for the drop in spending, which must be attributed mainly to nonmonetary factors (including overbuilding of too many residential and nonresidential structures in the 1920s and the impact of the 1929 stock market crash on consumption). But after September 1931, the contraction was caused mainly by monetary factors, including the enormous loss of lifetime savings in bank failures.

---

[7]Robert J. Gordon and James A. Wilcox, "Monetarist Interpretations of the Great Depression: An Evaluation and Critique," in Karl Brunner, ed., *Contemporary Views of the Great Depression* (Hingham, Mass.: Martinus Nijhoff, 1981), pp. 49–107.

Prices and the Output Ratio in the Great Depression

Does the behavior of output and the price level in the Great Depression support the Keynesian assumption of rigid nominal wages or the classical interpretation of a self-correcting economy? If the classicists are correct, we should find evidence of the economy's self-correcting forces at work through price deflation. Turning back to the right frame of Figure 7-11, we would expect that when price deflation works in a stabilizing direction, the economy would slide down an *AD* curve to the southeast, as from point *A* to point E_1.

Now compare this theoretical diagram to a graph of the actual data plotted in the top frame of Figure 7-12. The horizontal axis is measured as the ratio of actual to natural real GDP. Starting on the vertical *LAS* schedule at natural real GDP in 1929, with a price index of 100 (on a 1929 base), the economy moved rapidly to the southwest until 1933. Then a recovery to the northeast began, interrupted briefly in 1938.

Absence of Self-Correction.   The story of the Great Depression appears to lie in shifts in the *AD* curve to the left and then back to the right. There is no evidence at all of a movement southeast along a given *AD* curve, as would

Figure 7-12
The Price Level *(P)* and the Ratio of Actual to Natural Real GDP *(Y/Y^N)* During the Great Depression, 1929–41

The upper frame illustrates the actual values of the implicit GDP deflator *(P)* and an estimate of the ratio of actual to natural real GDP during the Great Depression era, 1929–41. The remarkable fact in the top frame is that the economy returned to natural output in 1941 with a price level that was almost as high as in 1929, despite the intervening decade that should have pushed the price level much lower. The bottom frame illustrates a hypothetical interpretation of what happened. (*Source:* Appendix A.)

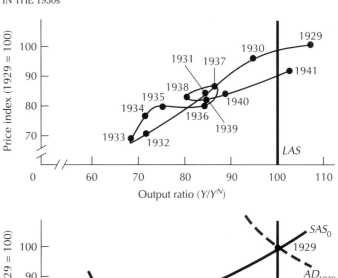

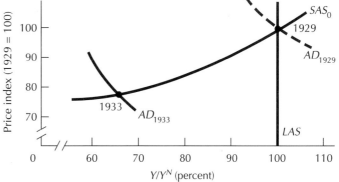

have occurred had price deflation played a major role in stimulating the recovery. Particularly important is the fact that there was no deflation between 1936 and 1940, even though Y/Y^N remained at or below 86 percent throughout that five-year interval.

Despite the absence of perfect price flexibility, the price level was not rigid during the Great Depression and did drop 24 percent between 1929 and 1933. The path from northeast to southwest to northeast reflects a regularity, as if the *AD* curve were following a well-marked highway. The bottom frame of Figure 7-12 represents a hypothetical interpretation of what happened. The *AD* curve in 1929 was close to the vertical *LAS* schedule, but by 1933 it had moved well to the left as business and consumer confidence collapsed. The actual location of the economy in 1933 suggests that the economy's aggregate supply schedule looks like SAS_0 of Figure 7-11, and so we have drawn in a positively sloped SAS_0 curve in the bottom frame of Figure 7-12.

Behavior of Nominal and Real Wage Rates.   The interpretation of the Great Depression contained in Figure 7-12 raises an obvious question: Why did the aggregate supply curve fail to shift downward to bring the economy to its long-run equilibrium level of output along the vertical *LAS* line at a lower price level? A fixed *SAS* curve requires a rigid nominal wage rate. Data on the nominal wage rate are included in Table 7-1, column 9.

The year 1930 provides a particularly important example of nominal wage rigidity. Despite a decline of real GDP of 9 percent between 1929 and 1930, one of the steepest declines ever recorded, *the nominal wage rate did not decline at all.* A decline occurred in 1931–33, but then in 1934 the nominal wage rate jumped by 12 percent despite an unemployment rate in 1934 of 22 percent! By 1937 the nominal wage rate was back to the 1929 level, despite an unemployment rate of 14 percent. Thus, it is an exaggeration for the Keynesian model to treat the nominal wage rate as absolutely rigid. A decline did occur in 1931–33. But the nominal wage rate did not exhibit the continued decline after 1933 that would have been necessary to bring the economy back to natural real GDP through the classical mechanism of self-correction.

Column 10 of Table 7-1 exhibits the real wage rate. The rise in the nominal and the real wage rate after 1933, despite high unemployment, is attributed by some economists to government intervention. During 1934 and 1935 the National Industrial Recovery Act (NIRA) explicitly attempted to raise wages and prices, setting forth industry-specific codes that required law-abiding employers to raise wage rates. Although the NIRA was declared unconstitutional in 1935, it was succeeded in 1935 by the Wagner Act (National Labor Relations Act), which favored union membership.

Nevertheless, many economists are skeptical that government policy can fully account for the failure of nominal wage rates to continue falling in the last half of the 1930s in light of the continuing high rate of unemployment. This is just one of the puzzles about the behavior of wages and prices that continue to fascinate economists. In Chapter 17 we examine the new Keynesian theories that address some of these puzzles.

And in the next chapter we explore the relationship between inflation and output that lies at the heart of U.S. macroeconomic behavior and plays a large role in the decisions of policymakers.

SUMMARY

1. The aggregate demand curve shows the different combinations of real output and the price level that are consistent with equilibrium in the commodity and money markets. The position of the aggregate demand curve depends on planned spending and on the money supply.

2. A shift in aggregate demand may change the level of real output, the price level, or both. With a horizontal aggregate supply curve, only real output changes. With a vertical aggregate supply curve, only the price level changes. With a positively sloped aggregate supply curve, both real output and the price level change.

3. The short-run aggregate supply curve slopes upward because a higher price level reduces the real wage. This induces firms to hire more workers, and the resulting increase in output raises real GDP.

4. The equilibrium real wage rate is located where the labor supply and demand curves cross. If a shift in demand changes the price level, and hence pushes the real wage rate away from the equilibrium real wage rate, there is pressure for change in the nominal wage rate.

5. The position of the short-run aggregate supply curve for the economy depends on the nominal wage rate. When changing demand conditions raise the nominal wage rate, the short-run aggregate supply curve shifts up.

6. In the short run, a fiscal or monetary expansion raises both real output and the price level. However, the short-run change in real output puts pressure for change on the nominal wage rate and causes the short-run aggregate supply curve to shift. This pressure for change is eliminated only when real output returns to the value that occurred prior to the fiscal or monetary expansion.

7. The economy is in long-run equilibrium only at a single level of natural real GDP, where there is no upward or downward pressure on the nominal wage rate. In the long run, any change in aggregate demand changes the price level without causing a change in real GDP.

8. Classical economists believed that cycles in aggregate demand mainly affected the price level, not real output. The economy's self-correcting forces of price flexibility protected real output from fluctuations.

9. Keynes criticized the classical economists on two grounds. The first was that the aggregate demand curve might be vertical rather than negatively sloped, due to a failure of planned spending to respond to the interest rate (vertical *IS* curve), or to a failure of a higher real money supply to lower the interest rate (horizontal *LM* curve), or both. Pigou countered that falling prices raise wealth and spending, guaranteeing a negatively sloped aggregate demand curve.

10. Keynes also criticized the classical economists because he believed that nominal wages were rigid, preventing prices from adjusting sufficiently to return real GDP to the level of natural real GDP.

CONCEPTS

aggregate demand curve
short-run aggregate supply curve
comparative statics
equilibrium real wage rate
long-run aggregate supply curve *(LAS)*
short-run equilibrium
long-run equilibrium
countercyclical variable
self-correcting forces
quantity theory of money

monetary impotence
rigid wages
Pigou or real balance effect
Keynes effect
expectations effect
redistribution effect
persistent unemployment
market-clearing model
non–market-clearing model

QUESTIONS AND PROBLEMS

Questions

1. Explain the difference between the aggregate demand curve developed in this chapter and the demand curve for a product (e.g., movies) used in microeconomics.

 How will the *AD* curve be affected if, all other things remaining equal, (a) the interest responsiveness of the demand for money becomes larger? (b) the income responsiveness of the demand for money becomes larger?

3. All other things remaining equal, which of the following changes would cause the *AD* curve to shift to the right? To the left? Make it flatter? Make it steeper? Leave it unchanged (that is, cause a movement along the *AD* curve)? (*Hint:* Explain how each change affects the *IS* or *LM* curves that lie behind the *AD* curve.)
   (a) an increase in the nominal money supply
   (b) an increase in autonomous exports
   (c) an increase in the marginal tax rate
   (d) an increase in the marginal propensity to consume
   (e) a decrease in the responsiveness of investment to changes in the interest rate
   (f) an increase in the price level
   (g) an increase in government spending
   (h) a decrease in the exchange rate

4. Explain the importance of the assumption of fixed *nominal* wages in the determination of the short-run aggregate supply curve.

5. Explain why every point on the *SAS* curve is a profit-maximizing point for the firm(s).

6. Describe whether the following variables increase or decrease when real GDP (*Y*) increases above Y_0 in Figure 7-5.
   (a) the price level
   (b) the nominal wage rate
   (c) the real wage rate
   (d) the level of employment
   (e) the demand for labor
   (f) the quantity of labor demanded

7. Do the following events increase or decrease the equilibrium real wage?
   (a) an increase in worker productivity due to the introduction of new computerized machinery
   (b) a decrease in worker productivity in response to higher oil prices as firms "retire" machinery that is very energy-intensive
   (c) an increase in unemployment benefits
   (d) an increase in immigration of workers who are willing to work for less than present American workers.

8. Is the actual real wage equal to the equilibrium real wage at every point on the *SAS* curve?

9. Assume that the aggregate demand curve shifts to the right by an equal amount through *either* increased government spending or increased nominal money supply. Assuming that the position, but not the shape, of the *AD* curve changes, compare the effects on the economy of the two expansionary policies. How does each action affect the government budget deficit and the foreign trade deficit?

10. Is sustainable long-run equilibrium always reached when the *AD* and *SAS* curves intersect? Why or why not?

11. According to the view of the classical economists, there should have been a movement down the *AD* curve during the 1930s. Explain why this type of movement would require a shifting *SAS* curve. Did the *SAS* curve shift during the Great Depression in the way expected by the classical economists?

12. What is meant by the term *monetary impotence?* According to Keynes, what two conditions could lead to monetary impotence? Were either of these conditions present during the Great Depression?

13. Explain the role played by the interest rate in the Pigou effect.

14. Why does the existence of a potent Pigou effect guarantee a negatively sloped *AD* curve?

15. Does the Pigou effect alter the average propensity to consume in the economy?

16. If policymakers were trying to decrease output in a period of continuing inflation, would the existence of the Pigou effect have any impact? Can you explain, under these circumstances, how the redistribution effect and the expectations effect might affect the economy?

17. Given the existence of a Pigou, or real balance, effect, what do you predict will happen to the *IS* and *AD* curves if the economy experiences an unexpected increase in autonomous exports? (Assume that the economy begins in a long-run equilibrium position where *AD* crosses *LAS.*)

18. The whole controversy regarding the location of the *IS* curve and the potency of the real balance effect becomes irrelevant if nominal wages are rigid downward. Why is this so? Use the *AD-SAS* model to explain your answer.

Problems

1. The *IS* and *LM* curves for the economy have the following equations:

$$IS:\ Y = k(A_0 - 50r)$$

$$LM:\ Y = 3(M^s/P) + 300r$$

where $k = 4$, $A_0 = 1200$, $M^s = 600$, and $P = 1.00$. For the purpose of this question, which aims solely at

deriving the *AD* curve, assume away the *SAS* and *LAS* curves.
   (a) Find the equilibrium level of real output and the equilibrium interest rate.
   (b) What is the equilibrium real output when the price level equals 0.8? When it is 1.2? When it is 1.5? Plot the aggregate demand curve based on your answers to these questions.

(c) Assume that A_0 is now 1000. What is the equilibrium real output when the price level equals 0.8, 1.0, 1.2, and 1.5? Plot the aggregate demand curve for this case.

2. Using the information in problem 1(a) and assuming that an upward-sloping *SAS* curve intersects the *AD* curve at $Y = 3600$ and $P = 1.00$, explain what will

happen in the economy if the natural real output is 3600.

3. Using the information in problem 1(c) and assuming that an upward-sloping *SAS* curve intersects the original *AD* curve at $Y = 3600$ and $P = 1.00$, explain what will happen in the short run to actual real output, the price level, and the real wage.

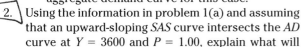

SELF-TEST ANSWERS

p. 198 When the *LM* curve is steep, an increase in the real money supply causes output to increase more than when the *LM* curve is flat (compare the top and bottom frames of Figure 5-1). Thus, when the *LM* curve is steep, a given price reduction (which raises the real money supply) leads to a greater output increase and a *flatter AD* curve than when the *LM* curve is flat.

p. 202 A union concession shifts the *SAS* curve down. A discovery of a giant oil field shifts the *SAS* curve down. An increase in the money supply shifts the aggregate demand *(AD)* curve upward and thus causes a movement *along* the *SAS* curve.

p. 210 All these events cause an upward shift in the aggregate demand *(AD)* curve. In long-run equilib-

rium, the price level and nominal wage level must increase by the same percentage, while the level of real GDP does not change.

p. 217 The Pigou effect stabilizes the economy when demand is high; rising prices reduce the value of real balances and real wealth, which in turn reduce consumption. The expectations and redistribution effects destabilize the economy. The expectations effect causes people to spend sooner, since they expect future prices to be higher. This boosts demand when demand is already high. Similarly, the redistribution effect causes income to be redistributed from savers who spend little to borrowers who spend much, thus boosting demand when demand is already high.

CHAPTER 8

Inflation: Its Causes and Cures

Why is our money ever less valuable? Perhaps it is simply that we have inflation because we expect inflation, and we expect inflation because we've had it.

—*Robert M. Solow*[1]

8-1 Introduction

We are now ready to study the fundamental causes of inflation and the determinants of the responsiveness of inflation to shifts in aggregate demand and supply. Does faster growth in the money supply cause faster inflation instantly, or only after some time has passed? Does the government, through its monetary and fiscal policy, bear the blame for the faster inflation experienced in the United States between 1965 and 1982? Does government policy deserve credit for achieving low inflation in the mid 1990s?

The *AD-SAS* model of Chapter 7 suggests that any event that can cause a *single upward shift* in the economy's aggregate demand schedule (*AD* curve) can cause at the same time a *single upward jump* in the price index. But **inflation** is a continuous increase in the price index, not a single jump. Thus, sustained inflation requires a continuous increase in aggregate demand. To focus on the determinants of inflation, we now shift from the diagrams of Chapter 7, which measure the level of the price index on the vertical axis, to related diagrams that measure vertically the percentage rate of change of the price index—that is, the inflation rate itself. In Chapter 7 a continuous inflation results in a steady upward movement of the economy's equilibrium position, so that the economy eventually moves off the upper edge of the page. Now, in the diagrams of this chapter, the equilibrium position of an economy experiencing a steady inflation of, say, 6 percent remains fixed on the page.

In this chapter we will study the relationship between inflation and the level of real GDP. We will see that in the absence of supply shocks, shifts in aggregate demand are the main cause of swings in real GDP and in the rate of inflation. A level of real GDP above the natural level of real GDP cannot be sustained permanently without continuously accelerating inflation. We will also examine the unfortunate corollary to this fact, that a reduction of inflation cannot be achieved by aggregate demand policy without also involving a transition period of recession, with real GDP below natural real GDP. We then turn to an analysis of inflation caused by supply shocks, such as the sharp increase in the price of oil in 1974 and 1979.

Inflation is a sustained upward movement in the aggregate price level that is shared by most products.

---

[1]*Technology Review* (December/January 1979), p. 31.

8-2   Real GDP, the Inflation Rate, and the Short-Run Phillips Curve

A *continuous* increase in demand pulls the price level up *continuously*. This kind of inflationary process is sometimes called demand-pull inflation, describing the role of rising aggregate demand as the factor "pulling up" on the price level, a phenomenon depicted in Figure 8-1. Here the top frame repeats the aggregate demand and supply schedules from Chapter 7, with minor changes: for expositional simplicity, we have drawn both curves as straight lines, and we have introduced specific numbers on the vertical and horizontal axes. For instance, the natural level of real GDP is assumed to be 100 on the horizontal axis, and the economy is assumed to be at that level of output initially at point E_0, where the AD_0 and SAS_0 curves cross. The initial values of the price index (P_0) and an index of the nominal wage rate (W_0) are both 1.0. The real wage rate (W_0/P_0) is initially at its equilibrium value of 1.0.

The short-run aggregate supply curve *(SAS)* has a positive slope, meaning that a higher level of output raises the price level. Each *SAS* curve is drawn for a particular nominal wage rate, shifting upward when the nominal wage rate increases, just as in Chapter 7. The long-run aggregate supply curve *(LAS)* has a vertical slope at the point where actual real GDP *(Y)* equals rational real GDP (Y^N).

As we learned in Chapter 7, there is upward pressure for an increase in the wage rate (and thus for an upward shift in the *SAS* curve), whenever actual real GDP *(Y)* exceeds natural real GDP (Y^N). This occurs whenever the economy operates to the right of the vertical *LAS* curve. However, despite this upward pressure, we shall assume throughout this chapter that the wage rate does not jump instantaneously when the economy moves to the right of *LAS*. Why? Most workers receive wage increases only once or twice a year, and the wages of some union workers are set for as long as three years. Due to the importance of these long-term wage contracts and agreements (some formally written down, and others an informal understanding between business firms and their workers), the wage rate increases gradually, not instantly, whenever the economy is operating to the right of the vertical *LAS* curve. As a result, the economy can enjoy a boom, during which Y exceeds Y^N, that lasts several years. Similarly, the economy can suffer through a slump that lasts several years, during which Y is less than Y^N and the economy remains to the left of the vertical *LAS* curve.

Effects of an Increase in Aggregate Demand

An increase in aggregate demand shifts the *AD* curve upward from AD_0 to AD_1. The economy moves initially to point E_1, where the price level is 1.03. The higher price level puts upward pressure on the nominal wage rate to rise. Everywhere to the right of the *LAS* curve, including point E_1, there is upward pressure on the nominal wage rate, so gradually the *SAS* curve will shift up. When this occurs, we move to the new SAS_1 curve, which assumes that the nominal wage rate is 3 percent higher than it was along the original SAS_0 curve.

Figure 8-1

Relationship of the Short-Run Aggregate Supply Curve (SAS) to the Short-Run Phillips Curve (SP)

In the top frame the economy starts in long-run equilibrium at point E_0. When aggregate demand shifts up from the AD_0 curve to the AD_1 curve, the price level moves to point E_1. The economy can stay to the right of the LAS line only if aggregate demand shifts up continuously from AD_1 to AD'_1 to even higher levels of aggregate demand. The nominal wage rate adjusts upward whenever the economy is in the area to the right of LAS. Aggregate demand must keep ahead of the upward adjustment of the nominal wage rate, shown by the vertical path marked by red arrows. This continuous inflation of 3 percent per period is represented directly below in the lower frame at point E_1.

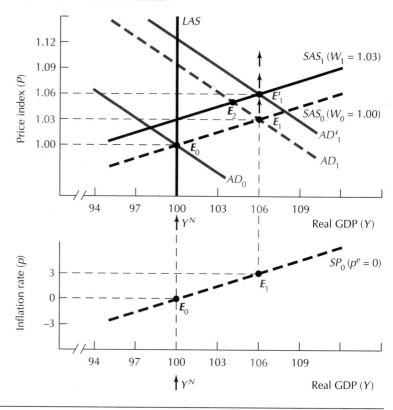

HOW A CONTINUOUS INCREASE IN AGGREGATE DEMAND CAUSES CONTINUOUS INFLATION

How Continuous Inflation Occurs

What happens to real GDP and the price level as the result of the upward shift from SAS_0 to SAS_1? There are two possibilities, both illustrated in the top frame of Figure 8-1.

A One-Shot Increase in Aggregate Demand. The first possibility is that aggregate demand stays at the level indicated by the AD_1 schedule. Then the upward shift of the supply curve to SAS_1 would shift the economy from E_1 northwest to point E_2. What must happen to prevent the level of output from declining? The aggregate demand schedule AD must shift upward by exactly the same amount as the supply schedule SAS. Thus, if the nominal wage rate increases from 1.00 to 1.03, shifting supply up from SAS_0 to SAS_1, output can remain fixed *only if the demand curve shifts up* again, this time from AD_1 to AD'_1. Once again, however, the price level of 1.06 at point E'_1 has raced ahead of the wage rate of 1.03, and there will again be upward pressure on the nominal wage rate.

A Continuous Increase in Aggregate Demand. To keep output from declining, aggregate demand must increase continuously, the economy will move straight upward along the path depicted by the red arrows in the top frame. The bottom frame shows the same process in a much simpler way. The horizontal axis is the same as in the top frame, but now the vertical axis measures not the price level but its rate of change, the inflation rate. Thus, in the top frame when the price level is fixed in long-run equilibrium, as at point E_0, the percentage rate of change of prices (or inflation rate) in the bottom frame is zero, as at point E_0. Throughout the book we will write percentage rates of change as lowercase letters, p in the case of the inflation rate; thus the vertical axis measures the zero rate of inflation occurring at point E_0 as $p = 0$.

The maintenance of a higher level of output requires a continuous increase in aggregate demand and in the price level, as depicted by the vertical path of the red arrows in the top frame. This same process of continuous inflation in the bottom frame is illustrated by *the single point E_1*, where each period the rate of change of the price level is 3 percent (just as in the top frame the price level rises by 3 percent between points E_1 and E'_1).

The *SP* Curve

In the bottom frame of Figure 8-1 the upward-sloping line connecting points E_0 and E_1 is called the *SP* line. It shows that to maintain real GDP *(Y)* above natural real GDP *(Y^N)*, aggregate demand must be raised *continuously* to create a *continuous* inflation (3 percent at point E_1).

Thus point E_1 in the lower frame, and indeed all points to the right of Y^N, share the characteristic that the economy is not in a long-run equilibrium because the price level is constantly racing ahead of the nominal wage rate. The reason for the continuous upward pressure for higher wages is that contracts fail to *anticipate further inflation, and, as a result, they specify in advance the wage increases needed to keep up with inflation.* Such wage contracts are said to have an **expected rate of inflation** of zero. This is abbreviated $p^e = 0$ and is included as a label on the *SP* line, which is based on the assumption that people do not anticipate further inflation when they negotiate wage contracts.

The term *SP curve* is used as an abbreviation for the term **short-run Phillips curve,** which is named after A. W. H. Phillips, who first discovered the statistical relationship between real GDP and the inflation rate.[2] The *SP* curve slopes upward for the same reason that the *SAS* curve slopes up in Chapter 7 (a negatively sloped demand for labor). There are additional reasons for the upward slope of the *SP* curve. As output increases, the economywide inflation rate tends to rise, due to the sensitivity of raw materials prices to higher aggregate demand, and due to the tendency of business firms to boost prices more rapidly when aggregate demand is high.

The **expected rate of inflation** is the rate of inflation that is expected to occur in the future.

The schedule relating real GDP to the inflation rate achievable given a fixed expected rate of inflation is the **short-run Phillips curve.**

---

[2]Phillips showed that over 100 years of British history the rate of change of wage rates was related to the level of unemployment. Because the change in wage rates, in turn, is related to inflation, and unemployment is related to real GDP, the research of Phillips popularized the idea, depicted by the *SP* curve in Figure 8-1, that a high level of output is associated with a high inflation rate. See A. W. H. Phillips, "The Relation Between Unemployment and the Rate of Change of Money Wage Rates in the United Kingdom, 1861–1957," *Economica* (November 1958), pp. 283–299. The curve should actually be called the Fisher curve, since the relationship between the unemployment and inflation rates had been pointed out much earlier in Irving Fisher, "A Statistical Relation Between Unemployment and Price Changes," *International Labour Review* (June 1926), pp. 785–792, reprinted in *Journal of Political Economy* (March/April 1973), pp. 596–602.

The **expectations-augmented Phillips curve,** or *SP* curve, shifts its position whenever there is a change in the expected rate of inflation.

The position of the *SP* curve is fixed by the rate of inflation that was expected at the time current wage contracts were negotiated (p^e), assumed in Figure 8-1 to be zero. Because the position of the *SP* curve depends on expectations, it is sometimes called the **expectations-augmented Phillips curve.**

SELF-TEST

From what you have learned so far, can you generalize about the accuracy of the expected rate of inflation in the bottom frame of Figure 8-1? In what area is actual inflation greater than expected inflation? In what area is actual inflation less than expected inflation? Where in the diagram does the expected rate of inflation turn out to be exactly right?

8-3 The Adjustment of Expectations

The remarkable thing about the inflation process illustrated in Figure 8-1 is that it presupposes that people never learn to *anticipate* inflation when they negotiate their informal wage and price agreements and their formal labor contracts. Each period the price level races ahead of the nominal wage rate along the path shown by the red arrows, but people fail to build this inflation into their price and wage agreements *ahead of time.*

Changing Inflation Expectations Shift the *SP* Curve

Once negotiators anticipate inflation in advance, the short-run Phillips curve shifts, as illustrated in Figure 8-2. There the lower SP_0 short-run Phillips curve is copied directly from the bottom frame of Figure 8-1. Everywhere along the SP_0 curve no inflation is expected. At point E_0 the actual inflation rate is just what is expected—zero—and the economy is in a long-run equilibrium position with the price level completely fixed. At point E_1 no inflation is expected $(p^e = 0)$ either, but the actual inflation rate turns out to be 3 percent.

When an expected 3 percent inflation occurs $(p = p^e = 3)$, the long-run equilibrium position occurs at point E_3. The entire short-run Phillips curve has shifted upward by exactly 3 percent, the degree of adjustment of the expected inflation rate. The excess of Y over Y^N has led firms to raise their prices, and workers have obtained larger wage increases in newly negotiated contracts. Now a real GDP greater than Y^N cannot be achieved along the new SP_1 schedule unless the actual inflation rate exceeds 3 percent, in which case the actual inflation rate would again exceed the expected inflation rate.

The economy is in long-run equilibrium only when there is no pressure for change. Point E_1 certainly does not qualify, because the actual inflation rate of 3 percent at point E_1 exceeds the zero inflation rate expected along the SP_0 curve when people made their long-term wage agreements. There is pressure for people to adjust their erroneous expectation $(p^e = 0)$ to take account of the continuing inflation. At point E_3 the pressure for change ceases because expected inflation has been boosted enough $(p^e = 3)$. Wage agreements allow *in advance* for a 3 percent inflation. This keeps employment and output unaffected by inflation.

Thus point E_3 qualifies as a point of long-run equilibrium, because expectations turn out to be correct, just as does E_0. There is no need for further revi-

Figure 8-2

Effect on the Short-run Phillips Curve of an Increase in the Expected Inflation Rate (p^e) from Zero to 3 Percent

The lower SP_0 curve is copied directly from the bottom frame of Figure 8-1 and shows the relation between output and inflation when no inflation is expected $(p^e = 0)$. But when people begin fully to expect the 3 percent inflation, the 3 percent actual inflation yields only the level of real GDP at E_3. The short-run Phillips curve has shifted upward by exactly 3 percent, the amount by which people have raised their expected inflation rate. The vertical LP line running through points E_0 and E_3 shows all the possible positions of long-run equilibrium where the actual and expected inflation rates are equal $(p = p^e)$.

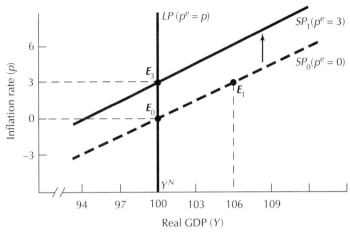

THE RELATION BETWEEN OUTPUT AND INFLATION DEPENDS ON THE RATE OF EXPECTED INFLATION (p^e)

sion of price markups or to build the expected inflation rate into wage contracts. The only difference between points E_0 and E_3 is the inflation rate that is correctly expected, zero at E_0 versus 3 percent at E_3. Otherwise the two points share the correctness of expectations and the same real GDP level of 100, equal to natural real GDP (Y^N).

The *LP* "Correct Expectations" Line

The vertical LP line connects E_0 and E_3 and shows all possible points where the expected inflation rate turns out to be correct. The term *LP line* stands for *Long-run Phillips* curve and can be thought of as the "correct expectations" line. Everywhere to the right of the LP line inflation turns out to be higher than expected and the expected inflation rate will be raised. Everywhere to the left inflation turns out to be lower than expected and the expected inflation rate will be reduced. The vertical LP line showing all possible positions of long-run equilibrium is analogous to the vertical *LAS* long-run supply schedule of Chapter 7. Its message is the same: real GDP (Y) cannot be pushed permanently away from its long-run natural level (Y^N).

How should we interpret the state of the economy to the right of the LP line? Anywhere in that area the actual inflation rate (p) turns out to be faster than was expected (p^e) at the time contracts were negotiated. However, we do not assume that workers are unable to observe the inflation that is occurring, or that they have some informational disadvantage compared to firms.

Instead, p^e represents the inflation that *both* workers and firms expected at the time of the last contract negotiation, say last year. Now, this year, there may be a shift in aggregate demand that pushes up the actual inflation rate above what *both* expected. If the wage contract does not expire for several months or years, both workers and firms may *accurately observe* the actual increase in the inflation rate but be unable to react to it until it is time for the

LEARNING ABOUT DIAGRAMS: *The Short-Run (SP) and Long-Run (LP) Phillips Curves*

The Phillips curve depicts the relationship between inflation and output.

Diagram Elements and Reasons for Slope

Both the *SP* curve and *LP* curve are plotted with real GDP on the horizontal axis (the same as for the *SAS* and *LAS* curves) and with the inflation rate on the vertical axis (in contrast to the price level for the *SAS* and *LAS* curves).

The *SP* curve slopes upward because higher output boosts inflation through the same mechanisms that cause the short-run aggregate supply curve to slope upward in Chapter 7.

The *LP* curve shows the level of output when inflation is accurately anticipated $(p = p^e)$. The *LP* curve is a vertical line, because accurate anticipations can occur only at a single level of output, that is, natural real GDP (Y^N).

What Shifts the *SP* Curve and *LP* Curve?

The crossing point of the *SP* curve with the *LP* curve shows the rate of anticipated inflation (p^e). An increase in p^e will shift the *SP* curve up, and a decrease in p^e will shift the *SP* curve down.

The *LP* curve cannot shift up or down. However, the *LP* curve could shift to the left or right if there were a change in natural real GDP. Various kinds of supply shocks can change natural real GDP, and we will learn in Chapter 12 that natural real GDP can be increased if a way if found to equip unskilled workers with the skills needed to qualify for particular job openings.

What Is True at Points Off the Curves?

A point below the *SP* curve represents an inflation rate below that chosen by firms and workers, given the anticipated rate of inflation and the level of output. A point above the *SP* curve represents the opposite.

A point to the right of the *LP* curve but on the *SP* curve represents a situation in which actual inflation exceeds expected inflation. In such a situation there is upward pressure on the expected rate of inflation. A point to the left of the *LP* curve but on the *SP* curve represents a situation in which actual inflation is less than expected inflation, putting downward pressure on expected inflation.

---

contract to be renegotiated. For instance, in 1988 the U.S. inflation rate accelerated as the result of higher aggregate demand. Existing wage contracts, which had been negotiated in 1986 and 1987, were based on a substantially lower inflation rate.

SELF-TEST | Assume that the economy is initially at point E_3 in Figure 8-2. There is a decline in aggregate demand, and real GDP declines from 100 to 94. What happens subsequently to the expected inflation rate and to the position of the *SP* curve?

8-4   Nominal GDP Growth and Inflation

Once we have determined the value of p^e, the average inflation rate expected at the time contracts were negotiated, we know which *SP* curve applies to today's economy. But we still have a major question remaining if we are to understand the determination of real GDP and the inflation rate: *where will the economy's position be along the current SP curve?* For instance, along SP_0, will the economy be at point E_0, point E_1, or some other point?

To answer this question, we need to know the relationship between nominal GDP and both real GDP and the inflation rate. Recall from Chapter 2 that nominal GDP *(X)* is defined as the price level *(P)* times real GDP *(Y)*:

$$X = PY \qquad (8.1)$$

Just as real GDP is determined in the *IS-LM* model of Chapter 4 by such factors as real government spending and the real money supply, so nominal GDP is determined by nominal government spending and the nominal money supply. In addition, nominal GDP is determined by any other *disturbance* to aggregate demand discussed in the preceding chapters, including changes in tax rates, autonomous net taxes, the autonomous component of net exports, and the shifts in business and consumer optimism.[3]

In this chapter we are interested in the *growth rate* of the price level, that is, the rate of inflation. We can convert (8.1) into a relationship that directly includes the rate of inflation if we recall a simple piece of arithmetic: the growth rate of any product of two numbers, such as *P* times *Y* in equation (8.1), is equal to the sum of the separate growth rates of the two numbers.[4] Writing the growth rates of variables in (8.1) as, respectively, *x, p,* and *y,* implies

$$x = p + y \qquad (8.2)$$

In words, this equation says that the growth rate of nominal GDP *(x)* equals the inflation rate *(p)* plus the growth rate of real GDP *(y)*.

If the level of nominal GDP starts out at 100, as in period 0 in Table 8-1, then a growth rate of 6 percent will bring the level to 106 in period 1. As shown in Table 8-1, several different combinations of inflation and real GDP growth are compatible with a 6 percent growth rate for nominal GDP *(x = 6)*.

Alternative B shows that if inflation is 6 percent, higher prices will absorb all of the 6 percent growth of nominal GDP so that nothing will remain for real GDP growth. Real GDP remains constant, then, at its initial level of 100. Inflation "uses up" all of nominal GDP growth.

---

[3]We can take our basic equation for the aggregate demand *(AD)* curve, developed in the appendix to Chapter 5, and repeat it here:

$$Y = k_1 A_0 + k_2 M^s / P$$

This states that real GDP *(Y)* equals an autonomous spending multiplier times the value of *real* autonomous planned spending at a zero interest rate (A_0), plus a monetary multiplier times the real money supply (M^s/P). When multiplied through by the price level *(P)*, this becomes an expression that determines nominal GDP *(X)* as equal to the autonomous spending multiplier times *nominal* autonomous spending at a zero interest rate (PA_0), plus a monetary multiplier times the *nominal money supply* (M^s).

[4]The formal way to show this is to take the logarithm of the product of two terms, such as *PY:*

$$\log X = \log P + \log Y$$

Then the derivative of both sides is taken with respect to time:

$$\frac{d \log X}{dt} = \frac{d \log P}{dt} + \frac{d \log Y}{dt}$$

This is the same as equality in equation (8.2), since *x* is defined as *(d log X)/dt* and likewise for *p* and *y*.

Table 8-1   **Alternative Divisions of 6 Percent Nominal GDP Growth Between Inflation and Real GDP Growth**

	Period	Nominal GDP (X)	Real GDP (Y)	GDP Deflator (P)	Nominal GDP (x)	Real GDP (y)	GDP Deflator (p)
		Level of Variable			*Growth Rate of Variable Between Periods 0 and 1*		
Alternative A:							
Inflation at 9 percent	0	100	100	1.00	6	−3	9
	1	106	97	1.09			
Alternative B:							
Inflation at 6 percent	0	100	100	1.00	6	0	6
	1	106	100	1.06			
Alternative C:							
Inflation at 3 percent	0	100	100	1.00	6	3	3
	1	106	103	1.03			

Alternative C shows that if inflation is only 3 percent, then half of the 6 percent growth in nominal GDP will remain for real GDP to grow by 3 percent, from 100 initially to 103 in period 1. Here inflation uses up only half of nominal GDP growth.

Finally, alternative A shows that if inflation is 9 percent, then nominal GDP growth of 6 percent will not be sufficient to maintain real GDP constant at 100. Real GDP growth must be *minus* 3 percent, forcing the level of real GDP to fall from 100 in period 0 to 97 in period 1. Here inflation uses up more than the available rate of nominal GDP, forcing real GDP to fall.

Example: When inflation is less than the growth rate of nominal GDP, real GDP must rise, just as in alternative C. When inflation is greater than the growth rate of nominal GDP, real GDP must fall, just as in alternative A.

		x	$=$	p	$+$	y
Years like Alternative C						
	1977	10.82	=	6.08	+	4.74
	1984	10.47	=	3.87	+	6.60
	1996	4.40	=	1.94	+	2.46
Years like Alternative A						
	1974	7.94	=	8.31	+	− 0.36
	1982	3.97	=	6.14	+	− 2.17
	1991	2.97	=	3.94	+	− 0.98

8-5   Effects of an Acceleration in Nominal GDP Growth

Now we are ready to see how changes in nominal GDP growth (x) affect real GDP (Y) and the inflation rate (p). We shall assume that initially the economy is in a long-run equilibrium in Figure 8-3 at point E_0. The actual and expected inflation rates are both zero $(p = p^e = 0)$. Thus the SP curve that applies is SP_0, which assumes $p^e = 0$ and is copied from Figure 8-2.

Figure 8-3
The Adjustment Path of Inflation and Real GDP to an Acceleration of Nominal GDP Growth from Zero to 6 Percent When Expectations Fail to Adjust

The economy initially is at point E_0, with actual and expected inflation of 0 percent. A 6 percent acceleration in nominal GDP growth moves the economy in the first period to point F. If the expected rate of inflation ($p^e = 0$) fails to respond to faster actual inflation (an unrealistic assumption), the economy eventually arrives at point E_2.

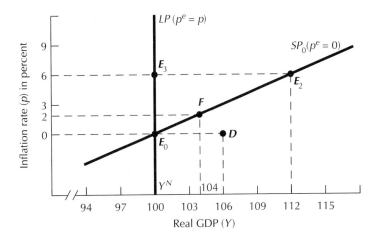

THE IMPACT ON INFLATION AND REAL GDP OF FASTER NOMINAL GDP GROWTH

If nominal GDP growth is also zero $(x = 0)$, then the economy can stay at point E_0, since $x = p$. Why? As we can see by subtracting p from both sides of equation (8.2), when $x = p$, the growth rate of output (y) must be zero:

$$y = x - p \tag{8.3}$$

$$0 = 0 - 0 \text{ (the specific values at point } E_0)$$

As long as $x = 0$, point E_0 is a long-run equilibrium, meeting the three conditions (1) that the economy is on the *SP* curve, (2) that $x = p$ (so $y = 0$), and (3) that expectations are accurate $(p^e = p)$.

Now let us assume that nominal GDP growth (x) accelerates permanently from 0 to 6 percent. What happens? The economy can no longer stay at E_0 because it is no longer true that $x = p$. Instead, the 6 percent value of x exceeds the 0 percent initial value of p, and real GDP must grow. With no price increases at all, firms respond to rising expenditures by producing more goods and services. If real GDP (Y) grows, that makes the *growth rate* of real GDP (y) positive. Equation (8.3) teaches us the following key rule about the adjustment of real GDP and inflation:

Real GDP must grow; that is, the growth rate of real GDP is positive (y > 0), whenever nominal GDP growth exceeds the inflation rate (x > p).

Now it might seem that as the result of an acceleration of x from 0 to 6, the economy must go to point D in Figure 8.3, where inflation (p) is zero but real GDP (Y) has grown from 100 to 106, so that the *growth rate* of real GDP is 6 percent $(y = 6)$:

$$y = x - p \text{ (in this case at point } D)$$

$$6 = 6 - 0$$

However, there is a problem with point D: *It does not lie on* SP_0, which shows the combinations of output and the inflation rate that are consistent with profit-maximizing behavior by businesses and zero expected inflation. We must find a point along SP_0 that also satisfies equation (8-3). This is point

F, where the inflation rate is 2 percent *(p = 2)*, while real GDP has grown from 100 to 104 *(y = 4)*:

$$y = x - p$$

$$4 = 6 - 2 \text{ (the specific values at point } F)$$

Thus, starting from E_0, an acceleration in nominal GDP growth from zero to 6 percent will slide the economy up the fixed positively sloped schedule SP_0, since people initially expect an inflation rate of zero *($p^e = 0$)*. This extra 6 percent of nominal GDP growth is divided between inflation and output growth, according to equation (8.3). In this example, 2 percentage points of the total 6 percentage point acceleration in *x* are devoted to higher inflation at point *F*, and the remaining 4 percentage points are devoted to output growth, that is, raising real GDP from 100 to 104. Point *F* is a position of *short-run equilibrium*, since it is on *SP* and it also satisfies equation (8.3).

The Continuing Adjustment.   What happens next? The economy cannot stay at point *F*, because *F is not a position of long-run equilibrium*. It violates two of the three requirements stated earlier for long-run equilibrium—that *x = p* and that expectations be accurate. First, if nominal GDP growth is 6 percent forever, and the inflation rate is only 2 percent at point *F*, then equation (8.3) tells us that real GDP growth must be positive and real GDP must increase, moving us to the right of point *F* in Figure 8-3. This means the economy cannot stay at point *F*. Second, *expectations have turned out to be incorrect.* Instead of the zero inflation expected along the SP_0 curve, inflation has turned out to be 2 percent.

Let us deal with the first of these issues and temporarily put aside the second. What happens if workers and firms who are negotiating contracts fail to react to the inaccuracy of their expectations? This means that the expected rate of inflation remains at zero *($p^e = 0$)* and that we remain on the *SP* curve. But we still have the first problem, that real GDP grows whenever nominal GDP exceeds the inflation rate, that *y > 0* when *x > p* as in equation (8.3). Since we have assumed that nominal GDP growth has accelerated permanently to 6 percent, this means that *real GDP must keep growing until inflation "uses up" all of nominal GDP growth,* that is, until *x = p = 6*. This occurs only at point E_2, where the inflation rate (plotted on the vertical axis) is equal to 6 percent, the same as the assumed permanent growth rate of nominal GDP.

But point E_2 is not satisfactory because it fails to satisfy the second condition for long-run equilibrium—that expectations be accurate. Granted E_2 is a position of short-run equilibrium, lying on the *SP* curve and satisfying equation (8.3). And real GDP has stopped growing because *x = p*. However, the economy cannot stay at E_2 because this point has inflation racing along at 6 percent, while expectations of inflation *(p^e)* remain at zero. It is inevitable that labor contract negotiations will take the ongoing 6 percent inflation into account. As the rate of wage increase is raised to take account of the unfortunate reality of 6 percent inflation, the *SP* curve will shift upward. Thus, point E_2 is not a position of long-run equilibrium.

The *SP* curve will stop shifting upward only when the economy reaches a long-run equilibrium, satisfying the three requirements that (1) the economy is on the *SP* curve, (2) *x = p* (so output stops growing), and (3) expectations are accurate *($p^e = p$)*. While the first two conditions are met at point E_2, the third is satisfied only along the vertical *LP* line. And where along the *LP* line do we satisfy the second condition, $x = p$? Given the assumed growth rate of nominal GDP $(x = 6)$, this occurs only at point E_3, where $x = p = 6$.

8-6 Expectations and the Inflation Cycle

Forward-Looking, Backward-Looking, and Adaptive Expectations

How high can real GDP be pushed by the acceleration in nominal GDP growth, and for how long? Just as high as point F? or all the way out to point E_2? Everything depends on the speed at which p^e (the average rate of inflation expected when current wage and price contracts were negotiated) responds to higher inflation. This speed of adjustment depends on numerous factors.

Forward-looking expecta-tions attempt to predict the future behavior of an economic variable, using an economic model that specifies the interrelationship of that variable with other variables.

Forward-Looking Expectations. First, are expectations forward-looking or backward-looking? **Forward-looking expectations** attempt to predict the future behavior of an economic variable, like the inflation rate, using an economic model that specifies the interrelation of that variable with other variables. Contract negotiators with forward-looking expectations might reason, for instance, that an acceleration of nominal GDP growth from zero to 6 percent implies 6 percent inflation in the long run, and immediately raise the expected rate of inflation to 6 percent. The growth rate of the nominal wage rate would speed up by 6 percent, and this would shift the *SP* curve directly upward by 6 percent. The economy would move *immediately* from point E_0 to point E_3, without any period at all with real GDP (Y) greater than natural real GDP (Y^N).

Backward-looking expec-tations use only informa-tion on the past behavior of economic variables.

The Rationality of Backward-Looking Expectations. Another alternative, **backward-looking expectations,** does not attempt to calculate the implica-tions of economic disturbances *in advance,* but simply adjusts to what has *already* happened. For instance, the backward-looking approach bases expec-tations of inflation on the past behavior of inflation, without any attempt to guess the future path of nominal GDP growth or its implications. There are two important reasons why rational workers and firms may form their expec-tations by looking backward rather than forward.

1. People may have no reason to believe that an acceleration in nominal GDP growth will be permanent. Nominal GDP growth has fluctuated before, making individuals reluctant to leap to the conclusion that the change is permanent. They may prefer just to wait and see what happens.

2. Even if the acceleration of nominal GDP growth were permanent, the exis-tence of long-term wage and price contracts and agreements, both formal and informal, would prevent *actual* inflation from responding immedi-ately. Since people know about these contracts and agreements, they know that changes in wages and prices will adjust *gradually* to the accel-eration in nominal GDP. The exact speed of adjustment cannot be pre-dicted in advance, since it depends on many factors, including the average length of wage and price contracts and agreements. Further, *one* set of contract negotiators may have no idea whether *other* negotiators

expect future nominal GDP growth to be 6 percent, 0 percent, or some other number.

Adaptive expectations
base expectations for
next period's values on an
average of actual values
during previous periods.

The most popular form of backward-looking expectations, and one that has been widely studied and verified, is called **adaptive expectations.**[5] The idea is simply that when people find that actual events do not turn out as they were expected to, they adjust their expectations to bring them closer to reality. Here is a particularly simple example of adaptive expectations. Assume that the expected inflation rate is always set equal to what actually happened last period. In Figure 8-3, the acceleration of nominal GDP growth from zero to 6 percent, which raises actual inflation from zero to 2 percent as the economy moves from point E_0 to point F, would cause the next period's expected inflation rate to rise by the same amount, to 2 percent. Here is the simple relation to remember:

This period's expected inflation rate equals last period's actual inflation rate, or $p^e = p_{-1}$.

Adjustment Loops

The economy's response to higher demand growth depends on the adjustment of expectations. In Figure 8-4 two responses are plotted. The black line moving straight northeast from point E_0 through point F to E_2 duplicates Figure 8-3. Expectations do not adjust at all and the economy remains on its original SP_0 curve.

The red line shows full adjustment with a one-period lag. In each period the SP curve shifts upward by exactly the previous period's increase in actual inflation. Because actual inflation increases by 2 percentage points in going from E_0 to point F, in the next period the SP curve shifts upward by 2 per-

---

Figure 8-4
Effect on Inflation and Real GDP of an Acceleration of Demand Growth from Zero to 6 Percent

When expectations do not adjust at all, the economy follows the black path northeast from E_0 to E_2, exactly as in Figure 8-3. When expectations adjust fully to last period's actual inflation, the economy moves upward along the red path going northwest from point H.

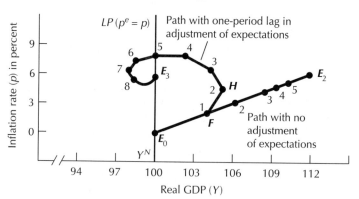

HIGHER NOMINAL GDP GROWTH RAISES INFLATION PERMANENTLY BUT RAISES REAL GDP ONLY TEMPORARILY

[5]The idea of adaptive expectations was first used in macroeconomics in a now-classic paper, Phillip Cagan, "The Monetary Dynamics of Hyperinflation," in Milton Friedman, ed., *Studies in the Quantity Theory of Money* (Chicago: University of Chicago Press, 1956), pp. 25–117.

centage points and takes the economy northward from *F* to *H*. But then expectations adjust upward again, because at *H* inflation has risen above the 2 percent people expected. Eventually, after looping around the long-run equilibrium point E_3, the economy arrives there. (The appendix to this chapter shows how to calculate the exact location of the economy in every time period along this path.)

The red path exhibits several basic characteristics of the inflation process.

1. An acceleration of demand growth (as in Figures 8-3 and 8-4) raises the inflation rate and real GDP in the short run.
2. In the long run, if expectations adjust to the actual behavior of inflation, the inflation rate *(p)* rises by exactly the same amount as *x*, and any increase in *Y* along the way is only temporary. The economy eventually arrives at point E_3.
3. Following a permanent increase in nominal GDP growth *(x)*, inflation *(p)* always experiences a temporary period when it overshoots the new growth rate of nominal GDP. For instance, in Figure 8-4, *x* increases from 0 to 6, and eventually inflation settles down to 6 percent at point E_3. But along the adjustment path the final equilibrium value of 6 percent inflation is temporarily exceeded. Along the red path, for instance, inflation reaches 8 percent in periods 4 and 5. Overshooting occurs along this path because the economy initially arrives at its long-run inflation rate *(p = 6)* in period 3 before expected inflation has caught up with actual inflation. The subsequent points that lie above 6 percent reflect the combined influence on inflation of (1) the upward adjustment of expectations and (2) the continued upward demand pressure that raises actual inflation above expected inflation whenever the economy is to the right of its *LP* line.

SELF-TEST   Look at the red adjustment loop in Figure 8-4. Why is the line from point 1 to point 2 steeper than from E_0 to point 1?

8-7 **Recession as a Cure for Inflation**

How to Achieve Disinflation

Disinflation is a marked deceleration in the inflation rate.

In the theoretical model summarized in Figure 8-4, an increase in nominal GDP growth causes an acceleration of inflation. Now we need to find out how to achieve **disinflation,** that is, a marked deceleration in the inflation rate. It seems obvious that the most straightforward way of eliminating inflation would be to set in reverse the process that created the inflation. By causing demand growth *(x)* to slow down, the government could cause inflation to decelerate.

The "Cold Turkey" Remedy for Inflation

The response of inflation to a slowdown in nominal GDP growth is explored in Figure 8-5. This figure is identical to Figure 8-3, except that here we begin with 10 percent inflation. On the horizontal axis we plot actual real GDP *(Y)* and

Figure 8-5
**Initial Effect on Inflation and Real GDP
of a Slowdown in Nominal GDP Growth
from 10 Percent to 4 Percent**

Initially the economy is in a long-run
equilibrium at point E_4 with expected
inflation (p^e) equal to the actual inflation
rate (p) of 10 percent. When nominal
GDP growth slows down suddenly and
permanently from 10 percent to 4 percent, the economy initially moves to
point K in the first period. Notice that
the *drop* in real GDP and inflation
between points E_4 and K in this figure is
exactly equal to the *increase* in real GDP
and inflation between E_0 and F in Figures
8-3 and 8-4.

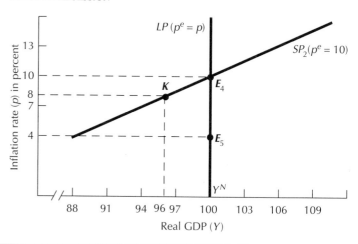

SLOWING NOMINAL GDP GROWTH INITIALLY
CAUSES A RECESSION

The **cold turkey** approach
to disinflation operates by
implementing a sudden
and permanent slowdown
in nominal GDP growth.

assume that natural real GDP (Y^N) remains fixed at a value of 100. Expected
inflation is assumed to be 10 percent along the SP_2 line.

In Figure 8-5 we assume that the government introduces a policy, sometimes called **cold turkey,** that suddenly reduces demand growth (x) from 10
to 4 percent. If the position of the SP_2 curve remains fixed, with people expecting inflation of 10 percent because inflation last period was 10 percent, then
the economy will move initially to point K. The government's policy cuts inflation from 10 percent at point E_4 to 8 percent at K, but at the cost of a recession as real GDP falls from 100 to 96.

Notice that the move from E_4 to point K in Figure 8-5 represents an exact
reversal of the adjustment from E_0 to point F in Figure 8-3. In both cases, the
initial reaction of the economy to the 6 percent change in nominal GDP
growth is divided into two percentage points of adjustment of inflation and
four percentage points of adjustment in real GDP.

The Process of Adjustment to the New Long-Run
Equilibrium

The process of adjustment finally comes to an end when inflation is equal to
the new growth rate of nominal GDP $(p = x = 4)$, and when the expected inflation rate has declined to its long-run equilibrium value of four $(p^e = 4)$. Recall
that the vertical LP line shows all the different combinations of inflation and
real GDP when expectations are correct. One such point on LP is E_5, where
inflation is 4 percent and thus is compatible in the long run with a nominal
GDP growth of 4 percent. But to reach E_5, the SP line must go through that
point, which requires that expected inflation fall to 4 percent, and, with adaptive expectations, this is unlikely to occur until people see that the inflation
rate has actually declined to 4 percent.

Because individual households and firms are likely to take a "show me"
attitude, refusing to believe that inflation will slow down until they see such a
slowdown actually occurring, the cold turkey cure for inflation is likely to be

a long and drawn-out process. The economy's arrival at point E_5 could take more than a decade, as illustrated in Figure 8-6. Please note that Figure 8-6 does not display actual data but rather hypothetical adjustment paths implied by our theoretical model. Actual data are plotted subsequently in Figure 8-7.

The Downward Spiraling Loop.   In Figure 8-6 the economy starts at point E_4, the same point as in the previous diagram. Nominal GDP growth, actual inflation, and expected inflation are all 10 percent at point E_4 $(x = p = p^e)$. The red loop running southwest from point E_4 shows what would happen if the rate of nominal GDP growth (x) were suddenly slowed down from 10 percent in 1980 and prior years to 4 percent in 1981 and all future years. The economy's initial reaction is to go to the point marked 1981, with inflation of 8 percent and real GDP that falls from 100 to 96 percent. *The point marked 1981 is exactly the same as point* K *in Figure 8-5.*

For 1982 and the following years, the economy follows the red path. This downward spiraling loop, which shows the effects of a permanent deceleration of x from 10 to 4, is the *mirror image* of the upward spiraling loop in Figure 8-4, which showed the effects of a permanent acceleration of x from 0 to 6. The economy overshoots, with inflation falling temporarily below the 4 percent permanent growth rate of nominal GDP (x).

A Fatter Loop.   The red path in Figure 8-6 is not the only possible outcome. The shape of the loop and the length of the adjustment period depend on the slope of the *SP* curve. The black line in Figure 8-6 shows an alternative outcome when the *SP* curve is only half as steep as we have assumed thus far in this chapter.[6] The assumption of a flatter *SP* curve results in a fatter loop in

---

Figure 8-6
Adjustment Path of Inflation and Real GDP to a Policy that Cuts Nominal GDP Growth from 10 Percent in 1980 to 4 Percent in 1981 and Thereafter

The red line between 1980 and 1981 traces exactly the same path as between E_4 and K in Figure 8-5 and shows what happens in subsequent years. The black line, as an alternative, assumes that the *SP* line is only half as steep as in previous diagrams in this chapter. The flatter the *SP* line, the longer it takes for the economy to approach long-run equilibrium.

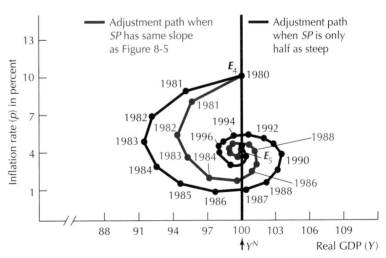

THE ECONOMY ADJUSTS TO A COLD TURKEY POLICY

---

[6]That is, the slope of the *SP* curve is assumed to be ½ in drawing the red line and ¼ in drawing the black line. The slope of the diagrams earlier in the chapter is ½, because the *SP* line rises by one percentage point of inflation for every two percentage points of increase in real output.

Figure 8-6, with a deeper recession, during which real GDP falls to a minimum of 91.6 percent instead of a minimum of 94.7 percent as it does along the red line, and a longer recession, with the economy returning to $Y = 100$ only in 1987, instead of 1985.

SELF-TEST

Why does the slope of the *SP* curve affect the economy's adjustment path in response to a slowdown in nominal GDP growth?

The Output Cost of Disinflation

The two paths depicted in Figure 8-6 share in common the cold turkey approach to disinflation, that is, a sudden drop in nominal GDP growth from 10 percent in 1980 to 4 percent forever afterward. The cost of disinflation is a slump in output, with real GDP declining by a greater amount if the SP curve is relatively flat.

What policy would avoid the decline in output illustrated by the two paths in Figure 8-6? One alternative would be to do nothing or live with inflation policy. This would require that the economy stay permanently at point E_4 in Figure 8-6. Nominal GDP growth and inflation would remain permanently at 10 percent. This would maintain real GDP growth at zero, as contrasted with the negative real GDP growth that is required as part of the disinflationary process shown by the loops in Figure 8-6.

The Sacrifice Ratio.   The model that generates the disinflation loops of Figure 8-6 can be used to assess the costs and benefits of a cold turkey policy compared to a live with inflation policy. With a cold turkey policy, over the six years 1981–86 the total amount by which real GDP falls below natural real GDP is 35.5 percent, or an average of 5.9 percent per year for six years. A con-

The **sacrifice ratio** is the cumulative loss of output incurred during a disinflation divided by the permanent reduction in the inflation rate.

venient measure of the cost of disinflation is the **sacrifice ratio,** the ratio of the *cumulative* output lost to the permanent reduction in the inflation rate created by a disinflationary policy like the cold turkey approach shown in Figure 8-6. With the cold turkey policy, the sacrifice ratio is a loss of output of 35.5 percent to obtain a permanent reduction of inflation of 6 percent, or a sacrifice ratio of 5.9 (35.5/6).

Thus the issue addressed by the sacrifice ratio is How important is it to reduce the inflation rate permanently? Would citizens endorse a policy of permanently reducing the inflation rate by 1 percent if they knew this would require a loss of output (implying lost income and jobs) equal to 5.9 percent of one year's GDP, which amounts to about $450 billion or $1700 for every adult and child in the country? We return to this issue in Chapter 12, where we assess the relative costs of inflation and unemployment.

8-8   CASE STUDY: Why Inflation Declined in the 1980s and 1990s

A good test of our theory is to compare its predictions from the experience of the United States during the past 15 years, when the inflation rate (as measured by the GDP deflator) fell from almost 10 percent in 1980 to only 2 percent in 1996. Can this "disinflation" be explained by the theoretical adjustment loop depicted in Figure 8-6?

1981–82: A Classic Disinflation

To compare actual events with the predictions of our theory, Figure 8-7 plots actual data on a graph that looks just like the theoretical Figure 8-6, with the inflation rate on the vertical axis and the output ratio (Y/Y^N) on the horizontal axis. In 1981 and 1982 there was a sharp deceleration in nominal GDP growth (achieved by tight monetary policy and an unprecedented sharp increase in short-term interest rates). Just as predicted by our theory, the economy moved to the southwest, with a declining output ratio and declining inflation as well. The output ratio declined to below 94 percent. As shown subsequently in Figure 8-8, the unemployment rate increased to 10.7 percent in 1982:Q4—the highest rate experienced by the economy since the Great Depression of the 1930s.

How closely did the actual events correspond to the theoretical adjustment path in Figure 8-6? Notice that the inner loop in Figure 8-6 has a decline of the inflation rate from 1980 to 1982 of roughly 5 percent, and an output ratio in 1982 of about 94 percent. The actual events depicted in Figure 8-7 correspond very closely to the inner loop of Figure 8-6.

Disinflation and the Revival of Inflation During the 1982–90 Expansion

After 1983 the actual events plotted in Figure 8-7 differ from the inner loop of the theory shown in Figure 8-6. Why? Recall that the theoretical adjustment was based on a *permanent* slowdown in nominal GDP growth from 10 to 4 percent. But in the real world of Figure 8-7, nominal GDP growth did not remain permanently lower. Instead, nominal GDP growth accelerated sharply in 1983–84, causing the output ratio to recover more rapidly than in the theoretical diagram, and also bringing the decline of the inflation rate to an end. Another difference is that inflation dropped temporarily in 1986 from the path it would otherwise have followed in response to a sharp decline in oil prices.

Figure 8-7
The Inflation Rate and the Output Ratio, 1980–1996

Notice how slower growth in nominal GDP was divided between slower inflation and slower real GDP growth. Because real GDP *(Y)* fell while natural real GDP (Y^N) continued to rise, the output ratio fell from 98 percent in 1981:Q1 to below 94 percent in 1982:Q4. A revival in demand growth allowed the output ratio to increase between 1983 and early 1989. The inflation rate decelerated during 1984–86, accelerated during 1987–90, and decelerated again as the output ratio fell in 1990–92. Inflation stayed low during the 1992–96 expansion because the output ratio never appreciably exceeded 100 percent.

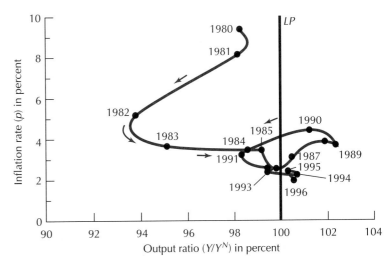

DID THE ECONOMY FOLLOW THE TEXTBOOK ADJUSTMENT PATH?

THE NATURAL RATE OF UNEMPLOYMENT FELL IN THE 1990s

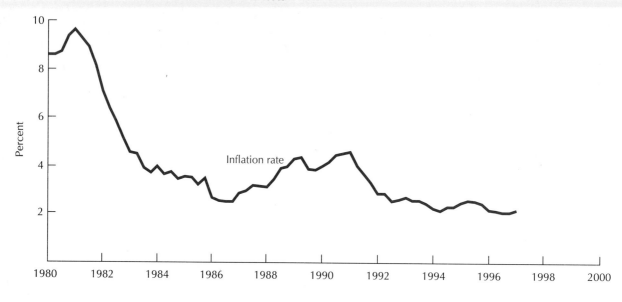

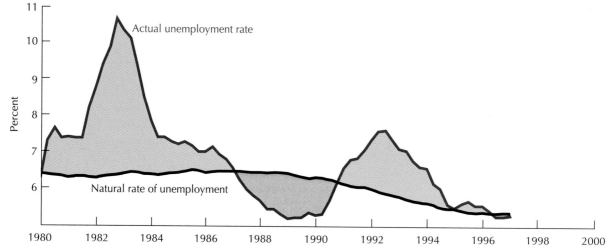

Figure 8-8   **The Inflation Rate, The Actual Unemployment Rate, and the Natural Rate of Unemployment, 1980–97.**

A comparison of the top and bottom frames shows that the inflation rate slowed down during 1980–86 when the actual unemployment rate was above the natural rate of unemployment. Inflation speeded up during 1987–90 when the actual unemployment rate fell below the natural rate and then slowed again during 1990–93 when the actual unemployment rate once again rose above the natural rate. Inflation was approximately constant during 1994–96, corresponding to the fact that the actual unemployment rate was quite similar to the natural rate of unemployment.

Starting in 1987, the continued rapid growth in nominal GDP caused the output ratio to rise above 100 percent. As predicted by our theory, the inflation rate accelerated, and the economy went through another loop. Reacting to higher inflation in 1988–90, the Fed tightened monetary policy, nominal GDP growth slowed, and the economy had a brief and mild recession in

1990–91, during which the output ratio fell from about 102 percent to about 98 percent. As shown in the bottom frame of Figure 8-8, the unemployment rate increased from 5.3 percent in early 1990 to a peak of 7.7 percent in the summer of 1992. As predicted by the theory, the inflation rate decelerated in response to the recession and the interval during which the output ratio was below 100 percent between 1990 and 1993.

Comparing the Actual and Natural Rates of Unemployment

Figure 8-8 in its top frame displays the same data on the inflation rate as in Figure 8-7, but plots the inflation rate against time on the horizontal axis, rather than against the output ratio. In the bottom frame the actual unemployment rate is plotted along with the natural rate of unemployment. Recall from Chapter 1 (p. 10) that the actual and natural unemployment rates are equal at any time that the actual and natural levels of real GDP are equal, that is, when the output ratio is 100 percent. The bottom frame of Figure 8-8 shows that this situation of equality between the actual and natural rates of unemployment (along with an output ratio of 100 percent) occurred in early 1980, late 1986, late 1990, late 1994, and early 1996.

    Our theory in this chapter has been developed as a relationship between the inflation rate and the output ratio. But since the actual unemployment rate falls below the natural rate of unemployment by definition whenever the output ratio rises above 100 percent, the same theory predicts that inflation should accelerate when the actual unemployment rate falls below the natural rate of unemployment. Likewise, the inflation rate should decelerate whenever the actual unemployment rate rises above the natural rate of unemployment. Comparing the top and bottom frames of Figure 8-8, we see that inflation slowed down during 1980–86, when the unemployment rate was above the natural rate, then accelerated during 1987–90 when the unemployment rate was below the natural rate, and then decelerated again during 1990–93 when the unemployment rate was above the natural rate.

Steady Inflation During 1994–96

From 1994 to 1996 the economy remained close to an output ratio of 100 percent, and the unemployment rate remained close to the natural rate of unemployment. As shown in Figures 8-7 and 8-8, the inflation rate showed no significant speeding up or slowing down. If anything, inflation seemed to slow down slightly in 1996, despite an output ratio that was slightly above 100 percent.

    The business expansion of the mid-1990s was significantly different from that in the late 1980s. In the earlier episode, the actual unemployment rate fell close to 5 percent, and this caused inflation to accelerate significantly. Yet in 1996 the actual unemployment rate was similar to that in 1988–89, but inflation did not accelerate. Why? The natural rate of unemployment fell from above 6 percent in the 1980s to only about 5.3 percent in 1996. Thus the same actual unemployment rate that had caused inflation to accelerate in 1988–89 did not cause any acceleration of inflation in 1996.

INTERNATIONAL PERSPECTIVE

Did Disinflation in Europe Differ from That in the United States?

Most industrial nations have been experiencing relatively low rates of inflation in the mid-1990s. But this is a new phenomenon. Only a few years ago inflation rates were much higher and differed widely among the major nations.

The figure compares the inflation rate for the United States, beginning in 1975, with the four largest European nations—France, Germany, Italy, and the United Kingdom. Until the 1990s Germany had the lowest inflation rate of all, and its inflation rate rose relatively little during the time of the 1979–81 oil shock. Germany's success in maintaining relatively low inflation is attributable to the relatively tight monetary policy conducted by the German central bank, the Deutsche Bundesbank.

During the early 1980s the other three European countries had higher inflation rates than the United States and more than double the inflation rate experienced by Germany. These countries did not follow the same tight monetary policy as did Germany; instead, monetary and fiscal policies were much looser, allowing nominal GDP to rise much faster than in Germany. In 1980 the inflation rate in Italy reached 20 percent per year and in the United Kingdom was almost as high.

Clearly, something important changed after 1980. While the United States achieved a substantial disinflation between 1981 and 1986, the amount by which the inflation rate fell was even greater in Italy and the United Kingdom. The key ingredient in the European disinflation was the establishment of the European Monetary System (EMS) in 1979. Member nations attempted to maintain their exchange rates within a relatively narrow band around that of the German currency, the deutsche mark, or DM.

Clearly, at first the British and Italian exchange rates could not be held fixed for very long, since their inflation rates were so much higher than Germany's. At a fixed exchange rate, high inflation meant that British and Italian export prices rose rapidly compared to German prices, and these countries became uncompetitive. Hence, the EMS allowed for periodic adjustments of exchange rates for nations with high inflation rates. But the U.K. and Italy committed themselves to reducing inflation, primarily through tight monetary policies (aided by the decline in the real price of oil, as displayed in Figure 8-9). By 1987 they had made sufficient progress and could commit to maintaining their exchange rates within a narrow band relative to the deutsche mark. However, the price of this progress was that unemployment rose to levels that were much higher than those in the United States. For instance, the unemployment rate in France never fell below 9 percent after 1985 and was above 12 percent in 1996–97.

The era of fixed exchange rates for

Why Did the Natural Rate of Unemployment Decline in the mid-1990s?

Academic research has only begun to address the question of why the natural rate of unemployment declined in the 1990s. Several factors combined to reduce the inflation rate that occurs at a given actual rate of unemployment, thus reducing the natural rate of unemployment. In the language developed in the next section, these events operated as "beneficial supply shocks":

● The falling prices of computers (that is, *negative* inflation for computers) began to pull down the overall inflation rate as computers became a larger part of total spending in the economy.

the major European nations within the EMS lasted from 1987 to 1992, when it broke down. Italy, the U.K., and several other countries, including Spain and Sweden, devalued their exchange rates relative to the DM, while France and several other countries maintained parity with it. Observers expected the inflation rates in Italy and the U.K. to increase after 1992, since their exchange rate devaluation made goods and services imported into Italy and Britain from France and Germany go up in price. But as the figure shows, by 1996 there had been no upsurge of inflation in Italy and the U.K.

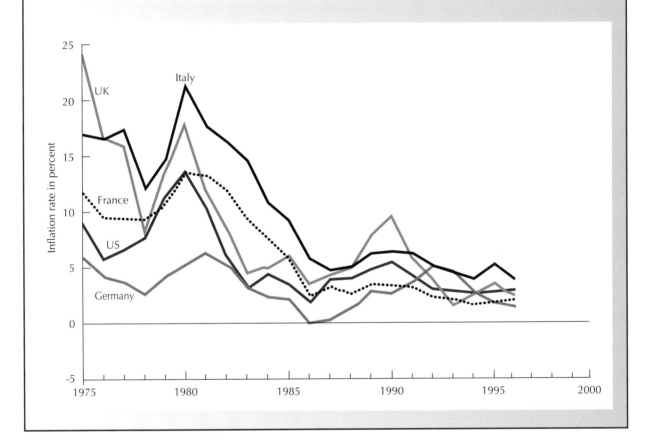

- A drastic decline in the inflation rate for medical care services (including hospitals and doctors) occurred, partly as a result of the transition to managed care organizations like HMOs (Health Maintenance Organizations). This spontaneous disinflation in a major sector of the economy helped hold down overall inflation.

- The bargaining position of labor had become weaker. Labor unions covered a smaller percentage of the workforce, the real minimum wage was lower than in the early 1980s, and workers generally felt insecure about their jobs after waves of well-publicized layoffs and corporate downsizing.

- Finally, global competition in many industries made firms more resistant to worker demands for wage increases and made firms reluctant to raise prices.

As we shall see in the rest of this chapter, events that change the inflation rate occurring at a given unemployment rate are called *supply shocks*. These shocks harmed the economy in the 1970s and early 1980s, but helped hold down inflation both in the mid-1980s and mid-1990s.[7]

8-9 The Importance of Supply Disturbances

Demand inflation is a sustained increase in prices that is preceded by a permanent acceleration of nominal GDP growth.

Supply inflation is an increase in prices that stems from an increase in business costs not directly related to a prior acceleration of nominal GDP growth.

So far in this chapter we have studied **demand inflation,** which is inflation caused by an acceleration of the growth rate of nominal aggregate demand—that is, nominal GDP. Demand inflation can be caused by changes in any of the demand factors studied earlier in the book—consumer and business confidence, the money supply, government spending, tax rates, transfers, and net exports. Now we turn to a second reason for changes in the inflation rate, that is, **supply inflation.** As we see in Figure 8-9, during the decade between 1971 and 1981, fluctuations in nominal GDP growth were a poor guide to the timing of fluctuations in the inflation rate; the U.S. inflation rate exhibited volatile accelerations and decelerations that were not preceded by changes in nominal GDP growth in the same direction. *In fact, the lowest nominal GDP growth of the decade was experienced in early 1975, when the inflation rate was the fastest.* Shifts in supply inflation also help us understand why inflation was so low in 1986, why it accelerated in 1987–89, and why it was again so low in 1994–96.

Types of Supply Shocks

Supply inflation stems from sharp changes in business costs that are not related to prior changes in nominal GDP growth. The most important single cause of supply inflation in the 1970s and early 1980s in most industrialized countries in the world was a sharp increase in the price of oil, shown in the bottom frame of Figure 8-9. A sharp decline in the price of oil in 1986 reversed some of the earlier harm done by supply inflation. The rise in the real price of oil during the Iraqi invasion of Kuwait in 1990 is another example of an adverse supply shock. Supply inflation can also result from an increase in the prices of other raw materials, particularly farm products, if they are sufficiently important.

Sometimes the *weather* causes supply shocks, as in the case of a crop failure that causes a sharp increase in farm prices. Usually supply shocks caused by the weather are *temporary,* lasting only a year or two, after which condi-

---

[7]Estimates of the natural rate of unemployment that vary over time, as in Figure 8-8, are developed in Robert J. Gordon, "The Time-Varying NAIRU and its Implications for Economic Policy," *Journal of Economic Perspectives,* vol. 11 (winter, 1997), pp. 11–32.

BETWEEN 1971 AND 1981 INFLATION AND NOMINAL GDP GROWTH MOVED IN
OPPOSITE DIRECTIONS

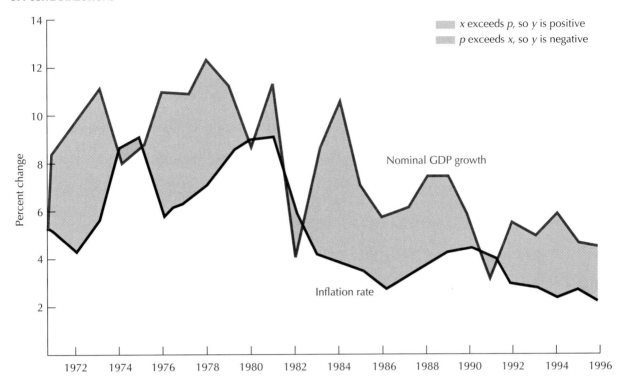

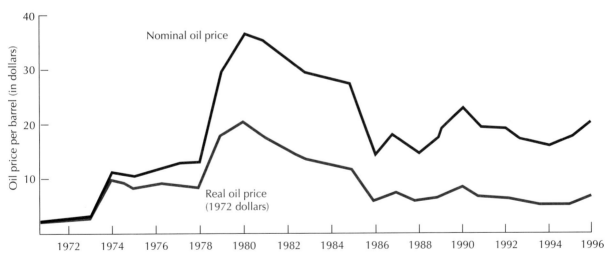

Figure 8-9   **Four-Quarter Growth Rates of the GDP Deflator and Nominal GDP and the Level
of Nominal and Real Oil Prices, 1970–96**

The top frame compares the inflation rate *(p)* with nominal GDP growth *(x)* beginning in 1970:Q1. The red areas show periods of positive real GDP growth *(y)*, and the
gray areas show periods of negative real GDP growth. In the bottom frame the nominal price of oil is compared with the real price of oil, using 1972 as a base year.
Notice the upsurge in inflation in the top frame at the times of the two oil shocks in
the bottom frame.

tions return to normal. The OPEC oil shocks, however, were considered *permanent,* causing an increase in the real price of oil that lasted from 1974 to 1986.

Supply shocks can be either *adverse* or *beneficial.* An adverse supply shock is one that makes inflation worse while causing real GDP to fall, as in the case of sharp increases in oil or farm prices in the early 1970s. A beneficial supply shock is one that reduces inflation while causing real GDP to rise, as in the case of the sharp decline in oil prices in 1986.

A new type of beneficial supply shock occurred in the mid-1990s, particularly during 1994–96. This occurred for two reasons. First, a major component of consumption spending, that on medical care services, experienced a sharp slowdown in its inflation rate that was independent of the level of aggregate demand, the output ratio, or the unemployment rate. A revolution in the U.S. medical care industry occurred, with a massive shift to "managed care" providers, e.g., Health Maintenance Organizations (HMOs). These organizations could provide medical care at significantly lower costs than under the previous system, and this accounted for the fact that medical care inflation slowed down from well above the average rate of inflation to somewhat below the average rate.

A second and unrelated reason for the beneficial supply shock of the mid-1990s was the role of computers. For several decades, computer prices have been falling in nominal terms. But for many years this did not affect the behavior of the overall inflation rate, since computers were such a small share of total spending. However, in the mid-1990s the share of computer spending increased rapidly, and so the negative inflation rate of computers (sometimes proceeding at *minus* 25 or *minus* 35 percent per year) began to pull down the overall inflation rate. This occurred in just the same way that the average batting average of a baseball team would be pulled down if it hired 10 new players whose individual averages were only .100, compared to a .300 average for the rest of the team.

Whether adverse or beneficial, supply shocks pose a difficult challenge for the makers of monetary and fiscal policy. Adverse supply shocks impose unpleasant choices on policymakers, who can avoid extra inflation only at the cost of higher unemployment, or vice versa. But even beneficial supply shocks may require policymakers to make choices.

Supply Shocks and the Macroeconomic Puzzles

PUZZLE 1: WHY HAS UNEMPLOYMENT BEEN SO HIGH AND SO VARIABLE?
PUZZLE 2: WHY HAS THE INFLATION RATE AT TIMES BEEN SO HIGH AND SO VARIABLE?

Supply shocks help explain the first two puzzles introduced at the beginning of the book. The first two puzzles ask why the unemployment and inflation rates in the United States have been so high and so variable at certain times, particularly in the 1970s and early 1980s, and lower and less variable at other times, as in the 1990s.

We have now learned that the *SP* curve can be shifted by an adverse supply shock like a boost in oil prices or farm prices. By altering the position of the *SP* curve, supply shocks can make inflation, real GDP, and the unemployment rate more unstable. But supply shocks can also be beneficial, as occurred in the mid-1990s as a result of lower medical care inflation and the increasing role of deflation in computer prices.

8-10   The Response of Inflation and Real GDP to a Supply Shock

In Figure 8-9 we examined the relationship between oil price shocks and the U.S. inflation rate. There we saw that increases in the *level* of the real price of oil caused a change in the aggregate *rate of inflation.* How can this response of the rate of inflation be explained in terms of the *SP* diagram?

Effects of Supply Shocks on the Price Level and on the Rate of Inflation

Earlier we noted that supply shocks may be temporary or permanent. We can distinguish between the effects of each type of shock on the *price level,* as compared to the effect of each type on the *rate of inflation.*

Temporary Supply Shock.   One example of a temporary supply shock is a crop failure, caused by an untimely freeze or drought. The result is likely to be a temporary increase in the level of prices, followed by a return of the price index to its previous level. This occurred in the summer of 1988 when an unusually severe drought ruined much of the nation's wheat, corn, and soybean crop, causing an increase in prices in the fall and winter of 1988. But then normal weather returned in 1989 and the price index for these products dropped to its initial level. The following diagram assumes that initially the inflation rate is zero.

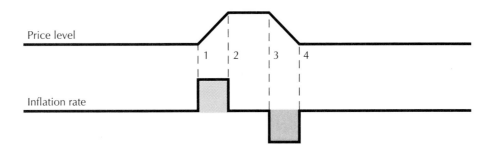

   In the diagram, at time 1 the price level begins to rise, increasing the rate of inflation (which is, after all, just the rate of change of the price level). At time 2 the price index levels off, so that the rate of inflation returns to zero. At time 3 the price level begins to fall, so that the rate of inflation becomes negative, and finally both the price level and rate of inflation return at time 4 to their initial values. This type of supply shock is unlikely to cause any adjustment of the expected inflation rate, because most people will correctly view the initial inflation (indicated by the red shaded area) as a temporary phenomenon.

Permanent Supply Shock.   Examples of a permanent supply shock were the OPEC oil price increases of 1974 and 1979, which affected the economy for more than a decade until oil prices finally fell in 1986. Increasing energy prices pushed up the rate of inflation as firms adjusted to the higher price of oil, but then no further direct impact was felt on the price level. This type of permanent supply shock can be depicted as follows:

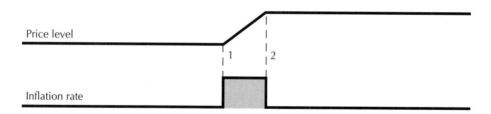

This diagram duplicates the previous one for the first two time periods, during which the price index rises to a new, higher level. The difference is that no subsequent drop in the price level occurs; the OPEC oil cartel did not allow the price of oil to return to its pre-1974 level until 1986, a long, 12-year interval, unlike corn and soybean farmers who raised production promptly in 1989 after the 1988 drought had ended.

Supply Shocks and the Short-Run Phillips Curve *(SP)*

To see how the rate of inflation reacts, we must use the short-run Phillips curve *(SP)*. The SP_2 curve in Figure 8-10 assumes that the expected rate of inflation is 6 percent. The vertical axis plots the aggregate rate of inflation, while the horizontal axis plots the output ratio—the ratio of actual to natural real GDP (Y/Y^N).

Supply Shocks Shift the *SP* Schedule.   As long as the real price of oil remains constant, the only factor that could make the *SP* curve shift would be a change in the expected rate of inflation (p^e). But if a supply shock changes the real price of oil, then we have a second reason why the *SP* curve might shift up.

Point E_3 in Figure 8-10 depicts a situation of long-run equilibrium. Actual inflation is 6 percent, and initially the rate of nominal GDP growth is assumed to be 6 percent. Since SP_2 assumes that expected inflation (p^e) is 6 percent, the condition $p^e = p$, required for long-run equilibrium, is satisfied.

Now let us assume that OPEC suddenly doubles the price of oil over the course of a year, as occurred in 1979, and let us assume that its action is sufficient *to add three extra percentage points to the inflation rate at any given level of real GDP.* The three extra points of inflation are reflected in the upward shift of the *SP* schedule from SP_2 to SP_3. Where will the economy move along the new SP_3?

Policy Responses to Supply Shocks

The response of the economy to the adverse permanent supply shock depicted in Figure 8-10 *depends on the response of nominal GDP growth.* The

Figure 8-10

The Effect on the Inflation Rate and the Output Ratio of an Adverse Supply Shock that Shifts the *SP* Curve Upward by 3 Percent

The economy is initially at point E_3, with an output ratio of 100 percent and both actual and expected inflation rates of 6 percent. The supply shock shifts the *SP* curve upward to SP_3. The movement of the economy depends on the policy response. With an accommodating policy the economy moves from E_3 to point *N*, with a neutral policy to point *L*, and with an extinguishing policy to point *M*.

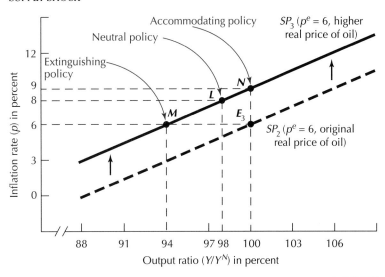

THE FED'S UNPLEASANT CHOICES AFTER AN ADVERSE SUPPLY SHOCK

Neutral, Accommodating, and Extinguishing Policy Responses. There are three possible policy responses. The first is called a **neutral policy.** Such a policy would attempt to keep nominal GDP growth unchanged from the original rate (6 percent). This is shown by point *L* in Figure 8-10. Since real GDP growth, by definition, must be equal to nominal GDP growth minus the inflation rate $(y = x - p)$, *a neutral policy makes the output ratio decline by the same amount as inflation increases.* Thus, at point *L*, the output ratio falls by 2 percent (from 100 to 98) and inflation rises by 2 percentage points (from 6 to 8 percent).[8] The sum of −2 and +2 is precisely zero, the assumed zero change in the growth rate of nominal GDP.

> Following a supply shock a **neutral policy** maintains nominal GDP growth so as to allow a decline in the output ratio equal to the increase of the inflation rate.

Does the government have any way to escape the simultaneous worsening of inflation and decline in the output ratio shown at point *L*? It can keep the output ratio fixed only if it is willing to accept more inflation. Or, it can keep inflation from accelerating above 6 percent only if it is willing to accept a greater decline in the output ratio.

> Following a supply shock an **accommodating policy** raises nominal GDP growth so as to maintain the original output ratio.

An **accommodating policy** attempts to maintain the output ratio intact at point *N*. To do this, inflation must be allowed to rise by the full extent of the vertical shift in *SP,* so that inflation jumps from 6 to 9 percent per year. This acceleration of inflation requires an acceleration of nominal GDP growth.

government can implement policy measures to alter nominal GDP growth. These policy actions determine where the economy moves along the new SP_3 schedule.

[8]The text discussion of the graphical example in Figure 8-10 ignores the decline in Y^N that is likely to occur. The precise definition of a neutral policy is one involving no change in the excess of nominal GDP growth over the growth rate of natural real GDP from its initial value, assumed to be 6 percent $(x - y^N = 6)$. This more precise definition is developed in the appendix to this chapter.

Following a supply shock an **extinguishing policy** reduces nominal GDP growth so as to maintain the original inflation rate.

An **extinguishing policy** attempts to eliminate entirely the extra inflation caused by the supply shock.[9] This requires cutting nominal GDP growth by enough to take the economy to point M, where the inflation rate is 6 percent, but the output ratio has fallen from 100 to 94 percent (instead of to 98 percent at point L). Why is the extra four-point decline in the output ratio necessary? To extinguish the extra two percentage points of inflation that occur at L compared to M, the output ratio must be cut by four percentage points, since the slope of the SP curve is assumed to be 1/2 (two units in a vertical direction for each four units in the horizontal direction).

What Happens in Subsequent Periods

If the hypothetical supply shock occurs for just one period, then in Figure 8-10 the *SP* curve shifts down to its original position *(SP$_2$)* after one period at position SP_3. The economy would then be free to return to the original output ratio and the original inflation rate. The indirect effect on the output ratio (Y/Y^N) and on the rate of inflation would last for just one period.

But the *SP* curve returns to position SP_2 only if the expected inflation rate *remains at 6 percent.* The expected inflation rate must not respond to the one-period increase in the actual inflation rate that occurs at points *L* and *N* in Figure 8-10. Is this plausible? The response of the expected inflation rate depends on whether people view the supply shock as temporary or permanent (discussed above) and on whether labor contracts incorporate cost-of-living agreements (COLAs) that automatically boost wages by a percentage that is related to the inflation rate.

Why are COLAs crucial? Without COLAs, contract negotiators will recognize that it is possible for the economy to return to its original position (point E_3 in Figure 8-10) after the one-period effect of the supply shock. But with COLAs, the one-period increase of inflation (to point *L* or *N*) will be incorporated automatically into a faster growth of nominal wage rates *next period.* Contract negotiators in subsequent periods will see that COLAs have raised the rate of change of the nominal wage and will realize that this makes it impossible for the economy to return to point E_3. Their expected rate of inflation will shift up above the original 6 percent, and the *SP* curve will shift to a position above the original SP_2 in subsequent periods.

The Policy Dilemma.   Thus we see that COLAs create a dilemma for the makers of monetary policy. COLAs imply that a permanent supply shock will permanently raise the inflation rate *unless an extinguishing policy response to the initial impact of the supply shock prevents any increase at all of inflation and thus prevents any increase at all in the rate of change of nominal wage rates.*

What should the Fed do when presented with this dilemma? It faces the classic trade-off between inflation and lost output. With even partial COLA protection for workers, a permanent adverse supply shock will permanently raise the inflation rate in the absence of an extinguishing policy. But this does not mean that the Fed should actually pursue such an extinguishing policy.

---

[9]The phrase *extinguishing policy* was introduced in Edward M. Gramlich, "Macro Policy Responses to Price Shocks." *Brookings Papers on Economic Activity,* vol. 10, no. 1 (1979), pp. 125–178.

The social costs of the loss in output may be severe, as Y/Y^N declines to point M in Figure 8-10, while the social costs of permanently higher inflation following a neutral or accommodating policy response may be relatively small. We examine those social costs in Chapter 12.[10]

Effects of Favorable Supply Shocks

So far our discussion has been concerned solely with adverse supply shocks like the oil price increases of the 1970s. But supply shocks can be beneficial as well. An obvious example is the sharp decline in oil prices in 1986. Similarly, an unusually abundant harvest can cause food prices to drop, creating a beneficial shock as emphasized above. Slower inflation in medical care prices, together with the growing importance of computers (which experience negative inflation), created a favorable supply shock in the mid-1990s. Finally, government-mandated price controls, like those in effect during the 1971–74 period, can be interpreted as having the same effect as a beneficial supply shock, shifting down *SP* at any given output ratio.

The policy options in response to a beneficial shock are the same as those for an adverse shock. An accommodating policy requires a reduction in nominal GDP growth, so that the entire impact of the beneficial shock reduces the inflation rate and none spills over to boost the output ratio. In contrast, an extinguishing policy would keep the inflation rate constant and allow the full impact of the shock to boost the output ratio.

SELF-TEST

Imagine that the relative price of oil falls by half within a single year and exhibits no change thereafter. Under what circumstances will the inflation rate be reduced by this event in the year of the change? Thereafter?

8-11 Inflation and Output Fluctuations: Recapitulation of Causes and Cures

At the beginning of the book we introduced six puzzles of macroeconomic behavior. The first two puzzles were a high and variable rate of unemployment and a rate of inflation that, at times, is high and variable. We learned early in the book that fluctuations in unemployment are a direct mirror image of fluctuations in the output ratio. In this chapter we have gained a considerable understanding of our first two macroeconomic puzzles. We have learned that an acceleration of inflation can be caused by excessive nominal GDP growth and by supply shocks. Supply and demand inflation are interrelated because the extent and duration of the acceleration of inflation following a supply shock depends on the response of nominal GDP growth, which is controlled in part by policymakers.

---

[10]The analysis of supply shocks in this chapter was introduced in two papers. See Robert J. Gordon, "Alternative Responses of Policy to External Supply Shocks," *Brookings Papers on Economic Activity,* vol. 6, no. 1 (1975), pp. 183–206, and Edmund S. Phelps, "Commodity Supply Shocks and Full-Employment Monetary Policy," *Journal of Money, Credit, and Banking,* vol. 10 (May 1978), pp. 206–21. The separate models in these two papers were merged and summarized in Robert J. Gordon, "Supply Shocks and Monetary Policy Revisited," *American Economic Review Papers and Proceedings,* vol. 74 (May 1984), pp. 38–43.

A Summary of Inflation and Output Responses

Figure 8-11 provides a highly simplified summary of our analysis in this chapter. The figure presents four cases corresponding to (a) demand shifts alone, (b) supply shifts alone, (c) demand and supply shifts in the same vertical direction, and (d) demand and supply shifts in opposite vertical directions. In our discussion we identify examples from U.S. history that illustrate the four cases.

Case A: Demand Shifts Alone.   When we observe a marked increase in the output ratio with a modest or small increase in the rate of inflation, we can infer that there has been an acceleration of nominal aggregate demand growth with little if any shift in the *SP* curve. Expectations of inflation (p^e) remain roughly constant, and there are no supply shocks. The economy exhibited this type of response during 1963–66, when tax cuts and the beginning of Vietnam War spending, supported by monetary accommodation, boosted nominal GDP growth. A similar movement to the northeast occurred in 1987–89. An example of a shift in a southwestern direction, with a deceleration of nominal GDP growth, occurred in the first few quarters of the 1981–82 recession, when there was a sharp decline in Y/Y^N with little downward response of the inflation rate.

Case B: Supply Shifts Alone.   The United States experienced a straight northwestward movement in 1973–74, when food and energy supply shocks sharply boosted the inflation rate, with a relatively small change in the rate of nominal GDP growth. As a result, the inflation rate and the output ratio moved in opposite directions and by about the same amount. In 1979 and 1980 a second supply shock had roughly the same impact. The only example of a southeastward movement occurred during the first few months of the Nixon price control period in late 1971, when the rate of inflation fell without much change in nominal GDP growth.

Case C: Demand and Supply Shifts in the Same Vertical Direction.   When we observe the economy move straight north on the diagram, with an acceleration of inflation but little change in the output ratio, we can infer that there is a simultaneous demand and supply shift. For instance, between 1967 and 1969 nominal GDP growth accelerated while the *SP* curve shifted upward in response to accelerating inflationary expectations. As a result of this, inflation accelerated while the output ratio remained constant. The economy made a small southward movement in the first few quarters after the beneficial 1986 oil shock.

Case D: Demand and Supply Shifts in Opposite Directions.   The economy can move straight to the right when nominal GDP growth accelerates and cancels out the effect of a downward *SP* shift. This occurred in 1972, when the effect of the Nixon price controls program in holding down the inflation rate was offset by rapid nominal GDP growth. A leftward movement can occur when nominal GDP growth decelerates while the *SP* curve is shifting upward. This occurred during the 1969–70 recession, when nominal GDP growth slowed while the *SP* curve was shifting upward as the expected inflation rate (p^e) continued its slow and delayed adjustment to the acceleration of actual inflation during 1966–69. This interpretation helps us understand why

A SUMMARY OF INFLATION AND OUTPUT RESPONSES

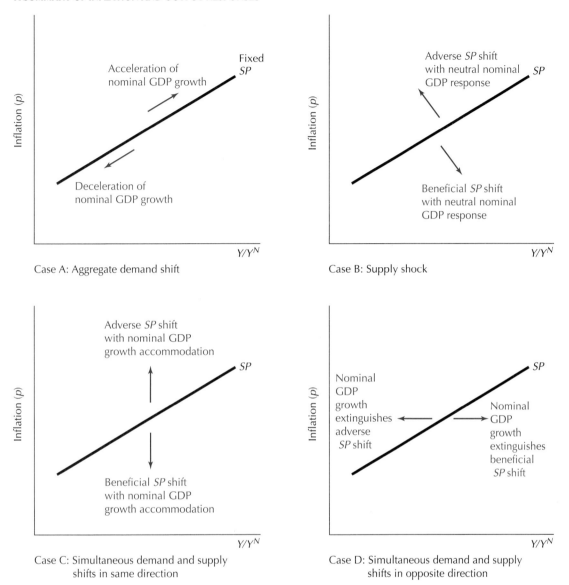

Figure 8-11   **Responses of the Inflation Rate *(p)* and the Output Ratio *(Y/Y^N)* to Shifts in Nominal GDP Growth and in *SP***

In Case A an aggregate demand shift moves the economy to the southwest, or to the northeast if there is no supply shift. In Case B a supply shift moves the economy to the northwest, or to the southeast when nominal GDP growth is unchanged (a neutral policy response). Case C illustrates the northward or southward movement that occurs with an accommodative policy response to a supply shift. Case D illustrates the westward or eastward movement that accompanies a supply shift with an extinguishing supply response.

inflation in early 1971 was still as rapid as in 1969 despite an intervening decline in the output ratio. The same pattern was repeated in 1989–90.

SELF-TEST | In Figure 8-11, which plots the inflation rate against the output ratio, it is possible for the economy to move in any direction. Can you explain why the economy would move in each possible direction: north? northeast? east? and so on for each other possible direction?

Cures for Inflation

Just as excessive nominal GDP growth and adverse supply shocks are the fundamental causes of inflation, the basic cure for inflation is to turn these causes on their head. The reverse of fast nominal GDP growth is obviously slow nominal GDP growth. A decision to reduce the inflation rate by restricting the growth rate of nominal GDP can be both effective and costly, as in 1981–82 or, to a lesser extent, in 1990–1992. Inflation can be cut markedly, but only at the cost of a substantial and prolonged slump in the output ratio and a substantial increase in the number of jobless workers.

But government policy against inflation is not limited to creating a deceleration of nominal GDP growth. Whether there are adverse supply shocks or not, the government can attempt to create beneficial supply shocks by eliminating or weakening price-raising or cost-raising legislation, and by creative tax and subsidy policy.

Such cost-cutting government policies were recommended as a method of reducing the inflation rate *without* the massive loss of output and extra amount of unemployment that the economy actually experienced after 1981. Instead, government cost-cutting policies could have been used to shift the *SP* downward, while restrictive aggregate demand policy could have been used to reduce the growth rate of nominal GDP. By *coordinating* cost-cutting supply policies with aggregate demand policies, a disinflation could have been engineered without a substantial loss in output. In Figure 8-11 the economy would have experienced a straight southward movement, like that in case C.

Sometimes government policymakers are just plain lucky. They get lucky when a beneficial supply shock occurs. The decline in oil prices in 1986 was one example of such a beneficial shock, and so was the role of medical care and computer prices in holding down inflation in 1994–96.

SUMMARY

1. The fundamental cause of demand inflation is excessive growth in nominal GDP. In long-run equilibrium, when actual inflation turns out to be exactly what people expected when they negotiated their labor contracts, the pace of that inflation depends only on the growth rate of nominal GDP.

2. In the short run, actual inflation may be higher or lower than expected, and real GDP can differ from long-run equilibrium natural real GDP. An acceleration of nominal GDP growth in the short run goes partially into an acceleration of inflation, but also partly into an acceleration of growth in real GDP. But when expectations of inflation catch up to actual inflation, the economy will return to its level of natural real GDP.

3. The response of inflation to an acceleration in demand growth depends on the slope of the short-run Phillips curve *(SP)* and the speed with which expectations of inflation respond to changes in the actual inflation rate. The flatter is *SP,* the longer it takes for inflation to respond to faster nominal GDP growth, and the longer the temporary expansion of real GDP.

4. A permanent end to inflation requires that nominal GDP growth drop to the growth rate of natural real GDP, assumed in the text to be zero. But this will cause a temporary recession in actual real GDP, the length and intensity of which will depend on the slope of the *SP* curve.

5. The highly variable inflation experience of the United States since the 1960s cannot be explained solely as the consequence of previous fluctuations in the growth rate of nominal GDP. Instead, supply shocks caused inflation to accelerate and decelerate independently of the influence of nominal GDP growth.

6. The main effect of an adverse supply shock is the impact on the inflation rate and on the ratio of actual to natural real GDP. Policymakers cannot avoid a worsening of inflation, a decline in the output ratio, or both. An accommodating policy keeps real GDP at its previous level, but causes inflation to accelerate by the full impact of the supply shock; an extinguishing policy attempts to cancel out the acceleration of inflation, but at the cost of a reduction in real GDP.

7. Accommodation would be an attractive policy if the upward shift in *SP* were expected to be temporary, and if expectations of inflation did not respond to the temporary jump in the inflation rate. But accommodation may cause a permanent increase of inflation if wage contracts have cost-of-living adjustment clauses that incorporate the supply shock into wage growth.

8. The low and stable inflation rate experienced by the United States in the mid-1990s reflected in part the role of beneficial supply shocks, created by favorable developments in the medical care and computer industries.

CONCEPTS

inflation
expected rate of inflation
short-run Phillips curve
expectations-augmented Phillips curve
forward-looking expectations
backward-looking expectations
adaptive expectations
disinflation

cold turkey
sacrifice ratio
demand inflation
supply inflation
neutral policy
accommodating policy
extinguishing policy

QUESTIONS AND PROBLEMS

Questions

1. In what ways are the *SAS* curve and the *SP* curve similar? In what ways do they differ?
2. If the equilibrium real wage remains constant, what happens to the nominal wage when the actual inflation rate exceeds the expected inflation rate?
3. If the government chooses a more expansionary policy and workers and their negotiators realize that there will be an increase in inflation for the coming year, does the expected inflation rate change? Why or why not?
4. What are the three conditions for long-run equilibrium? Explain what happens if each of the conditions is violated.
5. Why can't the economy move from point E_0 to point *D* in Figure 8-3 when the level of real GDP increases?
6. Distinguish between forward-looking and backward-looking expectations. Which type of expectations would rational workers and firms be most likely to use? Explain why.

7. Suppose that when nominal GDP growth changes, workers and firms immediately adjust their inflation expectations so that $p^e = x$. Is this an example of forward-looking or backward-looking expectations? How does it alter the adjustment loops in Figures 8-4 and 8-6? How does it affect the output cost of disinflation?
8. Assume the economy is at Y^N and that the level of Y^N does not change over time. If p^e remains constant and Y increases, what happens to the rate of inflation?
9. How would you answer question 8 if Y^N were increasing?
10. Explain the role played by the slope of the *SP* curve in determining the path taken by the economy when there is a deceleration of nominal GDP growth.
11. What data suggest that the fluctuations in the inflation rate that took place during the 1970s were not examples of demand inflation?

12. What differentiates accommodating, extinguishing, and neutral policy responses to an adverse supply shock? What happens to the rate of inflation and the real output ratio in each of the three cases?

13. Under what conditions would a permanent supply shock cause a temporary increase in the inflation rate? If these conditions exist, are there any permanent effects of the supply shock on the economy?

14. Did policymakers choose an accommodating, neutral, or extinguishing policy during the price controls of 1971–74? What was the result of the chosen policy?

15. Give at least one example of a beneficial supply shock that occurred in the 1980s. In the 1990s.

Problems

1. In answering the following questions, assume that $P = 1.20$ and $W = 300$ in period 0, which is a long-run equilibrium.
   (a) Assume that $p^e = 0$. What would be the expected price levels in periods 1 through 3?
   (b) Assume that $p^e = 4$. What would be the expected price levels in periods 1 through 3?
   (c) What is the actual real wage in period 0?
   (d) What is the equilibrium real wage in period 0?
   (e) If the equilibrium real wage remains constant and the labor market is always in equilibrium, what would be the nominal wage in periods 1 through 3 when $p^e = 0$? When $p^e = 4$?
   (f) Assume that $p = 5$. What is the price level in periods 1 through 3? What would be the actual real wage in periods 1 through 3 if $p^e = 0$? If $p^e = 4$?
   (g) What is the relationship between Y and Y^N in part (f) of this question? Explain how you know what the relationship will be.

2. The following questions are based upon the relationship between the growth rate of nominal GDP (x), the inflation rate (p), and the growth rate of real GDP (y). [See equations (8.1) and (8.2).]
   (a) If the price level (P) equals 1.00 and the level of real GDP (Y) equals 2000, what is the level of nominal GDP (X)?
   (b) If Y increases by 4 percent and P remains the same, what is the new X?
   (c) If Y is the same as in part (a) of this question and P increases by 4 percent, what is X?
   (d) If $Y = 2000$ and $P = 1.00$, and both P and Y increase by 2 percent, what is the new X?
   (e) Explain why your answers to parts (b) through (d) of this question are related as they are.
   (f) Complete the following table.

3. Assume the SP curve for the economy is the same as shown in Figure 8-3. Assume, as in Figure 8-3, that $x = 6$ and that Y^N remains fixed at 100. In period 1, the economy is at point F in Figure 8-3 ($Y = 104$ and $p = 2$). Given this information, answer the questions or respond to the statements given below.
   (a) Assume that labor negotiators use an adaptive-expectations approach to setting expectations such that $p^e = p_{-1}$. What is p^e in period 2?
   (b) Draw a new SP curve based upon your answer to part (a) of this question.
   (c) What will be the new Y if policymakers want no further increase in the inflation rate (i.e., keep $p = 2$)? What is y under these circumstances? What will policymakers have to do to achieve this result?
   (d) Assume that instead of following the policy in part (c) of this question, policymakers want to keep Y at 104. What would Y and p be under this circumstance? How would policymakers achieve this result?
   (e) Assume that rather than following the policies described in parts (c) and (d) of this question, policymakers again allowed nominal GDP to grow at 6 percent (i.e., $x = 6$). What would Y and p be under this circumstance?

4. Assume that the price level in period 0 is 1.00 and that there has not been any inflation prior to this period. Because of a widespread infestation in the Midwest, the supply of farm products decreases dramatically. As a result, the overall price index rises by 5 percentage points in period 1. Because the infestation is short-lived, the price index falls back to its normal level of 1.00 in period 2.
   (a) What will be the price level in period 1 through period 3?
   (b) What will be the inflation rate in periods 1 through 3?
   Assume that the infestation causes permanent damage to the soil and that farm prices remain at their new higher levels permanently.
   (c) What will be the price levels in periods 1 through 3?
   (d) What will be the inflation rate in periods 1 through 3?

Alternatives	Period	X	Y	P	x	y	p
A: 0 percent inflation	0	3900	3000	1.30			0
	1	4056					
B: 2 percent inflation	0	3900	3000	1.30			2
	1	4056					
C: 6 percent inflation	0	3900	3000	1.30			6
	1	4056					

(e) Explain why your answers to these two pairs of questions differ.

Assume that in period 0 there had been an existing 4 percent inflation rate.

(f) What would have been the price level in period 1 if the infestation had not occurred? If the infestation caused the overall price index to rise by an additional 5 percentage points, what would have been the price level in period 1? What would have been the rate of inflation in period 1?

(g) If in periods 2 and 3 the economy had moved back to its preinfestation equilibrium, what would have been the price levels in periods 2 and 3?

5. Assume that for every increase of 1 percentage point in the rate of inflation, firms are willing to increase output by 1 percentage point and that the level of output in the economy is currently at 200 (the natural level of output) and that the rate of inflation is 4 percent.

(a) Based upon the above information, draw the *SP* curve.

(b) What is the level of nominal GDP growth in the economy?

An adverse supply shock rocks the economy such that the inflation rate associated with every level of output increases by 4 percentage points.

(c) Draw the new *SP* curve.

(d) The government chooses to follow a neutral policy in response to this shock. What will be the level of nominal GDP growth? What will be the new rate of inflation? What will be the new level of real GDP?

(e) If the government chose to follow an accommodating policy, what would be the new inflation rate? The level of real GDP? The level of nominal GDP growth?

(f) If the government chose to follow an extinguishing policy, what would be the new inflation rate? The level of real GDP? The level of nominal GDP growth?

SELF-TEST ANSWERS

p. 230 Everywhere to the right of Y^N actual inflation is greater than expected inflation (for instance, actual inflation of 3 percent at E_1 is greater than expected inflation of $p^e = 0$ along the SP_0 line). Everywhere to the left of Y^N actual inflation is less than expected inflation. Only at Y^N is expected inflation correct.

p. 232 A decline in aggregate demand moves the economy to the left of point E_3, down along the SP_1 curve. When real GDP declines from 100 to 94, the actual inflation rate drops to zero, and is now below the 3 percent inflation rate expected everywhere along the SP_1 curve. Eventually the expected inflation rate will decline as well, shifting the SP curve downward.

p. 239 Why in Figure 8-4 is the red line from point 1 to 2 steeper than from E_0 to point 1? The line is steeper because inflation is higher at point 2 than at point 1, because the expected rate of inflation (p^e) has shifted up in response to the actual inflation that occurred at point 1. And, since nominal GDP growth (x) is the same at point 1 and point 2, but inflation (p) is higher, the growth of real GDP $(y = x - p)$ must be less from 1 to 2 than from E_0 to point 1. Similarly, since inflation is even higher at point 3, real GDP growth must be even lower, and in fact is negative, going from point 2 to point 3.

p. 242 The slope of the *SP* curve determines how a slowdown in nominal GDP growth is divided between a decline in the inflation rate (p) and a decline in real GDP growth (y). The flatter the *SP* curve, the larger is the decline in real GDP and the smaller is the decline in actual inflation. With backward-looking (adaptive) expectations, a smaller decline in the actual inflation rate produces a smaller decline in the next period's expected inflation rate. Smaller declines in expected inflation make the economy's adjustment path longer: it takes more time for the economy to return to long-run equilibrium. Conversely, the economy's adjustment path is shorter the steeper the *SP* curve and the faster the decline in actual and, hence, in expected inflation.

p. 255 The inflation rate will fall in the year of the decline in the relative price of oil, except in the case of an extinguishing policy which raises nominal GDP growth sufficiently to cancel out the oil price effect. And, if the inflation rate declines in the first year, it will also decline in subsequent years if the expected rate of inflation declines and/or if COLA agreements cause lower inflation in the first year to cause lower wage changes in subsequent years.

p. 258 *North:* an adverse supply shock accommodated by an increase in nominal GDP growth. *Northeast:* an acceleration of nominal GDP growth, causing inflation during the period prior to the adjustment of expectations. *East:* a beneficial supply shock extinguished by an increase in nominal GDP growth. *Southeast:* a beneficial supply shock accompanied by an unchanged rate of nominal GDP growth. *South:* a beneficial supply shock accommodated by a reduction in nominal GDP growth. *Southwest:* a deceleration of nominal GDP growth, causing disinflation prior to the adjustment of expectations. *West:* an adverse supply shock extinguished by a reduction in

nominal GDP growth. *Northwest:* an adverse supply shock accompanied by an unchanged rate of nominal GDP growth.

APPENDIX TO CHAPTER 8

The Elementary Algebra of the *SP-DG* Model

Throughout Chapter 8 we have located the short-run equilibrium rate of inflation and level of real GDP along an *SP* curve, as at point E_3 of Figure 8-10. Now we learn how to draw a second line—the *DG* line—which shows where the economy will operate along the *SP* schedule. We also learn how to calculate the inflation rate and level of real GDP without going to the trouble of making drawings of the *SP* and *DG* lines. We do this by solving together the equations that describe the *SP* and *DG* lines, just as we did in the appendix to Chapter 5, where we learned the equivalent in algebra to the *IS* and *LM* curves. We use *SP-DG* diagrams to show that either the algebraic or graphical method leads to the same answer.

The centerpiece of our model in this appendix is the deviation of the output ratio from 100 percent. One way to write this deviation is:

$$100 \, (Y/Y^N) - 100$$

This deviation is zero when the output ratio (Y/Y^N) equals 1.0, which occurs when actual output (Y) equals natural output (Y^N).

Calculations in the model are more accurate and straightforward when we use logarithms. Since the logarithm of 1.0 is zero, the log of the output ratio is zero when the output ratio is unity. Thus, a second way of expressing the deviation of the output ratio from 100 percent is the "log output ratio" expressed as a percentage.

$$\hat{Y} = 100[\log(Y/Y^N)]$$

The following table shows that $\hat{Y}$ is very close in value to the deviation $100(Y/Y^N) - 100$:

Y/Y^N	$100(Y/Y^N) - 100$	$\hat{Y}$
0.90	−10	−10.5
1.00	0	0.0
1.05	5	4.9

In the rest of this appendix, a value of $\hat{Y}$ of zero corresponds to 100 on the horizontal axis of those diagrams in Chapter 8 that plot output or the output ratio against the inflation rate.

Equation for the *SP* Curve

The *SP* curve can be written as a relationship between the actual inflation rate (p), the expected inflation rate (p^e), and the log output ratio $(\hat{Y})$.

General Linear Form

$$p = p^e + g\hat{Y} + z \qquad (1)$$

Numerical Example

$$p = p^e + 0.5\hat{Y}$$

Here the z designates the contribution of supply shocks to inflation, and initially in the numerical example we assume that the element of supply shocks is absent $(z = 0)$, so that we can concentrate on demand inflation. The numerical example also assumes that the slope of the *SP*, designated g in the general linear form, is 0.5 in the numerical example. Thus $g = 0.5$ indicates that the *SP* line slopes up by 1 percentage point in extra inflation for each 2 percentage points of extra real GDP relative to natural real GDP. We also note that when $\hat{Y} = 0$, the economy is on its vertical *LP* line where actual and expected inflation are equal $(p = p^e)$.

In order to understand what makes the *SP* curve shift, we assume the expectations of inflation (p^e) are formed adaptively as a weighted average of last period's actual inflation rate (p_{-1}) and last period's expected inflation rate (p^e_{-1}), where j is the weight on last period's actual inflation rate (j must be between 0 and 1).

General Linear Form

$$p^e = jp_{-1} + (1 - j)p^e_{-1} \qquad (2)$$

Numerical Example

$$p^e = p_{-1}$$

The numerical example assumes that $j = 1$; that is, that expected inflation depends simply on what the inflation rate actually turned out to be last period, with the subscript -1 indicating "last period." This was also assumed in drawing Figures 8-4 and 8-6.

When we substitute (2) into (1), we obtain a new expression for the *SP* line that depends on two current-period variables $(\hat{Y}$ and $z)$ and two variables from last period $(p_{-1}$ and $p^e_{-1})$:

General Linear Form

$$p = jp_{-1} + (1 - j)p^e_{-1} + g\hat{Y} + z \qquad (3)$$

Numerical Example

$$p = p_{-1} + 0.5\hat{Y}$$

Equation for the *DG* Line

But we need more information than that contained in (3) to find both current inflation *(p)* and the current log output ratio *(Ŷ)*. In other words, we have two unknown variables and one equation to determine their equilibrium values. What is the missing equation? This is the *DG* line and is based on the definition that nominal GDP growth *(x)* equals the inflation rate *(p)* plus real GDP growth *(y)*, all expressed as percentages:

$$x \equiv p + y \qquad (4)$$

In the theoretical diagrams of Chapter 8 the natural level of real GDP (Y^N) is constant. But now we want to be more general an allow Y^N to grow, as it does in the real world. We subtract the growth rate of natural real GDP (y^N) from each side of equation (4):

$$x - y^N \equiv p + y - y^N \qquad (5)$$

Let us give a new name, "excess nominal GDP growth" *(x̂)*, to the excess of nominal GDP growth over the growth rate of natural real GDP $(\hat{x} = x - y^N)$. We can also replace the excess of actual over natural real GDP growth $(y - y^N)$ with the change in the log output ratio *(Ŷ)* from its value last period $(\hat{Y}_{-1})$.[1] When these replacements are combined, (5) becomes

$$\hat{x} \equiv p + \hat{Y} - \hat{Y}_{-1} \qquad (6)$$

Combining the *SP* and *DG* Equations

Now we are ready to combine our equations for the *SP* line (3) and *DG* line (6). When (6) is solved for the log output ratio $\hat{Y}$, we obtain the following equation for the DG line:

$$\hat{Y} \equiv \hat{Y}_{-1} + \hat{x} - p \qquad (7)$$

This says that the *DG* relation between $\hat{Y}$ and *p* has a slope of -1, and that the relation shifts when there is

---

[1]This replacement relies on the definition of a growth rate from one period to another as the change in logs (here we omit the "100" that changes decimals to percents):

$$y = \log(Y) - \log(Y_{-1})$$
$$y^N = \log(Y^N) - \log(Y^N_{-1})$$

Subtracting the second line from the first, we have
$$y - y^N = \log(Y) - \log(Y^N) - [\log(Y_{-1}) - \log(Y^N_{-1})] = \hat{Y} - \hat{Y}_{-1}$$

any change in $\hat{Y}_{-1}$ or $\hat{x}$. Now (7) can be substituted into the *SP* equation (3) to obtain:

$$p = jp_{-1} + (1 - j)p^e_{-1} + g(\hat{Y}_{-1} + \hat{x} - p) + z \qquad (8)$$

This can be further simplified if we factor out *p* from the right-hand side of (8).[2]

General Linear Form

$$p = \frac{1}{1 + g}[jp_{-1} + (1 - j)p^e_{-1}$$
$$+ g(\hat{Y}_{-1} + \hat{x}) + z] \qquad (9)$$

Numerical Example

$$p = \frac{2}{3}[p_{-1} + 0.5(\hat{Y}_{-1} + \hat{x})]$$

Now we are ready to use equation (9) to examine the consequences of any event that can alter the inflation rate and log output ratio in the short run and long run. One focus of Chapter 8 was the consequences of accelerations and decelerations in nominal GDP growth *(x)*, so let us use equation (9) to reproduce the path of adjustment plotted in Figure 8-4 following an acceleration in *x* from zero to 6 percent per annum. Now, however, we shall perform the analysis for adjusted nominal GDP growth *(x̂)*, thus allowing it to remain valid for any value of y^N.

Example When *x̂* Rises from Zero to 6 Percent

We start out initially with zero inflation and with an output ratio of 100 percent, as at point E_0 in Figure 8-4. This means that the log output ratio *(Ŷ)* is zero. We also assume that there are no supply shocks *(z = 0)*. Thus our initial situation begins with:

$$p_{-1} = p^e_{-1} = \hat{x} = \hat{Y}_{-1} = 0$$

Substituting into the numerical example version of (9), we can confirm that these values are consistent with an initial value of zero inflation:

$$p = \frac{2}{3}[0 + 0.5(0 + 0)] = 0$$

Now there is an assumed sudden jump in *x̂* to 6 percent per year. What happens to inflation in the first period? Substituting $\hat{x} = 6$ into the numerical example, we have:

$$p = \frac{2}{3}[0 + 0.5(0 + 6)] = \frac{2}{3}(3) = 2$$

---

[2]To obtain (9) from (8), add *gp* to both sides of equation (8). Then divide both sides of the resulting equation by $1 + g$.

The new log output ratio can be found by using equation (7):

$$\hat{Y} = \hat{Y}_{-1} + \hat{x} - p = 0 + 6 - 2 = 4$$

Thus we have derived the combination of p and $\hat{Y}$ plotted at point F in Figure 8-4—that is, inflation of 2 percent and a log output ratio of 4.[3]

The adjustment continues in future periods. We can compute the values of p and $\hat{Y}$ in the next few periods by substituting the correct numbers into the numerical example version of (9), using a pocket calculator. These values correspond exactly to the path labeled "Path with one period lag in adjustments in expectations" in Figure 8-4:

Period	p_{-1}	$\hat{Y}_{-1}$	$\hat{x}$	p	$\hat{Y}$
0	0.00	0.00	0	0.00	0.00
1	0.00	0.00	6	2.00	4.00
2	2.00	4.00	6	4.67	5.33
3	4.67	5.33	6	6.89	4.44
4	6.89	4.44	6	8.07	2.37

Exercise 1: Using the same numerical example, calculate what happens for the first four periods when the economy is in an initial long-run equilibrium at point E_4 in Figure 8-5, with $\hat{x} = p = p^e = 10$ and $\hat{Y} = 0$, and suddenly the adjusted growth rate of nominal GDP $(\hat{x})$ falls to a new permanent value of zero. How is your answer changed if the coefficient of adjustment of expectations is assumed to be $j = 0.25$ instead of $j = 1.0$?
(*Hint:* This requires that you substitute $j = 0.25$ and $g = 0.5$ into the General Linear Form version of equation (9) above.)

Learning to Shift the *SP* Curve and *DG* Line

In this section we learn how to draw graphs in which the *SP* curve and *DG* lines are accurately shifted, so that the economy's adjustment path can be traced out. In an example we will see how to trace out the path in Figure 8-4 marked "path with one period lag in adjustments in expectations," showing how the economy reacts to a permanent 6-percentage-point acceleration in nominal GDP growth.

---

[3]In Figure 8-4 we assumed for simplicity that natural real GDP was not growing. Thus any change in Y/Y^N became simply a shift in Y itself, in this case a 4 percent increase from 100 to 104 in Figure 8-4.

Shifting the *SP* Curve. The two *SP* curves plotted in the left frame of Figure 8-12 are based on the numerical example of equation (1), repeated here for convenience:

$$p = p^e + 0.5\hat{Y} \tag{1}$$

The lower, SP_0 curve assumes that $p^e = 0$. Thus, it shows that inflation (p) is zero when $\hat{Y} = 0$. When $\hat{Y}$ is 4, inflation is 2 percent. In our numerical example the inflation rate in period 1 is shown by point F on SP_0. If $j = 1$, so the expected rate of inflation always equals last period's actual rate of inflation $(p^e = p_{-1})$, then there is an easy rule for drawing the new *SP* line for the subsequent period:

> **Rule for shifting *SP* when $j = 1$:** If the economy is at point F in period 1, then the *SP* curve for period 2 can be drawn as intersecting the *LP* line at the same vertical coordinate as point F, shown by the point F'.

Thus, in the example the *SP* curve for period 2 is SP_1, shown as having the same slope as SP_0, but intersecting *LP* at point F'. The vertical coordinate of the point where *SP* intersects *LP* tells us what expected rate of inflation (p^e) is being assumed along that *SP*. Along SP_1, for instance, p^e must be 2 percent, since the vertical coordinate of point F' is 2 percent.

Shifting the *DG* Line. The *DG* lines plotted in the right frame of Figure 8-12 are based on equation (7), repeated here for convenience:

$$\hat{Y} = \hat{Y}_{-1} + \hat{x} - p \tag{7}$$

Since p and $\hat{Y}$ are on the two axes, to plot a *DG* line we need to know the values of $\hat{x}$ and $\hat{Y}_{-1}$. The DG_1 line in the right frame of Figure 8-12 assumes that $\hat{x} = 6$ and $\hat{Y}_{-1} = 0$. This line has a slope of minus 45 degrees, sloping down 1 percentage point vertically for every percentage point in the horizontal direction.

When the economy is at point F in period 1 in our example, with an inflation rate of 2 percent and an output ratio of $\hat{Y} = 4$, we must draw a new *DG* line for period 2. To develop a general rule for shifting *DG*, we draw a horizontal line, *CY*, which stands for "constant output." The *CY* line is always horizontal, and its vertical coordinate is the assumed growth rate of $\hat{x}$, in this case 6 percent. It shows that if inflation were equal to $\hat{x}$, then by equation (7) the output ratio would be constant, $\hat{Y} = \hat{Y}_{-1}$, hence the name constant output, or *CY* line. Now we can write a general rule for shifting *DG*:

> **Rule for shifting *DG*:** Start from the economy's position in period 1, point F in this example. Then draw a horizontal *CY* line at a vertical coordinate corresponding to the assumed value of $\hat{x}$, in this case 6 percent. Then the *DG* line for period 2 will be a line

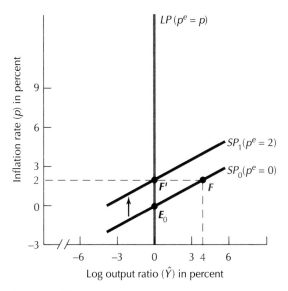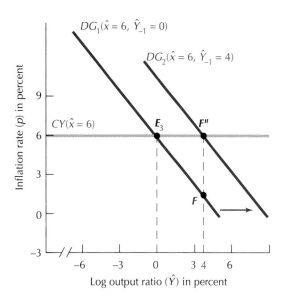

Figure 8-12

with a slope of minus 45 degrees intersecting the *CY* line at the same horizontal coordinate as point *F.* This point of intersection is labeled point *F'''* in the right frame of Figure 8-12.

Thus, in the example the *DG* line for period 2 is DG_2, shown as parallel to the DG_1 line but intersecting *CY* at point *F'''.* Note that the rule also applies to the DG_1 line. Since the economy in the previous period (period 0) was at a log output ratio of 0, the DG_1 line intersects the *CY* line at point E_3, which has a horizontal coordinate of 0.

Another, equivalent way to remember the rule for shifting the *DG* line is simple. When $\hat{x}$ increases, the *DG* line shifts up *vertically* by the amount of the change in $\hat{x}$, for example, up by 6 percentage points to the line DG_1. But when $\hat{Y}_{-1}$ increases, the *DG* line shifts to the right *horizontally* by the amount of the change in $\hat{Y}_{-1}$, for example, by 4 percentage points between the lines DG_1 and DG_2.

Tracing the Economy's Adjustment with Shifts in *SP* and *DG*. Now we are prepared to draw a graph tracing the economy's adjustment to a permanent 6 percent acceleration in $\hat{x}$, from an initial value of zero to a new value of 6. In Figure 8-13 the economy starts at point E_0 on SP_0 drawn for the initial assumed expected rate of inflation $(p^e = 0)$, and on the DG_0 line drawn for $\hat{x} = 0$ and an output ratio last period $\hat{Y}_{-1}$ of 0.

The permanent acceleration of $\hat{x}$ fixes the *CY* line at a vertical position of 6. We draw a new DG_1 line intersecting *CY* directly above point E_0. The *SP* does not shift in period 1, because expectations of inflation adjust with

a one-period lag. Thus in period 1 the economy moves from E_0 to *F*, with an inflation rate *(p)* of 2.0 percent and an output ratio $(\hat{Y})$ of 4.0 percent. Then in period 2 both *SP* and *DG* shift. We draw the new SP_1 line, as in Figure 8-13, as intersecting the *LP* line at the same vertical coordinate as point *F.* We draw a new DG_2 line, as in Figure 8-13, as intersecting the *CY* line at the same horizontal coordinate as point *F.* The two new lines, SP_1 and DG_2, intersect at point *H,* where the inflation rate *(p)* is 4.67 percent and the log output ratio is 5.33 percent. This is the same as the economy's position in period 2 calculated by the algebraic method in the preceding section.

The adjustment in period 3 is also shown in Figure 8-13. A new SP_2 curve is drawn as intersecting the *LP* at the same vertical coordinate as point *H.* A new DG_3 line is shown as intersecting the *CY* line at the same horizontal coordinate as point *H.* The economy's new position in period 3 is at the intersection of the SP_2 curve and DG_3, labeled in Figure 8-13 as point *I.* Inflation has now risen to 6.89 percent and the log output ratio has fallen to 4.44 percent.

The general principles developed in this section can be used to show the economy's adjustment to either a shift in $\hat{x}$ or a supply shock. General characteristics of the adjustment process, shown in the example of Figure 8-13, are as follows:

The *SP* line always shifts up in the subsequent period when the economy's position in the current period is to the right of *LP,* and it shifts down when the economy is to the left of *LP.* The *DG* line always shifts to the right in the subsequent period when the

Figure 8-13

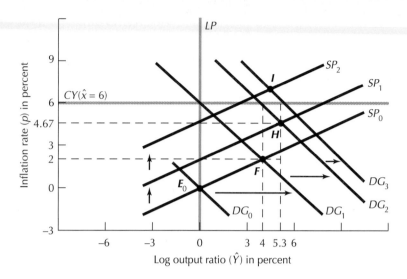

economy's current position is below the *CY* line, that is, when inflation is less than $\hat{x}$. And the *DG* line shifts to the left in the subsequent period when the economy is above the *CY* line. Thus, in the example of Figure 8-13, the *DG* line drawn for period 4 would intersect the *CY* line at the same horizontal coordinate as point *I* and thus would be to the left of the DG_3 line.

The Consequences of a Supply Shock

We have examined the effect on inflation of an acceleration of growth in nominal GDP. But another source of inflation may be a supply shock, such as an increase in the relative price of food or energy. Let us assume that we start in long-run equilibrium at point E_3 in Figure 8-10, with $\hat{x} = p = p^e = 6$ and $\hat{Y} = 0$. Initially the supply-shock variable z is equal to zero. But now let us assume there is a jump in the relative price of oil that boosts z to a value of 3 for two periods, followed by a return after that to $z = 0$.

The discussion of supply shocks emphasized that two crucial factors determine how the economy reacts to a supply shock. First, is $\hat{x}$ increased, decreased, or left the same by policymakers following the shock? Second, do expectations adjust to the temporary shock? Cost-of-living adjustment clauses in wage contracts are equivalent to an adjustment of expected inflation for the influence of the supply shock.

The simplest case to analyze is one in which there is no response of either demand growth ($\hat{x}$) or expected inflation (p^e). To trace the path of inflation and the log output ratio, we simply use the general formula (9) with $\hat{x}$ assumed to be permanently fixed at 6, and $j = 0$ (representing the failure of expectations to respond at all to

actual inflation). The general form for this case becomes:

$$p = \frac{1}{1 + g} [p^e_{-1} + g(\hat{Y}_{-1} + \hat{x}) + z] \qquad (10)$$

$$= \frac{2}{3} [p^e_{-1} + 0.5(\hat{Y}_{-1} + \hat{x}) + z]$$

Now, starting in the initial situation, we substitute the required elements into this formula for each period in succession.

Period	p^e_{-1}	$\hat{Y}_{-1}$	$\hat{x}$	z	p	$\hat{Y}$
0	6	0.00	6	0	6.00	0.00
1	6	0.00	6	3	8.00	−2.00
2	6	−2.00	6	3	7.33	−3.33
3	6	−3.33	6	0	4.89	−2.22
4	6	−2.22	6	0	5.26	−1.48
5	6	−1.48	6	0	5.51	−0.99

This adjustment path shows what would happen to the economy with a two-period supply shock of $z = 3$, with a neutral aggregate demand policy that maintains steady excess nominal GDP growth, and with no response of expectations to the effects of the supply shock. A good example of this is the temporary 1990–91 oil shock after the Iraqi invasion of Kuwait. In period 1 the inflation rate jumps from 6 to 8, exactly duplicating the movement from point E_3 to point *L* in Figure 8-10. In the next period inflation diminishes somewhat, since the position of the *DG* line depends on the current period's starting value of $\hat{Y}$, which has fallen from 0 to −2. Thus the intersection of *DG* and *SP* slides southwest down the stationary SP_3 line to $p = 7.33$ and $\hat{Y} = −3.33$.

Then the supply shock ends, z returns to its original zero value, and the economy gradually climbs back up the SP_2 line to its long-run equilibrium position, $p = 6.0$ and $\hat{Y} = 0$.

Exercise 2: What rate of adjusted nominal growth should policymakers choose if they want to pursue an accommodating policy? An extinguishing policy? (*Hint:* An accommodating policy means that $\hat{Y}$ remains fixed at 0, which requires that $\hat{x} = p$. Substitute p for $\hat{x}$ in equation (10) and, in addition, note that $\hat{Y}_{-1} = 0$, thus obtaining $p = p^e_{-1} + z$. For an extinguishing policy, take (10) and set the left-hand side (*p*) equal to 6; then solve for the required $\hat{x}$.)

Exercise 3: For a neutral policy response, calculate the adjustment path of inflation and $\hat{Y}$ in the first four periods when expectations respond fully to the extra inflation caused by the supply shock. That is, assume now that $j = 1$ instead of $j = 0$ as in the previous exercise. Next, maintaining the assumption that $j = 1$, calculate the same adjustment path when the policy response is accommodative. (See the hint for Exercise 2.) How would you describe the disadvantages of an accommodative policy when $j = 1$?

The Behavior of the Unemployment Rate

The unemployment rate (*U*) is very closely related to the log output ratio (*Ŷ*), as we learned in Chapter 2. Corresponding to the natural level of real GDP (Y^N), defined as the level of real GDP at which expectations of inflation turn out to be accurate, there is a natural rate of unemployment U^N. When real GDP is above Y^N, and inflation is accelerating, we also find that the actual unemployment rate (*U*) is below the natural rate of unemployment (U^N). This relationship can be written:[4]

General Linear Form

$$U = U^N - h\hat{Y} \tag{11}$$

Numerical Example

$$U = U^N - 0.4\hat{Y}$$

How is this relationship to be used? First, we must determine the value of the natural rate of unemployment. In the United States in the early 1980s this appeared to be approximately $U^N = 6.0$ percent. Then

we take alternative values for $\hat{Y}$ and substitute these values into equation (11). Here are two examples:

Example 1: $\hat{Y} = -5$
Since $U^N = 6.0$, we use (11) to determine the unemployment rate:

$$U = 6.0 - 0.4(-5) = 8.0$$

In other words, there is an unemployment rate of 8.0 percent.

Example 2: $\hat{Y} = 5$

$$U = 6.0 - 0.4(5) = 4.0.$$

The unemployment rate is 4.0 percent. Thus we see that for every 5 percentage points by which $\hat{Y}$ exceeds 0, the unemployment rate lies 2 percentage points below U^N, the natural unemployment rate of 6.0 percent. And for every 5 percentage points by which $\hat{Y}$ falls short of 0, the unemployment rate lies 2 percentages points above the natural unemployment rate of 6.0 percent.

There is also a simple short-cut way of calculating the *change* in the unemployment rate from last period (U_{-1}) to this period (*U*).[5]

General Linear Form

$$U = U_{-1} - h(y - y^N) \tag{12}$$

Numerical Example

$$U = U_{-1} - 0.4(y - y^N)$$

Thus, starting with $U_{-1} = 6.0$, a value of $y - y^N$ of 1.0 will cause the unemployment rate to fall to $U = 5.6$.

Exercise 4: Go back through the previous exercises and calculate the unemployment rate for each period corresponding to that period's value of $\hat{Y}$.

---

[4]*Caution:* In the appendix to Chapter 5 we used h to designate the income responsiveness of the demand for money. In Chapter 17 h designates the slope of the Lucas-Friedman supply curve.

---

[5]How can (12) be derived from (11)? Let us write down (11) and then subtract from it the value of (11) for last period:

$$U = U^N - h\hat{Y}$$
$$-U_{-1} = U^N_{-1} - h\hat{Y}_{-1}$$

If there is no change in U^N from one period to the next, then this difference is:

$$U - U_{-1} = -h(\hat{Y} - \hat{Y}_{-1})$$

But now we can substitute $y - y^N$ into this expression,

$$U - U_{-1} = -h(y - y^N)$$

To see why this substitute is valid, look back at appendix footnote 1.

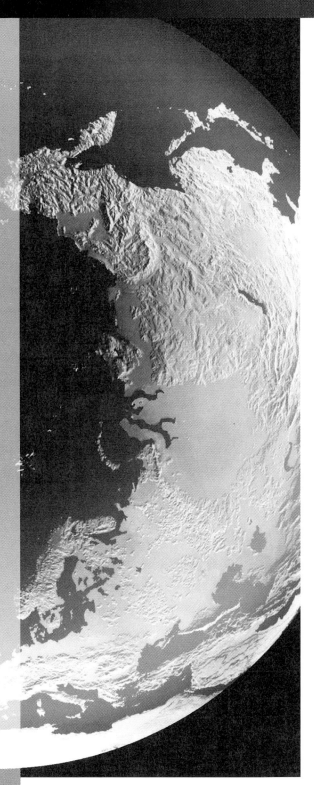

PART FOUR

Macroeconomics

in the Long Run:

Growth and the

Public Debt

CHAPTER 9

The Theory of Economic Growth

In essence the question of growth is nothing new but a new disguise for an age-old issue, one which has always intriguted and preoccupied economics: the present versus the future.

—*James Tobin*[1]

9-1 The Importance of Economic Growth

As we learned in Chapter 1, a fundamental task of macroeconomics is to determine the sources of economic growth. By economic growth we usually mean the growth rate of real GDP per person (or per capita). The achievement of rapid economic growth is one of the most (if not *the* most) important distinguishing features of a successful economy. It is the fact that the U.S. economy grew more rapidly than those of the industrialized nations of Europe during the century between 1850 and 1950 that allowed Americans to enjoy a higher standard of living than most residents of Europe throughout the postwar era.

The profound importance of growth comes from the power of compound arithmetic. Even apparently small differences in growth rates make a huge difference in the standard of living over, say, a period of fifty years. Consider an average income of $40,000 in 1998. At a growth rate of 2 percent, that income would grow over fifty years to $108,700 in the year 2048. At a growth rate of 2.5 percent, that income would grow to $139,600 in 2048, a difference of $30,900, or more than three-quarters of the initial income level!

The welfare gains resulting from even minor increases in the rate of economic growth are enormous. In the oft-quoted words of Nobel Prize–winning University of Chicago economist Robert E. Lucas, Jr., "the consequences for human welfare are simply staggering. Once one starts thinking about them, it is hard to think of anything else."[2] This is true because small differences in the rate of economic growth can make a huge difference in the welfare of the average citizen when compounded over 50 or 100 years.

The newly industrializing countries of Southeast Asia (South Korea, Taiwan, Hong Kong, and Singapore) are widely admired for their success in achieving very rapid economic growth over the past thirty years. Although South Korea had about the same level of real income per capita as the Philippines in 1960, by 1990 (thanks to its stunning achievement of rapid economic growth) South Korea's real income per capita was *seven times* that of the Philippines. Other Asian economies, including China, Thailand, Malaysia, and Indonesia, are also growing very rapidly and steadily improving the standard of living of their citizens.

---

[1]Economic Growth as an Objective of Government Policy," *American Economic Review,* vol. 54 (May 1964), p. 1.
[2]Robert E. Lucas, Jr., "On the Mechanics of Economic Development," *Journal of Monetary Economics,* vol. 22 (July 1988), p. 5.

Americans are used to economic progress. Real income per capita has grown at almost 2 percent per year over the last century, enough to double the standard of living every thirty-five years. This growth in real income per capita primarily reflects growth in labor productivity, that is, output per hour. But a significant problem has developed for the American economy. The growth rate of labor productivity has fallen by more than half since the early 1970s. Although a similar slowdown in the rate of productivity growth has also occurred in most other countries, the growth rate of productivity in the United States has been slower than in any other major industrialized nation during the past twenty-five years.

Why is productivity growth in the United States so slow? This is the third puzzle introduced at the start of the book. This is a question of utmost concern for today's generation of college students. For, without the advance in per capita income made possible by productivity growth, today's college students may be the first generation in American history that fails to achieve a standard of living in their adult lives that exceeds the standard of living of their parents.

Economic growth has become a critical macroeconomic problem. Accordingly, we begin here a three-chapter discussion of economic growth and related issues. In this chapter we examine the theory of economic growth and its relation to growth in population, in the capital stock, and in the types of investments that tend to favor growth, including education, research, and development. We identify puzzling aspects of the differences between rich and poor countries which cannot be explained by the traditional theory of economic growth, and which have led economists in the past decade to develop new theories and new sets of factors that seem to differentiate successful and unsuccessful economies.

Then, Chapter 10 inquires into the causes of the slowdown in productivity growth and in the growth of real income in the United States. Why have real wages stagnated so much more in the United States than in Europe or Japan? Is slow productivity growth the main cause of slow real wage growth? Or does the causation work in reverse as well—do low real wages for unskilled workers induce firms to hire extra workers, thus holding down productivity? We investigate the connections between slow productivity growth in the United States and high unemployment in Europe. Different labor market institutions and regulations may lead to higher wages for unskilled workers in Europe, leading to fewer unskilled jobs, higher productivity for those lucky enough to obtain jobs, and higher unemployment for unskilled workers than in the United States.

One cause of slow economic growth is an inadequate rate of national saving, that is, the sum of private saving by households and business firms, and of public saving by the government. Whenever the government runs a budget deficit, the public saving rate is negative. This reduces the national saving rate and hinders economic growth because private saving is diverted into financing the government budget deficit and thus is unavailable to finance private investment spending, which is a source of economic growth. As the final component of this three-chapter part, Chapter 11 reviews the measurement and causes of the budget deficit. It examines the implications of the increasing public debt and the debate over whether the government budget should be balanced or in surplus rather than in deficit, as it has been with unusual persistence in the United States since the early 1980s.

9-2 Standards of Living as the Consequence of Economic Growth

The Poor United Kingdom

In economics, **economic growth** is the study of the causes and consequences of sustained growth in natural real GDP per person.

In 1870 average real GDP per person in the United Kingdom was about 28 percent higher than in the United States. But by 1994 average real GDP per person in the United States was 41 percent higher than that in the United Kingdom. How was this possible? Faster **economic growth,** meaning a higher average annual growth rate of real GDP per person, allowed the United States to overtake the United Kingdom in 1890 and to move ahead by a growing distance between 1890 and 1950. Although the United Kingdom kept pace with the United States after 1950, the United Kingdom was never able to close the gap. This was a race between the tortoise and the hare, in which the tortoise never caught up.

The gap between the average real GDP per person in the two countries makes an enormous difference in their relative standards of living. The comparisons are made in a way that holds constant the prices of goods and services in the two countries.[3] Thus the average American can purchase all the goods and services bought by the average U.K. resident and still have 41 percent more left over for additional spending. And this difference is the result of a seemingly puny and insignificant difference in the U.S. economic growth rate between 1870 and 1996—1.83 percent per year for the United States as compared to 1.36 percent for the United Kingdom.

> *Minor differences in economic growth rates sustained over a long period build up into substantial differences in relative living standards. As another example, in 1955 the United Kingdom enjoyed a living standard that was 10 percent higher than that of West Germany. But a West German economic growth advantage between 1955 and 1996 of 2.67 percent compared to 1.99 percent for the United Kingdom converted the 1955 situation into a totally different relationship in 1996, when the West German average per person real GDP level was 18 percent higher than that in the United Kingdom.*

Economic Growth: Something for Nothing?

It is easy to see why economic growth is such a fascinating topic. High rates of economic growth make it possible to have more of everything—higher health spending and welfare benefits, with plenty left over for more private

---

[3]The "bible" for comparisons of living standards across nations, as in the table and figure in the International Perspectives box in this section, is an immense body of data collected by economists at the University of Pennsylvania. See Robert Summers and Alan Heston, "The Penn World Table (Mark 5): An Expanded Set of International Comparisons, 1950–88," *Quarterly Journal of Economics* (May 1991), pp. 1–41. As a simple example of what the Penn project involves, let us assume that if Japanese output is translated from yen to dollars at today's exchange rate, Japanese output per person is $30,000 while U.S. output is just $20,000. If every good in Japan costs twice as many dollars to buy as the same goods in the United States, then the true Japanese standard of living must be divided by 2 and becomes $15,000 ($30,000/2), or just 0.75 of the U.S. standard of living. The Penn project makes such comparisons of the cost of living for many different goods in more than 100 countries over a long period of time.

INTERNATIONAL PERSPECTIVE

The Growth Experience of Seven Countries over the Last Century

The accompanying figure shows the level of per person GDP in seven leading industrial countries for selected years over the last 126 years. The figures are expressed in 1996 U.S. dollars and are based on a careful study that bases the prices actually paid by inhabitants of other countries on the average paid in all industrialized countries. The table summarizes some of the most important information contained in the figure, including the values, in 1996 U.S. prices, of per person GDP in both 1870 and 1996, as well as the growth rates of per person GDP during selected intervals. In the table, countries are listed in order of 1996 per person GDP. Several major conclusions can be drawn from an inspection of the figure and companion table:

1. All nations have enjoyed substantial growth in per person GDP; in the United States it increased by a factor of exactly 10, from $2,853 in 1870 to $28,554 in 1994.

2. The figure is plotted on a logarithmic scale. This means that the slope of each line indicates the economic growth rate; a steep line means fast growth and a flat line indicates slow growth. For most countries 1955–73 was the period of fastest growth, and all countries have experienced a growth slowdown since 1973.

3. Differing growth rates among countries have led to changes in relative positions. Japan has had the most rapid growth, particularly between 1955 and 1973, when it reached the incredible rate of 8.1 percent per

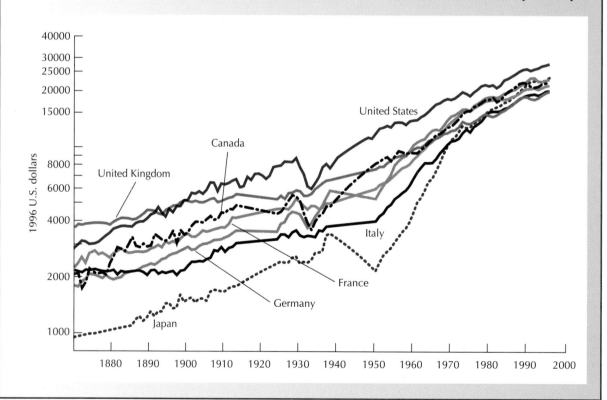

annum. Japan overtook Italy in 1970, the United Kingdom in 1980, and Germany in 1994.

4. The United Kingdom's loss of relative position has been continuous over the entire century. In each subperiod listed in the table, the United Kingdom had a growth rate at the bottom or next to the bottom of the group. The United Kingdom was overtaken by the United States in 1901, by France and Germany in 1960, and by Japan in 1980.

5. The United States is something of a "has-been" in the growth race, owing its high living standard to its superior growth performance before 1950. In particular, the United States gained an advantage in its freedom from wartime destruction as compared to some European nations. But since 1950 the U.S. advantage has eroded, with the United States at or near the bottom of the growth league during 1955–73 and 1973–94.

TYPES OF ECONOMIC CHANGE

The figure displays not only the process of economic growth that raises the standard of living decade after decade, but two types of shorter-term movements. The first of these is wartime destruction, which is clearly visible in the sharp drop in the living standards of Germany and Japan from 1940 to 1950. Making up for wartime destruction explains much of the rapid economic growth in these two countries in the 1950s and early 1960s.

The second type of short-term economic change is the business cycle. The data for each country are annual, so the alternation of business recessions and expansions is visible, most notably during the depression years of the 1930s. The figure also highlights the unique nature of the Great Depression in the United States and Canada, where per person real GDP declined much more than in the other countries.

Level and Growth Rate of per Capita Real GDP in 1996 Dollars for Seven Countries, 1870–1996

	Level in 1996 U.S. dollars		Average Annual Growth Rate in Percent				
	1870	*1996*	*1870–1996*	*1870–1913*	*1913–55*	*1955–73*	*1973–96*
United States	2853	28,554	1.84	2.01	1.68	2.12	1.50
Japan	937	24,108	2.58	1.48	1.31	8.07	2.59
Germany	1708	23,554	1.96	1.62	1.65	3.88	1.60
Canada	2062	22,641	1.92	2.01	1.47	2.94	1.60
France	2229	21,869	1.82	1.46	1.28	4.35	1.45
Italy	2165	20,470	1.78	0.80	1.31	4.57	2.25
United Kingdom	3665	20,290	1.34	1.00	1.09	2.48	1.67

consumption of goods and services. In contrast, a society with a low rate of economic growth suffers continual strife as difficult choices must be made about the allocation of a slow-growing pie. In this unfortunate society, more spending on health or education may mean higher taxes or a cut in Social Security benefits. No wonder that exploration of economic growth has moved to the forefront as a central topic of macroeconomics.

9-3 The Production Function and Economic Growth

The traditional theory of economic growth (often called the "neoclassical" theory) has filled many academic journals with highly mathematical articles. Yet the basic ideas are very simple. The theory divides output growth into two categories: (1) growth of **factor inputs,** such as labor and capital, and (2) growth in output relative to growth in factor inputs. Thus the theory converts the question of how to achieve faster output growth into two subquestions: how to achieve faster growth in factor inputs, and how to achieve faster growth in output relative to inputs.

The economic elements that directly produce real GDP are **factor inputs.**

Throughout most of this book we have examined the causes and consequences of changes in the ratio of actual real GDP to natural real GDP, which we have called the output ratio (Y/Y^N). But now we are interested in changes in economic conditions over long periods during which the output ratio may be expected to be roughly constant. Thus our theory of economic growth refers to the growth of natural real GDP.

The Production Function

How much real GDP (Y) can be produced at any given time? This depends on the total available quantity of the two main factor inputs, capital (K) and labor (N), and also the behavior of output per average available factor input, which the neoclassical theory calls A (for the "autonomous" growth factor).[4]

The **production function,** *a relationship usually written algebraically, shows how much output can be produced by a given quantity of factor inputs.*

The **production function** states the relationship between $Y, A, K,$ and N.

$$Y = A\,F(K, N) \qquad (9.1)$$

In words, real GDP equals an autonomous growth factor (A), expressed as an index, multiplied by a function of an index of capital input (K) and labor input (N). The appendix to this chapter provides background information on the general functional form used in equation (9.1) and a popular numerical example often used to illustrate the workings of the production function.

Output per Person and the Capital-Labor Ratio.   We need to isolate those factors that determine the increase in per person real GDP, which can be writ-

---

[4]The use of the symbol A in this context and the decomposition of real GDP growth into growth in labor, capital, and the "residual" A date back to the seminal paper by Robert M. Solow, "Technical Change and the Aggregate Production Function," *Review of Economics and Statistics,* vol. 39 (August 1957), pp. 312–20. The symbol A stands for autonomous growth factor and should not be confused with A_p or A_0, the symbols for autonomous planned spending in Chapters 3–7.

ten as follows when the production function is divided through by the amount of labor input (N).[5]

$$\frac{Y}{N} = Af\left(\frac{K}{N}\right) \qquad (9.2)$$

This important relationship states that there are just two sources of growth in the standard of living, or real GDP per person (Y/N). These are the autonomous growth factor (A), and the ratio of capital to labor input (K/N), or "capital per person." (In this chapter we simplify by treating "persons" and "employment" as synonyms, ignoring changes in the ratio of employment to the population.)

Equation (9.2) is the per person version of the production function. It is illustrated in Figure 9-1. This production function is drawn by assuming that the autonomous growth factor is fixed at A_0. Like the production functions presented in Chapter 7, which plotted output against labor input, this one exhibits diminishing returns. Thus, any addition to the per person stock of capital (K/N) yields less and less of an increase in per person output (Y/N). In the diagram, point B represents one possible level of production, with capital input per person $(K/N)_0$ producing output per person $(Y/N)_0$.

SELF-TEST | **What happens to the ratio of output to capital (Y/K) as more capital per person is accumulated?**

The production function in Figure 9-1 is just a start toward an adequate theory of economic growth. So far our analysis tells us simply that the main sources of growth in the standard of living are an autonomous factor (A) and growth in capital per person (K/N). But this does not explain why these two sources of growth differ among countries or among historical eras. We do not yet know why the autonomous growth factor in Figure 9-1 is A_0 rather than some other amount, nor do we know what determines the level of K/N.

Our study of what determines the autonomous growth factor is deferred until later. Here, we focus on the determinants of growth of capital per person (K/N). We begin by reviewing the basic relationships between investment, the growth in capital, and saving.

Saving, Investment, and the Growth in Capital per Person

How is growth in K/N related to total national saving? This relationship is important, since it represents the link between the government's fiscal policy

---

[5]How can (9.2) be derived from (9.1)? There are two intermediate steps. First, we multiply and divide K by N in equation (9.1):

$$Y = A \, F(NK/N, N) \qquad (9.1')$$

If the function F displays constant returns to scale (see appendix to this chapter), then there is a unit elasticity of Y with respect to an increase in N (which appears in the numerator of the first term inside the parentheses as well as in the second term), and this fact allows us to factor out the N term and rewrite (9.1) as follows:

$$Y = A \, N f(K/N, 1) \qquad (9.1'')$$

Notice here that we have given a new name (f) to the function. Equation (9.2) in the text is obtained by dividing through both sides of (9.1'') by N.

Figure 9-1

A Production Function Relating per Person Output to per Person Capital Input

The production function shows how much output per person can be produced by different amounts of capital per person. One possible position for the economy is point *B*, but other positions are possible as well. We cannot tell from this diagram how large the economy's per person capital stock will be. The slope of the production function is the marginal product of capital $(\Delta Y/\Delta K)$, showing the extra amount produced by raising capital, when the amount of labor is held constant.

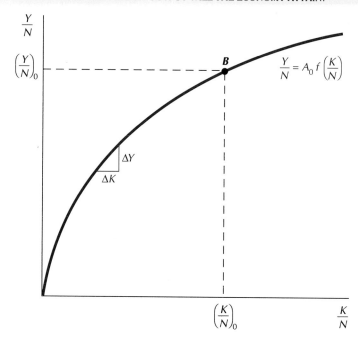

WHAT LEVEL OF PER PERSON OUTPUT WILL THE ECONOMY ATTAIN?

and the long-run growth of output per person. The concept of saving *(S)* that matters for economic growth is not the household saving of Chapter 3, but rather total national saving, *including the saving of households, corporations, and the government.* If we assume that net exports are zero, total *national* saving *(S)* equals private investment *(I)*.[6]

$$S = I \qquad (9.3)$$

Our task is to determine how the growth in capital is related to investment, and hence to total national saving *(S)*.

The basic link between investment and the growth in capital is simple. Spending on investment goods *(I)* either causes the capital stock to grow *(ΔK)* or it replaces old capital that wears out or becomes obsolete *(dK):*

$$I = \Delta K + dK \qquad (9.4)$$

Here we make the assumption that replacement investment can be represented by a fixed depreciation rate *(d)* times the capital stock *(K)*. The depreciation rate indicates what fraction (say, 0.06) of the capital stock is replaced each year due to wear and tear or to obsolescence.

---

[6]Rearranging equation (2.4), which shows the relation of private saving *(S)* to government saving *(T − G)*, private investment *(I)*, and net exports *(X)*, we have:

$$S + (T - G) = I + NX$$

When *S* is redefined to include both private saving and government saving, we have:

$$S = I + NX$$

This is the same as equation (9.3) in the text, where *NX* is set equal to zero.

We want to know how saving and investment are related to the rate of change of the capital stock *(ΔK/K)*. To express equation (9.4) in terms of the growth rate of capital, we multiply and divide *ΔK* by *K*, as follows:

$$I = \frac{K\Delta K}{K} + dK = \left(\frac{\Delta K}{K} + d\right)K \tag{9.5}$$

In words, this states that investment equals the growth rate of capital *(ΔK/K)* plus the depreciation rate, both times the capital stock.

Saving and Investment in the Steady State

A **steady state** is a situation in which output and capital input grow at the same rate, implying a fixed ratio of output to capital input.

A **steady state** occurs when output *(Y)* and capital input *(K)* grow at the same rate, implying a fixed ratio of output to capital. A particularly simple case occurs when the autonomous growth factor *(A* in equation 9.2) is constant, so that the economy stands still at a point like *B* in Figure 9-1. This occurs when the growth of both *Y* and *K* are equal not only to each other but to the growth in labor input *(N)*, implying that the economy stands still at a fixed value of the vertical axis *(Y/N)* and of the horizontal axis *(K/N)*.

As in previous chapters, we use lowercase letters to designate growth rates, including the growth rate of output *(y = ΔY/Y)*, the growth rate of capital *(k = ΔK/K)*, and the growth rate of labor input *(n = ΔN/N)*. Thus the condition for a steady state, in which capital per person *(K/N)* is constant, can be written as:

$$k = n \tag{9.6}$$

In commonsense terms, (9.6) states the condition necessary for the economy to stand still at a point like *B* in Figure 9-1. Since we already have a relationship between investment and the growth of capital *(ΔK/K)* in equation (9.5) we can represent the behavior of investment in a steady state by replacing the growth of capital in (9.5) by the growth of labor input *(n)*:

$$I = (n + d)K \tag{9.7}$$

Since saving equals investment from (9.3), we can set saving equal to the right-hand side of (9.7):

$$S = (n + d)K$$

This implies that

$$s\frac{Y}{K} = n + d \tag{9.8}$$

To obtain the final line of (9.8), we redefine total national saving *(S)* as the ratio of national saving to output *(s = S/Y)* times output *(Y)*, and then divide both sides of the equation by *K*. In words, the final line of (9.8) states that saving per unit of capital must equal the sum of the growth rate of labor input and the depreciation rate, which in turn is the amount of steady-state investment per unit of capital.

SELF-TEST

There are four components of equation (9.8), *s, Y/K, n,* and *d*. Which, if any, of these components changes its value as we move along the production function in Figure 9-1?

9-4 Solow's Theory of Economic Growth

Robert M. Solow (1924 –).
*Solow, 1987 Nobel Prize
winner, invented both the
modern theory of economic
growth and the standard
method for empirically
distinguishing the roles of
capital and technological
change in the growth process.*

Can an increase in the ratio of national saving to output *(s)* create a permanent increase in the growth rate of output? The answer is no. This was the most surprising result of the "neoclassical" theory of economic growth originally developed in the 1950s by MIT's Robert M. Solow,[7] a theory for which he was awarded the Nobel Prize in 1987. We have already developed the major building blocks of Solow's theory. These are the per person production function of equation (9.2) and Figure 9-1, and the relationship between saving and steady-state investment in equation (9.8).

Solow's Insight

The algebra of equation (9.8) had been worked out in the 1940s by Sir Roy Harrod, an English economist, and Evsey Domar, who later taught at MIT. In their Harrod-Domar model of economic growth, all of the elements of (9.8) are constant. But then, why does the left side of (9.8) equal the right side? This equality seems an unlikely coincidence, since the elements of (9.8) depend on totally unrelated factors. The ratio of national saving to output *(s)* on the left-hand side of the equation is determined by the saving decisions of households, business firms, and the government, while the ratio of output to capital *(Y/K)* is determined by technological factors. And the growth rate of labor input *(n)* and depreciation rate *(d)* on the right-hand side of (9.8) are determined by totally different considerations—birth rates, death rates, immigration, and the rate at which old capital wears out or becomes obsolete. In Solow's words, describing a simple version of (9.8) in which *d* is omitted:

> Discomfort arose because . . . all three of the key ingredients—the saving rate, the rate of growth of the labor force, and the capital-output ratio— were given constants, facts of nature. The saving rate was a fact about preferences; the growth rate of labor supply was a demographic-sociological fact; the capital-output ratio was a technological fact. . . . The possibility of steady growth would be a miraculous stroke of luck. Most economies, most of the time, would have no equilibrium growth path. The history of capitalist economies should be an alternation of long periods of worsening unemployment and long periods of worsening labor shortage.[8]

In Solow's words again, "I began tinkering with the theory of economic growth, trying to improve on the Harrod-Domar model . . . I thought first about replacing the constant capital-output (and labor-output) ratio by a richer and more realistic representation of the technology."

What Solow did, in short, was to marry the per person production function of equation (9.2) to the saving-investment relation in (9.8). To do this we simply multiply both sides of equation (9.8) by *K* and divide both sides by *N*:

$$s \frac{Y}{N} = (n + d) \frac{K}{N} \qquad (9.9)$$

[7]Robert M. Solow, "A Contribution to the Theory of Economic Growth," *Quarterly Journal of Economics,* vol. 70 (February 1956), pp. 65–94.

[8]Robert M. Solow, "Growth Theory and After," *American Economic Review,* vol. 78 (June 1988), p. 307.

On the left-hand side we have total national saving per person, which is the national saving rate *(s)* times output per person *(Y/N)*, and this, in turn, is given by the per person production function of equation (9.2). On the right-hand side of (9.9), we have the amount of steady-state investment per person, that is, the amount of investment needed to equip each new population member with the same capital per person as the existing population, and to replace worn-out or obsolete capital.

The Solow Model in Pictures

The two sides of equation (9.9) can be plotted separately, as in Figure 9-2. In the left frame, the upper red line is a copy of the per person production function from Figure 9-1, plotting the output-labor ratio *(Y/N)* as a function of the capital-labor ratio *(K/N)*. When we multiply this line by the fixed saving rate *(s)*, we obtain the lower red line, national saving per person *(sY/N)*. The distance between the two lines indicates consumption per person. The right-hand frame plots steady-state investment per person, which rises steadily to the right, since a larger *K/N* raises the amount of investment needed to equip new population members and replace worn-out and obsolete capital.

Now in Figure 9-3 we put together the two parts of Figure 9-2, omitting for clarity the per person production function. The steady state occurs at point E_0, where the capital-labor ratio is $(K/N)_0$. Why is this a steady state? At any point to the left of E_0, say point *C*, saving and investment are higher than the investment required to maintain *K/N* at a fixed level. This extra investment makes *K/N* grow, moving the economy rightward from point *C* to the steady-

SAVING AND INVESTMENT ARE THE OUTCOME OF SEPARATE DECISIONS

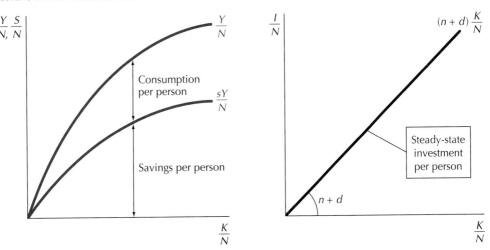

Figure 9-2 **Output, Saving, and Steady-State Investment per Person**
The upper curved line in the left frame copies the per person production function from Figure 9-1. Multiplying it by the saving rate *(s)* produces the lower curved line showing per person saving. Consumption per person is the distance between the two lines. The right frame shows steady-state investment per person, the amount needed to replace old capital and equip new workers for each capital-labor ratio *(K/N)*.

Figure 9-3

Equilibrium of Saving and Investment in the Solow Growth Model

This figure superimposes the two frames of Figure 9-2. The saving line crosses the steady-state investment line at point E_0. At any point to the left, like C, saving and actual investment exceed steady-state investment (the amount needed to keep K/N constant), and accordingly K/N grows until the economy reaches point E_0. At any point to the right, like D, saving and actual investment are less than steady-state investment and K/N shrinks back to E_0.

THERE IS PRESSURE FOR K/N TO GROW OR SHRINK AWAY FROM STEADY-STATE EQUILIBRIUM

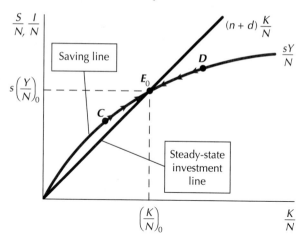

state equilibrium E_0. Similarly, starting at point D, saving and investment are below the required amount, meaning that not enough is being invested to equip new members of the population and replace worn-out and obsolete capital. Hence starting from point D, the economy moves leftward back down the red line to the steady-state equilibrium at point E_0.

Effects of a Higher Saving Rate

To understand the startling implication of the Solow growth model that a change in the ratio of national saving to output does not create a permanent change in the growth rate of output, let us see how an increase in the saving rate affects the economy. In Figure 9-4 we begin by copying the steady-state investment line (which remains unchanged in the examples of Figures 9-2, 9-3, and 9-4, but could change as in the self-test on p. 283) and the "old saving line" directly from Figure 9-3. The economy's initial position is at point E_0, just as it was in that figure.

Now we introduce a sudden increase in the saving rate from s_0 to s_1, which shifts the red saving line up. The distance between point F along the new red saving line and point E_0 along the old red saving line represents *additional saving available to fuel growth in per person capital.* The economy moves to the right up the new saving line, since there is extra saving available to equip new members of the population with a higher capital-labor ratio, and as well to provide for the added depreciation of old capital at that higher ratio. Eventually the economy arrives at point E_1 along the new saving line. But once at E_1, the capital-labor ratio is fixed at the new higher ratio, per person saving and output are fixed, and the growth in output is once again equal to the growth rate of labor input (at E_1 as at E_0, $y = k = n$).

Thus the saving rate matters, but not as people had believed prior to the development of Solow's model. An increase in the saving rate raises the standard of living, since the higher capital-labor ratio at E_1 produces a higher output-labor ratio. To achieve this higher standard of living, the growth rate

Figure 9-4
The Effect of a Higher Saving Rate on Capital and Income per Person

The lower "old saving line" is copied from Figure 9-3. A higher saving rate implies the higher "new saving line." The economy's position immediately jumps from E_0 to F. Now saving and actual investment are above steady-state investment, and so K/N grows until the economy reaches point E_1.

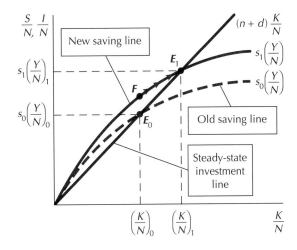

A HIGHER SAVING RATE BOOSTS CAPITAL AND INCOME PER PERSON

of output is *temporarily* raised above the growth rate of N. But the higher saving rate does not create a permanently higher growth rate of output, which depends only on population growth. In the steady state Y/N is fixed, so that Y and N must grow at the same rate. Intuitively, the extra saving finances only a higher *level of* the capital stock per person *(K/N),* not continuing *growth* in the capital stock per person. The extra saving is "eaten up" by the extra replacement investment implied by the higher capital stock, and the extra net investment required to equip each worker with the higher level of capital stock per person.

SELF-TEST

What is the effect of a reduction in the rate of population growth *(n)?* Is there a change in the growth rate of output?

One aspect of this theory may seem puzzling. We learned in Chapter 3 that an increase in the saving rate *(s)* depresses the economy by reducing consumption spending. How can we be so sure here that an increase in the saving rate will stimulate the growth of per person capital? The answer is that *the Solow model is intended for long-run analysis* (decades, not months or years) *and assumes continuous full employment and flexible prices.* Thus, when the saving rate rises in this model, consumption and the price level both decline. The interest rate falls by enough to stimulate sufficient investment to guarantee that saving and investment will remain equal along the economy's path between E_0 and E_1.

9-5 Technology in Theory and Practice

At first glance the Solow growth model seems to contain a major flaw. As presented thus far, the model implies that the permanent growth rate of output should be the same as the growth rate of the population, and that the standard of living *(Y/N)* should be fixed. How, then, does the theory explain the sharp increase in the standard of living that has occurred over the last century in each of the major industrialized nations?

Two Types of Technological Change

Solow used two methods to make the model consistent with history. Both methods introduce an added element into the story: growth in technology in all its forms, including better schooling, improved organization, and all the fruits of innovation and research. The two methods for introducing technological change into the Solow growth model are to assume (1) that technology makes each worker more efficient, and (2) that technology shifts the production function relating per person output to per person capital.

Labor-Augmenting Technological Change.   This approach leaves our previous discussion of the Solow growth model, including the diagrams, completely intact. We simply need to adopt a broad definition of growth in "labor input." Instead of just counting the number of bodies at work, we count effective labor input, taking into account improved education and the storehouse of technology that makes today's workers more efficient than workers a century ago. We now interpret N as effective labor input, and n as the growth rate of effective labor input. In the steady state, output can grow at 3 percent ($y = 3$) if effective labor input grows at 3 percent ($n = 3$), leaving the ratio of output to effective labor input (Y/N) fixed. Now K/N remains fixed if the capital stock grows at 3 percent. Effective labor input growth of 3 percent exceeds population growth of, say, 1 percent, allowing the standard of living (Y per person) to grow at 2 percent.[9]

Neutral Technological Change.   One problem with the first approach is that it assumes that technology only makes workers more efficient, with no impact on capital input. A more realistic assumption is that technology makes *both* labor and capital input more efficient. This neutral type of technological change simply means that the autonomous growth factor *(A)* in equations (9.1) and (9.2) grows over time. Here we copy (9.2) for convenience:

$$\frac{Y}{N} = Af\left(\frac{K}{N}\right) \tag{9.2}$$

If education, innovations, and research raise the value of A every year, then per person GDP can increase steadily. The growth rate of per person GDP *(y − n)* is:

General Form	Numerical Example	
$y - n = a + b(k - n)$	$y - n = a + .025(k - n)$	(9.10)

Here a is the growth rate of the autonomous growth factor, and b is the elasticity of output with respect to capital input, assumed to be 0.25 in the numer-

---

[9]Labor-augmenting technical change can be introduced into our original production function from equation (9.1) by defining effective labor input as a technological factor *(T)* times the population:

$$Y = F(K, TN)$$

When T enters in this form, it is sometimes called "Harrod-neutral" technical change.

ical example. An economy might, for instance, have values of $a = 1.5$ and $k - n = 2$, which would be consistent with a steady state in which

$$y - n = a + b(k - n) = 1.5 + 0.25(2) = 2.0$$

In this example, there is a steady state, because per person output and per person capital are growing at the same rate, allowing Y/K to remain fixed. After introducing neutral technological change into the diagrams of the Solow growth model, the production function shifts upward steadily, thus shifting the saving line up and to the right along a fixed steady-state investment line. Y/N and K/N rise in the steady state, but at the same rate.

SELF-TEST

Calculate the percentage growth rate of real GDP per person $(y - n)$ from the numerical example of equation (9.10), assuming that b always equals 0.25, for the following combinations of the rates a, k, and n:

a	k	n	$y - n$
0	0	4	____
0	4	4	____
4	0	0	____
4	4	4	____

The "Solow Residual"

Soon after Solow developed his theory of growth, he applied the theory to the measurement of the autonomous growth factor (a) in (9.10). His idea was to turn (9.10) around, so that a could be calculated from the other components:

$$a = (y - n) - b(k - n) \qquad (9.11)$$

Since data were available on the growth rates of output (y) and of both capital and labor input $(k$ and $n)$, the only trick in determining the value of a was to identify the elasticity b. Here Solow's idea was to apply the theory of profit maximization in a competitive firm. Solow pointed out that such firms would also set the return on capital equal to the marginal product of capital, which implies that the elasticity b can be measured by the share of capital income in total GDP.[10]

Solow's finding was controversial. Fully seven-eighths of the growth in output per hour of work $(y - n)$ over the period he studied (1909–57) was attributed to "technical change in the broadest sense," including education, research, innovations, and other improvements, while only the remaining one-eighth was attributed to growth in the capital stock per hour of work $(k - n)$. But this is not a very satisfactory outcome. Knowing that some mysterious a factor was important in the growth process does not tell us, for instance, what caused a to grow more slowly after 1973.

Some skeptics believe that a should not be given a name like "technological change," which implies we know precisely what determines a. They sug-

---

[10]Let r be the rate of return to capital. Then competitive firms will set r equal to the marginal product of capital (MPK). The share of capital in GDP is rK/Y, which competitive firms will set equal to $(MPK)(K/Y)$, which is equal to the elasticity of output with respect to capital, $(dY/dK)(K/Y) = (dY/Y)(dK/K)$.

The **residual** is the amount that remains after subtracting from the rate of real GDP growth all of the identifiable sources of economic growth.

The growth in **multifactor productivity,** or **total factor productivity,** is the growth rate of output per hour of work, minus the contribution to output of the growth in the quantity of other factors of production per hour of work, notably capital but sometimes including energy, raw materials, or other factors of production.

Solow's residual is the same as growth in multifactor productivity.

gest that we call *a* instead the **residual** or, more frankly, "the measure of our ignorance." Government agencies like the U.S. Bureau of Labor Statistics, which now routinely calculate *a,* describe *a* as the growth in **multifactor productivity,** or **total factor productivity.** In recent years macroeconomists have come to describe *a* as **Solow's residual.**

The simplified version of Solow's growth model summarized in the previous section (Figures 9-2, 9-3, and 9-4) illustrated one key implication of his model, that a change in the saving rate would cause only a temporary, rather than a permanent, increase in output per unit of labor input. That simplified version could not explain steady growth of output—a defect that we have remedied in this section by introducing technological change. And we have seen that Solow's own empirical research identified technological change (broadly defined) as a much more important source of economic growth than increases in capital input per unit of labor input. In the past decade, however, the Solow growth model has received substantial criticism. In the next section we identify several puzzles that his model cannot explain, and in the following section, we learn about recent developments in growth theory.

9-6   Puzzles That Solow's Theory Cannot Explain

In recent years economists have become increasingly dissatisfied with Solow's neoclassical theory of economic growth, for two primary reasons. First, the theory makes economic growth depend primarily on "Solow's residual," which remains unexplained. Thus we are left with very little understanding of why the world's standard of living stagnated until the industrial revolution that occurred around the year 1800, why it grew rapidly from then until the early 1970s, and why in some countries like the United States the standard of living has grown much more slowly in the last 25 years. Second, we are left with little understanding of differences among nations—why some are rich and some remain poor, and why some grow rapidly while others stagnate.

The critics of neoclassical growth theory go beyond claiming that the theory provides an inadequate explanation of growth. They point to widely observed phenomena in the world that *conflict* with the predictions of the theory. In this section we review these conflicts:

Conflict 1: Income per Capita Varies Too Much Across Countries.   Real income per capita in a rich country like the United States is more than ten times as high as in a poor country like India or Bangladesh. Yet this fact conflicts with the neoclassical theory. Why? The theory states that there are only two reasons for differences in per capita income, the vertical axes in Figures 9-3 and 9-4. One reason could be a difference in saving rates, since, as shown in Figure 9-4, an increase in the saving rate raises income per capita *(Y/N).* Another could be a difference in the slope of the steady-state investment line *(n + d).* However, even very large differences in the saving rate or rate of population growth cause only small variations in per capita income, not the large variations observed in the world. To take one example, quadrupling the saving rate and reducing the rate of population growth by two-thirds would boost per capita income only from 1.0 to 1.7, whereas in the real world we observe countries differing in per capita income by magnitudes on the order of 1.0 to 10.0.[11]

A flaw in the neoclassical theory is to assume that all countries have the same production function (equation 9.2). Poor countries are assumed to operate at the same level of technology and knowledge as rich countries. To see that the production function is at fault, consider a specific version of equation (9.2) called the Cobb-Douglas production function (see the appendix to this chapter).

General Form	Numerical Example
$Y/N = (K/N)^b$	$Y/N = (K/N)^{0.25}$

Accounting for the tenfold difference in per capita income observed in the real world would require a difference of a factor of $10^{1/b}$ in capital per capita *(K/N)* or, in the numerical example, 10^4, which is a factor of 10,000. Yet there is no evidence of such huge differences among nations in *K/N*. In fact, a regular feature of real-world economies is a roughly constant ratio of *K/Y*, not ratios of *K/Y* that are hugely greater in rich countries than poor countries (by 10,000/10 or 1,000 times greater in the example).

Conflict 2. Poor Countries Do Not Have a Higher Rate of Return on Capital. The neoclassical theory describes the difference in per capita income between poor countries and rich countries simply as a result of differing levels of per capita capital, which in turn result from differences in the three parameters that appear in equation (9.9)—the saving rate *(s)*, population growth rate *(n)*, and depreciation rate *(d)*. As shown in Figure 9-5 a poor country is at a position like point *P*, with a low capital-labor ratio $(K/N)_P$, while a rich country is at a position like point *R*, with a high capital-labor ratio $(K/N)_R$.

But this leads to an unrealistic implication. The slope of the per person production function in Figure 9-5 is the marginal product of capital $(\Delta Y/\Delta K)$, and this is much higher on the left side of the diagram for the poor country than on the right side of the diagram for the rich country. A simple numerical example shows that the marginal product of capital should be as much as 1,000 times higher in a poor country than in a rich country when per capita

---

[11]To see this, let us combine equation (9.9) with the Cobb-Douglas production function (explained in the appendix to this chapter):

$$s\left(\frac{Y}{N}\right) = (n + d)\left(\frac{K}{N}\right) \tag{i}$$

$$\left(\frac{Y}{N}\right) = \left(\frac{K}{N}\right)^b \tag{ii}$$

By solving equation (ii) for *(K/N)*, substituting into equation (i), and simplifying, we obtain:

$$\left(\frac{Y}{N}\right) = \left(\frac{s}{n + d}\right)^{\frac{b}{1-b}} \tag{iii}$$

Using as examples $s = 0.1$, $n = 0.03$, $d = 0.07$, and $b/(1 - b) = 1/3$, we can calculate that $Y/N = 1^{1/3} = 1$. Quadrupling the saving rate to 0.4 would raise Y/N from 1 to $4^{1/3} = 1.59$. Reducing the rate of population growth from 0.03 to 0.01 (assuming the saving rate remains at 0.4) would raise Y/N further from 1.59 to $(0.4/0.08)^{1/3} = 1.7$.

Figure 9-5

A Production Function Relating Per-Person Output to Per-Person Capital Input

The per person production function is the same as in Figures 9-1 and 9-2. The poor country has a capital-labor ratio of $(K/N)_P$ and produces at point P. The rich country has a capital-labor ratio of $(K/N)_R$ and produces at point R. The marginal product of capital is given by the slope of the production function, $\Delta Y/\Delta K$. Because of the curvature of the per person production function, this slope is clearly larger for the poor country than for the rich country. The text discusses reasons why this diagram makes the erroneous prediction that the marginal return to capital is higher in poor countries than in rich countries.

WHY THE MARGINAL RETURN TO CAPITAL SHOULD BE HIGHER IN POOR COUNTRIES

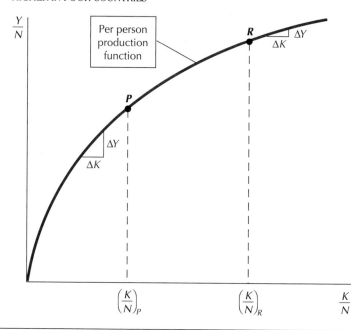

income is ten times as high.[12] The implied high marginal product of capital in the poor country implies that the rate of return on capital in poor countries should be much higher than in rich countries, *and that there should be massive flows of capital from rich countries to poor countries to earn this higher rate of return.* Yet we do not observe high rates of return on capital, or massive capital inflows, in many of the poorest countries of the world. Some less-developed countries enjoy substantial inflows, but others do not.

How can we explain why the rate of return on capital in very poor countries is not substantially higher than in rich countries? The poor countries may not be operating on the same production function as the rich countries, unlike the single production function drawn in Figure 9-5.

Conflict 3. The Facts About Immigration Differ from the Model's Implications. If the neoclassical model cannot explain differences in per capita income by observed differences in capital per person, then what explanation remains? Here the model is forced to point to differences among countries in the effectiveness of labor. As discussed above, labor is measured in units of effective labor, and most of the observed rate of output growth must be attributed to labor-augmenting technical change, that is, the quantity of effective

---

[12]With the Cobb-Douglas production function, the marginal product of capital *(MPK)* is

General Form	Numerical Example

$$MPK = b(K/N)^{b-1} \qquad MPK = 0.25(K/N)^{-0.75}$$
$$= b(Y/N)^{(b-1)/b} \qquad MPK = 0.25(Y/N)^{-3.0}$$

Thus, if Y/N is ten times greater in a rich country, the marginal product of capital in the numerical example would be 10^{-3} or 1/1000 times smaller.

labor embodied in each person. This approach must attribute most observed differences between rich and poor countries to their quantities of effective labor per person, since we do not observe enormous differences in capital per person or in the rate of return to capital.

However, this interpretation of labor runs into a substantial difficulty. When people immigrate from a poor country to a rich country, their income instantly increases by an amount that is far greater than can be explained by any plausible change in their quantity of effective labor in the brief period between the day they arrive in the rich country and the day they start working on their first job. Even if a recent immigrant makes only half of the average income in a rich country, that income may be four or five times higher than the income that same person received prior to departing from the poor country.

What is it about the process of production in a rich country that allows a recent immigrant to have a much higher marginal product and earn a much higher wage than previously in his or her poor country? There are many possible factors of production that matter but which are omitted from the neoclassical model, including skills and education of the work force, cultural attitudes toward work, how well the legal system protects property rights, the presence or absence of crime, and infrastructure in the form of highways, airports, and the like.

Conflict 4. Convergence Has Not Been Uniform.   The neoclassical model predicts that poor nations should "converge" to the income levels of the rich. That is, nations that are initially poor should have faster growth rates than nations that are initially rich. This occurs for three reasons. First, nations that are below their steady-state growth paths (for instance, at point F in Figure 9-4) will grow faster until they reach the steady state (at point E_1 in Figure 9-4). Second, as noted above, the neoclassical model predicts that the rate of return is much higher in poor countries, causing capital to flow from rich to poor countries and thus boosting the capital stocks of poor countries. Third, whatever the barriers that prevent poor countries from fully utilizing the production technology, the passage of time should allow poor countries to learn how to use the productive techniques of the rich countries.

Economists have devoted much attention in recent years to the issue of convergence, and the subject is controversial.[13] There has been convergence among the major industrialized countries, e.g., Japan has caught up substantially to the per capita income levels of Europe and the United States. There has also been convergence among the income levels of states within the United States, and among regions within Western Europe. However, in the world at large convergence has not been uniform. Many nations of Africa and some of the poorer nations of Asia have fallen further behind the advanced countries over the past fifty years, and the relative income levels of major Latin American nations have fallen relative to Western Europe and the United States.

---

[13]A pioneering study of cross-country differences in growth rates is Robert J. Barro, "Economic Growth in a Cross Section of Countries," *Quarterly Journal of Economics,* vol. 106 (May 1991), pp. 407–33. Another influential study is N. Gregory Mankiw, David Romer, and David N. Weil, "A Contribution to the Empirics of Economic Growth," *Quarterly Journal of Economics,* vol. 107 (May 1992), pp. 407–37.

How is this conflict to be resolved? The answer is related to the previous conflict involving immigration. The income level of a new immigrant depends on many attributes of the new country, including not just physical capital but cultural attitudes, infrastructure, the legal system, and other factors. In the same way, some nations possess some or most of these attributes and have succeeded in converging rapidly to the income levels of the advanced nations, while the economies of other nations have continued to stagnate.

9-7 Endogenous Growth Theory

Ever since the development of Solow's neoclassical growth model in the 1950s, economists have been uneasy about several of its implications. We have now reviewed several implications of the model that conflict with important facts about the real world. As we have seen, a primary problem is that technical change (*a,* the autonomous growth factor) is *exogenous,* dropping from the sky totally unexplained. Thus, a nation desiring to boost its growth rate of output gains no insight into how to achieve *A,* just the pessimistic conclusion that a policy-induced increase in the saving rate will raise the growth rate of output only temporarily.

In the late 1980s there was an explosion of activity in what is now called "endogenous growth theory," so named because it attempts to explain technical change as the outcome of market activity in response to economic incentives rather than just assuming that technical change drops exogenously from the sky. The chief inventors of endogenous growth theory are Paul Romer of Stanford University and his Ph.D. thesis adviser at the University of Chicago, Robert E. Lucas, Jr. (also the inventor of the new classical macroeconomics and pictured in Chapter 17). Much of the writing on endogenous growth theory is highly technical; here we summarize some of the main ideas at a non-technical level.[14] As the early ideas of Romer and Lucas continue to be subjected to critical reviews and reconsidered, the theory is still evolving.

The Interpretation of Capital

Endogenous growth theory begins from the awkward fact that, as we have seen, the standard of living in many advanced countries is as much as ten times higher than that in many less-developed countries. But if technical change is freely available to all nations, then *all* of this huge superiority in standards of living must be attributable to a capital-labor ratio that is higher by a factor of 10,000. This would imply very little capital in less-developed countries and a huge rate of return to additional investment, since this would be guaranteed to bring these countries up toward the level of advanced

---

[14]Frequently cited academic papers include Paul M. Romer, "Increasing Returns and Long-Run Growth," *Journal of Political Economy,* vol. 94 (1986), pp. 1002–37; the same author's "Endogenous Technological Change," *Journal of Political Economy,* vol. 98 (1990), pp. S71–103; and Robert E. Lucas, Jr., "On the Mechanics of Economic Development," *Journal of Monetary Economics,* vol. 22 (1988), pp. 3–42. The summary in this section is partly based on Paul M. Romer, "Increasing Returns and New Developments in the Theory of Growth," in W. A. Barnett, et al., eds, *Equilibrium Theory and Applications,* Cambridge University Press, 1991, pp. 83–100.

nations. As a consequence, we should observe massive flows of capital from advanced countries to poor countries, but in fact we do not.

Romer's initial idea was to reject diminishing returns to capital (assumed in the curvature of the production function of Figures 9-1 and 9-2). This would allow the return to additional investment to be as high in advanced countries as in less-developed countries. Examples were developed showing that it was even possible for capital to flow from poor to rich countries. But this idea still assumed that all capital was alike and freely mobile between countries, which did not seem realistic.

Lucas improved the analysis by adding a third factor input, "human capital" (the sum of all a nation's human knowledge), which is distinguished from "physical capital" (i.e., structures and business equipment). Funds for investment in physical capital are able to move between countries but, ignoring migration, human capital is not. A poor country with little human capital cannot become rich just by accumulating physical capital, and its rate of return on investment in physical capital may be lower than in rich countries. This approach makes improved education (and indeed any kind of training or research that adds to human knowledge in a given country) the key to achieving economic growth.

But, as we have seen, consideration of immigration leads to basic problems for the Lucas approach, as it does for the concept of "effective labor" in the neoclassical model. Both these models imply that immigrants to a rich country from a poor country with, say, 1/10 the output per person and 1/10 the human capital per person, upon arrival in the rich country should earn only 1/10 as much as native citizens. But many immigrants to the United States and other rich countries soon achieve the same high average standard of living as native residents.

The Production of Ideas

Endogenous growth theorists thus have been led to focus on what are the characteristics of a rich society that not only make its native residents rich but also seem automatically to equip immigrants from poor countries with much higher incomes than they earned before. They have built models in which the key to growth is the development of ideas for new goods. To solve the incentive problem of how these ideas get produced, the models rely on monopoly power that is reinforced by patents and copyrights. International trade also plays an important role, since each country can concentrate on developing the ideas to produce a few new goods and then trade them with other countries, so that consumers can enjoy all of the new goods produced anywhere in the world. For instance, American households enjoying video rental movies are benefiting from early research on the VCR that took place in Europe and the United States, together with product development in Japan that made the VCR inexpensive to buy and relatively repair-free.

When the concept of ideas is applied broadly, it helps explain not only the introduction of new goods but also the development of better production techniques and higher quality in older goods like automobiles and household appliances. Rich countries use ideas and techniques that produce more and better goods per person. Furthermore, most of these ideas won't work without associated investment in physical capital and human capital. Even if a poor country like Bangladesh obtained piles of instruction manuals for making automobiles and personal computers, these manuals would be useless without educated people, factories, and equipment. This approach simultaneously explains why poor people clamor to migrate to rich countries, and also why poor nations are so eager for foreign investment by companies from rich countries, companies that can bring with them the required equipment and educated engineers and managers.

Empirical Studies and Policy Implications

As endogenous growth theory has developed, so has research on a wide variety of rich and poor countries, looking for correlations between growth rates and other variables. The conclusion is that faster growth is associated with a higher rate of investment by either the private or government sector, a lower share in GDP of government consumption spending, higher school enrollment rates, greater political stability, and lower fertility (i.e., fewer children per female of child-bearing age). And if the influence of all these factors is taken into account, a poor country tends to grow more rapidly than a rich country.

Unfortunately, all these factors are not the same in rich and poor countries. Poor countries have lower rates of investment, lower school enrollment rates, higher fertility rates, and less political stability. The implication of this research is that government policies can affect growth rates by taxing consumption, subsidizing investment and research, and shifting resources from government consumption to government investment.

Overall, endogenous growth theory has taken economists a long way from the original Solow model, with its pessimistic implications that a higher national saving rate alters economic growth only temporarily, and that technological change is exogenous, falling from the sky with no potential for policy effects. However, endogenous growth theory has been useful mainly in understanding differences between rich and poor countries. It has little to say about the main puzzle affecting the rich countries themselves, which is the slowdown in productivity growth in the last two decades as compared to the period before 1973.[15]

9-8   CASE STUDY: The Economic Miracle of the Four Tigers

Endogenous growth theory contributes some suggestive ideas as to the source of differences between rich and poor countries but nevertheless leaves economic policymakers in poor countries wishing to achieve rapid economic growth with a difficult set of choices. Can we learn more about the "secrets of growth" by examining the behavior of nations that have achieved rapid growth over the last thirty years?

The growth experience of east Asian countries during the last few decades is remarkable but highly variable. The worst-performing country was the Philippines, experiencing a growth rate during 1960–90 quite similar to

---

[15]Readable overviews of endogenous growth theory are provided in a symposium in the winter 1994 issue of the *Journal of Economic Perspectives.* See especially Paul Romer, "The Origins of Endogenous Growth," pp. 3–32, and Robert M. Solow, "Perspectives on Growth Theory," pp. 45–54.

that of non-Asian countries, about 2 percent per year in per capita real income. Five other east Asian countries (China, Japan, Indonesia, Malaysia, and Thailand) achieved growth rates in the range of 3 to 5 percent. This impressive performance was exceeded by the truly phenomenal achievement of Hong Kong, South Korea, Taiwan, and Singapore. These countries, which have come to be known as the Four Tigers, achieved growth rates in excess of 6 percent per year. The magnitude of this achievement can be summarized by the following remarkable fact: While the average resident of a non-Asian country in 1990 was 72 percent richer than his or her parents were in 1960, the corresponding figure for the average South Korean is no less than 638 percent!

Figure 9-6 shows in the top frame the average annual growth rates during 1960–90 of China, Hong Kong, Japan, South Korea, Taiwan, and the average for countries in the rest of the world outside Asia. And, as you can see in the lower frame, the rapid growth rates achieved by Japan and Hong Kong allowed them to overtake and exceed the average level of per capita income of the non-Asian countries, while Taiwan's rapid growth allowed it to catch up to the non-Asian countries. China's average growth rate over the entire 1960–90 period does not appear to be particularly impressive, but the data used for the averages chart slow growth in the period prior to 1980 with a much faster growth rate after 1980.

Naturally, the growth experience of the Four Tigers and other east Asian countries has attracted the attention of economists interested in economic growth. What lessons can be learned to benefit economic policy in other countries? There are several debates about the Asian growth miracle.

1. Growth in Factor Inputs or in Multifactor Productivity? The biggest debate about the east Asian growth experience is whether it was driven primarily by growth in factor inputs (extensive growth) or by multifactor productivity (intensive growth). The proponents of the extensive growth hypothesis claim that east Asian growth has been driven by very high saving rates and extraordinarily rapid capital accumulation. Growth in multifactor productivity contributed substantially less to total per capita income growth than in the advanced countries over the same 1960–90 time interval. However, these results are controversial, and recent research shows that, while rapid capital accumulation was important, growth in multifactor productivity was still very rapid—about 3 percent per year in the Four Tigers as compared to about 1 percent a year in the advanced industrial nations and just one-half percent a year in the United States over the last two decades.[16] Thus, a reasonable compromise is to conclude that the Four Tigers achieved an outstanding record both in capital accumulation and in multifactor productivity growth.

2. Did Public Policy Play a Role? One interpretation of the east Asian growth experience is that it provides an example of the virtues of free markets. The role of the government should be to provide infrastructure and enforce property rights, not to intervene on behalf of particular industries. Proponents of this view point to the beneficial role of government in

---

[16]See Michael Sarel, "Growth in East Asia: What We Can and What We Cannot Infer from It," in Palle Andersen et al., eds., *Productivity and Growth* (Sydney: Reserve Bank of Australia, 1995), pp. 237–59.

Figure 9-6

Levels and Growth Rates of GDP per person, Selected Asian Countries and Non-Asian Average, 1960–90

The top frame contains bars indicating the average annual growth rates of GDP per person over the period 1960–90 for China, Hong Kong, Japan, South Korea, Taiwan, and an average of non-Asian countries. The bottom frame displays the levels of GDP per person for the same nations and the average of non-Asian countries. Notice that Hong Kong and Japan started well behind the non-Asian average but by 1990 were well ahead.

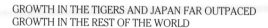

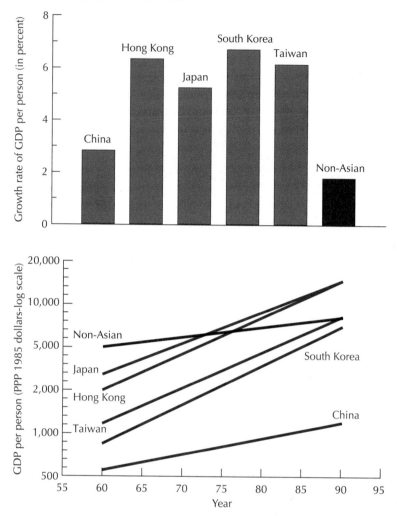

establishing favorable conditions in which free markets could operate, including policies that promoted primary and secondary education, encouraged foreign investment, and kept taxes low.

The contrary view states that governments adopted specific policies that went far beyond infrastructure and education. In Taiwan and South Korea, for instance, there were tax incentives that subsidized investment and exports while encouraging saving. Generally, profits were favored at the expense of wages, while exports were promoted and imports were curtailed. The problem in evaluating the role of these interventions is that the experience of each of the Four Tigers differed from the others. South Korea was highly interventionist, while Hong Kong was noninterventionist. South Korea promoted very large firms producing many different products, while Taiwan emphasized small, entrepreneurial firms. This diversity of experience makes it hard to draw lessons from the experience of the Four Tigers, although a few common elements emerge.

3. Should Policy Promote Investment and Exports? The view that investments and exports have been central to the success of the Four Tigers reflects the very high ratio of investment to GDP in these economies, and the rapid growth in exports achieved by all of the Tigers. Doubt is cast on this proposition by comparing a variety of nations, including the Four Tigers and other less-successful economies, in 1960 prior to the rapid growth period. For instance, in 1960 South Korea had a low ratio of investment to GDP and a relatively poor export performance. The achievement of high investment rates and rapid export growth came as growth started to occur, rather than being a precondition of growth.

What, then, were the unique features of the Four Tigers at the beginning at their growth spurt around 1960? Recent research focuses on several positive factors present in the Tigers in 1960, including good primary education, relative equality of income distribution, and relatively equal distribution of land. In terms of education and equality, the Four Tigers and most other east Asian nations had better initial conditions than most other countries at the same income level in 1960.

What should we conclude? Education and equality seem to have helped the growth process of the Four Tigers get started, but subsequent policies to promote saving, investment, and exports clearly helped. It will be interesting to learn over the years whether other east Asian nations will be able to sustain rapid growth rates for as long as the Four Tigers managed to do so, and whether other nations outside east Asia can learn from the success of the Tigers.[17]

9-9 Conclusion: Are There Secrets of Growth?

The theory of economic growth has come a long way since the original Solow growth model, which tended to minimize the role of capital accumulation and maximize the role of an unexplained rate of technological change. An important development in the new growth theory has been to broaden the definition of capital, so that it includes research and development, human capital (i.e., education), government-financed infrastructure (e.g., highways and airports), and more generally, the "capital" needed to protect liberty and property rights.

Despite these developments, however, much remains unexplained. Those studying the four east Asian tigers are hard-pressed to relate these special accomplishments to particular economic theories. The former chairman of the Council of Economic Advisers, Joseph Stiglitz (now of the World Bank),

---

[17]An important overview of the East Asian growth experience, on which this section is partly based, is provided in Joseph Stiglitz, "Some Lessons from the East Asian Miracle," *The World Bank Research Observer,* vol. 11, no. 2 (August 1996), pp. 151–77. A controversial skeptic's account is in Paul Krugman, "The Myth of Asia's Miracle," *Foreign Affairs,* vol. 73 (November-December 1994), pp. 62–78. Influential papers arguing that some East Asian countries, especially Singapore, have experienced very slow growth in multifactor productivity, have been written by Alwyn Young. See his "Tale of Two Cities: Factor Accumulation and Technical Change in Hong Kong and Singapore," *NBER Macroeconomics Annual 1992,* pp. 13–54 and "Lessons from the East Asian NICs: A Contrarian View," *European Economic Review,* no. 38 (April 1994), pp. 964–73.

argues that it is necessary to go far beyond traditional economic theories and into political science to understand the growth miracle of East Asia:

> No single policy ensured success, nor did the absence of any single ingredient ensure failure. There was a nexus of policies, varying from country to country, sharing the common themes that we have emphasized: governments intervened actively in the market, but used, complemented, regulated, and indeed created markets, rather than supplanted them. Governments created an environment in which markets could thrive. Governments promoted exports, education, and technology; encouraged cooperation between government and industry and between firms and their workers; and at the same time encouraged competition. The real miracle of East Asia may be political more than economic: Why did governments undertake these policies? Why did politicians or bureaucrats not subvert them for their own self interest? . . . The recognition of institutional and individual fallibility gave rise to a flexibility and responsiveness that, in the end, must lie at the root of sustained success.[18]

The verdict of Stiglitz in the preceding quote is humbling for economists, because it implies that the successful countries had a particular talent for "just doing the right thing," and the definition of the right thing varied across countries.

Other economists have taken a broader view and have tried to identify and quantify the specific factors that account for the difference in outcomes of rich and poor countries. An interesting framework is presented by Robert E. Hall and Charles Jones, both of Stanford University.[19] Successful economic growth performance, according to their analysis, requires the following ingredients:

- A favorable infrastructure in the form of rules and institutions within which workers and firms operate. Achieving such a favorable infrastructure is the key role that government must play.
- "Minimizing diversion." The concept of diversion includes outright thievery and criminality, as well as corruption within government. Ironically, the government can be both the biggest source of corruption and also the essential enforcer of law and order that prevents criminality such as Mafia-type extortion.
- Openness to foreign trade. Policies to prevent free trade, including tariffs and quotas, provide incentives to corruption by government officials and monopoly rents by private firms. Economies that allow themselves to remain open to trade and foreign investment appear to be more productive and grow faster.
- Language. Hall and Jones find that countries that do not communicate in one of the eight major international languages (Arabic, Chinese, English, French, German, Portuguese, Russian, and Spanish) have less contact with "international communication." Skeptics might note that countries with traditionally high levels of productivity, e.g., Scandinavia or the

---

[18]Joseph E. Stiglitz, "Some Lessons from the East Asian Miracle," *World Bank Research Observer*, vol. 11, no. 2 (August 1996), pp. 151–77.

[19]Robert E. Hall and Charles Jones, "The Productivity of Nations," paper presented to NBER Economic Fluctuations research meeting, January 31, 1997.

Czech Republic, have vastly higher levels of productivity than some countries where the primary language is one of the top eight, e.g., Haiti, where French is the dominant language.

- Climate. Countries in temperate climates appear to be more productive. The explanation of this relationship between productivity and climate originates in agriculture, since high-value crops such as wheat, corn, and soybeans can only be grown in temperate climates (not in the tropics), and in turn these crops provide feed for livestock. Also, the heat and humidity in tropical climates are enervating and may decrease the energy of workers there.

Overall, the Hall-Jones results add richness to the traditional explanations of high productivity and economic growth, which emphasize high levels of physical capital, human capital, and productivity. But they go beyond any of the formal theories discussed in this chapter by emphasizing government institutions that favor production over "diversion," the role of free trade, the ability of citizens of a country to speak an international language (which is a form of human capital), and the role of a temperate climate. While their study raises as many questions as it answers, it helps to demonstrate the complexity and richness of recent analyses of economic growth, and how the puzzles of economic growth performance have pushed economists into examining factors that lie outside the bounds of traditional macroeconomics.

SUMMARY

1. Divergences between the economic growth rates of individual nations, sustained over long periods of time, can create substantial differences in living standards. Although Britain had the highest level of real GDP per capita in 1870 among the major industrialized nations, by 1996 Britain was at the bottom as a consequence of its slow rate of economic growth in the twentieth century.

2. The production function explains real GDP as depending on the quantity of factor inputs (capital and labor) and on an autonomous growth factor that reflects the influence of research, innovation, and other factors. An increase in the growth rate of real GDP per person requires either an increase in the growth rate of capital per person or an increase in the growth rate of the autonomous growth factor.

3. National saving is the sum of government saving (which equals the government surplus or deficit) plus private saving. National saving equals private investment, which is equivalent to the change in the capital stock plus the investment expenditures required to replace capital goods that wear out or become obsolete.

4. An equilibrium called the "steady state" occurs when output, capital, and labor input are all growing at the same rate. If per person saving exceeds steady-state investment per person, the capital-labor ratio will grow until the per person steady-state investment is high enough to halt the growth in the capital-labor ratio. At this point the economy reaches a new steady state with a constant capital-labor ratio.

5. In the Solow model of economic growth, the economy's growth rate of output in the long run depends only on its rate of population growth, or, more broadly, on the growth rate of "effective" labor input (which takes account of improvements in education, skills, and technology). An increase in the saving rate does not change the economy's steady-state growth rate of output.

6. There are four facts that conflict with the predictions of the Solow growth theory. First, income per capita varies too much across countries. Second, poor countries do not have a higher rate of return on capital as the theory predicts. Third, the model cannot explain why people are able to raise their incomes by so much when emigrating from poor countries to rich countries. Fourth, poor countries have not uniformly converged to the income level of rich countries, as the theory predicts.

7. The endogenous theory of economic growth criticizes the Solow model for making technical change exogenous and unexplained and for providing no explanation of what profit opportunities would induce people and firms to invent new goods and better techniques of production and why (if technical change falls from the sky) poor nations do not rapidly catch up to the standard of living of rich nations.

8. Endogenous growth theory emphasizes the interactions between the production of ideas, investment in physical capital, and investment in human capital (education) to explain why poor countries cannot instantly boost their standard of living up to the level of rich countries. It takes many years of investment in physical and human capital for the ideas developed in the rich countries to benefit the poor countries.

9. Solow's growth model states that an increase in the national saving rate cannot permanently boost the growth rate of output, but there are two reasons to believe that this theoretical result is misleading. First, the strong relationship between saving rates and growth rates in different countries over long periods of time suggests that saving and growth are related in a way not explained by the Solow growth model. Second, endogenous growth theory suggests several ways in which a higher rate of saving and investment might generate faster growth in ideas, human capital, and physical capital.

CONCEPTS

economic growth
factor inputs
production function
steady state

residual
multifactor productivity
Solow's residual

QUESTIONS AND PROBLEMS

Questions

1. In terms of the theories of growth presented in this chapter, is it important to distinguish between growth of output and growth of per person output?
2. If the production function is characterized by constant returns to scale, what happens to real GDP (Y), capital per person (K/N), the ratio of output to capital (Y/K), and output per person (Y/N) when labor and capital inputs both double? What happens when labor and capital inputs double and the autonomous growth factor (A) also doubles?
3. What is the "steady state" in the Solow growth model? How is it reached from an initial situation in which the conditions required for the steady state are not satisfied?
4. Assuming the autonomous growth factor (A) remains unchanged, explain why the gains in output per worker associated with an increase in the capital labor ratio inevitably fall following increases in the level of investment.
5. What is the most important implication of the Solow growth model? Does it imply that an increase in the rate of private saving is useless as a means to increase the standard of living in the long run?
6. Explain why, in spite of the suggested steady-state outcome of Solow's model, the national saving rate is treated in this chapter as playing such an important role in determining the rate of economic growth.
7. Many people advocate policies to raise the U.S. national saving rate (s). According to the Solow growth model, should a low saving rate be a matter of national concern? What policies might be implemented to raise it?
8. The record of economic growth in the leading industrialized countries over the past century hardly represents the steady state described and predicted by the Solow model. What is added to the model to account for the long-term improvement in output per person these countries have experienced?
9. What is the "Solow residual" and why is it problematic for theorists of economic growth?
10. The three big problems with the Solow model can be labeled *exogeneity, incentives,* and *non-convergence.* Carefully explain each italicized term.
11. What is endogenous growth theory? What weaknesses of the Solow growth model led to its development?
12. Distinguish between *human capital* and *physical capital.* Why are both important to a country's economic growth?

Problems

1. Assuming that the United States' output is characterized by a Cobb-Douglas production function with constant returns to scale and that the share of capital income to total GDP is 0.25, consider the follow-

ing five cases, where n = growth rate of labor, k = growth of capital, and a = growth rate of the autonomous growth factor:

Case I: $n = 1\%$, $k = 4\%$, $a = 2\%$
Case II: $n = 2\%$, $k = 3\%$, $a = 0.75\%$
Case III: $n = 1\%$, $k = 5\%$, $a = 2.4\%$
Case IV: $n = 3\%$, $k = 3\%$, $a = 0\%$
Case V: $n = 0\%$, $k = 0\%$, $a = 3\%$

  (a) In each case, what is the elasticity of output with respect to the capital input? Explain.
  (b) In each case, what is the rate of growth of output?
  (c) In each case, what is the rate of growth of per person output?
  (d) Assuming that the autonomous growth factor is a "neutral" type of technological change, which case or cases are consistent with steady state growth?

2. Recalculate your answers to Problem 1 if the elasticity of output with respect to the *labor input* were 0.6.

3. If a country's income has been growing at 3.1 percent per year for the past 25 years, while the labor input has been growing at 1.5 percent per year and the capital input has been growing at 2.5 percent per year, what part of the total growth is accounted for by autonomous growth factors? Assume the economy is characterized by the following production function: $Y = AK^{0.25}N^{0.75}$.

4. Consider an economy characterized by the following production function: $Y = AK^{1/3}N^{2/3}$, with a capi-tal stock of $3,000 billion and current net investment of $120 billion.

  (a) If the growth rate of autonomous factors is zero and the growth rate of labor is 1 percent, what is the current growth rate of per person output? Is this a steady state situation?
  (b) If the government wanted to increase the growth rate of per person output by an extra percentage point through tax and subsidy policies that affected capital growth alone, by what percentage would it have to raise investment?
  (c) In the unlikely event that the government successfully stimulated the required investment, at what rate of growth in output would the economy arrive in the steady state according to the implications of the Solow growth model? Does the text accept this assumption? Why or why not?

5. You are given the production function, $Y = AK^{1/3}N^{2/3}$. Convert this to a function relating Y/N to K/N. Now consider two countries that have access to the same information on technology, have the same quality of labor and capital, and the same production function given above. Suppose that one country has per person output 10 times as high as the other country. In the context of these assumptions, to what factor is the difference attributable? Can you quantify the difference between the countries with respect to that factor?

SELF-TEST ANSWERS

p. 277 Y/K declines as K/N increases. This result follows from diminishing returns to capital per person in the per person production function (equation 9.2). Because additions to output per person decrease in size with constant increases to capital per person, output per person grows more slowly than capital per person, and the ratio of output to capital declines. This can be seen by drawing a straight line from the origin (lower-left corner) of Figure 9-1 to point B. The slope of this line is the Y/K ratio. As K/N increases, we move to the right along the production function, and the slopes of lines from the origin to points on the production function decrease.

p. 279 Only Y/K varies as we move along the production function in Figure 9-1, which plots Y/N against K/N. The other parameters s, n, and d are all held constant and are not introduced into the graphical analysis until Figure 9-2.

p. 283 A decline in the growth rate of population (n) causes the growth rate of output (y) to decline by exactly the same amount, after which the economy reaches a new steady rate. But the lower rate of population growth raises the standard of living (Y/N). Be sure that you can explain why: Start from point E_0 in Figure 9-3, assume that the old saving line remains valid, and rotate the steady-state investment line downward to the right, as required by the decline in the growth rate of population (n).

p. 285 The following are the growth rates of real GDP per person $(y - n)$ corresponding to the four blanks $-1.0, 0.0, 4.0, 4.0$.

APPENDIX TO CHAPTER 9

General Functional Forms and the Production Function

Until this point, we have used only "specific linear" forms for the behavioral equations. For instance, the demand for money in the appendix to Chapter 5 was written as:

$$\left(\frac{M}{P}\right)^d = hQ - r$$

This equation can be stated in words as: The real demand for money $(M/P)^d$ is equal to a positive number (h), times real GDP (Y), minus another number (f), times the interest rate (r). The equation tells specifically how the real demand for money depends on real GDP and the interest rate.

The production function can also be written in a specific form called the Cobb-Douglas production function.[1]

General Form	Numerical Example
$Y = A\,K^b N^{1-b}$	$Y = AK^{0.25} N^{0.75}$

In words, this states that real GDP (Y) is equal to an autonomous growth factor (A), multiplied by a geometric weighted average of an index of capital (K) and of labor (N). The weights, b and $1 - b$, represent the elasticity (or percentage response) of real GDP to an increase in either factor.[2] For instance, in our numerical example if all variables are indexes initially at 1.0, a 4 percent increase in labor input will cause a 3 percent increase in real GDP. Initially:

$$1.0 = 1.0(1.0^{0.25}\,1.0^{0.75})$$

After a 4 percent increase in labor input:

$$1.03 = 1.0(1.0^{0.25}\,1.04^{0.75})$$

Thus the elasticity of real GDP with respect to a change in labor input is 0.75 (= 3/4).

Several other characteristics of the production function are evident. First, an equal percentage increase in both factors, capital and labor, raises real GDP by the same percentage. This characteristic, called **constant returns to scale,** occurs because the sum of the weights (b and $1 - b$) is unity. When both factor inputs increase by 4 percent, we have:

$$1.04 = 1.0(1.04^{0.25}\,1.04^{0.75})$$

after a 4 percent increase in both K and N.

A second characteristic is the direct one-for-one response of real GDP to the autonomous growth factor A. If A increases by 4 percentage points, while capital and labor input remain fixed at 1.0, real GDP increases by the same four percentage points:

$$1.04 = 1.04(1.0^{0.25}\,1.0^{0.75})$$

after a 4 percent increase in A.

The Cobb-Douglas production function is only one of many ways in which real GDP might be related to A, K, and N. Often in economics we want to make the simple statement that "Y is related to A, K, and N," but without restricting the particular form of the relationship. To accomplish this, we sometimes use a *general functional form*. An example of such a general form for the production function is:

$$Y = F(A, K, N)$$

In words, this states simply that real GDP (Y) depends on an autonomous growth factor (A), an index of capital input (K) and an index of labor input (N). The capital letter F and the parentheses mean *depends on,* and any alphabetical letter can be used.

Why is it interesting to know simply that one variable depends on others? By writing an alternative equation, one could state the *alternative hypothesis* that there is no role for an autonomous growth factor:

$$Y = F(K, N)$$

This states that real GDP depends *only on* capital and labor input.

Sometimes it is desirable to make a specific assumption about the form in which one variable enters, but not the others. This occurs in equation (9.1) in the text, which states that the elasticity of real GDP with respect to the autonomous growth factor is unity, but does not restrict the form of the relationship between real GDP and the other inputs, capital and labor:

$$Y = AF(K, N)$$

Without further information one cannot look at these general functional forms and learn whether the assumed relationship is positive or negative. The posi-

---

[1] The function is named after an Amherst mathematics professor, Charles W. Cobb, and a University of Chicago economics professor (later U.S. senator), Paul H. Douglas, and is described in a book by the latter, *The Theory of Wages* (New York: Macmillan, 1934), especially Chapter V.

[2] *Elasticity* is a term introduced in most elementary economics courses and refers to the percentage change in one variable in response to a 1 percent change in another variable.

tive relationship between real GDP and both capital and labor inputs can be written in either of two ways:

$$\text{Method 1: } Y = A\,F(K,\,N)$$
$$(+)(+)$$

$$\text{Method 2: } Y = A\,F(K,\,N); \quad F_K > 0,\, F_N > 0.$$

The terms to the right of the semicolon in method 2 can be put into these words: the response of real GDP to a change in capital input (F_K) and in labor input (F_N) is positive (> 0).

Exercise:　Consider a general functional form for the demand for money:

$$\left(\frac{M}{P}\right)^d = L(Y,\, r)$$

State in words what this function states about the relationship between the real demand for money $(M/P)^d$ and real GDP (Y) and the interest rate (r). Use both methods 1 and 2 to write down the facts that the real demand for money depends positively on real GDP and negatively on the interest rate.

CHAPTER 10

Explanations of Slow Growth in Productivity and Real Wages

Production is not the application of tools to materials,
but logic to work.
—*Peter Drucker, 1965*

10-1 America's Greatest Economic Problem?

In the mid-1990s the United States achieved an unusually favorable combination of low unemployment and low inflation, as we learned in Chapter 8. Despite that achievement, there remained a nagging economic problem—real wages and real family incomes were barely growing. This slow growth rate of real wages distinguished the United States from most other industrial nations, where the growth rate of real wages was substantially faster. This flaw in U.S. economic performance affected college graduates, who experienced difficulty in finding high-paying jobs and who in many cases were forced by economic circumstances to move back in with their parents. College students wondered whether they might be the first generation in U.S. history that would fail to achieve a standard of living higher than their parents'.

The slow growth in real wages is closely related to slow growth in productivity, that is, in output per hour. Only by raising its total output per hour can an economy sustain a higher hourly real wage for the average worker. Since the early 1970s productivity growth in the United States has been much slower than in the previous half century. And productivity growth has been considerably slower than in other industrial countries. The productivity growth slowdown has challenged the attention of a generation of economists, but as yet no single overall explanation has emerged.

The perception of inadequate U.S. economic performance extends beyond the growth rates of specific measures of real wages and of productivity. There are other problems that have caused journalists to write mountains of articles with titles like "The New, Ruthless Economy," "The Age of Anxiety," "Winter of Discontent," "Where Have the Good Jobs Gone?" and "America, Land of the Shaken." It seems that every week some corporation announces thousands of layoffs as it struggles to cut costs, restructure, and downsize. Other thousands of managers and staff workers lose their jobs as a result of mergers. Despite a relatively low overall unemployment rate, the fear of job loss creates a sense of anxiety and insecurity.

Adding to concerns about job insecurity and slow growth in the *average* real wage was a clear disparity between the income gains of average citizens and those who were best off. Data are available for average family income for the bottom 20 percent (quintile) of families, the top quintile, and those in the middle. Between 1977 and 1992, the change in average family real income for the bottom quintile was −17 percent, for the middle three quintiles it was +1 percent, and for the top quintile it was +28 percent. An even starker disparity was at the very top, where the top 1 percent of families enjoyed an average family income gain of +91 percent. The average chief executive officer

(CEO) earned compensation 41 times higher than that of an average American worker in the mid-1970s; by the early 1990s the average CEO compensation was 225 times as high. Since much of the growth in real income earned by Americans accrued to those at the top of the income distribution, Americans at the bottom and in the middle experienced real wage growth even slower than that for the nation as a whole.

In this chapter we study the interrelated issues of slow growth in real wages and in productivity. Which is the chicken and which the egg? Does slow productivity growth cause slow growth in real wages, or is it the other way around? How are productivity and real wage growth measured, and why do available measures differ so widely in how they report growth rates? Can the slowdown in productivity and real wage growth be explained by the growth theory developed in Chapter 9, particularly by capital accumulation and technological change, the central elements in the Solow growth model? What other factors caused the slowdown, and do any of them explain why growth in productivity and in real wages have been slower in the United States than in other countries? Finally, does the anxiety and insecurity noted by journalists have an economic explanation, and can economists explain the increasing inequality of incomes between bottom and the top?

10-2   Concepts of Productivity and the Real Wage

In Chapter 9 we were introduced to two alternative concepts of productivity. The first is labor productivity, or output per hour *(Y/N)*. The growth rate of labor productivity is simply the growth rate of total output minus the growth rate of total hours of work *(y − n)*.

The second concept introduced in Chapter 9 is multifactor productivity (MFP), which we also called Solow's residual. The concept of MFP differs from labor productivity in that it expresses the amount of output produced relative to *both* labor and capital inputs; in contrast, labor productivity expresses the amount of output produced relative to labor input only. The contribution that capital makes to output is measured by the elasticity of output to capital (*b*), which we will continue, as in Chapter 9, to assume is 0.25 in our numerical examples. The elasticity of output to capital and labor input together is unity (1.0), and so the elasticity of output to labor is the remaining amount not attributable to capital (1 − *b*), or 0.75 in the numerical example.[1]

The growth rate of MFP (for which we use, as before, the symbol *a*) can be written as the growth rate of output *(y)* minus the contribution of capital *(bk)* minus the contribution of labor [(1 − *b*)*n*]:

$$a = y - bk - (1 - b)n \qquad (10.1)$$

Thus, to measure the growth rate of multifactor productivity, we need to know four facts—the growth rates of output, capital, and labor (*y, k,* and *n*), and the elasticity of output with respect to capital (*b*). As Robert Solow

---

[1]As we saw in Chapter 9, the assumption that the elasticity of output to capital and labor sums to unity is called "constant returns to scale." If the two elasticities sum to a number greater than unity, this implies "increasing returns to scale," and a number less than unity implies "decreasing returns to scale."

showed in the 1950s in part of the work that earned him the Nobel Prize in economics, this elasticity can be measured by the share of capital in national income, including corporate profits, depreciation, rent, interest, and the portion of the income of the self-employed that is attributable to capital.[2]

How are the growth rates of multifactor productivity (a) and labor productivity ($y - n$) related to each other? Equation (10.1) can be rearranged to show their relationship:

General Form   Numerical Example

$$a = (y - n) - b(k - n) \qquad 2.25 = (4 - 1) - 0.25(4 - 1)$$

In words, the growth rate of multifactor productivity is equal to the growth rate of labor productivity minus b times the growth in the ratio of capital input to labor input. Since growth in the ratio is almost always positive, the growth of MFP is almost always slower than that of labor productivity.

SELF-TEST

The definition of MFP growth in equation (10.1) has five elements: y, a, k, n, and b. Assuming that b always equals 0.25, any of the four remaining elements can be calculated if the other three are known. Fill in the blanks:

y	a	k	n
—	4	4	1
4	3	4	—
3	0	—	1

For each example in the table above, which is higher: labor productivity growth or MFP growth? Why should this be the case?

How the Real Wage Is Related to Productivity

If labor productivity (Y/N) grows slowly, the real wage (W/P) tends to grow slowly. We have already learned in equation (10.1) that an ingredient in the measurement of multifactor productivity (MFP) is labor's share in national income ($1 - b$). This central concept, called labor's share, can be defined in a way that connects labor productivity with the real wage:

$$\text{Labor's share} = 1 - b = \frac{WN}{PY} = \frac{W/P}{Y/N} \tag{10.2}$$

The first expression states that labor's share is equal to the total compensation of labor (the nominal wage rate *(W)*, times the quantity of labor input *(N)*), divided by total income in nominal terms *(PY)*. The second expression states that this is exactly the same as the real wage divided by labor productivity.

Equation (10.2) helps us see that if labor's share in national income is constant, then the real wage must grow at the same rate as labor productivity. As usual, we employ lower-case symbols to represent growth rates, and we can use the familiar relationship that the growth rate of any ratio equals the growth rate of the numerator minus the growth rate of the denominator. This implies that the growth rate of labor's share equals the growth rate of the real wage ($w - p$), minus the growth rate of labor productivity ($y - n$):

---

[2]Solow's idea of linking the elasticity of output to capital with capital's share in national income is explained in Chapter 9, footnote 10.

$$\text{Growth rate of labor's share} = (w - p) - (y - n) \qquad (10.3)$$

This leads us to a very important conclusion about the growth rate of the real wage. If labor's share is constant (so that the growth rate of labor's share is zero), then *the growth rate of the real wage must be exactly equal to the growth rate of productivity.*

Condition if the growth rate of labor's share is zero

$$w - p = y - n \qquad (10.4)$$

As we shall see, labor's share of national income in the United States has been virtually constant for the past twenty-five years. As a result, the real wage must have grown at the same rate as labor productivity. We shall examine the facts in the next section.

Before doing so, we should note that so far we have used a particular definition for the growth of the real wage, namely the growth in the nominal wage rate *(w)* minus the growth rate of the price deflator for total GDP *(p)*, sometimes called the **real product wage,** since the deflator used to convert nominal wages into real wages is the deflator for total domestic *product.* However, there is no reason for workers to care about the growth of their real wage using the GDP deflator. They care about the growth in the ability of their nominal wage rate to purchase *consumer goods.* Thus workers care about the **real consumption wage,** defined as the growth in the nominal wage rate *(w)* minus the growth rate of the deflator for personal consumption expenditures *(c).* These two concepts of the real wage can differ if the two deflators grow at different rates:

The **real product wage** is the nominal wage rate, divided by the price index for total output, such as the GDP deflator.

The **real consumption wage** is the nominal wage rate divided by the price deflator for personal consumption expenditures.

General Form   Numerical Example

$$w - c = w - p - (c - p) \qquad 0 = 1 - (3 - 2) \qquad (10.5)$$

As shown by the numerical example, it would be possible for the real consumption wage *(w − c)* to exhibit a zero growth rate while the real product wage *(w − p)* grew at 1 percent per annum, if the price index for consumption expenditures *(c)* grew 1 percent faster than the GDP deflator *(p)*—for instance at 3 percent compared to 2 percent. As we shall see in the next section, this divergence between the two deflators helps explain why growth in the real consumption wage has been so slow in the United States.

10-3 CASE STUDY: Behavior of Real Wages and Productivity in the United States

Thus far we have learned several important relationships linking labor productivity, multifactor productivity (MFP), the real product wage, and the real consumption wage. In this section we see how these concepts have performed in the United States, both during the postwar period and over a longer period of time.

The Startling Facts About the Productivity Growth Slowdown

It is possible to calculate MFP growth for the United States using equation (10.1) and data on *y, k, n,* and *b* that extend all the way back to 1870. We can take the resulting yearly data on MFP growth and cumulate it into an index number for the *level* of MFP.[3] Such an index, shown on a base of 1972 equals 100, is displayed in Figure 10-1. The MFP line is plotted on a logarithmic scale. As we learned in Chapter 1, the growth rate of a variable plotted on a logarithmic scale is given by the slope of the line.

At first glance the United States' record of achieving productivity growth is impressive. In 1994 MFP was more than *triple* its value in 1900, more than *double* its value in 1929, and more than 40 percent higher than its value in the late 1940s after World War II. But a closer look suggests that something has gone badly wrong. MFP in 1994 was only 2 percent higher than in 1972, implying virtually no growth in the intervening two decades. Stated another way, the slow growth rate of MFP beginning in the late 1960s is shown by the very

MFP GROWTH: ONE BIG WAVE?

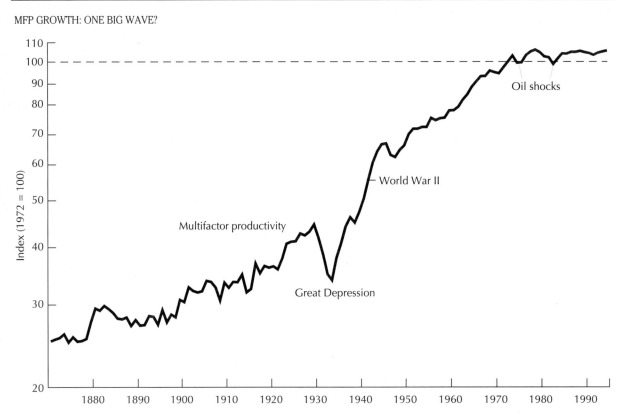

Figure 10-1   Multifactor Productivity in the United States, 1870–1994

The line plots multifactor productivity (MFP) on a log scale, so that the intervals with the steepest line segments enjoyed the fastest MFP growth. MFP grew slowly not only after 1972 but also during the latter part of the nineteenth century, when the growth rate was less than 1 percent per year in the four decades after 1870.

---

[3]If a_t is the annual logarithmic growth rate of MFP, then we can calculate an index for MFP from the sum of the growth rates:

$$A_t = 100e^{\left(\sum_{t=1871}^{1994} a_t\right)}$$

This gives us an index of MFP on a base of 1870 = 100. The MFP index plotted in Figure 10-1 is the same index divided by its 1972 value and multiplied by 100.

flat slope of the MFP line in the 1970s, 1980s, and 1990s, as contrasted to the much steeper slope extending between the early 1920s and the late 1960s.

Most economists discuss the productivity slowdown only in the context of the post–World War II period, that is, the years since 1948.[4] The period between 1948 and 1973 is often called a "golden age" because of the rapid MFP growth that occurred during this interval. Yet the broader view of the 120-year period contained in Figure 10-1 casts doubt on this interpretation. If we skip over the Great Depression and World War II, and draw a line connecting, say, 1928 and 1950, we find that this interval registered faster MFP growth than the so-called golden age.

Some of the ups and downs of MFP are caused by the business cycle, since the economy tends to be more productive in booms and less productive in recessions. To assess properly the historical behavior of MFP, we want to make comparisons between years when the economy was in a normal condition, neither in boom nor recession but operating close to its natural rate of unemployment and natural level of output. This is carried out in Table 10-1, which computes the growth rate of output, inputs, and MFP over intervals between years of normal economic activity. The top half of the table calculates growth rates over nine relatively short intervals spanning 1870–1994, and the bottom part displays the same growth rates over three longer intervals spanning the same time period. The numbers are based on the same data plotted in Figure 10-1, but they are more meaningful, because they exclude the ups and downs of MFP due to business cycles and wars.

Table 10-1   **Annual Percentage Rates of Growth, Output, Inputs, and Multifactor Productivity (MFP) in the United States, Selected Intervals, 1870–1994**

Interval	*Output*	*Labor*	*Capital*	*MFP*
Short-Term Trends				
1870–1891	4.41	3.56	4.49	0.39
1891–1913	4.43	2.93	3.68	1.13
1913–1928	3.11	1.45	2.20	1.40
1928–1950	2.68	0.93	0.41	1.96
1950–1964	3.53	1.41	3.53	1.23
1964–1972	4.16	1.58	4.95	1.56
1972–1979	3.49	2.16	4.39	0.67
1979–1987	2.60	1.86	4.40	0.01
1987–1994	2.26	2.07	2.36	0.10
Long-Term Trends				
1870–1913	4.42	3.24	4.17	0.77
1913–1964	3.05	1.21	1.79	1.60
1964–1994	3.14	1.90	4.07	0.60

Note: All data refer to the nonfarm private business sector.

Source: 1870–1964. Robert J. Gordon, "American Economic Growth: One Big Wave?" Working paper, March 1993; 1964–1994. U.S. Bureau of Labor Statistics.

---

[4]While World War II ended in 1945, comparisons involving 1946 or 1947 are usually avoided, as these were years when economic activity was distorted by the need to convert from wartime to peacetime production.

One Big Wave?

The growth rates of MFP displayed in the right-hand column of Table 10-1 provide detailed numbers to confirm the general impression of Figure 10-1: MFP growth started slowly in the late nineteenth century, then accelerated to a crescendo in the period 1928–50, and has gradually slowed down since. Thus the much-discussed U.S. productivity growth slowdown goes back to 1972 and raises an important question that is rarely asked.

> *Which is the unusual phenomenon to be explained, slow MFP growth in 1972–94 or fast MFP growth during 1913–72? The fact that MFP growth after 1972 slowed to roughly the same rate experienced before 1913 suggests that there may have been something unusually favorable about the years 1913–72.*

The data presented in Figure 10-1 and Table 10-1 point to a limited set of facts that are widely accepted. First, MFP growth subtracts out the growth in the capital stock, and thus the productivity slowdown of the last three decades cannot be due mainly to lower investment and the resulting slow growth of capital. Second, MFP growth does not proceed steadily decade after decade. Whatever made MFP growth so rapid between 1913 and 1972 needs to be explained. While the new endogenous growth theory has done a good job of clarifying those factors that prevent poor nations from quickly becoming rich nations, it has contributed little that would help us understand the "one big wave" phenomenon identified for the United States in this section.

Why does Real Wage Growth Lag Behind That of Labor Productivity?

So far we have examined the behavior of MFP over the past 125 years. Now we are ready to look at the behavior of labor productivity and real wages over a shorter period, that since 1960.

Figure 10-2 plots labor productivity as the red line and the real consumption wage as the solid black line. While both grew at roughly the same annual rate until the early 1980s, the two lines began to diverge around 1983. By 1996 the growth of the real consumption wage had fallen behind that of labor productivity by almost 9 percent.

The information illustrated in Figure 10-2 is given also in Table 10-2 in the form of annual growth rates. Line 1 shows that labor's share was virtually constant between 1972 and 1996, rising slightly in 1979 and 1987, and then falling back to roughly the 1972 level. The remaining lines in the table show annualized growth rates over the previous interval. For instance, line 2 shows that the growth rate of labor productivity between 1960 and 1972 was 3.00 percent per year, but by the 1987–96 interval it had slowed to 0.79 percent per year. Notice that the productivity slowdown has been getting worse, with each successive interval in line 2 recording an ever-lower growth rate.

The relationship between the growth in the real wage and in labor productivity is shown by comparing lines 3 and 4 with line 2. Here we see that growth in the real product wage $(w - p)$ was roughly the same as that of labor productivity $(y - n)$, but that growth in the real consumption wage $(w - c)$, line 4, lagged behind by an increasing amount.

Why did this slow growth in the real consumption wage occur? In Section 10-2 of this chapter, we learned that the growth rate of the real consumption

THE REAL WAGE FALLS BEHIND PRODUCTIVITY

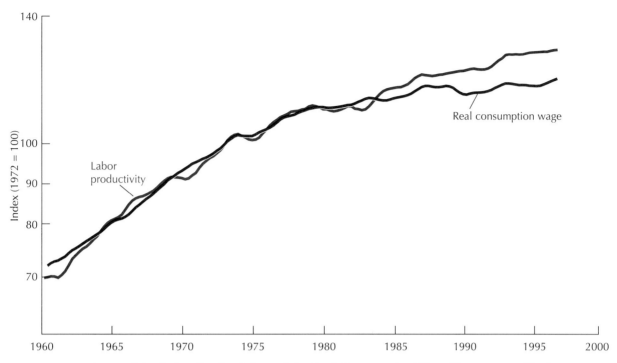

Figure 10-2   **Labor Productivity and the Real Consumption Wage, Four-quarter Moving Average, 1960–96**

The red line displays labor productivity, that is, output per hour in the U.S. private nonfarm business economy. The black line displays the real consumption wage, defined as nominal compensation per hour divided by the deflator for personal consumption expenditures. Between 1960 and 1983 the two lines move very closely together, but after 1983 the real consumption wage grew more slowly than labor productivity. As explained in the text, this occurred because the prices of consumption goods rose slightly faster than the prices of output as a whole.

Table 10-2   **Level of Labor's Share (in percent) and Annual Growth Rates of Productivity and Real Wages, Selected Intervals, 1960–96**

	1960	*1972*	*1979*	*1987*	*1996*
1. Labor's share (percent of national income)	69.6	72.7	73.2	73.0	72.3

Annual percent growth rate over previous interval		*1960–72*	*1972–79*	*1979–87*	*1987–96*
2. Labor productivity $(y - n)$	—	3.00	1.40	1.16	0.79
3. Real product wage $(w - p)$	—	2.78	1.62	1.01	0.85
4. Real consumption wage $(w - c)$	—	2.64	1.46	0.68	0.31
5. Consumption deflator minus product deflator $(c - p)$	—	0.14	0.16	0.33	0.54

Source: U.S. Bureau of Labor Statistics and National Income and Product Accounts.

Note: Labor's share is defined as total compensation divided by national income. The real product wage is compensation per hour in the nonfarm private business sector divided by the implicit deflator for the nonfarm business sector. The real consumption wage is the same compensation measure divided by the implicit deflator for personal consumption expenditures.

wage could differ from that of labor productivity for two main reasons. First, the real consumption wage could lag behind if labor's share declined. But this was not a factor, since the level of labor's share (line 1) was constant between 1972 and 1996.[5] Second, the real consumption wage could lag behind both labor productivity and the real product wage if the price index of consumption expenditures were to rise more rapidly than that of total output. This indeed has happened, as shown on line 5, which displays the *difference* in the growth rate between the price indexes for consumption expenditures and total output. Since the early 1980s there has been a growing disparity between the inflation rates of consumer expenditures and the economy as a whole.

Looking for Culprits

Thus far we have learned that, indeed, the malaise expressed by many journalists has a solid foundation in the facts about the performance of the American economy. In contrast to the period 1960–72, when the real consumption wage increased at 2.64 percent per year, during 1987–96 the increase was only 0.31 percent per year, less than *one-eighth* as much. Another way to express the contrast is that if the 1960–72 rate had continued forever, the real consumption wage would double every 26 years. But if the 1987–96 rate were to continue forever, it would take *224 years* for the real consumption wage to double! No wonder that this generation of college students fears it will be the first to fail to exceed the standard of living of its parents.

So far we have identified some of the most important relationships among the major productivity and real wage concepts, but we have emerged with more questions than answers. The main questions can be expressed as follows:

1. Did Slower Productivity Growth Cause Slower Real Wage Growth or Vice Versa?   Most discussions of slow real wage growth assume that the fundamental cause is slower productivity growth. But some recent analyses suggest that the causation may, at least partly, work in reverse. If real wages are low and workers are cheap to hire, then many workers will be hired for a given set of tasks and the level of productivity will be low. Similarly, if the growth rate of real wages is slow, then the growth of employment will be rapid and the growth rate of productivity will be slow.

2. What Caused the Productivity Growth Slowdown?   As we have seen, the growth in MFP and labor productivity slowed substantially after 1972. The slowdown has become progressively worse. What are the explanations of the slowdown?

3. Why Have Prices for Consumption Expenditures Risen More Rapidly Than for Total Output?   Table 10-2 shows that since 1987 the real

---

[5]Labor's share rose between 1960 and 1972, indicating that the real product wage should have grown faster than labor productivity over this interval. Instead, the relationship in lines 2 and 3 of Table 10-2 goes in the opposite direction. The reasons for this have to do with minor differences in definition between the total economy and the nonfarm private business sector which have been ignored in the simplified definition in equation (10.4).

consumption wage has grown less than half as rapidly as labor productivity. The table also shows that this has occurred because of more rapid growth in the price index for consumer expenditures than in the price index for total output. Why has this discrepancy in the price indexes occurred?

10-4 Does Slow Productivity Growth Cause Slow Real Wage Growth, or Vice Versa?

It is frequently assumed that the problem of slow real wage growth in the United States must be caused by slow productivity growth. Indeed, we can use the standard labor market diagram, first introduced in Figure 7-7 on p. 205, to illustrate this assumption.

An Adverse Productivity Shock Reduces the Real Wage, Hours, or Both

The top frame of Figure 10-3 plots the real wage on the vertical axis and the level of labor input (measured in hours) on the horizontal axis. The initial labor demand curve is shown as the dashed line (N_0^d) and slopes downward, reflecting the decline in the marginal product of labor that occurs when more labor input is added while the quantity of other factors of production (not just capital, but also energy and imported materials) remains constant.

Instead of staying in its initial position, two events could cause the labor demand curve to shift downward to a position like N_1^d. First, this shift could occur if the quantity of the other factors of production (in addition to labor) were to decline instead of staying constant. Second, such a downward shift could occur even if the quantity of these other factors of production remained constant—for example, if MFP were to decline (i.e., if less output were produced by a given quantity of factors of production). In either case, the new lower labor demand curve is shown by the same solid line in the top frame of Figure 10-3. The original level of employment (N_0) could be maintained only at point Z, where the real wage is shown to fall in the same proportion as the vertical downward shift in the labor demand curve.

Is there any escape from the logic that an autonomous decline in labor productivity must cause an equiproportionate decline in the real wage rate, as occurs at point Z? If for some reason the real wage were completely rigid, as at point X, employment could not be maintained at point N_0 but instead would decline to point N_1. Some analysts believe that this outcome occurred in Europe during the 1970s and early 1980s at the time of the adverse supply shocks, and that this helps to explain why unemployment increased so much in Europe relative to the United States during that period.[6]

The Possibility of Feedback from Low Real Wages to Low Productivity

The top frame of Figure 10-3, as we have seen, shows how an adverse shock to labor productivity can cause a decline in the real wage. However, the

---

[6]See Section 12-11 on p. 389.

Figure 10-3

The Effect on the Labor Market of an Adverse Productivity Shock and a Downward Shift in Labor Supply

In the top frame the economy is initially at point B. An adverse productivity shock shifts the labor demand curve downward. If the amount of labor input remains unchanged, the economy moves to point Z, where the real wage is lower than at point B. Another possibility is that the real wage is held fixed, possibly by union contracts, in which case the economy goes to point X, and labor input falls to point N_1. In the bottom frame a downward shift in the labor supply curve, for reasons suggested in the text, would move the economy from point B to point C along a fixed labor demand curve. Labor input would rise from N_0 to N_2, while the real wage would fall from $(W/P)_0$ to $(W/P)_1$. The marginal product of labor is lower at point C than at point B, implying that average labor productivity is lower as well.

REAL WAGES AND PRODUCTIVITY: WHICH IS THE CHICKEN AND WHICH THE EGG?

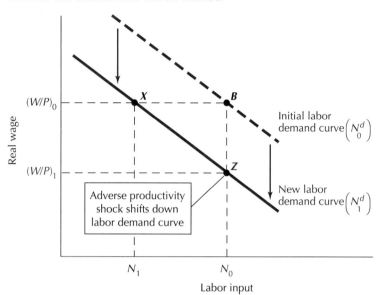

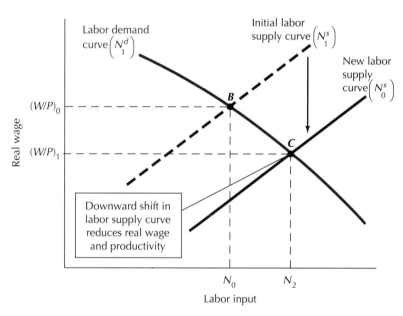

relation can work in reverse. The bottom frame of Figure 10-3 shows a fixed labor demand curve, which assumes a fixed quantity of factors of production (other than labor) and a fixed level of MFP. Now let us assume that there is a downward shift in the labor supply curve.[7]

---

[7] An upward sloping labor supply curve was introduced in Figure 7-7 on p. 205.

What factors might cause such a downward shift? This could be caused by any event that increases the supply of labor, such as a larger work force caused by more immigration. Another factor causing such a shift would be any event that reduces the wage at which a given quantity of labor input is willing to work, including a reduction in the power of unions or a reduction in the real minimum wage (which may tend to depress wages for unskilled workers). Increased anxiety by workers about job security might also cause such a shift.

If the labor supply curve shifts downward along the labor demand curve, the real wage will decline, but so also will labor productivity.[8] The economy will shift from point *B* to point *C,* and the decline in both the real wage and productivity will have been caused by a shift in the labor supply curve rather than a shift in the labor demand curve.

While Figure 10-3 shows why a downward shift in the *levels* of labor productivity and the real wage are related, caused either by a downward shift in labor supply or labor demand, the same logic applies to the growth rates of labor productivity and the real wage. For instance, growth in labor productivity and the real wage could be held down by inadequate growth in capital input, whether that takes the form of slow growth in physical capital, in forms of human capital such as education and training, or in government-financed infrastructure such as highways and airports.

Similarly, any event that stimulates the *growth* of labor supply can hold down the growth rates of labor productivity and the real wage, including steady growth in the labor force caused by immigration, or a shift in labor's bargaining position resulting from a decline in the strength of labor unions. Some observers interpret the steady increase in foreign trade, sometimes called the globalization of the world economy, as having the effect of creating competition between foreign workers and domestic U.S. workers, thus weakening the position of U.S. workers. This would directly slow the growth of the real wage and indirectly, as in the bottom frame of Figure 10-3, slow the growth rate of productivity.

Since we observe in Figure 10-2 and Table 10-2 that growth in both labor productivity and in the real wage have been much slower in the past decade than in the 1960s, either adverse productivity shocks or labor supply shocks may have been responsible. More likely, some combination of both types of shocks may have caused the slowdown. In the next two sections we will review some of the specific types of shocks that have been suggested as a cause of the slowdown.

SELF-TEST

> For each of the following events, indicate whether it shifts the labor demand curve or the labor supply curve, and whether the shift is up or down: (a) College tuition becomes more expensive, causing some students to drop out and look for work; (b) tighter rules prevent immigration of unskilled workers; (c) the real price of oil declines; (d) a tax on equipment investment makes it more expensive to purchase equipment.

---

[8]The labor demand curve is drawn on the assumption that the real wage equals the marginal product of labor. When the marginal product of labor declines, as from point *B* to point *C* in the bottom frame of Figure 10-3, the average product of labor *(Y/N)* declines as well. In the special case of the Cobb-Douglas production function, the change in the average product of labor is proportional to that of the marginal product.

10-5   Sources of Adverse Productivity Shocks

We have now seen that, at least in principle, the growth slowdown in productivity and in real wages may have been caused by adverse productivity shocks, labor supply shocks, or both. In this section we will examine some of the adverse productivity shocks that have been suggested by economists who have been struggling for more than two decades to explain the productivity growth slowdown. As we shall see, a combination of several causes is plausible; certainly, no single cause has yet emerged as the convincing explanation.

Dimensions of the Productivity Slowdown

Table 10-3 allows us to focus on a sharp contrast in performance between the manufacturing and nonmanufacturing sectors. In the top half of the table we see that after experiencing slower growth between 1972 and 1979, manufacturing revived sufficiently so that, on balance, there is only a negligible post-1972 productivity slowdown. Not shown in the table is the main source of the manufacturing revival. Manufacturing is divided between durable goods (such as autos, steel, machines, and computers) and nondurable goods (food, apparel, tobacco, and chemicals). The revival has been much stronger in durables than in nondurables, and most of the revival in durables has been attributable to the computer industry. The nonmanufacturing part of the economy, which is about four times larger than manufacturing, reveals extremely slow productivity growth since 1972 and a larger slowdown than that for the economy as a whole.

The bottom half of Table 10-3 displays the growth rate of multifactor productivity (a) for the same time periods and sectors of the economy. These growth rates of MFP, which subtract out the growth of capital input as well as labor input, show almost as rapid a slowdown as for labor productivity growth in the top half of the table. This suggests that slower growth in capi-

---

Table 10-3   Average Annual Aggregate Productivity Growth, 1950–94, Selected Periods (percent per year)

Measure	*1950–72*	*1972–79*	*1979–87*	*1987–94*	*Change, 1950–72 to 1972–94*
Output per hour $(y - n)$					
Business	3.12	1.50	1.41	1.03	−1.78
Nonfarm business	2.65	1.30	1.21	0.91	−1.50
Manufacturing	2.62	2.17	3.01	2.10	−0.15
Nonmanufacturing	2.65	1.10	0.74	0.56	−1.84
Multifactor productivity (a)					
Business	1.93	0.85	0.21	0.17	−1.52
Nonfarm business	1.64	0.67	0.01	0.03	−1.40
Manufacturing	1.54	0.33	1.65	0.57	−0.64
Nonmanufacturing	1.66	0.76	−0.41	−0.12	−1.60

Source: U.S. Bureau of Labor Statistics.

tal accumulation accounts for very little of the slower growth in overall productivity.

In assessing alternative hypotheses, we must keep in mind that the productivity slowdown has now lasted more than twenty-five years, and that it is concentrated in the nonmanufacturing sector. Here we review some of the leading explanations, starting with those that center on slower growth in inputs. Then we turn to hypotheses that try to explain the slowdown in MFP, the Solow residual that remains after the quantity and quality of inputs have been taken into account.

Slower Growth in Measured and Unmeasured Inputs

Measured Capital per Labor Hour.   The growth of measured capital per labor hour slowed in the United States after 1973, both because the growth of the capital stock slowed down, and because the growth of labor hours increased in response to a massive movement by women from home activity into labor force participation. One hypothesis to explain slower growth is the fact that the rules of the U.S. tax system are set partially in nominal rather than real terms. When the rate of inflation accelerates, saving by corporations and individual households is overtaxed, and saving is discouraged. The weakness of this hypothesis is that capital growth was even lower in the 1980s and 1990s than the 1970s (Table 10-1), even though both inflation and tax rates were lower, not higher, in the 1980s and 1990s.

There is another explanation for the slowdown in the growth of capital per labor hour which concentrates on the fact that the growth rate of labor hours speeded up after 1973 in the United States but not in other countries. The real wage rate in the United States declined substantially in response to the supply shocks of 1973–74 and 1979–80. Yet in Europe real wage rates grew substantially faster than productivity in the 1970s, finally moderating only in the 1980s. As a result labor was relatively cheap in the United States after 1973 and relatively expensive in Europe. The German economist Herbert Giersch has pointed to this difference in real wage behavior to explain why European countries enjoyed faster productivity growth and suffered higher unemployment than in the United States.

Raw Materials and Energy.   The late Michael Bruno, of Hebrew University in Jerusalem, and Jeffrey Sachs of Harvard believe that the worldwide character of the productivity slowdown after 1973 (see the International Perspectives box) suggests the likelihood of a common cause. Bruno and Sachs stress the direct effect of the higher relative prices of energy and raw materials, together with restrictive macroeconomic policies that were introduced in response to those increases in relative prices.[9] A serious problem with the Bruno-Sachs analysis is that the increase in oil prices and raw materials prices was reversed in the 1980s and 1990s, yet productivity growth revived only in manufacturing, not in the rest of the economy.

---

[9]Michael Bruno and Jeffrey Sachs, *Economics of Worldwide Stagnation* (Cambridge, Mass.: Harvard University Press, 1985).

Decline in Labor Quality.   The role of labor quality in the productivity slowdown is still debated. The percentage of teenagers and adult women in the labor force rose after 1973, yet their average wages still lag behind those of adult men. Consequently, analysts who measure the relative productivity of groups of workers by their relative wages conclude that the quality of the workforce declined as its age-sex composition shifted toward a greater share of adult female workers and teenagers of both sexes. However, other economists believe that the low relative wages of women reflect, at least in part, the effects of discrimination rather than lower productivity. Economists also note the decline in scores on the SAT and other standardized tests that occurred in the 1970s and 1980s, and the more general problem that the U.S. school system is not training enough graduates with the skills needed to cope with the demands of modern technology.

Infrastructure

Infrastructure is public investment in roads, sewers, airports, and more broadly, even includes education. It is any investment that provides widespread benefits to consumers and raises the return on private investment.

Endogenous growth theory (reviewed in Section 9-6) stresses that private and public investment are equally important to an economy. Rich nations differ from poor nations by having more spending on education, sewers, highways, railroads, airports, and other types of **infrastructure** investment. Recently, inadequate public investment in infrastructure has been cited as the major cause of the productivity slowdown in the United States.[10] However, this conclusion is controversial, and another study over a longer historical time period and comparing a number of industrialized nations finds little systematic relationship between productivity growth and the share of output devoted to infrastructure investment.[11]

Problems of Particular Industries

One aspect of the productivity slowdown that seems to point in the direction of "death by a thousand cuts," that is, a multipart explanation, is the diversity of the experience of major industries. We have seen in Table 10-3 that manufacturing has done much better than nonmanufacturing. In the United States, for instance, three major nonmanufacturing industries have experienced a productivity growth slowdown that is about triple the average of other industries. One extreme case is the mining industry. Here most of the slowdown appears to have been caused by a reduced rate of finding new and productive oil wells.

The construction industry is also an extreme case, with a *negative* growth rate of productivity since 1965. Productivity in the construction industry has fallen back to the levels of the early 1950s. Faulty U.S. data may be a source of error here, since Canada has better statistics and has not experienced a similar decline in construction productivity.

---

[10]See David A. Aschauer, "Is Public Expenditure Productive?" *Journal of Monetary Economics,* vol. 23 (March 1989), pp. 177–200.

[11]See Robert Ford and Pierre Poret, "Infrastructure and Private-Sector Productivity," *OECD Economic Studies,* no. 17 (Autumn 1991), pp. 63–89.

Public utilities compose the third extreme industry, with most of the problem concentrated in electricity generation. Several hypotheses come together here. Government regulation has required costly investment in antipollution equipment. The lack of advances since the 1960s in equipment design have also slowed productivity growth. In fact, we have gone backward. Billions of dollars have been wasted on the construction of nuclear power plants that have never been put into service. The complexity of the diagnosis of the productivity problem in this industry suggests that we should be skeptical of simple hypotheses that attribute all of the problem to one cause and promise a solution with a single proposed policy change.

Running Out of Resources and Ideas

Because the productivity slowdown has been so pervasive and longlasting, some economists believe that the fundamental cause goes beyond slower growth in factor inputs. William Nordhaus has helped popularize the depletion hypothesis, which is a much more pessimistic approach than those reviewed earlier in the section.[12] One aspect is the depletion of natural resources, in particular the decline in the rate of finding new productive oil wells in the United States. This has reduced productivity growth, since there are more people engaged in searching for less and less available oil.

But the depletion hypothesis involves more than oil wells. The facts shown above are highlighted in Figures 10-1 and Table 10-1, which show that MFP growth was much faster during 1913–72 than either before or after.[13] Perhaps the MFP slowdown since 1972 is just a return to the normalcy of the nineteenth century, and the task of economists is not to explain why productivity growth was so slow after 1972, but why it was so fast during the golden era of 1913–72. Could the slowdown be explained by the fact that in the first few decades of the twentieth century an unusually large number of important inventions changed productive techniques, as well as the lives of individuals, in a more dramatic way than anything that has happened in the past 25 years? These inventions included the electric motor (which revolutionized manufacturing and allowed the development of consumer appliances), motor transport, air transport, radio, television, plastics, and other petrochemicals. This was the era which saw the emergence of the suburb, the supermarket, and the superhighway.

Is the main invention of the last part of the twentieth century, the electronic computer, as significant as those earlier inventions? Computers seem to have boosted productivity growth in manufacturing (both because computers are part of manufacturing and because computers have increased productivity growth in other manufacturing industries), which has been quite rapid in the past two decades (as shown in Table 10-3). But any productivity payoff from computers in the large nonmanufacturing sector is almost invisible.

---

[12]The Nordhaus approach is set out in William D. Nordhaus, "Economic Policy in the Face of Declining Productivity Growth," *European Economic Review,* vol. 18 (May/June 1982), pp. 131–58.

[13]Robert J. Gordon, "America's Economic Growth: One Big Wave?" working paper, March 1993.

Is the Slowdown Partly an Illusion?

Some economists are not convinced by the depletion hypothesis. When they see corporations pouring billions of dollars of investment in computers into the nonmanufacturing (predominantly service) sector of the economy with no apparent productivity payoff (as is apparent in Table 10-3), they do not conclude that the billions of investment have been a waste of money. Corporate profits in the mid-1990s were high, the stock market was booming, and foreign firms considered their American counterparts to be formidable competitors. Perhaps, suggest these critics, the productivity data are wrong, and the computers have been producing benefits that have not been measured in the form of increased output.

Zvi Griliches of Harvard University has suggested that the measured productivity slowdown results, at least in part, from the difficulties of measurement rather than any actual slowdown in productivity growth. Productivity, suggests Griliches, may still be growing at a healthy rate, but because the economy's output is shifting into sectors where output and productivity are hard to measure, the achievement of the overall economy is increasingly missed. Griliches makes his case by separating the various sectors of the economy into those in which output is easy to measure and those where it is hard to measure.[14] Among those whose output is easy to measure are agriculture, manufacturing, mining, transportation, and utilities. Hard-to-measure sectors include construction, trade, finance, other services (including medical care), and government. As the service sector has grown in importance, the economy has become harder to measure. Specifically, Griliches estimates that the hard-to-measure sectors grew from 51 to 69 percent of total output between 1947 and 1990.

Griliches' hypothesis helps to deal with an immediate criticism of the idea that the productivity slowdown is an illusion because of mismeasurement. This seems implausible on its face, because it would require that slower measured productivity growth after 1972 be accompanied by a *greater degree of mismeasurement.* Why should government statistics have become worse instead of better? The reason, suggests Griliches, is that the economy is becoming harder to measure.

> The major answer to this puzzle is very simple: over three-quarters of [computer] investment has gone into our "unmeasurable" sectors, and thus its productivity effects, which are likely to be quite real, are largely invisible in the data.[15]

Many of the benefits of computers, including cash stations, comprehensive asset-management accounts, and other financial innovations are not included in our national productivity statistics at all. Neither are such consumer conveniences as shorter checkout lines and itemized receipts made possible by laser bar-code scanners, and free trips accrued through frequent flyer mileage plans.

---

[14]Zvi Griliches, "Productivity, R & D, and the Data Constraint," *American Economic Review,* vol. 84 (March 1994), pp. 1–20.
[15]Ibid., p. 11.

Overall, there is no simple answer to the puzzle posed by the productivity growth slowdown. There is probably an element of truth to several of the ideas explored above, including the depletion hypothesis, the Griliches hard-to-measure hypothesis, and the problems experienced by specific industries. The absence of a single simple answer to the puzzle is perplexing to policymakers, because the lack of a single explanation makes it hard to devise government policies to boost productivity growth.

SELF-TEST

> How have each of the following contributed to the slowdown in labor productivity growth: (a) the increase in women's labor force participation rate; (b) the increase in energy prices during the 1970s; (c) the growth of services as a share of total output?

10-6 Can Labor Supply Shifts Contribute an Explanation?

Most of the literature on the productivity slowdown centers on the search for various adverse productivity shocks (as depicted in the top frame of Figure 10-3) that have caused both productivity and real wages to grow slowly. There has been much less discussion of the hypothesis that labor supply shocks may have made some contribution to the slow growth of both real wages and productivity.[16]

The Contrast Between Europe and the United States

American travelers to several of the more prosperous European countries, including France, Germany, and Sweden, notice interesting differences. For instance, it is much less common in Europe for supermarkets to employ baggers in addition to checkout cashiers. Parking lots are more likely to be fully automated than to employ attendants. The bus boy occupation—clearing and setting tables—that is so prevalent in American restaurants at the middle-price and high-price level is largely absent in similar restaurants in these European countries.

These observations are symptoms of a broader set of differences in the evolution of the economies of the United States and leading European nations over the last two decades. Table 10-4 summarizes some of these differences. As shown on line 1, Europe has achieved considerably faster growth in real compensation per employee. Europe's faster growth in the hourly compensation of manufacturing production workers is even more marked, as shown on line 2.

But while the United States lags behind Europe in the growth of real wages and in productivity (as shown in the box on p. 320), the United States has a

---

[16]The ideas in this section are developed more fully in Robert J. Gordon, "Is There a Tradeoff Between Unemployment and Productivity Growth?" in D. Snower and G. del la Dehesa, eds., *Unemployment Policy: Government Options for the Labour Market* (Cambridge, UK: Cambridge University Press, 1996), pp. 433–63.

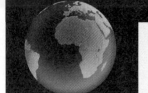

INTERNATIONAL PERSPECTIVE

*Is the U.S.
Productivity
Slowdown
Unique?*

The slow growth in labor productivity and in the real wage in the United States has challenged economists to find one or more causes and to search for policies to achieve faster growth. One obvious way to study this question is to compare the United States with other industrialized countries. Is their level of labor productivity higher or lower than that in the United States? Has their rate of productivity growth experienced a slowdown, as in the United States? Is the slowdown more or less severe? If these countries are enjoying faster productivity growth than in the United States, will they catch up to and exceed the level in the United States, or have they already done so? Finally, does their experience provide the United States with any lessons in how to make productivity grow more rapidly?

Answers to some of these questions are provided by the figure. Here we see the level of labor productivity plotted as the red line, just as in Figure 10-2. The middle line (solid black) displays the

average level of labor productivity for the four largest European countries—France, Germany, Italy, and the United Kingdom. The bottom line (gray) is for Japan. As in any such diagram on a logarithmic scale, the growth rate is shown by the slope of the line. Because the line for Europe rises more steeply than the U.S. line throughout the period shown, we can conclude that productivity growth in Europe has been more rapid throughout. Indeed, by 1994, the last point plotted, Europe had virtually caught up to the U.S. level of labor productivity.

Japan seemed in the 1960s and 1970s to be catching up to the U.S. level of labor productivity at a spectacular rate. But then Japan experienced a slowdown even more significant than that in the United States. Between 1990 and 1994, Japan's labor productivity grew more slowly than in the United States, so that it was no longer narrowing the productivity gap. The ratio of labor productivity in Japan to that in the United States

**Levels of Labor
Productivity,
1961–94**

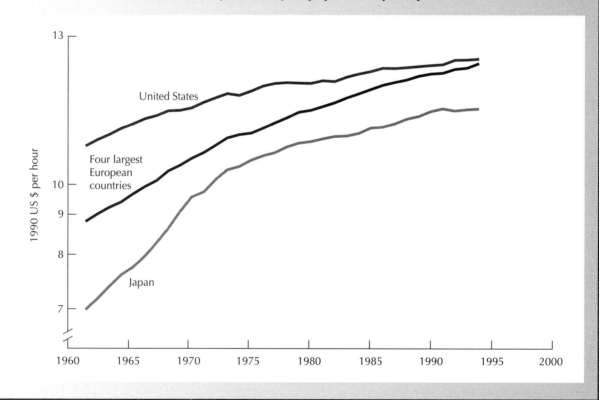

was 72 percent in 1990, but had fallen back to 70 percent by 1994 (as compared to 30 percent in 1961).

The figure in this box makes an interesting contrast with Figure 9-1 on p. 278, which shows a similar comparison of income per capita among industrial countries. The figures differ because income per capita is not the same as income per hour (i.e., productivity), since hours of work per member of the population differ widely across countries. In the comparison shown in Figure 9-1, Japan does much better relative to the United States (with a ratio of about 83 percent), while the same European countries do much worse, with an average of about 75 percent. Why does Japan achieve a level of income per capita closer to the United States than it does when the measure is output per hour, as in this figure? Why does Europe's ranking change in reverse?

The answer is simply that the average employee in Japan works about 10 percent more hours per year than U.S. workers, while the average employee in Europe works about 20 percent fewer hours. This reflects longer workweeks and fewer vacations in Japan, and shorter workweeks and much longer vacations in Europe. In essence, European workers have chosen to "spend" some of their higher productivity on leisure rather than on the consumption of market goods and services, while Japanese workers are compensating for some of their lower productivity by working longer hours and enjoying less leisure.

The table shows growth rates of output per hour over three decades, as well as the slowdown in productivity growth between the first decade and the last. Each of the five other countries had faster productivity growth than the United States, in both the first period and the last period, but all the other countries except for the United Kingdom experienced a more severe productivity growth slowdown than did the United States.

This comparison raises numerous interesting questions. Why was productivity growth in the other countries so rapid in the 1960s, and why did it then slow down so much thereafter? Why did productivity growth in the other countries continue to proceed at a more rapid pace than in the United States even in the final 1984–94 period (except in Japan after 1990)? These questions remain to be answered by economists.

Growth Rate of Labor Productivity, Selected Intervals

	1964–74	*1974–84*	*1984–94*	*Slowdown, 1984–94 vs. 1964–74*
United States	2.20	1.42	0.96	−1.24
Japan	7.95	2.43	1.81	−6.14
France	4.98	2.97	1.86	−3.12
Germany	4.97	2.63	2.76	−2.21
Italy	6.17	3.42	1.77	−4.40
United Kingdom	3.42	3.03	2.61	−0.81

Sources: U.S.: Bureau of Labor Statistics and National Income and Product Accounts. Other countries: See Appendix C.

Table 10-4   **Comparisons of United States with the European Community**

	U.S.	*Europe*
Annual growth rates, 1979–95		
1. Real compensation per employee	0.2	1.0
2. Real hourly compensation, manufacturing production workers	−0.4	1.6
3. Employment level	1.7	0.2
4. Unemployment rate in 1996	5.4	11.5

Sources: Lines 1 and 2: Laurence Mishel, et al., *The State of Working America,* Tables 8.3 and 8.4; Lines 3 and 4: *IMF World Economic Outlook,* October 1996, Table A4. Line 4: Bureau of Labor Statistics.

much superior record in achieving growth in jobs and maintaining a relatively low unemployment rate. As shown on line 3, the percentage growth rate of U.S. employment was 1.7 percent per year, more than 8 times the tiny 0.2 percent growth rate in Europe. And the 1996 unemployment rate in the United States was 5.4 percent, less than half the 11.5 percent unemployment rate in Europe.

Why should the United States experience such rapid growth in employment with such slow growth in real wages? The labor supply shock hypothesis suggests that the United States and Europe have chosen different policies, and these have had the effect of creating a weak bargaining situation for U. S. labor and a somewhat stronger bargaining situation for European labor. Ingredients in this difference for the United States include relatively weak unions, a relatively low and declining real minimum wage, and substantial competition for low-skilled jobs from legal and illegal immigrants. In some countries like France it is very expensive for shopkeepers and restaurant owners to hire service workers, because of the role of unions and the minimum wage, and also because supplementary employer payments for Social Security and medical care tend to be much higher.

The result of these differences is that it is relatively cheap to hire workers in the United States, and therefore many are hired. Because so many are hired to perform given tasks in the service sector, service employment has grown rapidly, but service productivity and real wages have grown slowly. As a counterpart to these differences, European nations have suffered from stagnant employment, high unemployment, and bleak job prospects for youth, particularly those with low skills.

The contrast between the United States and Europe points to differences in labor market policies as a possible cause of the differences shown in Table 10-4. European governments tend to protect workers, particularly low-skilled workers, which keeps their wages relatively high and penalizes firms for firing them. American policies tend to be more laissez-faire and leave labor market arrangements to employers. Proponents of the American approach praise the "flexibility" of U.S. labor markets, pointing to high unemployment (especially for youth) as an inevitable cost of the European system. Proponents of the European approach praise greater job security and greater income equality, and some liken the American free-market approach to a chaotic jungle.

Clearly, both the American and European approaches have advantages and disadvantages. There is little sign that American policymakers want to move toward a more European-like system, or that European policymakers want to make their labor markets more like those in the United States. What emerges for the main topic of this chapter, however, is that the "system" can make a difference: Some component of slow growth in U.S. productivity and real wages may be contributed by the weak bargaining position of labor, which makes it easy and cheap for American firms to hire workers. Slow real wage growth and slow productivity growth are simultaneously determined by the labor market system, rather than reflecting a simple one-way causation from productivity growth to real wage growth.

SELF-TEST | Which, Europe or the United States, is best described by the following statements: (1) Higher unemployment, (2) faster employment growth, (3) faster productivity growth, (4) slower real wage growth, (5) weak unions.

10-7 The Role of Growing Inequality

The stagnation of real wages in the United States since the early 1970s stands in contrast to the more robust growth of real wages prior to 1972 and also to the more rapid growth of real wages in Europe in the last several decades. But, unfortunately, the data we have been examining overstate the growth of real wages for most Americans, because *average* real wage growth has exceeded *median* real wage growth.

Median Real Wage Growth Falls Short of Average Real Wage Growth

To understand this distinction, imagine that there are 100 families, each earning $100. Ten years later, 99 of the families continue to earn $100 while the one-hundredth family enjoys a jump in income from $100 to $1,000. Total income for the 100 families rises from $10,000 (100 × 100) to $10,900 (99 × 100 + 1,000). The *mean* of income has increased from $100 to $109, a 9 percent increase. Yet the *median* family (the family ranked 50th out of 100) has an income increase of zero.

A less extreme case of this example has occurred in the American economy since 1973, as shown in Figure 10-4. The solid red line and the solid black line contrast labor productivity and the mean real consumption wage, just as in Figure 10-2, and show that the real consumption wage increased somewhat more slowly than did the level of labor productivity. However, the dotted black line shows that the median real wage did not increase at all, and the gray line shows that the median real wage for males actually declined.[17] As a result, the median worker did not enjoy any increase in real wage rates, even though the mean real wage increased. Why did this occur?

High and Increasing Inequality

The basic reason for the difference between average and median real wage growth is that all of the real wage gains accrued to workers with above-

---

[17]Both median real wage indexes use the same price index as the average real wage index. This is the CPI-V-X1, a version of the CPI that uses an improved treatment of housing before 1983.

A GROWING SPLIT BETWEEN PRODUCTIVITY AND THE MEDIAN WAGE

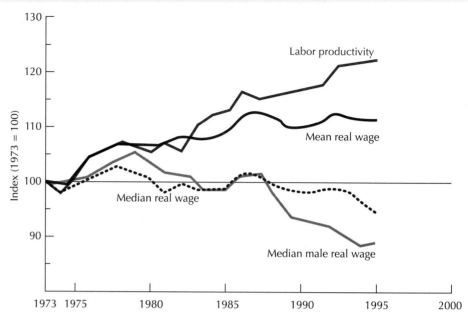

Figure 10-4   **Labor Productivity and Three Concepts of the Consumption Real Wage: Mean, Median, and Median Male, 1973–95**

The solid red line plots labor productivity and the solid black line plots the mean real consumption wage, the same two series as were plotted in Figure 10-2. The dotted black line shows that the median real wage has fallen behind the mean real wage, and the gray line shows that the median real wage for males has fallen even further behind.

Source: Lawrence Mishel, Jared Bernstein, and John Schmitt, *The State of Working America 1996–97.* Armonk, N.Y.: M. E. Sharpe Publishers. Figure 3J, p. 167. Reprinted with permission from M. E. Sharpe, Inc., Armonk, NY 10504.

median real wages. As high-wage workers gained relative to low-wage workers, inequality increased.

Data for inequality refer mainly to family income, rather than to real wages. Figure 10-5 shows one measure of inequality of family income, the ratio of average family income in the top 5 percent of the population to that in the lowest 20 percent. Inequality decreased from 1947 to 1973, with the ratio dropping from 14 to 11.3. Then from 1973 to 1995 inequality increased, and the ratio went from 11.3 to 18.2. For example, in 1995 average family income of the bottom 20 percent was a mere $9,000, in contrast to an average of $163,800 for the top 5 percent.

Figure 10-6 contrasts the relatively even growth of real family income across the different income groups during the period from 1947 to 1973 (left frame), a period when income growth for the poorest fifth was actually somewhat more rapid than for the richest fifth. This situation changed dramatically in the 1973–94 period (right frame), when almost all of the income gain went to the richest fifth. The two lowest categories actually lost ground, and saw a decline in median family income.

Income inequality is much greater in the United States than in most other industrial countries, as shown in Figure 10-7. This measure is different than that in Figure 10-5. Instead of comparing average income in the top 5 percent

Figure 10-5
Ratio of Family Income of the Top 5 Percent of Families to the Bottom 20 Percent, 1947–95

The bar shows the ratio of family income in the best-off 5 percent of families to that in the poorest 20 percent of families. From 1947 to 1973 the ratio fell from 14.0 to 11.3. But then it rose from 11.3 in 1973 to 18.2 in 1995. As an example, if the bottom 20 percent of families earned $10,000 in 1995, the top 5 percent earned $182,000. *Source:* Lawrence Mishel, Jared Bernstein, and John Schmitt, *The State of Working America 1996–97.* Armonk, N.Y.: M. E. Sharpe Publishers. Figure 1C, p. 54. Reprinted with permission from M. E. Sharpe, Inc., Armonk, NY 10504.

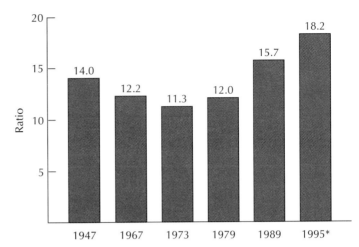

INEQUALITY HAS INCREASED SHARPLY SINCE THE 1970s

* Part of the increase in inequality in 1995 is attributable to changes in data collection methodology.

CONVERGENCE FOLLOWED BY DIVERGENCE

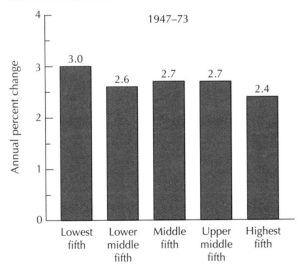

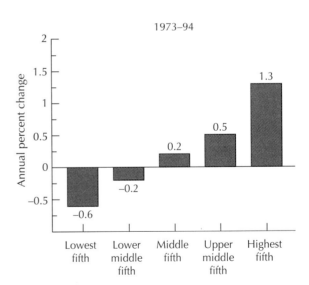

Figure 10-6   **Annual Growth Rate of Real Family Income, by Quintile (Fifth), 1947–73 Contrasted with 1973–94**

The left frame shows the annual growth rate of real family income of five groups of American families, ranked from the poorest 20 percent (on the left) to the best-off 20 percent (on the right). Real income growth for 1947–73 was actually faster for the poorest than for the best-off, leading to the increased equality shown in Figure 10-5. After 1973 the reverse occurred, with a drop in real income for the poorest contrasting markedly with a substantial increase in real income for the best off. *Source:* Lawrence Mishel, Jared Bernstein, and John Schmitt, *The State of Working America 1996–97.* Armonk, N.Y.: M. E. Sharpe Publishers. Figure 1D, p. 57. Reprinted with permission from M. E. Sharpe, Inc., Armonk, NY 10504.

INCOME INEQUALITY IS FAR HIGHER IN THE
UNITED STATES THAN IN OTHER ADVANCED NATIONS

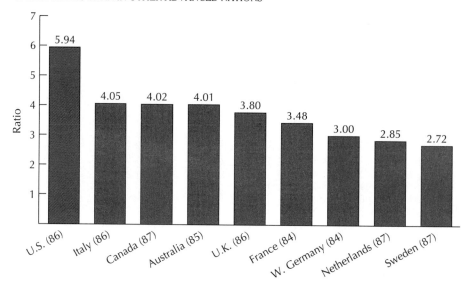

Figure 10-7   **Ratio of Family Income in 90th Percentile to that in 10th Percentile, Mid-1980s**
Each bar represents the ratio of the family income at the 90th percentile (the family 90 percent of the way from the poorest to the richest) to the family income at the 10th percentile. The ratio of 5.94 for the United States in the mid-1980s is much higher than in other countries, which range from 2.72 to 4.05. *Source:* Anthony Atkinson, Lee Rainwater, and Timothy M. Smeeding. *Income Distribution in OECD Countries: Evidence from the Luxembourg Income Study.* Paris: OECD, 1995. Used with permission.

with the bottom 20 percent, we arrange all families in order from the richest to the poorest. Figure 10-7 takes the ratio of the family income 90 percent of the way from poorest to richest (90th percentile) to the family income 10 percent of the way from poorest to richest (10th percentile). The ratio of 5.94 for the United States in the mid-1980s is much higher than in other countries, which range from 2.72 to 4.05.

Sources of High and Growing Inequality

A major explanation of high income inequality in the United States is the flexibility of U.S. labor markets, the same set of factors cited in Section 10-6 to help explain why the United States differs from high-income European nations in having slower growth in real wages and productivity, but much faster growth in employment and a much lower unemployment rate. Labor markets in Europe tend to bolster the incomes of low-wage workers by promoting stronger unions, a higher minimum wage, and more generous unemployment and disability benefits. At the same time, wages at the top echelon in Europe do not reach the extremely high levels observed in the United States. For instance, as noted at the beginning of this chapter, the ratio of compensation of chief executive officers to their average employee tends to be very high in the United States.

Why has U.S. inequality increased? While there is no consensus, most analyses point to two important factors. The first is the role of technology in raising the demand for high-skilled workers. Well-educated workers with good technical skills tend to be in high demand. In contrast, less educated, low-skilled workers find less demand for their services. The second factor is an increased relative supply of low-skilled workers. Americans with little education and low skills face growing competition, directly from low-skilled immigrants and indirectly from low-skilled workers in foreign countries that produce cheap imports that destroy some low-skilled American jobs.

10-8 Is Real Wage Stagnation a Figment of Measurement Error?

While the contrast between the median and average real wage in Figure 10-4 appears to make the situation of the median U.S. worker look worse than in the standard data on real wages examined earlier in this chapter, another factor works in the opposite direction and makes the situation look better.

Alternative Real Wage Indexes

The government produces several different measures of real wages. We have focused in this chapter on the real consumption wage, plotted again as the solid black line in Figure 10-8. It shows modest growth in real wages after 1972. Another government index of real average hourly earnings shows a much more pessimistic story, with a continuous *decline* in the real wage since 1972 and, indeed, no net increase in the real wage since the early 1960s.

Why do these two official real wage indexes differ? They use different measures of nominal wages and different price indexes. The more pessimistic index uses a wage index called average hourly earnings, which excludes fringe benefits and many types of compensation (e.g., sales commissions and bonuses) which are included in the more optimistic index. Further, the more optimistic index uses a more accurate price deflator to convert nominal wages into real wages. The pessimistic index is based on the Consumer Price Index (CPI), while the optimistic index is based on the deflator for personal consumption expenditures (PCE deflator), and the latter price index rises about 10 percent less over the period shown, thus yielding a real wage index that rises 10 percent more.

Biased Price Indexes

But both the optimistic and pessimistic real wage indexes in Figure 10-8 may be too pessimistic, because both the price deflators used to construct them (the CPI and the PCE deflator) are generally believed to overstate inflation. In late 1996 a commission established by the U.S. Senate and chaired by Michael J. Boskin of Stanford University concluded that the CPI in recent years has been biased upward, i.e., has overstated inflation, by 1.1 percent per year. The CPI tends to overstate inflation because it is based on an out-of-date market basket of goods and services and does not adequately reflect changes in consumer behavior as they shift to products that experience a decline in relative price, to outlets like Wal-Mart that sell goods at lower prices, and to new

OPTIMISM OR PESSIMISM ABOUT THE REAL WAGE?

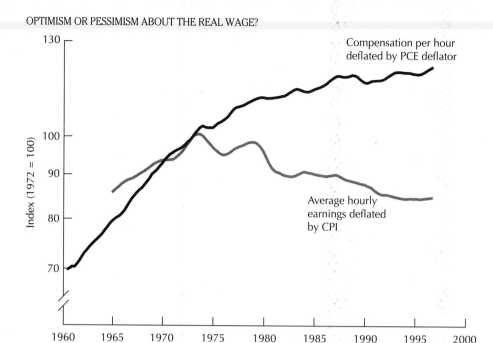

Figure 10-8   Two Alternative Indexes of the Real Consumption Wage, 1960–96

The solid black line calculates the real consumption wage as the ratio of compensation per hour to the deflator for personal consumption expenditures (PCE deflator). The gray line computes the same concept as the ratio of average hourly earnings divided by the Consumer Price Index. The former index provides a more optimistic interpretation of real wage growth, for reasons discussed in the text.

products like VCRs, large-screen television sets, and personal computers. Most of the reasons for the upward bias in the CPI apply to the PCE deflator as well. As a result, even the more optimistic real wage index in Figure 10-8 rises too slowly and understates gains in real wages enjoyed by the average American worker.

If the price index used to compute the real wage overstates inflation by 1.1 percent per year, then the growth in real wages is understated by 1.1 percent per year. This understatement, compounded between 1972 and 1997, implies that the real consumption wage has not grown at 0.77 percent per year (the average rate implied by line 4 of Table 10-2), but at a much healthier 1.87 percent per year.[18] Most of the understatement of real wage growth also applies to growth in labor productivity and multifactor productivity.

A Balanced Assessment

In this section and in the last one we have examined two forms of misstatement of real wage growth that point in opposite directions. It is certainly true

---

[18]The figure of 0.77 percent per annum cited in the text is a weighted average of the figures shown in Table 10-2, line 4, over the three periods 1972–79, 1979–87, and 1987–96.

that the median real wage has grown more slowly than the average real wage (Figure 10-4), so that the average real wage overstates gains experienced by the median worker. But the overstatement of inflation by the CPI and PCE deflator works in the opposite direction, indicating that the average real wage understates gains experienced by the median worker.

Errors in price data make the overall performance of the U.S. economy look better than is shown by the official statistics, but they do not change several of the problems identified in this chapter. First, it is unlikely that errors in price data have become so much worse since 1972 that they can explain more than a small fraction of the productivity slowdown, which in Table 10-3 amounts to −1.8 percent for labor productivity and −1.5 percent for MFP. Second, price statistics are irrelevant to data on inequality, since inflation affects all income groups in roughly the same way. Third, other countries have similar problems with their price indexes, and so improved price statistics would apply to all countries and leave us with the fact that real wages have been growing more slowly in the United States than elsewhere.

10-9 Conclusion: What Policies Are Available to Boost Growth?

The public policy debate over slow productivity growth has centered on measures that would boost saving and investment. Yet we already know that inadequate saving and investment are not the main cause of the productivity growth slowdown. Why? Simply because, as shown in Table 10-3, the slowdown in MFP has been almost as great (−1.5 percent per year) as it has been for labor productivity itself (−1.8 percent per year).

As we shall see in the next chapter, most debates about growth involve the federal budget deficit. For the nation to save more, the government must borrow less. Many proposals to boost growth would work in the opposite direction, including tax cuts that would boost the government budget deficit. Instead, policies to increase national saving would need to include some combination of tax increases and expenditure reductions. We examine the debate over the budget deficit more closely in the next chapter.

We have seen that productivity growth has been slow and real wage gains, especially for workers with low skills and little education, have been even less. This has suggested that a central policy to boost productivity growth should be public investment in education. James Heckman of the University of Chicago has estimated that it would take a huge increase in federal government spending on education, from $30 billion to $130 billion, to raise productivity growth by even 0.1 percent per year (and this would have to be balanced by a $100 billion cut in other expenditures to keep the government budget deficit from worsening).

Other proposals include redesigning and scaling back the regulatory apparatus of the federal government. Some critics claim that some environmental laws and regulations impose economic costs that exceed the value of the benefits. Many economists suggest that the government should rely less on detailed rules and more on monetary incentives (e.g., pollution taxes) to control environmental pollution.

Policies to promote faster growth in productivity are controversial, and no consensus has emerged. Perhaps the least controversial statement with which to end this chapter is that part of the U.S. problem of slow economic growth lies in flaws in the economic statistics, caused both by the bias in the CPI and the problem identified by Griliches in capturing the economic benefits of computers. Improved economic statistics can be achieved at relatively low cost compared to many other proposals for boosting economic growth.

SUMMARY

1. The slow growth in productivity and in the real wage has been called the greatest macroeconomic problem faced by the United States.
2. Labor productivity is the ratio of output to labor input. Multifactor productivity is the ratio of output to a weighted average of labor and capital input.
3. If labor's share in total income is constant, the real wage rate grows at the same rate as labor productivity. The real wage rate can grow faster or slower than labor productivity if labor's share rises or falls, respectively.
4. Multifactor productivity growth in the United States was faster between 1913 and 1964 than before or since, raising the question as to whether it was that period that was unusual, or the period of the productivity slowdown since the mid 1960s.
5. Slower growth in both productivity and the real wage rate can be caused either by adverse shocks to productivity or shocks to labor supply that have the effect of reducing the wage rate at which people are willing to work.
6. Among the adverse shocks to productivity suggested as explanations are slower growth in capital per hour, higher prices of energy, a decline in labor quality, slower growth of infrastructure, problems of particular industries, running out of resources and ideas, and problems of measurement in the service sector.

7. Factors that could account for a shock to labor supply are the declining influence of unions, a declining real minimum wage, low-skill immigration, and the role of global competition and an increase in labor force participation by females.
8. Income inequality is relatively high in the United States and has been rising. One implication is that the median real wage has risen less rapidly than the average real wage.
9. Measurement problems tend to overstate the rate of inflation and understate the growth rate of the real wage. However, they are unlikely to explain much of the productivity slowdown, and they explain none of the rise in income inequality.
10. Economic performance in the leading European countries has differed significantly from that in the United States. The same factors that account for high unemployment and slow employment growth in Europe also help to explain faster growth in productivity and real wages, as well as a more equal distribution of income.
11. Policies to boost growth are elusive. They include reducing the government budget deficit, putting more government resources into education and training, and reforming government regulation, including environmental regulation.

CONCEPTS

real product wage
real consumption wage

infrastructure

QUESTIONS AND PROBLEMS

Questions

1. Describe the quantitative dimensions of the slowdown in productivity and real wage growth in the United States since the early 1970s. How does the United States' experience over this period compare with earlier periods in U.S. history and with the experience of other industrialized countries over the past three decades?
2. Distinguish between labor productivity and multifactor productivity. How are the growth rates of these productivity measures related? Which one

typically has the higher growth rate? Why?

3. Under what conditions will labor's share of national income grow? Decline? Remain constant over time?

4. Distinguish between the real consumption wage and the real product wage. Which of these real wage measures has grown more slowly? Why?

5. What is the relationship between real wages and labor productivity? How would real wages and labor productivity be affected by:

   (a) an increase in the quantity of other productive factors (such as capital, energy, and raw materials) used in production;

   (b) a decline in the size of the work force resulting from lower rates of population growth and immigration?

   Is the cause-and-effect relationship between real wages and productivity the same in each case? Explain in terms of shifts in the labor demand and labor supply curves.

6. Lester Thurow argues that the productivity slowdown experienced by the United States since 1973 has been like "death from a thousand cuts." Explain.

7. In what ways could the oil crisis of the 1970s and the resulting price of energy have affected the growth rate of real GDP per person? What is the problem with such an explanation?

8. In your opinion, what are the most likely causes of the slowdown in the growth rate of labor productivity in the United States since 1973?

9. "Restrictive monetary policy will lower the rate of labor productivity growth. Restrictive fiscal policy, on the other hand, will raise it." Is this statement true, false, or uncertain? Explain.

10. Describe the changes in income distribution in the United States since the early 1970s. How does the United States' experience over this period compare with income distribution patterns in other industrial countries?

11. What role has education played in the productivity growth slowdown and in the increasingly unequal distribution of income in the United States?

12. Convinced that strong measures must be taken to stimulate productivity growth, Senator Progrowth introduces a bill to increase federal government spending on education by $150 billion. Why might those who agree with the senator about the importance of economic growth nonetheless question the wisdom of this legislation?

13. Evaluate the argument advanced by some economists that the apparent slowdown in labor productivity and real wage growth is merely illusory, a result of errors in measuring economic variables rather than any actual deterioration in economic performance since the early 1970s.

14. Since the early 1970s, many Western European economies have enjoyed faster growth of labor productivity and real wages than the United States has. What accounts for their superior performance in these measures? Does it signify that those economies have been more successful than the United States in meeting the challenge of the growth slowdown?

15. At the time of German unification, average labor productivity in the East lagged behind that in the West. Despite this productivity differential, government policy promoted a relatively rapid rise in the wages of Eastern workers to levels matching those of their Western counterparts. How do you think this affected measured growth in real wages and productivity as well as unemployment in Germany? Why?

Problems

1. Calculate the growth rates of output (y) and labor productivity $(y - n)$ in each of the following scenarios. Assume that the share of capital in total income (b) is 0.25.

(a)

	y	a	k	n	$y - n$
	—	2.5	2	1	—
	—	2.0	2	1	—
	—	1.5	2	1	—
	—	1.0	2	1	—

(b)

	y	a	k	n	$y - n$
	—	2.5	2.0	1	—
	—	2.5	1.5	1	—
	—	2.5	1.0	1	—
	—	2.5	0.5	1	—

(c)

	y	a	k	n	$y - n$
	—	2.5	2.0	1.0	—
	—	2.5	2.0	1.5	—
	—	2.5	2.0	2.0	—
	—	2.5	2.0	2.5	—

Based on your calculations, what happens to output growth and labor productivity growth as MFP growth declines, capital input growth declines, and labor input growth increases, holding the other variables constant? Are these the results you would expect? Why?

2. Suppose that nominal wages are growing 4 percent per year and labor productivity is growing 1 percent per year.

(a) If the price deflator for GDP is growing 2 percent per year, what is happening to real wages and labor's share of total income?

(b) If the price deflator for personal consumption expenditures is growing 4 percent per year at the same time that the price deflator for GDP is growing 2 percent per year, what are workers likely to think is happening to their real wages? Why?

SELF-TEST ANSWERS

p. 304 $y = 5.75$; $n = 0$; $k = 9$. In each case labor productivity growth $y - n$ exceeds MFP growth a, because in each case the growth of capital per worker $k - n$ is positive. The growth of capital per worker increases the growth of output relative to labor input, which is what labor productivity growth measures, but it does not increase the growth of output relative to *all* inputs, which is what MFP growth measures.

p. 313 (a) More workers will be available at any given real wage rate, so the labor supply curve shifts down (to the right), representing an increase in labor supply.   (b) Fewer workers will be available at any given real wage rate, so the labor supply curve shifts up (to the left), representing a decrease in labor supply. (c) With greater availability of energy resources, more workers will be demanded at any given real wage rate, so the labor demand curve shifts up (to the right), representing an increase in labor demand. (d) With less investment in new equipment that increases labor productivity, fewer workers will be demanded at any given real wage rate, so the labor demand curve shifts down (to the left), representing a decrease in labor demand.

p. 319 (a) and (b) both increase the growth rate of labor inputs relative to that of capital and other inputs, which reduces the growth of output relative to labor input (labor productivity).   (c) reduces measured productivity growth by increasing the share of hard-to-measure sectors in total output.

p. 323 (1) Europe, (2) U.S., (3) Europe, (4) U.S., (5) U.S.

CHAPTER 11

The Government Budget and the Public Debt

In contrast to the original notion of activist fiscal stabilization policy, the budget decisions are now regarded as important because of their long-term effects on resource allocation.

—Martin S. Feldstein, 1988

11-1 Introduction: The Debate over the U.S. Budget Deficit

This chapter is about the long-run aspects of fiscal policy. Should the government budget be balanced every year, on average over the business cycle, or not at all? Does a persistent government budget deficit, as has occurred in the United States and many other countries during the past two decades, have adverse economic consequences? What are these consequences, and are they serious? Can high budget deficits cause the public debt to explode without limit? Finally examine such topical issues as the proposal for a balanced budget amendment to the U.S. Constitution.

The role of fiscal policy in the determination of real GDP and the interest rate was provided by the *IS-LM* model of Chapters 4 and 5. Fiscal and monetary policy were portrayed as alternative tools available to influence the level of real GDP. We learned that a desirable level of real income, that is, natural real GDP (Y^N), could be achieved with a variety of different combinations of monetary and fiscal policy. A given level of Y^N could be achieved with a high level of interest rates if monetary policy were relatively tight and fiscal policy relatively easy. The opposite situation, with relatively easy monetary policy and relatively tight fiscal policy, would lead to lower interest rates.

Most economists now agree that monetary policy is better suited than fiscal policy for controlling short-run fluctuations in real GDP, because the Federal Reserve is able to make decisions about monetary policy much faster than Congress and the administration can make decisions about fiscal policy. If monetary policy succeeds in stabilizing real GDP at the desired level of output—that is, at Y^N—then fiscal policy by default becomes responsible for the level of real interest rates. This is seen in the analysis of the mix of monetary and fiscal policy in Figure 5-5 on p. 132.

Stated another way, as we learned in Section 5-10 monetary policy has a *short-run orientation* toward the smoothing of business cycles in real GDP. In contrast, fiscal policy has a *long-run orientation* toward the level of real interest rates, which in turn have a major influence on the long-run growth rates of productivity and real output per person. This means that the government can use fiscal policy as a key tool to influence the economy's long-run growth rate, which, as we learned in Chapter 10, has been slow and disappointing since the early 1970s.

This chapter begins by reviewing the basic economics of the government budget deficit and the public debt. Does the debt impose a future burden on society? How large can the deficit become without causing the debt to

333

explode? What is the history of the debt in the United States, and is it unusually high compared to that of other industrialized nations? What are some of the alternative positions in the debate over the budget deficit? In the 1990s economists are debating not only solutions to the deficit problem, but also whether there is, in fact, a problem at all. Some say, in essence, the gain from eliminating the deficit is not worth the cost. Another group claims that the deficit is improperly measured and does not really exist. Others view any deficit as a disaster.

Throughout the chapter we focus on the long-run effects of fiscal policy on the government debt and the rate of economic growth. We conclude by examining both sides of an important topical debate. What are the economic arguments for and against a balanced budget amendment?

11-2   Long-Run Effects of Fiscal Policy on Economic Growth and Welfare

Already in Chapter 5 we have discussed the economy's *short-run* response to changes in fiscal policy, that is, in government expenditures and tax rates. Now we are ready to study the impact of fiscal policy on the rate of *long-run* economic growth. The key link between fiscal policy and long-run growth comes through the effect of a persistent budget deficit in reducing the national saving rate (data on budget deficits and national saving were discussed on pages 135–41).

In Chapter 9 we concluded that an increase in the national saving rate is likely to stimulate economic growth, at least in the intermediate run of, say, the next decade or so. In this case, then, society must decide whether or not to save more, which requires the sacrifice of consumption *now* to obtain extra consumption *in the future*. This choice depends on society's **rate of time preference**, the extra amount people would be willing to pay to have consumption goods now instead of in the future. For instance, if people are willing to pay $1.10 to obtain a good today that they could have for $1.00 one year from now, then they are said to have a rate of time preference of 10 percent.

> The **rate of time preference** is the extra amount a consumer would be willing to pay to be able to obtain a given quantity of consumption goods now rather than a year from now.

Raise Saving or Do Nothing?

Figure 11-1 illustrates two of the choices open to society, paths A and B. Path A reflects a do-nothing policy that maintains the growth rate of per person consumption after time t_0 at the same rate as before. Path B reflects a policy that deliberately raises the incentive to save and invest at time t_0 while reducing the incentive to consume. Initially consumption along path B drops below path A by an amount shown by the red shading. But then the higher rate of investment makes the capital stock grow faster, thus increasing future output and income. Consumption begins to grow faster along path B than path A, eventually catching up at time t_1 and moving ahead thereafter. The question for growth policy is: Which path is better, A or B?

If the rate of return on extra capital investment is greater than society's rate of time preference, then $1 shifted from present consumption to investment will yield enough future consumption to be worthwhile. For instance, if

Figure 11-1
Two Alternative Paths of Consumption per Person

Before time t_0 both paths involve exactly the same consumption per person. Along path *A*, consumption per person continues to grow at the same steady rate after time t_0. But along path *B* a policy decision is made to consume less in order to save and invest more. At first, between time t_0 and t_1, consumption along path *B* drops below path *A* by an amount shown by the red shading. Then, after t_1 (and forever thereafter), consumption along path *B* exceeds that along path *A*, as shown by the gray shading.

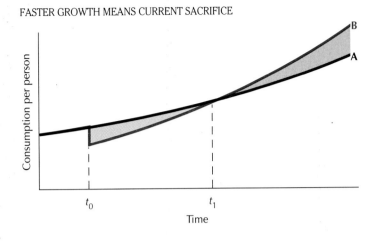

FASTER GROWTH MEANS CURRENT SACRIFICE

the rate of return is 10 percent, $1 less of consumption today will yield $1.10 next year. If the rate of time preference is less than 10 percent, say 5 percent, then people are equally happy with $1.05 next year and $1 this year, so that clearly they would prefer $1.10 next year to $1 this year. In this situation, with a rate of return higher than the rate of time preference (sometimes called the rate at which individuals "discount" future consumption), society should save more and consume less, as along path B. This principle can be stated as follows:

> *The United States saves too little if the rate at which individuals discount future consumption is less than the rate of return on private investment.*

In recent years the real rate of return on private investment in the corporate sector has been about 12 percent, and the rate of time preference of individuals is less than that. How much less? We know that the *real* interest rate on corporate bonds was roughly 5 percent in the mid-1990s (Figure 1-10 on p. 19). Many individuals have been willing to save despite the relatively low real interest rates available to them. Thus it is accurate to say that the United States now saves too little, because a dollar diverted from present consumption to present saving could earn a real return of about 12 percent, more than the real return after taxes now earned by most savers. People would want to save more if they were offered a real return of 12 percent than they save now at a real return of 5 percent or less.

National Saving, Economic Growth, and the Government Budget Deficit

National saving is the sum of private saving and government saving.

To boost the growth rate of output and productivity, fiscal policy must raise the rate of national saving, which in turn would boost the growth rate of output. By definition, **national saving** is simply the sum of private saving and government saving. A government budget surplus is the same as government saving, while a government budget deficit is treated as *negative* government saving. Thus at any given amount of private saving, the larger the government budget deficit, *the more is subtracted from private saving—that is, the lower is the national saving rate.* We learned in Section 5-9 on pp. 142–46 that the U.S. national saving rate fell to historically low levels in the 1980s and 1990s, largely as a result of persistent government budget deficits.

A government budget deficit reduces national saving, and a reduction in national saving in turn reduces the rate of economic growth, at least in the intermediate run of a decade or more. To stimulate growth, the national saving rate needs to be raised, which means either that private saving must be raised or the government budget deficit must be reduced.

In choosing methods to reduce the government budget deficit, policymakers should take care that the smaller deficit is not accompanied by a reduction in private saving. For instance, attempting to cut the government budget deficit by raising income tax rates will reduce the after-tax return to private saving. The beneficial boost to national saving caused by the lower budget deficit will be partly or largely offset by a decline in private saving, leaving little net increase in national saving. To achieve an increase in national saving, a preferable method to cut the government deficit would be to raise taxes on consumption (rather than income), or reduce government expenditures.

The ultimate aim of policies to boost the rate of national saving is to increase the rate of investment, i.e., the ratio of investment to real GDP. However, the types of investment that contribute to growth include not just private expenditures on machines and structures, but also government investment. Thus policymakers attempting to boost growth by reducing the government deficit should either boost taxes on consumption or cut expenditures on government consumption (e.g., transfer payments, subsidies to farms and corporations, and defense outlays) rather than cutting government investment (e.g., education and highways).

In short, cutting the government deficit may or may not boost the rate of economic growth. How the deficit is reduced is just as important as whether it is reduced. To boost growth, tax increases should be targeted to protect private saving, and this means that tax increases should be applied to consumption rather than income. Similarly, cuts in government expenditures designed to reduce the budget deficit should be directed toward government consumption rather than government investment.

SELF-TEST

> Would the following events raise or lower national saving as a percent of GDP? (a) An increase in federal spending on military aircraft without any change in tax rates; (b) an increase in sales taxes on food; (c) a reduction in income taxes.

11-3 The Future Burden of the Government Debt

We have already learned that a higher government budget deficit reduces national saving, holding other factors constant. Whenever the government spends one dollar more than it receives in tax revenues, it must finance its deficit by issuing one more dollar of government debt. We ask in this section whether this extra government debt is harmful. How do we assess the burden placed by extra dollars of government debt on the well-being of future generations?

Government investment projects, such as the construction of hospitals, schools, and public universities, generate a future rate of return, consisting of the benefits to future generations created by the project. Some recent economic research suggests that government investment spending, particularly on infrastructure, is highly productive in yielding future benefits to society.

Whether or not the government debt is a burden depends partly on whether the extra dollars of government debt pay for government expenditures on investment goods or for consumption goods. There is no burden if the government deficit finances productive government investment projects. In this case the government acts just like a private corporation, say AT&T, which pays for much of its new plant and equipment by selling bonds to the public. But there is a burden if the extra dollars of government debt pay for consumption goods that yield no future benefits. Such expenditures would include, for instance, ammunition fired at target practice by soldiers, or groceries purchased by recipients of Social Security benefits. These consumption expenditures have value for their recipients at the current time but not in the future.

The Burden of the AT&T Debt

What is the difference between the "burden of the AT&T debt" and the "burden of the government debt"? No one has ever accused AT&T of creating a burden on future generations by issuing bonds, and for good reason. Like any other corporation, AT&T is in business to make a profit for its stockholders. It attempts to estimate the future rate of return on each planned investment project, that is, the annual future profit likely to be contributed by each project divided by its cost. When each project is ranked in order of its rate of return, AT&T is ready to make its investment decisions. Projects with rates of return greater than the interest rate that AT&T must pay to sell bonds (AT&T's borrowing rate, say r_0) are approved. Projects with a rate of return below the borrowing rate (r_0) are rejected.

The contribution to revenue and expenses of the marginal AT&T project is summarized on the first line of Table 11-1. Net of all operating expenses (labor, materials, fuel, and so forth), the marginal project generates a rate of return (r_0) just equal to the borrowing rate (r_0), and thus contributes zero to net profit.[1] There is no burden on present or future generations. Individuals make voluntary purchases of AT&T bonds without compulsion. Thus in the present generation everyone acts voluntarily in his or her own best interests, and there is no burden on anyone.

In future generations the bondholders receive the interest payments that induced them to purchase the bonds in the first place. Where does AT&T obtain the money to pay the interest payments? By definition the marginal investment project creates exactly enough revenue (over and above operating costs) to pay the interest costs.

If the government chooses to invest only in projects yielding future benefits to society that on an annual basis equal or exceed the government's

---

[1]This discussion neglects explicit consideration of corporation and personal income taxes. The AT&T rate of return on line 1 can be calculated after payment of corporate income taxes. Although personal income taxes must be paid on interest payments to individuals by both AT&T and the government, this factor makes no essential difference in the discussion.

Table 11-1   **Comparison of Consequences of AT&T Debt with Those of Public Debt**

	(1) Rate of Return	(2) Interest Payment	(3) Net of Interest Return
1. AT&T marginal investment project	r_0	r_0	0
2. Government marginal investment project	r_0	r_0	0
3. Government deficit-financed consumption expenditure	0	r_0	$-r_0$

borrowing rate, then the bonds floated to finance government investment projects are exactly analogous to AT&T bonds. Stated another way, it is fair and equitable to finance government investment projects by deficit spending, since this will ensure that those who receive some of the benefits from the projects in the future help pay some of the costs (through their future tax payments). As illustrated on line 2 of Table 11-1, the marginal government investment project generates a rate of return in the form of future benefits to society that just suffice to pay the interest on the government bonds. If the interest rate on government bonds—like that on AT&T bonds—is r_0, and the social rate of return of the government investment project is the same rate r_0, there are no future burdens on society. The AT&T bond and the government bond are identical.

True Burdens of the Debt

The true burden on future generations is created by government deficit spending that pays for goods that yield no future benefits, or benefits less than their social opportunity cost—for example, meals currently consumed by members of the armed forces. As illustrated on line 3 of Table 11-1, absolutely nothing is generated in the future as a rate of return; all benefits accrue in the present. The government must pay interest to keep bondholders happy, just as AT&T must pay interest, yet in current government deficit-financed consumption there is no future benefit or income to pay the interest. Future taxpayers are forced to hand over extra payments to the government to cover the interest cost on the debt, and the taxpayers receive no benefit in return. Similarly, investment projects such as highways may impose a burden if their benefits are less than their social opportunity costs, such as for a little-used highway.

Debt Owed to Foreigners.   The United States ran large budget deficits in the 1980s and 1990s, and the high real interest rates caused by these deficits attracted a large flow of capital from foreigners desiring to buy U.S. securities. This is part of the capital inflow that has offset the persistent U.S. current account deficit over the same period, as we learned in Chapter 6. As a result, a substantial portion of the additional federal government debt over this period is held by foreign investors, and the interest payments on this debt will flow abroad for as long as they hold this debt.

The analysis of debt held by foreigners is similar to that for debt held by domestic residents, since the extent of the burden depends on whether the debt was originally created to finance consumption or investment projects. If the federal government creates debt to build a beneficial long-lasting project, then the return on the project is available to cover the interest payments to foreigners. If the debt is created to pay for current consumption, there is no future return to balance the extra taxes needed to pay the interest to foreigners.

11-4 Will the Government Remain Solvent?

Is the government budget deficit too low or too high? In this section we take a different approach to answer this question. What matters, according to this approach, is not whether the deficit is zero, but rather the criterion of stabilizing the ratio of the outstanding nominal federal debt *(D)* to nominal GDP *(PY)*. The federal deficit can be quite large, yet the *D/PY* ratio can nevertheless remain stable instead of rise.

This paradox seems less mysterious when we recognize that the nominal government budget deficit is equal to the change in the debt *(ΔD)*. How large can the deficit be and keep the debt-GDP ratio, *D/PY,* constant? It will remain constant as long as the *growth rate* of the debt-GDP ratio is zero.

Thus, our task is to determine what size deficit will keep the growth rate of the debt-GDP ratio equal to zero. We begin by noting that the growth rate of the debt-GDP ratio *(D/PY)* is the difference between the growth rate in debt *(d)* and the growth rate in nominal GDP *(p + y)*:

$$d - (p + y)$$

For stability in the debt-GDP ratio we need the growth rate of debt *(d)* equal to the growth rate of nominal GDP *(p + y)*:

$$d = p + y \tag{11.1}$$

When we multiply both sides of (11.1) by the size of the debt *(D)*, we obtain the allowable deficit (that is, addition to debt) that is consistent with keeping the debt-GDP ratio constant:

General Form	Numerical Example	
$dD = (p + y)D$	$(0.05)(\$4000 \text{ billion}) = \$200 \text{ billion}$	(11.2)

This simple expression (11.2) leads to a surprising conclusion: *the debt-GDP ratio remains constant if the deficit equals the outstanding debt times the growth rate of nominal GDP.* In the numerical example, federal government debt in 1997 was about $4000 billion; that times an assumed growth rate of nominal GDP in 1997 of about 5 percent, equals an "allowable deficit" of $200 billion.[2]

---

[2]The assumed 5.0 percent growth rate of nominal GDP *(p + y)* in this example is the sum of the rate of inflation *(p)* that seemed likely to occur in the 1997–98 period, assumed to be 2.5 percent, plus the growth rate of natural real GDP *(y^N)* of 2.5 percent. The debt of $4000 billion in 1997 refers to the debt held by the public (excluding debt held by the Federal Reserve and government trust funds).

INTERNATIONAL PERSPECTIVE

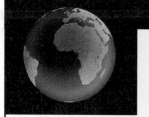

The Debt-GDP Ratio: How Does the United States Compare?

As shown in the accompanying figure, the debt-GDP ratio more than doubled in the United States between the mid-1970s and 1996. How does this experience compare with other countries? The figure displays debt-GDP ratios for two European countries, Germany and Italy. The ratio for Germany is smaller than in the United States, but it began to grow rapidly in the early 1990s.

In Italy the ratio is not only much higher than in the United States but is also growing faster, having tripled since 1970. The rapidly growing ratio reflects persistent government deficits that are at least twice as large as those in the United States (again, expressed as a share of GDP). One reason for the large deficits in Italy is the political system; because political support is splintered among numerous parties, under the parliamentary system it is possible to form a government only through a coalition among several parties. The neces-

sary political compromises tend to prevent tough action to raise taxes or cut spending.

Nevertheless, the burgeoning debt-GDP ratio in Italy is not as serious a problem as it might appear. Italy offsets its government deficit with a very high private saving rate, so that its national saving rate is more than double that in the United States. As a result, high private saving creates a large demand for the bonds that the government must constantly issue to cover its deficit.

How do these countries compare to other industrialized nations? Debt-GDP ratios in 1994 covered a wide range, from 46 percent in the United Kingdom to 136 percent is Belgium. Among the larger countries, the ratio in France is similar to that in Germany, and Britain is similar to the United States. The ratio in Japan jumped from 70 to 83 percent as a result of stagnation in the Japanese economy.

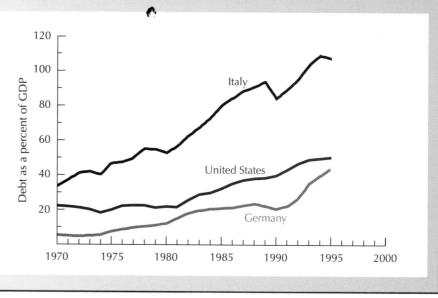

Since the deficit was below this amount, the debt-GDP ratio fell in 1997. But a stable debt-GDP ratio would be feasible if the federal deficit were held to the allowable deficit of $200 billion.

But what is the optimum debt-GDP ratio? Should the ratio be stable? Is there any reason why the debt-GDP ratio should not be allowed to rise, as it did between 1981 and 1993?

The Solvency Condition

Surely there is a limit to the size of the government debt, expressed as a percentage of GDP. The government must pay interest on the debt held by the public in the form of bonds. Does not the obligation to pay interest set a limit on the size of the government debt? Some observers have pointed out that it is possible for the government to pay the interest on its outstanding debt by issuing more bonds. A typical bondholder holding $100,000 in bonds, let us call her Claudia R. Asset, would expect to earn $5000 in interest each year when the overall economywide interest rate is 5 percent. Surely the government could simply issue $5000 in extra bonds to meet its interest obligations, without needing to levy taxes on future generations to pay this interest bill.

The government can meet its interest bill by issuing more bonds without increasing the debt-GDP ratio *only if the economy's real growth rate of output equals or exceeds its real interest rate.* Let us assume, unrealistically, that the real growth rate is 5 percent and the real interest rate is 5 percent. Then each year the government could issue 5 percent additional debt, raising Claudia's holdings from $100,000 to $105,000, without raising the ratio of outstanding debt to GDP (which also has grown 5 percent by assumption). In this case, Claudia would receive the $5000 payment that she expects, but the government would not have to levy additional taxes.

Clearly, if the real growth rate of output is less than the real interest rate, this method of financing the government debt is not available. If the real interest rate is 5 percent, Claudia expects to receive her $5000, but with a real growth rate below 5 percent any issuance of $5000 of extra debt *will raise the ratio of debt to GDP.* Next year, another $5000 of interest will be due. To finance this interest obligation by printing more debt, the government will further raise the ratio of debt to GDP. Eventually, the ratio of debt to GDP will grow and grow, approaching infinity.

The Real-World Solvency Condition in the 1990s

The government faces the solvency condition whenever the real interest rate exceeds the economy's real growth rate. The relevance of the solvency condition in 1997 depended on how much the government could finance at the short-term real interest rate (roughly 3 percent) and how much at the long-term real interest rate (roughly 5 percent). The average of these two real interest rates is above the economy's real growth rate of natural real GDP (y^N) of about 2.5 percent. This implies that the government must keep its deficit below the amount shown in equation (11.2) above. Because the average real interest rate exceeds the economy's real growth rate, the debt-GDP ratio will increase if the government chooses to issue new bonds to pay the interest on its outstanding debt.

SELF-TEST   Calculate the allowable deficit that maintains a fixed debt to GDP ratio for the following situations:

	Real Growth Rate	Inflation Rate	Existing Debt
(a)	.01	.10	$4000 billion
(b)	.03	.00	$4000 billion
(c)	.03	.00	$1000 billion

11-5   CASE STUDY: Historical Behavior of the Debt-GDP Ratio Since 1790

Figure 11-2 exhibits the ratio of the U.S. federal government debt held by the public (excluding government bonds held by the Federal Reserve and other government agencies) since 1790. From this figure we can draw several significant generalizations.

Wars and Depressions

The most consistent feature of the historical record is the tendency of the debt ratio to jump during wars and to shrink during succeeding years until the next war breaks out. The Revolutionary War, the Civil War, World War I, and World War II all created major jumps in the debt ratio, while in most other periods the debt ratio fell. Less visible, but also important, is the effect of economic recessions and depressions in raising the public debt through the effect of automatic stabilization (which reduces government revenue automatically as Y/Y^N falls, requiring an increase in the public debt to finance ongoing government expenditures). The most important example of this was the decade of the Great Depression, when the debt ratio rose from 15 percent in 1929 to 43 percent in 1939.

The New Regime of the 1980s and 1990s

The bottom frame of Figure 11-2 magnifies the period since 1955 in order to exhibit the debt ratio more clearly over the past four decades. Until 1974 the debt ratio fell. From 1974 to 1976 the ratio rose, but then leveled off at about 27–28 percent until 1981. From 1981 to 1987 the ratio rose sharply, indicating that the federal budget deficits were sizeable enough to make the government debt grow much faster than nominal GDP.

In 1987–89 the debt ratio stabilized temporarily at about 42 percent, both because the deficit fell somewhat as a percent of GDP and because there had been a rise in the allowable size of the deficit. As we can see on the right-hand side of equation (11.2), the allowable deficit (that is, one that is consistent with a constant debt-GDP ratio) is the nominal debt times the growth rate of nominal GDP. In the late 1980s the nominal debt was increasing, but so was the growth rate of nominal GDP.

The stability of the debt-GDP ratio in the late 1980s was a temporary phenomenon. The recession of 1990–91 reduced government revenues, thus raising the deficit, while the growth rate of nominal GDP slowed. In 1992, the worst year, the federal deficit reached a peak of $290 billion, and the deficit was well above the allowable level of about $200 billion for four straight years, 1990–93. This succession of high deficits caused the debt-GDP ratio to shoot up again to 50 percent, its highest level since the late 1950s.

After 1993 the deficit began to decline, and in 1996–97 was well below the "allowable level" of $200 billion (i.e., the amount that would keep the debt-GDP ratio unchanged). As a result, the debt-GDP ratio stabilized in 1994–95 and fell slightly in 1996–97. The decline in the deficit during the mid-1990s was partly a by-product of prosperity, since the buoyant economy, with relatively low unemployment and a relatively high output ratio (Y/Y^N), generated

WAR CAUSES SPIKES IN THE DEBT-GDP RATIO

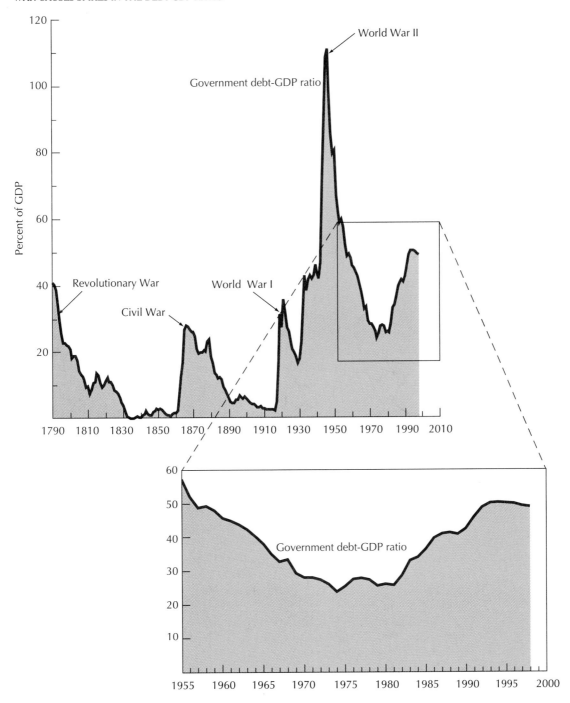

Figure 11-2   **The Ratio of U.S. Government Debt to GDP, 1790–1998**
The ratio of debt to GDP has ranged widely throughout U.S. history, rising during
wartime and falling between wars. During peacetime periods the debt-GDP ratio
increased only during the Great Depression decade of the 1930s and during the high
deficit period of 1981–93.

robust revenues for the government. In addition, legislation adopted in 1993 raised income tax rates and introduced other changes that had the consequence of boosting federal revenue. In fact, federal income tax revenues increased by more than one-third between 1992 and 1996.

11-6 Sources of the Deficits and the Debate over the Size of Government

Do Official Deficit Measures Exaggerate the Problem?

By the mid-1990s the debt-GDP ratio had stabilized at roughly 50 percent and had begun to decline slightly. This improved behavior did not, however, diminish the debate over the budget deficit. Many politicians and other prominent figures argued that the only "correct" level of the deficit is zero, and they pushed for a balanced budget amendment (see pp. 351–53). Obviously, if the "allowable deficit" of about $200 billion is consistent with a stable debt-GDP ratio, then it follows that a balanced budget (deficit of zero) would imply a rapid decline in the debt-GDP ratio, as occurred prior to 1974.

Another group of economists argue that the deficit problem is greatly exaggerated and that there is no need for a balanced budget amendment. We will review some of their arguments about the amendment later in this chapter. Here, we will review some of the factors that, it is claimed, cause official measurements of the deficit to be exaggerated.

In a widely noticed book and several articles, Robert Eisner of Northwestern University has called attention to numerous issues that lead him to conclude that the federal deficit is not measured correctly.[3] First, he claims that we should deduct from the deficit an inflation component, due to the fact that the real value of the federal debt erodes at the rate of inflation, but we have already taken this into account more generally by allowing the total debt to grow at the same rate as nominal GDP. This amounts to correcting the deficit not only for inflation but also for real growth.

Next, Eisner has argued that the bailout of the thrift institutions that boosted the deficit in the 1990–93 period should not be counted as part of the deficit, since this was a one-shot event that reinstated the deposits that people always thought they owned (so no change in household behavior is implied by the bailout). This factor ceased to be important after 1993.

Third, Eisner notes that the final deficit measure should adjust for state-local government surpluses. Indeed, in the mid-1990s the state and local government sector was running an annual surplus of about $100 billion, offsetting most of the federal deficit.

The final Eisner adjustment is for the fact that some of the government deficit represents net investment. Indeed, we should not worry about government budget deficits that finance net investment, just as we should not worry about AT&T debt (p. 337) if it finances net investment that has a payoff equal to the rate of interest paid on the investment. However, no adjustment

---

[3]See especially Robert Eisner, *How Real Is the Federal Deficit?* (New York: Free Press, 1986).

is called for by this item, because we have already taken it into account by making our criterion of the allowable deficit that which will keep the debt-GDP ratio from growing. Just as AT&T would not want its outstanding debt to rise as a fraction of its sales, so we do not want the federal debt to rise as a fraction of GDP, even if some of that federal debt is incurred to finance investment spending.

Overall, the only Eisner argument that affects our discussion in this section concerns the state and local government surplus. With the state and local government surplus running at around $100 billion, the drain on national saving caused by the federal government deficit is partly or largely offset. However, despite the state and local government surplus, there is no denying that the rate of national saving in the United States declined dramatically during the 1981–96 period as contrasted with the three decades before 1981. Thus, those who favor reducing the federal government deficit in order to boost national saving and the rate of economic growth are unconvinced by Eisner's arguments that we should not be concerned with the federal deficit.

Behavior of Revenue and Expenditure Ratios

What contributed to the radical change in fiscal policy in the period after 1980, as illustrated by the increase in the debt-GDP ratio evident in Figure 11-2? Some U.S. economists point to the three-year phased introduction of substantial personal and business tax cuts enacted in 1981, while others claim that the problem is excessive government spending. Figure 11-3, which exhibits ratios to GDP of federal receipts and expenditures, seems consistent with the latter claim. In 1991–96 federal expenditures averaged 23.3 percent of GDP, an increase of 2.2 points from the 21.1 percent average of 1970–79. In contrast, federal receipts in 1991–96 averaged 19.7 percent of GDP—*almost the same* as the 1970–79 average.

In examining the line for receipts in Figure 11-3, we notice a zigzag pattern in which receipts creep up over the years and then fall sharply. This reflects

---

Figure 11-3
Federal Government Revenues and Expenditures as a Percent of GDP, 1960–96

The federal revenue share in GDP has been amazingly stable at about 19 percent, although in 1995–96 it jumped to almost 21 percent. The expenditure share gradually increased until 1992, when it reached almost 24 percent, although by 1996 it was back down below 23 percent.

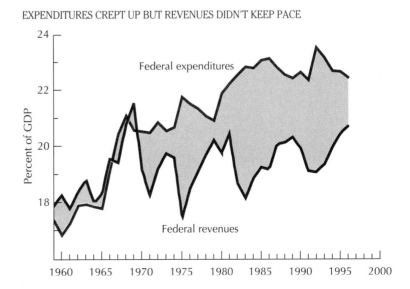

EXPENDITURES CREPT UP BUT REVENUES DIDN'T KEEP PACE

"bracket creep" (an elasticity of tax revenues to nominal GDP of greater than unity), together with periodic legislative tax cuts (1964, 1970–71, 1975, 1982–84) that offset the creep. The fact that the ratio of receipts to GDP has remained in the 19 percent range may reflect the "revealed preference" of the political process, although politicians have hardly been idle, since they increased the share of payroll taxes from 2.1 to 8.1 percent of GDP from 1960 to 1996, while reducing the percentage for all other taxes from 16.4 to 12.8 percent.

In contrast, politicians allowed an upward creep in the ratio of expenditures to GDP until 1992. The expenditure percentage was 18.1 in 1955–59, 20.1 in 1960–69, 21.1 in 1970–79, and 23.2 in 1980–96. The left hand giveth and the right hand taketh away at different rates (or, the right hand doesn't know what the left hand is doing).

Categories of Spending

What has caused the upward drift in the percentage of expenditures in GDP? As illustrated in Figure 11-4, virtually all of the increased share of government spending in GDP can be attributed to transfer payments, mainly Social Security and Medicare, which went from 2.3 percent of GDP in 1960 to 10.1 percent in 1996. As the figure shows, "non-defense plus grants and subsidies programs" were cut somewhat, from 6.3 percent in 1980 to 5.5 percent in 1996, and the share of defense spending fell from 9.7 percent in 1960, to 5.1 percent in 1980, and to 3.3 percent in 1996.

A central cause of U.S. fiscal problems is an unintended increase in the well-being of Social Security recipients in the 1970s that neither Congress nor the administration has the courage either to finance or to reverse. During the 1970s, Social Security benefits per retiree rose 50 percent after adjustment for inflation, while average real earnings per employee did not increase at all, amounting to a substantial redistribution of income from workers to the

---

Figure 11-4
Components of Federal Government Expenditures as a Percent of Natural GDP, 1959–96

The diagram has five "slices" corresponding to the shares in GDP of the five major types of federal government spending. The sum of the five slices is the share of total federal government spending in GDP. The increase in the share of federal government spending in GDP is mainly accounted for by transfer payments throughout the period and by net interest payments in the 1980s. The share of national defense declined until 1979, rose in the early 1980s, and then declined substantially after 1987. Grants and subsidies rose until 1978 and then declined.

THE COMPONENTS OF FEDERAL GOVERNMENT EXPENDITURES AS A PERCENT OF GDP, 1959-96

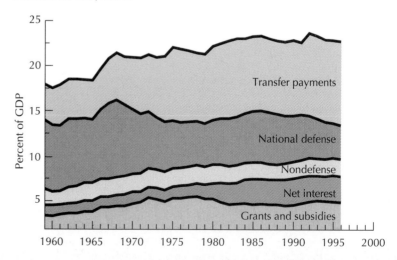

elderly. This occurred because generous indexation clauses more than compensated retirees for inflation (which itself was exaggerated by measurement errors in the Consumer Price Index, see pp. 52–53), while most workers outside of the unionized sector had little or no formal indexation protection. An important by-product was a marked reduction in the percentage of the elderly who have incomes below the official poverty line, from 35.2 percent of the over-65 population in 1959 to just 11.7 percent in 1994.

11-7   Alternative Views of Fiscal Policy: Supply-Side Economics

With the enactment of President Reagan's budget and tax packages in August 1981, the stage was set for the most dramatic shift in fiscal policy of the postwar era. We studied in Chapters 5 and 6 the effects of this program on the natural employment deficit (NED), interest rates, the value of the dollar, and net exports. And we have seen in this chapter that the result was a doubling in the ratio of debt to GDP between 1981 and 1996.

Supply-Side Argument for Reagan Tax Cuts

The Reagan program differed from previous episodes of fiscal policy stimulus, because its primary motive was *not* a belief that the economy was so weak, nor unemployment so high, nor monetary policy so impotent that the government needed to apply a fiscal stimulus. Instead, the Reagan administration believed that tax rates were simply too high and that the government sector was too large. According to the doctrine called **supply-side economics** embraced by the Reagan administration, high tax rates stifled individual initiative and saving.

Supply-side economics predicts that a reduction in marginal income tax rates will create an increase in the supply of output, that is, in natural real GDP.

The supply-side theory makes one uncontroversial statement, and two controversial claims:

1. Income taxes reduce the after-tax reward to work and saving.

2. An increase in the after-tax reward to work and saving would create a *significant increase in the amount of work and saving.*

3. The resulting increase in work and saving would be so significant that after the tax cuts the federal government would collect more revenue than before the tax cuts.

Response of Work Effort and Saving. The first statement is uncontroversial, because everyone admits that taxes reduce the after-tax reward to work and saving. In the second statement, the supply-siders argue that reductions in personal income taxes, such as those implemented by the Reagan tax package in 1981, will lead people to work longer hours, will encourage more people to take second ("moonlighting") jobs, and will allow and encourage people to save more. Many economists were skeptical of these claims, however, and present evidence indicates that their skepticism seems justified. At the time of the original 1981 debate about supply-side economics, Charles Schultze (chairman of the Council of Economic Advisers under President

Carter during 1977–81) quipped that "There's nothing wrong with supply-side economics that division by ten couldn't cure."

As it turned out, even Schultze's skeptical assessment may have been too optimistic. When we compare the economy four years before to the economy after the Reagan tax cuts, we find that the amount of work effort, as measured by the labor-force participation rate, grew more slowly after 1981 than before, and the personal saving rate fell after rising during 1977–81. The only bit of support for supply-side doctrines is that hours per employee fell more slowly after 1981 than before.

PUZZLE 3: WHY HAS PRODUCTIVITY GROWN SO SLOWLY?

Response of Productivity Growth.   Some supply-side advocates also predicted a rebound in productivity growth. Everyone agreed in 1981 that the U.S. productivity growth record had been dismal since 1973—a slowdown that no one fully understood. The post-1973 productivity slowdown, which we studied in Chapter 10, is the third puzzle introduced at the beginning of this book.

If the supply-side advocates were correct, we would expect productivity growth to have been more rapid after 1981 than before. But it was not; productivity growth was slower after 1981 than before.

	1960–72	1972–81	1981–96
Private nonfarm output per hour (annual growth rate in percent)	3.0	1.4	1.0

The Laffer Curve.   The third supply-side claim, that tax cuts raise government revenue, is even more controversial than the second. This claim was widely touted in 1981 during the debate about the Reagan tax cuts, because critics had claimed that such large tax cuts would create unprecedented government budget deficits. Supply-side proponents argued that the tax cuts would "pay for themselves."

The proponents' argument was illustrated by the famous Laffer curve, which Arthur Laffer of Pepperdine University in California had drawn on a

---

Figure 11-5
The Laffer Curve

The curve shows that total government tax revenue depends on the tax rate. With either a zero or 100 percent tax rate, the government collects no revenue. Maximum revenue occurs at point *C*. If tax rates are cut starting from point *B*, government revenue declines, but if tax rates are cut starting from point *D*, government revenue increases.

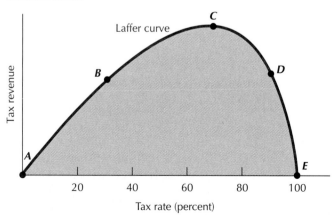

WILL A TAX CUT REDUCE GOVERNMENT REVENUES OR RAISE THEM?

napkin in a Washington restaurant in an inspired moment in 1974. The Laffer curve, reproduced in Figure 11-5, starts from the obvious point that the government will raise no tax revenue at all if tax rates are zero, as at point *A,* and if tax rates are 100 percent, as at point *E.* In between, as the tax rate rises from zero to 100 percent, tax revenues will first rise and then fall. If the government introduces a tax cut (like the 1981 Reagan package) starting from point *B,* the economy would move leftward along the Laffer curve and government revenue would fall. But a tax cut starting from point *D* would cause a leftward movement that would raise government revenue.

Was the economy at point *B* or point *D* in 1981? Clearly, one can draw a Laffer curve with its peak at any tax rate—20, 50, or 80 percent. The peak at 70 percent in Figure 11-5 is completely arbitrary. The fact that the United States entered an era of persistent deficits after the Reagan tax cuts suggests that it moved from a point like *C* to *B* in the 1980s, not from *D* to *C.*

SELF-TEST

> Looking at the Laffer curve in Figure 11-5 and assuming that government spending is fixed, does a reduction in tax rates starting from point *B* raise or lower the government budget deficit? Starting from point *D?* Which point, *B* or *D,* was believed to describe the position of the U.S. economy in 1981 by the following: Arthur Laffer? President Reagan? critics of supply-side economics?

11-8 Alternative Views of Fiscal Policy: The Barro-Ricardo Equivalence Theorem

Robert J. Barro (1944–   )
Barro's fame stems from his theory of fiscal policy, the Keynesian non-market-clearing model (Chapter 17), and his recent research on new models of economic growth (Section 9-7).

We have seen in the previous section that supply-siders depart from the traditional Keynesian analysis of fiscal policy by predicting a large effect on supply (Y^N), not just on demand. Another attack on the traditional Keynesian analysis of fiscal policy was launched in 1974 by Robert J. Barro of Harvard University.[4] Because Barro's approach echoed a theme originally proposed by the classical economist David Ricardo in the early nineteenth century, his point has become known as the "Barro-Ricardo equivalence theorem."

Barro's theory denies the efficacy of discretionary fiscal policy that takes the form of tax changes, because tax cuts are balanced by an increase in saving rather than an increase in consumption. Why? Barro points out that any tax cut is financed by deficit spending, which requires future tax payments to meet the interest on the public debt. People who see their taxes cut will tell themselves, "This just means lower taxes today and higher taxes in the future when the government needs to pay the interest on the debt; I'll save today in order to build up a savings account that will be needed to meet those future taxes."

---

[4]Robert J. Barro, "Are Government Bonds Net Wealth?" *Journal of Political Economy,* vol. 82 (November/December 1974), pp. 1095–1117.

Bequests Imply Concern About Children

While economists had recognized that taxpayers might perceive their future obligation to meet government interest payments, most had not taken seriously the possibility that people would view higher future taxes as *completely equivalent* to lower current taxes (hence the name "equivalence theorem"). Economists had previously pointed out that much of the future interest burden of the higher public debt would occur after today's taxpayers are dead. Barro's contribution was to argue that people leave bequests to their children, implying that they care about their children and hence, indirectly, about the tax burden that they face. His striking deduction was that *today's taxpayers, reacting to a tax cut today, would raise their saving so as to increase their bequests to their children in order to pay for future taxes levied by the government.*

In other words, today's holdings of government bonds do not represent net wealth. When the government prints an additional one-dollar bond to pay for a tax cut, bondholders feel richer by one dollar, but taxpayers feel poorer by the same dollar, since they recognize that one dollar's worth of future taxes will have to be levied to pay the interest on the bonds.

Criticism of the Equivalence Proposition

Barro's ingenious argument let loose a torrent of criticism. The link between bequests and concern for children was doubted. Decision horizons of private individuals are often quite short. Some parents do not care about their descendants. Perhaps more important, the absence of "perfect" rental markets for consumer housing and household possessions means that almost every homeowner is likely to die with a significant positive net worth in the form of housing and furnishings, which will be bequeathed to some heir even if the deceased does not care about the exact standard of living that the heir achieves.

A separate criticism pointed out that most individuals pay a substantially higher interest rate to borrow than does the government (for example, 18 percent on credit cards compared to a long-term government bond rate in late 1997 of 6 percent). This means that people apply a much higher discount rate to future government tax levies than the interest rate the government has to pay on its bonds. This point applies with special force when it is recognized that the typical adult consumer has an expected life span of about 35 years. If the government cuts taxes by raising the public debt, most of the burden of servicing or repaying the debt will be borne within that 35-year lifetime. Only a very small portion of the debt burden will be passed on to future generations, making moot the debate about the motives for bequests.

Evidence from the 1981 Tax Cuts

Most of the skepticism about the Barro-Ricardo equivalence theorem emerged immediately after the 1974 publication of Barro's article and was based on general principles. However, saving behavior after the 1981–83 tax cuts provided additional reason for doubt. If consumers had behaved in the forward-looking way postulated by the Barro proposition, consumption would have remained unaffected while saving would have jumped to pay for the future tax burden created by the extra federal debt. However, the personal saving rate *fell* after 1981, from 7.5 percent of disposable personal income in 1981 to an average of 5.9 percent in 1982–85. To set aside sufficient saving to pay for the future tax burden of the extra debt, households should have raised their saving rate from 7.5 percent in 1981 to roughly 11 percent in 1985, but *actual behavior went in the opposite direction.* (In Chapter 15 we return to the puzzle of the low saving rate in the 1980s and 1990s.)

11-9 Pros and Cons of a Balanced Budget Amendment

In the mid-1990s a coalition in Congress formed to support a balanced budget amendment to the U.S. Constitution. In this section we will divide the case for and against such an amendment into two parts. First, what is the case to be made for balancing the budget? Second, if the case for budgetary balance is strong, what are the arguments for amending the Constitution rather than relying on the political process to achieve balance?

The Case for Budgetary Balance

As we have seen, the basic economic argument for budgetary balance is to boost the rate of economic growth. Balancing the budget eliminates the drain from the budget deficit on the rate of national saving. Stated another way, balancing the budget enhances economic growth because it permits resources that are currently devoted to consumption to be allocated instead to investment. In the near term, the share of output that is consumed will fall, as will the level of consumption. In the longer term, as shown in Figure 11-1, the level of consumption will eventually become higher because the greater rate of investment will boost total output.

It has been estimated by the Congressional Budget Office (CBO) that only about 20 percent of the reduction in the federal government deficit will find its way into increased private investment. Because there will be some decline in private saving, part of the deficit reduction will not raise national saving. Also, the stimulus to investment will be less than the increase in national saving, since borrowing from foreigners will decline. As indicated in Chapters 5 and 6, budget deficits tend to increase the extent of borrowing from foreigners, and a reduction in the budget deficit will reduce our dependence on foreign borrowing. However, less borrowing from abroad for investment will reduce the amount of interest paid to foreigners, and this will boost American living standards.[5]

What are the channels by which deficit reduction tends to boost economic growth? First, balancing the budget would lower interest rates. While there is a great deal of uncertainty about the quantitative effects, the CBO

---

[5]Stated another way, the benefit of deficit reduction is greater for GNP than for GDP (GNP includes income received from U.S. foreign investments, less income paid to foreigners; GNP rises relative to GDP if our net indebtedness to foreigners decreases; see pp. 36–37).

estimates that balancing the budget by the year 2002 would reduce interest rates in that year by 0.7 percent. Deficit reduction has no impact on the inflation rate, since it is assumed that the rate of inflation depends on the success of monetary policy in maintaining the actual unemployment rate equal to the natural unemployment rate. Thus, with no impact on inflation, the decline in the real interest rate would be the same as that in the nominal interest rate, say 0.7 percent as assumed by the CBO.[6]

How much would balancing the budget raise the growth rate of real GDP and GNP? The CBO assumes that by the year 2005 a policy of balancing the budget would boost real GDP by 0.4 percentage points and real GNP by 0.6 percentage points. Thus, the difference in the annual growth rate over the decade 1996–2005 is very small, only 0.04 percentage points for real GDP and 0.06 percentage points for real GNP. Nevertheless, the boost in real income that is achieved by balancing the budget helps to "pay" for part of the deficit reduction. By 2005 the CBO estimates that the increase in economic growth will contribute $56 billion annually in the form of higher federal revenues and lower federal expenditures.

If a slight increase in the rate of economic growth is the main benefit of a balanced budget, what are the costs? The answer, obviously, is that some government programs must be cut, and/or some tax rates must be raised in order to put together the $137 billion in program changes (i.e., changes in expenditures or tax rates) that the CBO estimates will be required to balance the budget by the year 2002. Social Security recipients may have their benefits reduced, recipients of government subsidies (such as farmers and urban transit systems) may find their subsidies cut, and taxpayers may pay more in income and payroll taxes. Balancing the budget is not painless, and the political pressure to avoid painful expenditure cuts and tax increases helps to explain why the federal government has run such large deficits since 1981, and why the national debt has increased so much as a ratio to GDP (Figure 11-2).

The Case For and Against an Amendment

The case for a balanced budget amendment is simple. For years the political process in Washington has attempted to reach an agreement between successive congresses and administrations to achieve a balanced budget, but the political process has failed. The amendment is necessary simply to force politicians to achieve what they cannot seem to accomplish without it.

The arguments against an amendment are threefold:

1. An amendment would require balancing the budget every year, no matter what. But in years of recession and slow growth the deficit balloons as revenues fall, and the debt-GDP ratio tends to rise (as in 1990–93 in Figure 11-2). A balanced budget amendment would thus require tax increases or expenditure cuts, thereby aggravating the recession. Some versions of the balanced budget amendment deal with this argument by allowing Congress, by say a two-thirds majority, to declare the amendment temporarily nonbinding during a serious recession.

---

[6]All quantitative estimates in this section come from Congressional Budget Office, *The Economic and Budget Outlook: Fiscal Years 1998–2007* (Washington, D.C., January 1997), Chapter 4.

2. There is no magic in a balanced budget. As we have learned, a budget deficit of about $200 billion per year is consistent with a stable debt-GDP ratio so long as nominal GDP grows at about 5 percent annually. This is not really an argument against the amendment, but against the virtues of budget balancing in general. Proponents of this argument point out that the tiny increase in the nation's rate of economic growth (0.04 percent as estimated by the CBO) is hardly worth all the pain of expenditure cuts and tax increases needed to reach budgetary balance.

3. The final argument is that, almost alone among industrialized nations, the United States does not separate out current from capital expenditures in calculating the deficit. A balanced budget could discourage the government from borrowing for capital expenditures that might have a high social rate of return. Most state governments, which are required to balance their current operating budgets (and, in fact, have achieved substantial surpluses in recent years), are allowed to finance capital expenditures by borrowing.

What should we conclude? The main argument for a balanced budget is that the United States needs a higher rate of national saving, but unfortunately the CBO calculations cited in this section suggest that there will be minimal improvement in the U.S. rate of economic growth as a result of a balanced budget. Further, the urgency of passing a balanced-budget amendment decreased in 1996–97 as the actual budget deficit declined well below the level consistent with a stable debt-GDP ratio. As a result, that ratio declined in 1996–97. Finally, the balanced-budget amendment does not make an appropriate distinction between government consumption and investment. Cutbacks in government investment (like education) in the struggle to achieve a balanced budget could reduce economic growth instead of increasing it.

11-10 Conclusion: The Debate Between the Termites and Pussycats

Charles Schultze of the Brookings Institution has clarified the debate over persistent U.S. federal budget deficits by distinguishing "termites" from "pussycats." Termites view persistent deficits as insidious, slowly but steadily undermining the foundations of the U.S. economy. Pussycats view the deficits as benign, and nothing to worry about. Termites are led by Schultze and other economists at the Brookings Institution. The pussycat group finds such unlikely soulmates as liberal Keynesian economist Robert Eisner of Northwestern University and conservative monetarist Milton Friedman.

Termites analyze the slow productivity growth of the past two decades and conclude that more domestic private investment is required to boost growth, and that this strategy requires an increase in national saving. In turn, the most direct way for the government to boost national saving is to reduce its own *dissaving*. It is undeniable that net domestic private investment fell as a share of GDP in the 1980s (see Figure 5-10), although this decline was caused as much by a collapse of private saving as by persistent government deficits. Furthermore, even if investment does not fall, the drop in national saving implies that investment would have to be financed by foreign borrowing, which imposes on future citizens the burden of making interest payments to foreigners.

Pussycats have four responses. First, investment did not fall in the 1980s. Second, a sizeable deficit can be tolerated. Third, borrowing from foreigners in the 1980s was a sign of strength in the economy, not a weakness. Fourth, the deficit put political pressure on the government to cut spending and avoid implementation of new programs, a desirable situation from the point of view of those pussycats who desire a smaller government.

Was investment high or low? The figures shown in Figure 5-10 are for net investment, after allowing for replacement of worn out and obsolete capital. Net investment undeniably fell, while gross investment (the measure preferred by pussycats) did not. Explaining this discrepancy is a shift in the 1980s and 1990s to shorter-lived equipment, especially computers, which have to be replaced more often than other types of capital. Since only net investment boosts capital input and contributes to growth, most economists believe that net investment (which did decline) is the better measure.

The second issue concerns the allowable deficit that is consistent with a stable debt-GDP ratio. We learned in Section 11-5 that in 1997 a substantial deficit of about $200 billion could be sustained without implying any increase in the ratio of the national debt to GDP.

The third issue concerns the interpretation of foreign borrowing. Pussycats believe that foreigners were attracted to invest in the United States (creating large foreign borrowing in the 1980s and 1990s) by the potential to make high profits from a booming U.S. economy. Furthermore, despite 15 years of foreign borrowing, in 1996 the United States still earned almost as much from its holdings of foreign assets as it paid as interest to foreigners. Also, there is a huge supply of saving in other countries (due to higher saving rates abroad), and there is nothing wrong if a share of this saving is invested in the United States. Put another way, U.S. indebtedness to foreigners can grow at a moderate rate without raising the ratio of such debt to world nominal GDP. However, the growth in foreign debt in the 1980s and 1990s was much faster than can be sustained without creating an ever-growing drain of interest payments to foreigners.

Finally, Milton Friedman believes that the persistent deficits have been the only effective restraint on ever-growing federal spending. One can doubt this proposition on the ground that the deficits of the 1980s did not prevent the ratio of federal spending to GDP from rising (see Figure 11-4). Furthermore, the debate over whether more or less government is desirable is political, taking us out of the realm of positive macroeconomics into the sphere of normative macroeconomics, where value judgments are required.

It would be safe to conclude by noting, as emphasized by Eisner and others, that the absence of separate current and capital budgets for the federal government makes our official national saving concept a misnomer. If states and localities can keep separate accounts, balancing their operating budget and borrowing for new buildings and facilities, why can't the federal government do the same thing? The new endogenous growth theory of Chapter 9 emphasizes the role of education and other forms of public investment in generating economic growth. To the extent that government investment in infrastructure, education, preventive medicine, and research have a payoff that is equal to or greater than private domestic investment, trying to reduce the fiscal deficit by reducing public investment would retard rather than enhance economic growth. Instead, any attempt to boost private investment by cutting the fiscal deficit should be achieved by cutting government consumption or boosting tax rates.

SUMMARY

1. A budget deficit reduces national saving and lowers the rate of economic growth.
2. The two methods for stimulating national saving and hence economic growth are for policymakers to create incentives that raise private saving or to run a larger government surplus (or smaller deficit).
3. Deficits that raise the future level of the public debt create a burden on future generations if the deficits finance government consumption expenditures that yield no future benefits to balance the burden of taxes required to pay the interest on the debt.
4. The government faces a solvency condition, which states that it cannot run a deficit in the long run if the real interest rate exceeds the economy's growth rate of real output.
5. The U.S. ratio of public debt to GDP fell throughout the postwar period until 1974, rose between 1974 and 1987, then briefly stabilized, rose again in 1990–93, and stabilized again during 1994–97. The deficits in the 1980s and 1990s were due to a higher ratio of government spending to GDP, not to a lower ratio of tax revenue to GDP. In turn, most of the higher spending was due to an increase in transfer payments.

6. The Laffer curve predicts that if initial tax rates are high enough, a cut in tax rates raises government tax revenue. Supply-side economists predicted in the early 1980s that tax rate cuts would not only raise government tax revenues but would also stimulate saving and work effort. The predicted effects did not occur.
7. The Barro-Ricardo equivalence theorem states that deficit-financed tax cuts will stimulate saving rather than consumption, because individuals will try to build up their savings accounts to pay the future taxes required to service the higher government debt.
8. Maintaining a balanced budget instead of a deficit around $200 billion would modestly boost the rate of economic growth. The main argument for a constitutional amendment to balance the budget is to tie the hands of politicians who have not managed to balance the budget on their own.
9. "Termites" insist that the federal deficit should be cut in order to boost national saving and private investment. "Pussycats" argue that the size of the deficit is exaggerated as is the harm done by the deficit.

CONCEPTS

rate of time preference
national saving

supply-side economics

QUESTIONS AND PROBLEMS

Questions

1. Economic policymakers are concerned with both economic growth and economic stabilization. Explain the distinction between them. Are different policies used for the two purposes? Give some examples.
2. What is national saving? Under what circumstances would it be appropriate to increase the level of national saving?

3. If the level of real GDP is held fixed by monetary policy at some given amount, which of the following will provide the greatest stimulus to saving?
   (a) An increase in the personal income tax rates paid by the rich.
   (b) An increase in the personal income tax rates paid by the poor.
   (c) The introduction of a federal retail sales tax.

4. "Unnecessary fears of the rising government deficit have restricted desirable government spending." Explain.

5. We rarely hear concern about the "burden" of privately held debt, yet many people share a concern about the public debt. Why is this so? Is the concern about the public debt reasonable?

6. Many people are less concerned with the absolute size of the government debt than they are about its size relative to GDP. Such people would not worry about the size of government deficits if the ratio of government debt to GDP remained equal to some "appropriate" level.
   (a) Explain the conditions under which it is possible for the debt-GDP ratio to be a constant.
   (b) Don't people who hold the view described above have to worry about the future solvency of the government?

7. What have been the main causes of the upward drift in government expenditures as a percentage of GDP?

8. The supply-side argument for tax cuts is based on one uncontroversial claim and two controversial claims. What are they? Is the empirical record consistent or inconsistent with the controversial claims? Explain.

9. When analyzing the effects of price changes, microeconomists consider how consumers' behavior will respond to changes in relative prices (the "substitution" effect) and to changes in real purchasing power (the "income" effect). Substitution and income effects also occur when tax rates change.

Not only do tax changes affect disposable income, but they also change the relative "prices" of certain types of behavior.
   (a) What is the opportunity cost of leisure? What happens to leisure's opportunity cost (its "price") following a tax rate cut? Describe the substitution and income effects on people's decision to consume leisure. Do these effects reinforce or offset one another?
   (b) Do the proponents of supply-side economics see the substitution effect or the income effect having the dominant impact on decisions to consume leisure following a tax rate cut? Explain.

10. State and critique the Barro-Ricardo equivalence theorem.

11. Evaluate each of the following statements in terms of the Barro-Ricardo equivalence theorem's implications for saving.
   (a) "Retirement benefits promised by Social Security reduce workers' incentives to save and thus diminish private saving in the economy."
   (b) "Social Security is solvent now, but over the next 35–40 years it will likely go broke unless taxes are raised or benefits are reduced."

12. What is the balanced budget amendment? What are the main arguments for and against it?

13. Are you a "termite" or a "pussycat" in the debate over the government budget deficit? To answer, compare your views with those associated with "termites" and "pussycats," presented in the text.

Problems

1. In 1990 a country had real GDP of $500 million, a government debt of $200 million, and a real interest rate of 2.5 percent. The country's growth rate of real GDP was 2.5 percent.
   (a) What was the value of the ratio of government debt to GDP for this country in 1990?
   (b) What was the amount of interest paid on the country's debt in 1990? What was the interest payment as a percentage of real GDP in 1990?
   (c) If the government issued new debt in 1991 to cover the interest charges on the 1990 debt, what was the new level of government debt in 1991? How much interest had to be paid in 1991 on the government debt, assuming the real interest rate was still 2.5 percent?
   (d) What was the level of real GDP in 1991? Compare the percentage of real GDP going for interest payments in 1991 to that for 1990. Compare the ratio of government debt to real GDP for the two years. Is the ratio of govern-

ment debt to real GDP equal in the two years? If so, why? If not, why not?
   (e) Assume that the real interest rate was actually 5 percent, not 2.5 percent, for both years. How does this change affect your answers to (b)–(d)?

2. Assume that the current rate of inflation is 4 percent and that nominal GDP is $5000 billion and growing at 2 percent per year. If the current government deficit is $100 billion and the debt-GDP ratio is 20 percent, and the government wants to maintain it at that level, then by how much should the government increase or decrease the deficit next year?

3. Study the following relationship:

$$T_B = 4480 - 4480t$$

Here, T_B is the federal government tax base in billions of dollars and t is the tax rate. Tax revenue is the product of the tax rate and the tax base:

$$T = tT_B$$

Here, T is federal tax revenues in billions of dollars. Define the tax-rate elasticity of the tax base, η, as

$$\eta = -\% \, \Delta T_B / \% \, \Delta t = -(t/T_B)(\Delta T_B / \Delta t)$$

(a) If $t = 0.50$, what are T_B, T, and η?

(b) If $t = 0.75$, what are T_B, T, and η?

(c) If $t = 0.25$, what are T_B, T, and η?

(d) On the basis of these calculations, can you formulate a relationship between T and η?

(e) If $t = 0.75$, would cutting the tax rate raise or lower T?

SELF-TEST ANSWERS

p. 336 By looking at the impact on national saving as a percent of GDP, we are able to ignore the multiplier effects of these fiscal policies. Since national saving is the sum of government saving and private saving, for each item we must determine the effect on each. (a) Government saving declines (deficit rises) with no impact on private saving, so national saving declines. (b) Government saving increases (deficit falls) while private saving may also increase due to the higher price of food, so national saving increases. (c) Government saving declines (deficit rises), while the increase in personal disposable income is split between higher private saving and higher consumption; thus national saving declines because govern-

ment saving declines more than private saving increases.

p. 341 (a) $440 billion; (b) $120 billion; (c) $30 billion

p. 349 A reduction in tax rates moves the economy to the left in Figure 11-5, the Laffer curve diagram. Thus, starting from point B, tax revenues fall as we move to the left, raising the government deficit if government expenditures are fixed. Starting from point D, tax revenues rise and the government deficit declines. Arthur Laffer and President Reagan believed that the 1981 economy was at point D, and critics of the supply-side economists believed that the 1981 economy was at point B.

PART FIVE

Stabilization Policy in an Open Economy

CHAPTER 12

The Goals of Stabilization Policy: Low Inflation and Low Unemployment

The government fighting inflation is like the Mafia fighting crime.
—Laurence J. Peter

This book began by introducing six major concepts of macroeconomics. The first three of these—unemployment, inflation, and growth in per person output—are also the three major goals of macroeconomic policy, namely, to achieve low unemployment, low inflation, and rapid growth in per-person output. In Chapter 1 we learned why growth in output is desirable; simply put, more is better, allowing society to have everything it now produces (and more) without the need to sacrifice something currently produced. In Chapter 9 we studied some of the theories of how economic growth is determined.

Now we inquire into the two other major goals of economic policy, beginning with low inflation in the first part of this chapter and ending with low unemployment in the last part. As we learned in Chapter 8, in order to achieve a lower inflation rate by restrictive monetary or fiscal policies, policymakers must be willing to accept a transition period during which unemployment is higher. Is the goal of achieving lower inflation worth the cost of lost jobs in the period during which inflation is reduced? This depends on the costs of inflation—just what is it that society loses if inflation proceeds at a rate of 5 percent per year instead of 2 percent?

In the last part of the chapter we inquire into the costs of unemployment. Is unemployment of a teenager seeking a part-time job as costly to individuals and society as unemployment of an adult head of household? Why can't the unemployment rate be pushed down to zero percent? Why are some people unemployed even in a prosperous economy?

12-1 The Costs and Causes of Inflation

Inflation is widely viewed as a social evil, although the degree of its seriousness is debated. At one extreme, inflation is considered as serious a problem as unemployment. This view was popularized by Arthur Okun, who defined the "misery index" as the sum of the inflation and unemployment rates. This index implies that the social value of a reduction of inflation by one percentage point (say from 3 to 2 percent) exactly offsets the social cost of an increase in the unemployment rate by one percentage point (say from 6 to 7 percent), leaving the economy with an unchanged level of "misery."

Others think that the harm done by inflation is minimal. James Tobin has written that "inflation is greatly exaggerated as a social evil." As we learned in Chapter 8, policymakers desiring to reduce the inflation rate must reduce the growth rate of nominal GDP, and such action is likely to cause a temporary drop in output and an increase in unemployment. Many economists like Tobin do not regard the benefits of lower inflation as worth the sacrifice of lost output and jobs necessary to achieve it.

In Chapter 8 we also learned that the basic cause of inflation is excessive growth in nominal GDP. In this chapter we ask why governments inflate; that is, why they allow excessive nominal GDP growth to occur. We then examine the costs of inflation, asking whether they are serious enough to warrant stopping inflation, even though doing so may require policies that cut output and cause millions to lose their jobs. This question is highly topical. In the late 1980s the Bank of Canada formally adopted a policy of gradually reducing the Canadian inflation rate from 5 percent to zero by the mid-1990s. As of 1997, inflation had fallen substantially, but Canadian unemployment was above 9 percent. Will the benefits of the Canadian policy be worth its cost, and should the United States follow in Canadian footsteps?

Hyperinflation is a very rapid inflation, sometimes defined as a rate of more than 22 percent per month, or 1000 percent per year, experienced over a year or more.

Any debate about the costs of inflation must distinguish between moderate (crawling) inflation and extreme inflation, usually called **hyperinflation.** One traditional definition of hyperinflation is an inflation rate of 50 percent per month, or 12,975 percent per year.[1] We shall use as our definition an inflation rate of 1000 percent per year or above; a rate of 1000 percent per year (or 22 percent per month) afflicts a society with all the problems usually associated with hyperinflation. Argentina, Brazil, Nicaragua, Peru, and Poland all suffered from inflation rates of over 1000 percent per year for one or more years in the late 1980s or early 1990s.[2]

Everyone agrees that hyperinflation is a severe plague, and we will learn how economic policymakers have managed to stop hyperinflations in several specific cases. Then we will turn to the social costs of moderate inflation, such as that experienced by the United States. We will see that there are quite different costs associated with an inflation that is fully anticipated (crawling along at roughly the same rate year after year) and of an inflation that is a "surprise," changing in an unpredictable way.

12-2 Money and Inflation

In Chapter 8 our model of inflation showed that a permanent increase in the growth rate of nominal GDP would lead to a permanent increase in the inflation rate. Since nominal GDP growth is so important in determining the inflation rate, we need to understand its determinants.

---

[1]Why is a 50 percent monthly inflation equivalent to an annual rate of 12,875 percent? This occurs because of compounding. Starting at 100, after one month prices are up to 150, after two months they are at 225, after three months they are at 338, and after twelve months they are at 12,975. Although these simple geometric changes are widely cited in the literature, they become increasingly misleading at high rates of inflation; a better measure is the logarithmic price change, which in this example is 40.5 percent per month, or 487 percent per year. See Problems 1 and 2 at the end of the chapter.

[2]The 1000 percent cutoff for episodes of "extreme" inflation is suggested in R. Dornbusch et al., "Extreme Inflation: Dynamics and Stabilization," *Brookings Papers on Economic Activity,* 1990, no. 2, pp. 1–84.

Definitions Linking Money, Velocity, Inflation, and Output

A convenient starting point for understanding the determinants of inflation is provided by the quantity equation of Section 7-8:

$$M^s V \equiv X \equiv PY \tag{12.1}$$

This equation is familiar; it duplicates equation (7.1). The right side of the equation states that nominal GDP *(X),* by definition, is equal to the price index, or the GDP deflator *(P),* multiplied by real GDP *(Y).* The left side states that nominal GDP is also equal, by definition, to the money supply *(M^s)* multiplied by velocity *(V).*[3] Thus nominal GDP must rise if there is an increase in either the money supply or in velocity.

Equation (12.1) is a good beginning, but it concerns the price *level.* How can we convert equation (12.1) into a relationship that shows the determinants of the rate of *inflation,* that is, the rate of change of the price level? As we learned in Chapter 8, the growth rate of any product of two numbers, such as *P* times *Y* in equation (12.1), is equal to the sum of the separate growth rates of the two numbers. This allows us to take (12.1), a relationship among *levels* (written as uppercase letters), and restate it as a relationship among *growth rates* (written as lowercase letters):

$$m^s + v \equiv x \equiv p + y \tag{12.2}$$

In words, this states that the growth rate of the money supply *(m^s)* plus the growth in velocity *(v)* equals the growth rate of nominal GDP *(x),* which in turn is divided between the inflation rate *(p)* and the growth rate of real GDP *(y).* The formula immediately allows us to classify the determinants of inflation, when we rewrite (12.2) with inflation on the left side:

$$p \equiv x - y \equiv m^s + v - y \tag{12.3}$$

If we are interested in the long-run determinants of inflation, we can assume that the growth rate of real output *(y)* is fairly constant, roughly fixed by the growth rate of the population and of productivity. This leads to the same conclusion as we reached in Chapter 8.

> *In the long run the inflation rate equals the excess growth rate of nominal GDP, that is, the difference between nominal GDP growth and the long-run growth rate of real GDP.*

The right-hand terms in equation (12.3) provide additional insight into the causes of inflation. In the long run the inflation rate must equal the excess growth rate of money plus velocity, relative to the long-run growth rate of real GDP (which in the long run grows at the same rate as natural real GDP).[4]

---

[3]Why is the left side true by definition? As we learned in Chapter 4 on p. 113 velocity is defined as $V \equiv PY/M^s$, or $V \equiv Y/(M^s/P)$.

[4]In the appendix to Chapter 8, we subtracted the long-run growth rate of natural real GDP (y^N) explicitly from both nominal and real GDP growth. Applying the same subtraction to equation (12.3), we have

$$p \equiv (x - y^N) - (y - y^N) \equiv (m^s + v - y^N) - (y - y^N)$$

This states that in the long run when $y - y^N$ is zero, inflation equals the excess growth of nominal GDP relative to that of natural real GDP, and inflation also equals the excess growth of money plus velocity relative to that of natural real GDP.

Thus, to understand the determinants of inflation, we need to know what determines the excess growth of money plus velocity. The growth rate of the money supply is controlled by the central bank (in the United States by the Federal Reserve, in Canada by the Bank of Canada, and by similar institutions in other countries). Velocity changes whenever there is a change in real GDP relative to the real money supply (M^s/P). In Chapter 4 we learned that anything that shifts the *IS* curve will change velocity, including changes in business and consumer confidence, government spending, tax rates, autonomous net taxes, autonomous net exports, or the foreign exchange rate. Further, if the demand for money changes for reasons independent of changes in income, then velocity will change. For instance, velocity could change, following the introduction of credit cards that allow households to economize on their holdings of money.

While the growth rate of velocity can be highly volatile in the short run, over the long run velocity growth tends to be quite stable. For the United States the average annual growth rate of velocity has been almost exactly zero over the last three decades.[5] Thus if we assume $v = 0$ in equation (12.3), the determinants of inflation become extremely simple:

> *In the long run the inflation rate equals the excess growth rate of the money supply, that is, the difference between the growth rate of the money supply and the long-run growth rate of real GDP. If the central bank allows the money supply to grow rapidly, rapid inflation will result. The key to attaining zero inflation is for the central bank to allow the money supply to grow no faster than the long-run growth rate of real output.*

SELF-TEST

Assume that over a decade the growth rate of the money supply is constant at 5 percent per year, and the growth rate of velocity is constant at 3 percent per year. In the first half of the decade, the growth rate of output is 4 percent per year, then, because of a slowdown in productivity growth, it is only 2 percent for the last half of the decade. The growth in money and velocity are not affected by the productivity growth slowdown. What is the inflation rate in the first half of the decade? In the last half of the decade?

Why Do Central Banks Allow Excessive Monetary Growth?

The previous section identified excessive monetary growth as the fundamental cause of inflation *in the long run*. If the growth rate of velocity is zero in the long run (it was roughly zero in the U.S. since 1961), then excessive nominal GDP growth and excessive monetary growth are identical. Why do governments and central banks allow excessive monetary growth to occur?

Three basic factors can lead to excessive nominal GDP and monetary growth. The first two were examined in Chapter 8, and the third will be introduced in Section 12-4. As shown in Chapter 8, a permanent increase in nominal GDP growth leads to a *temporary* increase in output along with a permanent increase in the inflation rate. A permanent decrease in nominal

---

[5]The velocity of the money supply concept M2 (defined in Chapter 13) was 1.62 in 1961 and 2.03 in 1996, for an annual growth rate of -0.6 percent.

INTERNATIONAL PERSPECTIVE

Money Growth and Inflation

Equation (12.3) in the text $(p = m^s + v - y)$ states that the inflation rate (p) is equal to the rate of monetary growth (m^s) plus the difference between velocity growth and real GDP growth $(v - y)$. If this difference is positive, then inflation exceeds the rate of monetary growth, and vice versa.

The graph plots the inflation rate over the period 1990–96 against the rate of monetary growth for twelve countries. The diagonal 45-degree line shows all the points with equal rates of inflation and monetary growth, i.e., with $v = y$. In most of the low-inflation countries, the plotted points lie below the 45-degree line, indicating that velocity growth was less than real GDP growth. For instance, in the United States veloc-ity growth was roughly zero, less than output growth of about 2.5 percent per year. These plotted points illustrate that the relationship between inflation and monetary growth is relatively close, supporting the theme of the text that the key to understanding inflation is to understand why some governments choose much higher rates of monetary growth than others.

The scale in the graph is logarithmic, and one of the countries plotted (Brazil) had an inflation rate of over 1000 per-cent over the period. In some years these and other countries had inflation rates of 2000 percent or more. Later in this chapter we look more closely at the causes of high inflation and its basic cause, rapid monetary growth.

Inflation vs. Money Growth, 1990–96

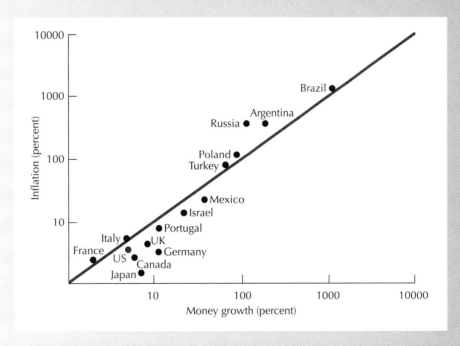

GDP growth leads to a *temporary* decrease in output along with a permanent decrease of the inflation rate. This analysis underlies the first reason govern-ments cause inflation:

Temptation of demand stimulation Governments and central banks may set off inflation when they attempt to raise output and reduce unem-ployment. While Chapter 8 indicated that such policies can boost inflation with only a temporary benefit to output, governments may think (erroneously) that the benefits of higher output will last forever, or (perhaps correctly) at least long enough to benefit the government at the next election. In some countries the central bank is controlled directly or indirectly by the government. Even in the United States, with its relatively independent central bank, it is widely believed that the Fed boosted monetary growth in 1972 to help reelect President Nixon.

The corollary to the first reason is the fact that stopping inflation usually causes a temporary drop in output and loss of jobs. Thus, an implication of the first reason for higher inflation is that governments are reluctant to stop inflation once it gets started:

Fear of recession and job loss   An economy must sacrifice a substantial amount of lost output in order to reduce the inflation rate permanently. The size of this output sacrifice (measured by Chapter 8's sacrifice ratio) is highly controversial and differs among countries. One estimate for the United States is that a permanent decrease in the inflation rate of one percentage point would require a one-time loss of about 6 percent of a year's GDP, or about $480 billion. The sacrifice required in some countries may be higher, in others lower. Politicians and central banks may be reluctant to impose this sacrifice on citizens, and as a result inflation tends to persist year after year.

Chapter 8 also introduced adverse supply shocks as a second cause of higher inflation. When higher food or oil prices raise business costs, the inflation rate rises unless the central bank introduces an extinguishing policy that offsets the extra inflation with a massive recession. Thus the second reason for higher inflation is

Adverse supply shocks   Any sharp increase in the price of oil, such as those that occurred in 1973–74 and 1979–80, poses a distasteful choice for central banks. An extinguishing policy reaction can offset extra inflation only at the cost of extra unemployment. An accommodative policy calls for the central bank to "print the extra money to pay for the inflation," and this is likely to create a permanent upsurge of inflation following an adverse supply shock. Even a neutral policy, which leaves the growth rate of nominal GDP and the money supply unchanged, will cause a temporary upsurge of inflation.

Thus, according to the Chapter 8 model, inflation results from the temptation of demand stimulation, with related fears of recession and output loss, and the effect of adverse supply shocks. Subsequent sections of this chapter introduce an important third reason for inflation, the requirements of government finance.

Financing government deficits by printing money   In our analysis of the *IS-LM* model of Chapter 4, we learned that governments can run deficits (by boosting expenditures or cutting taxes) in two ways. First, they can hold the real money supply steady and issue bonds to pay for the deficit, which usually requires an increase in the interest rate. Or they can hold the interest rate steady by raising the money supply sufficiently, a policy previously described as monetary accommodation of a fiscal stimulus. However, many countries lack markets in which the government can sell bonds; in such countries virtually the only source of finance for government deficits is an increase in the money supply (often called financing deficits by "printing money"). Thus, governments with excessive spending or insufficient tax revenues can cause inflation *(p)*, according to equation (12.3), by boosting the growth rate of the money supply *(m^s)*.

In summary, we have learned that the basic reasons why central banks allow excessive monetary growth are the temptation of demand stimulation together with the related fear of recession and output loss, the partial or complete accommodation of adverse supply shocks, and the effect of government deficits in boosting monetary growth.

12-3 Interest Rates and Inflation

If a temporary period of lost output and higher unemployment must be experienced in order to reduce inflation, then policymakers need to be convinced that it is harmful for them to allow inflation to continue. At first glance, worry about inflation may appear misplaced. When inflation is zero, wages may increase at 1 percent a year. When inflation proceeds at 6 percent annually, wages may grow at 7 percent annually. Workers have little reason to be bothered about the inflation rate *(p)* if the growth in their wages *(w)* always stays the same distance ahead, as in this example:

	No inflation	6 percent annual inflation
Growth rate of nominal wages *(w)*	1	7
Growth rate of price deflator *(p)*	0	6
Growth rate of real wages *(w − p)*	1	1

However, even if real wage growth is unaffected by inflation, it is still possible for inflation to impose substantial costs on society. Inflation is felt primarily by owners of financial assets. The distinction between surprise and fully anticipated inflation is central to understanding the costs of inflation and the suggested methods for reducing those costs. In this section we distinguish between nominal expected real and actual real interest rates, and show how both surprise and fully anticipated inflation affects savers and borrowers.

The **nominal interest rate** is the market interest rate actually charged by financial institutions and earned by bondholders.

The **expected real interest rate** is the nominal interest rate minus the expected rate of inflation.

The **actual real interest rate** is the nominal interest rate minus the actual inflation rate.

Nominal and Real Interest Rates

Even in countries with moderate inflation, people learn the difference between nominal and real interest rates, even if they have not been taught the following economists' jargon (which we first introduced in Section 1-6 on pp. 18–19).

The **nominal interest rate** (i) *is the rate actually quoted by banks and negotiated in financial markets. The* **expected real interest rate** (r^e) *is what people expect to pay on their borrowings or earn on their savings after deducting expected inflation* (r^e = i − p^e). *The expected real interest rate is what matters for investment and saving decisions. The* **actual real interest rate** *is the nominal interest rate minus the actual rate of inflation* (r = i − p).

The nominal interest rate can differ greatly in two countries with different inflation rates, or in one country at different moments in history. But investment and saving decisions will be the same in the two situations as long as the expected real interest rate is the same, and as long as all other determinants of investment besides the expected real interest rate are held constant.

Consider two situations, both with a real expected interest rate (r^e) of 3 percent. In the first situation expected inflation is zero and the nominal interest rate is 3 percent:

General Form   Numerical Example

$$r^e = i - p^e \qquad r^e = 3 - 0 = 3 \qquad\qquad (12.4)$$

In the second situation there is an expected inflation rate of 6 percent and a nominal interest rate of 9 percent. The real interest rate is the same value, 3 percent:

General Form   Numerical Example

$$r^e = i - p^e \qquad r^e = 9 - 6 = 3 \qquad\qquad (12.5)$$

Why is the incentive to save and invest the same in each situation? In the second situation savers face the prospect that one year later prices will be higher by 6 percent, but they receive an interest rate on their saving of 9 percent, of which 3 percent compensates them for their willingness to save (just as in the zero-inflation situation), while the additional 6 percent compensates them for inflation, that is, the fact that goods they plan to consume with their saving will be 6 percent more expensive one year later. Investors react similarly; the fact that they can sell their products for 6 percent more after one year of 6 percent inflation compensates them for having to pay a nominal interest rate of 9 percent.

This example creates the impression that inflation does not matter, since the nominal interest rate will adjust to maintain the same incentives for savers and investors at a 6 percent inflation rate as at a zero inflation rate. However, this example makes several important assumptions, none of which are validated in the real world:

1. Inflation is universally and accurately anticipated.
2. All savings are held in bonds, stocks, or savings accounts earning the nominal interest rate (i); no one holds money in accounts with an interest rate held below the market nominal interest rate.
3. An inflation of p_0 percent raises the market nominal interest rate (i) for both saving and borrowing by exactly p_0 percent above the no-inflation interest rate.
4. Only real (not nominal) interest income is taxable, and only the real cost of borrowing is tax deductible.
5. Inflation raises the prices of all goods by the same percent (that is, inflation causes no changes in the relative prices of goods).

Interest Rates in a Surprise Inflation

Now let us violate condition 1 in the preceding summary list, that is, that inflation is accurately anticipated. In several episodes in the United States, such as in 1966–69, 1973–74, 1978–80, and 1987–90, the actual inflation rate accelerated well above the rate expected by most people.

Now imagine that at the beginning of the year, everyone expects zero inflation and savers are offered an interest rate of 3 percent, but at the end of the year, the price of goods jumps by 6 percent. Savers' hopes have been dashed, because their savings have been eroded by an **unanticipated inflation.**

Unanticipated inflation occurs when the actual inflation rate *(p)* differs from the expected (or anticipated) inflation rate (p^e).

When actual inflation (p = 6 percent in the example) differs from expected inflation (p^e = 0 in the example), the actual real interest rate differs from that which was expected. In the example a 3 percent real interest rate was expected (r^e = 3), but after the fact *(ex post)* the actual real interest *(r)* turned out to be much less:

General Form   Numerical Example

$$r = i - p \qquad\qquad r = 3 - 6 = -3 \qquad\qquad (12.6)$$

Deflation Hurts Debtors.   The basic case against unanticipated inflation, then, is that it redistributes income from creditors (savers) to debtors without their knowledge or consent. Conversely, an unanticipated deflation does just the opposite, redistributing income from debtors to creditors. Throughout history, farmers have been an important group of debtors who have been badly hurt by unanticipated deflation. The interest income of savers hardly fell at all between 1929 and 1933, but farmers, badly hurt by a precipitous decline in farm prices, saw their nominal income fall by two-thirds, from $6.2 to $2.1 billion. Because their nominal income fell by so much but their nominal interest payments did not fall, many farmers were unable to afford to purchase seed, fertilizer, and other necessities. As a result, many lost their farms through foreclosures of their mortgages.

Gainers from Surprise Inflation.   Clearly, all savers lose from a surprise inflation. Who gains? The gainers from unanticipated inflation are those who are heavily in debt but have few financial assets, owning mainly physical assets whose prices rise with inflation. Private individuals who have just purchased houses with small down payments are among the classic gainers from an unanticipated inflation.

Interest Rates, Expected Inflation, and the Fisher Effect

Irving Fisher (1867–1947)
Fisher, a pioneering mathematical economist, developed theories on interest rates, intertemporal choice, and money and prices. His work forms the basis of much of today's macroeconomics.

We have previously defined the expected real interest rate (r^e) as the nominal interest rate *(i)* minus the expected inflation rate (p^e). The same relation can be rearranged to show that the nominal interest rate is the sum of the expected real interest rate and the expected inflation rate:

$$i = r^e + p^e \qquad\qquad (12.7)$$

Thus the nominal interest rate can rise either if the expected real interest rate rises or if the expected inflation rate rises.[6] Among a group of nations that

---

[6]The *IS-LM* model of Chapter 4 showed how real output and the real interest rate were determined. Recall that in the *IS-LM* model the real interest rate rises as a result of any event that shifts the *IS* curve to the right (higher government spending, lower tax rates, etc.) or any event that shifts the *LM* curve to the left (a reduction in the supply of money or an increase in the demand for money).

have roughly the same expected real interest rate, we would expect those that have a history of rapid inflation to have high nominal interest rates. This relation between expected inflation and the nominal and real interest rate is called the **Fisher equation,** so named for the famous Yale University economist Irving Fisher (1867–1947).[7] The implication that a one percentage point increase in the expected inflation rate causes a one percentage point increase in the nominal interest rate is called the **Fisher effect.**[8]

The **Fisher equation** states that the nominal interest rate equals the expected inflation rate plus the expected real interest rate.

If expectations are accurate in the long run $(p^e = p)$, then the Fisher equation can be combined with the growth rate version of the quantity equation (12.3) to show how growth in the money supply affects the nominal interest rate in the long run:

$$i = r^e + m^s + v - y \qquad (12.8)$$

The **Fisher effect** predicts that a one percentage point increase in the expected inflation rate will raise the nominal real interest rate by one percentage point, leaving the expected real interest rate unaffected.

According to the Fisher analysis, the expected real interest rate (r^e), velocity growth (v), and output growth (y) are all unaffected by a change in monetary growth (m^s). This implies that a one percentage point increase in the growth rate of the money supply raises the nominal interest rate by one percentage point.

The Fisher analysis predicts that nations with rapid monetary growth will experience both rapid inflation and high nominal interest rates.

12-4 The Government Budget Constraint and the Inflation Tax

We are now ready to investigate the third reason cited above to explain why policymakers sometimes allow excessive growth in the money supply. This reason is simple—government spending must be financed by some combination of tax revenues, bond creation, or money creation. When there are obstacles to raising sufficient tax revenue and when bond financing is not possible, the government has no option other than money creation, that is, turning on the printing press.

A household must withdraw its savings or borrow if its expenditures exceed its income; the same is true of the government. The options open to the government for financing its expenditures are summarized in the **government budget constraint.** This divides government spending into two parts, spending on goods and services (G) and spending on interest payments (iB), where i is the nominal interest rate on government bonds and B is the dollar amount of government bonds outstanding. Government revenue sources are tax revenue net of transfer payments (T), the issuance of additional bonds (ΔB), and the issuance of additional government monetary liabilities (ΔH).

The **government budget constraint** relates government spending to the three sources available to finance that spending: tax revenue, creation of bonds, and creation of money.

---

[7]Fisher also popularized other important ideas in economics, including the theory that deflation feeds on itself by cutting the buying power of debtors, e.g., farmers in the Great Depression.

[8]More sophisticated analyses show that an increase in the inflation rate tends to reduce the real interest rate, so that the nominal interest rate does not rise one-for-one with the inflation rate. This is sometimes called the "Mundell effect," stemming from a famous paper by Robert Mundell, "Inflation and Real Interest," *Journal of Political Economy,* vol. 71 (June 1963), pp. 280–83.

Government monetary liabilities, which consist of currency held by the public and bank reserves, are called high-powered money and are abbreviated *H*. Both *B* and *H* are part of the government debt; the only difference is that bonds pay interest and high-powered money does not.

The Government Budget Constraint Equation

The government budget constraint can be expressed in a simple formula:

$$\underbrace{G - T}_{\text{basic deficit}} + \frac{iB}{P} = \frac{\Delta B}{P} + \frac{\Delta H}{P} \tag{12.9}$$

Here $G - T$ is called the basic deficit, that is, the deficit that the government would run excluding its interest payments on outstanding bonds. In the last few years in the United States, the federal government has run both a basic deficit and a basic surplus. Compare the following two situations—in the first the government ran a basic deficit, while in the second it ran a basic surplus, that is, a negative basic deficit. As in equation (12.9) above, the data are expressed in real terms (in 1992 prices):

	Basic Deficit	+	Interest Cost	=	Total Deficit
1992	91.0	+	199.4	=	290.4
1996	−122.0	+	219.8	=	97.8

Stated another way, the total federal deficit in 1996 was more than accounted for by total interest costs, which far outweighed the basic surplus in all other categories of federal revenue and expenditure (a negative deficit of $ −122 billion is, of course, the same as a surplus of $ + 122 billion). However, even if the federal government runs a basic surplus, as in 1996, the total budget deficit that must be financed is the amount of the total deficit, $97.8 billion in the right-hand column.

Bond Creation Versus Money Creation

The right-hand side of equation (12.9) shows the two methods available to finance the total government budget deficit. These are the issuance of additional government bonds, represented by ΔB, and the issuance of additional high-powered money, represented by ΔH. When the government raises *H*, the total nominal money supply *(M)* tends to increase.

An increase in *H* raises aggregate demand more than an increase in *B*, because a higher *H* raises the money supply and eliminates the crowding out effect of Chapter 4. Because a deficit financed by *H* is more stimulative to the economy, the government may want to finance its budget deficit by issuing more *H* when the economy is weak and by issuing more *B* when the economy is strong.

In the United States the size of the government deficit is determined by the administration and Congress, while the choice between bond and money creation is made by the Federal Reserve. Since the Fed controls *ΔH*, and since there is a large, well-organized market for government bonds, the Fed can respond to a larger government deficit by raising ΔH, reducing ΔH, or leaving ΔH unchanged. However, not every nation is able to choose between bond and monetary finance of government deficits. Developed nations like the United States, Japan, Canada, and the more prosperous European nations have sophisticated capital markets where the government can sell bonds. But less developed nations lack these markets, so their governments have little latitude to finance their government deficits by selling bonds. As a result, in many countries a higher government deficit *automatically* requires raising ΔH, which boosts the growth rate of the money supply and (according to equation 12.3) the rate of inflation.

Effects of Inflation

Inflation may seem to aggravate the government's problem of financing its basic deficit, since according to the Fisher effect, inflation raises the nominal interest rate (i) that appears on the left-hand side of (12.9). However, inflation also eases the government's problem. This is not evident in equation (12.9), where the inflation rate (p) does not appear. However, we can slightly rearrange (12.9) by multiplying the first term on the right-hand side by B/B and the second term by H/H. This converts (12.9) into:

$$G - T + \frac{iB}{P} = \frac{\Delta BB}{BP} + \frac{\Delta HH}{HP} \qquad (12.10)$$

The reason for this step may seem unclear, since the inflation rate (p) still does not appear in (12.10). But $(\Delta BB/BP)$ is the percentage change in bonds $(\Delta B/B)$ times the amount of real bonds outstanding (B/P), and $(\Delta HH/HP)$ is the percentage change in high-powered money $(\Delta H/H)$ times the amount of real high-powered money (H/P) outstanding. Clearly, if B/P and H/P are to remain stable, then the percentage growth rate of B, represented by a lower-case b, and the growth rate of H, designated by a lowercase h, will each have to equal the inflation rate (p):

$$\Delta B/B = b = \Delta H/H = h = p \qquad (12.11)$$

This equation says simply that the growth rate of bonds (b) and the growth rate of high-powered money (h) equals the rate of inflation. If that is true, then the real value of bonds (B/P) and the real value of high-powered money (H/P) will remain fixed. (This criterion is chosen simply to prevent the B/P and H/P ratios from growing without limit.)

Our aim is to determine the nature of the government's budget constraint that would keep the real value of bonds and high-powered money fixed. Since equation (12.11) gives the condition $(b = h = p)$ that will allow this situation to persist, we need to substitute the inflation rate (p) into equation (12.10), replacing the term there for the growth rate of bonds $(\Delta B/B)$ and also replacing the term for the growth rate of high-powered money $(\Delta H/H)$. In arriving at this final statement of the government budget constraint, we also move the term representing real interest payments (iB/P) from the left-hand side of equation (12.10) to the right-hand side of equation (12.12):

$$G - T \quad = \quad \frac{pH}{P} \quad - \quad \frac{(i - p)B}{P} \qquad (12.12)$$

basic deficit = seignorage — real interest
or on bonds
inflation tax

The first term on the right-hand side of equation (12.12), namely *(pH/P)*, represents the inflation rate times real high-powered money, that is, the revenue that the government receives when it creates just enough *H* to maintain fixed the real quantity of high-powered money *(H/P)*. This revenue that the government gets from inflation is called **seignorage;** from the point of view of private households and firms that must add to their nominal quantity of *H* enough to keep real *H/P* constant, this same revenue is called the **inflation tax.**

Stated simply, if *pH/P* were the only term on the right-hand side of equation (12.12), it would indicate the amount of the deficit that the government could run by creating the right amount of nominal high-powered money *(H)* that would be consistent with keeping the real quantity of high-powered money constant. If the inflation rate is not zero, then this amount is not zero, and the government can run a deficit and still maintain real high-powered money constant. Subsequently we will see that the inflation tax is a cost of inflation to households, the exact counterpart of the benefit that inflation provides to the government.

Inflation does not eliminate the government's obligation to pay interest on its outstanding bonds held by private households and firms. But the second right-hand term *[(i − p)B/P]* in equation (12.12) illustrates that the government only has to worry about paying the *real* interest expense of servicing the bonds. While it pays bond holders the nominal interest rate *(i)*, bond holders have to give part of *i* back to the government to purchase sufficient additional bonds to keep their real bond holdings *(B/P)* constant.

To see how this works in an example, imagine that we start with $100 of bonds, a 5 percent inflation rate per year, an 8 percent nominal interest rate, and a 3 percent real interest rate. The government must pay $8 in interest. But, to keep the real quantity of bonds *(B/P)* constant, the government sells $5 in new bonds to the public, raising the value of outstanding bonds to $105. The government's net interest expense is just $3 (the real interest rate of 3 percent times the original $100 of bonds). Why? Because the government *pays* $8 in interest but *receives* $5 as a payment by the public for the new bonds.[9]

Thus the government benefits from inflation in two ways. First, it obtains an extra source of revenue, called seignorage or the inflation tax. The government can then lower ordinary taxes or increase spending more than it could otherwise. Second, the government may gain if inflation raises the nominal interest rate by less than inflation itself. Sharp increases of inflation, particularly such as those during the oil shock periods of the 1970s, are often accompanied by an increase in the nominal interest rate of less than one-for-one, thus reducing the real interest rate (see Figure 1-10 on p. 19). And, as shown in equation (12.12), it is the real interest rate that matters for government finance.

Seignorage is the revenue the government receives from inflation and is equal to the inflation rate times real high-powered money.

The **inflation tax** is the revenue the government receives from inflation and is the same as seignorage, but viewed from the perspective of households.

---

[9]To simplify the presentation, both equation (12.12) and the numerical example in this paragraph neglect the taxation of interest earnings, which further reduces the government's net real interest expense.

SELF-TEST   Assume that after centuries of a zero budget deficit and a zero debt, the nation of Abstinia runs a one-year deficit equal to 1 percent of GDP, which it finances by creating H/P equal to 1 percent of GDP. If inflation over the next decade occurs at 5 percent per year, what must be true of the basic deficit and the level of H for Abstinia to end the decade with the same level of H/P equal to 1 percent of GDP?

12-5 Starting and Stopping a Hyperinflation

We have already defined hyperinflation as an inflation rate of 1000 percent or more per year. If an inflation of 1000 percent per year were to occur in the United States, a Big Mac would increase in price from around $2.50 to $27.50! Clearly, such an inflation rate would be disruptive if wages and salaries did not grow as rapidly, and if interest rates on savings accounts were less than the inflation rate.

As shown in Table 12-1, in 1986–90 four of the listed countries experienced annual inflation rates that averaged over 1000 percent per year. In all of those countries inflation was more rapid than it had been in the previous period. In fact, all of these countries (excepting Argentina) had inflation rates below 100 percent in the first period shown, 1975–80.

In the most recent period (1990–95) three of these countries—Brazil, Nicaragua, and Peru—continued to experience annual inflation rates above 1000 percent, while in Argentina the inflation rate during the most recent period fell to 421 percent per year. Not shown in the table is that Argentina's poor inflation performance all occurred in 1990–91. In the twelve months ending in March 1997, Argentina's inflation rate was only 1 percent, an incredible improvement. Brazil, which had an inflation rate of over 2000 percent per year as recently as 1994, achieved an inflation rate in the year ending March 1997, of only 9 percent, an even more remarkable achievement.

Since there are more than 100 countries for which records are available, the fact that only five countries experienced inflation rates greater than 1000 percent per year over the periods shown in Table 12-1 suggests that hyperinflations are unusual events. But, like the Great Depression of the 1930s, such unusual events are nevertheless worth studying for what they can teach us

Table 12-1   **Annual Rates of Inflation in Selected High Inflation Countries, 1975–95**

	1975–80	1980–86	1986–90	1990–95
Argentina	206	300	1192	421
Bolivia	16	1969	68	13
Brazil	48	142	1056	1548
Israel	61	177	24	14
Mexico	20	61	76	19
Nicaragua	18	150	4811	1749
Peru	46	95	2342	1341
Poland	6	29	180	129

Source: International Monetary Fund, *International Financial Statistics,* February 1997.

about macroeconomic behavior, and because the memory of these events may continue to influence economic theories and the beliefs of policymakers.

How a Hyperinflation Begins

Wage indexation calls for an automatic increase in the wage rate in response to an increase in a price index. It is the same as cost of living agreements (see Section 17-9).

What factors cause a hyperinflation to take off?[10] The first factor is familiar from Chapter 8. There we learned that accommodation of an adverse supply shock by more rapid nominal GDP growth can cause inflation to accelerate. What converts a mild acceleration into a hyperinflation is frequent (e.g., monthly) **wage indexation.** Such indexation sets off a rapid inflationary spiral in which wage indexation leads to wage increases, which set off further price increases, which make a nation's goods less attractive to foreigners, in turn reducing the demand for its currency and causing a depreciation of the exchange rate, which in turn raises import prices and acts as a further supply shock. For instance, Argentina, Brazil, and Israel all had experienced relatively rapid inflation in the late 1970s and had in place systems involving frequent wage indexation. This system facilitated the countries' transition to more rapid inflation in the 1980s (although Israel never reached the hyperinflation stage). The combination of supply shocks, monetary accommodation, and frequent wage indexation is an "unholy trinity" that can lead to hyperinflation. In a hyperinflation, wage indexation occurs more frequently, aggravating the destructive power of the unholy trinity.

The other classic cause of hyperinflation is deficit financing, particularly as a result of wars (when government spending rises far more than revenues from conventional taxes). Hyperinflations do not generally occur while wars are being fought, since price controls are often used to suppress the inflationary pressure caused by deficit financing (a situation called "repressed inflation").[11] But when price controls are lifted after wars, the consequence of deficit finance can cause an explosion of monetary growth. Classic postwar hyperinflations far exceeded the rate of 1000 percent per year, or 22 percent per month, that defines a hyperinflation. The average *monthly* inflation rate during the German hyperinflation of 1922–23 was 322 percent, while the "mother of all hyperinflations" occurred in Hungary between August 1945 and July 1946, when the average monthly inflation rate was 19,800 percent!

In thinking about hyperinflations, we should not be satisfied with the simple conclusion that a supply shock or a government budget deficit causes hyperinflation, as if the supply shock or budget deficit were totally exogenous. Instead, the essence of a hyperinflation is its cumulative dynamic character, best characterized as a vicious circle. Hyperinflation can create continuous supply shocks if there is a flight from a nation's currency, by causing a real exchange rate depreciation. Hyperinflation can cause the real budget deficit to worsen by giving citizens a strong incentive to delay tax payments as long as possible. Government must then finance the growing budget deficit by an ever-increasing rate of monetary growth. The labor market also adapts to hyperinflation by increasing the frequency of wage indexation, pouring more fuel on the inflationary fire.

---

[10]This section summarizes several of the important conclusions of the Dornbusch et al. source cited in footnote 2.

[11]However, during the U.S. Civil War prices doubled in the North and toward the end of the war rose at a near-hyperinflationary rate in the South.

How to End a Hyperinflation

The steps a government must take to end a hyperinflation are sometimes called a stabilization strategy. The key ingredient is to achieve a sharp reduction in the budget deficit, by cutting government expenditures and subsidies and by raising taxes. In countries where tax evasion is a tradition, this fiscal reform may involve shifting to a broad-based tax that is easy to enforce, like the value-added tax.[12] At least in the short run, it is necessary to cut through the wage-price spiral by introducing some type of controls on wages, often called an **incomes policy.** This policy may involve reducing the frequency of wage indexation or obtaining an agreement between firms and workers to reduce real wages.

Incomes policy is an attempt by policymakers to moderate increases in wages and other income, either by persuasion or by legal rules.

One by one, the nations that have experienced hyperinflation have achieved successful stabilizations, including Bolivia in 1985, Israel in 1986, Mexico in 1989, Argentina in 1991–92, and Brazil in 1995–96. The successive failures of past attempts at reform, particularly in the cases of Argentina and Brazil, suggest that stopping a hyperinflation is a complex and difficult task. Much depends on the **credibility** of the government, that is, the public's belief that budget deficits and monetary growth are really going to stop. It may take several dramatic actions all at once to achieve credibility. The monumental achievement of stopping inflation in Argentina in 1991 required a drastic plan that combined every possible ingredient—fiscal correction, suspension of indexation, a fixed exchange rate, and international support. Since Brazil's achievement of relatively low inflation is quite recent, it remains to be seen whether its stabilization plan will be successful, as has been the case in most of the other nations that have experienced very rapid inflation.

Credibility is the extent to which households and firms believe that an announced monetary or fiscal policy will actually be implemented and maintained as announced.

12-6   Costs of a Fully Anticipated Inflation: Creeping Inflation Versus Hyperinflation

As we learned in Section 12-3, the key distinction in understanding the costs of inflation is between surprise and fully anticipated inflation. If a sudden upsurge of inflation occurs, as in the United States during the supply shock era of the 1970s and early 1980s, then it is likely to be a surprise. We have already seen in Section 12-3 that such an inflation is likely to benefit debtors and hurt savers.

However, the effects of a fully anticipated inflation are quite different. If interest rates adjust, so that the real interest rate is unaffected by inflation, then the main cost of inflation relates to the reduced use of money, particularly currency and those types of checking and savings accounts that pay relatively low interest rates. In this section we first look at the costs of creeping (mild) anticipated inflation, like that experienced by the United States in the last 15 years. Then we turn to the more serious costs of an anticipated hyperinflation like those that have occurred in several Latin American countries.

---

[12]A value-added tax, which does not exist in the United States, is common in Europe and was introduced in Canada in 1991. This tax has the same effect as a universal sales tax on all goods and services and is collected on the value that is added at each stage of production, that is, a firm's sales minus its expenditures on materials and supplies (which have already been taxed).

THE WIZARD OF OZ AS A MONETARY ALLEGORY

The famous movie *The Wizard of Oz,* originally produced in 1939 and an annual television ritual for the last three decades, is based on a 1900 book *(The Wonderful Wizard of Oz)* by L. Frank Baum. Recently economists have recognized that the book is an allegory for the major economic and political issues in the late nineteenth century United States, the battle over free silver, which involved a debate about whether deflation or inflation was desirable.[a]

The three decades after the Civil War (1865–95) were characterized by a steady deflation that reduced the overall price level by about 40 percent and the price of farm products by about 55 percent. As we have learned in this chapter, inflation benefits

borrowers at the expense of savers, and deflation does the opposite, benefiting savers at the expense of borrowers. Some of the losers from the 1865–95 deflation were farmers (who not only were debtors but were particularly hard hit by the decline in farm prices).

The main cause of the deflation was slow monetary growth, which in turn was due to the gold standard (which essentially limited the growth in the money supply to growth in the supply of gold). Farmers and other borrowers supported the free coinage of silver, which, if adopted, would have boosted the money supply and, perhaps, converted the deflation into an inflation. The gold standard was seen as benefitting the eastern United States, home of the creditors and savers.

What are some of the references in the book? Dorothy represents America; her dog Toto represents the Prohibition Party (the name is short for "teetotaler"); and Oz is the abbreviation for ounce (as in ounce of gold or silver). Dorothy's house lands on the Wicked Witch of the East (stronghold of the gold standard), who dries up completely, leaving only her silver shoes (symbolizing the triumph of silver, but changed to ruby slippers in the movie); the yellow brick road (symbol of the gold standard) leads to the Emerald City (Washington, D.C.). The Scarecrow is the western farmer; the Tin Woodsman is the workingman whose joints are rusted due to unemployment in the depression of the 1890s; and the Cowardly Lion is William Jennings Bryan, leader of the free-silver movement (a lion, as the symbol of one of America's greatest orators; a coward, because he later retreated from support of free silver after economic conditions improved in the late 1890s). In the end the Wicked Witch of the West melts when Dorothy pours a bucket of water on her, symbolizing the power of water (rain) to solve the problems of the western farmers, and the Wizard is unmasked as an ordinary man who, like a dishonest politician, has been fooling the people.

[a]This box is a very brief summary of Hugh Rockoff, "The 'Wizard of Oz' as a Monetary Allegory," *Journal of Political Economy,* vol. 98 (August 1990), pp. 739–60. Readers interested in the full richness of the references in the *Wizard of Oz* should consult this fascinating article.

Costs of a Fully Anticipated Creeping Inflation

What are the costs to society of allowing inflation to continue at a steady moderate rate like 3, 5, or 10 percent, as long as everyone accurately anticipates that rate? Our previous analysis of the effects of anticipated inflation enumerated five conditions that must be satisfied for inflation to have no effect. The first of these was accurate anticipation, which we will assume throughout this section. The other four conditions are (2) no one holds money earning any interest rate below the market interest rate, (3) inflation raises the nominal interest rate by 1 percent for each 1 percent of inflation, (4) only real interest income is taxable and the real cost of borrowing is tax deductible, and (5) inflation causes no changes in relative prices. Each of these conditions is violated in the real world, and the following discussion of the effects of anticipated inflation is organized into categories corresponding to the violation of these conditions—the effects of money holding, effects of nonadjustment of nominal interest rates, effects of the tax system, and effects of inflation on relative prices. This section examines the effects of inflation on money holding and the inconvenience that inflation creates to money holders, as well as the relationship between inflation and changes in relative prices. In the next section we examine the effects of regulations that prevent the adjustment of nominal interest rates and effects of the tax system.

Welfare Cost of Lower Real Money Balances

The market rate of interest is not paid on money for three main reasons. First, currency pays no interest. Second, banks earn no interest on the reserves (deposits) they are required to keep at the Federal Reserve banks, so banks cannot afford to pay the market rate of interest on deposits. Third, bank deposits enjoy the protection of deposit insurance, and customers are willing to accept lower interest rates on deposits because they are protected from loss by deposit insurance. The fact that the market rate of interest is not paid on money has several consequences for society.

The **extra convenience services** of money are the services provided by holding one extra dollar of money instead of bonds.

People Demand Money for Its Convenience Services.   The main reason that a fully anticipated creeping inflation imposes welfare costs on society is that people do not desire money for itself, but rather for the **extra convenience services** that it provides. Inflation causes people to hold less money, so they suffer inconvenience. Money provides convenience to the consumer because purchases can be made instantly. If no money were held (that is, no currency and no checking accounts), then the consumer would have to suffer the inconvenience of going to the bank to make a savings deposit withdrawal, or—even less convenient—to sell a stock or bond before the purchase could be made.

People hold currency even though it pays no interest. The reason they are willing to hold currency paying zero interest, instead of holding a savings certificate paying 5 percent interest, *must be* that the money provides them with at least 5 percent more convenience services than the certificate. How is this related to inflation? When the inflation rate increases, the nominal interest rate on all assets other than currency tends to increase. If the inflation rate rose by 5 percent, then the nominal interest rate on certificates would tend to rise from 5 percent to 10 percent, that is, to a rate 5 percent higher than before. Thus people would cut back on their money holdings until the extra convenience services of money rose from 5 to 10 percent. They would hold less cash in their pockets, retain cash only for those expenditures where only cash is accepted (as for taxi rides and bus fares), and would hold less cash for nonessential purposes.

The "Shoe-Leather Cost" of Inflation.   The effect of higher inflation and higher interest rates in causing people to hold less cash is sometimes called the "shoe-leather cost" of inflation. Why? Higher interest rates cause people to hold less cash in their pockets at any given moment, so they must go more often to the bank to obtain cash by making withdrawals from savings accounts and other interest-paying assets. The inconvenience and loss of productive time that people suffer while making these trips to the bank figuratively wear out their shoes, hence the saying shoe-leather cost.

Financial deregulation has allowed the banking system to pay interest on most types of checking accounts. Thus, it is only currency (and the nonpayment of interest on bank reserves at the Federal Reserve banks) that accounts for money's shoe-leather costs. Taking account of the payment of interest on bank checking accounts, it has been estimated that the value of convenience services lost from a 10 percent inflation in the United States is just 0.25 percent of GDP, or $20 billion at 1997 prices. This loss is very small in comparison to the costs of the recession that would be needed to eliminate permanently a 10 percent fully anticipated inflation, which has been estimated at 6 percent of GDP per 1 percent permanent reduction of inflation, or 60 percent of GDP for a 10 percent permanent reduction of inflation. And it could be reduced even further if the Federal Reserve System paid interest on bank reserves.

Costs of an Anticipated Hyperinflation.   The inconvenience cost of inflation becomes much larger in a hyperinflation, like that which occurred in Germany in 1922–23. In 1919 a farmer sold a piece of land for 80,000 marks as a nest egg for old age. All he got for the money a few years later was a woolen sweater. Elderly Germans can still recall the terrible days in 1923.

> People were bringing money to the bank in cardboard boxes and laundry baskets. As we no longer could count it, we put the money on scales and weighed it. I can still see my brothers coming home Saturdays with heaps of paper money. When the shops reopened after the weekend they got no more than a breakfast roll for it. Many got drunk on their pay because it was worthless on Monday.[13]

Interest Rates and Taxation

For fully anticipated inflation to have no impact on saving and investment decisions, a number of assumptions must be made. One of these, that money pays the market interest rate, is clearly violated in the real world. We have already analyzed the effect of zero interest on money—a shoe-leather cost of anticipated creeping inflation and, in hyperinflation, a major flight from the

---

[13]Alice Segert, "When Inflation Buried Germany," *Chicago Tribune,* November 30, 1974.

use of money, which is highly inefficient because people devote so much time to reducing their real monetary holdings.

Three other assumptions are violated as well in the real world, and these violations create additional costs of a fully anticipated inflation.

We previously assumed that all assets pay the market interest rate, but in fact checking accounts pay less, adding to the shoe-leather cost.

We previously assumed that inflation raises the nominal interest rate one-for-one, but in many episodes the nominal interest rate has failed to rise sufficiently, creating a redistribution away from savers similar to that in a surprise inflation.

We previously assumed that only real interest is taxable. But in many nations nominal interest is taxable, so an increase in the inflation rate (and nominal interest rate) raises tax payments. This adds to the damage for savers and the benefit for borrowers (who can deduct the interest paid).

Summary: Costs of Inflation

The main cost of a surprise inflation is a redistribution from savers (or creditors) to borrowers (or debtors). This occurs when an upsurge of inflation is not anticipated in advance. Similarly, a surprise decline in the inflation rate creates a redistribution from borrowers (like farmers) to savers. The main costs of an anticipated inflation are the shoe-leather cost (cost of lost time) in reducing holdings of real money balances to a bare minimum; in some extreme hyperinflations this time cost has been enormous, as people have given up on the use of money and resorted to barter. Other possible costs of anticipated inflation are changes in relative prices, and a redistribution from savers to borrowers due to the possible failure of nominal interest rates to rise one-for-one with inflation, as well as the fact that some countries tax nominal rather than real interest.

SELF-TEST   If financial deregulation occurs and allows payment of interest on checking accounts, what effect does this event have on the shoe-leather costs of fully anticipated inflation?

12-7 Indexation and Other Reforms to Reduce the Costs of Inflation

There is a strong case for the institution of reforms that can cut substantially the costs imposed by inflation. These reforms fall into three categories: the elimination of government regulations that redistribute income from savers to borrowers, the creation of an indexed bond to give savers a secure place to save, and a restatement of tax laws to eliminate the effects of inflation on real tax burdens.

Decontrol of Financial Institutions

Much of the distortion caused by the U.S. inflation of the 1970s resulted from federal government-imposed interest rate ceilings on commercial banks and savings institutions. Financial deregulation solved this problem. By 1985 all regulations on the payment of interest on checking, savings, and time-deposit accounts had been lifted. Thus, inflation in the future will not have as great a redistributive effect as in the past, since all individuals, rich and poor alike, will be able to receive a return close to the market rate of interest on their checking and savings accounts.

Even if all checking and savings accounts paid a nominal interest rate that included a full inflation premium, savers would still suffer an erosion of purchasing power on their pocket cash. Inflation still causes people to incur shoe-leather costs as they work harder to keep their cash balances at a minimum.

Indexed Bonds

Even though the lifting of government interest-rate ceilings on savings and checking accounts has substantially cut the costs of inflation, many economists recommended that the government issue an indexed bond that would fully protect savers against any unexpected movements in the inflation rate. Finally, in early 1997 the U.S. government responded to these recommendations by issuing an indexed bond.

An **indexed bond** pays a fixed real interest rate; its nominal interest rate is equal to this real interest rate plus the actual inflation rate.

An **indexed bond** protects savers from unexpected movements in the inflation rate by paying a fixed real interest rate (r_0) plus the actual inflation rate (p). Thus the saver's nominal interest rate would be

General Form	Numerical Example
$i = r_0 + p$	(a) $3 = 3 + 0$
	(b) $13 = 3 + 10$

In numerical example (a), savers would receive a 3 percent return if the inflation rate were zero. If inflation suddenly accelerated to 10 percent, as in example (b), savers would find that the nominal return (i) rose to 13 percent, and they would be just as well off as if there had been no inflation.

Indexed Tax System

Another important reform made effective in 1985 is the partial indexation of the personal income tax system. This now raises the dollar amounts of tax credits, exemptions, standard deductions, and tax rate brackets each year by the amount of inflation that has been experienced. Without an indexed tax system, inflation would raise individual incomes and push taxpayers into higher tax brackets.

But the government must do more than index credits, exemptions, deductions, and tax brackets in order to achieve a fully inflation-neutral tax system. It must end present rules that discriminate against savers and favor borrowers by taxing real rather than nominal interest and capital gains. Just as savers should be taxed only on real interest income and real capital gains, borrowers should be allowed to deduct from their taxable income only the real portion of the interest they pay on loans. These reforms would eliminate the present effect of inflation in the U.S. tax system of discouraging saving and encouraging borrowing and spending.

INTERNATIONAL PERSPECTIVE

The Indexed Bond Has Arrived

Following the lead of Canada, the United Kingdom, and other countries, the U.S. Treasury has introduced inflation-indexed bonds to investors. These bonds protect the savings of investors from being eroded by unanticipated increases in the inflation rate.

Unlike a conventional bond, an indexed bond promises to pay its holder a fixed real rate of return. If the inflation rate were always accurately anticipated, then there would be no difference in the real return on a conventional bond and an indexed bond. But an indexed bond maintains its promised real rate of return even if inflation suddenly accelerates by 5, 10, or even 20 percent relative to the inflation rate that was expected when the saver purchased the bond.

Beginning in early 1997, the U.S. Treasury started to issue a 10-year indexed bond. It is structured like a similar bond available since 1991 in Canada. Semiannual interest payments will be calculated by adjusting the principal for inflation (using the CPI) and applying the fixed real interest rate (determined at the auction at which the bonds were first issued) to the inflation-adjusted principal. The table in this box lists the main countries that have already introduced an indexed bond, the year of adoption, the inflation rate in the year prior to the introduction of the

bond, and the share of indexed bonds as a percentage of total marketable government debt. It appears that only in Israel have indexed bonds become a majority of total outstanding bonds.

The benefits for the U.S. Treasury are several. Indexed bonds could reduce the risk premium that the government must pay to savers who fear that their returns on bonds will be eroded by future unanticipated inflation. By eliminating the risk of loss from future unanticipated inflation, the Treasury should be able to reduce its average borrowing costs, thus reducing the interest component of the federal government deficit. An additional benefit is that the process of issuing indexed bonds will provide information about the inflation expectations of investors, measured as the difference in market-determined interest rates on conventional and indexed bonds of the same maturities.

A problem with the U.S. tax system is that it taxes the total nominal returns on bonds, not just the real returns. The inflation component of the return on indexed bonds will be taxed. This means that savers who purchase indexed bonds will be subject to a large tax liability if there is a surge of unanticipated inflation. For this reason, it is expected that the main demand for indexed bonds will come from tax-deferred retirement accounts.

Country of issuance	Year of adoption	Inflation rate before introduction	Indexed bonds as a % of total marketable debt
Israel	1955	12.3%	86.0%
United Kingdom	1981	14.0	15.3
Australia	1985	4.5	3.8
Canada	1991	4.8	1.2
Sweden	1994	4.4	3.2
New Zealand	1995	2.8	< 1.0

Source: Adopted from John Y. Campbell and Robert I. Shiller, "A Scorecard for Indexed Government Debt," *National Bureau of Economic Research, Working Paper No. 3587,* April 1996. Used by permission.

12-8 Why the Unemployment Rate Cannot Be Reduced to Zero

Thus far in this chapter we have concentrated on the causes and costs of inflation. The other major goal of macroeconomic policy (besides achieving as high as possible a growth rate in output per person) is to maintain the unemployment rate as low as possible. The analysis of unemployment appears to be simpler than that of inflation, because everyone agrees that more jobs are better. The only obstacle to reducing the unemployment rate to zero, according to our analysis of Chapter 8, is that too high an output ratio (which causes too low an unemployment rate) would cause the inflation rate to accelerate, thus exacerbating the costs of inflation.

In the rest of this chapter we learn some of the other reasons (besides higher inflation) why maintaining too low an unemployment rate is undesirable. There are good reasons why the overall unemployment rate is not zero, and these emerge from the efficient operation of a well-functioning economy.

Distinguishing the Types of Unemployment

Cyclical unemployment is the difference between the actual unemployment rate and the natural rate of unemployment.

The actual rate of unemployment consists of the natural rate of unemployment, estimated to be roughly 5.5 percent in the United States in the late 1990s, and **cyclical unemployment,** which is simply the difference between the actual unemployment rate and the natural rate of unemployment. When the actual rate of unemployment is relatively high, say 7.7 percent as in mid-1992, then cyclical unemployment is roughly 2.0 percent, the difference between the actual and natural rates of unemployment. Cyclical unemployment can be negative when the actual rate of unemployment is below the natural rate, as occurred in October 1997, with an actual unemployment rate of 4.7 percent.

Turnover unemployment is another name for frictional unemployment. It is one of the two components of the natural rate of unemployment.

Why is the natural rate of unemployment a number like 5.5 percent, rather than zero? When the economy is operating at the natural rate of unemployment, it experiences two types of unemployment. One is called **turnover unemployment,** sometimes also called frictional unemployment. Turnover unemployment occurs in the normal process of job search by individuals who have voluntarily quit their jobs, are entering the labor force for the first time, or are reentering the labor force. Any economy can expect to have a moderate amount of turnover unemployment, and we shall see that there are good reasons for the United States to have more turnover unemployment than some other countries.

Mismatch unemployment is another name for structural unemployment. It is one of the two components of the natural rate of unemployment.

Mismatch unemployment is the second component of the natural rate of unemployment. Sometimes also called structural unemployment, it occurs when there is a mismatch between the skill or location requirements of job vacancies and the present skills or location of members of the labor force. For an unemployed individual, mismatch unemployment tends to last much longer than turnover unemployment, since more time is required for people to learn new skills or to move to new locations.

To summarize, the actual unemployment rate is divided up into cyclical, turnover, and mismatch unemployment. When the actual unemployment rate is equal to the natural rate of unemployment, then cyclical unemployment is zero and all unemployment is accounted for by the turnover and mismatch components. Cyclical unemployment can be eliminated by stimulative monetary policy that expands the economy when cyclical unemployment is positive and by restrictive monetary policy that reduces aggregate demand when cyclical unemployment is negative. In the remainder of this chapter we are concerned with the remaining two types of unemployment, turnover and mismatch, and the factors that tend to make them high or low.

12-9   Sources of Mismatch Unemployment

Vacancies and Unemployment in an Imaginary Economy

We can better understand the mismatch component of the natural unemployment rate (U^N) if we think of an imaginary society in which U^N is zero. All jobs are completely identical in their skill requirements, and all are located at exactly the same place. All workers are completely identical, with skill requirements perfectly suited for the identical jobs, and all workers live in the same location as the jobs. We can imagine a 10-mile-high combined factory-office-apartment skyscraper with very fast elevators at the corner of State and Madison streets in Chicago.

In this imaginary economy it is impossible for vacancies and unemployment to exist simultaneously. Why? Imagine that initially some workers are unemployed, and that the government pursues expansive monetary and fiscal policies that stimulate aggregate demand. Additional jobs open up, but the unemployed workers are in exactly the right place and possess the right skills, so that they instantly zoom up or down the speedy elevators in the 10-mile-high skyscraper to the job's location. Each job vacancy disappears immediately, and unemployment declines.

Eventually all the unemployed will have found jobs. Any further job vacancies caused by an additional demand stimulus will not disappear because there are no available jobless people to fill them. Further aggregate demand stimulus will just expand the number of job vacancies.

Skill Differences Among Jobs Can Cause Structural Unemployment.   To be slightly more realistic, let us now assume that there are two types of jobs and workers in the 10-mile-high skyscraper, typists and computer programmers. As the economy expands, it gradually uses up its supply of trained computer programmers. Once all the computer programmers have jobs, all of the unemployment consists of jobless typists. If the government further stimulates aggregate demand, we assume that an equal number of job vacancies is created for programmers and typists. The typist vacancies disappear immediately as available typists are carried by elevator to fill the job openings. But there are no computer programmers left, and so the programmer job openings remain. *Vacancies and unemployment exist simultaneously because firms refuse to hire typists to fill programmer vacancies.* The costs of training are just too high.

In reality the actual economy is divided into numerous separate labor markets that differ in location, working conditions, and skill requirements. Any increase in aggregate spending generates job openings in some labor markets, while many people remain unemployed in other markets. Some unemployed are able to fill developing job vacancies. But others are prevented from qualifying by the cost of moving to the locations of the job openings, by the cost of acquiring the required skills, and even by the "cost of information" involved in finding out what jobs are available.

Vacancies and Upward Pressure on Wage Rates.   In the imaginary economy, with all jobs and workers alike and located at the same place, policymakers could use aggregate demand stimulus to push the unemployment rate to zero. There would be no job vacancies and no tendency for firms to boost wage rates to fill empty job slots. Thus it would be possible to experience zero unemployment without upward pressure on wages.

But in the real-world economy, with numerous separate labor markets, vacancies and unemployed workers can coexist. There may be unfilled job openings for hotel workers in Iowa, while aircraft factory workers may be unemployed in Los Angeles. In other words, structural or mismatch unemployment exists. Any attempt to use aggregate demand policy to push the total unemployment rate to zero will create numerous job vacancies for the types of skills that are in short supply and in the locations where labor is scarce. Firms will be desperate to fill the job vacancies and will boost wage rates, hoping to steal workers away from other firms. Higher wages will raise business costs and cause price increases. *Thus a situation with a low unemployment rate and lots of job vacancies maintained by rapid demand growth is one in which the inflation rate will continuously accelerate.*

Causes of and Cures for Mismatch Unemployment: Mismatch Skills

All groups in the labor force, including adult men, adult women, and teenagers, are victims of mismatch between their own skills and locations, and the skill and location requirements of available jobs. Why does this worker-job mismatch occur? We begin with causes of skill mismatch, add some suggested policy remedies, and then turn to the causes of and remedies for location mismatch.

Lack of Job Training.   Vacant jobs often have specific skill requirements. Sometimes firms are willing to train workers when the skills are specific to the particular job; for example, an administrative assistant needs to know the filing system in a particular office. But some training, for example, how to use a personal computer, is general in nature. Firms may be unwilling to train employees in general skills for fear that the employees will quit before the firm's training investment can be repaid. Yet schools may not be able to provide the training because they lack either the equipment or properly trained instructors.

Solutions for low skills fall into three basic categories—better public education, subsidies for firms to train workers, and government-financed training programs. Better public education is essential, particularly for students from disadvantaged backgrounds, since training subsidies and programs will not work if teenagers and young adults cannot read or perform arithmetic.

Inflexibility of Relative Wages.   Elementary economics teaches that a surplus of a commodity develops when its price is too high. In the same way, many economists have argued that high unemployment of some groups, particularly teenagers, signals an excessive real wage for that group. In the United States there is a uniform minimum wage for both adults and teenagers, but teenage unemployment is higher than adult unemployment, and some people have proposed a lower minimum wage for teenagers.

Discrimination.   Some employers will not hire women, minorities, or teenagers. Much discrimination stems from long-standing customs and from social pressure. We observe that most administrative assistants, telephone operators, elementary school teachers, nurses, and typists are women, and that black workers are pushed into relatively unpleasant occupations. Despite the gains of the civil rights movement and antidiscrimination legislation, less-educated blacks and women are still in many cases prevented from entering unions in blue-collar trades.

Several Western European nations have helped reduce discrimination against women by subsidizing maternity leaves and providing subsidized child care, thus allowing women with children to maintain more stable job records. A case could be made for similar subsidies in the United States. Some barriers, particularly the limitation of many blue-collar craft unions to white males, may require legal rather than economic remedies.

Causes of and Cures for Mismatch Unemployment: Mismatch Location

Often job vacancies and unemployment are very unequally distributed. Despite a prosperous economy in 1996–97, the unemployment rate in California and in parts of the Northeast United States was substantially higher than in the Midwest and much of the South.

Several solutions, other than a better employment service, have been proposed to reduce the locational source of mismatch unemployment. One suggestion is subsidies to help unemployed workers pay the costs of relocating to areas with ample job openings. Another suggestion is to establish enterprise zones, a system of tax incentives or similar incentives to induce manufacturers to move their factories to depressed areas. While the United States has little experience with such programs, several European nations have attempted to "bribe" firms to locate in depressed areas. A successful example is a new electronics area called Silicon Glen between Glasgow and Edinburgh, Scotland, but similar programs in southern Italy have been largely unsuccessful.

12-10   Turnover Unemployment and Job Search

We have now examined the sources of mismatch unemployment, one of the two components of the natural unemployment rate. A second component is turnover unemployment. What is the difference between mismatch and turnover unemployment? The barriers that stand between vacant jobs and workers unemployed due to mismatch are serious and require substantial investments in training or moving to eliminate. But the barriers that stand between vacant jobs and those unemployed due to turnover are less serious, involving the costs of job search for a relatively short period in the local community for a suitable job.

One way of differentiating mismatch and turnover unemployment is the length of unemployment episodes ("spells"). In a year like 1996 when the economy was operating close to the natural rate of unemployment, half of all weeks of unemployment occurred in spells of at least four months' duration. Thus some of the unemployed found jobs quite rapidly, in a month or two, suggesting turnover unemployment. Many other individuals took much longer, suggesting mismatch unemployment. Thus turnover and mismatch unemployment are not in conflict; both occur at the same time, to different people.

Reasons for Turnover Unemployment

As we learned in Section 2-9 on pp. 53–56, Census Bureau workers ask a number of questions in order to determine whether individual household members are unemployed. These questions allow the unemployed to be broken down into five groups:

1. Persons laid off who can expect to return to the same job.
2. Persons who have lost jobs to which they cannot expect to return.
3. Persons who have quit their jobs.
4. Reentrants who are returning to the labor force after a spell of neither working nor looking for work.
5. New entrants who have never worked at a full-time job before but are now seeking employment.

Frictional unemployment consists primarily of individuals in categories 3, 4, and 5, although reentrants and new entrants may spend a long time in futile search if their skills and location are mismatched with job vacancies.

Some reasons for unemployment are concentrated in particular demographic groups. For instance, job loss tends to be most concentrated among adult males. Reentry unemployment is felt mainly by adult females, teenagers, and college students. New entry unemployment, of course, is mainly experienced by teenagers and college-age youth.

Table 12-2 shows how the types of unemployment are divided among the major demographic groups. The month illustrated is January 1997, when the economy was operating at a rate close to its natural rate of unemployment. To simplify the table, the categories of temporary and permanent job loss are consolidated. Overall, perhaps the most striking contrast is between the large percentage of adult male unemployment caused by the "lost job" category (67.6 percent on line 1) as opposed to the small share of teenage unemployment caused by job loss (19.4 percent). Thus in a year like 1997 it would be fair to conclude that adult males experience mostly mismatch unemployment, while teenagers experience mostly turnover unemployment.

The Economics of Job Refusal.   The basic reason for turnover unemployment is explained by the theory of "search" unemployment, which develops the idea that an unemployed person may sometimes do better to refuse a job offer than accept it! Why? Imagine a teenager who quits school and begins to look for his first job. He walks down the street and soon encounters a restaurant displaying a sign "Dishwasher Wanted." An inquiry provides the

Table 12-2   **Unemployment Rates by Reason, Sex, and Age in January 1997**

	Unemployment Rate				Percentage of Group Unemployment			
	Adult Men	*Adult Women*	*Teenagers*	*All Groups*	*Adult Men*	*Adult Women*	*Teenagers*	*All Groups*
Job losers	3.7	3.7	2.1	3.0	67.6	43.2	19.4	50.8
Job leavers	0.6	0.6	1.3	0.6	10.6	12.7	7.1	10.8
Reentrants	1.1	2.0	8.6	1.9	19.9	40.0	47.8	31.8
New entrants	0.1	0.2	4.6	0.4	1.9	4.1	25.6	6.6
Total for group	5.5	6.5	16.6	5.9	100.0	100.0	100.0	100.0

Source: Bureau of Labor Statistics, *Employment and Earnings,* February 1997, Table A-29.

information that the dishwasher opening is available immediately and pays $6.00 per hour. Will the teenager accept the job without further search? Refusal may benefit the teenager if he is able to locate a job with higher pay or better working conditions.

Job search theory treats unemployment as a socially valuable, productive activity. Unemployed individuals "invest" in job search. The cost of their investment is the cost of the search itself plus the loss of wages that could be earned by accepting a job immediately. The payoff to their investment is the prospect of earning a higher wage for many months or years into the future. Because people do not always want the first available job and prefer to search, the only ways for the government to bring down turnover unemployment are (1) to provide better employment agencies that provide information that shortens the period of job search, (2) to lessen job search by reducing the motivation for quitting, reentry, and initial entry, or (3) to change the economic incentives that unnecessarily prolong the search, particularly unemployment benefits and high taxes on the income of the employed, both of which cut the net earnings of taking a job immediately rather than remaining unemployed.

Effects of Unemployment Compensation.   Some economists blame the government for making frictional unemployment higher than necessary and advocate measures to reduce the duration in weeks of an average episode (spell) of unemployment, as well as reducing the number of episodes per worker.

The incentive for temporary layoffs given by the unemployment compensation system occurs not only in recessions but also when the economy is operating at its natural rate of unemployment. The economy may be in equilibrium, with no tendency for inflation to accelerate or decelerate, yet a firm may find that its sales have dropped temporarily. The unemployment compensation system provides an incentive for the firm to adjust by laying off workers rather than by cutting hours per employee or simply by allowing inventories to grow.

SELF-TEST   Would the following events raise or lower the amount of turnover unemployment? (1) A change in rules allowing the unemployed to earn unemployment benefits for one year instead of the present six months. (2) A reduction in the personal income tax rate. (3) A decrease in the fraction of the working-age population consisting of teenagers. (4) An increase in the price of pay telephone calls.

The Human Costs of Recessions

In assessing the costs of reducing inflation by creating a temporary recession, we need to consider not only the hundreds of billions of dollars of lost output, but also the human costs of recessions. The basic difference between the costs of unemployment and inflation is that the unemployment of a household head hits the family like a hammer, whereas the costs of inflation are milder and spread more broadly across the entire population.

The human costs of unemployment are tragic. Researchers have found that with every 1 percent increase in the U.S. unemployment rate, 920 more people commit suicide, 650 commit homicide, 500 die from heart and kidney disease and cirrhosis of the liver, 4000 are admitted to state mental hospitals, and 3300 are sent to state prisons. In total, a 1 percent increase in unemployment is associated statistically with 37,000 more deaths, including 20,000 heart attacks. Unemployed workers are also more likely to experience dizziness, rapid heart beat, troubled sleep, back and neck pain, and high blood pressure.[14]

Common among the psychological costs of unemployment is a sense of being condemned to uselessness in a world that worships the useful. Just as serious are the long-term consequences. Many people have been deprived of medical insurance as a consequence of unemployment, since such insurance is a job benefit typically paid in part or wholly by employers. Physical and mental health deteriorates, and this is exacerbated by alcoholism. The health of children also suffers, particularly when parents take out their frustration and rage on their children in the form of child abuse.

All these factors taken together strengthen the case for government stabilization policies that maintain the actual unemployment rate close to the natural rate, and for a vigorous pursuit of policies to reduce turnover and mismatch unemployment in order to reduce the natural unemployment rate.

12-11 New Theories to Explain High European Unemployment

While structural and cyclical unemployment are important problems in the United States, the unemployment rate is even higher in some other countries. In Chapter 1 (p. 24) we first learned that Japan outperforms the U.S. by three measures—inflation, unemployment, and productivity growth. When Europe is compared to the United States, Europe does better on productivity growth, about the same on inflation, but worse on unemployment. As discussed in the box on the next page, the great mystery is why the natural rate of unemployment in Europe should have *quintupled* between the 1960s and 1990s, while the natural rate hardly changed at all in the United States.

The puzzle of high unemployment in Europe has stimulated an outpouring of new theories of inflation and unemployment behavior. In this brief

---

[14]Barry Bluestone and Bennett Harrison, *The Deindustrialization of America* (New York: Basic Books, 1982), Chapter 3.

INTERNATIONAL PERSPECTIVE

The Divergence of Unemployment Rates in the United States and Europe

The behavior of U.S. inflation and the output ratio seems to be well explained by the theory developed in Chapter 8. The disinflation experienced by the United States during 1982–86, the reacceleration of inflation during 1987–90, and the slowdown of inflation in 1990–93, all follow the theory's predictions.

European Unemployment in the 1980s

But the behavior of European unemployment is another story. As shown in the top frame of the figure, unemployment in Europe remained considerably above the American rate after 1983, after being much lower in the 1960s and 1970s. And, unlike the short duration of most U.S. unemployment, European unemployment is long-lasting and therefore much more serious. *In many European countries more than half of the unemployed have been out of work for more than one year.*

The accompanying table displays historical unemployment data for individual European countries. Here two remarkable facts stand out. First, the unemployment rate for the group labeled European Economic Community has increased steadily, from 2.2 percent in 1961, to 3.3 percent in 1972, to 5.7 percent in 1979, to 10.8 percent in 1986, and after an improvement in 1989,

to 10.7 percent in 1993 and 11.3 percent in 1997. Second, unemployment rates vary among the individual European countries, ranging in 1997 all the way from 4.0 percent in Norway to 21.3 percent in Spain (not shown in the table).

European Inflation and the Natural Rate Hypothesis

If the United States and Europe had the same natural rate of unemployment, then we would expect that the high level of European unemployment would have caused inflation in Europe to slow down much more than in the United States. But this did not happen. As shown in the bottom frame of the figure, between 1980 and 1986, European inflation slowed down by about the same amount as in the United States and inflation behavior during 1987–95 was almost identical in Europe and the United States. Yet according to the natural rate hypothesis, when there are no supply shocks, a steady rate of inflation occurs only when the economy is operating at its natural rate of unemployment, so Europe's natural rate must have been at or slightly above its already high actual unemployment rate in 1993–95. Thus in 1993–95 the natural rate of unemployment in Europe must have been around 11 percent. Yet inflation was steady in Europe in the early 1960s, when the actual and natural

Unemployment Rates in North America, Japan, and Europe, Selected Years, 1961–93

Country	1961	1972	1979	1986	1989	1993	1997
United States	6.7	5.5	5.8	6.9	5.2	6.7	4.9
Canada	7.1	6.2	7.4	9.5	7.5	11.1	9.4
Japan	1.4	1.4	2.1	2.8	2.3	2.5	3.1
European Economic Community	2.2	3.3	5.7	10.8	9.0	10.7	11.3
France	1.2	2.7	5.8	10.4	9.4	11.7	12.8
Germany	0.8	0.8	3.2	6.4	5.6	6.1	11.3
Italy	5.1	6.3	7.6	10.5	10.9	10.2	12.3
United Kingdom	1.5	4.0	5.0	11.2	7.2	10.3	6.0

Sources: All data for 1961–93 are OECD standardized unemployment rate definitions. Data for 1997 are estimates from IMF *World Economic Outlook*, May 1997, Table A4.

unemployment rates were just 2 percent. Thus Europe seems to be stuck at a high natural rate of unemployment of about 11 percent, more than five times higher than the 2 percent natural unemployment rate of the early 1960s. The mystery of high European unemployment can be summarized in this puzzle:

How could the natural rate of unemployment have quintupled in Europe since the early 1960s, while in the United States it hardly changed at all? This puzzle forms the basis for the debate between the hysteresis and structuralist theories as discussed in this section.

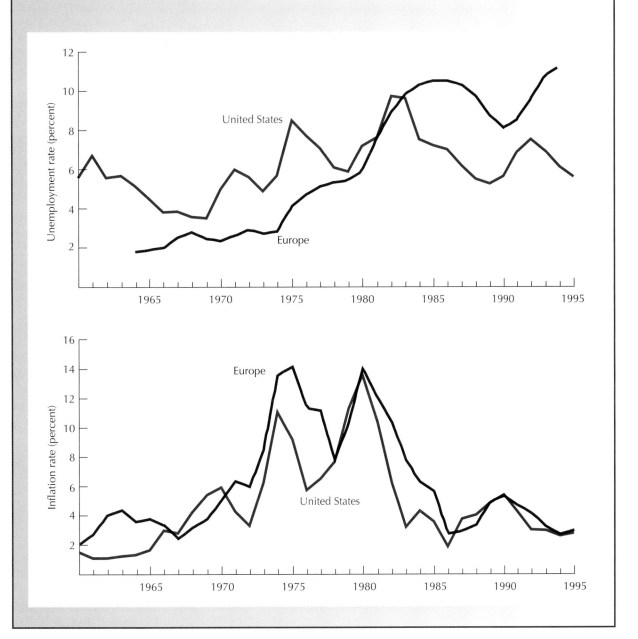

The **structuralist hypothesis** holds that European unemployment is high because of specific impediments in the operation of the economy, including excessive real wages, high unemployment benefits, excessive government spending and regulation, high marginal tax rates, regional imbalances, and others.

The **hysteresis hypothesis** holds that the natural rate of unemployment follows automatically in the path of the actual unemployment rate; if the actual rate were lowered by stimulative policy, the natural rate would also decline automatically.

introduction we look at the two main competing explanations, the **structuralist** and **hysteresis** hypotheses.[15] The structuralist hypothesis holds that European unemployment is high because specific impediments in the operation of the economy, particularly the labor market, have raised the natural unemployment rate. Among the structural causes of the high natural rate are excessive real wages, high unemployment benefits, excessive government spending and regulation, high marginal tax rates, and regional imbalances. Because the natural unemployment rate is high as a result of one or more of these causes, the actual unemployment rate cannot be reduced without either (1) an accelerating inflation or (2) changes in government policy that eliminate the structural impediments.

The **hysteresis hypothesis** holds that the natural rate of unemployment follows automatically in the path of the actual unemployment rate; if the actual rate were lowered by stimulative policy, the natural rate would automatically decline as well. The hysteresis view shares the prediction of the structuralist view, that stimulative demand policy designed to reduce the actual unemployment rate will cause inflation to accelerate. But the hysteresis view is more optimistic than the structuralist view, believing that the resulting acceleration of inflation will end after the economy settles down to a new and lower level of unemployment. In contrast, the structuralist view holds that inflation will accelerate forever if unemployment is allowed to decline from its current level. In the context of our model of Chapter 8, inflation will continue to accelerate because, as inflationary expectations adjust upwards, the government must raise nominal GDP growth to keep unemployment below the natural rate of unemployment.

The Structuralist and Hysteresis Views in Pictures

Both views agree that Europe is today operating close to its natural unemployment rate. What they disagree about is the cause of the high natural rate and its implications for the future: Will stimulative demand policy cause inflation to accelerate forever, or not? Figure 12-1 depicts the basic idea of both views, with the structuralist interpretation on the left and the hysteresis view on the right. Unemployment is plotted in the top frame and inflation in the lower frame, just as in the figure in the box on p. 391. In all frames three time periods are marked out. Time t_0 marks a point in the past that marked the end of the period of decelerating inflation, t_1 is the current period (now), and t_2 is a hypothetical future period.

During the time prior to t_0, corresponding roughly to the interval 1980–87 in Europe, inflation was decelerating. In the absence of supply shocks, this implies that the actual unemployment rate was above the natural unemployment rate, as shown in both the left and right frames. During the time between

---

[15]The most complete assessment of the structuralist hypothesis is Robert Z. Lawrence and Charles L. Schultze, eds., *Barriers to European Growth: A Transatlantic View* (Washington: Brookings, 1987). The most widely cited paper introducing the hysteresis interpretation is Olivier J. Blanchard and Lawrence H. Summers, "Hysteresis and the European Unemployment Problem," in S. Fischer, ed., *NBER Macroeconomics Annual 1986*, pp. 15–77. The two views are compared, with an application to the experience of the United States in the late 1930s, in Robert J. Gordon, "Back to the Future: European Unemployment Today Viewed from America in 1939," *Brookings Papers on Economic Activity*, vol. 19 (1988, no. 1), pp. 271–304.

HYSTERESIS MAKES A MORE OPTIMISTIC PREDICTION FOR THE FUTURE

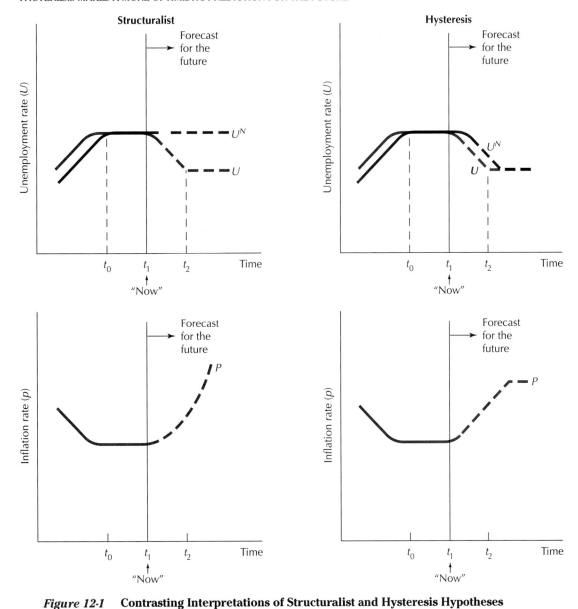

Figure 12-1   Contrasting Interpretations of Structuralist and Hysteresis Hypotheses

The left two frames describe the interpretation of the structuralist hypothesis; the right two frames the hysteresis hypothesis. Both agree that prior to time t_0 the natural rate of unemployment U^N increased enough to equal the actual rate of unemployment (U), thus explaining why inflation stopped declining. The structuralist hypothesis predicts that U^N will remain high unless remedies for specific structural impediments are found. As a result, any decline in U will cause accelerating inflation, as shown by the dashed line in the lower left frame. The hysteresis hypothesis suggests that such a decline in U will cause U^N to follow along behind, thus stopping the acceleration of inflation at time t_2.

t_0 and t_1, corresponding roughly to the interval 1987–97, inflation stopped decelerating and unemployment changed little. This implies that the natural unemployment rate must have risen and caught up with the actual unemployment rate, as shown in both frames.

The differences come to the right of t_1, which shows the consequences of a hypothetical decline in actual unemployment traced by the red dashed line. The structuralist view is based on the idea that specific impediments hold up the natural rate, and that it will not decline. As a result, the decline of the actual unemployment rate will cause inflation to accelerate for as long as unemployment stays below the natural rate. The more optimistic hysteresis view holds that the natural rate automatically follows the actual rate. Thus, the black dashed line in the upper right frame declines as the natural rate falls in response to the decline in the actual unemployment rate. Eventually the natural rate catches up to the actual rate, and as a result the inflation rate stops accelerating.

Assessing the Structuralist Hypothesis

The structuralist hypothesis advances specific reasons for the increase in Europe's natural unemployment rate between the 1960s and the 1990s. These fall into two groups, those that involve government regulation and the welfare state, and those that emphasize excessive real wages.

Eurosclerosis.   Some writers describe Europe as suffering from a disease they call *Eurosclerosis,* the effects of excessive government regulation and the welfare state in impeding the efficient operation of the labor market. Europeans often describe themselves as trapped in webs of government regulation. Among the most frequently cited examples of restrictive legislation are layoff regulations, plant-closing laws, and shop-opening hours. Some critics doubt that regulation is an important cause of the European problem, because regulations vary widely among individual countries and in some places seem little more burdensome than in the United States. Limitations on shop-opening hours, on the other hand, may be a legitimate complaint. By hindering the opening of convenience stores like "7-11," such regulations prevent the growth of low-wage jobs of the types that have blossomed in the United States.

Much blame for high European unemployment has been ascribed to generous unemployment benefits, which insulate the jobless against income loss. Yet careful studies have shown that European unemployment benefits have, if anything, become *less* generous during the period that unemployment has been rising. A similar skeptical verdict seems warranted for the claim that there is a worsening mismatch between the locations of vacant jobs and the long-term jobless in Europe; quantitative measures find no evidence of this.

A more serious problem may be high European tax rates, which may hinder entrepreneurship and stifle the opening of small business firms, prime sources of job growth in the United States. Yet European tax rates are not as high as the top-bracket U.S. rate of 70 to 90 percent in effect during the 1950s and 1960s, and such high rates did not prevent the United States from achieving growth in jobs and productivity during that period.

High Real Wages.   Ever since the Great Depression, excessive real wages have been blamed for high unemployment. Indeed, in Chapter 7 we criticized the original Keynesian model for requiring real wages to move countercyclically, rising in recessions. However, after 1979, growth in European real wages slowed markedly, and labor's share of the national income declined back to the levels of the early 1970s. Thus, most observers find that excessive real wages cannot be blamed for high unemployment in Europe.

Assessing the Hysteresis Hypothesis

The term *hysteresis* means that which "comes after" or "is behind," and comes from the Greek word for "to be behind." In the right frame of Figure 12-1, the natural unemployment rate "follows behind" the actual unemployment rate.[16] We have already seen in Figure 7-12 how a self-correcting downward movement of the U.S. aggregate supply curve was notably missing in the late 1930s. Both Europe in the 1980s and the United States in the 1930s displayed unemployment and inflation behaviors that are consistent with the hysteresis hypothesis. When unemployment is high, the natural rate "follows behind" and becomes high as well, thus eliminating any continuous downward pressure on the inflation rate.

Proponents disagree on the best theoretical explanation of the hysteresis phenomenon. Something happens to prevent the unemployed from bidding down wages. Some believe that long-term unemployment causes a decline in skills, so that the unemployed can no longer compete with those who have jobs. Others prefer the "insider-outsider" model. Instead of claiming that insider job holders have better skills than the long-term unemployed outsiders, the insider-outsider model emphasizes the monopoly market power of the insiders to hold up wages. Why don't firms fire insiders? Two reasons are costs of hiring and training outsiders and the threat of strike actions by insiders. A final explanation of hysteresis is that the economy's capacity falls during a period of high unemployment, reducing the level of capacity to the level of actual output.

All the explanations of hysteresis imply that a stimulus to aggregate demand will raise the inflation rate. If the unemployed lack skills, firms will often raise wages to steal trained workers from other firms rather than retrain the unemployed. If the insiders have market power, they will insist on wage increases in response to more rapid demand growth. Furthermore, insufficient capacity may lead to shortages of some goods, which in turn could cause inflation. But the three explanations also imply that the inflation will stop accelerating once unemployment settles at a new lower level, since by then the unemployed will have regained their skills, the outsiders will have become insiders, and new investment will have added the needed capital. This optimistic verdict for the future contrasts sharply with the structuralist approach.

---

[16]For an intellectual history, see Rod Cross and Andrew Allan, "On the History of Hysteresis," in Rod Cross, ed., *Unemployment, Hysteresis, and the Natural Rate Hypothesis* (Oxford and New York: Basil Blackwell, 1988), pp. 26–38.

INTERNATIONAL PERSPECTIVE

Is a European Expansion Being Stifled by the Drive to Monetary Union?

The prospect for a sustained demand expansion in Europe has been postponed by the drive toward European Monetary Union (EMU), proposed to begin in 1999. The countries that join EMU will give up their own national currencies, e.g., the deutsche mark and French franc, and will instead conduct all their transactions in a new currency to be called the *euro*. European nations agreed in 1992 at Maastricht (a small city in the Netherlands) that three criteria must be met for a country to be eligible to join EMU. These three Maastricht requirements include a specified inflation rate and ratios of government deficit and debt to GDP.

How does the approach of EMU hinder demand expansion in Europe? Many countries have been trying to meet the Maastricht requirements by restrictive fiscal policies (in order to reduce their ratios of deficit and debt to GDP) and restrictive monetary policies (to reduce their inflation rates). Several important countries, particularly France, have chosen to keep their foreign exchange rate tied to that of the deutsche mark, thus eliminating the possibility of domestic policies that would cause the French economy to expand faster than the German economy. And the rate of expansion of the German economy is held down both by the restrictive monetary policies of the German central bank (Bundesbank) and the restrictive fiscal policies needed to meet the Maastricht criteria.

Does demand expansion cause inflation to accelerate, as the structuralists predict? France is prevented from finding out as long as it ties its exchange rate to that of Germany. But an interesting experiment has occurred as a result of the decision in 1992 and 1993 of several important countries to devalue their currencies and drop any attempt to keep their exchange rates aligned with the deutsche mark (these countries include Italy, Portugal, Spain, Sweden, and the United Kingdom). Devaluation is a policy that expands aggregate demand by making a country's exports cheaper and imports more expensive, thus boosting net exports. This policy experiment was very successful, since on average the five devaluing countries experienced no increase in the inflation rate at all compared to the countries that did not devalue (Austria, Belgium, France, Germany, and the Netherlands), while real GDP grew faster and unemployment fell.

In particular, by 1997 the unemployment rate in the United Kingdom had fallen below 6 percent without any substantial increase in inflation, while unemployment in France had almost reached 13 percent, even though the unemployment rates in the two countries had been exactly the same in 1991. This suggests that the hysteresis hypothesis, which is more optimistic about the consequences of demand expansion than the structuralist hypothesis, may have received substantial support from the policy experiment carried out by those countries that chose to devalue in 1992.

Implications of the Debate for Macroeconomics

The debate between the structuralists and those who support hysteresis is not yet settled. While the various structural factors seem to go in the wrong direction, or to be insufficiently powerful to explain the high level of the European natural unemployment rate, the hysteresis approach also rests on a flimsy foundation. No one yet has adequately explained why hysteresis should have been prevalent in the United States in the 1930s and Europe in the 1980s and 1990s, but not in the postwar United States. The argument that skills and capital depreciate during a period of high unemployment would seem to apply equally to Europe and the United States. And if the entire support for the hysteresis idea rests on the insider-outsider distinction, then one wonders what explains hysteresis in the United States in the 1930s, when labor unions were barely established and company-hired strikebreaking was common.

The only event that would provide a definitive test in Europe between the structuralist and hysteresis approaches would be a sustained demand expansion that brought the unemployment rate down significantly and then held the unemployment rate at the new lower level for a number of years. Then, if the inflation rate steadily accelerated, the structuralists would be vindicated; the hysteresis view would be supported if inflation increased but then leveled off at a new higher rate rather than continuing to accelerate.

12-12 Conclusion: Solutions to the Inflation and Unemployment Dilemma

Both inflation and unemployment are costly, but economists differ widely in their assessment of the relative costs. All agree that a steady inflation is less costly than a highly variable surprise inflation. And all agree that a hyperinflation is far more costly than a steady creeping inflation of, say, 3 percent per year. But there the agreement stops. Some economists consider it important to reduce the inflation rate to zero, whereas others consider the costs of a steady 3 percent inflation to be trivial. Indeed, the costs of a steady creeping inflation have probably declined as a result of financial deregulation that allows banks to pay interest on checking accounts, so that the only shoe-leather cost of inflation involves extra effort needed to minimize holdings of currency. And the ever-spreading use of credit cards makes it easier for people to hold a minimum amount of currency.

As we have seen also in this chapter, the costs of turnover unemployment are quite low, and turnover unemployment usually lasts only a few weeks. But the costs of mismatch unemployment can be very large, leading to family breakdown, mental illness, loss of health insurance, and an erosion of job skills. For this reason many economists believe that the costs of mismatch unemployment swamp the costs of a steady creeping inflation of, say, 3 percent.

We have learned that four options are available to reduce the costs of inflation: (1) restrictive monetary and fiscal policies that reduce output and raise unemployment temporarily, (2) price and wage controls, (3) cost-reducing policies like reducing the burden of financial regulation, and (4) issuance of an indexed bond and reform of the tax system to make it inflation-neutral.

What are the corresponding options to reduce the unemployment rate? There is little need for policies to reduce turnover unemployment, since this generally lasts such a short time and results from the free flow of people back and forth from home and school to jobs. Many people believe that it is a virtue of American society (in contrast to some European countries) that young people have so many alternatives to continuing their education, even if it means that they suffer short spells of unemployment when they move from school to the labor market. Nevertheless, sensible suggestions to reduce turnover unemployment include creating an efficient computerized information service that makes listings of job openings widely available, and perhaps reform of the unemployment insurance system.

Responsibility for the avoidance of cyclical unemployment lies mainly with the central bank (Federal Reserve), which should conduct monetary policy to maintain the unemployment rate close to the natural rate of unemployment. As we shall learn in Chapter 14, the Fed did a good job of eliminating cyclical unemployment in the mid-1990s.

This leaves mismatch unemployment, which results from a mismatch of job openings and available unemployed workers by skill and location. The quickly shifting economic fortunes of regions of the United States in recent years suggest that the government should not devote large resources to programs to move jobs to people or people to jobs; New England's overheated economy of 1985–88 became an economic basket case in 1990–92, only to recover to the national average experience of zero cyclical unemployment in 1996–97. Recent research also suggests that migration of workers between states and regions quickly eliminates unusually high or low unemployment rates in particular states without the need for government intervention.

Thus the main focus for policymakers is reducing the natural rate of unemployment by reducing the mismatch of jobs and workers by skill. The increasing technical, educational, and skill requirements of many jobs help to explain why structural unemployment has persisted and perhaps worsened, as well as why incomes of college graduates and people with graduate degrees increased substantially in the 1980s and 1990s, while incomes stagnated for high school dropouts and those with only high school diplomas.

Numerous programs have been suggested to help reduce the job-worker skill mismatch. Among these are widely available student loans for college (to be repaid by subsequent earnings or community service), adult learn-to-read programs, better prenatal care, improved funding of such programs as Operation Headstart and the Job Corps, and perhaps national standards and testing to raise the overall educational level of U.S. schools. The choice among such programs goes beyond macroeconomics, into such disciplines as labor economics, sociology, and political science.

SUMMARY

1. In the long run the inflation rate equals the excess growth rate of nominal GDP, that is, the difference between nominal GDP growth and the long-run growth rate of real GDP.

2. Money growth equals the growth rate of nominal GDP minus the growth rate of velocity. Since velocity is not greatly affected by inflation, the long-run inflation rate equals the excess of the growth rate of the money supply minus the long-run growth rate of real GDP.

3. Governments allow excessive monetary growth for several reasons: (1) the temptation to boost demand before an election, (2) the output loss required to stop inflation, (3) adverse supply shocks require extra monetary growth if higher unemployment is to be avoided, and (4) inflation provides the government an added

opportunity to finance expenditures without resorting to unpopular taxes.

4. The costs of unanticipated inflation are primarily felt by savers, while the benefits of such inflation primarily accrue to borrowers. Unanticipated deflation works in the opposite direction, benefiting savers while hurting borrowers.

5. The Fisher effect is the one-for-one increase in the nominal interest rate in response to an increase in the expected rate of inflation, implying that the real rate of interest is unaffected by inflation.

6. In an ideal world, with inflation-neutral taxes and an operative Fisher effect, fully anticipated inflation would affect only holders of money earning less than the market interest rate, particularly holders of currency.

The struggle by such holders to reduce their holdings of money is the shoe-leather cost of inflation and becomes particularly important in a hyperinflation.

7. In practice the Fisher effect has not been validated, so that the real interest rate tends to drop even when inflation accelerates over a sustained period. This implies that even an anticipated inflation redistributes income and wealth from savers to borrowers.

8. The government budget constraint states that government spending and interest payments on government bonds must be financed by some combination of conventional taxes, money finance (the inflation tax), and bond finance. In many countries bond finance is not feasible, so that an upsurge of expenditures or a decline in conventional tax revenues implies increased reliance on money finance, implying a higher inflation rate.

9. A hyperinflation can begin with the unholy trinity of adverse supply shocks, monetary accommodation, and frequent wage indexation. A hyperinflation can also result from a shock that sharply boosts government spending or cuts conventional tax revenue.

10. Reforms to reduce the cost of inflation include decontrol of financial institutions (which had largely occurred in the United States by the mid-1980s), indexed bonds, and an indexed tax system.

11. The main reason for high unemployment in the United States is that the natural rate of unemployment is not zero but in the vicinity of 5.5 percent. Roughly half of the natural unemployment rate consists of turnover unemployment; the rest consists of mismatch unemployment.

12. Mismatch unemployment is caused by an imbalance between the high skill requirements of available jobs and the low skills possessed by many of the unemployed. In an economy with flexible relative wages, the unskilled would be able to find jobs more easily but would receive lower wage rates. Any real cure for the problems of the unskilled—whether high unemployment, or low wages, or both—requires an increase in their skills and better matching of their locations with the locations of available job openings.

13. Turnover unemployment is another component of the natural rate. The barrier that maintains turnover unemployment is the absence of perfect information, making necessary an investment in job search to locate job openings that offer higher wage rates or better working conditions.

14. Policy solutions to reduce turnover unemployment include an improved employment service to provide better information, as well as changes in the present system of unemployment compensation, which provides a subsidy to workers who turn down job offers and continue to search or to remain at home awaiting recall to their old jobs.

15. One explanation for high European unemployment is called *structuralist* and emphasizes the adverse effects of government regulations, the welfare state, and excessive real wages. Another explanation is called *hysteresis,* which states that the natural rate of unemployment automatically moves up and down in response to changes in the actual rate of unemployment.

CONCEPTS

hyperinflation
nominal interest rate
expected real interest rate
actual real interest rate
unanticipated inflation
Fisher equation
Fisher effect
government budget constraint
seignorage
inflation tax

wage indexation
incomes policy
credibility
extra convenience services
indexed bond
cyclical unemployment
turnover unemployment
mismatch unemployment
structuralist hypothesis
hysteresis hypothesis

QUESTIONS AND PROBLEMS

Questions

1. What is the misery index? What major criticism or criticisms can you make of it?
2. Distinguish between a hyperinflation and a moderate (crawling) inflation.
3. Do you agree that, as measures of the inflation rate, simple percentage changes become increasingly misleading at high rates of inflation? Why or why not?

4. What does "excess nominal GDP growth relative to natural real GDP growth" mean? Under what conditions is it equal to the inflation rate?

5. What are the three main reasons for inflation?

6. Explain the distinction among the following: the nominal interest rate, the expected real interest rate, and the actual real interest rate. Which of these interest rates is the most relevant to saving and investment decisions? Which of the rates has the most impact on determining the distribution of income?

7. What are the primary determinants of who wins and who loses in an unanticipated inflation? Using your answer as a starting point, explain why the major redistributional effect of unanticipated inflation is to transfer real wealth from the rich to the middle class.

8. Distinguish between the Fisher equation and the Fisher effect. Which one is true by definition, and which one provides a testable hypothesis? Do you think the hypothesis is verified? Why or why not?

9. Explain term-by-term the government budget constraint of equation (12.9).

10. "In the steady state, the government benefits from inflation." Explain.

11. What are the two ways of financing a government deficit? Explain the conditions under which the financing of the deficit would be inflationary.

12. Explain the relationship between wage indexation and hyperinflation.

13. What should a government do to stop a hyperinflation?

14. Explain why people want to hold money up to the point where extra convenience services are equal to the nominal interest rate. How can this observation help us understand the net social loss to society of an inflation?

15. "Policymakers may reduce temporarily the natural rate of unemployment by pursuing an expansionary monetary policy." Do you agree with this statement? Explain your answer.

16. How can vacancies and unemployed workers coexist? If policymakers pursue an expansionary policy to increase real GDP, what will happen to the number of unemployed workers? What will happen to the number of vacancies as real output increases?

17. Explain how your answer to Question 16 helps us understand why wages tend to rise faster as real output increases (i.e., why the *SP* curve is upward sloping).

18. Explain why the length of unemployment episodes is one way of differentiating between structural and frictional unemployment.

19. In what way can unemployment be considered a socially valuable experience?

20. What is the primary evidence suggesting an increase in the European natural rate of unemployment between the 1960s and the 1990s?

21. Summarize the alternative theories that purport to explain this phenomenon.

Problems

1. Let P_0 be the initial price level (say, a price index such as the CPI). Let p be the inflation rate per period.
   (a) If P_t is the price at the end of period t, show that

   $$P_t = P_0(1 + p)^t$$

   (b) If $P_0 = 1.00$ and $p = 50$ percent per month, calculate P_{12}.
   (c) Given P_{12}, calculate the percentage change from P_0, i.e., the annual rate of inflation when the monthly rate is 50 percent.

2. If inflation is a continuous process (i.e., prices rising daily or even hourly, as in a hyperinflation), calculating inflation rates at discrete intervals (such as months, quarters, and years) may be misleading. We desire a continuous analogue to the equation in Problem 1. In

   $$P_t = P_0 e^{pt}$$

   let e represent the base of natural logarithms, p the instantaneous rate of inflation, and the other variables remain as defined earlier.

   (a) Prove that p is the instantaneous rate of inflation in the preceding equation. *Note:* This requires the use of calculus. You're trying to prove the following: $p = (1/P_t)(dP_t/dt)$.
   (b) The logarithmic price change is given by

   $$p = (lnP_t - lnP_0)/t.$$

   Derive this equation from the immediately preceding one.
   (c) If $P_0 = 1.00$, $P_{12} = 129.75$, and the time interval between these periods is twelve months, find p, using the log price change formula.
   (d) For (c), you should have gotten $p = 40.5$ percent per month. Now calculate the instantaneous rate of inflation *per year* equivalent to the instantaneous rate of inflation of 40.5 percent per month. Hint: Use the equation for log price change, but this time let $P_1 = 129.75$ and $t = 1$.

3. Assume an individual is willing to save $1500 if the real rate of interest is 6 percent.
   (a) If that individual is expecting a rate of inflation

of 3 percent, what does the nominal interest rate have to be to induce the individual to save?

(b) If the nominal interest is at the rate found in (a), what is the nominal return (in dollars) from one year of saving?

(c) If this individual's expectations are correct, what is the real return (in dollars) from that year of saving?

(d) If the individual's expectations are not fulfilled and the actual inflation rate turns out to be 6 percent, what is the real return (in dollars)?

4. Bill borrows $200,000 for three years from Larry and agrees to pay Larry 8 percent interest, compounded annually. The entire amount of the loan plus interest will be paid at the end of the third year. The price level at the time of the loan is 1.00.

(a) What is the amount that Larry will receive at the end of the third year? If the price level is 1.00 at the end of the third year, what is the real value of the payment received by Larry?

(b) Assume that the inflation rate in the economy is 3 percent per year for each of the three years. What is the price level at the end of the third year? What is the real value of the payment received by Larry?

(c) Again, assume that the inflation rate in the economy is 3 percent per year for each of the

three years. In this case, however, Larry had indexed the loan to protect himself from inflation. What would be the nominal interest rate for each year of the loan? What is the nominal amount of the payment received by Larry at the end of the third year? What is the real value of the payment?

5. Suppose the relationship between H/P and p is given by

$$H/P = 8 - 0.8p$$

Here, H/P is real high-powered money, in billions of dollars, and p is the rate of inflation, in percent. Define the inflation elasticity of real high-powered money, η, as

$$\eta = -\% \, \Delta(H/P)/\% \, \Delta p = -(p/[H/P])(\Delta[H/P]/\Delta p)$$

(a) If the current rate of inflation is 5 percent, what are H/P, pH/P, and η?

(b) If p falls to 4 percent, what are H/P, pH/P, and η?

(c) If p rises to 6 percent, what are H/P, pH/P, and η?

(d) On the basis of these calculations, can you formulate a relationship between pH/P and η?

SELF-TEST ANSWERS

p. 364 The inflation rate in the first half of the decade is 4 percent per year and for the last half is 6 percent per year.

p. 374 If inflation occurs at 5 percent per year for a decade, then the price level grows at 5 percent per year. To keep H/P constant, H must grow at 5 percent per year. Seignorage, the pH/P term in equation (12.12) is equal to 5 percent ($p = 0.05$) times 1 percent of GDP ($H/P = 0.01$ times GDP), or 0.05 of 1 percent of GDP. Thus the government must run a basic deficit of 0.05 of 1 percent of GDP in order to end the decade with a fixed level of H/P.

p. 380 Financial deregulation, which allowed the payment of interest on checking accounts, made the demand for money (that is, checking accounts plus currency) less responsive to an increase in the interest rate. Hence an increase in the nominal interest rate caused by higher inflation causes less shifting away from money than prior to deregulation, thus

reducing the shoe-leather cost of fully anticipated inflation.

p. 388 (1) An extension of the time to earn unemployment benefits would reduce the cost of refusing a job and hence would extend the period of search and raise the turnover unemployment rate. (2) A reduction in the personal income tax rate would raise the cost of refusing a job, since it would increase the after-tax pay for any given pretax wage rate, and hence would reduce the period of search and the turnover unemployment rate. (3) Fewer teenagers would imply less turnover, since teenagers often engage in search unemployment when they look for after-school or summer employment, or work during years off from school. (4) A higher price of phone calls would raise the cost of search and hence would reduce the amount of search and reduce the turnover unemployment rate.

CHAPTER 13

Money and Financial Markets

Money is what the state says it is. The state claims the right not only to enforce the dictionary, but also to write the dictionary.
—*John Maynard Keynes, 1925*

13-1 Money in a World of Many Financial Assets and Liabilities

Over the last three decades monetary policy has emerged as the major tool of stabilization policy, at least in the United States. Policymakers realize that discretionary fiscal policy is severely flawed as a means of controlling the economy over the short run (a year or two). There are two main reasons for this: Fiscal policy changes require debate in Congress, which can last a long and unpredictable amount of time, and *temporary* income tax changes tend to have small and unpredictable effects. Further, in the 1980s fiscal policy became caught up in an ideological and political battle over the size of the government. This led to a government deficit, as we learned in Chapters 5 and 11, whose persistence was unprecedented in peacetime.[1] In the 1990s the consensus that the government budget be balanced precluded using discretionary fiscal policy to stabilize the economy. As a result, monetary policy has become the primary tool of stabilization policy.

In this chapter we study money—the definition of the money supply, the determinants of the money supply, and the determinants of money demand. We discuss the components of the two most common definitions of the money supply, M1 and M2. Earlier in this book (Chapters 4 and 5) we developed the *IS-LM* model and assumed that the Federal Reserve could control the nominal money supply precisely. In this chapter we learn that, in practice, the Fed's control is not exact. We shall see that the process of **financial deregulation** has allowed more and more types of assets to serve as money. This has made it difficult to find a definition of "money" for which demand is reliably related to income and interest rates.

Financial deregulation
Deregulation of U.S. financial markets began in the 1970s and continues today. One of the first changes was permitting banks to pay interest on checking accounts to pay interest.

We will learn that a reliable, or stable, demand for money is required for changes in the money supply to lead to predictable changes in the *AD* curve, and thus in nominal GDP. We will see that, unless the demand for money is stable, the *LM* curve will shift unpredictably, which in turn will translate into unpredictable shifts in the *AD* curve and therefore in nominal GDP.

Many different assets and liabilities are part of the financial markets. We learn which of them are included in the various definitions of the money sup-

---

[1]Nations with political institutions that are different from those in the United States may still be able to use fiscal policy as a tool of stabilization policy. For instance, in the United Kingdom the chancellor of the exchequer (equivalent to the U.S. secretary of the treasury) gives an annual budget speech in mid-March in which changes in tax rates go into effect the very day they are announced.

ply, and which are not. We also learn how the Fed controls the money supply through its instruments of monetary control, and why its control over the money supply is not precise.

Next, we turn to the major theories of the demand for money. These theories explain why the demand for money is related to income, to the interest rate, and to other variables, and why the demand for money appears to be stable at some times and unstable at others. We use these theories to show how the deregulation of financial markets contributed to interest rate volatility in the 1980s. And we conclude this chapter by learning why the instability of the demand for money has led the Fed to focus on interest rates rather than the money supply.

13-2 Financial Institutions, Markets, and Instruments

Some economic units currently spend more than they earn and need to borrow funds. Others currently earn more than they spend and need a place to keep their savings. Financial markets and financial intermediaries perform the essential function of channeling funds from those with surplus funds (savers) to those in need of funds (borrowers).

Reasons for Saving and Borrowing

On balance, businesses are borrowers and households are savers (or lenders). A newly opened Burger King needs funds for its building and equipment before it can earn a single dollar selling hamburgers. Even long-established businesses like Boeing Aircraft Company may borrow when a surge of orders creates a temporary need for cash to buy materials and components. And farmers frequently borrow money in the spring in order to purchase seed and fertilizer, repaying the loans when their crops are sold in the fall. Because businesses need to borrow funds, financial markets that allow the efficient exchange of funds between savers and borrowers are essential.

Individuals save for many reasons: for their retirement, for their children's education, or simply for a rainy day. Many people save and borrow at the same time, setting funds aside for long-term needs like retirement while borrowing funds to purchase a car, a home, and other goods and services. The total saving of the household sector, however, greatly exceeds its borrowing.

What about the other two major economic units, the government and the foreign sector? We have gotten used to thinking of the government sector and foreign sector as perennial net borrowers; historically, however, each sector has alternated between saving and borrowing.

Because borrowers have profitable uses for borrowed funds, they are willing to pay interest on them. And savers are happy to save when the interest they receive exceeds the benefit they would receive by spending the funds immediately. Thus, fluctuations in the interest rate help create an equilibrium between the funds available from savers and those demanded by borrowers. And the Fed, through its control of monetary policy, can influence interest rates by its control over the money supply.

Financial Institutions and Financial Markets

Financial markets are organized exchanges where securities and financial instruments are bought and sold.

Financial intermediaries make loans to borrowers and obtain funds from savers, often by accepting deposits.

Funds are channeled from savers to borrowers, either directly or indirectly. The direct channel is through **financial markets,** exchanges where securities or financial instruments are bought and sold. Financial markets provide direct finance when borrowers issue securities directly to savers. The securities, such as General Motors stock or bonds, are a liability or debt of the borrower (General Motors) and an asset of the saver (security holder).

The indirect channel operates through **financial intermediaries,** such as Citibank, which issue liabilities in their own name. The intermediaries balance their liabilities (for example, savings accounts) with assets (for example, loans).

What determines whether savers channel their funds through financial markets or through intermediaries? The simple answer is that savers are only willing to purchase securities through the direct channel—that is, via financial markets—from borrowers *large enough* to have established a reputation for paying back borrowed money. Most large business firms and units of government issue securities directly through financial markets. But most individuals cannot do so because they do not have established reputations: Individuals may be willing to entrust their savings to Citibank, but they are unlikely to accept IOUs issued by other individuals.

Financial intermediaries *spread risk* and *collect information efficiently.* Thus, Citibank makes loans to many borrowers, only a small fraction of whom will fail to repay their loans. To cover the losses from borrowers who do not repay, Citibank sets aside a contingency fund and adds the cost of this fund to the rates charged to borrowers. Because Citibank is large enough to hire specialists to assess credit risks, it is less risky for it to lend to individuals than it is for individuals to lend to each other.

Figure 13-1 illustrates the role of financial markets and institutions. The gray box on the left represents savers, and the gray box on the right represents borrowers. The upper red box represents the financial intermediaries, and the lower red box, the financial markets. The red lines connecting the boxes indicate the flows of funds from savers to borrowers. Notice that financial intermediaries not only provide funds directly to borrowers (loans to individuals) but also purchase financial market instruments. Banks and other intermediaries hold billions of dollars worth of bonds, mostly issued by the government, in addition to loans granted directly to borrowers.

Categories of Financial Institutions and Instruments

Table 13-1 displays some of the breadth and size of U.S. financial intermediaries and instruments issued. Shown in the top half of the table are the three main categories of intermediaries, which correspond to the three categories indicated in the top red box in Figure 13-1. Shown in the bottom half are financial market instruments corresponding to the bottom red box in Figure 13-1.

Depository Institutions.   Commercial banks comprise by far the largest category of depository financial intermediary. Commercial banks issue deposit accounts, both checkable and savings, hold government securities (or bonds), and grant a wide variety of loans, including business loans, home mortgages, installment loans, and credit card loans. Savings and loan institu-

Figure 13-1
The Role of Financial Intermediaries and Financial Markets

Shown on the left are the savers—any economic unit with surplus funds. These funds can be held as currency, deposited in a financial intermediary, or used to purchase a money market instrument, stocks, or bonds directly from the financial markets. Financial intermediaries both purchase financial market instruments and also lend to borrowers. So borrowers have two sources of funds: loans from intermediaries and funds that come from issuing financial market instruments.

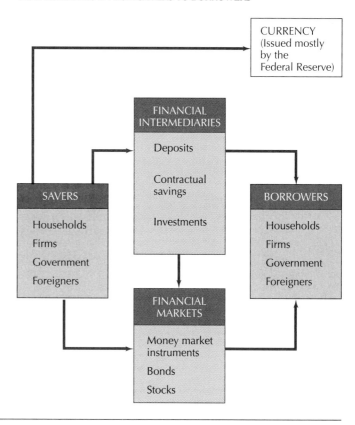

HOW FUNDS FLOW FROM SAVERS TO BORROWERS

---

tions (S&Ls), notorious for their many failures in the 1980s, historically have been required by regulation primarily to make home mortgage loans. Savings banks are similar to S&Ls. Credit union loans and deposits are limited to the members of the credit union. Credit unions draw their members from specific groups, such as employees of a particular firm, and are owned by their members. Together, S&Ls, savings banks, and credit unions are called **thrift institutions.** Financial deregulation has allowed thrift institutions to issue a far wider range of loans and deposits than they used to. Now, like commercial banks, they have checking accounts and real estate and business loans.

Thrift institutions include two types of financial intermediaries, savings and loan institutions and savings banks, that used to obtain most of their funds from savings deposits and make most of their loans in the form of mortgages. Credit unions historically accepted household deposits and made consumer loans. In recent years thrifts have been allowed to become more like commercial banks.

Contractual Savings Institutions.   A primary form of saving for many households consists of contributions to retirement plans. Usually these contributions are deducted from the paycheck in a fixed amount previously determined as part of a written or unwritten contract between employer and employee.

Thus retirement contributions and other similar forms of saving are called "contractual savings." Contractual savings institutions are classed as financial intermediaries, and include insurance companies (particularly life insurance companies), private pension funds, and state and local government retirement funds. These institutions receive contributions and pay out benefits upon retirement.

Table 13-1   **The Main Financial Intermediaries and Instruments**

Type of Financial Intermediary	Value of Assets, March 1995 ($ billions)
Depository institutions	
Commercial banks	4,261
Savings institutions	1,017
Credit unions	299
Contractual savings institutions	
Insurance companies	3,605
Private pension funds	2,491
State and local government retirement funds	1,236
Investment intermediaries	
Finance companies	759
Mutual funds (bonds and stocks)	1,773
Money market mutual funds	633

Type of Financial Market Instruments	Amount of Outstanding, End of 1995 ($ billions)
Money market instruments	
Large-denomination negotiable certificates of deposit	417
Commercial paper	437
Repurchase agreements	179
Eurodollars	91
Banker's acceptances	12
U.S. Treasury bills	761
Capital market instruments	
Corporate bonds	2,766
U.S. Treasury notes and bonds	2,503
U.S. government agency securities	808
State and local government bonds	1,307
Corporate stocks (market value)	8,345
Consumer loans	1,132
Mortgages	4,716

Sources: Balance sheets for the U.S. Economy, 1945–94 (published by Board of Governors of the Federal Reserve System) (June 1995); *Federal Reserve Bulletin* (September 1996); *Economic Report of the President* published by USGPO (February 1997).

Investment Intermediaries.   These intermediaries differ from banks in the types of assets they hold, the types of liabilities they owe, or both. Finance companies make consumer loans but raise funds they lend not from depositors but from the financial markets, especially through the issuance of commercial paper. Mutual funds raise funds from investors and invest these funds in corporate stocks and bonds. Closest to banks are money market mutual funds, whose shareholders, like bank depositors, can write checks. Balances in these funds are not deposits but rather shares in the pool of money market instruments purchased by the fund.

Financial Market Instruments

As shown in Figure 13-1, savers can purchase financial market instruments not only directly, but also indirectly through financial intermediaries like

Sold in financial markets, **money market instruments** are assets that have short maturities, usually less than one year, small fluctuations in price, and minimal risk of default.

Sold in financial markets, **capital market instruments** are assets that have relatively long maturities, can experience large fluctuations in price, and often expose investors to more risk of default.

banks and money market mutual funds. Financial market instruments fall into two categories, **money market instruments** and **capital market instruments.** Money market instruments have short maturities, usually less than one year, small fluctuations in price, and minimal risk of default. Capital market instruments have longer maturities, larger fluctuations in price, and often greater risk of default.

Money Market Instruments. Negotiable large-denomination (at least $100,000) certificates of deposit are issued by depository institutions and are called "negotiable" because, once issued, they can be traded like shares of stock. They are held by other financial institutions and by households. Commercial paper is a type of short-term, fixed-interest-rate, uncollateralized but high-quality bond that is usually issued by banks and large corporations. Banker's acceptances are often used in connection with international trade, where the buying and selling parties may know little about each other. Importers may arrange in effect for a loan by getting a banker's acceptance, which obligates the bank to pay for imported goods. Repurchase agreements are equivalent to very short-term loans from corporations to banks. Eurodollars are dollar deposits in foreign banks. Finally, Treasury bills are short-term securities issued by the U.S. government, similar to the commercial paper issued by private corporations. They are the most actively traded and safest of all money market instruments.

Capital Market Instruments. More familiar are long-term capital market instruments, including stocks and bonds. Bonds are typically issued by large corporations and by the government. Because they generally offer a fixed nominal payment, called a coupon, bond prices move in the opposite direction of interest rates. Stocks are claims on the dividends of private corporations. They are riskier than bonds because bondholder interest is paid first and stockholders have a claim only on what is left over. Loans to business firms and consumers and mortgages are also considered capital market instruments.

SELF-TEST

Without looking at Table 13-1, answer the following. Which is the largest single type of financial intermediary? For each of the following, state whether it is classified as a financial intermediary, money market instrument, or capital market instrument: money market mutual funds, state government bonds, state government retirement funds, corporate bonds, and commercial paper.

13-3 Definitions of Money

In Chapter 4 we learned that households and firms value money for its usefulness in carrying out transactions and that they value bonds for the interest they pay. In the previous section we were introduced to a wide range of assets that pay interest. These assets differ in their time to maturity, in their risk of default, and in many other dimensions. Deciding whether a financial asset should be considered a bond or a part of the money supply is not always easy

M1 is the U.S. definition of the money supply that includes only currency, transactions accounts, and traveler's checks.

M2 is the U.S. definition of the money supply that includes M1; savings deposits, including money market deposit accounts; small time deposits; and money market mutual funds.

because the asset may pay interest and may also be used to carry out transactions. Faced with this practical difficulty, the Federal Reserve compiles several measures of the money supply. The two most important of these are **M1,** which corresponds roughly to the medium-of-exchange function of money, and **M2,** which adds to M1 some but not all assets that can be used solely as a store of value. Financial deregulation has blurred the former distinction between M1 and M2, the distinction between the medium-of-exchange and store-of-value functions of money, by allowing interest to be paid on some checkable deposits and allowing checks to be written on some non-M1 categories of M2.

The M1 Definition of Money

Table 13-2 shows the various components of the Fed's M1 and M2 definitions of the money supply. Each of the categories of assets in M1 can be used directly for transactions.

1. **Currency** (cash) includes coins and paper currency, consisting of notes ranging in denomination from $1.00 to $100.00, that is held outside the Fed and vaults of depository institutions.
2. **Transactions accounts** include demand deposits, which are prohibited by law from paying interest, at commercial banks, and other deposits on which checks can be written. Demand deposits were traditionally the major deposit component of M1. There are now numerous types of "other checkable deposits," which are permitted to pay interest. These include negotiable orders of withdrawal (NOW) accounts and "super NOW" accounts at thrift institutions; automatic transfer service (ATS) accounts at commercial banks, which allow automatic transfers to checking from savings accounts to cover overdrafts; and similar accounts at savings institutions and credit unions.

Table 13-2   **Components of the M1 and M2 Measures of the Money Supply, December 1996 ($ billions)**

	Component of M1	Component of M2
Currency	$395.2	
Transactions accounts		
Demand deposits	402.4	
Other checkable deposits	274.8	
Traveler's checks	8.6	
Equals M1		$1,081.0
Savings deposits, including money market		
deposit accounts		1,271.1
Small-denomination time deposits		944.4
Money market mutual funds (retail only)		536.6
Equals M2		$3,833.1

3. **Traveler's checks** outstanding have been purchased from a bank or other financial institution but have not yet been used for purchases.

The M2 Definition of Money

The major components of M2 are:

1. **M1.** Everything included in M1 is also included in M2.
2. **Savings deposits** include passbook savings accounts, as well as savings accounts that allow deposits and withdrawals to be made by mail. Included in this category are *money market deposit accounts* that allow the writing of a limited number of checks per month, pay a rate of interest comparable to money market mutual funds (category 4 below), and because they are deposits qualify for deposit insurance.
3. **Time deposits** with balances under $100,000 are included in M2. They have maturities ranging from six months to several years and may have either fixed or variable interest rates.
4. **Money market mutual funds** allow an unlimited number of checks over a certain minimum value to be written.

Which financial market instruments are excluded from the M2 definition of the money supply? Comparing Tables 13-1 and 13-2 we can see that M2 mainly consists of liabilities of depository institutions and investment intermediaries (money market mutual funds, but not stock or bond mutual funds). None of the money market or capital market instruments are included in M2.

Money Supply Definitions and the Instability of Money Demand

Because M2 omits several financial assets, for example stock and bond mutual funds, the demand for M2 may shift unpredictably when these omitted assets become more attractive relative to the assets that are included in M2. The demand for M1 is even more likely to be unstable, because some of the assets, like super NOW accounts, that are included in M1 are very similar to some of the assets, like money market deposit accounts, that are excluded from M1.

The availability of these close substitutes creates severe difficulties for *monetarists,* who endorse a constant growth rate rule (CGRR) for "*the* money supply." To implement the CGRR, they have to decide which money supply measure should have its growth rate held constant. The notion of a stable money demand function that links "money" to "income" is a central theme of the theories of the demand for money that we shall survey later in this chapter.

SELF-TEST

For each of the following, state whether the event raises or lowers the demand for M1 and whether it raises or lowers the demand for M2: (1) the introduction of money market mutual funds; (2) the introduction of smart cards; (3) the introduction of money market deposit accounts.

SMART CARDS, E-MONEY, AND THE MONEY SUPPLY

Cash transactions in most countries represent a large share of the number of retail transactions (e.g., putting a few coins in vending machines or buying milk at a convenience store), but a very small share of the value of retail transactions—less than 1 percent in the United States. The overwhelming majority of the value of retail transactions is made by credit cards and checks. Thus far, only a few retail payments are made with electronic substitutes for cash, called "smart cards," but that may be about to change.

Some subway systems, corporations, regional phone companies, and universities issue prepaid, or stored-value, cards, which are usually purchased with cash and use a magnetic strip to record the balance remaining on the card. These cards can be used only to purchase the goods and services that the card issuer sells. University-issued prepaid cards often are used to pay for photocopying, dormitory meals, or books at campus outlets, but they cannot be used for movies, pizza, or clothes at off-campus outlets. Smart cards are prepaid cards that allow additional funds to be added to the card's balance and are accepted at a wide range of outlets. Though the smart card market is still in its formative years, consumers will probably be able to replenish or "load up" the balances on

their smart cards by ATM, by phone, or by computer. Smart cards are most likely to be issued by depository institutions, and will probably resemble plastic credit cards, but contain a computer chip that tracks the remaining balance on the card and enables the card to serve as an ATM card, a debit card, and a credit card. Smart cards may also allow balances to be transferred into Internet accounts so that purchases can be made in cyberspace.

After using your computer to connect to your institution and placing your smart card in a card reader, suppose you increase the balance on your smart card by $20. Your balance in an account already established at your financial institution then goes down by the same amount. Your demand for money is unchanged: The transactions balance on your smart card is $20 larger, which you might regard as electronic money, or e-money, and the balance in your transactions account is $20 smaller. Thus, e-money will presumably not much affect the demand for money, if the money supply is defined to include smart card balances. This is another example of how financial innovation can change what financial assets should be included in the definition of the money supply in the future. When you load up your smart

13-4 High-Powered Money and Determinants of the Money Supply

Regardless of what definition of the money supply we select, the basic mechanism for "creating" the money supply is the same. In this section we show how the Fed and depository institutions "create" money and learn that the Fed's actions have a multiplier effect on the money supply. Though the Fed can control the longer-run average growth rate of the money supply, we will see that in practice the Fed cannot always control the money supply precisely over shorter periods.

Money Creation on a Desert Island

The role of the Fed in the money supply process is best understood by starting with a simple banking system where there is no Fed. We begin with the

card, no funds actually leave the institution—and this is where loading up your smart card differs from using it as an ATM card to withdraw $20 in cash. Instead, when your institution deducts $20 from your account, it credits $20 to its own account, where the $20 credit remains until you use the card. The amount of reserves in your institution is not affected by your transfer of funds from one account to the other. When you make purchases with the card, simultaneously the balance on the card declines and instructions are sent electronically to your institution to transfer funds from its smart card account to the seller's account at the seller's depository institution.

Widespread acceptance of smart cards will depend on their benefits and costs to consumers, businesses, and to card-issuing depository institutions. Consumers are likely to find smart cards convenient, especially for the large number of small-value purchases they make. With smart cards—and vendors that accept them—consumers will not need coins. Who hasn't stood at a bus stop or in front of a vending machine or newspaper rack without the correct change! Using a smart card may require entering a personal identification number, or PIN, just as ATM cards do now. Unlike cash, smart cards that require PINs will not be attractive to thieves. Like cash, however, if you lose your card, you will probably lose the balance remaining on it. Merchants are likely to appreciate the speed and accuracy of purchases made with smart cards, the reduced risk of employee theft of cash, and the speed and accuracy with which the funds move into their own accounts. Whether purchases will be traceable or whether merchants will be able to accumulate and use data associated with smart card purchases remains to be seen. To the extent that consumers move balances to zero-interest-bearing smart cards from interest-bearing accounts, smart card issuers will benefit. The reduced handling of cash is also likely to reduce issuers' costs. On the other hand, since purchases made with bogus cards will trigger payments from smart card issuers to merchants, issuers will incur losses if smart cards are successfully counterfeited.

---

[a]For much of this and more information on smart cards, see John Wenninger and David Laster, "The Electronic Purse," *Current Issues in Economics and Finance,* Federal Reserve Bank of New York, 1(1), April 1995.

First Desert Island Bank, which is started by a banker who receives a deposit of 100 gold coins. Initially the bank holds the gold as an asset and has deposits of 100. However, the banker is missing an opportunity to make a profit: 100 gold coins earn no interest sitting in the vault. Because the depositor rarely withdraws more than 10 coins, the banker decides to keep "reserves" equal to just 10 percent of total deposits and to grant loans equal to the remaining 90 percent of total deposits.

Required Conditions for Money Creation

Depositing and lending the coins starts the process of money creation. Suppose the loan of 90 coins is redeposited in the bank by a merchant, say, a used-raft dealer, who sold a raft to the person who borrowed the 90 coins. This raises total deposits to 190, consisting of the initial deposit of 100 and the new deposit of 90. Because the used-raft dealer has redeposited the 90 gold coins that were borrowed to pay for the raft, the bank again has the original 100 gold coins. At this point, the banker again decides to hold as reserves

10 percent of "total" deposits. Since the banker decides to hold only 10 percent of 190 for reserves, the remaining "excess" reserves of 81 gold coins can be loaned out.

The banker can continue making loans of excess reserves until total deposits equal 1000. At that point, the banker's actual reserves (100) equal required reserves (100 = 10 percent of 1000) and excess reserves equal zero. Thus the original deposit of 100 gold coins leads to the creation of 1000 units of money, all in the form of bank deposits. The First Desert Island Bank has succeeded in creating an additional 9 units of money for every gold coin that it initially received.

How has this magic occurred? Four conditions are necessary for the banker to turn 100 gold coins into a money supply of 1000.

1. **Equivalence of coins and deposits.** Paper receipts representing ownership of bank deposits, i.e., checks, must be accepted as a means of payment on a one-for-one basis. That is, checks must be treated as equivalent to payment of gold coins.

2. **Redeposit of proceeds from loans.** Any consumer or business firm receiving a cash or check payment must deposit it into an account at the same bank. We assumed in the example that the used-raft dealer redeposited the 90 gold coins received as the proceeds of the first loan.

3. **Holding of cash reserves.** The bank must hold some fraction of its reserves in the form of cash (10 percent in gold coins in this example).

4. **Willing borrowers.** Someone must be willing to borrow from the bank at an interest rate that covers the bank's cost of operation. If the First Desert Island Bank stopped lending its excess reserves, the process of money creation would stop.

The Money-Creation Multiplier

When these four conditions are met, then the entire process of money creation can be summed up in a simple equation. We let the symbol H denote **high-powered money,** that is, the type of money that is held by banks as reserves. In the example, H consists of the 100 gold coins, which are high-powered because they generate the multiple expansion of money by the First Desert Island Bank. The symbol D represents the total bank deposits. The symbol e represents the fraction of deposits that banks hold as reserves. In equilibrium, the *demand* for high-powered money to be held as reserves *(eD)* equals the *supply* of high-powered money *(H):*

High-powered money is the sum of currency held outside depository institutions and the reserves held inside them.

General Form	Numerical Example	
$eD = H$	$0.1\,(1000) = 100$	(13.1)

The same equation can be rearranged (dividing both sides by e) to determine the amount of deposits (D) relative to the quantity of high-powered money (H) and the bank reserve-holding ratio (e):

General Form	Numerical Example	
$D = \dfrac{H}{e}$	$1000 = \dfrac{100}{0.1}$	(13.2)

Comparison with Income-Determination Multiplier. The money-creation multiplier is $1/e$, or $1/0.1 = 10$ in the numerical example. This is the second usage of the word *multiplier* in this book. In Chapter 3 we examined the factors that determined the income-determination multiplier. In its simplest version, that multiplier in Chapter 3 was:

$$\frac{\text{Income-determination}}{\text{multiplier } (k)} = \frac{\text{autonomous planned spending } (A_p)}{\text{marginal propensity to save } (s)}$$

An increase in autonomous planned spending (A_p) is multiplied because spending creates income, a fraction of which *leaks out* into saving and taxes and the remainder of which goes into additional spending. The multiplier process ends only when the total of extra induced leakages equals the original increase in A_p.

The intuition behind the money-creation multiplier is the same. An increase in high-powered money (H) is multiplied (13.2) because the initial deposit of H becomes reserves, a fraction of which *leaks out* into required reserves and the remainder of which is lent out and comes back as additional deposits of the households and business firms that receive the loan proceeds. The money-creation multiplier process continues until the extra induced leakages into required reserves equal the original increase in H.

Comparison with Real-World Conditions. In reality, some of the four conditions required to obtain the simple money-creation multiplier may not hold.

Condition (2) required that any seller receiving a payment from the proceeds of a loan redeposit it into the bank. If not, the multiplier process of money creation cannot occur at that bank. If the cash is redeposited at another depository institution, then the second institution will find itself with excess reserves, allowing the multiplier process to proceed. Thus, condition (2) can be revised to apply to, say, all the banks within the United States. As long as sellers who receive loan proceeds in the form of either cash or checks redeposit the funds in a U.S. bank, the money-creation multiplier in equation (13.2) remains valid for the U.S. banking system as a whole.

Cash Holding. The money-creation multiplier is changed, however, if households or businesses want to hold not only checkable deposits but some pocket cash as well. Imagine that everyone wants to hold a fixed fraction (c) of his or her deposits, say 15 percent, in the form of cash.[2] This demand for currency adds an extra amount (cD) to the total demand for high-powered money. In a revised desert island example, the demand for gold coins, the only form of high-powered money, might be 10 percent of deposits for bank reserves $(eD = 0.1D)$, plus 15 percent of deposits for pocket cash $(cD = 0.15D)$.

The total demand for high-powered money $(eD + cD)$ can be equated to the total supply (H):

[2]The cash fraction c has nothing whatsoever to do with the marginal propensity to consume (c) of Chapter 3. Nor does the reserve holding ratio (e) have anything to do with the foreign exchange rate (e) of Chapter 5. At this stage we have run through the alphabet and are asking some letters to perform double duty. See the guide to symbols provided on the inside back cover.

General Form	Numerical Example
Demand = Supply	Demand = Supply
$eD + cD = H$	$0.1D + 0.15D = 100$

or

$$(e + c)D = H \qquad\qquad 0.25D = 100 \qquad\qquad (13.3)$$

Dividing both sides by $(e + c)$, we can solve for deposits:

$$D = \frac{H}{e + c} \qquad\qquad D = \frac{100}{0.25} = 400 \qquad\qquad (13.4)$$

In words, total deposits equal the supply of high-powered money (H) divided by the fraction of deposits that leaks into reserves (e) plus the fraction that leaks into cash (c).

Remember that the total money supply (M) includes not only deposits (D) but also currency:

$$M = D + cD = (1 + c)D \qquad\qquad (13.5)$$

Substituting for D in (13.5) from (13.4), we obtain

$$M = (1 + c)D = \frac{(1 + c)H}{e + c} = \frac{1.15(100)}{0.25} = 460 \qquad\qquad (13.6)$$

The ratio of the money supply (M) to high-powered money (H) is called the **money multiplier** (M/H). In equation (13.6), the money multiplier is equal to $(1 + c)/(e + c)$. In the next two sections we will learn that the money multiplier is volatile due to additional factors omitted from (13.6).[3]

The **money multiplier** is the ratio of the money supply to high-powered money, that is, M/H. There is a separate money multiplier for each definition of the money supply.

Gold Discoveries and Bank Panics

The supply of money depends only on the three terms that appear in (13.6): the supply of high-powered money (H), the cash-holding ratio (c), and the ratio of reserves to deposits (e). When only gold can serve as high-powered money (H), the total supply of money depends on the demand for and supply of gold. Because a sustained increase in monetary growth causes higher inflation in the long run, gold discoveries have caused some episodes of inflation. For instance, inflation was higher immediately following the gold discoveries in California in 1848 and in Alaska in 1898.

Before the establishment of the Federal Reserve in 1913 and the introduction of federal deposit insurance in 1934, the U.S. economy was at the mercy of capricious changes in the money supply, stemming not only from the influence of gold discoveries on the growth of H, but also from episodes in which the cash-holding ratio (c) and the reserve ratio (e) fluctuated dramatically. During banking panics, which occurred about once a decade and culminated in the serious panic of 1907, depositors feared for the safety of their deposits and withdrew their deposits as cash. This raised the cash-

---

[3]Students interested in a more detailed treatment of the money supply process should consult Frederic S. Mishkin, *The Economics of Money, Banking, and Financial Markets*, 5e (Reading, MA: Addison Wesley Longman, 1998), Chapters 16 and 17.

holding ratio *(c)* and thereby lowered the money supply. To deal with the tide of withdrawals, banks began to bolster their reserves by raising the reserve ratio *(e),* which further reduced the money supply.[4] In the pre–Federal Reserve era, there was no way for the government to raise *H* to offset panic-induced increases in *c* and *e.* Panics caused a drop in the money supply and in aggregate demand, cutting both output and prices.

SELF-TEST

Assume that high-powered money is 500, the fraction of deposits held as currency is 0.25, and the fraction of deposits held as reserves is 0.15. Answer the following: (1) Calculate the value of deposits and the money supply; (2) calculate the new value of deposits and the money supply if the currency-holding fraction changes from 0.25 to 0.35; (3) calculate the new value of deposits and the money supply if the reserve-holding fraction changes from 0.15 to 0.25 (while the currency-holding fraction remains at the original 0.25).

13-5   The Fed's Three Tools for Changing the Money Supply

Suppose the Federal Reserve wants the economy to have a given money supply *M.* The Fed must predict the public's desired cash-holding ratio *(c),* over which the Fed has no control. Then the Fed can adjust the two remaining variables in equation (13.6), *H* and *e,* to make its desired *M* consistent with the public's chosen *c.* The Fed uses three tools to accomplish this task; the first two control *H* and the last influences *e.* This section helps us understand which real-world events change *H* and *e.*

First Tool: Open-Market Operations

The first tool is by far the most important. The Fed can change *H* by purchasing and selling government securities like Treasury bills. When it buys Treasury bills in the open market, the Fed (electronically) receives the Treasury bills from the seller and pays for them with high-powered money. The Fed pays for the Treasury bills it has bought simply by raising (electronically) the account balance of the seller at the seller's bank and the reserve balance of the seller's bank at the seller's bank's Federal Reserve Bank. This addition to *H,* brought about by the Fed's **open-market operations,** leads to an even larger increase in *M* through the money multiplier.

Open-market operations are purchases and sales of government securities made by the Federal Reserve in order to change high-powered money.

Federal Reserve monetary policy is decided by the Federal Open Market Committee at meetings scheduled eight times each year. The meetings of the FOMC are held in a large and imposing room at the Federal Reserve Board in Washington, D.C., and are attended by the seven governors of the Federal Reserve Board and the twelve presidents of the regional Federal Reserve

---

[4]Notice in equation (13.6) that any increase in e reduces the quantity of money *(M).* Although *c* appears in both the numerator and denominator, an increase in *c* reduces the money supply as long as the reserve-holding ratio *(e)* is less than 1.0.

banks.[5] The FOMC also discusses monetary policy at other times by phone and can change policy at any time. After its meetings, the FOMC often issues a statement indicating generally what policy it has decided to follow. The FOMC also issues a directive to the Fed's open-market manager at the Federal Reserve Bank of New York, a position held in 1997 by Peter Fisher.

H Is Created out of Thin Air.   Let us say that Mr. Fisher's directive from the FOMC calls for continued moderate growth in the money supply, and that he has decided that the time has come for a $100 million increase in high-powered money *(H)*. All Mr. Fisher has to do is pick up the phone and buy $100 million in U.S. Treasury bills from a government bond dealer, say Salomon Brothers. *H* is created out of thin air when the Fed electronically gives a credit of $100 million to the reserve account at the bank, say Bank of America, where Salomon Brothers has a checking account.[6] At the same time, the Fed notifies Bank of America that it should give a $100 million credit to the Salomon Brothers checking account.

This transaction has given Bank of America an additional liability of $100 million of deposits and an additional asset of $100 million of reserves, which earn no interest. Suppose that Bank of America chooses to hold $10 million of reserves against the additional $100 million deposit. It then has $90 million of excess reserves that it can use to make interest-bearing loans. Borrowers usually get loans so that they can spend the funds. When the proceeds of the loans are spent, some will be redeposited in a depository institution someplace. That institution will then have excess reserves that it can lend out, just as Bank of America did. Note that depository institutions no longer have excess reserves once all the funds have been loaned out and they are withdrawn to be spent. Thus, another way to view the money-creation process is that it continues until no depository institution has excess reserves it is willing to lend out.

By buying Treasury bills with electronic credits, Mr. Fisher has "created" more high-powered money, *H.* Salomon Brothers transferred Treasury bills to the Fed, but Fed regulations do not permit Treasury bills to be counted toward reserves. Thus, the transfer of Treasury bills did not lower *H* or reserves, but the Fed's paying for the Treasury bills did raise reserves. That is why the Fed's open-market purchase produced an increase in *H.* Mr. Fisher also created a multiple increase in the money supply. The total money supply rises each time funds are deposited. As the money-creation multiplier showed us, the money supply is likely to rise by a sizeable multiple of the original value of Treasury bills purchased by the Fed on the open market.

Effect on Interest Rates.   Mr. Fisher's purchase influences not only the total supply of money but also the interest rate. When he demands $100 million of Treasury bills, the price of Treasury bills rises, thereby lowering the return, or interest rate, they pay.

---

[5]All twelve regional presidents attend, but only five may vote. The New York Fed president always has a vote and the other four votes are rotated. All Governors are entitled to vote at every FOMC meeting.

[6]In spite of its name, the Bank of America is a San Francisco-based commercial bank and should not be confused with a central bank, like the Bank of England or the Bank of Japan.

Sometimes the Fed must engage in open-market operations even when it has no desire to raise or lower the money supply. For instance, during the Christmas shopping season, the public needs more cash for transactions and raises its desired cash-holding ratio *(c)*. Without action by the Federal Reserve, this increase in the denominator of the money-supply equation (13.6) would reduce the money supply by a multiple of the public's cash withdrawals from deposit accounts. The Fed can prevent this decline in the money supply and the associated leftward shift of the *LM* curve by conducting a "defensive" open-market purchase of Treasury bills. To prevent a decline in the money supply, the Fed would raise *H* enough to offset the effect of the higher *c*.

Second Tool: Discount Rate

The **discount rate** is the interest rate the Federal Reserve charges depository institutions when they borrow reserves.

Depository institutions' incentives to borrow from the Fed rise when market interest rates rise relative to the **discount rate,** the interest rate that the Fed charges them when they borrow reserves. Depository institutions' so-called discount-window borrowings tend to be high when the interest rates they can earn on money market instruments, like Treasury bills, are substantially above the discount rate that the Fed has set.

Because $100 million in Fed loans provides banks with the same $100 million in bank reserves as a $100 million open-market purchase, the Fed can control high-powered money *(H)* either by varying the discount rate or by conducting open-market operations. Monetary control can be achieved with either instrument and does not require both. The primary justification for allowing discount-window borrowing at the Fed is the need for immediate help by individual banks suffering from an unexpected rush of withdrawals. Such cases are rare and can be handled individually. Many economists have criticized the Fed for keeping the discount rate low enough to induce banks to borrow substantially. The unpredictability of this borrowing reduces the Fed's day-to-day control over *H*.

Third Tool: Reserve Requirements

Required reserves are the reserves that Federal Reserve regulations require depository institutions to hold.

Reserve requirements are the rules that stipulate the minimum fraction of deposits that must be held as reserves.

Unlike the desert island, where the banker chose *voluntarily* to keep 10 percent of the bank's deposits on hand in the form of gold coin reserves, in the United States all depository institutions must hold reserves equal to 10 percent of transactions balances as **required reserves.** Reserves can be held in reserve accounts at the Fed or as vault cash (currency and coin). **Reserve requirements** apply only to transactions accounts.

As is evident in equation (13.6), the Fed can raise the money supply by reducing bank reserve requirements *(e)*. Thus, a reduction in *e* produces the same increase in the money supply as an open-market purchase of the appropriate amount. Why does the Fed retain its control over reserve requirements? One reason is that setting reserve requirements at a high level can come in handy in wartime, when the government needs to run a large budget deficit. In World War II, for instance, the government would have been required to pay very high interest rates to induce the public to voluntarily finance its entire deficit. To avoid this problem, the government sold a large quantity of bonds to the Fed, causing H to double between 1940 and 1945. To minimize the inflationary pressure created by the large wartime increase in H, the Fed maintained bank reserve requirements at a level much higher than at present. The high required reserve ratio kept the money-creation multiplier, and thus the money supply, lower than it would have been otherwise. Another reason that the Fed retains reserve requirements is that they help the Fed control the money supply. Even without reserve requirements, depository institutions would hold some reserves. Institutions hold vault cash because customers control the depositing and withdrawing of cash and their deposits and withdrawals are somewhat unpredictable. Because the 10 percent required reserve ratio is a considerably higher ratio of reserves to transactions deposits than most depository institutions need to satisfy their customers' cash withdrawals, depository institutions typically hold no more reserves than they are required to hold. That is, depository institutions typically face a binding reserve ratio constraint and hold few, if any, excess reserves when the required reserve ratio is high. A high required reserve ratio then means that the reserve ratio, e, stays close to it. In the absence of binding reserve requirements, however, depository institutions would have lower and less predictable (excess) reserve ratios. As we can see from equation (13.6), low and unpredictable reserve ratios unpredictably change the money-creation multiplier and the money supply by sizeable amounts.

SELF-TEST   Be sure you can answer these questions without looking back at the preceding text: If the Fed wants to reduce the money supply, does it conduct an open-market purchase of bonds or sale of bonds? Why might lowering the discount rate lead to a larger money supply?

Why the Fed Can't Control the Money Supply Precisely

This chapter focuses on two problems faced by the Fed: Why it can't control the money supply precisely, and why an unstable demand for money can break the link between changes in the money supply and changes in nominal GDP. We have now learned that the Fed can use its three instruments—open-market operations, the discount rate, and changes in reserve requirements—to achieve control of the money supply (as in equation 13.6 above). Why, then, is its control imprecise?

Multiple Definitions of Money.   There are many types of financial assets included in M2 that are not included in M1. Both savings deposits and time deposits are included in M2 but excluded from M1. An increase in the attractiveness of these deposits relative to transactions accounts, for example, would raise the level of M2 relative to M1. In that case, the Fed will not be able to precisely control M1 and M2 simultaneously.

The Public Chooses the Amount of Currency.   The Fed controls two elements in the money supply equation (13.6): high-powered money *(H)* and the reserve ratio *(e)*. It does not control the ratio of currency to deposits *(c)*, which is controlled by firms and households. If the Fed cannot predict precisely when c will change, it cannot control the money supply precisely. As we will see later in this chapter, shifts in the demand for U.S. currency by foreigners further complicate attempts to control the money supply in the United States.

Other Factors.   Equation (13.6) simplifies the money supply process, omitting other factors that can interfere with precise Fed control. The equation does not take into account that transactions accounts have reserve requirements, while other accounts do not. And since money market mutual funds are not actually deposits, they are also free from reserve requirements. A consequence of these differing reserve requirement ratios is that shifts of funds across accounts will change the average reserve ratio, *e*.

Taken together, these factors make the money multiplier hard to predict and thus make it hard to control precisely the *LM* curve. These **money-multiplier shocks** play a central role in our discussion of monetary policy later in this chapter.

A **money-multiplier shock** is any event that causes the money multiplier to change, such as a change in the public's demand for currency relative to deposits, or a shift between deposits having different reserve requirements.

13-6   Theories of the Demand for Money

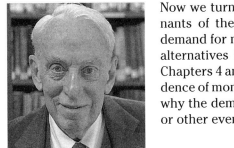

James Tobin (1918–   )
Tobin, 1981 Nobel Prize winner, is famous both as one of the most articulate advocates of policy activism and for his theories of the transaction and portfolio demands for money.

Now we turn from the determinants of the supply of money to the determinants of the demand for money. Our first aim is to understand why the demand for money depends on the interest rates available on assets that are alternatives to money. This is a central assumption in our *IS-LM* model of Chapters 4 and 5, and we need to examine the theories that explain the dependence of money demand on the interest rate. Our second aim is to understand why the demand for money might shift in response to financial deregulation or other events.

Interest-Responsiveness of the Transactions Demand for Money

In the early 1950s William J. Baumol of Princeton and New York University and James Tobin of Yale demonstrated that the transactions (i.e., medium-of-exchange) demand for money depends on the interest rate.[7] The funds people hold for transactions, to "bridge the interval between the receipt of income and its disbursement," can be placed either in M1 (currency and transactions accounts, which are assumed by Baumol and Tobin to pay no interest) or in savings deposits (which do pay interest but offer less transaction service). The higher the interest rate, the more individuals shift their transactions balances into interest-bearing savings deposits and other components of M2 that do not serve as a medium of exchange.

Baumol analyzes the money-holding decision of a hypothetical individual who receives income at specified intervals but spends it steadily between paydays. An example is given in the left frame of Figure 13-2, where the person is assumed to be paid $900 per month *(Y)* on the first of each month. How will the person decide whether to convert all of the paycheck into currency

---

[7]William J. Baumol, "The Transactions Demand for Cash: An Inventory Theoretic Approach," *Quarterly Journal of Economics* (November 1952), pp. 545–56; James Tobin, "The Interest-Elasticity of the Transactions Demand for Cash," *Review of Economics and Statistics* (August 1956), pp. 241–47.

THE HOLDING OF CASH DEPENDS INVERSELY ON THE ATTRACTIVENESS
OF HOLDING SAVINGS DEPOSITS

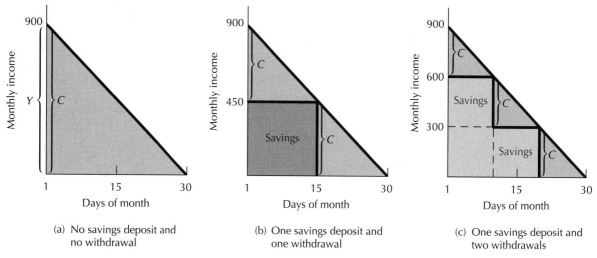

(a) No savings deposit and
    no withdrawal

(b) One savings deposit and
    one withdrawal

(c) One savings deposit and
    two withdrawals

Figure 13-2   Alternative Allocations of an Individual's Monthly Paycheck Between Cash and Savings Deposits

In the left frame the individual holds the entire paycheck in the form of cash, indicated by the gray triangle, which shrinks as the paycheck is spent on consumption purchases. In the middle frame only half as much cash is held, initially and on average, because the individual finds it advantageous to hold half the paycheck in a savings account for half the month. In the right frame even less cash is held, because initially two-thirds of the paycheck is deposited in a savings account.

and transactions accounts (M1), which bear no interest, or to deposit part of the paycheck in a savings deposit that pays a monthly interest rate r?[8]

Costs and Benefits of Holding Money.   The individual compares the costs and benefits of holding M1 instead of the savings deposit. The cost of M1 is its opportunity cost, the interest forgone on savings *(r)* when M1 is held instead of savings deposits. The main benefit of holding M1 is the avoidance of what Baumol calls the "broker's fee" of b dollars charged every time *(T)* cash is obtained, either by cashing the original paycheck or by obtaining cash at the depository institution. The broker's fee in real life includes the time and transportation expense required to make an extra trip to the bank to obtain cash from a savings account.

The number of times the broker's fee is incurred equals the size of the paycheck *(Y)* divided by the average amount of cash *(C)* obtained on each trip. For instance, the left frame of Figure 13-2 involves no savings account; the paycheck of $900 *(Y)* is cashed at the beginning of the month *(C = 900)*, and the broker's fee is incurred only one time $(T = Y/C = 1.0)$.

---

[8]Throughout this section we assume that no interest is paid on transactions accounts, in contrast to the real world, where interest is paid on some components of M1 and M2 that can be used for transactions. Our analysis remains valid as long as a higher interest rate on non-money assets raises the average interest rate paid on M1 less than proportionately, thus reducing the demand for M1.

In the middle frame half the paycheck is cashed on the first of the month ($C = 450$); the other half is deposited in a savings deposit. Interest forgone equals the interest rate times the value of the average amount held in cash, which is half the value of the cash withdrawal ($rC/2$). Why? In the first half of the month the individual starts with $450 in cash, winding up with zero on the fifteenth of the month, for an average holding of $225. Then the person converts the remaining savings deposit into cash, incurring a second broker's fee. The $450 of cash dwindles again to zero on the last day of the month. The average cash holding during the last half of the month is again $225. Total interest forgone is the interest rate times $C/2$, or $225 in this example.[9]

In the right frame only one-third of the paycheck is initially cashed ($C = 300$), while the other two-thirds are deposited in the savings deposit. On the tenth and on the twentieth, withdrawals are again made, so that the broker's fee is incurred three times ($T = Y/C = 900/300 = 3$). The interest income forgone by holding cash is once again $rC/2$.

How Many Trips to the Bank?   How should the individual behave—as in the left frame, the middle frame, or the right frame, or should even more trips be made to the bank? The answer is that the combined cost of broker's fees (bT) and interest income foregone ($rC/2$) should be minimized:

$$\text{cost} = bT + \frac{rC}{2} \tag{13.7}$$

or

$$= b\frac{Y}{C} + \frac{rC}{2}$$

It can be shown that the average value of the cash withdrawal (C) that minimizes cost is[10]

$$C = \sqrt{\frac{2bY}{r}} \tag{13.8}$$

This equation says that the average cash withdrawal equals the square root of the following: two times the broker's fee, times income, divided by the interest rate. A higher broker's fee (b) raises cash holdings by discouraging trips to the bank, each of which incurs the broker's fee.

Conversely, as equation (13.8) indicates, a higher interest rate on savings deposits lowers average cash holdings. The higher interest rate makes it

---

[9]What is the area of the gray triangle in the left frame? The formula for the area of a triangle is one-half times the height, times the length, or $1/2(900)(1)$, where the length is expressed in months. This equals 450. In the middle are two gray triangles, each with an area $1/2(450)(1/2)$, or $1/2(450)(1)$ for both triangles. This equals 225. On the right are three triangles, each with an area $1/2(300)(1/3)$, or $1/2(300)(1)$ for the three triangles. This equals 150.

[10]Here elementary calculus is required. Cost is minimized by choosing C to make the derivative of cost with respect to C equal to zero:

$$\frac{\partial(\text{cost})}{\partial C} = \frac{-bY}{C^2} + \frac{r}{2} = 0$$

When this is solved for C, we obtain the square-root expression shown as equation (13.8).

optimal to go to the bank more frequently and make smaller withdrawals, thereby leaving more on average in the interest-earning savings accounts. The smaller withdrawals mean that on average cash holdings are smaller. The extra broker's fees incurred by going to the bank more frequently are compensated for by the extra interest earned on the larger savings account balances at the higher interest rate. Equation (13.8) also shows that the transactions demand for money rises with increases in income. Just as with interest rates, the Baumol model implies specifically that the transactions demand for money is related to the square root of income.[11]

Summary: The Baumol-Tobin contributions are of major importance. They show that the interest sensitivity of the demand for money is based on a transactions motive that is shared by almost everyone. Their theories underpin the positive slope of the *LM* curve, which implies that changes either in private spending desires or in fiscal policy will change both real output and the interest rate, at least in the short run.

The Portfolio Approach

At about the same time as the Baumol-Tobin contributions, several articles highlighted another source of the demand for money, as a store of value. In particular, James Tobin, in another classic article, showed that people diversify their portfolios by holding several categories of assets.[12]

Tobin's Contribution.   Some assets, particularly those in M1 and M2, have nominal values that do not change when interest rates change and thus are "safe" or "riskless."[13] The prices of other financial assets, like those of stocks or long-term bonds, vary all the time and thus are "risky" assets. If investors dislike the risk that the prices of the assets they own will fluctuate, they will hold risky assets only when those assets are expected to provide higher returns than riskless assets do. Without this risk premium on risky assets, risk-averse investors would not hold them.

Faced with various safe and risky assets, with the former paying less interest than the latter, most investors compromise, diversifying their portfolios of assets. Holding only risky assets yields a high average interest return but exposes investors to much risk. Holding only safe assets eliminates risk completely, but yields a low average return. A mixed, or diversified, portfolio is usually the best approach.

---

[11]The Baumol theory's "square root hypothesis" of money holding can be tested against the data. In that case, both the output elasticity and the interest rate elasticity of real money demand should be one-half. Why? Let us rewrite (13.8) in exponential form:

$$C = (2bY)^{1/2}(r)^{-1/2}$$

Thus a 1 percentage point change in Y raises C by 1/2 percent. For a more advanced treatment that allows the theoretical elasticities to differ from 1/2, see Edi Karni, "The Transactions Demand for Cash: Incorporation of the Value of Time into the Inventory Approach," *Journal of Political Economy,* vol. 81 (September/October 1973), pp. 1216–25.

[12]James Tobin, "Liquidity Preference as Behavior Towards Risk," *Review of Economic Studies,* vol. 25 (February 1958), pp. 65–86.

[13]"Riskless" is placed in quotes because M1 is not free of risk when prices are flexible, since inflation reduces the real value of nominal holdings of M1. This is one of the costs of inflation emphasized in Chapter 12.

Although the Tobin approach gives a very appealing reason for diversifying portfolios, it does not explain why anyone holds currency or non-interest-bearing checking accounts when safe, interest-bearing assets are available. The major contribution of the portfolio approach is to explain why most households hold both safe, interest-bearing components of M1 and M2, and risky stocks and bonds.

Friedman's Version.   At roughly the same time that Tobin was writing, Milton Friedman developed a similar approach to the demand for money.[14] Friedman's theory was a generalization of the older quantity theory of money, in which he treated money as one among several assets, including bonds, equities (stocks), and goods. Friedman emphasized that, in principle, any category of spending on GDP could be a substitute for money and might be stimulated by an expansion of the real money supply. Because he viewed a wider range of assets as being substitutes for money than did Tobin, Friedman viewed monetary policy as having more potent effects on spending.

The portfolio approach pioneered by both Tobin and Friedman makes the demand for money a function of both income and wealth, not just income. The response of the demand for money to wealth has an implication for the efficacy of fiscal policy. A stimulative fiscal policy financed by deficit spending raises real wealth if people treat government bonds as part of their wealth (see Chapter 11). The increase in wealth, in turn, raises the demand for money and shifts the *LM* curve to the left, reducing the fiscal policy multipliers below those we calculated in Chapter 5, where the wealth effect on the demand for money was ignored.[15]

SELF-TEST

According to the Tobin and Friedman versions of the portfolio theory, would an increase in the supply of M1 tend to raise or lower prices in the bond market? In the stock market?

13-7   CASE STUDY: How Financial Deregulation and Innovation Steepened the *IS* and *LM* Curves

This chapter began by introducing the wide variety of financial instruments that are available. We showed which assets are included in the major definitions of the money supply. It can be difficult to decide whether a particular type of asset should be included in M2, for example. Before the 1980s money market mutual funds were not included in M2. Now they are, because they are regarded as being close substitutes for other types of assets in M2, like money market deposit accounts and other interest-bearing checkable deposits. The

---

[14]Friedman's approach is explained in more detail in his "The Quantity Theory of Money—a Restatement," in Friedman (ed.), *Studies in the Quantity Theory of Money* (Chicago: University of Chicago Press, 1956), pp. 3–21.

[15]A formal analysis of the wealth effect in the demand-for-money function is the subject of Alan S. Blinder and Robert M. Solow, "Analytical Foundations of Fiscal Policy," in *The Economics of Public Finance* (Washington, D.C.: Brookings Institution, 1974), pp. 45–57. See also Benjamin M. Friedman, "Crowding Out or Crowding In? Economic Consequences of Financing Government Deficits," *Brookings Papers on Economic Activity,* vol. 9 (1978), pp. 593–641.

definitions of the money supply can also change because deregulation and innovations alter the menu of assets that are available for households and businesses to hold. Next, we show how the deregulation of financial markets can increase the volatility of interest rates.

Until 1986 **Regulation Q** put ceilings on interest rates on certain types of deposits.

Effects of Regulation Q.   Until 1986 federal regulations put ceilings on the interest rates that could be paid on various categories of deposits at banks and thrift institutions. When interest rates on money-market instruments, like Treasury bills increased, either because of a rightward shift of the *IS* curve or a leftward shift of the *LM* curve, a substantial gap could open up between the interest rates on money-market instruments and the deposit interest rates that were *held down by regulations*.

Large gaps between the interest rates on Treasury bills and on passbook savings accounts caused massive withdrawals of funds from commercial banks and thrift institutions, each of which are depository institutions. The resulting reduction in loans made by thrifts had a disproportionately depressing effect on the housing market, because thrifts were required by law to hold almost all their assets in the form of mortgages. The supply of mortgage finance declined for purchasers of both new and used homes. The shift toward bonds, Treasury bills, and money market mutual funds, and away from depository institutions was called **disintermediation.** An outflow of funds from the thrifts, a drop in mortgage finance, and a decline in housing expenditure occurred in every postwar episode of high interest rates before 1983.

Disintermediation was the withdrawal of funds from financial intermediaries like thrift institutions when market interest rates rose above the interest rate ceilings on savings and time deposit accounts.

Financial Deregulation and the *IS* Curve

Financial deregulation and innovation beginning in the late 1970s, including the introduction of new interest-sensitive deposits at the thrifts, the removal of deposit-rate and loan-rate ceilings, and the development of mortgage-backed securities, largely eliminated the incentive for disintermediation and its effects on mortgage finance. Another innovation was the **adjustable-rate mortgage** (ARM). Interest rates on ARMs tend to adjust to the interest rates in the open market, rising and falling about the same amount as interest rates on Treasury bills, for example.

An **adjustable-rate mortgage** has an interest rate that can change frequently in response to changes in short-term interest rates, in contrast to a fixed-interest mortgage.

Prior to financial deregulation and innovation, purchases of new homes and of consumer durables declined sharply when interest rates in the open market rose. They declined because disintermediation reduced the funds that depository institutions had available to lend. At the same time, regulations prevented some loan and mortgage rates from rising as much as other rates rose. Thus, construction of new houses declined dramatically even though mortgage rates rose relatively little when disintermediation reduced the funds that depository institutions had available to lend out. With the removal of virtually all ceilings on deposit and loan interest rates, depository institutions are free to raise deposit rates to prevent disintermediation and keep mortgage rates in line with other interest rates. Because disintermediation no longer stymies spending, larger increases in interest rates are now required to reduce spending by the same amount.

Recall that the *IS* curve displays all the combinations of real output *(Y)* and the market rate *(r)* that are consistent with equilibrium in the commodity market. The slope of the *IS* curve indicates how much an increase in the interest rate reduces interest-sensitive spending, and thus reduces real output. Changes in financial markets have made the *IS* curve steeper, shown in the left frame of Figure 13-3, because a larger increase in the interest rate on financial assets is required to reduce spending by the same amount.

Why the *LM* Curve Became Steeper

Chapter 4 showed that the *LM* curve normally slopes up because the demand for M1 responds to the interest rate paid on bonds and other nonmonetary assets. That interest rate (r) is plotted on the vertical axis in Figure 13-3. Our previous analysis, and the curve in Figure 13-3 labeled "old *LM* curve," assumed that the interest rate paid on M1 (r_m) was zero. Thus an increase in r raised $r - r_m$ by the same amount and increased the incentive for individuals to reduce their holdings of M1.

This analysis is still valid for holdings of currency, which pays no interest. But financial reforms have allowed banks to offer interest-bearing checking NOW and super NOW accounts. The interest rate on these accounts is variable, tending to rise and fall with the interest rate paid on nonmonetary assets (r). Thus r_m, which is an average of the zero interest rate on currency and the positive interest rate paid on NOW and super NOW accounts, responds partially to changes in r. Thus, the difference, $r - r_m$, now rises by less than the amount of any increase in r, providing less of an incentive than previously for individuals to reduce their checking account balances. As a result, the demand for money function, and thus the *LM* curve, has become steeper in the right frame of Figure 13-3.

FINANCIAL DEREGULATION TILTS THE *IS* AND *LM* CURVES

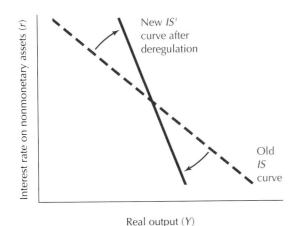 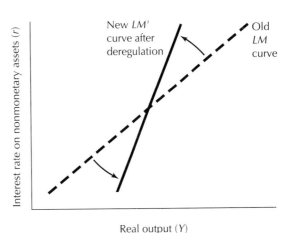

Figure 13-3 **The Effect of Financial Deregulation in the Commodity and Money Markets**
In the left-hand frame deregulation caused the *IS* curve to become the steeper line, *IS'*. This was the result not only of the discontinuation of Regulation Q, but also of the introduction of new types of deposits at depository institutions with flexible interest rates, the development of mortgage-backed securities, and the introduction of adjustable-rate mortgages. In the right-hand frame the *LM* curve became the steeper line *LM'*, because a given increase in the interest rate in financial markets does not cause as much of a reduction of the demand for M1 as previously, since depository institutions are now able to raise the rates they pay for deposits.

Effects on Interest Rates

Now we can put our analysis into action and learn why the main effect of deregulation is likely to be increased volatility of interest rates. In Figure 13-4 both frames show the *LM* curve shifting to the left by the same horizontal distance, as the result of a decision by the Fed to tighten monetary policy. The difference between the frames is that the left-hand frame shows the economy before deregulation, with the flatter "old *IS* curve" and "old *LM* curve" copied from Figure 13-3. The right-hand frame shows the economy after deregulation, with the new curves *IS'* and *LM'*, also copied from Figure 13-3. The economy moves from point *A* to *B* in the left frame and from point *A* to *B'* in the right frame, with a much greater increase in the interest rate under the new deregulated environment.

PUZZLE 4: WHY WERE INTEREST RATES IN THE 1980s HIGHER THAN EVER BEFORE?

This analysis helps explain the fourth macroeconomic puzzle introduced in Chapter 1, which involved interest rates. And it shows that deregulation can have adverse side effects that may partially offset the benefits of greater efficiency and fairness when prices (that is, interest rates) play the main role in balancing supply and demand in financial markets.

WHY DEREGULATION MAKES INTEREST RATES MORE VOLATILE

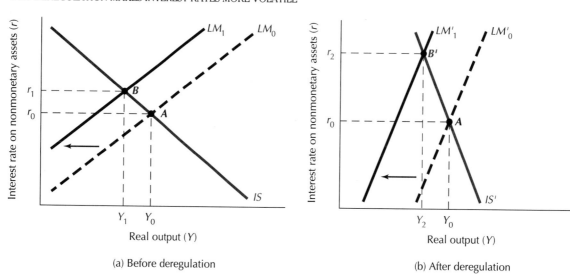

(a) Before deregulation

(b) After deregulation

Figure 13-4   **The Effect of a Lower Money Supply on Interest Rates and Output**
Both frames show the effect of the same leftward horizontal shift in the *LM* curve as the result of a decision by the Fed to tighten monetary policy. In both frames the *IS* curve remains fixed. The difference is that the left frame uses the flatter *IS* and *LM* curves from the period before deregulation of financial markets, copied from Figure 13-3. The right frame uses the new steeper *IS'* and *LM'* curves, also copied from Figure 13-3. As a result of the steeper curves, a given leftward shift in the *LM* curve creates a much larger increase in the interest rate in the right frame than in the left frame. We cannot tell whether output fell more in the right frame than in the left frame.

13-8 Why the Federal Reserve "Sets" Interest Rates

We have just seen how financial deregulation and innovation can alter the slopes of the *IS* and *LM* curves. The effects, and even the occurrence, of financial deregulation and innovation will not always be predictable. In addition, the *IS* and *LM* curves will sometimes shift unpredictably for reasons unrelated to financial deregulation and innovation.

Pervasive deregulation and innovation in financial markets were apparently major contributors to the frequent instability of the demand for money since the mid-1970s. But even after the fact, it has been difficult to redefine the money supply or change the list of factors that affect the demand for money so that there is a stable relation between the amount of money demanded and measures of income and interest rates. In the 1970s, for example, the growing use of credit cards was suspected as a reason that the demand for money was inexplicably weak. However, considering definitions of the money supply that included credit card balances, or in some other way allowing for the possibility that households held lower checking account balances when they had the option of making purchases with credit cards, did not explain the instability. Similarly, the official redefinition of M2 in 1980 to include money market mutual funds did not produce a stable demand for money then or in the years that followed. Nor did a stable demand for money result in the 1990s when researchers considered adding balances in stock and bond mutual funds to the other assets in M2.[16]

Whether financial deregulation and innovation will continue at the same pace through the 1990s and beyond is uncertain. Further deregulation may allow insurance companies and investment banks to conduct activities formerly prohibited to them. Further innovation may lead to the widespread use of e-money and of electronic home banking. The experience since the 1970s suggests that even knowing whether these changes in regulation and technology will take place, however, will not tell us how much the demand for money will be affected. The large, frequent, and apparently continuing instability of the demand for money led the Fed in 1993 to reduce its focus on the money supply and to concentrate more on interest rates in its conduct of near-term monetary policy.

In this section we use the *IS-LM* model of Chapter 4 to explain why the unpredictability, or instability, of the demand for money led the Federal Reserve to shift its policies toward setting interest rates. Reports in the media and announcements from the Fed that the FOMC has decided to change interest rates often give the (incorrect) impression that the Fed sets interest rates directly. It is important to remember that the Fed can only affect the nominal federal funds interest rate indirectly. When the Fed wants to raise short-term interest rates, it undertakes open-market sales of bonds, which reduce reserves and thus the money supply. When the Fed sells the right amount of bonds, the *LM* curve shifts leftward and intersects the *IS* curve at the higher interest rate that the Fed seeks.

---

[16]For a complete evaluation of the issues and evidence regarding stock and bond mutual funds and the demand for money, see Athanasios Orphanides, Brian Reid, and David H. Small, "The Empirical Properties of a Monetary Aggregate That Adds Bond and Stock Funds to M2," *The Federal Reserve Bank of St. Louis Review,* vol. 76, no. 6 (November/December 1994).

As in Chapter 4, Figure 13-5 illustrates the working of the *IS-LM* model with a diagram that plots the interest rate on the vertical axis and the level of real output on the horizontal axis. As in Chapter 4, we assume that the expected inflation rate is zero, so that the nominal and real interest rates are the same; both are labeled simply as the "interest rate" on the vertical axis. A constant price level is an acceptable assumption when long-term wage and price contracts in the real world limit the flexibility of the price level in the short run. In such a case, the shifts in the *IS* or *LM* curves of Figure 13-5 mainly influence the level of real output in the first few months or quarters after the shift.

The *IS* curve shows all the combinations of the interest rate and real output that maintain equilibrium in the commodity market, while the *LM* curve shows the combinations that maintain equilibrium in the money market. The position of the *IS* curve can be shifted by changes in business and consumer optimism, by changes in net exports, and by changes in government spending, autonomous net taxes, and tax rates. When *commodity demand is unstable* because of swings in optimism, net exports, or government policy, the *IS* curve shifts back and forth as shown in the left-hand frame of Figure 13-5. The

---

WHICH MONETARY POLICY TARGET MINIMIZES OUTPUT VARIABILITY
DEPENDS ON THE SOURCE OF INSTABILITY

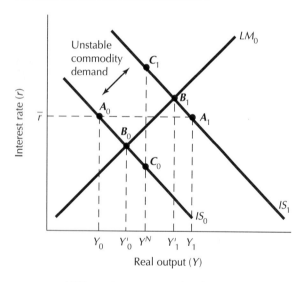

(a) Target the money supply when commodity
demand is unstable

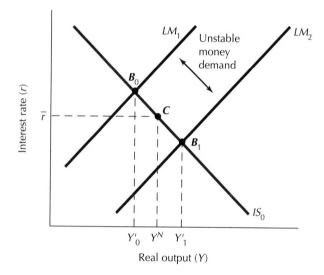

(b) Target the interest rate when money
demand is unstable

Figure 13-5   **Effects on Real Output of Policies That Either Stabilize the Interest Rate or Stabilize the Real Money Supply When Either Commodity Demand or Money Demand Is Unstable**

In the left frame the demand for commodities is unstable, fluctuating unpredictably between IS_0 and IS_1. A policy that maintains a fixed real money supply and a fixed LM_0 curve leads to smaller fluctuations of output than an alternative policy that stabilizes the interest rate at r by shifting *LM.* A third policy, which stabilizes real GDP at Y^N, causes interest rate instability between points C_0 and C_1. In the right frame, the demand for money is unstable. In this case a policy of stabilizing the interest rate at $\bar{r}$, will stabilize real GDP. When the real money supply is held fixed, unstable money demand shifts the *LM* curve from LM_1 to LM_2 and causes output to fluctuate between Y_0' and Y_1'.

position of the *LM* curve can be shifted by a change in the real money supply; the LM_0 curve in the left-hand frame assumes that the real money supply is fixed.[17] The *LM* curve will also be shifted when the demand for money is unstable. A sudden increase in the demand for money brought on by a financial panic would shift the *LM* curve leftward.

Implications of Unstable Commodity Demand.   William Poole of Brown University first popularized the use of the *IS-LM* model to compare targeting of the money supply with the alternative of targeting the interest rate.[18] Unstable commodity demand, shown by the shifting *IS* curve in the left-hand frame of Figure 13-5, calls into question the wisdom of targeting the interest rate. When the real money supply is held constant and the *LM* curve remains fixed at LM_0, the economy moves back and forth between positions B_0 and B_1. In the left-hand frame, and real output moves over the limited range between Y_0' and Y_1'.

With unstable commodity demand, fixing the *LM* curve by targeting the money supply is superior to a policy of maintaining stable interest rates. When commodity demand is high (as along IS_1), a stable interest rate policy means that the real money supply must be allowed to rise to prevent the interest rate from increasing. The Federal Reserve must increase the money supply to accommodate the additional demand for money that occurs when commodity demand is high. The stable interest rate policy causes the economy to fluctuate between points A_0 and A_1, and it allows real output to vary over the wide range between Y_0 and Y_1.

Instead of targeting interest rates or the money supply, an alternative approach for the Fed would be to target real GDP itself. The policy of targeting real output is illustrated in the left-hand frame of Figure 13-5 by the points C_0 and C_1. Fluctuations in commodity demand would have to be offset by fluctuations in the supply of money in the *opposite* direction. If the *LM* curve can be promptly moved in the opposite direction of the shift in the *IS* curve, then the economy could remain at its natural real GDP (Y^N). And, as we learned in Chapter 8, keeping the economy at Y^N is consistent with steady inflation in the absence of supply shocks.

The Analysis with Unstable Money Demand.   The right-hand frame of Figure 13-5 assumes that commodity demand is fixed, so that the *IS* curve remains fixed at IS_0. But, here the demand for money is assumed to be unstable. When the real money supply is fixed, *an unstable demand for money causes the* LM *curve to move about unpredictably between* LM_1 *and* LM_2. A constant money supply policy leads to fluctuations in the economy between points B_0 and B_1, with output varying between Y_0' and Y_1'. A superior policy is to change the money supply in order to maintain a constant interest rate. When the demand for money rises, the interest rate is prevented from rising by raising the money supply. This constant interest rate policy keeps the

---

[17]A fixed real money supply *(M/P)* and a fixed *LM* curve can be achieved either with a constant nominal money supply *(M)* and a fixed price level *(P)*, or with the money supply growing at the same rate as the price level $(m = p)$

[18]William Poole, "Optimal Choice of Monetary Policy Instruments in a Simple Stochastic Macro Model," *Quarterly Journal of Economics*, vol. 84 (May 1970), pp. 197–216. A little-known earlier reference is M. L. Burstein, *Economic Theory* (New York: Wiley, 1966), Chapter 13.

INTERNATIONAL PERSPECTIVE

Where in the World Is All the U.S. Currency?

Section 13-8 shows us why the stability of the demand for money relative to the stability of commodity demand influences whether the Fed is likely to target interest rates or the money supply. Section 13-7 showed us that financial deregulation and innovation in the United States contributed to the instability of the demand for money. That instability may also stem importantly from unstable demand for the money of the United States by those outside the United States. At least since the 1980s the foreign demand for U.S. currency has been large and volatile. To the extent that the foreign demand for U.S. currency is unpredictable, it adds another source of instability to the total demand for money. Here we discuss how much U.S. currency is outstanding, where it all is, and why. We also show measures of the "cash-intensity" of the U.S. and several other countries.

Though checks, credit cards, and e-money have each been predicted to replace it, old-fashioned cash seems as popular as ever. Though cash transactions often involve small dollar amounts, they are more numerous than any other type of transaction. About 20 percent of the dollar amount of household expenditures are made with cash, and at the end of 1995, U.S. currency totaled $380 billion, or nearly $1400 per inhabitant of the United States. Currency is the sum of the coins and paper Federal Reserve notes that are held outside the vaults of depository institutions. (Remember that the reserves held by depository institutions are not counted in the definition of the money supply. At the end of 1995, U.S. depository institutions held $42 billion of currency in their vaults. [They also held $20 billion as reserves in deposits in their respective Federal Reserve Banks.]) Of the $380 billion of U.S. currency outstanding, coins accounted for $23 billion. The six billion $1 bills make them the most numerous denomination, but the approximately $240 billion worth of $100 bills outstanding constitute by far the largest share of currency by value. Although wider use of automatic teller machines, or ATMs, has raised the demand for $20 bills, the value of $100 bills outstanding is still three times that of $20 bills.

The table shows that the amount of currency outstanding per inhabitant varies widely across countries around the world. Using the exchange rate we have translated these values into U.S. dollar equivalents. Although the Canadian economy resembles that of the United States, on a per capita basis there are fewer than half as many Canadian as American dollars. There are even fewer British pounds. On the other hand, the Japanese, who use relatively few paper checks, have far more currency outstanding than do other developed countries. The middle column in the table shows the ratio of currency to GDP. Japan and Germany have above-average amounts of currency

Currency Holdings and ATMs in North America, Japan, and Europe, 1995

Country	Currency per Inhabitant ($US)	Currency-GDP Ratio (Percent)	ATMs per 1 Million Inhabitants (Number)
Canada	662	3.4	595
France	891	3.7	395
Germany	2025	6.9	436
Italy	1082	5.5	378
Japan	3873	10.4	1013
United Kingdom	528	2.8	358
United States	1443	5.2	467

Source: Bank for International Settlements, Basle, December 1996.

outstanding relative to their populations and relative to the amounts of their economic activity. The United States' currency-to-GDP ratio of 5.2 percent is about average for this group of countries.

The right column of the table shows the number of ATMs per one million inhabitants in each country. Consistent with its strong demand for currency, Japan leads the way, with more than twice as many ATMs as most other countries. In general, in countries where ATM transactions are fewer, the average size of the transactions are larger. For example, in Japan, where ATM transactions per capita are about one-tenth as frequent as in the United States, the average ATM transaction is about $450. At the 120,000 ATMs in the United States, the average currency withdrawal is about $70.

Both firms and households would be expected to optimize the amount of zero-interest-bearing currency they hold, balancing opportunity costs against transaction costs, as in the Baumol-Tobin models presented in Section 13-6. The large amount of U.S. currency has long seemed at odds with everyday experience. Though some currency is held by retail businesses like grocery stores and gas stations, most currency is thought to be held by households. Currency is rarely used for payments by businesses or government. Speculation about who was holding and using so much U.S. currency, and why, often conjured up hypotheses about drug-dealing, tax evasion, and other illegal activities. In general, the amounts of currency outstanding seem very large relative to the presumed extent of such activities.

Recent research points to an answer to this puzzle: It indicates that about 60 percent of all U.S. currency isn't even in the United States.[a] (That is why the example in Section 13-4 did not use the actual currency-to-deposits ratio of 45 percent, but a ratio that is only one-third as large—15 percent.) The study suggests that about $225 billion of U.S. currency is now abroad. It also estimates that whereas in the late 1970s only about 1 out of 4 of the additional U.S. dollars outstanding went abroad, during the first half of the 1990s about 3 out of every 4 additional dollars issued went abroad.

Paper money is cheap to make, which is the allure of counterfeiting. In the mid-1990s, currency had an average production cost to the U.S. government of about $0.04 per note, regardless of denomination. The new $100 bills, which first appeared in 1996 and have a number of anticounterfeiting features, cost the U.S. Bureau of Printing and Engraving about $0.05 each to produce. Pennies cost about 8/10 of a cent to produce. Selling a product—in this case $100 bills—for $100 when it costs only a nickel to produce can be very profitable. For example, the flow of currency abroad during the early 1990s provided nearly $20 billion of net revenue annually to the U.S. government.

Households and businesses in high-inflation countries often use U.S. dollars in order to avoid the impact of inflation on their home currencies. Households and businesses in politically unstable countries also demand U.S. dollars, which are regarded worldwide as being a secure store of value. Thus, it is not surprising that in recent years the demand for U.S. currency has been strong in Latin America, in eastern Europe, and in the republics of the former Soviet Union. Demand has been especially strong in Argentina and Russia. The increased foreign demand for U.S. dollars, then, explains at least partly why the total demand for U.S. currency has been so strong at a time when financial deregulation and innovations over the past two decades would

---

[a]Ruth A. Judson and Richard D. Porter, "The Location of U.S. Currency: How Much Is Abroad?", *Federal Reserve Bulletin* (October 1996), pp. 883–903.

have been expected to reduce the demand for currency.

The demand abroad for U.S. currency is concentrated in $100 bills, the largest U.S. denomination that has been issued for many years. Such bills are easier to travel with and to use for large-scale transactions. In Argentina, for example, U.S. dollars are used to pay for cars and houses. The reason is that you get more bang-per-buck, or rather bucks-per-ounce, with $100 bills. (As your experience probably tells you, you can fit about $1 million of $100 bills in a briefcase!)

Finding that the foreign demand for U.S. currency has been strong helps us explain why there is so much U.S. currency outstanding. In addition, the dependence of foreign demand on unpredictable forces like political upheaval alerts us to another reason why the U.S. economy may not perform well under a constant growth rate rule (CGRR) for the money supply. It is the total demand, foreign and domestic, for U.S. currency that is included in the demand for money. To the extent that foreign demand for U.S. currency is unstable, the total demand for money will be unstable, and the case for the Federal Reserve to target interest rates or GDP rather than the money supply is strengthened.

economy pinned to point C, with a fixed interest rate $\bar{r}$ and a fixed output level Y^N. In this diagram, an interest rate target and a natural real GDP (Y^N) target amount to the same thing.

The Case for a GDP Target

In the left-hand frame of Figure 13-5, an unstable demand for commodities makes a real GDP target superior to a money supply target, which in turn is superior to an interest rate target. In the right-hand frame, with an unstable demand for money, a real GDP and interest rate target are the same, and both are superior to a money supply target. If, as is likely, there is instability in both commodity and money demand, a real GDP target is superior to an interest rate target.

In a world with no supply shocks of the types we studied in Chapter 8 (such as sharp changes in the price of oil), there would be no difference between targeting real GDP at the level of natural real GDP (Y^N) and targeting nominal GDP to grow at a constant rate. If the economy were initially operating at Y^N, with excess nominal GDP growth $(x - y^N)$ equal to the rate of inflation, a policy of maintaining $Y = Y^N$ would be the same as maintaining nominal GDP growth equal to the present inflation rate plus the growth rate of natural real GDP $(x = p + y^N)$.

Supply shocks, however, make nominal GDP targeting different from real GDP targeting. A policy that fixes the growth rate of nominal GDP would, in the aftermath of an adverse supply shock, allow real GDP to fall below natural real GDP, as at point L in Figure 8-10 on p. 253. In contrast, a policy of maintaining $Y = Y^N$ would require an accommodating monetary policy and an acceleration of nominal GDP growth in response to an adverse supply shock. Because of the likelihood that accommodation of an adverse supply shock would lead to a permanent acceleration of inflation, many activists recommend that the Fed target nominal GDP growth rather than the growth rate of real GDP.

SELF-TEST | Using the *IS-LM* model analysis of Figure 13-5, which neglects both lags and inflation, rank three types of policies (money supply rule, interest rate rule, real GDP rule) by their ability to maintain stable real GDP under two sets of circumstances: (1) unstable commodity demand and (2) unstable demand for money. In each case, rank as first the policy that is most likely to maintain stable output, then the next best policy, and then the third best.

SUMMARY

1. Surplus funds from savers are channeled to borrowers by way of financial intermediaries and financial markets. The main types of financial intermediaries are depository institutions, contractual saving institutions, and investment intermediaries. The main types of financial market instruments are money market and capital market instruments.

2. The United States has two major definitions of the money supply. M1 includes currency, balances in transactions accounts, and traveler's checks. M2 comprises M1 plus other assets, including savings deposits, small time deposits, and retail money market mutual funds.

3. A set of banks in a closed economy—one with no transfers of funds to the outside—can "create money" by a multiple of each dollar of cash that is initially received. This is true for a single bank on a desert island or for all banks in the United States taken together.

4. The deposit-creation multiplier is 1.0 divided by the fraction of the initial cash receipt that is held as reserves or currency. The money multiplier is then the deposit multiplier times 1.0 plus the currency-holding fraction. The money supply is equal to high-powered money times the money multiplier.

5. The Fed uses three tools for changing the money supply: open-market operations, the discount rate, and reserve requirements.

6. Several theories have been developed to explain the relation between the demand for money, income, wealth, and the interest rate. The transactions demand

for money depends on the interest rate; people will take the trouble to make extra trips to the bank and keep more of their income in savings accounts (and other interest-earning assets) when the interest rate is higher.

7. The portfolio approach emphasizes the household decision to allocate its wealth among money, savings accounts, bonds, and other assets. Any event that raises wealth, such as a stimulative fiscal policy, will tend to raise the demand for money.

8. Deregulation and innovation in financial markets has made both the *IS* and *LM* curves steeper, so that a given change in the supply of money now has a larger effect on interest rates.

9. In earlier chapters we assumed that the growth of aggregate demand could be controlled precisely by policymakers. We now recognize that in the real-world economy, policy shifts cannot instantly or precisely offset the effects on aggregate demand of shocks to *IS* or *LM* curves.

10. When commodity demand is unstable and money demand is stable, a money supply target is superior to an interest rate target, but a real GDP target is superior to both. When money demand is unstable and commodity demand is stable, both real GDP and interest rate targets are superior to a money supply target.

11. The ongoing instability of the demand for money has led the Fed to target interest rates rather than the money supply.

CONCEPTS

financial deregulation
financial markets
financial intermediaries
thrift institutions

money market instruments
capital market instruments
M1
M2

high-powered money
money multiplier
open-market operations
discount rate
required reserves

reserve requirements
money-multiplier shock
Regulation Q
disintermediation
adjustable-rate mortgage

QUESTIONS AND PROBLEMS

Questions

1. What is meant by the term *financial markets*? Given the existence of financial markets, why do we have financial intermediaries?
2. Distinguish among the three types of financial intermediaries: depository institutions, contractual saving institutions, and investment intermediaries.
3. Distinguish between money market instruments and capital market instruments.
4. What are the two most important functions of money? Give examples of assets that perform both functions. Give examples of assets that perform one of the functions but not the other.
5. What is the main distinction between the M1 and M2 definitions of money?
6. What is high-powered money? Explain why *both* reserves and cash held by the public are considered to be high-powered money.
7. What are the required conditions for money creation? In the Great Depression of the 1930s, many bank failures occurred in part because one or more of these conditions was no longer met. Which are the most likely candidates to explain the failure of the banking system to operate properly in the depths of the Depression?
8. Explain what happens when the Fed conducts an open-market purchase of $200 billion in bonds. How do the banks get involved? What is the ultimate effect on the level of high-powered money and on the money supply?
9. Explain how the money-creation multiplier is similar to the income-determination multiplier of Chapter 3.

10. What are the major ways in which the supply of money can change? If it is that simple, why couldn't the Fed effectively control the money supply in the past?
11. Explain the significance of the Baumol-Tobin analysis of the transactions demand for money.
12. In what ways are the portfolio approaches developed by Tobin and Friedman similar? In what ways do they differ?
13. What is meant by the term *disintermediation*? What impact did deregulation of financial markets have on the process?
14. How have financial deregulation and innovation since the early 1980s affected the *IS* and *LM* curves and the results to be expected from monetary and fiscal policy?
15. Many people advocate the supremacy of rules over discretion in the Fed's conduct of monetary policy, but there is less agreement as to what kind of rule the Fed should follow. A money supply rule, an interest rate rule, and a real GDP rule have all been suggested. Discuss the advantages and disadvantages of each type of rule.
16. Approximately 60 percent of all U.S. currency is held outside the United States. What factors account for large holdings of U.S. dollars abroad, and how does the foreign demand for U.S. currency affect the administration of monetary policy?

Problems

1. Suppose the ratio of deposits that banks hold in the form of reserves is 7 percent. Suppose further that people want to hold 8 percent of their deposits in the form of cash. Then, if the Fed wants the money supply to be $800 billion, what is the necessary level of high-powered money?
2. Assume an economy in which the reserve ratio is 15 percent, people hold 10 percent of their deposits in the form of cash, and there are no other leakages.

(a) If the current level of high-powered money is $100 billion, what is the money supply in this economy?
(b) How much does the money supply change if the Fed buys $5 billion of U.S. government treasury bills from a government bond dealer? How about if banks' borrowings of reserves from the Fed decline by $2 billion?
(c) If the Fed set a target money supply of $560 bil-

lion, what would it have to do to achieve that target?

3. Suppose you earn and spend $2400 per month. You receive your paycheck on the first day of the month and must decide how much of it to hold as cash or in a non-interest-earning checking account and how much to deposit in your savings account. The savings account pays 5 percent interest; however, the bank charges you $2 for each withdrawal you make during the month.
   (a) What will be your average demand for money over the month?
   (b) If the interest rate rose to 10 percent, what would be your average demand for money over the month? Is this change consistent with your expectations about the demand for money?

4. The following equations summarize the structure of the commodity market both before and after deregulation of the financial system.

$$C = a + 0.75\,(Y - T) \qquad G = 400$$
$$a = 50 - 5r \qquad\qquad T = 200 + 0.2Y$$
$$I_p = 200 - 5r \qquad\quad NX = 150 - 0.1Y$$

The demand for money before deregulation is $(M/P)^d = 0.4Y - 36r$, and the demand for money after deregulation is $(M/P)^d = 0.3Y - 12r$. The money supply both before and after deregulation is 300. Using the above information, answer the following questions:
   (a) What is the equation of the *IS* curve?
   (b) What is the equation of the *LM* curve before deregulation?
   (c) What is the equation of the *LM* curve after deregulation?
   (d) What are the equilibrium levels of Y and r before deregulation?
   (e) What are the equilibrium levels of Y and r after deregulation?
   (f) How do your answers to (b) through (e) differ before and after deregulation?
   (g) Before deregulation, if the money supply increased to 350 from 300, what would Y and r be?
   (h) After deregulation, if the money supply increased to 350 from 300, what would Y and r before?
   (i) Are these results consistent with the text's explanation of the effect of deregulation on the variability of interest rates?

SELF-TEST ANSWERS

p. 407 Commercial banks are the largest single type of financial intermediary. Money market mutual funds are financial intermediaries; state government bonds are capital market instruments; state government retirement funds are financial intermediaries; corporate bonds are capital market instruments; and commercial paper is a money market instrument.

p. 409 (1) This new type of account, which allows interest to be earned and checks to be written, is part of M2, and so its invention raises the demand for M2 and lowers the demand for M1; (2) This new product lowers the demand for M1, unless M1 is redefined to include the balances on smart cards, because some households will prefer to hold balances on their smart cards rather than in their transaction actions. If M1 is redefined to include smart card balances, the demand for M1 is unlikely to change much; (3) same as (1).

p. 415 (1) $D = H/(e + c) = 500/0.4 = 1250$
$M = (1 + c)D = (1.25)1250 = 1562.5$
(2) $D = 500/0.5 = 1000$
$M = (1.35)1000 = 1350$
(3) $D = 500/0.5 = 1000$. $M = (1.25)1000 = 1250$

p. 418 The short answer is that the Fed sells bonds when it wants to reduce high-powered money (and hence the money supply through equation 13.6), and it buys bonds when it wants to raise the money supply. To pay for the bonds they bought, the purchasers send high-powered money to the Fed, thereby reducing the amount of H remaining in the economy. Lowering the discount rate, the interest rate that they pay on their discount window borrowings, makes it more attractive for depository institutions to borrow H from the Fed. An increased stock of H in the economy raises the money supply.

p. 423 Starting from an initial equilibrium, an increase in the supply of M1 creates an excess supply of M1. According to Tobin and Friedman, M1 is a substitute for both bonds and stocks, and so some of the M1 that is in excess of the initial demand will be used to purchase bonds and stocks, causing prices to rise in both markets. (Strictly speaking, the Tobin version makes stocks and bonds a substitute only for the interest-bearing part of M1, not non–interest-bearing currency and checking deposits.)

p. 433 (1) With unstable commodity demand, a real GDP rule is most capable of maintaining stable real GDP and the interest rate rule is least likely to maintain stable real GDP. (2) With unstable money demand, the real GDP and interest rate rules are equally capable of maintaining stable real GDP, while the money supply rule will result in unstable real GDP.

> *Economic forecasting is the occupation that makes astrology respectable.*[1]
> —*David Dremas, 1982*

14-1   The Central Role of Demand Shocks

Unrealistic Precision of Policy Control in Previous Chapters

Demand shocks include unexpected changes in business and consumer optimism, changes in net exports, and changes in government spending or tax rates (for example, in wartime) not related to stabilization policy.

Policy activism purposefully changes the settings of the instruments of monetary and fiscal policy to offset changes in private sector spending.

In earlier chapters we assumed that aggregate demand could be controlled exactly. But in the real world, life is more difficult for policymakers. Exogenous **demand shocks** can shift the *AD* curve and thus the level of nominal GDP, but policymakers cannot neutralize these shocks totally because nominal GDP reacts to policy changes with a lag and by an uncertain amount. As a result, many economists argue against **policy activism,** that is, the use of monetary and fiscal policy to offset exogenous demand shocks.

In this chapter we take into account those aspects of the real-world economy that make successful policy activism elusive. We contrast the real world with the idealized world of the simple *IS-LM* model (Chapters 4–5), where policymakers could compute the exact policy response (taking the form of a change in the money supply, government spending, autonomous net taxes, or tax rates) needed to offset fully any shift in the *IS* or *LM* curves. In that model there was no obstacle to an instant response by policymakers and of the economy to prevent output and unemployment from being affected by changes in consumer or business confidence, net exports, or other demand disturbances.

Similarly, our dynamic inflation model of Chapter 8 was driven by the assumption that nominal GDP was exogenous and could be set exactly by policymakers. In that model the cure for inflation was straightforward, if painful—inflation could be reduced permanently by any required amount at the cost of a temporary, but perhaps sizable, decline in output and increase in unemployment.

The supply side of the economy can also be hit by shocks. In Chapter 8 we saw how adverse supply shocks, such as the sudden increases in the price of oil during the 1970s, can raise inflation and lower output simultaneously. Whether policymakers respond to adverse supply shocks with accommodating or extinguishing policies depends on their perceptions of the costs to society of temporarily higher inflation relative to the costs of temporarily higher unemployment. Different policymakers are likely to make different judgments about these relative costs and thus recommend different amounts of accommodation in response to adverse supply shocks.

---

[1]David Dremas, "The Madness of Crowds," *Forbes,* September 27, 1982, p. 201.

There is much less disagreement on the demand side. In general, economists recommend that aggregate demand grow steadily. Suppose the economy were to start from its natural level of output. If autonomous net exports declined or the natural employment government budget surplus rose, the widespread (but not universal) consensus among economists to the resulting negative shock to aggregate demand would be that policy should attempt to offset that shock. In the absence of supply shocks, stabilizing nominal demand will stabilize output. Thus in this chapter we discuss the real-world complications that influence the success of activist policies and of rules-based policies in stabilizing the growth rate of nominal aggregate demand.

The Economy as Supertanker

Unfortunately, policymakers cannot steer the economy back and forth as easily as a driver steers an automobile. Changing aggregate demand is much more like steering a giant supertanker. Even if the captain gives the signal for a hard turn, it takes a mile or so to see a change in the supertanker's direction, and 10 miles before the supertanker completes the turn. In the same way, the real-world economy has a momentum of its own, and policy shifts cannot control aggregate demand precisely.

Chapter 13 on money demand and supply introduced several of the reasons why monetary control is so difficult. The Fed does not control the money supply precisely. Rather, money multiplier shocks occur because the link between the Fed's instruments and the money supply depends in part on factors over which the Fed has no direct control, such as the public's demand for currency. Furthermore, shifts in the demand for money loosen the links between the money supply and nominal GDP.

A **policy rule** can call for a fixed path of a policy instrument like the discount rate, of an intermediate variable like the money supply, or a target variable like inflation or unemployment. A rule can also call for a specified response of a policy instrument in response to a given change in a target variable.

In this chapter we contrast policy activism with an alternative approach based on **policy rules.** We examine specific rules that fix the growth rate of high-powered money or the money supply, and discuss the pros and cons of policy rules in general. We then examine in detail some of the problems associated with activist policies, including lags, forecasting errors, uncertainty about responses, and the need to maintain credibility. We see that the policy debate is less about the general merits of rules than about *which of many alternative rules should be implemented.* Many proposed rules, such as those that fix the growth rate of nominal GDP or the price level, are just as vulnerable to the pitfalls of lags, forecasting errors, and response uncertainty as are activist policies. We also look into two monetary policy rules that have been much discussed internationally: targeting the exchange rate and maintaining a single European currency.

14-2 Stabilization Targets and Instruments in the Activists' Paradise

This section sets forth the traditional analysis of stabilization policy favored by the proponents of policy activism and explains why activists feel that multiple policy instruments are needed, and also how they perceive the roles of monetary and fiscal policy. We then focus on the concerns of those who advocate policy rules and oppose activism. Their opposition is highlighted by a number of idealized assumptions that would be necessary for policy activism to work promptly and precisely, an unrealistic ideal called (for ease of reference) the "activists' paradise."

The Need for Multiple Instruments

In attempting to reach a given destination, the driver of a car is trying to hit two targets: a particular latitude (north-south position) and a specific longitude (east-west position). To hit these two targets, the driver needs two basic instruments: an engine to move the car forward or backward and a steering wheel to move it left or right. Just as hitting two location targets in a car requires two instruments, hitting two policy targets requires at least two instruments of stabilization policy. For instance, Chapter 5 showed that changes in the real money supply could not simultaneously achieve both a target level of real GDP and a target interest rate. Both monetary and fiscal policy must be manipulated to achieve an intersection of the *IS* and *LM* curves at a given combination of the interest rate and real GDP.

The *IS-LM* analysis assumed that the price level was fixed. Monetary and fiscal policy together control the growth rate of nominal and real GDP and the real interest rate in the short run. Now that we have learned to allow for inflation, we recognize that monetary policy involves control of the growth rate only of a nominal variable (like high-powered money or the money supply). In the long run, when actual and natural real GDP growth are the same, monetary policy controls the inflation rate (nominal minus real GDP growth) and fiscal policy controls the growth of real GDP.

Monetary, Fiscal, and Structural Employment Policies.   The natural rate of unemployment is beyond the control of monetary and fiscal policy. A permanent reduction in unemployment requires a permanent drop in the natural rate of unemployment, which in turn requires a separate policy instrument. That instrument is the mixture of structural employment policy tools discussed in Chapter 12—training subsidies to firms, and so on. Also, sometimes lucky events, like the sharp decline in medical care inflation in the mid-1990s, can reduce the natural rate of unemployment without the need for any action by policymakers (as we learned in Section 8-8).

Policy instruments for monetary policy are high-powered money and the Fed's discount rate; for fiscal policy they are government spending and tax rates.

But we have not finished adding to our list of policy instruments. Fiscal policy really consists of two types of **policy instruments:** government spending and tax rates. A given government deficit can be achieved with high spending and high tax rates or low spending and low tax rates. Thus, given any level of the natural employment deficit, another target of policy is the size of government spending and revenue relative to natural real GDP.

So far we are up to five instruments and five targets:

Instruments	*Targets*
Structural employment policy	Unemployment rate
High-powered money	Inflation rate
Discount rate	Inflation rate
Government spending	Size of government
Tax rates	Long-run growth in real GDP per person

Figure 14-1 gives a more complete illustration of the principles of economic policy. The goal of economic policy is economic welfare, represented by the box in the upper right corner. Economic welfare can be thought of as simply happiness, the things that individual members of society want—stable prices, full employment, and a high standard of living.

Targets, Instruments, and Structural Relations

Target variables are the economic aggregates whose values society cares most about—society's goals.

Directly to the left of the economic welfare box in Figure 14-1 we find a box that lists the main policy **target variables** that influence economic welfare. Some are more important than others. The distribution of income is quite different from the other targets; any policy shift that raises the income of one group at the expense of others (rich versus poor; creditors versus debtors) is bound to be controversial and lead to political conflict.[2]

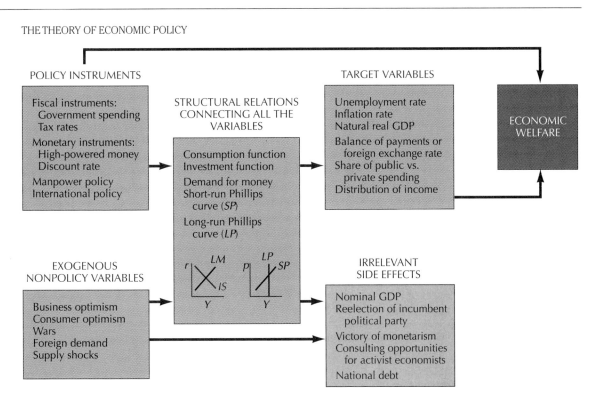

Figure 14-1   **A Flowchart Showing the Relationship Between Policy Instruments, Policy Targets, and Economic Welfare**

Both policy instruments and exogenous nonpolicy variables are fed into the structural relations that connect the exogenous (policy and nonpolicy) variables with the endogenous (target and nontarget) variables. Total economic welfare at the upper right depends on the achieved values of the target variables, and thus it depends on policymakers' decisions about the settings of policy instruments.

---

[2]An introduction to these and other targets is Arthur M. Okun, "Conflicting National Goals," in Eli Ginzberg, ed., *Jobs for Americans* (Englewood Cliffs, N.J.: Prentice-Hall, 1976).

In the upper left corner of Figure 14-1 is a list of some of the policy instruments that the government can use to try to achieve its targets. Linking the instrument box with the upper right target box is the large central box, which contains the structural relations that link the variables. The *IS* and *LM* curves of Chapter 4 and *SP* and *LP* curves of Chapter 8 summarize the main relations that link money, taxes, and government spending to unemployment and inflation. But as shown in the lower left box, those curves can also be shifted by several exogenous factors not under the direct control of policymakers, such as a burst of business or consumer optimism or higher export sales (shifting the *IS* curve upward) or an adverse supply shock (shifting the *SP* curve upward). Wars are also listed in the exogenous box rather than in the instrument box, because the level of wartime government spending is presumably set in accord with the goals of military strategy rather than economic stabilization.

When the values of the exogenous and instrument variables are fed into the structural economic relations in the middle box, they produce the values of the target variables—unemployment, inflation, and the others. Other variables, shown in the lower right box, are also affected, but these are called irrelevant variables because they are not major determinants of economic welfare.

Rules Advocates and the Activists' Paradise

The framework supporting activist policy intervention, as set out in Figure 14-1, evokes a skeptical response from economists who advocate policy rules. Rules advocates feel that activists are unrealistically optimistic about how successful their policies are likely to be. By contrast, policy rules advocates believe that activist stabilization policy may actually do more harm than good. "Activist economists," they claim, "require a utopian set of assumptions about the economy for activist stabilization policy to do more good than harm."

The utopian "activists' paradise" is a hypothetical world in which activist policy achieves almost perfect control over aggregate demand. It dramatizes the optimistic set of assumptions required for policy activism to be accepted without question. The activists' paradise has these main characteristics:[3]

1. Policymakers forecast accurately future changes in the private demand for and supply of goods and services.

2. Policymakers forecast accurately the future effect of current changes in monetary and fiscal policy.

3. Policymakers possess policy instruments that powerfully affect aggregate demand.

4. Policymakers can change policy instruments without incurring any costs, economic or social.

5. No political constraints affect the use of the policy instruments.

---

[3]The term *activists' paradise* and its major characteristics originate in Arthur M. Okun, "Fiscal-Monetary Activism: Some Analytical Issues," *Brookings Papers on Economic Activity,* vol. 3 (1972), pp. 123–163. In this, as in many other areas of economics (see Okun's law, p. 56), Okun had the unique ability to capture an issue in clear and vivid language. The author's tribute to the unique talents of Okun appears in *Brookings Papers on Economic Activity,* vol. 11 (1980), pp. 1–5.

RULES VS. ACTIVISM IN A NUTSHELL: *The Optimism-Pessimism Grid*

The artificial assumptions of the activists' paradise help to crystallize the debate between the policy activists and rules advocates. The table in this box sorts out a wide variety of issues in this debate. Activists' beliefs are presented in the top line. Activists are relatively pessimistic about the stability of the private economy. This pessimism stems from their concern that the private (i.e., nongovernment) economy is subject to substantial business fluctuations, of which the most prominent example is the Great Depression of the 1930s (pp. 219–222). Such fluctuations are sometimes the result of a wave of business and consumer pessimism, as in the 1930s, or of a collapse and subsequent boom of net exports (due to the sharp appreciation of the dollar during 1980–85 and subsequent depreciation during 1985–87). Business fluctuations may result also from government actions, as when military spending exploded during wartime (1940–45, 1950–53, 1965–68, or during peacetime [1980s]), then collapsed afterward. Through multiplier effects, wars and postwar readjustment periods can create instability in the private economy.

While the activists are pessimistic about the stability of the private economy, they are optimistic about the feasibility of stabilizing the economy through government policy. This reflects their belief that the activists' paradise, while a caricature designed to exaggerate the conditions needed for successful policy activism nevertheless contains a kernel of truth.

As shown in the table, the activists' position is disputed on both counts by policy rules advocates. This group optimistically views the private economy as inherently self-correcting, due in part to the belief (based on the permanent income hypothesis, which is explored in depth in Chapter 15) that demand disturbances are partly or largely absorbed by changes in private saving and do not create the traditional (Chapter 3) multiplier effect. And policy rules advocates are pessimistic about stabilization policy, believing it can do more harm than good, due to lags, forecasting errors, uncertainty, and the other problems discussed in this chapter.

	Belief Regarding Automatic Self-Correcting Properties of Private Economy?		Belief Regarding Efficacy of Government Stabilization Policy?
Activists	Pessimistic		**Optimistic**
Rules Advocates	**Optimistic**		Pessimistic

The activists' paradise is an extreme set of positions that no economist actually believes, but those positions rather set the stage for the debate over activism versus rules. *The core of the activists' paradise is a deep faith in the power of macroeconomics as a science. The activists' paradise requires policymakers to be able to forecast accurately not just future changes in demand, but also the future effects of current changes in policy.*

The other characteristics of the activists' paradise can be summarized as requiring policy to have powerful effects, but no side effects. Activist proponents must therefore be a special blend of pessimist and optimist, remaining pessimistic about the ability of the private economy to remain close to its natural level *(of Y^N or U^N)* while being firmly optimistic about the power of macroeconomic forecasting and policy. Activist policymakers need to be able with some confidence to identify the economy's natural rate *(Y^N or U^N)*, so that any particular level of real GDP or of the unemployment rate can be regarded as "too high" or "too low" and the appropriate offsetting policy response can be identified.

As shown in the box on page 441, one easy way to think about the rules-versus-activism debate is to note the contrast between where the two groups place their optimism and pessimism. Policy activists are pessimistic about the self-correcting powers of the private economy and optimistic about the efficacy of stabilization policy. In contrast, rules advocates are optimistic about the underlying stability of the private economy but pessimistic about the efficacy of stabilization policy.[4]

SELF-TEST

Classify the following as policy instruments or target variables: (1) the inflation rate, (2) the personal income tax rate, (3) the Federal Reserve discount rate, (4) the unemployment rate, (5) high-powered money.

14-3 Policy Rules

Discretionary policy treats each macroeconomic episode as a unique event, without any attempt to respond in the same way from one episode to another.

A **rigid rule** for policy sets a key policy instrument at a fixed value, as in a constant growth rate rule for the money supply.

A **constant growth rate rule (CGRR)** stipulates a fixed percentage growth rate for the money supply, in contrast to the variable growth rate recommended by policy activists.

The great debate over policy rules primarily concerns monetary policy. In the 1930s University of Chicago economist Henry Simons posed a stark contrast between a totally discretionary monetary policy and a fixed rule that takes away all discretion from the central bank.[5] In reality, there is a continuum in monetary policy between completely **discretionary policy** at one extreme and a **rigid rule** at the other extreme.

The most extreme form of rigid rule would be for the Fed to carry out a specified set of open-market operations, e.g., to buy exactly enough securities to make high-powered money (*H,* the sum of currency and reserves) grow by, say, 5 percent per year. However, as we learned in the last chapter (see equation [13.6] on p. 414), such an action would not lead to steady growth in the money supply, since the money supply depends not only on *H* but also on the reserve ratio and the public's currency-holding ratio. Even if growth in *H* is kept absolutely rigid, choices by the public to raise or lower its holdings of currency could lead to major swings in the money supply. Another form of rigid rule would be for the Fed to conduct whatever open-market operations are required to maintain absolutely constant a short-term interest rate like the federal funds rate.

The best-known proposal for a policy rule, a **constant growth rate rule (CGRR)** for the money supply, was made in the late 1950s by Milton Friedman, then at the University of Chicago. Just as maintaining a fixed growth rate for *H* does not insure a fixed growth rate for the money supply, due to variations

---

[4]Traditionally, macroeconomics textbooks have interpreted the rules versus activism debate as about the strength of policy multipliers. An extended statement that attempts to reorient the monetarist debate is Franco Modigliani, "The Monetarist Controversy, or Should We Forsake Stabilization Policy?" *American Economic Review,* vol. 67 (March 1977), pp. 1–19. An earlier paper is Milton Friedman, "Why Economists Disagree," in *Dollars and Deficits* (Englewood Cliffs, N.J.: Prentice-Hall, 1968), pp. 1–16. Friedman on pp. 6–9 shares the same orientation as this chapter, although on pp. 10–16 he places considerably more weight than we do here on the influence of money on inflation.

[5]Henry C. Simons, *Economic Policy for a Free Society* (Chicago: University of Chicago Press, 1948). Simons originally wrote on rules versus discretion in the mid-1930s.

in the money multiplier *(M/H),* the reverse is true as well. Maintaining a CGRR for the money supply would require the Fed to manipulate H actively in order to offset changes in the money multiplier.

In addition to rules calling for a fixed growth rate of H or the money supply, many other types of rules have been proposed. Some involve not a monetary variable like H or the money supply, but rather a target variable like the price level or output. Other rules fall under the category of **feedback rules,** which systematically change monetary variables like the money supply or interest rates in response to actual or forecasted changes in target variables like inflation or unemployment.

The most famous school of thought advocating a rule for monetary policy is called **monetarism.**[6] This approach combines the key elements in the box on p. 141—optimism regarding the stability of the private economy and pessimism regarding the efficacy of discretionary policy—with a specific policy proposal advocating a CGRR for the money supply.[7] The key elements of monetarism, and its critique of activism, were developed in the 1950s and 1960s by Milton Friedman, the late Karl Brunner of the University of Rochester, and Allan Meltzer of Carnegie-Mellon University.

A **feedback rule** sets stabilization policy to respond in a systematic way to a macroeconomic event, such as an increase in unemployment or inflation.

Monetarism is a school of thought that opposes activist or discretionary monetary policy and instead favors a fixed rule for the growth rate of high-powered money or of the money supply.

The Positive Case for Rules

The case for rules takes two forms. One is a positive case based on the advantages of rules themselves, and the other is a negative case based on the defects of a completely discretionary policy.

The main arguments for rules as set forth by Milton Friedman are three.[8] First, a rule insulates the central bank from political pressure, which might, for instance, take the form of pushing the central bank to overstimulate the economy in the year before an election. Second, a rule allows the performance of the central bank to be judged by the government and the public. For instance, a central bank charged with a CGRR for the money supply would be judged to be a failure if in reality the money supply gyrated wildly or grew at an average rate different from the one specified in the rule. Third, a rule reduces uncertainty, since firms, workers, and consumers are able to gauge accurately what the central bank will be doing over the next several years.

However, as suggested by Stanley Fischer of MIT, there are weaknesses in each of these arguments.[9] First, it is not necessarily desirable for the central bank to operate independently of political pressure; a central bank, in its attempts to achieve or maintain low inflation, might be more willing to sacrifice jobs in the short run than the general public is. The merits of the second and third arguments fail as a general support for rules, since their validity

---

[6]The term *monetarism* was introduced in Karl Brunner, "The Role of Money and Monetary Policy," *Federal Reserve Bank of St. Louis Review,* no. 50 (1968), pp. 9–24.

[7]See Milton Friedman, *A Program for Monetary Stability* (New York: Fordham University Press, 1959).

[8]Ibid.

[9]Stanley Fischer, "Rules versus Discretion in Monetary Policy," in Benjamin Friedman and Frank Hahn, eds., *Handbook of Monetary Economics,* vol. 2 (Amsterdam: Elsevier Science Publishers, 1990), pp. 1156–84.

depends on what variable the central bank chooses to target. For instance, the public has no reason to care directly about the quantity of high-powered money or the money supply, since the target variables that concern the public are inflation, unemployment, and productivity growth. Whether the Fed hits its target for, say, the money supply is irrelevant to the public if such a policy creates a poor record on inflation and/or unemployment. Further, if inflation and unemployment are volatile because they are only loosely linked to the money supply, it is of little value to the public to know that the money supply will grow steadily in the future.

In short, it is hard to make a general case for rules without specifying the exact nature of the rule. As in the saying "there are many slips between cup and lip," there are many sources of slippage between the Fed's policy instruments, particularly open-market operations, and the most important target variables, that is, inflation, unemployment, and productivity growth. These slippages include money multiplier shocks (Chapter 13), money demand shocks (Chapter 13), commodity demand shocks (anything discussed in Chapter 4 or 5 that can shift the *IS* curve), and supply shocks (Chapter 8).

The proponents of rules face a dilemma: A rigid rule for a policy instrument that the Fed can actually control directly (like *H*) may lead to undesirable behavior on the part of target variables. But a rigid rule for a target variable may require activist management of policy instruments and may lead to conflicts among the target variables themselves, as for instance when an unemployment target that is unrealistically low leads to accelerating inflation, or when a low target for inflation leads to high unemployment.

As shown in the box on p. 441, rules advocates are optimistic about the stability of the private economy. Stated another way, they believe that the sources of slippage between the policy instruments and the target variables are of minor importance, so that a rule for high-powered money or the money supply can achieve a satisfactory outcome for the target variables.

The Negative Case for Rules

The negative case for rules consists of a criticism of activism. As shown in the box on p. 441, rules advocates are pessimistic about activist (discretionary) policy, believing that such measures can do more harm than good. Much of the rest of this chapter looks in detail at their case by examining the many reasons why the activists' paradise is unrealistic—lags, uncertainty, forecasting errors, and other issues.

However, just as the merits of the positive case for rules depend on the particular type of rule being considered, so does the negative case for rules. For instance, lags and uncertainty may create so much slippage between the Fed's policy instruments and the economy's target variables that it becomes infeasible for the Fed to carry out a rule involving a target, such as the proposal that the Fed maintain a stable price level or a CGRR for nominal GDP.

14-4 Policy Pitfalls: Lags and Uncertain Multipliers

The core of Milton Friedman's case against policy activism and in favor of a monetary rule has always been that there are what he called "long and variable" lags between changes in monetary policy instruments and the ultimate response of target variables like inflation and unemployment. In this section we distinguish five types of lags for monetary policy and attempt to estimate the length of these lags.

The Five Types of Lags

Lags prevent either monetary or fiscal policy from immediately offsetting an unexpected shift in the demand for commodities or in the demand for money. There are five main types of lags. Some are common to both monetary and fiscal policy; others are more important for one policy than the other:

1. The data lag
2. The recognition lag
3. The legislative lag
4. The transmission lag
5. The effectiveness lag

To explain the meaning of each lag and to estimate its length, let us take the example of the "double dip" in the recession of 1990–91. After appearing to be on the road to recovery in the spring and summer of 1991, economic activity slumped in late 1991. Some analysts have called this episode a "double dip" recession, treating the initial slump in the fall of 1990 and winter of 1991 as the first dip and the decline in late 1991 as the second. What were the lags that intervened between the beginning of the second dip and the time that the economy could have responded to a policy stimulus by the Fed?

1. **The data lag.** Policymakers do not know what is going on in the economy the moment it happens. Although the economy had been flat from May to October 1991, with virtually no growth in employment or production, the first news of the second dip did not arrive until mid-December, after a November drop in employment and industrial production were announced. Typically, an economic change that starts at the beginning of one month, say November, is not fully evident in the data until the middle of the next month, so that the data lag is about 1.5 months.

2. **The recognition lag.** No policymaker pays much attention to reversals in the data that occur for only one month. One reason for this caution is that data for real economic aggregates, unlike data for stock prices and interest rates, are revised over time as the government's data collection agencies receive more complete information. Although the revised data for December 1991 eventually showed a small increase in employment, at the time, the data for January 1992 showed a third consecutive month of decline in employment and production. The revised December 1991 data were not available until mid-February 1992.[10] Thus, the recognition lag may add about two months.

---

[10]While the table on p. 448 sets the recognition lag at 2.0 months, in this particular episode the Fed acted with unusual speed when it received the news of the economy's weak performance in November, dropping the discount rate by a full percentage point on December 20, 1991.

3. **The legislative lag.** Although most changes in fiscal policy must be legislated by Congress, an important advantage of monetary policy is the short legislative lag. Once a majority of the Federal Open Market Committee (FOMC) decides that a monetary policy stimulus is needed, only a short wait is necessary, since the FOMC has eight regularly scheduled meetings annually and can meet by phone anytime. This brings us to March 1992.

4. **The transmission lag.** The transmission lag is the time interval between the policy decision and the subsequent change in policy instruments. Like the legislative lag, this lag is a more serious obstacle for fiscal policy. Once the FOMC has given its order for the open-market manager to make open-market purchases, the short-term (federal funds) interest rate declines immediately. Often the Fed signals that it has shifted policy by changing the discount rate; there is no transmission lag at all for such an action.

5. **The effectiveness lag.** Most of the controversy about the lags of monetary policy concerns the length of time required for an acceleration or deceleration in the money supply to influence real output. As we have seen, Milton Friedman has argued that the effectiveness lag is long and variable.

Evidence on the Effectiveness Lag

The most difficult lag to measure, as well as the longest, is the effectiveness lag between the change in monetary policy and the response of the economy. Estimates of this lag differ for numerous reasons, including the use of different measures of monetary policy (e.g., money supply vs. interest rates) and different indicators of the economy's response (e.g., a monthly index of production or employment or a quarterly index of real GDP).

In determining the length of the effectiveness lag, it is useful to measure the change in monetary policy by the change in short-term interest rates, since the Fed can change those interest rates almost immediately after a meeting of the FOMC (thus eliminating the transmission lag). One set of estimates of the effectiveness lag is presented in Figure 14-2. This figure plots for three alternative intervals the response of real GDP to a change in the short-term interest rate, specifically the Treasury bill rate.[11]

As shown by Figure 14-2, in all three intervals (1962–69, 1970–82, and 1983–96) real GDP declined following an increase in the short-term interest rate. But the change in GDP is very spread out over time, distributed over more than two years. Because the economy's response is so spread out, the best measure of the effectiveness lag is not obvious. One sensible measure of this lag is the length of time necessary for *half of the ultimate effect* to be felt.

---

[11]For those readers trained in econometrics, the details lying behind Figure 14-2 are as follows. The annualized percentage change in quarterly real GDP over the indicated intervals was regressed on a constant and lags 2 through 9 of the quarterly changes in the nominal Treasury bill rate. Lag lengths of 10 quarters or greater were statistically insignificant and were omitted. The current change and the first lag were omitted because their coefficients are positive, indicating the presence of simultaneity.

THE ECONOMY'S RESPONSE TO MONETARY POLICY HAS BECOME WEAKER AND MORE STRETCHED OUT

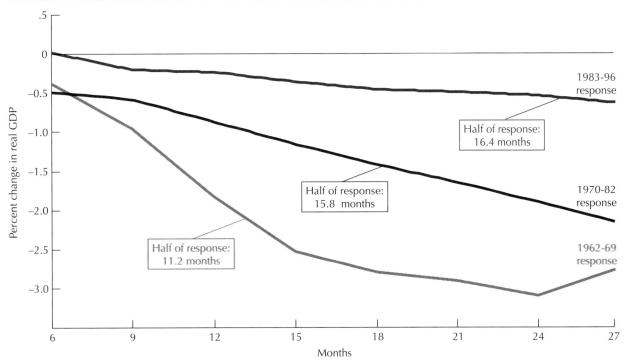

Figure 14-2   **The Percent Change in Real GDP Following a 1 Percentage Point Change in the Treasury Bill Rate, Three Intervals, 1962–96**

Following a 1 percentage point change in the short-term (Treasury bill) interest rate, real GDP changes in the opposite direction by the percentages shown by the plotted lines drawn for each of three intervals, 1962–69, 1970–82, and 1983–96. The lines show, for instance, that after 12 months real GDP would have dropped by about 2 percent during the 1962–69 interval, but by about 1 percent in 1970–82 and by less than 0.5 percent during 1983–96. The boxed labels show how many months were required for half of the ultimate impact on real GDP to occur.

As shown by the small boxes in the figure, this lag was 11.2, 15.8, and 16.4 months respectively. Notable also is the fact that the total responses in the more recent intervals were much smaller than in the first; we explain this shift in a subsequent section.

Another measure of the policy lag, one that does not rely on interest rate data, can be extracted from recent research by David and Christina Romer of the University of California, Berkeley. They read the minutes of the FOMC to identify the months when the Fed "made a decision to try to cause a recession to reduce inflation,"[12] identifying six such episodes between 1947 and 1979. They ran a statistical test similar to that in Figure 14-2 to examine the response of industrial production in the three years after the Fed's policy

---

[12]Christina D. Romer and David H. Romer, "Does Monetary Policy Matter? A New Test in the Spirit of Friedman and Schwartz," in O. J. Blanchard and S. Fischer, *NBER Macroeconomics Annual 1989* (Cambridge, Mass.: MIT Press), p. 152.

shift. For their six episodes, their estimated effectiveness lag averages 19 months, even longer than the lags of 7 to 11 months in Figure 14-2.[13]

Adding the Lags Together

To summarize this section on lags, let us add up the total delay between an unexpected economic event and the economy's reaction to a monetary policy action taken in response to such an economic event.

Type of lag	Estimated length (months)
1. Data	1.5
2. Recognition	2.0
3. Legislative	0.5
4. Transmission	0.0
5. Effectiveness	16.0
Total	20.0

Thus the first half of the economy's reaction to the Fed's policy response to the economic slowdown that began in November 1991 would not have been felt until July 1993 (plus or minus a few months, reflecting the variability of the effectiveness lag). By then employment had already risen for over a year.

Multiplier Uncertainty

Chapters 3 and 4 developed a set of multiplier formulas indicating the size of the change in real GDP that would result from a change in a policy instrument, such as tax rates, government spending, or the money supply. But the *IS-LM* model summarized in those chapters was very simple. This section shows that we do not know nearly as much about the values of the multipliers as the simple *IS-LM* model initially led us to believe.

Figure 14-2 illustrates **dynamic multipliers** that show the response of real GDP to a change in the interest rate over several intervals. We noted that the multipliers were much larger in 1962–69 than after 1970. Also, even for a given time period economists differ widely regarding the size of the monetary and fiscal multipliers.[14] This **multiplier uncertainty** creates a dilemma for policymakers. Even if they could forecast perfectly that the economy needs a policy stimulus now to add 2.0 percent to real GDP four quarters from now, there remains the question as to what exact policy action should be taken. Should the interest rate be dropped today by 0.5, 1.0, or 2.0 percentage

Dynamic multipliers are the amount by which output is raised during each of several time periods after a given change in the policy instrument.

Multiplier uncertainty concerns the lack of firm knowledge regarding the change in output caused by a change in a policy instrument.

---

[13]Romer and Romer, ibid., Table 1, p. 153. The maximum effect of their monetary policy variable (defined as unity in one of the six months when the Fed changed policy and zero otherwise) is reached 32 months after the policy change. Half of the total effect occurs after 18.8 months. This estimate is approximate, as it omits the impact of the lagged dependent variable in their equation.

[14]Many years ago a study showed a wide range of fiscal multipliers estimated by different economists, ranging from 0 to 2.5 for the effect on real GDP five quarters after a $1 billion increase of government nondefense spending. See Gary Fromm and Lawrence R. Klein, "A Comparison of Eleven Econometric Models of the United States," *American Economic Review*, vol. 63 (May 1973), p. 391.

points? Any of these numbers might be correct, depending on the policy multiplier.[15]

Why Have Monetary Policy Multipliers Changed?

Three aspects of Figure 14-2 make life especially difficult for policymakers—these are the length of the lag, the change in the lag, and the change in the multiplier (that is, the total effect of an interest rate change on real GDP). We have already noted the fact that the effectiveness lag is long, with half of the effect taking 16 months during 1983–96. Why is this lag longer now than it was in the 1960s?

Activist policymaking is even more difficult when the underlying structure of the economy changes. The structure of the economy can be altered by changes in government regulations; business practices; technology; the extent and speed of the effect of other economies on the domestic economy; and other factors. Such changes can change the response of the economy to shocks and to changes in policy by unpredictable amounts. Thus, changes in the underlying structure of the economy are likely to increase the uncertainty about multipliers.

Three changes in the structure of the economy since the 1960s help explain why lags are now longer and multipliers are now smaller than they were in the 1960s. The first change concerns thrift institutions and housing. In earlier decades housing expenditures took the brunt of tight monetary policy, declining quickly in response to upward movements in interest rates. After the late 1970s this channel of influence on housing became less important, because deregulation lifted the ceilings on interest rates paid to depositors by thrifts. Also, other types of financial institutions that were not subject to interest rate ceilings began to participate more in mortgage markets, further insulating the housing sector from the impact of tightened monetary policy.

The second major change is the reduced impact of changing interest rates on consumer spending. More consumer borrowing now occurs on credit cards, but interest rates on credit cards are very insensitive to monetary policy.

The third major change was the adoption of flexible exchange rates in 1973, previously examined in Chapter 6. This added a major channel of influence of monetary policy, as changing interest rates cause changes in the foreign exchange rate and, after a long lag, changes in net exports. It takes two years or more for net exports to respond fully to changes in the foreign exchange rate, which helps to explain the longer effectiveness lag observed since the 1960s.[16]

---

[15]See William Brainard, "Uncertainty and the Effectiveness of Policy," *American Economic Review,* vol. 57 (May 1967), pp. 411–25. Brainard's formula suggests that the expected gap between actual and target GDP should be closed by only a fraction of the gap, but that fraction depends on correlations that we are most unlikely to know. An earlier analysis is Milton Friedman, "The Effects of a Full-Employment Policy on Economic Stability: A Formal Analysis," *Essays in Positive Economics* (Chicago: University of Chicago Press, 1953), pp. 117–32.

[16]For more on the changing monetary policy multipliers and lags, see Eileen Mauskopf, "The Transmission Channels of Monetary Policy: How Have They Changed?" *Federal Reserve Bulletin* (December 1990), pp. 985–1008; also George A. Kahn, "The Changing Interest Sensitivity of the U.S. Economy," *Federal Reserve Bank of Kansas City Review* (November 1989), pp. 13–34.

Summary: The effectiveness lag of monetary policy has become longer, and the multiplier of real GDP response to a change in interest rates has become smaller, because the prompt channel working through housing finance has become weaker, while the time-consuming channel working through exchange rates and net exports has become stronger.

SELF-TEST

For each of the following statements, indicate whether it relates to multiplier uncertainty or lags, and if your answer is "lags," indicate which of the five types of lags is most closely related to the statement:

(1) Congress debated President Johnson's proposal for an income tax surcharge for 18 months, from late 1966 to mid-1968. (2) Interest rate ceilings on savings accounts were eliminated by financial deregulation. (3) A record-setting snowstorm in Washington delays publication of the Consumer Price Index by two weeks. (4) Flexible exchange rates were adopted in 1973.

14-5   CASE STUDY: How Accurate Are Forecasts?

Among other criticisms, rules advocates fault the proponents of activism for making overly optimistic assumptions about the ability of forecasters to foresee future demand and supply disturbances. The ability to look into the future is required by the lag of monetary policy, examined in the last section. Thus *policymakers must be able to look ahead to determine whether future output is likely to be too high or too low.*

In this section we learn that U.S. forecasters have experienced some dramatic failures since 1970, as illustrated in Figure 14-3. The diagram compares the actual growth rates of real GDP *(y)*, the GDP price deflator *(p)*, and the level of the unemployment rate *(U)*, with their changes predicted nearly a year in advance of the designated quarter by five well-known forecasting organizations. Most of these forecasters sell their forecasts to business firms and have every incentive to take account of all relevant factors that might affect the economy in the coming year.

For example, in the middle frame of Figure 14-3 we see that over the four-quarter interval ending in the first quarter of 1971 the inflation rate was actually 4.9 percent (the red actual *p* line), whereas the median one-year inflation forecast (the black predicted *p* line) for that interval, made in the second

Figure 14-3   **Actual and Predicted Values of the Unemployment Rate *(U)* and of the Growth Rates of Real GDP *(y)* and the GDP Deflator *(p)*, 1971–96**

The most important forecasting errors were an underprediction of inflation throughout 1973 and 1974, and of nominal and real GDP in 1982. Note that between 1973 and 1976 most of the errors in forecasting inflation caused errors in forecasting real output in the opposite direction. The predictions shown are the median of five forecasts. *(Source:* Stephen S. McNees, "How Large Are Economic Forecast Errors?" *New England Economic Review* (July/August 1992) and updated data provided by Stephen S. McNees.)

FORECASTERS DO NOT LOOK BACK FONDLY ON THEIR PERFORMANCE

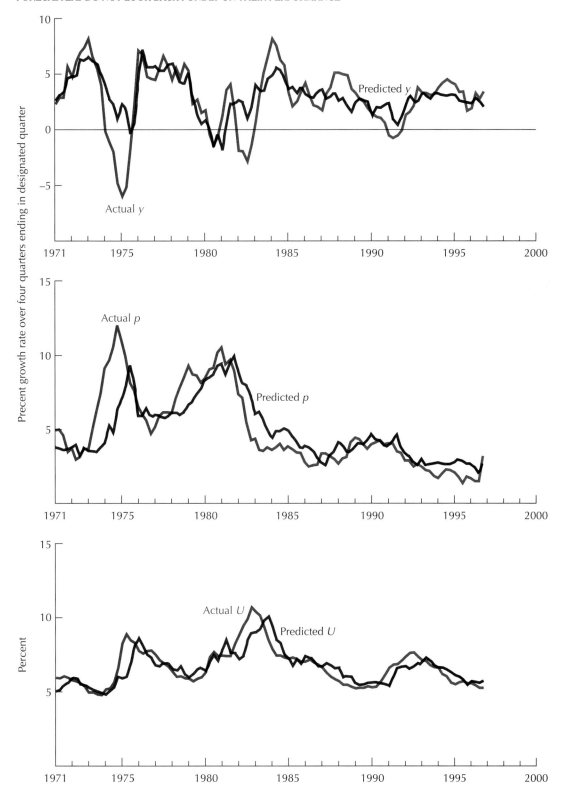

quarter of 1970, predicted that inflation would be 3.8 percent. Inflation forecasts made for 1972 (when price controls were in effect) were quite accurate. Actual inflation, however, far exceeded forecasted inflation from mid-1973 through mid-1975 (when price controls were being removed and a severe, adverse supply shock in the form of higher oil prices struck).

Forecasting Failures

The 1974–75 Debacle.   Prior to the 1974–75 period, forecasters had not been required to deal with a major supply shock and the sharp jump in oil prices and subsequent recession took them completely by surprise. As a result they greatly overpredicted real GDP growth and underpredicted inflation and unemployment.

The 1979–80 Supply Shock and 1981–82 recession.   The largest forecasting error of this period, the collapse of real GDP growth in 1981–82, was completely missed, and as a result so was the increase in unemployment. The initial upsurge of inflation in 1978–79 was missed, and in addition forecasters were surprised at how rapidly inflation dropped in 1982–86.

The Expansion of the 1980s.   While unemployment was forecasted relatively well, forecasters did not predict the weakness of real GDP growth in 1986 nor its strength in 1987 or 1988.

The 1990–91 Recession and the Recovery of the 1990s.   Since the 1990–91 recession was relatively short, forecasting errors in this episode were smaller than in 1974–75 and 1981–82. But forecasters missed both the recession of 1990–91 and the weakness of the recovery in 1991–92. They also failed to foresee the strength of the expansion after 1993, when unemployment was below its forecasted level for several years in a row.

Reasons for Forecasting Errors

Why do forecasting errors occur? No matter how sophisticated their forecasting models, economists must still make guesses about two of the key ingredients in any forecast.

1. First, they must guess the settings of the various policy instruments. Often forecasters make several forecasts: first an initial control forecast that assumes that policy remains unchanged, then additional forecasts that vary these policy assumptions in specified ways.
2. Second, they must guess the values of the nonpolicy exogenous variables. Among these, as shown in Figure 14-1, are export demand, supply shocks, and business and consumer optimism, each of which can shift aggregate demand or supply.

An **econometric model** is a set of equations with statistically estimated responses that can be solved to provide forecasts under alternative assumptions about policy instruments and nonpolicy exogenous variables.

There also must be a structural model that ties together exogenous variables, policy instruments, and target variables. In the first part of this book we developed a simple version of such a model. Modern forecasting uses **econometric models** that estimate the values of the responses by statistical study of past episodes. An important weakness of the models is that, inevitably, their estimated responses are based on a long historical period over which conditions may have changed. For instance, we saw in Section 14-4 that monetary policy multipliers were smaller in recent years than they were in the 1960s. The historical average responses may differ importantly from current responses.

Implications of Forecasting Errors for the Policy Debate

The record of forecasts suggests that the Fed may not receive accurate early warning signals of economic turning points, that is, of peaks and troughs of the business cycle.[17] Thus, forecasting the economy's future need for policy stimulus or restraint may not be successful.

The weakness of forecasting in past episodes constitutes more than a simple criticism of the activists' paradise and of discretionary policy. It also raises problems for policy rules based on targets such as nominal GDP or the price level. The success of a monetary policy that targets nominal GDP growth is likely to depend on the ability to forecast what would happen to nominal GDP in the absence of a policy change. Taken together, the top and middle frames of Figure 14-3 show that nominal GDP growth, the sum of real GDP growth and the inflation rate, was much lower than it was forecasted to be during the 1981–82 and the 1990–91 recessions. Since nominal GDP growth was surprisingly slow, the Fed could not be expected to have acted before the fact to offset it with more stimulative monetary policy. Thus, even had the Fed been trying to stabilize the growth rate of nominal GDP, it likely would not have prevented these recessions.

14-6 **CASE STUDY: Did the Federal Reserve Pilot a "Soft Landing"?**

We now know that it can be difficult in practice to conduct stabilization policy successfully. In Section 14-4 we learned that there is a substantial lag between the time a shock to aggregate demand or supply strikes the economy and the time policy changes begin to counteract the effects of the shock. We estimated the lag for monetary policy, for example, to be over a year. We also saw that changes in the structure of the economy can change the size of multipliers by uncertain amounts. As time passes, incoming data provide information about how much the structure of the economy and its multipliers have changed. To the extent that structural changes are ongoing, however, multipliers may be changing continually. Thus, policymakers' knowledge about the current condition of the economy and its multipliers may be seriously incomplete. The resulting uncertainty about the effects of policy and even about the economy's current condition should temper the recommendations of activist policymakers.

---

[17]The fact that forecasters do better at forecasting years of normal growth than predicting turning points is among the points made in Victor Zarnowitz, "Has Macro-Forecasting Failed?" NBER Working Paper 3867 (October 1991).

Section 14-5 reminded us that, by their very nature, *future* shocks to aggregate supply and demand cannot be forecasted. This, coupled with the lengthy lags associated with policy and the uncertain size of multipliers, adds to the difficulty of keeping output near its natural level. As we will see from the experiences of the 1990s that are recounted below, activist policymaking in a world fraught with all these uncertainties is a formidable challenge. We will see also that years later it can even be difficult to judge whether activist policymaking was successful.

Figure 14-4 plots quarterly actual and natural real GDP for the period 1960–96. In Chapter 9 we learned how natural real GDP rises over time as the number of people in the labor force, the size of the capital stock, or the level of technology embodied in the capital stock increases. The rate at which the economy accumulates additional capital, labor, and embodied technology determines the speed at which natural output grows, and thus puts a speed

UNTIL THE 1990s REAL GDP OFTEN DEVIATED FROM ITS NATURAL RATE FOR LONG SPANS OF TIME

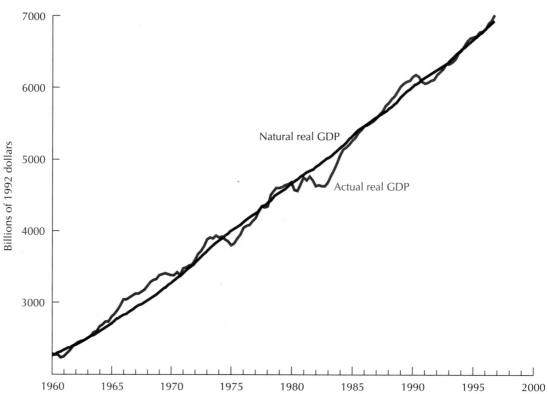

Figure 14-4   **Actual and Natural Real GDP, 1960–96**

The black line indicates an estimate of natural real GDP. The red line indicates actual real GDP. Natural real GDP rises over time when the economy's stocks of capital, labor, and the factors in the "residual" (including technology and education) grow. From the early 1960s through the early 1970s, output tended to exceed its natural level. As a result, inflation accelerated. In the first half of the 1980s, output was considerably below its natural level. As a result, inflation declined. The long expansion of the 1980s eventually carried actual real GDP above natural real GDP. Since the late 1980s, output has deviated relatively little from its natural level.

limit on how fast actual output can grow on average. During the 1990s the annual growth rate of natural real GDP was in the range of 2 percent to 2 1/2 percent. Uncertainty about the rate stems, in part, from uncertainty about how much additional output can be produced by the higher average level of technology embodied in the capital stock. Just as we cannot be sure of the growth rate of natural real GDP (and therefore cited its most likely range), we cannot be sure at any time of the *level* of natural real GDP. As we will see below, uncertainty about the level of natural output, and the associated natural rate of unemployment, makes it difficult to assess how successful policies have been at guiding the economy toward the level of natural output.

Soft Landings

Since the mid-1980s, the Federal Reserve's policies have often been described as intending to produce a soft landing for the economy. We can visualize the basic strategy of a soft landing for the economy by looking at Figure 14-4. A monetary policy designed to achieve a soft landing changes the nominal money supply so that, as time passes, actual real GDP glides smoothly onto the "runway" of natural real GDP. When output is below its natural rate, the goals of a soft landing policy are to have actual output grow faster than natural output and to have the actual growth rate taper down to the growth rate of natural output as output approaches its natural level.

A soft landing implies that actual real GDP avoids both overshooting and undershooting natural real GDP by large amounts. Of course, we could not expect the economy to touch down exactly on the runway of natural output. A soft landing, however, does mean that the economy avoids both overheating, by having output way above its natural level and inflation accelerating, and stalling, with output remaining far below its long-run equilibrium level. Regardless of the context, macroeconomic or not, the alternative to a soft landing, a crash landing, sounds like something to avoid! A soft landing of the economy conveys the idea that output approaches its natural level but avoids the crash landing of a recession.

Growth: Fast, Then Slow

Notice in Figure 14-4 that output was significantly below its natural level, and thus unemployment was significantly above its natural level, for long periods around the 1975, 1982, and 1991 troughs in economic activity. The recessions that ended with those troughs each lasted less than a year and a half. However, because it takes time for output to rebound to its prior level and because natural output continues to grow during recessions, output typically remained below its natural level for three or four years after those troughs. The long spans of time during which output persistently exceeds or falls short of its natural level give activists hope that they can undertake successful stabilization policy, even in the face of the difficulties noted above.

When output is significantly below its natural level, the economy is capable of growing much faster than the growth rate of natural output for a while. Indeed, in the years immediately following recessions output often grows very rapidly. For example, in the two years after the 1981–82 recession, output grew at an annual rate of 6 percent, far above the growth rate of natural output. Because actual output grew so much faster than natural GDP, the gap between them shrank, as we can see in Figure 14-4.

When output is below its natural level, the resources needed to produce more output are already available. To produce additional output in that case, it is fairly easy, fast, and cheap for businesses to hire unemployed workers and utilize the equipment and buildings they already own. By contrast, for output to grow once it has reached its natural level, the supply of labor, capital, and technology must be increased. It is far more difficult, more time-consuming, and more expensive to build new capital and obtain more workers once the existing stocks of those inputs are fully utilized.

Has the Economy Been Landing Softly?

When the level of output is appreciably above or below the level of natural output, achieving a soft landing suggests that output growth should taper off as the actual level of real GDP approaches natural output. Since the late 1980s, periods when output fell below its natural level have more usually been followed by faster growth rates of output, and periods when output exceeded its natural level have more usually been followed by slower growth rates of output.[18] In addition, since the late 1980s, growth rates have tapered off more when the economy deviated from its natural level.[19] This suggests that landings have been softer in recent years than they used to be.

The consensus reached in the late 1990s was that the Fed was responsible for the softer landings. Rather than waiting until the economy was clearly overheating or stalling, the Fed had been quicker to stimulate or restrain the economy when output fell short of or exceeded its natural level. A look at the record of the economy and the Fed's actions since the late 1980s shows why that consensus developed.

As we saw in Figure 14-4, the economy surged above its natural level of output in 1988–89. In response to the overheating of the economy, the Fed raised interest rates during 1988 and 1989. As we saw in Section 14-4, estimates of the effectiveness lag indicate that it may be a year or more before the economy responds strongly to a change in monetary policy. Thus, we would have expected output to respond significantly in 1989 and 1990 to the interest rate increases of 1988 and 1989. Although the Fed may have wanted to pilot a soft landing, in fact the economy slumped into recession in mid-1990.

Of course, monetary policy is rarely the only influence on the economy. Aggregate supply and demand can be buffeted by many different factors. In the late 1980s and early 1990s, a number of important contractionary shocks struck the economy. As a result, it is difficult to claim that any one factor was responsible for the relatively short 1990–91 recession.[20] Indeed, even if the Fed had not raised interest rates, the contractionary shocks that struck the

---

[18]In statistical terms, there has been a stronger negative correlation recently between the ratio of actual to natural output and the subsequent growth rates of actual output.

[19]In statistical terms, there has been a larger (in absolute value) negative response recently of subsequent growth rates of actual output to the ratio of actual to natural output.

[20]This 8-month recession lasted from July 1990 through March 1991. It was shorter than the average postwar recession, which lasted 11 months.

economy around 1990 might have been enough to drive the economy into a recession.

One contractionary factor was the adverse supply shock associated with the Iraqi invasion of Kuwait on August 2, 1990. Oil prices surged from $18 per barrel in June to $40 per barrel in October 1990. The success of Operation Desert Storm in early 1991 then reversed the upsurge in oil prices. This temporary supply shock sapped consumer buying power and consumer confidence, contributing to the decline in real GDP during this period.

Starting very near the end of the 1980s borrowers ran into a credit crunch in which banks reduced their willingness to lend.[21] The banks' reluctance to lend stemmed from several sources. One factor was that bank regulators apparently raised various standards by which banks are measured; another was that recent losses on loans had made banks shy about extending more of the same kind of credit. The resulting reduction in the amount of credit supplied by banks curtailed firms' abilities to invest and employ workers. The real estate and small business sectors were among those whose output was detectably reduced by the banks' difficulties.[22]

The top frame of Figure 14-5 shows how the 1990–91 recession compares with the 1973–75 and 1981–82 recessions. The top frame plots the output ratio for each of these three recessions, beginning with the quarter during which output peaked. The horizontal axis aligns the recessions so that the peak quarter is plotted at the same horizontal position. In each of these recessions the output ratio declined at about the same pace. The biggest difference in the most recent recession was its duration. Whereas output declined for five quarters in the earlier recessions, during the 1990–91 recession it declined for only two quarters.

The bottom frame of Figure 14-5 plots the output ratio beginning with the quarter during which the economy reached its trough for the recoveries that began after the three recessions. The most recent recovery, which began in March 1991 and seemed to be going strong in mid-1997, differs from the two earlier recoveries in at least two ways. First, the most recent recovery began from a considerably higher output ratio. Second, it proceeded at a much slower pace. In contrast to the rapid growth that took place immediately following the earlier troughs, during the first three years of the recovery that began in early 1991, output grew at an annual rate of slightly less than 2 1/2 percent.

Soft Landing in the Late 1990s?

The Fed has also been widely credited with having logged another soft landing in the mid-1990s. As Figure 14-4 shows, real GDP was near its estimated

---

[21]Issues and evidence related to the credit crunch of the early 1990s were first presented in Joe Peek and Eric N. Rosengren, "The Capital Crunch: Neither a Borrower Nor Lender Be," *Journal of Money, Credit and Banking,* vol. 27 (August 1995), pp. 625–38; and in Ben S. Bernanke and Cara Lown, "The Credit Crunch," *Brookings Papers on Economic Activity,* 1991:2, pp. 204–39. The credit crunch was apparently most severe in New England, where especially heavy losses on prior commercial real estate loans reduced the willingness and ability of banks to lend.

[22]See Diana Hancock and James A. Wilcox, "Bank Capital, Nonbank Finance, and Real Estate Activity," *Journal of Housing Research,* vol. 8, (1997), pp. 75–105; and Diana Hancock and James A. Wilcox, "The 'Credit Crunch'" and the Availability of Credit to Small Business," *Journal of Banking and Finance,* forthcoming 1998.

THE 1990–91 RECESSION WAS SHORT AND THE 1990s' RECOVERY WAS SLOW

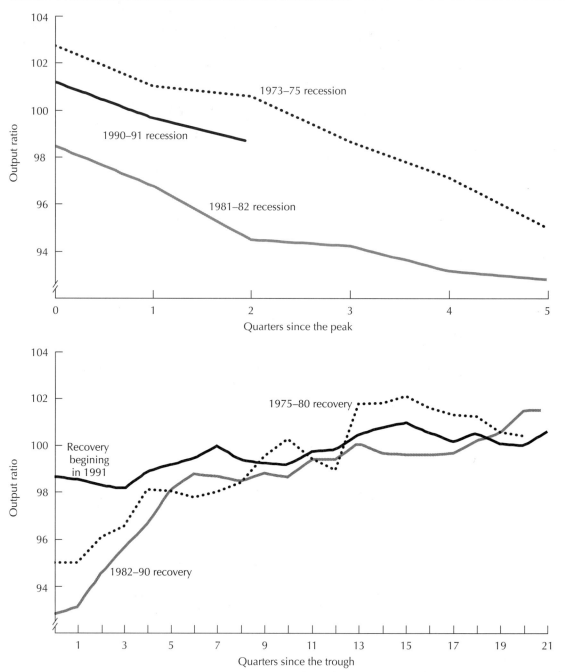

Figure 14-5   The Output Ratio in Three Recessions and in Three Recoveries

The top frame shows the output ratio in three recessions. The bottom frame shows the output ratio in the three recoveries that followed those recessions. The horizontal axis begins at the quarter in which quarterly real GDP reached its peak or trough. The 1990–91 recession started from a somewhat lower output ratio than the 1973–75 recession. During each of these three recessions output declined at about the same rate. However, the 1990–91 recession lasted only about half as long as the earlier recessions. The recovery that began in 1991 started from a higher output ratio than the other recoveries shown, but proceeded at a slower pace. Of the three recoveries shown, after five years the most recent recovery left the output ratio at its lowest level.

natural level in 1994 and 1995. The unemployment rate averaged 5.8 percent, which at that time was close to the consensus estimate of the natural rate of unemployment. There were few indications that inflation was rising.

By the first half of 1997, however, the unemployment rate dipped below 5 percent. Since few estimates available in the mid-1990s placed the natural rate of unemployment that low, some analysts suggested the economy had again landed briefly and quickly taken off again. They asked: Was the economy again on a touch and go path, as it had been a decade earlier? And if so, would it again culminate in rising inflation, followed by a recession? Others suggested that the natural rate of unemployment had inexplicably fallen below 5 1/2 percent, and that the economy in the late 1990s had glided smoothly onto the runway of natural output. As of mid-1997 this view was supported by the fact that inflation showed little sign of accelerating, even though the actual unemployment rate had, for quite some time, been far below the unemployment rates that previously had signaled rising inflation. Exactly how much and why the natural rate of unemployment had fallen so much so quickly was widely debated.[23]

Lags and Preemptive Strikes Against Inflation

The lag between changes in the Fed's interest rate target and large responses of output means that the Fed may want to raise interest rates before output recovers to its natural level—just as a plane decelerates long before the runway is in sight. Because the economy would still be operating below its natural level, inflation would still be falling and the unemployment rate would still be above its natural rate. Although such a forward-looking or preemptive monetary policy may be perfectly reasonable, to casual observers it may seem overly restrictive. When the Fed raised interest rates during 1994 and again in 1997, it was roundly criticized in the press and even in Congress for stifling the economy. But in a sense the Fed was trying to keep the economy from soaring too high: It was attempting to guide the economy to a soft landing, to avoid the accelerating inflation rates that would result if output climbed above its natural level.

To what extent in recent years has the Fed changed its interest rate target prior to the economy's overheating or stalling out? Figure 14-6 plots quarterly data for the years 1984–96 for the nominal federal funds interest rate and the output ratio. The Fed began raising interest rates in 1987, a bit before actual output attained its natural level, and then continued to raise interest rates as the economy rose above its natural level in 1988. Then, in 1989 while the economy was still overheated but showing some signs of weakening because of the contractionary shocks discussed above, the Fed began to lower interest rates. Conversely, in early 1994, when the economy neared and seemed headed above its natural level, the Fed raised the federal funds interest rate by about 3 percentage points. And even though output was still slightly above its natural level in 1995 and 1996, the Fed lowered rates slightly. Thus, the recent pattern of the Fed has been forward-looking. Because it recognizes the lengthy effectiveness lags involved in monetary policy, the Fed

---

[23]Numerous hypotheses to explain the mid-1990s' decline in the natural rate of unemployment were surveyed at the end of Section 8-8.

THE FED HAS ACTED IN ANTICIPATION OF THE ECONOMY'S OVERHEATING

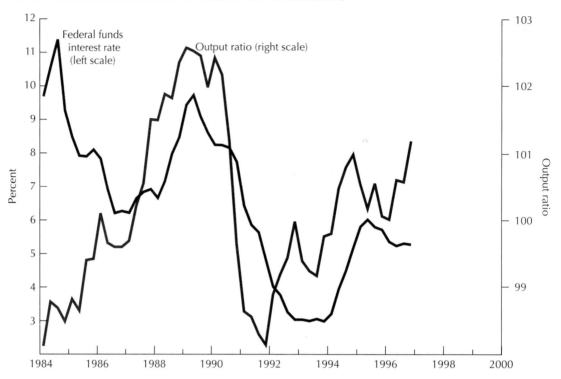

Figure 14-6   **The Federal Funds Interest Rate and the Output Ratio, 1984–96**

Since the 1980s the Fed has tended to raise and lower interest rates in anticipation of the economy's overheating or stalling out. In the late 1980s the Fed began to raise interest rates as the economy neared an output ratio of 100 percent. When signals began to suggest in 1989 that the output ratio would be falling appreciably below 100 percent in the near future, the Fed began lowering interest rates. The Fed raised interest rates in 1994 as the output ratio again seemed headed above 100 percent.

has tended to change policy in anticipation of the economy either overheating or stalling out. Compared to a policy that waits until there is clear evidence that the economy has overheated or stalled out, a forward-looking policy might reduce the amplitude of oscillations of output around its natural level.

14-7   Time Inconsistency, Credibility, and Reputation

We have already seen that one of the advantages that Milton Friedman claimed for policy rules was that firms, workers, and consumers would be able to form accurate expectations of future policy actions. Proponents of activism saw no merit in this claim, since any good rule could be adopted by a discretionary policymaker.

Time Inconsistency

In 1977 Finn Kydland of Carnegie-Mellon University and his colleague Edward Prescott (now at the University of Minnesota) introduced the concept of **time**

Time inconsistency
describes the temptations
of policymakers to devi-
ate from a policy after it is
announced and private
decisionmakers have
reacted to it.

inconsistency.[24] The basic idea is that discretionary policymakers decide on policy A because it is optimal at that time, and private decisionmakers make consumption, investment, and labor supply decisions based on that policy. However, once private decisionmakers have done so, it may be optimal for policymakers to shift to policy B, thus invalidating the expectations on which private decisionmakers acted.

The simplest example arises in the classroom. Professors want their students to learn but hate to make up tests and grade them. Time inconsistency occurs when a professor announces that there will be a tough final exam. The students respond to policy A by studying hard, but then, just before the scheduled exam time, the professor announces policy B, that the exam has been canceled.

Other examples involve government incentives to encourage specified activity. Once that activity has occurred, the government may reverse the incentives in order to achieve other objectives. For instance, the government may promise a permanent subsidy to investment, but once a substantial increase in investment has occurred, government may revoke the subsidy to help reduce its budget deficit. Or the government may promise to protect inventors from competition through patent laws that are then revoked after inventions are on the market.

In macroeconomics the prominent example of time inconsistency involves the Phillips curve tradeoff between inflation and unemployment. For any given unemployment rate, the actual inflation rate will be low if expectations of future inflation are low. This gives the Fed an incentive to pursue policy A, vowing to achieve low inflation. But once inflation expectations have shifted down, the Fed is tempted to shift to policy B by a monetary stimulus that reduces unemployment, even though policy B will raise inflation and invalidate the low expectations of inflation held by workers and firms.

The implication of the time inconsistency argument is that economic performance may be better, on average, if private decisionmakers know that the central bank will adhere to a rigid rule to target monetary growth or, better yet, the inflation rate. Knowing that there is no discretion and thus no chance of a surprise monetary stimulus (policy B), expectations of future inflation will subside, making possible a lower actual inflation rate for any given unemployment rate.

Credibility and Reputation

In order to achieve the best possible economic performance, with low or even zero inflation combined with unemployment at the natural rate (U^N), it may pay a central bank to invest in its reputation. If the central bank succeeds year after year in avoiding the temptation to boost monetary growth in order to reduce unemployment (policy B), it will convince private decisionmakers

---

[24]The original reference is Finn E. Kydland and Edward C. Prescott, "Rules Rather Than Discretion: The Inconsistency of Optimal Plans," *Journal of Political Economy,* vol. 85 (June 1977), pp. 473–92. The most influential subsequent article was Robert J. Barro and David B. Gordon, "A Positive Theory of Monetary Policy in a Natural Rate Model," *Journal of Political Economy,* vol. 91 (August 1983), pp. 589–610.

Policy credibility is the belief by the public that the policymakers will actually carry out an announced policy.

that a future upsurge of inflation is unlikely. Once the actions of policymakers create this type of reputation, they are said to gain **policy credibility.**

Over the past decade economists have built sophisticated models of "reputational equilibrium."[25] These lead to the conclusion that *if* the policymaker has a long time horizon and *if* the policymaker has a low discount rate, then an equilibrium with zero inflation is possible. That is, the policymaker has an incentive to produce a time-consistent policy, and private decisionmakers adjust their expectations accordingly. However, such theoretical models are not very practical for real-world situations in which governments and central bankers do not last forever and in which governments face regular election campaigns. One interesting result is that central banks (like the German Bundesbank) that are relatively independent of government interference and hence of the need to worry about elections, manage to achieve a lower inflation rate than central banks (like the Bank of Italy) that tend to do the bidding of elected government officials.

Implications for Rules versus Discretion

The debate over time inconsistency focuses on the process by which private decisionmakers form expectations concerning the inflation rate. Other target variables, such as the unemployment rate, are ignored on the assumption that the natural rate hypothesis (p. 536) is valid, so in the long run policymakers have no power to make the actual unemployment rate deviate from the natural rate.

Like many other aspects of the rules versus discretion debate, much of the literature on time inconsistency ignores the variety of different rules that are possible. It ignores as well the many slippages that occur between the policy instrument most directly under the Fed's control (e.g., high-powered money, which the Fed can control from day to day through its open-market operations) and the target variable of central concern in the debate, that is, the inflation rate. Three main slippages may occur. First, money multiplier shocks create slippage between high-powered money and the money supply. Second, shocks to money demand and commodity demand create slippage between the money supply and nominal GDP.[26] Third, supply shocks can cause volatile changes in both real GDP growth and the inflation rate, even if nominal GDP growth is steady.

Because of these three slippages, no monetary policy based on rigid control of high-powered money is likely to produce a steady inflation rate. Only a policy rule that targets the inflation rate is likely to establish policy credibility, but all the problems with activism examined in this chapter apply as well to such a policy rule. To rigidly peg the inflation rate, the Fed would have to carry out Chapter 8's extinguishing policy, allowing large swings in output and employment in response to supply shocks, and, because of the long effectiveness lag, would have to be able to forecast long in advance any major

---

[25]See Fischer, "Rules versus Discretion . . . ," pp. 1175–78.

[26]Recall from Chapter 4 that anything that shifts the *IS* curve along a given *LM* curve—including changes in business and consumer confidence, government spending, tax rates, autonomous net taxes, and autonomous net exports—automatically alters the velocity of money, that is, the ratio of nominal GDP to the money supply.

changes in money demand or any major supply shocks. In short, the three slippages between the instruments of monetary policy and the inflation rate make it almost impossible to conduct a policy rule that would maintain policy credibility.

SELF-TEST   Are the following statements true, false, or uncertain? (1) For any given deceleration of nominal GDP growth created by a tight monetary policy, the recession will be shorter and less severe if the central bank possesses policy credibility with the public. (2) For any given deceleration of nominal GDP growth created by tight monetary policy, the recession will be shorter and less severe if the public believes that the central bank's policy is subject to time inconsistency. (3) Policy credibility increases the merits of a "cold turkey" disinflation as compared to a policy of "living with inflation." (4) The possibility of time inconsistency strengthens the case of discretionary policy against a policy rule that targets the growth rate of high-powered money.

14-8   CASE STUDY: Should Monetary Policy Target the Exchange Rate?

In Chapter 6 we learned how foreign exchange rates were determined. We saw that when a country has flexible exchange rates, its central bank is free to set policy to attain its objectives for the domestic economy. The more expansionary the monetary policy is, the more the exchange rate is likely to depreciate. The weaker currency stimulates exports and restrains domestic purchases of imported goods and services. Thus, the easier monetary policy is likely to raise that country's net exports, thereby shifting its *IS* curve to the right. By contrast, when a country chooses to fix its exchange rate in relation to some other currency or some other group of countries, its central bank surrenders the freedom to pursue domestic objectives; its central bank must use monetary policy to keep the exchange rate fixed. It cannot independently operate to attain other domestic objectives, like stimulating aggregate demand.

In Section 14-7 we saw that the prospect of time-inconsistent behavior by policymakers implied that a country's average inflation rate would be lower if the central bank were committed to a rigid rule for growth of the money supply. The reason is that rule commitment removes the central bank's opportunity to stimulate output temporarily by a surprise monetary stimulus. Knowing that the central bank doesn't have the option, the private sector will not need to incorporate the possibility of surprisingly easy monetary policy when forming its expectations of inflation. The resulting lower *SP* curve means that the central bank can then achieve lower inflation at the natural rate of output.

One way for the central bank to convey its commitment to a rigid rule is to fix the exchange rate. Fixing the exchange rate commits the central bank to keeping domestic interest rates in line with that of the country to which its currency is fixed, thereby precluding the possibility of the central bank adopting a more stimulative monetary policy. Facilitating international trade was a major reason why many advocated fixed exchange rates in the early postwar decades. Since the 1970s, however, the primary attraction of a fixed exchange rate policy seems to have shifted to its ability to keep inflation in check.

INTERNATIONAL PERSPECTIVE

A Single European Currency as a Monetary Policy Rule

Ever since the end of World War II, the nations of Western Europe have been moving toward closer relations. The formation of the NATO security alliance in 1949 was followed by the formation of an economic alliance, the European Economic Community in the 1950s. During the 1980s, economic policies were coordinated even more when the European Monetary System was formed to stabilize the exchange rates of its member nations. During the 1990s, a "single market" was created to permit the unfettered movement across national borders of goods and services, financial capital, and people. The 1992 Maastricht Treaty called for much greater economic integration in its proposal for a monetary union that would replace each member nation's currency with a single European currency.

The European Monetary Union (EMU) has been controversial. Interestingly, the most ardent group of EMU supporters has been politicians. Politicians across Europe have sought greater economic cooperation because in general, such cooperation seems to enhance the chances of having Europe remain prosperous and at peace. Economists as a group have been among the most vocal detractors of EMU.

FOR EUROPEAN MONETARY UNION

Some have argued that international trade within Europe would be enhanced by having a single currency, which would eliminate the costs and risks associated with exchange rates. The irony is that advances in financial markets now make it easier and cheaper than ever before for firms and financial institutions to manage risks associated with exchange rate fluctuations. In spite of that, it may still be expensive, especially for smaller firms and tourists, to deal with the numerous European currencies and the risks and uncertainties that they entail.

Since World War II Germany has kept its inflation rate low. Some support the EMU as a vehicle for other countries to "free-ride" on the German resolve and reputation for low inflation. If the European Central Bank (ECB), perhaps located in Germany for symbolic reasons, carries out monetary policy the way the Bundesbank does, then all of the EMU members would have low inflation, and the low interest rates that accompany it. Thus, EMU is favored by some as a vehicle for achieving the low inflation rates that Germany has had.

The EMU is a monetary union, but it may also provide fiscal discipline. You learned in Section 14-8 how countries that have very high inflation rates sometimes adopt fixed exchange rates in order to discipline both their monetary and their fiscal policies. Among the criteria for entrance to the EMU are that government deficits not exceed 3 percent of GDP and that government debt not exceed 60 percent of GDP in 1997. Other entrance criteria stipulate that inflation and interest rates not diverge too widely from those of the other countries entering the EMU. One reason why the entrance criteria for monetary union included limits on fiscal conditions is that the pressure on central banks to print money often emanates from fiscal imbalances. To reduce those pressures, deficit and debt limits were included among the criteria for participating in the EMU.

AGAINST EUROPEAN MONETARY UNION

Although we haven't delved into the relevant European *political* considerations, in Chapter 6 we did learn about some of the important *economic* costs and benefits of a fixed exchange rate regime like the EMU. Recall that when a nation chooses to fix its exchange rate, it surrenders the independence of its central bank. Its central bank is committed to use its one policy instrument, the money supply, to achieve its one goal, the exchange rate. In the case of the EMU, each member gives up its national currency and any independent monetary policy. The ECB monetary policy will determine the supply of euros, presumably based on conditions in Europe as a whole. In the face of a decline in consumer confidence in Sweden, for example, monetary policy will not be able to lower Swedish interest and exchange rates to revive aggregate demand in Sweden. As a result, output and employment in Sweden will fall.

To the extent that the macroeconomic shocks that strike Europe have similar effects on all EMU members, and that the members have similar preferences about how best to respond to such shocks, the ECB will be able to apply a European monetary policy to the entire EMU and that policy would also be appropriate to each member nation. On the other hand, to the extent that the effects or preferences tend to be more nation-specific, nations will probably have misgivings about the single European monetary policy.

Three sets of responses can help offset these misgivings about the single European monetary policy. First, as we learned in Chapter 7, the more flexible wages and prices are, the less likely it is that various shocks will push the economy away from its natural level. Second, the more mobile a nation's labor force is, the smaller the effect of a shock on its unemployment rate. Third, the larger are the transfer payments that flow into

a nation (from the other EMU members), the smaller the effects on spending and unemployment when a contractionary shock strikes.

There is reason to be concerned that these responses will not be large enough to prevent output from falling considerably short of its natural level in some countries when contractionary shocks strike. Wages and prices adjust gradually enough that output movements in Europe can be quite large. The language, cultural, and national differences across nations make it unlikely that unemployed workers in rural England would, for example, migrate to urban Italy. The rather stringent budget policies of the EMU itself make it likely that the size of transfers, say, from Spain, when its output ratio is high, to Germany, when its output ratio is low, will be small.

Having a single currency imposes a monetary policy rule on each of the member nations: No nation then has a central bank that can conduct monetary policy for itself; each nation accepts the European monetary policy, which will be set by the ECB. Monetary union does not necessarily impose a monetary policy rule on the ECB. In principle, the ECB could alter the supply of euros at will, rather than following a clearly specified monetary policy rule. The legislation that led to the formation of the ECB, however, mandated that the primary goal of monetary policy in the EMU should be to attain price stability. That may not compel the ECB to follow a specific monetary policy rule, but it does instruct it as to what the ends of ECB policy should be.

Evidence from developing countries suggests that adopting fixed exchange rates tends to reduce the average inflation rate in the future.

Countries do not casually inflate their economies. More often they print money out of desperation. Hyperinflations have almost always occurred among the vanquished following an international or civil war or other major calamity (Germany, Hungary, the Soviet Union, China, Nicaragua). The very high inflations in Latin America (Brazil, Argentina, Bolivia) occurred after the prices of commodities they exported collapsed, and energy prices and the interest rates they paid to foreigners soared. The very high inflations in Eastern Europe and the countries of the former Soviet Union occurred during the difficult transition to market economies, when their needs for public outlays were high and their ability to generate tax revenue was low (Poland, Russia). (For more on hyperinflation and rapid inflation, see Sections 12-4 and 12-5.)

Whether the commitment itself to maintain a fixed exchange rate is credible is also relevant. After all, a country that freely chooses to fix its exchange rate presumably is also free to change its mind and devalue its exchange rate or adopt a flexible exchange rate policy. In the absence of some outside constraint, it may be difficult for a country that still has the same problems that led it originally to print money, to convince the private sector that its government is committed to a fixed exchange rate. Having aid from international agencies depend on the maintenance of a fixed exchange rate is likely to bolster confidence in the commitment. Having resisted the temptation to change the exchange rate over a long period of time is also likely to inspire confidence in the commitment. How many years it would take to establish such credibility is unclear.

During the 1990s many of the countries of western Europe pledged to keep their exchange rates fixed relative to each other (but not relative to the United States or Japan). Though some of these European currencies have slipped relative to their initial exchange rates, a somewhat less rigid system of exchange rates remained in place into the late 1990s. This system was designed to serve as a precursor to the ultimate fixed exchange rate system, a single currency. European monetary union is discussed in the International Perspectives box on pp. 464–65.

14-9   Rules versus Discretion: An Assessment

A central theme of this chapter is that money multiplier shocks, money demand shocks, commodity demand shocks, and supply shocks loosen the links between the Fed's policy instruments and its targets for the economy. These shocks imply that a rigid rule for setting the growth rate of the supply of high-powered money (the only policy rule that the Fed is capable of achieving directly) may not achieve the nation's unemployment, inflation, and other targets. Similarly, these shocks may make a rule for a target variable like the inflation rate difficult to achieve. In fact, no policy rule can be perfect. There must be a compromise between tight control of a monetary policy instrument, which may not deliver desirable economic performance, versus better economic performance, which may be hard to achieve by manipulating monetary policy instruments.

A **nominal anchor** is a rule that sets a limit on the growth rate of a nominal variable, for instance, high-powered money, the money supply, the price level, or nominal GDP. A nominal anchor prevents inflation from accelerating without limit.

A second theme is that some policy rules provide a **nominal anchor** for the economy. That is, these rules target a nominal variable (high-powered money, the money supply, nominal GDP, or the inflation rate) and thus automatically place a limit on the ability of inflation to accelerate. A nominal anchor is inherently desirable because it increases the chance that inflation expectations will turn out to be accurate, thus facilitating financial planning by households and firms.

Rules for Policy Instruments

Table 14-1 assesses six policy rules. The first two rules set the values of the Fed's policy instruments, either high-powered money or the federal funds interest rate. A rule for high-powered money growth provides a nominal anchor but allows shocks to carry the economy away from its target. A nominal interest rate target does not provide a nominal anchor, and a positive commodity demand shock can lead to explosive inflation under a nominal interest rate rule.[27]

A Rule for the Money Supply

The money supply is neither directly under the control of the Fed nor is it a target variable. For this reason it is sometimes called an "intermediate variable." A money supply rule (like the monetarist CGRR) has only two advantages. In the first place, it provides a nominal anchor; in the second (as in Figure 13-5) it is superior to an interest-rate rule when commodity demand is unstable but money demand is stable. Otherwise, it combines the weakness of rules for targets (they are difficult to control) with the weakness of a high-powered money rule (money multiplier shocks, money demand instability, commodity demand shocks, and supply shocks can push the economy away from its targets).

Rules for Target Variables

The main target variables are inflation and unemployment. Unemployment moves inversely with the growth rate of real GDP, so a rule that targets unemployment is similar to a rule that targets real GDP growth. Because inflation plus real GDP growth equals nominal GDP growth, a nominal GDP growth rule has some of the characteristics of other rules for target variables, even though nominal GDP itself is not a target variable.

Rules for target variables avoid slippage between the instruments and the targets. In particular, all target rules (if successful) prevent instability in either commodity or money demand from causing undesirable fluctuations in target variables. These rules also suffer from a common disadvantage: It is difficult to control target variables because of policy lags, forecasting errors,

---

[27]This defect of a nominal interest rate rule was a major theme of Milton Friedman's 1967 Address to the American Economic Association. A positive commodity demand shift boosts the nominal interest rate; to maintain its target, the Fed must raise the money supply; this raises inflationary expectations and boosts the nominal interest rate again; again, the Fed must raise the money supply. Soon the Fed has caused a spiral of accelerating money growth and inflation. This phenomenon occurred when the Fed accommodated the fiscal stimulus of the Vietnam War during 1967–68.

Table 14-1   **Assessing Alternative Policy Rules**

Variable to Be Fixed by Policy Rule	Main Advantages	Main Disadvantages
Growth rate of high-powered money	Feasible for Fed to achieve; provides nominal anchor	May lead to variable inflation and unemployment rates
Nominal interest rate	Feasible for Fed to achieve (in short run)	Unstable commodity demand may lead to variable unemployment rate. Does not provide nominal anchor; hence inflation can increase without bound.
Growth rate of the money supply (monetarist CGRR)	Provides nominal anchor	Money supply hard to control; money demand instability may lead to variable inflation and unemployment rates.
Growth rate of nominal GDP	Provides nominal anchor; splits supply shock effect between output and inflation	Hard to control
Inflation rate or price level	Provides nominal anchor; if successful, most likely to stabilize inflation expectations and avoid time inconsistency	Hard to control; requires extinguishing reaction to supply shocks, creating highly variable unemployment rate
Unemployment rate or growth rate of real GDP	Avoids welfare cost of variable unemployment; allows households and firms to carry through on plans without making mistakes	Hard to control; requires accommodating reaction to supply stocks, creating highly variable inflation rate; does not provide nominal anchor

and multiplier uncertainty. As shown in Table 14-1, rules for target variables differ. Rules for nominal GDP growth or inflation provide a nominal anchor; rules for unemployment or real GDP growth do not.

The main advantage of a nominal GDP rule is that it requires no policy response to a supply shock (defined in Chapter 8 as a "neutral policy" response). In contrast, an inflation rule requires that the effect of supply shocks on the price level be extinguished, which raises the variability of output; whereas a real GDP or unemployment rule requires that the effect of supply shocks be "accommodated," which raises the variability of inflation. Because a nominal GDP rule represents a compromise response to supply shocks and provides a nominal anchor, numerous prominent economists over the past decade have come to advocate that the Fed adopt such a rule.

Is a Nominal GDP Rule Feasible?

While a nominal GDP rule has gained favor and a money supply rule lost support since the 1970s (largely due to the observed instability of the demand for money), there remain substantial questions about whether such a rule is feasible. Long lags and the difficulty of forecasting turning points in nominal GDP growth suggest that actual nominal GDP growth would fluctuate substantially around the Fed's chosen target path. The actual behavior of the economy since the early 1980s sends a mixed message about the feasibility of such rules. The good news is that the Fed generally succeeded in maintaining nominal GDP growth between about 5 and 8 percent, even though doing so required substantial variation in both interest rates and money supply growth. The bad news is that nominal (and real) GDP growth slumped considerably during 1991, culminating in a recession.

When monetary policy is carefully analyzed, we see that the debate between rules and discretion is misleading. There are a wide variety of economic variables that could be targeted by a rule, and only rules for policy instruments allow the Fed to escape the use of discretion. Implementation of a rule for nominal GDP growth or inflation inherently requires the Fed to use discretion in deciding which models and forecasts to use and how to resolve conflicts about the management of policy instruments. However, there is still a difference between a nominal GDP rule and pure discretion. The former provides the economy with a nominal anchor that would prevent a repeat of the accelerating inflation that plagued the U.S. economy in the late 1960s and again in the late 1970s, while pure discretion does not provide such a nominal anchor.

SUMMARY

1. In earlier chapters we assumed that the growth of aggregate demand could be controlled precisely by policymakers. We now recognize that in the real-world economy, policy shifts cannot control aggregate demand instantly or precisely.

2. Hitting several targets of stabilization policy, such as unemployment and inflation, requires several policy instruments. The conditions required for activist policy intervention to be effective (the "activists' paradise") are quite stringent, including accurate forecasting, possession of powerful tools, absence of costs of changing policy instruments, and absence of political constraints.

3. The general case put forth by advocates of policy rules is that rules insulate a central bank from political pressure, allow the performance of the central bank to be judged, and help private decisionmakers form cor-rect expectations. However, the strength of this case depends on which variable is being targeted by a rule.

4. Policy activists are pessimistic about the stability of the private economy, while they are optimistic about the feasibility of discretionary policy. Advocates of rules reverse the locus of their optimism and pessimism.

5. Five lags (data, recognition, legislative, transmission, and effectiveness) limit the speed at which policy can respond to a demand or supply shock. By far the longest for monetary policy is the effectiveness lag. Additional obstacles to effective activist policy, or to policy rules based on targets, are multiplier uncertainty and forecasting errors.

6. Time inconsistency suggests that discretionary policymakers may have an incentive to alter policies after private decisionmakers have reacted to previous policy announcements. To encourage decisionmakers to form low expectations of inflation, it may pay the central bank to target the inflation rate and achieve a reputation for succeeding in keeping the inflation rate low, thus establishing policy credibility.

7. The economy has come close to landing on the runway of natural real GDP since the mid-1980s. Long lags suggest that rather than waiting until output deviates appreciably from its natural level, the Fed should be forward-looking, changing interest rates when the economy is forecasted to overheat or stall out.

8. Fixing its exchange rate deprives a nation's central bank of discretionary monetary policy. In practice, that sometimes leads nations to redress their fiscal imbalances, as well as prevent the money growth that leads to inflation. European monetary union would permanently fix exchange rates between its members and cede monetary control to the European Central Bank, which would control the supply of euros, the new single European currency.

9. Proposed policy rules differ in the variables they propose to target. Rules targeting policy instruments may be successful but irrelevant for the achievement of desirable outcomes for target variables like inflation and unemployment, due to slippages coming from money multiplier shocks, money demand shocks, commodity demand shocks, and supply shocks. Rules for target variables may lead to better outcomes, in principle, but may be difficult to implement successfully.

CONCEPTS

demand shocks
policy activism
policy rule
policy instruments
target variables
discretionary policy
rigid rule
constant growth rate rule (CGRR)

feedback rule
monetarism
dynamic multipliers
multiplier uncertainty
econometric model
time inconsistency
policy credibility
nominal anchor

QUESTIONS

Questions

1. In the Appendix to Chapter 5, the equations of the *IS* and *LM* curves are given as follows:

$$IS: Y = k(A_0 - br)$$

$$LM: Y = [(M^S/P) - fr]/h.$$

Here, $k = 1/[s(1 - t_0) + t_0 + nx_0]$.
Let $A_0 = a_0 - cT_0 + I_{p0} + G + NX_0$, where a_0 is that part of consumption spending that is independent of both Y and r, I_{p0} is similarly defined, and the other terms are as defined in the Appendix to Chapter 3.
   (a) List the exogenous variables (and parameters) in this model. (See Chapter 5 to review the definition of this term.)
   (b) List the endogenous variables in this model. (See Chapter 3 to review the definition of this term.)
   (c) List the target variables in this model.
   (d) List the variables that make up the policy instruments in this model.

   (e) What is the relationship, if any, between endogenous variables and target variables in this model?
   (f) What is the relationship, if any, between exogenous variables and policy instruments in this model?
   Note: In answering this question, use only the variables in the *IS* and *LM* equations and the variables defining k and A_0. For example, don't include a variable such as structural employment policy as a policy instrument or the unemployment rate as a target variable; they are not variables in the above model, even though they are listed in the table in Section 14-2 as a policy instrument and target variable, respectively.

2. In the *IS-LM* model of the preceding question, what are the monetary policy variables? What are the fiscal policy variables?

3. In the model of Question 1, how many policy instruments are there? How many target variables? Is this

consistent with the text's statement that you need as many policy instruments as target variables to achieve the desired values of the target variables?

4. The case for activist intervention in the economy would work best in the activists' paradise. What are the characteristics of the activists' paradise?

5. What do advocates of policy rules think are the main objections to countercyclical activism?

6. Distinguish between a rigid rule and a feedback rule. Give an example of each.

7. One way of describing the rules-versus-activism debate is to compare the beliefs of each side regarding the self-correcting powers of the economy and the efficacy of stabilization policy. What does each side believe about these issues?

8. Under the constant growth rate rule (CGRR), the single target for the policymaker becomes the growth rate of the money supply. Does this statement suggest that those advocating the CGRR are not concerned with the level of real output and employment?

9. Explain why stability of the demand for money is so important to those advocating a constant growth rate rule for the money supply. What happens to the argument in favor of this rule if money demand is unstable?

10. In the 1980s, the growth of $M1$ proceeded at a faster rate than in the inflationary periods of the 1970s. What happened to the inflation rate in the 1980s? Does this result support or rebut the monetarist case?

11. Identify and describe the five main types of lags that affect the timeliness of monetary and fiscal policy.

12. What problems do long and variable lags present to the policymaker? If lags are long and fixed (rather than long and variable), do any problems remain?

13. Why does multiplier uncertainty create a dilemma for policymakers?

14. Figure 14-2 shows that the effectiveness lag of monetary policy increased during the period 1983–96, as compared to earlier periods, and that the interest rate multiplier declined in each of the successive periods, 1962–69, 1970–82, and 1983–96. What caused this trend toward diminished effectiveness of monetary policy?

15. During 1994 and again in 1996 the Fed used its control of high-powered money to increase the federal funds rate in a preemptive move against inflation. Citing the absence of any evidence of rising inflation, critics charged that this policy unnecessarily threatened to slow or halt economic growth. Does the presence of long and variable lags support the Fed or its critics in this controversy?

16. Assess the record of macroeconomic forecasting and explain its relevance to the policy debate.

17. What are the major limitations of monetary policy and how might they be overcome?

18. Suppose the output ratio is 100 and the inflation rate is 5 percent. Given these conditions, why will policymakers be more likely to pursue a zero inflation target if they have a long time horizon and a low discount rate rather than a short time horizon and a high discount rate?

19. What are the arguments for and against using monetary policy to target a currency's exchange rate?

20. What are the objectives of the European Monetary Union (EMU)? How are they to be achieved? What advantages and disadvantages are expected for EMU member countries and for economic conditions in Europe?

SELF-TEST ANSWERS

p. 442 (1) target, (2) instrument, (3) instrument, (4) target, (5) instrument.

p. 450 (1) Legislative lag. (2) Multiplier uncertainty. (3) Data lag. (4) Both the effectiveness lag and multiplier uncertainty.

p. 463 (1) True; the public will believe that the central bank will maintain low rates of growth of the money supply and the price level; (2) False; opposite of (1), (3) True; same as (1). (4) False; time inconsistency strengthens advocates of rules involving nominal variables such as the growth of high-powered money or the inflation rate.

PART SIX

Sources of Instability in the Private Economy

Instability in the Private Economy: Consumption Behavior

Economists become upset when they learn that we aren't spending money as they've planned for us.
—Eliot Marshall

15-1 Consumption and Economic Stability

In Part Five (Chapters 12–14), we studied the role of stabilization policy, which consists of monetary and fiscal policy. The most basic question about stabilization policy is whether "activist" policy intervention should be attempted or whether policy rules are preferable. If policy rules are preferable, what variable should be targeted by such rules? A central issue in making these choices is the set of shocks that can cause target variables to be unstable even if a policy instrument is successfully targeted by a rigid rule. These shocks include money multiplier and money demand shocks (Chapter 13), supply shocks (Chapter 8), and commodity demand, or spending, shocks.

We now turn to the nature of the shocks that destabilize consumption and investment demand. This chapter deals with the subject of consumption spending; the following chapter is devoted to investment spending. We start with consumption spending for the simple reason that it is by far the largest component of total spending, comprising two-thirds of GDP.

Consumption Spending and Shifts in the *IS* Curve

How did consumption spending enter into the basic theory of income determination earlier in the book? Chapter 3 introduced the simple Keynesian consumption function, which makes the level of consumption expenditures depend on disposable income and on an autonomous component. Shifts in this autonomous component, due to changes in consumer confidence or optimism, were cited as one of the factors that could shift the economy's *IS* curve. These shifts in the *IS* curve, amplified by the multiplier, cause fluctuations in real GDP as long as the *LM* curve is not completely vertical and the aggregate price level is not perfectly flexible. Further, the size of the multiplier is importantly affected by the size of the response of consumption to a change in disposable income, the marginal propensity to consume.

Forward-looking expectations are estimates of the future values of economic variables. They are generally based on the current and past values of several variables and an economic model that accounts for their behavior.

Forward-Looking Theories of Consumer Behavior

In this chapter we examine the determinants of consumption spending. The focus is a theory of consumer behavior that incorporates much more sophisticated consumer behavior than the Keynesian theory of Chapter 3. This theory states that consumers have **forward-looking expectations.** Because

475

consumers prefer stable as opposed to highly variable patterns of consumption, they assess whether changes in their incomes are likely to persist when deciding how much to change their consumption. Consumers behave quite differently in response to a change in disposable income that is expected to be temporary than they do in response to a change in disposable income that is expected to be permanent. Consumers can maintain their consumption when income changes temporarily by drawing down their accumulated savings. By contrast, if income is reduced permanently, consumption will fall more dramatically.

Introducing the PIH and LCH.   The hypothesis that consumption depends on forward-looking expectations was developed independently in the 1950s by two economists who have since won the Nobel Prize, Milton Friedman and Franco Modigliani. Friedman's version is usually called the **permanent-income hypothesis (PIH).** It predicts that consumption responds only to permanent changes in income, not to transitory ones. The PIH suggests that temporary changes in income will have minor effects on permanent income and, therefore, on consumption. As a result, the multiplier effect of a temporary change in autonomous spending is much smaller than the effect calculated in Chapter 3. In that case, the shifts in the *IS* curve are also much smaller than suggested in Chapter 4. (Remember that the horizontal shift of the *IS* curve equals the product of the change in A_p and the multiplier.) The resulting stability of consumption spending supports the view of rules advocates that the economy can be trusted to remain fairly close to natural output.

> The **permanent-income hypothesis (PIH)** holds that consumption spending depends on the long-run average (or permanent) income that people expect to receive.

Modigliani's version, called the **life-cycle hypothesis (LCH),** holds that consumers attempt to smooth out their consumption spending over their lifetimes. This version also implies that transitory blips of income will cause only a small response in consumption. The LCH also implies that consumption spending depends not just on disposable income but on the assets and liabilities of consumers as well. It implies, for instance, that major movements in stock market prices could affect consumption.

> The **life-cycle hypothesis (LCH)** implies that households base their current consumption on their expected total lifetime incomes and their wealth.

15-2   CASE STUDY: Main Features of U.S. Consumption Data

Before we study these two forward-looking theories of consumption behavior, we will examine data on aggregate consumption in the United States. Plotted in Figure 15-1 are total real consumption expenditures over the period 1959–96, as well as the behavior of the three main components of consumption: durable goods, nondurable goods, and services.

Note that the growth of total consumption spending, shown by the top line, has not been perfectly steady. Particularly sharp slowdowns in the growth of total consumption spending took place in 1974–75, 1980–82, and 1990–91. As we will see, the forward-looking theories emphasize that because consumers consider their permanent or lifetime incomes, they react to temporary declines in income (such as occur in a recession) primarily by reducing saving rather than consumption. Clearly, some consumers cut their consumption during recessions. They may not, for example, have enough savings to absorb the blow of losing a job. Also, banks typically will not lend to unemployed people, even though they may have good prospects of regaining their jobs and making an impressive total lifetime income.

Of the three components of consumption expenditures, spending on durable goods is by far the most volatile. Consumer durable expenditures, like the fixed-investment expenditures studied in the next chapter, are often made for big-ticket items that can be postponed. Many households buy new automobiles or TV sets simply because they want improved quality or new features; they can often postpone such purchases if income declines temporarily. Consumption of nondurable goods displays moderate cyclical volatility, while consumption of services tends to grow more smoothly.

Both durable goods and services spending grew much faster than spending on nondurable goods over the period shown in Figure 15-1. Percentages of total consumption for the three major categories of consumption expenditure at the beginning and end of the period depicted are:

	1959:Q3	*1996:Q4*
Durable goods	7.6	13.1
Nondurable goods	43.2	30.6
Services	49.2	56.3

CONSUMPTION DOES NOT ALWAYS GROW STEADILY

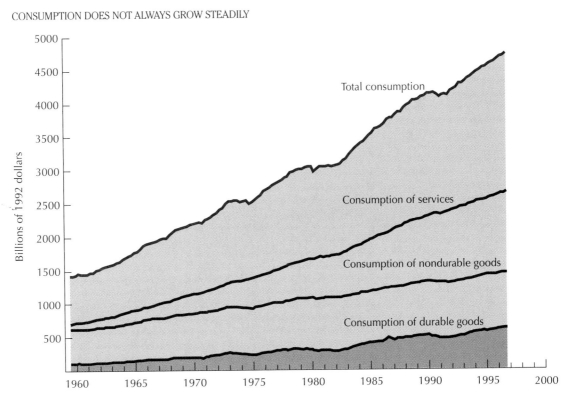

Figure 15-1   **Real Consumer Expenditure and Its Three Components, 1959–96**
The top line plots consumer expenditure and shows a marked pause in growth in 1974–75, 1980–82, and 1990–91. Consumption of durable goods is both the most volatile and fastest-growing component on average over this period. Consumption of services also has grown rapidly, but is much less volatile than expenditures on durable goods. Consumption of nondurable goods is the slowest-growing component and has moderate volatility.

The basic reason for the slow growth in nondurable goods purchases is that many such goods, particularly food and clothing, are necessities. Many types of durable goods (such as stereo equipment) and services (airline trips to Florida) are luxuries, which experience disproportionately fast growth in demand when incomes rise.

Have these trends made total consumption more or less stable? The shrinking segment, nondurable goods, has moderate cyclical volatility. The increases in the shares of high-volatility durable goods spending and low-volatility services spending have been roughly equal, implying that the overall volatility of total consumption spending did not change appreciably between 1959 and 1996.

15-3   Background: The Conflict Between the Time-Series and Cross-Section Evidence

One of the major innovations in Keynes's *General Theory* was the multiplier, which followed directly from the assumptions that consumption responds to income and that the marginal propensity to consume is less than unity: "The fundamental psychological law . . . is that men are disposed, as a rule and on the average, to increase their consumption as their income increases, but not by as much as the increase in their income."[1]

Keynes's second innovative idea was that there is a given amount, *a*, that individuals will consume no matter what their income, so that it is possible for saving to be negative if disposable income is very low. Denoting consumption as *C* and disposable income as Y_D, the Keynesian consumption function can be written:

$$C = a + cY_D \tag{15.1}$$

The hypothetical Keynesian consumption function and saving ratio are plotted in the top two frames of Figure 15-2. In the top frame, consumption *(C)*

Figure 15-2   The Relation Between Disposable Income (Y_D), Consumption Spending (C), and the Ratio of Saving to Income (S/Y_D)

The top frame repeats the consumption function introduced in Chapter 3. At levels of disposable income below (to the left of) Y_{D0}, people consume more than their income. To the right of Y_{D0} consumption is less than income, and the shaded red area, which represents the difference between income and consumption, that is, the amount of saving, is a steadily growing fraction of disposable income. In the middle frame the share of saving in disposable income is plotted as a negative fraction to the left of Y_{D0} and a positive and growing fraction to the right. The bottom frame plots actual data on the relation of saving to disposable income from a survey of consumers. Notice the close correspondence between the theoretical diagram in the middle frame and the actual data in the bottom frame. *Saving ratio is income after taxes minus average annual expenditures expressed as a percent of income after taxes. Real disposable income is expressed in 1996 dollars.*
(Source bottom frame: U.S. Bureau of Labor Statistics, *Consumer Expenditure Survey: Results from 1986,* Washington, D.C. April 1988, Table 2.*)*

---

[1]See John Maynard Keynes, *The General Theory of Employment, Interest and Money* (New York: Macmillan, 1936), Book III. The idea of the multiplier was first introduced by R. F. Kahn, "The Relation of Home Investment to Unemployment," *Economic Journal* (June 1931), but Keynes was the first to fit the multiplier into a general economic model of commodity and money markets.

PEOPLE WITH HIGHER INCOMES HAVE HIGHER SAVING RATES

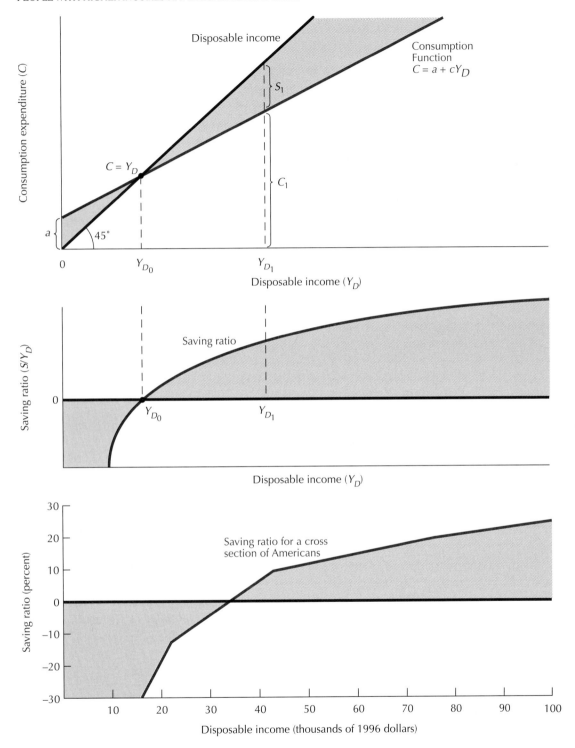

rises less rapidly than disposable income (Y_D), since the marginal propensity to consume (c) is less than 1.0. Consumption starts out greater than Y_D, equals Y_D at the income level Y_{D0}, and then is less than Y_D. Everywhere to the right of Y_{D0} the shortfall of consumption below disposable income allows room for a positive amount of saving. For instance, the income level Y_{D1} is divided into the consumption level C_1 and the saving level S_1.

Moving down to the middle frame of Figure 15-2, we find plotted the saving/income ratio, S/Y_D. To the left of the income level Y_{D0}, saving is negative; to the right of Y_{D0}, saving is positive. As income rises, according to the hypothetical Keynesian relation in the middle frame, a larger share of disposable income is saved.

A **cross section** consists of data for numerous units (for instance, households, firms, cities, or states) observed over a single period of time.

The actual data plotted in the bottom frame of Figure 15-2 confirm Keynes's hypothesis for a **cross section** of Americans who were polled in 1986 on their income, saving, and consumption behavior. Most people with low incomes do not save at all, but instead "dissave," consuming more than they earn by borrowing or by drawing on accumulated assets in savings accounts. As we move rightward from the poor to the rich, we find that the saving/income ratio increases, just as in the hypothetical relationship of the middle frame.

The Saving Rate: Short-Run Variability, Long-Run Constancy

Implicit in Figure 15-2 is a potentially serious problem for the economy. If individuals save more as their incomes rise, then the national saving rate will rise over time as natural real GDP rises with advances in technology and the other factors that raise natural real GDP over time. For output to remain close to natural real GDP requires the remaining components of spending (I, G, or NX) to rise, as a share of natural real GDP, by the same amount that the saving rate rises. If the other components of spending do not increase as much as the saving rate increases, then actual real GDP will sink below natural real GDP. Keynes's concern that the saving rate would rise as the years passed seemed particularly relevant during the Great Depression of the 1930s, when the world's actual real GDP was far below its natural level for many years and investment spending was very weak. The weakness of investment spending during the Great Depression led some to argue that government spending be used to raise output to its natural level.

A **time series** consists of data covering a span of time for one or more measures (for instance, disposable income or consumption spending).

But, has the saving rate, in fact, risen over time as natural real GDP has risen? Look now at Figure 15-3, which plots the actual historical **time-series** data for the average saving ratio for each major business cycle of the twentieth century. Between 1898 and 1899, the first observation plotted, and 1991–96, the last observation plotted, real income per person quintupled.[2] Yet there is little indication that the saving ratio trended upward over the twentieth century. Instead, the saving ratio has not changed dramatically over the twentieth century. If anything, in recent decades the saving ratio was lower than it was before World War I. The main longer-term variations in the saving ratio were the low saving ratio during the Great Depression of the 1930s and the high saving ratios during World War I and World War II.

---

[2]See page 481 for data source. Data for 1991–96 were used for the last observation.

Figure 15-3

Ratio of Personal Saving to Disposable Personal Income (S/Y_D), Averages over Business Cycles, 1898–1996

The low level of saving during the Great Depression is consistent with our theory (compare Figure 3-3). The high levels of saving during World War I and World War II were caused by the shortages of civilian goods and services. Leaving out these two extreme periods, the ratio of saving to disposable income was fairly constant. Observations plotted are averages over complete business cycles, except for the last observation, which is the average 1991–96 saving ratio. *(Sources: 1897–99:* Paul David and John Scadding, "Private Savings: Ultrarationality, Aggregation, and 'Denison's Law,'" *Journal of Political Economy* (March/April 1974). *1900–32: Historical Statistics of the United States, Series F 639 and F 9. 1933–96 National Income and Product Accounts.)*

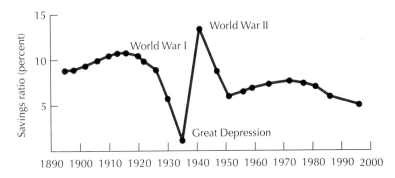

AMERICANS HAVE NOT SAVED A GREATER SHARE OF THEIR INCOME AS THEY HAVE GROWN RICHER

Keynes's consumption function implies that the saving ratio will decline in recessions and that in cross-section data those with higher incomes will tend to have higher saving rates. The data confirm both of these implications. Keynes's consumption function, however, does not explain why over the longer run the saving ratio is so nearly constant. The two most important hypotheses about consumption (and thus about saving) that can account for the long-run near-constancy of the saving ratio, as well as the short-run variability and the cross-section pattern of saving, are Friedman's permanent-income hypothesis and Modigliani's life-cycle hypothesis.

15-4 Forward-Looking Behavior: The Permanent-Income Hypothesis

A Theory of Steady Consumption

Imagine that you have a job and receive your take-home pay of $1000 on the first day of each month. Suppose you regard your income on the first day of each month as $1000, and your income on each of the remaining days of the month as zero. If you spend based on the simple Keynesian consumption function with a high marginal propensity to consume and a small autonomous component, you will do almost all your consumption spending on the first day of the month and consume very little over the rest of the month!

Of course people consume more steadily than that, setting aside part of their pay to buy groceries and other items during the rest of the month. Individuals who have variable income will be happier if they consume about the same amount each day rather than allowing their consumption to change each day with their changing income.

Permanent income is the average income that people expect to receive over a period of years in the future.

Milton Friedman first proposed the hypothesis that individuals consume a constant fraction (k) of their expected income, which Friedman called **permanent income** (Y^P).[3]

General Form	Numerical Example	
$C = kY^P$	$C = 0.9(\$10,000) = \$9000$	(15.2)

The individual marginal propensity to consume out of permanent income (k) depends on individual tastes and on the variability of income (farmers, salespeople, and others with variable income need higher saving to support themselves during bad years). In addition, k may depend on the interest rate. People may be willing to save more (and spend less) when interest rates are higher.[4]

Revising the Estimate of Permanent Income.   The permanent-income hypothesis summarized in equation (15.2) does not say that individuals consume exactly the same amount year after year. Every year new events occur that are likely to change individuals' guesses about their permanent income. For instance, an individual might find that in good years income has increased. Gradually the individual will revise his or her estimate of average expected income upward and will increase his or her stable-consumption level.

Friedman's permanent-income hypothesis consists of the assumption in equation (15.2) that individuals consume a constant portion of their permanent income. But this is not enough, because an additional assumption is required to indicate how individuals estimate the size of their permanent income. Friedman proposed that individual estimates of permanent income for this year (Y^P) be revised from last year's estimate (Y^P_{-1}) by some fraction (j) of the amount by which actual income (Y) differs from (Y^P_{-1}):

General Form	Numerical Example	
$Y^P = Y^P_{-1} + j(Y - Y^P_{-1})$	$Y^P = 10,000 + 0.2(15,000 - 10,000)$	(15.3)
	$= 11,000$	

Adaptive Expectations.   The behavior described in equation (15.3) is sometimes called the "error-learning" or "adaptive" hypothesis of expectation formation. This hypothesis implies that individuals will allow their consumption to respond modestly to changes in actual income because consumption depends on permanent income, and in turn permanent income in equation (15.3) depends only in part on this period's actual income. When we substitute (15.3) into (15.2), we obtain the following relationship between an individual's current consumption (C), this period's actual income (Y), and last period's estimate of permanent income (Y^P_{-1}):

General Form	Numerical Example	
$C = kY^P_{-1} + kj(Y - Y^P_{-1})$	$C = 0.9 Y^P_{-1} + 0.18(Y - Y^P_{-1})$	(15.4)

---

[3]Milton Friedman, *A Theory of the Consumption Function* (Princeton, N.J.: Princeton University Press, 1957).

[4]Because of the limitations of the alphabet we are once again forced to duplicate the use of letters. The k here is completely unrelated to the k used in Chapters 3 through 5 to represent the multiplier.

Exactly the same hypothesis for the formation of expectations was introduced in the appendix to Chapter 8 in the discussion of inflation expectations (see equation [8.2] on p. 233). Equation (15.3) can be rewritten in the form used there.

$$Y^P = jY + (1 - j)Y^P_{-1}$$

This says that permanent income in this period is a weighted average of actual income and last period's permanent income.

Two Marginal Propensities to Consume.   Equation (15.4) helps us see that Friedman's theory is based on a distinction between two concepts of the marginal propensity to consume (MPC). The *long-run* MPC is simply the coefficient *(k)* of permanent income in the original consumption function (15.2), and indeed k is the coefficient of the first term in (15.4). In our numerical example, the long-term MPC *(k)* is 0.9. The *short-run* MPC is the coefficient of a change in actual income, the coefficient kj (or $0.18 = 0.9$ times 0.2) in the second term in (15.4). When today's actual income *(Y)* increases, the second term in (15.4) shows that today's consumption goes up by the short-run MPC *(kj,* or 0.18).

The portion of today's income change that is not expected to be permanent is called **transitory income** in Friedman's theory. Transitory income *(Y^t)* is simply actual income minus permanent income:

Transitory income is the difference between actual and permanent income and is not expected to recur.

General Form	Numerical Example	
$Y^t = Y - Y^P$	$Y^t = Y - Y^P$	(15.5)
$\quad = Y - Y^P_{-1} - j(Y - Y^P_{-1})$	$\quad = 0.8(Y - Y^P_{-1})$	
$\quad = (1 - j)(Y - Y^P_{-1})$		

Friedman achieves his sharp distinction between the long-run and short-run MPC by assuming that the MPC out of transitory income is zero. Thus his consumption function (15.2) could be rewritten as:

$$C = 0Y^t + kY^P \qquad (15.6)$$

Reconciling the Conflict Between Cross-Section and Time-Series Data

The motivation for Friedman's PIH was the apparent conflict between the cross-section data in Figure 15-2, where high-income people were shown to have higher savings ratios than low-income people, and the long-run near-constancy of the saving ratio shown in Figure 15-3. The PIH contends that the high saving ratios of high-income people are due to their having atypically large, positive, transitory incomes (e.g., executives who received large bonuses after a good year; movie stars after the release of unusually popular films; or professional athletes, who have short-lived, high-income careers). Similarly, the PIH contends that low-income people dissave or have low saving ratios (as in Figure 15-2) because they are more likely than the average person to have actual incomes that are temporarily below their permanent incomes. (Examples of people with negative transitory income include farmers whose crops were ruined by drought, floods, or disease; executives who have just been fired; and college students who believe that their incomes will be higher in the future.) Thus, the PIH explains how, even when the longer-run savings ratio is constant across individuals and across time, cross-section data will record that high-income people have higher saving ratios.

The Two Consumption Functions Illustrated. Figure 15-4 illustrates the distinction between the long-run and short-run consumption functions. The solid red line running through points *A* and *F* is the long-run consumption function; its slope is the long-run MPC (*k*, or 0.9). It is called the long-run consumption function because it indicates the level of consumption only when actual income has remained long enough at a particular level for individuals to fully adjust their estimated permanent income to the actual level.

What happens in the short run, when actual income can differ from permanent income? The flatter dashed red schedule running between *A* and *B* is the short-run schedule and plots equation (15.4). When current income *(Y)* is exactly equal to last period's permanent income Y^P_{-1}, the short-run schedule intersects the long-run schedule at point *A*. But during an unusually good year, when an individual's income is at the high level Y_0, the current estimate of permanent income *(Y^P)* rises above last period's estimate Y^P_{-1} by a fraction *(j)* of the excess of actual income over last period's estimate. And the higher value of Y^P raises consumption by *k* times the increase in permanent income.

Thus consumption at point *B* lies vertically above point *A* by the fraction *kj* (18 percent in the numerical example) times the horizontal distance between Y^P_{-1} and Y_0. With the short-run marginal propensity to consume *(kj)* so far below the long-run propensity *(k)*, any short-run increase in income goes disproportionately into saving. If Y_0 comes to be regarded as permanent, the short-run consumption function will go through *F.*

To summarize, estimates of permanent income are continually raised as actual income outstrips previous levels, causing the relationship between

---

Figure 15-4
The Permanent-Income Hypothesis of Consumption and Saving

The long-run schedule shows that consumption is a fixed fraction of income in the long run, when actual and permanent income are equal. But short-run gains in actual income, as at point *B*, are not fully incorporated into permanent income. Thus consumption increases only a small amount (compare points *B* and *A*), and at *B* most of the short-run increase in income is saved. When the same gain in income is maintained permanently, the short-run schedule shifts upward, following the arrows along the long-run schedule to point *F.*

THE LONG-RUN CONSUMPTION FUNCTION IS MUCH STEEPER THAN THE SHORT-RUN FUNCTION

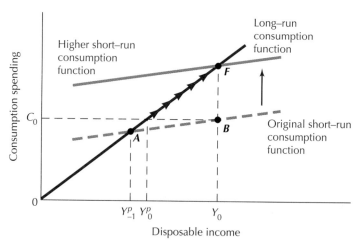

consumption and income to follow the long-run schedule, as marked by the arrows in Figure 15-4. Thus, in the long run the saving ratio is roughly constant. But in the short run a temporary increase in income raises the saving ratio and a temporary decrease in income reduces the saving ratio, because permanent income does not adjust completely to changes in actual income.

SELF-TEST   Determine whether actual income is above or below permanent income in each of the following situations and how consumption and saving compare to the values predicted by Friedman's theory if the income changes were permanent: (1) a stockbroker enjoying the best year of his or her career; (2) a North Dakota wheat farmer suffering from a severe drought; (3) the U.S. economy in a recession; (4) the U.S. economy in a period of unusually high real GDP.

15-5   Forward-Looking Behavior: The Life-Cycle Hypothesis

Franco Modigliani (1918–)
The 1985 Nobel Prize winner is best known for the life-cycle model of consumption behavior and for his articulate advocacy of policy activism.

About the same time that Friedman wrote his book on the permanent-income hypothesis, Franco Modigliani of MIT and collaborators devised a somewhat different way of reconciling the positive relation between the saving ratio and income observed in cross-section data and the constancy of the saving ratio observed over long periods in the historical time-series data.[5] Modigliani and Friedman both began with the perspective that individuals prefer to maintain a stable consumption pattern rather than allow consumption to rise or fall with every transitory oscillation of their income. But Modigliani carried the stable-consumption argument further than Friedman and suggested that people *would try to stabilize their consumption over their entire lifetimes.*

Because of its emphasis on the lifetime horizon of consumers, the Modigliani theory is called the life-cycle hypothesis (LCH). Since it stresses the way consumers smooth consumption over their lifetimes and save in preparation for their retirement years, the LCH falls into the category of theories based on *forward-looking expectations*. It shares with Friedman's theory the ability to reconcile a low short-run MPC with a high and stable long-run MPC. But the LCH adds a "lifetime budget constraint" to Friedman's theory, which is the condition that the consumption of households over their lifetimes equals their income plus their holdings of assets coming from sources other than work (for example, gifts from parents). This feature of the LCH provides a rigorous connection between consumption expenditures and the value of the assets held by consumers. As a result, the LCH *predicts that a stock market crash, like the one in 1987, will reduce consumption expenditures*

[5]Franco Modigliani and R. E. Brumberg, "Utility Analysis and the Consumption Function," in K. K. Kurihara, ed., *Post-Keynesian Economics* (New Brunswick, N.J.: Rutgers University Press, 1954). Also A. Ando and F. Modigliani, "The 'Life Cycle' Hypothesis of Saving: Aggregate Implications and Tests," *American Economic Review,* vol. 53 (March 1963), pp. 55–84.

and a stock market boom, like that of the 1990s, will raise consumption expenditures.

Lifetime Asset Holding: Modigliani's Asset Pyramid Illustrated

We now examine Figure 15-5, which shows how a simple version of Modigliani's theory predicts how income, consumption, saving, and asset accumulation will behave over the lifetime of the typical consumer. The horizontal axis shows various ages, with the age at retirement marked by R and the age at death marked by L. An individual is assumed to maintain a constant level of consumption (C_0) throughout life. Income, however, is earned only during the R working years. If there are no assets initially, as shown by the zero level of initial assets (A_0) in the bottom frame, then the only way individuals can manage to consume without any income during their retirement is to save during their working years. The amount saved, income minus consumption, is shown by the red shading during the period up to time R, and then the dissaving that occurs when consumption exceeds income during retirement is shown by the gray shading from time R through time L. In the bottom frame the accumulation of assets occurs steadily during the working years through time R, when assets reach their maximum level A_R. Assets decline thereafter and are zero at time L.

Figure 15-5
The Behavior of Consumption, Saving, and Assets Under the Life-Cycle Hypothesis

Under the life-cycle hypothesis particular attention is paid to the relation between the length of the lifetime (L) and an individual's age at retirement (R). The length of the retirement period is $L - R$. In the upper frame a constant amount (C_0) is consumed every year of one's life, as indicated by the red line. A constant amount of income Y_0 is earned each year until retirement. During the working years until R, income exceeds consumption, as shown by the saving that occurs in the red area. Then consumption exceeds the zero income during retirement and is financed by dissaving, as shown by the gray area. In the bottom frame the black line shows the growth of assets from the initial level (A_0) to the maximum level at retirement (A_R), followed by a decline in assets back to zero at death.

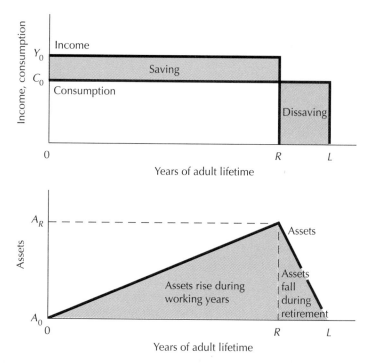

THE YOUNG SAVE DURING THEIR WORKING YEARS, AND THE OLD DISSAVE DURING RETIREMENT

No Initial Assets.   How are consumption and income related when there are no initial assets? Total lifetime consumption of C_0 per year for L years is constrained to equal total income Y_0 per year for R years:

$$C_0 L = Y_0 R \quad \text{or} \quad C_0 = \left(\frac{R}{L}\right) Y_0 \tag{15.7}$$

As Figure 15-5 is drawn, R is four-fifths of L, so consumption per year is limited to four-fifths of Y_0.[6]

The simple version of the life-cycle hypothesis can explain the positive association of saving and income, since the upward trend in per capita, natural real GDP raises both the saving and income of those of working age relative to those who are retired. The long-run constancy of the saving ratio can be explained by the fact that if the population in each historical era is divided into the same proportions of working and retired people, and each age group has the same saving behavior in generation after generation, then the long-run saving ratio will be constant.

The life-cycle hypothesis shares with Friedman's permanent-income hypothesis the implication that the saving ratio should rise in economic boom years and fall in recession years. A temporary increase in income today will be consumed over one's entire lifetime. For instance, imagine a person who believes he has forty years left to live and receives an unexpected increase in income this year of $4000 that he does not expect to receive again. His total lifetime consumption goes up by the $4000 and his actual consumption this year goes up by only 1/40 of that amount, a mere $100. In each succeeding year an additional $100 would be spent, for a total of $4000 over the remaining forty years of life.

Thus, in an economic boom widely expected to be temporary, an unexpected bonus of $4000 would lead to only $100 extra of current consumption and $3900 extra of saving. The short-run propensity to consume would be just 0.025, or 100/4000. By contrast, if the $4000 income increase is expected to be maintained for each of the next forty years, then $4000 extra can be consumed this year and again in each of the next thirty-nine years and the saving ratio will not rise.

The Role of Assets.   The Modigliani theory provides an important role for assets as a determinant of consumption behavior. Let us assume that initially a person has an endowment of assets of A_1, but plans to use these assets to

---

[6]There are several simplifications in Figure 15-5 and equation (15.7) involving the treatment of interest income. Assuming that interest is earned on asset holdings at the nominal interest rate i, then total income is equal to wage income in real terms (W/P) plus real interest income (rA), where r is the real interest rate. Then (15.7) becomes

$$C_0 L = (W/P)_0 R + \sum_{t=0}^{L} rA_t$$

Thus total income increases gradually through time R and then decreases to zero, but is nevertheless positive during the retirement period. To reflect the fact that consumption depends on total income, including both wage income and earnings from the holding of assets, the symbol Y (for total real income) rather than W/P is used in (15.7) in the text. The official definition of income overstates Y, since it includes the entire income from assets, including that portion of the nominal return $(i - r)$ needed to maintain intact the real value of assets.

raise consumption through his or her lifetime rather than to leave the assets to heirs. Then, as shown in Figure 15-6, consumption can be higher for a given level of income (Y_0), and saving can be lower, since the initial asset endowment provides more spending power. Now total lifetime consumption equals total lifetime income from work plus the available assets:

$$C_1 L = A_1 + Y_0 R$$

or

$$C_1 = \frac{A_1}{L} + \frac{R}{L} Y_0 \qquad (15.8)$$

The right-hand expression shows that consumption per year (C_1) depends not just on income (Y_0); it also depends on the ratio of available assets per year of life.

Figure 15-6 is oversimplified because it assumes that the initial endowment of assets is received at the beginning of the working life. In reality, however, increases in the value of assets occur throughout one's life, so one would expect the response of annual consumption to a change in asset value to be larger than is assumed in equation (15.8). Modigliani's empirical research has estimated that a \$1 increase in real asset values raised annual real consumption by about \$.06, which would indicate that people use a fifteen-year horizon over which to spend an increase in real assets.

Figure 15-6
Consumption, Saving, and Assets Under the Life-Cycle Hypothesis When There Is an Initial Stock of Assets

This diagram is identical to Figure 15-5, but here there is an initial stock of assets, A_1, in contrast to the initial stock of zero in the previous diagram. If we continue to assume that dissaving during retirement runs the stock of assets down to zero, then the existence of A_1 makes more total consumption possible with a smaller amount of saving. This is shown by an upward shift from the previous level of consumption (C_0) to a new higher level (C_1). The light red saving area is now smaller, as is the light red area in the bottom frame which shows the increase in assets due to saving.

AN INITIAL ENDOWMENT OF ASSETS RAISES CONSUMPTION AND REDUCES SAVING

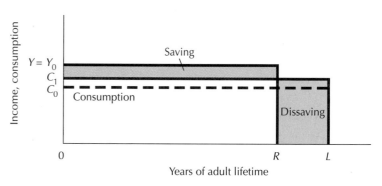

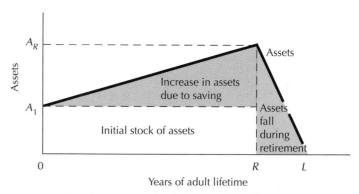

In Chapter 7 we learned that the economy's self-correcting forces are enhanced when real consumption spending depends on real assets or real wealth. If a drop in spending cuts the price level, the level of real wealth is raised, which helps arrest the decline in spending.[7] In the other direction, if an increase in spending raises the price level, the level of real wealth declines, which helps dampen the original stimulus to spending.

Thus, ironically, Modigliani's life-cycle hypothesis supports the optimism of rules advocates regarding the stability of the private economy, even though Modigliani is a prominent critic of policy rules. Private spending is stabilized because transitory increases in disposable income, those that are not expected to last very long, have only a modest influence on current consumption. In addition, the real-asset effect stabilizes the economy because higher prices cut the real value of assets and dampen spending. Overall, life-cycle considerations reduce the current marginal propensity to consume, cut the multiplier, and insulate the economy from unexpected changes in investment, net exports, or other types of spending.

SELF-TEST   Assume that an adult is making a consumption plan and anticipates a life of 40 more years, 30 of which will be spent in work and 10 in retirement. If income during the working years is $50,000, and the endowment of initial assets is zero, what will annual consumption expenditures be during the working years? During the retirement years? What will be the average propensity to consume *(C/Y)* during the working years? Now, assume instead that initial assets are $200,000. What will annual consumption expenditures be during the working years? During the retirement years? What will be the average propensity to consume during the working years?

15-6 Rational Expectations and Other Amendments to the Simple Forward-Looking Theories

In recent years consumption behavior has been one of the most active areas of research in macroeconomics. Much attention has been directed toward the implications of households using more sophisticated methods of forming their expectations about their future incomes than the simple adaptive expectations method shown in equation (15.3). The contrast between the predictions of the resulting theory and the actual cyclical behavior of consumption has highlighted the role of several additional factors that are not part of the pure PIH or LCH theories: liquidity constraints, consumer durables, bequests, and uncertainty.

Rational Expectations

Recall from equation (15.3) that in its original Friedman formulation, the PIH is combined with the adaptive or error-learning method of calculating

---

[7]Review the Pigou, or real balance, effect discussed in Section 7-9.

permanent income. Thus when actual income increases, people only *gradually* revise upward their estimate of permanent income. Though it provides a simple and convenient approximation to how households might form their expectations about their future incomes, the adaptive expectations hypothesis may be too simple. Among its drawbacks are that it mechanically extrapolates the past and that it does not explicitly allow for the effects of variables other than income on expectations of future income.

Rational expectations are forecasts of future economic magnitudes based on information currently available about the structure and past performance of the economy and future government policies.

The **rational expectations** hypothesis suggests that people use a more sophisticated method of forming their expectations about their future incomes. It posits that people use *all* the information that they have available about the economy to predict their future incomes. According to the rational expectations hypothesis, people incorporate a wide range of information about the past performance of the economy, about the structure of the economy (like its *IS, LM,* and *SAS* curves), and about likely future changes in government policies that could affect incomes.

The rational expectations version of the PIH continues to assume that consumption depends only on permanent income (as in equation [15.2]). The difference is in how people estimate their permanent income. Rational expectations assumes that expectations of future events are formed using all the information available. Thus, rational expectations implies that all the information that can be gleaned from the past and even from credible announcements about the future, like tax cuts that have been enacted but that have not yet taken effect, will be used to form estimates of permanent income. As a result, only *new* information will change estimated permanent incomes, which implies that consumption will change only if *unanticipated* events occur. Previously expected events provide no news and therefore no revisions to permanent income and no change in consumption.

Is Consumption Too Volatile or Too Smooth?   A controversy has developed over the empirical implications of the rational expectations version of the PIH. Everything depends on how consumers view the nature of new information about income. If a change in current income provides no information about income in the future, then estimates of permanent income change very little, and the marginal propensity to consume out of this change in current income should be close to zero.[8] However, our case study (Section 15-2) showed that consumption displayed visible responses to the decline of income in the 1974–75, 1981–82, and 1990–91 recessions. This points toward the conclusion that actual consumption responds too strongly to changes in actual income, that is, it is *excessively volatile* relative to the prediction of the theory.[9]

---

[8]In this case it can be shown in a specific mathematical model that the MPC would be $r/(1 + r)$, where r is the real rate of interest. Thus, depending on the asset used to measure r, the MPC would be between zero and 0.07. This result is developed in the excellent but mathematically advanced survey by Andrew B. Abel, "Consumption and Investment," in B. M. Friedman and F. Hahn, eds., *Handbook of Monetary Economics* (Amsterdam: Elsevier Science Publishers, 1990), pp. 725–78.

[9]The rational expectations approach to the study of consumption behavior was introduced in Robert E. Hall, "Stochastic Implications of the Life Cycle-Permanent Income Hypothesis: Theory and Evidence," *Journal of Political Economy,* vol. 86 (December 1978), pp. 971–87. The excess volatility argument is usually credited to Marjorie Flavin, "The Adjustment of Consumption to Changing Expectations About Future Income," *Journal of Political Economy,* vol. 89 (October 1981), pp. 974–1009.

However, another possibility is that changes in current income provide a good prediction of changes in future income. For instance, a person who loses a high-paying job may have very good reason to predict that future income will be lower, perhaps for many years. In the extreme case, if it were true that estimates of permanent income always responded by one dollar to any change in current income of one dollar (i.e., $j = 1$ in equations [15.3] and [15.4]), then the marginal propensity to consume out of current income would be k (simply because the marginal propensity to consume out of permanent income is k). But the data show clearly that consumption is smoother than current income. So by this contrasting approach, actual consumption is *too smooth* relative to the prediction of the theory.[10]

Thus far the debate over the cyclical behavior of consumption has not been settled. However, the initial conclusion that consumption was too volatile led to the realization that the simple versions of the PIH and LCH reviewed above, as well as the rational expectations updating of these theories, omit several important aspects of consumption behavior. Until these issues are adequately integrated into the theory, it is unlikely that the question of whether consumption is too volatile or too smooth will be resolved.

Consumer Durables

Both the permanent-income hypothesis and the life-cycle hypothesis are based on the desirability of maintaining a roughly constant level of enjoyment over time from consumption goods and services. If there is an increase in permanent income, people will not only want to increase their expenditures on services and nondurable goods, but will also want to increase their enjoyment of the services of durable goods. For consumer services and nondurable goods, such as haircuts and doughnuts, the enjoyment and the consumer spending occur at about the same time. Consumer durable goods are different. A television set is purchased at a single instant in time but produces enjoyment for many years thereafter. Thus the PIH and LCH suggest that it is not purchases of consumer durable goods that are kept equal to a fixed fraction of permanent income, but rather the flow of services (enjoyment) received from consumer durables. Consumers can keep the service flow at the same fixed fraction of permanent income by keeping the *stock* of consumer durable goods at the same fixed fraction of permanent income.

The essence of a durable good is that it provides service for many periods. New cars, for example, have service lives of ten years or more. Like any long-term asset, a durable good costs far more to purchase than the service it provides each period. A new car that sells for $25,000, for example, may provide only $2,000 worth of service each year. Thus, when a household decides that its higher permanent income warrants its annually consuming another $2,000 of car services, expenditure initially rises by $25,000. As a result expenditures for durables may surge temporarily as consumers raise their stocks of durables in proportion to the increase in their permanent incomes.

---

[10]See Angus Deaton, "Life-Cycle Models of Consumption: Is the Evidence Consistent with the Theory?" in T. F. Bewley, ed., *Advances in Econometrics Fifth World Congress* (New York: Cambridge University Press, 1987), pp. 121–48.

INTERNATIONAL PERSPECTIVE

Why Do Some Countries Save So Much?

We saw in Figure 15-3 that the *personal* saving rate in the United States has changed little over the past century. The worldwide average of *national* saving rates (as a share of GDP) has also been relatively stable over time, having stayed between 20 and 25 percent at least since 1970, with a slight tendency to drift lower over that time.[a]

While the world saving rate has remained relatively stable over the past few decades, saving rates differ by large amounts across countries and have fluctuated greatly within many countries. In general, saving rates in industrialized countries have been both lower and more stable than they have been in developing countries. National saving rates for industrialized countries have averaged about 20 percent since 1970, but they have averaged more than 25 percent in developing countries. In individual industrial countries the national saving rate has typically fluctuated within a 10 percentage point range, but the range within developing countries such as China, Egypt, Honduras, and Indonesia has been more than 15 percentage points.

In this chapter we have learned that consumption, and thus saving, responds to a number of factors: the stage of the life cycle, interest rates, and expectations about future income. In Chapter 11, we saw why increased private saving might offset reduced public saving through the Barro-Ricardo effect. If the offset were complete, the national saving rate would be unaffected by changes in government budget deficits. In practice how important are these various factors in explaining the differences in private saving rates across countries and across time?

The life-cycle model suggests that saving rates are lower for the young, who have recently embarked on their working lives and for the retired, who have left the labor force. Despite having current incomes that are low relative to lifetime incomes, both groups consume according to their lifetime incomes. Thus their savings rates are very low, and often negative. Workers, especially those near their peak earnings years, have considerably higher saving rates. That means that countries with higher dependency ratios, that is, with larger frac-

tions of the population not working, would save less. Empirical research at the International Monetary Fund indicates that the higher the dependency rate in a country, the lower its saving rate, both in industrial and in developing countries.[b]

Dependency ratios can vary dramatically across countries. A country may have a relatively high dependency ratio either because it has more retired people or because it has relatively more young people who have not yet reached working age. In Iran, for example, about 40 percent of the entire population is less than 15 years old. By contrast, only 22 percent of the population of the United States is less than 15 years old.

Over the next few decades, dependency ratios are expected to rise in developed countries (especially Japan), where the number of retired people will increase markedly as life expectancy continues to rise and the huge baby-boom generation retires. By contrast, dependency ratios are expected to fall in developing countries, which now have populations with low average ages. Over the next few decades, large numbers of young people in developing countries will move from being students to being workers, but relatively few people in those countries will attain retirement age.

As a consequence of these demographic shifts, the life-cycle model of consumption and saving predicts that saving rates will continue to fall in developed countries and continue to rise in developing countries—as they have generally since 1970. How big is this demographic effect? The shift in the average ages of their populations could raise the saving rate in developing countries by about 4 percentage points and lower it by about 1 percentage point of GDP in industrialized countries. On balance, this population shift could raise the world saving rate slightly.

Higher interest rates may either raise saving by raising income or lower it by making less saving necessary to achieve a targeted level of accumulated savings. The vast literature on this topic has not yet clearly signaled which effect is stronger. Typical of the mixed evidence is the IMF study, which reported that higher real interest rates raised private saving rates in industrialized countries, but did not raise them in developing countries.

Forward-looking consumers will raise their current spending, and thus reduce their saving out of current income, in response to an increase in their expected future incomes. One reason why consumers might not raise their spending as much as their permanent or life-cycle incomes justify is that they may not be able to borrow on the basis of expected future income. (Think about the expected future income of an undergraduate business major. Now think about how much that student can borrow while still a junior. The inability to borrow and spend in accordance with one's expected future income is an example of a borrowing, or liquidity, constraint.)

One measure of the availability of consumer credit is the maximum loan-to-value ratio: Higher ratios indicate that consumers can borrow a larger fraction of the funds needed for a purchase and need to save less ahead of time to purchase goods and services. The accompanying figure plots the maximum loan-to-value ratio and a measure of the saving rate for a number of European countries.[c] As expected, the figure shows that, when borrowing is more constrained, saving is higher because consumers have to save before they consume.

Do increased government deficits lead to increased private saving? If the Barro-Ricardo equivalence theorem holds, then an increase in the government deficit would generate an equal increase in private saving, which would offset the expected future tax burden associated with the increased deficit. The IMF study found that in both industrial and developing countries, the private saving rate typically rises only about half as much as the government deficit. Thus, the theorem does not hold in the real world. Higher deficits reduce national saving rates. The world budget deficit in the early 1990s was about 3 percent of GDP. Based on the IMF study estimates, if the world government deficit were reduced to zero, the world saving rate would rise by about 1.5 percent, which is about half of its decline since the early 1970s.

---

[a]For this and more information on saving around the world, see Paul R. Masson, Tamim Bayoumi, and Hossein Samiei, "Saving Behavior in Industrial and Developing Countries," *Staff Studies for the World Economic Outlook,* International Monetary Fund, September 1995, pp. 1–27.

[b]Ibid.

[c]See Tullio Jappelli and Marco Pagano, "Saving, Growth, and Liquidity Constraints," *Quarterly Journal of Economics,* February 1994, pp. 83–110 for more information and the data used in the figure. In the figure, the saving rate used is the 1971–80 average for national saving as a percent of net national product; the maximum loan-to-value ratio is the 1971–80 average of the maximum loan-to-value ratio.

Source: Tulio Jappelli and Marco Pagano, "Saving, Growth and Liquidity Constraints," *The Quarterly Journal of Economics,* 109:1 (February, 1994), pp. 83–109. ©1994 by the President and Fellows of Harvard College and the Massachusetts Institute of Technology. Used by permission.

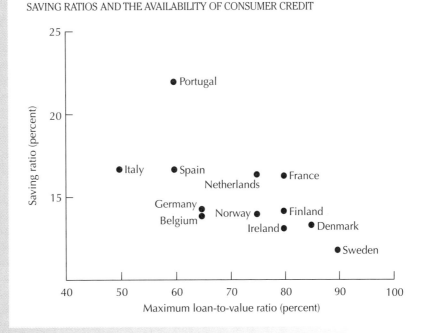

SAVING RATIOS AND THE AVAILABILITY OF CONSUMER CREDIT

As a result of the upsurge in purchases of consumer durables, total consumption expenditures may *rise* as a fraction of income when actual income rises, even though the PIH and LCH predict that consumption should *fall* as a fraction of income when actual income rises. Both the PIH and LCH predict that the saving ratio *falls* with higher income when consumer durables are counted as consumption expenditure but *rises* with higher income when consumer durables are counted as saving. Realization of the procyclical nature of consumer durable expenditures limits research on the validity of the PIH and LCH to consumer expenditures *excluding* durables—that is, including just services (haircuts) and nondurables (doughnuts).

Behavior of Consumer Durable Expenditures in Recessions.   Both the PIH and LCH predict that in a recession, when income exhibits a transitory decline, households should maintain their consumption expenditures *by cutting back on the ratio of saving to personal income (S/Y_P)*. Yet the saving ratio declines by only a small amount unless an adjustment is made for the procyclical nature of expenditures on consumer durables. In the following table the ratio of consumer durables expenditure to personal income declines more than the saving ratio in recessions, and the ratio of the sum of saving and consumer durables expenditure to personal income $[(S + C^D)/Y_P]$ declines more than either component separately:

Averages for Eight Recessions 1953–54 to 1990–91

Ratio to personal income	Peak	Trough	Peak to trough change
Personal saving	7.0	6.7	−0.3
Consumer durable expenditures	10.3	9.6	−0.7
Sum of personal saving and consumer durable expenditures	17.3	16.4	−1.0

Liquidity Constraints

The simple version of the LCH in Figure 15-5 assumes that consumption is constant over the lifetime and that labor income is constant until the date of retirement. Actually, however, labor income tends to rise with age, peaking a bit after age fifty. To achieve a constant level of consumption throughout their lifetimes, young people would need to borrow during their low-income years and repay the loans later in high-income years. But banks generally will not allow young people to borrow all they would like, which implies that the consumption expenditures of young people is subject to a **liquidity constraint.** A liquidity constraint may afflict people of any age who are suffering from a transitory loss of income; for instance banks may be unwilling to lend to a farmer who is close to bankruptcy after a year of poor growing weather, even though the weather can be expected to be better in the future.

A **liquidity constraint** prevents households from borrowing as much as they wish, even though there is sufficient expected future income to repay the loans.

People whose consumption can go no higher than their *current income* because of the unavailability of loans will have a much higher marginal propensity to consume in response to temporary changes in income than is predicted by the PIH or LCH theories. Economists have attempted to measure the importance of this so-called excess sensitivity of consumption to current changes in income. The consensus is that households whose consumption is subject to liquidity constraints account for about 15 percent of aggregate income. These households have MPCs out of transitory income of about 1. The remaining, unconstrained households behave roughly as predicted by the LCH: They have negligible MPCs out of transitory income.[11] Thus liquidity constraints do not seem to be prevalent enough to seriously weaken the implication of the LCH (and PIH) that the short-run MPC will be much lower than the long-run MPC.

Interest Rate Effects

Considerable controversy has arisen regarding the effect of interest rates on consumption, and thus on saving, behavior. A large response of saving to the after-tax real interest rate would give policymakers two instruments with which to influence the household saving rate—income tax rates and monetary policy. The high real interest rates of the 1980s provided a good test of the influence of interest rates, because the household saving rate should have risen, *both* because of higher real interest rates *and* because income tax rate cuts boosted the fraction of their interest income that savers could retain after paying income taxes.

However, the household saving rate in the 1980s did not rise in response to higher after-tax real interest rates. Research that focused on the 1980s' experience found no positive effect of interest rates on saving, but did find a substantial positive response of saving to inflation.[12] When inflation is high, people cut back on consumption and raise their saving rate, perhaps because they expect the Federal Reserve to react to higher inflation with a tight monetary policy that creates a recession and threatens them with a higher risk of job loss. In terms of our analysis of supply shocks in Chapter 8, this finding implies that an adverse oil price shock would not only boost the inflation rate but would also reduce aggregate demand as households cut their consumption in response to the higher inflation rate.

15-7 Bequests and Uncertainty

In both of our diagrams of the LCH (Figure 15-5 and 15-6), individuals are assumed *to consume all of their lifetime savings during retirement.* Their assets dwindle to zero on the date of death, and nothing is left in the form of bequests to heirs. In fact, however, people do leave bequests. It has been claimed that about 80 percent of asset accumulation by U.S. households is

---

[11]Estimates that the share of aggregate income accruing to liquidity-constrained households has been as high as 50 percent can be found in John Y. Campbell and N. Gregory Mankiw, "Consumption, Income, and Interest Rates: Reinterpreting the Time Series Evidence," *NBER Macroeconomics Annual 1989* (Cambridge, Mass.: The MIT Press), pp. 185–216.

[12]Barry Bosworth, "The Changing Impact of Monetary Policy," *Brookings Papers on Economic Activity,* vol. 20 (1989), pp. 77–110. The positive response of saving to inflation may also reflect tightened liquidity constraints on consumption associated with higher nominal interest rates. See James A. Wilcox, "Liquidity Constraints on Consumption: The Real Effects of 'Real' Lending Policies," Federal Reserve Bank of San Francisco *Economic Review,* Fall 1989, pp. 39–52.

transmitted to heirs rather than used for consumption during retirement.[13] This evidence seems to deny that the appropriate horizon to describe consumer behavior is the lifetime.

The Role of Bequests

As we learned in Section 11-7, the existence of bequests has been interpreted as support for a striking theory of fiscal policy, often called the Barro-Ricardo equivalence theorem. People are expected to leave bequests because they care about their children. Any event that leaves their children worse off will lead members of the present generation to increase saving in order to leave a larger bequest to their children. A prime example of such an event would be a deficit-financed tax cut that raises the taxes that must be paid by future generations (to pay the interest on the bonds issued to finance the debt). According to the Barro-Ricardo theorem, such a tax cut would not stimulate consumption because people would save all of the increase in their after-tax income in order to raise their bequests.

In Chapter 11, we reviewed some of the criticisms of the Barro-Ricardo theorem and noted that the U.S. household saving rate did not increase at all following the Reagan tax cuts of the 1980s, as the theorem would have predicted. In fact, as we have seen in Figure 15-3, the saving rate in the 1980s fell to its lowest level since the Great Depression. Thus it seems likely that the mere existence of bequests does not validate the kind of behavior postulated by the theorem—specifically the refusal of current households to raise their consumption in response to a tax cut.

Motives for Bequests

If parents do not adjust their bequests for every current event that changes their heirs' future tax liabilities, why does a large fraction of personal saving eventually flow to children in the form of bequests? Many think that the central issue is the uncertainty of the age of death. Benjamin Franklin's observation that "in this world nothing can be said to be certain, except death and taxes" omits the fact that the *timing* of death is quite uncertain. Contrary to the assumption of Figures 15-5 and 15-6, households cannot know the lengths of their lifetimes. They may believe there is a good chance that at least one spouse will live to an advanced age and may require expensive nursing home and other medical treatment that insurance does not completely cover. They may want to avoid relying on their children for support, and often they want to continue to live in their own homes.

---

[13]Laurence J. Kotlikoff and Lawrence H. Summers, "The Role of Intergenerational Transfers in Aggregate Capital Accumulation," *Journal of Political Economy,* vol. 89 (August 1981), pp. 706–32. This finding is very controversial. A lengthy scholarly debate on the Kotlikoff-Summers findings is contained in Franco Modigliani, "The Role of Intergenerational Transfers and Life Cycle Saving in the Accumulation of Wealth," and Laurence J. Kotlikoff, "Intergenerational Transfers and Savings," both in *Journal of Economic Perspectives,* vol. 2 (Spring 1988), pp. 15–40 and 41–58, respectively.

By this interpretation, *much saving is life cycle in nature, but only for a part of the lifetime and for medical care that does not occur for everyone.* Many people die before expensive nursing care treatment becomes necessary and thus have substantial wealth "left over" that goes as bequests to the children. Many of these bequests are houses and small businesses that parents do not want to sell before death. By this interpretation, bequests are primarily involuntary and are made because parents do not want to lose control of their assets and their living conditions prior to death, rather than because they calculate the effect of each dollar of bequest on their children's welfare.

Implications for the LCH Theory. The interpretation of bequests as primarily involuntary leaves the main predictions of the LCH intact. The only adjustment to the LCH is that the relevant horizon for most households extends beyond the actual age of death (as assumed in Figures 15-5 and 15-6) to the *oldest conceivable age of death.* For instance a 25-year-old may have a future life expectancy of 50 years, with 75 the most probable age of death, but may base consumption and saving decisions on the outside chance of living until age 90.

This amended version of the LCH would operate just like the version depicted in Figure 15-6, except the extended lifetime (L^*, say 90) replaces the most probable lifetime (L, say 75). Use of L^* instead of the lower L would imply an even lower MPC for temporary changes in income, and would imply that increases in wealth from the stock market would be consumed over the extended period until L^*. If parents are unwilling to move out of their homes (and are also unwilling to sell their homes to their children and pay them rent), then the gains parents make from higher housing prices may not be consumed over the lifetime but may be largely ignored and lead to a larger bequest.

SELF-TEST

Imagine a $1000 increase in the yearly personal income tax paid by every household in order to reduce the federal budget deficit. The tax increase is announced to be permanent. What would the following theories predict to be the effects on consumption? (1) Permanent-income hypothesis; (2) life-cycle hypothesis with certain lifetime; (3) life-cycle hypothesis that explains bequests as resulting from uncertain lifetimes; (4) Barro-Ricardo equivalence theory.

15-8   CASE STUDY: Do Tax Breaks Raise the Saving Rate?

Since the early 1980s, the saving rate in the United States has been considerably lower than it was in preceding decades. National saving as a share of GDP was lower in *every* year from 1990 through 1995 than in *any* year from 1959 through 1989. Higher federal government deficits beginning in the early 1980s were partly responsible for the decline in the national saving rate. To reduce this drag on national saving, both the Democratic Clinton administration and the Republican-led Congress proposed reducing the federal budget deficit to zero by fiscal year 2002.

The household, or personal, saving rate has also declined since 1980, as shown in Figure 15-7. While personal saving as a share of personal disposable

PERSONAL SAVING AS A SHARE OF DISPOSABLE PERSONAL INCOME 1959–96

Figure 15-7   **Personal Saving as a Share of Disposable Personal Income, 1959–96**

income averaged 8 percent during the 1970s, the average fell to 7 percent during the 1980s, and to only 5 percent during the first half of the 1990s.

To encourage households to save more, tax advantages were enacted for some kinds of saving. It was hoped that raising the after-tax return to saving by lowering the effective income tax rate on saving would increase personal saving. When households reduce their income taxes by making deposits in tax-advantaged accounts the government budget deficit rises, which reduces public saving. National saving would then increase if the increase in personal saving was greater than the decline in public saving.

Households can accumulate financial assets via two tax-advantaged programs: individual retirement accounts (IRAs) and 401(k) plans.[14] Annual contributions to IRAs generally are limited to $2,000 per employee. Earnings on balances in IRAs are exempt from income taxes until they are withdrawn, but withdrawals before age $59\frac{1}{2}$ are penalized. Though lower-income employees can deduct their annual IRA contributions from their taxable income, higher-income employees cannot. In spite of the relatively greater tax incentive given to lower-income employees to contribute to IRAs, most IRA contributors are higher-income employees. In practice, older households are also much more likely to contribute to IRAs than younger households.

---

[14]See Jonathan McCarthy and Han N. Pham, "The Impact of Individual Retirement Accounts on Savings," *Current Issues in Economics and Finance,* Federal Reserve Bank of New York, vol. 1, no. 6 (1995), and the Symposium on "Government Incentives for Saving" in *Journal of Economic Perspectives,* vol. 10, no. 4 (1996).

The 401(k) plans are available only to employees of firms that sponsor such plans. Employee contributions to 401(k) plans, as well as the earnings on past contributions, are exempt from income taxes until withdrawal. As with IRAs, early withdrawal penalties apply. Typically, contributions are made via payroll deductions. As a fringe benefit to their employees, some employers match their employees' contributions. Ceilings on annual employee contributions are generally in the $9,000–$10,000 range. Like IRAs, 401(k) plan balances can be invested in a wide range of financial assets, including stocks, bonds, and savings and time deposits.

Though they first became available in the 1970s, only small amounts were put into these accounts until eligibility and tax rules were clarified and eased. By 1984, however, about $50 billion of new contributions were flowing annually into these two types of tax-advantaged savings accounts. Saving in these accounts equals the flow of contributions each year, plus the interest and dividends earned on past contributions minus withdrawals. In keeping with standard measures of saving, capital gains and losses are not taken into account.[15] From the mid-1980s through the mid-1990s, saving in IRAs and 401(k) plans totaled between 1 and 2 percent of GDP. Thus, the tax incentives to put and retain funds in these accounts might have raised the household saving rate by up to 1 to 2 percent of GDP.

However, the saving rate has not risen, but instead has fallen since households began contributing to IRAs and 401(k) plans. Did tax-advantaged saving programs prevent the saving rate from falling even further? Or, were these programs actually a cause of the lower saving rate?

Using tax breaks to stimulate savings remains controversial because, so far, neither theory nor empirical studies clearly indicate whether tax-advantaged savings programs raise or lower national, or even personal, saving. Theory suggests that households face offsetting substitution and income effects when the after-tax returns on their saving rise. Higher returns encourage households to substitute more saving for consumption. On the other hand, earning higher returns provides households with more income from their past saving and thereby enables them to accumulate the same amount of wealth by doing less saving and more consumption. Theory does not tell us which effect is stronger.

In addition, there may be a "shuffling effect." When tax breaks are given for making contributions to designated accounts, taxpayers with funds in other accounts may merely shuffle funds from existing accounts into tax-advantaged accounts. In that case, households reduce their tax bill but the personal saving rate is unaffected. National saving, however, falls because reduced tax payments raise the government deficit. Once households have moved all of their existing balances into the tax-advantaged accounts, however, shuffling stops and only current saving generates tax breaks.

Unfortunately, empirical evidence has not decisively shown how much the personal saving rate is affected by tax-advantaged saving programs. Some

---

[15]Savers, of course, may well take capital gains and losses into account in judging how much wealth they have, and thus how much to spend and to save. To the extent that households feel wealthier when, for example, the value of their stock or their home goes up, they may spend more. Since conventional measures of income and saving do not include capital gains or losses, any resulting increase in household spending produces a lower measured saving rate. See Joe Peek, "Capital Gains and Personal Saving Behavior," *Journal of Money, Credit and Banking*, vol. 15, no. 1 (1983), pp. 1–23.

studies indicate that households increase their saving by about twice as much as the tax breaks they receive, which implies that the national saving rate rises by about half as much as their IRA contributions.[16] Other studies suggest the net effect on national saving of the IRA program is close to zero. McCarthy and Pham note that since IRA contributions have been only about 1 percent of GDP, the overall effect on the personal and national saving rates is likely to have been small. Studies that have simulated the long-run effects of saving programs like IRAs and 401(k) plans suggest that they raise the net national saving rate by about 1 percentage point.

15-9 Consumption and the Case For and Against Activism

If all consumption spending consisted of nondurable goods and services, the permanent-income hypothesis and life-cycle hypothesis both would strengthen the case of those who advocate policy rules and are optimistic that the private economy is basically stable if left alone by the government. Consumption would respond only partially to temporary bursts of nonconsumption spending, so that the economy's true short-run multipliers would be smaller than those calculated in Chapters 3 and 4.

On the other hand, the case for policy activism is strengthened by the procyclical fluctuations in consumer durable purchases, because this source of instability in the private economy may need to be offset by countercyclical government policy. The importance of erratic fluctuations in consumer spending is summarized by movements in the ratio of personal saving plus consumer durable expenditures to personal income. This ratio has fluctuated over a wide range during the postwar years. Part of these swings may reflect movements in consumer confidence, which are an important source of shifts in the *IS* curve. If a sustained improvement in consumer confidence cuts saving and boosts consumption, then an activist tightening of monetary and/or fiscal policy may be warranted, and a sustained decline in consumer confidence may warrant an easing of policy in order to stabilize real GDP.

SUMMARY

1. A major area of dispute between policy activists and advocates of policy rules concerns the stability of private spending decisions. Friedman's permanent-income hypothesis (PIH) and Modigliani's life-cycle hypothesis (LCH) are based on the assumption that individuals achieve a higher level of total utility (enjoyment) when they maintain a stable consumption pattern than when they allow consumption to rise or fall with every transitory fluctuation in their actual income. Individuals can achieve the desired stable consumption pattern by

consuming a stable fraction of their permanent or life-time income.

2. If all consumption consisted of nondurable goods and services, both the PIH and the LCH would strengthen the case of those who advocate policy rules, who claim that the private economy is basically stable if left alone by the government. Consumption would respond only partially to temporary fluctuations of nonconsumption spending, so that the economy's short-run multipliers would be smaller than the simple theoretical

---

[16]See McCarthy and Pham (1995), op. cit.

multipliers of Chapters 3 and 4. Consumers would dampen the decline of the economy in a recession by reducing their saving rate, and they would similarly moderate the subsequent economic expansion by raising their saving rate.

3. Both the PIH and the LCH can reconcile the observed cross-section increase in the saving ratio for higher incomes with the observed long-run historical constancy of the aggregate saving ratio.

4. Both hypotheses have important implications for fiscal policy. For example, a tax change announced as permanent should cause a bigger change in permanent income, and hence in consumption expenditures, than another equal-sized tax change announced as temporary. Thus temporary tax changes introduced to implement an activist fiscal policy may be rendered ineffective by offsetting movements in the saving ratio.

5. Numerous criticisms of the PIH and LCH have emerged in recent years. A large share of saving seems to be used not for consumption during retirement, but for bequests to children. Households may save more than they need, because they are uncertain about the date of death. Liquidity constraints imply that perhaps

15 percent of income is earned by households for whom the short-run marginal propensity to consume is much higher than implied by the PIH or LCH.

6. An additional consideration in explaining observed consumption and saving behavior is that consumer durable expenditures should be treated as a form of saving, not as current consumption. Sharp increases in income tend to go mainly into saving, which means that consumer durable expenditures treated as a form of saving may be very responsive to transitory income changes. Thus the PIH and LCH may be valid, but consumer durable purchases are still a source of instability in the private economy.

7. In spite of their intuitive appeal as a way to raise the saving rate, income tax breaks seem to have had only minor effects on household saving. Theory cautions that the disposable-income effects of tax breaks may offset the incentive of households to substitute saving for current consumption. Another reason why tax breaks may have limited effects on saving is that households may merely shuffle past saving into tax-advantaged accounts instead of increasing saving.

CONCEPTS

forward-looking expectations
permanent-income hypothesis (PIH)
life-cycle hypothesis (LCH)
cross section
time series

permanent income
transitory income
rational expectations
liquidity constraint

QUESTIONS AND PROBLEMS

Questions

1. The saving ratio has been remarkably stable since 1900. When we examine cross-section data, however, we find that the saving ratio tends to rise as incomes rise. How can these two observations be reconciled?
2. Why is a distinction made between a short-run marginal propensity to consume and a long-run marginal propensity to consume in the permanent-income hypothesis (PIH)?
3. Is permanent income permanent? If not, what causes it to change?
4. How does the existence of assets affect consumption and income in the life-cycle hypothesis (LCH)?
5. In what ways does the LCH support those advocating rules rather than activism?
6. Does the fact that many individuals leave bequests (i.e., do not consume their entire income over their lifetimes) invalidate the LCH?

7. Both the LCH and the PIH predict that the marginal propensity to consume out of transitory income is quite small (perhaps, even zero). Nevertheless, we observe many younger families spending a fairly large percentage of their transitory incomes. Is this observation consistent with the two hypotheses?
8. The PIH and LCH suggest that consumer durable expenditures should be considered separately from expenditures on nondurables and services. Why? How does this distinction alter the appearance of saving and consumption behavior? Why do some economists argue that consumer durables expenditures should be treated as saving rather than consumption?
9. Both the PIH and the LCH predict that consumers react differently to tax changes that are perceived to be permanent rather than temporary. Explain why

this is so. Has the empirical record of the past twenty years supported this prediction?

10. In the 1990s, stock prices rose dramatically. According to the LCH, what effect, if any, should this event have had on the saving ratio? Did the saving ratio behave as hypothesized? Explain your answer.

11. Suppose that evidence indicates that saving rises (and hence consumption falls) as the real interest rate increases. How would this behavior affect the slope of the *IS* curve and the relative effectiveness of monetary and fiscal policy?

12. Suppose that to eliminate the federal government budget deficit by 2002, the president and Congress remove the tax breaks to saving that exist under current tax laws. How would you expect this to affect the U.S. saving rate? Explain.

Problems

1. Assume that consumption and permanent income are derived as shown in equations (15.2) and (15.3). In those equations, let $k = 0.8$ and $j = 0.5$. Assume that 1997 actual income of $30,000 equals permanent income.
   (a) What would be the permanent income for 1998, 1999, and 2000 if actual income for those three years were $36,000, $45,000, and $30,000, respectively?
   (b) What would be consumption spending in those three years?
   (c) What would be the short-run marginal propensity to consume in each of those three years?
   (d) Using the distinction between permanent income and transitory income, explain why the short-run marginal propensity to consume would differ from the long-run marginal propensity to consume in 1998.

2. Assume that Gina's consumption decisions are consistent with the LCH. In 1997, Gina is 25 years old, expects to earn income until she is 65, and expects to consume until she dies at age 85.
   (a) If Gina earns $30,000 per year and wishes to consume an equal amount each year, how much will she consume each year?
   (b) What is the ratio of consumption to income for Gina? What is the saving ratio?
   (c) Assume that Gina had assets equal to $120,000 in 1997. Recalculate your answers for (a) and (b).
   (d) Assume that in 2017, Gina inherits $40,000. Now what are your answers to (c)?

SELF-TEST ANSWERS

p. 485 (1) A stockbroker enjoying his or her best year has actual income above permanent income and consumes less and saves more than he or she would if that income were permanent. (2) A wheat farmer suffering from a drought will have actual income below permanent income and will consume more and save less than he or she would if that income were permanent. (3) When the U.S. economy is in recession an unusually large number of people will experience below-permanent income and will consume more and save less than they would if they considered their recession-level income permanent. (4) When the U.S. economy is in a period of unusually high real GDP a large number of people will experience above-permanent income and will consume less and save more than they would if they considered their exceptionally high income permanent.

p. 489 Use the right-hand part of equation (15.7). If $A_1 = 0$, and $R/L = 30/40$, then consumption expenditures per year will be 30/40 times $50,000, or $37,500 during both the working and retirement years. C/Y

during working years will be $37,500/50,000, or 0.75, which of course equals R/L. With initial assets of 200,000, $A_1/L = 200,000/40 = 5,000$. Consumption expenditures by equation (15.8) will then be $5000 plus $37,500 = $42,500 during both the working and retirement years, and C/Y during working years will be $42,500/50,000 = 0.85$.

p. 497 (1) Since the tax increase is assumed to be permanent, it will reduce permanent income by $1000. Consumption will fall by k times $1000 per year. (2) According to the life-cycle hypothesis as set forth in equation (15.7), Y per year will fall by $1000, and consumption per year will fall by R/L^* times $1000. (3) According to the life-cycle hypothesis, with an uncertain lifetime L, consumption per year will fall by R/L^* times $1000. (4) According to the Barro-Ricardo equivalence theorem, consumption will not change at all, since saving will decline by the full amount of the tax increase (reflecting the lower anticipated tax liabilities).

Instability in the Private Economy: Investment

Whatever cannot go on forever must come to an end.
—Herbert Stein

If consumers purchased only nondurable goods and services, the permanent-income and life-cycle hypotheses predict that consumer behavior would stabilize the economy. An offsetting factor is the procyclical movement of consumer durable purchases. Although consistent with the PIH and LCH, such movement tends to aggravate booms and recessions. In this chapter we find that business fixed investment also fluctuates procyclically. Thus, both durable purchases by consumers and investment purchases by businesses introduce instability into the private economy, leading policy activists to claim that an activist stabilization policy is justified.

16-1 Investment and Economic Stability

In Chapter 15 we found that the permanent-income and life-cycle hypotheses of individual consumption behavior explain the partial insulation of aggregate consumption spending from changes in other types of spending in the short run. But what are the sources of changes in these other types of spending? Nominal GDP in 1996 was divided among the major types of expenditures as follows:

Personal consumption expenditures	68.0%
Gross private domestic investment	14.7
Government purchases of goods and services	18.6
Net exports	−1.3
	100.0

Having already considered government spending and other aspects of fiscal policy in Chapter 11, and net exports in Chapter 6, we concentrate here on private investment.

We will review a very simple theory that explains why investment spending is likely to exhibit more pronounced fluctuations than other types of spending. According to the permanent-income hypothesis, households try to maintain a constant ratio of their consumer durable stock to permanent income. This creates sudden bursts of durable purchases when an upward revision of permanent income causes the desired durable stock to increase. In this chapter we will see that investment spending on plant, equipment, inventories, and housing is driven by the same principle and therefore is also subject to sudden bursts of purchases.[1]

16-2   CASE STUDY: The Historical Instability of Investment

Total Investment Rises and Falls Dramatically and Procyclically

We begin by examining the historical record of investment spending since 1960. Figure 16-1 clearly shows that investment spending is far more variable than consumption spending (compare with Figure 15-1). The top line in the figure shows total real gross private domestic investment (GPDI). By any standard, the fluctuations in total investment are huge.

The following table shows how real GPDI has fluctuated since 1960.

	Quarters		*Percentage Change*	
Peak	*Trough*	*Peak*	*Peak to Trough*	*Trough to Peak*
1960:Q1	1961:Q1	1969:Q4	−23	+ 84
1969:Q4	1970:Q4	1973:Q4	−7	+ 47
1973:Q4	1975:Q1	1980:Q1	−29	+ 61
1980:Q1	1980:Q3	1981:Q3	−17	+ 25
1981:Q3	1982:Q4	1990:Q3	−22	+ 49
1990:Q3	1991:Q2	N/A	−13	N/A

Shown in the left part of the table are the dates of each successive business cycle peak and trough. We can see, for instance, that in the 1973–75 recession, GPDI fell 29 percent. Then GPDI more than recovered, growing 61 percent by the next peak in 1980:Q1. In the 1981–82 recession, GPDI also fell sharply, but by less than in 1973–75. After the 1991 trough, GPDI rose dramatically. Over the five-year period that ended in 1996:Q4, total real GPDI rose 44 percent.

Behavior of the Components of GPDI

GPDI is divided into two main parts, fixed investment and inventory changes. Fixed investment is further divided into residential and nonresidential, and in

---

[1]Examples of plant and equipment investment include:

Nonresidential plant (structures)	*Equipment*
Factories	Computers
Oil refineries	Jet airplanes
Office buildings	Trucks
Shopping centers	Cash registers
Private hospitals	Telecommunications hardware
Private universities	Tractors

The principles developed in this chapter apply also to residential investment, construction of both single-family homes and apartment buildings.

ALL TYPES OF INVESTEMENTS ARE VOLATILE OVER THE BUSINESS CYCLE

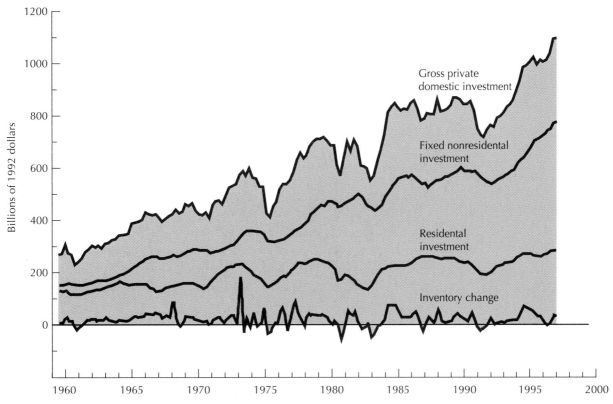

Figure 16-1 **Real Gross Private Domestic Investment and Its Three Components, 1959–96**

The top line plots real gross private domestic investment and shows substantial declines in recessions. All three components contribute to this volatility, but their timing is different. There is a marked tendency for residential investment to turn down earlier than nonresidential investment, and to recover earlier. Fluctuations in inventory investment are shorter-lived than fluctuations in either of the other two components.

turn nonresidential is divided into nonresidential structures and producers' durable equipment. For simplicity, Figure 16-1 distinguishes only fixed residential, fixed nonresidential, and inventory investment. Clearly all three of the major components contribute to the high volatility of GPDI. Each component has risen or fallen by more than $50 billion over a span of a year or less.

Examining the three components more carefully, we note several differences among them:

1. **Residential investment turns early.** Comparing the plotted lines for residential and nonresidential investment, we note that in almost every business cycle the downturn begins earlier for residential investment, as does the subsequent upturn. For instance, residential investment peaked about a year before fixed nonresidential investment in the 1973–75, 1981–82, and 1990–91 recessions. The slide of residential investment was startling in magnitude, −40 percent between 1973:Q1 and 1975:Q1 and −46 percent from 1978:Q4 to 1982:Q3. This component of investment fell sharply when monetary policy tightened in these two periods.

2. **Inventory change exhibits sharp but short-lived swings.** Inventory change appears as a series of small jagged mountain peaks, with an occasional deep valley. In the mid-1970s and again in the early 1980s, the level of inventories changed by over $100 billion over short periods. These sharp turns of inventory change help explain why forecasters did so poorly in 1982 (see Figure 14-3). But they also suggest that, since changes in inventory investment are usually unpredictable and short-lived, it will be difficult for the Federal Reserve Board to offset their effects. Given the lags in the operation of monetary policy, it is likely that the inventory swings will reverse before a change in monetary policy can take effect.

3. Fixed nonresidential investment was slightly larger than residential investment at the beginning of the 1959–96 period; by the end of the period it was nearly 3 times as large as investment in housing. Business purchases of equipment in particular soared during the 1990s. Investment in equipment during the 1990s was more than twice as large as business investment in structures.

   Because nonresidential investment constituted about 70 percent of GPDI over the last two decades, this chapter concentrates primarily on this component.

16-3 The Accelerator Hypothesis of Net Investment

Businesses must continually evaluate whether their buildings are the right size and have the right amount of equipment. Will they have too little capacity to produce the output they expect to be able to sell in the forthcoming year, causing lost sales and dissatisfied customers? Or will capacity be excessive in relation to expected sales, wasting expenses on maintenance workers and interest costs on unneeded plant and equipment? The **accelerator hypothesis** of investment relies on the simple idea that firms attempt to maintain a fixed ratio of their stock of capital (plants and equipment) to their expected sales.

The accelerator hypothesis states that the level of net investment depends on the *change* in expected output.

Estimating Expected Sales

Clearly the first key ingredient in a business firm's decision about plant investment is an educated guess about the likely level of sales. Table 16-1 provides an example of how a hypothetical firm, the Mammoth Electric Company, estimates expected output and determines its desired stock of electric generating stations. The estimate of expected sales (Y^e) is revised from the estimate of the previous year (Y^e_{-1}) by some proportion, j, of any difference between last year's actual sales outcome (Y_{-1}) and what was expected:

$$Y^e = Y^e_{-1} + j(Y_{-1} - Y^e_{-1}) \qquad (16.1)$$
$$= jY_{-1} + (1 - j)Y^e_{-1}$$

This so-called adaptive or error-learning method of estimating sales expectations is exactly the same one that we encountered earlier in the formation of expectations of inflation and of permanent income.[2]

---

[2]The formation of expectations of inflation was the subject of Section 8-3. The calculation of permanent income was discussed in Section 15-4.

The error-learning method is illustrated in Table 16–1, where j is assumed equal to 0.5. In period 1, sales (Y^e) were expected to be \$10 billion but actually turned out to be \$12 billion (Y). The revision of expected sales in period 2 can be calculated from equation (16.1):

$$Y^e = 0.5(Y_{-1}) + 0.5(Y^e_{-1})$$
$$= 0.5(12) + 0.5(10)$$
$$= 11$$

Thus, in period 2 expected sales are \$11 billion, as recorded on line 2. But then another mistake is made, because in period 2 actual sales turn out to be \$12 billion again instead of the expected \$11 billion. Once again expectations for the next period are revised, and they continue to be revised as long as actual sales differ from expected sales.

The Level of Investment Depends on the Change in Output

The next step in the accelerator hypothesis is the assumption that the stock of physical capital—that is, plant and equipment—that a firm desires (K^*) is a multiple of its expected sales:

General Form	Numerical Example	
$K^* = v^* Y^e$	$K^* = 4.0 Y^e$	(16.2)

For example, Mammoth Electric in Table 16-1 wants a capital stock that is always 4 times as large as its expected sales. Notice that the desired capital stock on line 3 of the table is always exactly 4.0 times the level of expected

Table 16-1   **Workings of the Accelerator Hypothesis of Investment for the Hypothetical Mammoth Electric Company**

	Period					
Variable	*0*	*1*	*2*	*3*	*4*	*5*
1. Actual sales (Y)	10.0	12.0	12.0	12.0	12.0	12.0
2. Expected sales $(Y^e = 0.5Y_{-1} + 0.5Y^e_{-1})$	10.0	10.0	11.0	11.5	11.75	11.87
3. Desired stock of electric generating stations $(K^* = 4Y^e)$	40.0	40.0	44.0	46.0	47.0	47.5
4. Net investment in electric generating stations $(I^n = K^* - K^*_{-1})$	0.0	0.0	4.0	2.0	1.0	0.5
5. Replacement investment $(D = 0.10K_{-1})$	4.0	4.0	4.0	4.4	4.6	4.7
6. Gross investment $(I = I^n + D)$	4.0	4.0	8.0	6.4	5.6	5.2

Note: All figures in \$billions.

sales on line 2. What determines the multiple υ^*, which relates desired capital to expected sales? As we will see, in calculating υ^*, firms pay attention to the interest rate and tax rates. Their chosen value of the multiple υ^* reflects all available knowledge about government policies and the likely profitability of investment.

Net investment (I^n) is the change in the capital stock (ΔK) that occurs each period.[3]

$$I^n = \Delta K = K - K_{-1} \tag{16.3}$$

In the example in Table 16–1, we assume that Mammoth Electric always manages to acquire new capital quickly enough to keep its actual capital stock (K) equal to its desired capital stock (K^*) in each period:

$$I^n = K - K_{-1} = K^* - K^*_{-1} \tag{16.4}$$

Equation (16.4) implies that net investment (I^n) is always equal to the change in the desired capital stock in each period, which from equation (16.2), is 4.0 times the change in expected sales:

$$I^n = K^* - K^*_{-1} \tag{16.5}$$
$$= \upsilon^*(Y^e - Y^e_{-1}) = \upsilon^* \Delta Y^e$$

The accelerator hypothesis says that the *level* of net investment (I^n) depends on the *change* in expected output (ΔY^e). When there is an acceleration in business and expected output increases, net investment is positive. If expected output stops increasing, net investment falls to zero. And if expected output were ever to decline, net investment would become negative as businesses undertook less gross investment than the amount by which their capital stocks depreciated.

Adding Replacement Investment.   Total business spending on plant and equipment includes not only net investment—purchases that add to the capital stock—but also replacement purchases, which simply replace plant and equipment that has become worn out or obsolete. Line 5 of Table 16-1 assumes that each year 10 percent of the previous year's capital stock needs to be replaced. The total or gross investment (I) of Mammoth Electric, the amount recorded in the national income accounts of Chapter 2, is the sum of net investment (I^n) and replacement investment (D), and is written on line 6 of the table.

Figure 16-2 illustrates the Mammoth Electric example from Table 16-1. The level of actual sales is plotted as the top red line. Underneath, total gross investment is shown as the zigzag line that rises from $4 billion to $8 billion, only to fall in period 3 and afterward back toward the original level. Replacement investment is initially at the level of $4 billion, rising gradually as the capital stock increases. Net investment is the red shaded area, which first increases in size and then shrinks. Overall, the accelerator theory

---

[3]This is an alternative but equivalent definition to the one we learned in Chapter 2, where net investment was defined as gross investment minus capital consumption allowances.

Figure 16-2
The Behavior of Actual Sales, Expected Sales, Gross Investment, Net Investment, and Replacement Investment for the Mammoth Electric Company Described in Table 16-1.

In period 1 actual sales increase, but expected sales are not revised until period 2. Net investment shoots up in period 2, as Mammoth Electric purchases equipment needed to service the higher expected level of sales. Expected sales continue to grow in periods 3, 4, and 5, but more slowly, so net investment actually declines from its peak in period 2.

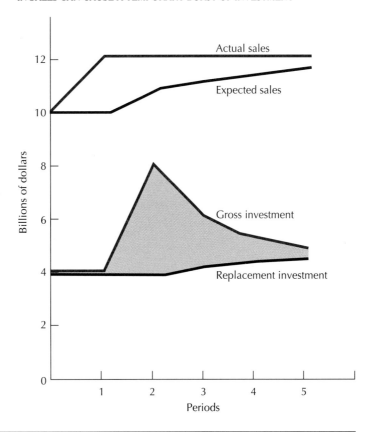

THE ACCELERATOR THEORY SHOWS HOW A PERMANENT INCREASE IN SALES CAN CAUSE A TEMPORARY BURST OF INVESTMENT

explains why a firm's gross investment is so unstable, at first rising and then falling, even when actual sales increase permanently.

SELF-TEST

Which is likely to be most stable from year to year, gross investment, net investment, or replacement investment? Least stable? Would gross investment in long-lived types of capital (like office buildings) be more or less stable than in short-lived capital (like computers)?

16-4   CASE STUDY: The Simple Accelerator and the Postwar U.S. Economy

The relation between gross investment *(I)* and GDP *(Y)* for the economy as a whole is, according to the accelerator hypothesis, the same as for an individual firm. In the special case when expected sales are always set exactly equal to last period's actual sales and therefore $j = 1$, $Y^e = Y_{-1}$, so that $\Delta Y^e = \Delta Y_{-1}$. This allows us to rewrite (16.5) as

$$I^n = v^*\Delta Y_{-1} \qquad (16.6)$$

Net investment *(I^n)* equals a multiple of last period's change in sales *(ΔY_{-1})*. Equation (16.6) is the simplest form of the accelerator theory and was invented when J. M. Clark in 1917 noticed a regular relationship between the level of boxcar production and the previous change in railroad traffic.[4]

> *This equation summarizes succinctly the inherent instability of the private economy. Any random event—an export boom, an irregularity in the timing of government spending, or a revision of consumer estimates of permanent income—can change the growth of real sales and temporarily (but significantly) change the level of net investment in the same direction.*

Assessing the Simple Accelerator

Figure 16-3 compares real net investment (I^n) with the change in real output (ΔY) in the U.S. economy since 1959.[5] Unfortunately, equation (16.6) is much too simple a theory to explain completely all historical movements in net investment in the United States. True, most peak years in net investment coincided with (or followed by one year) peak years in real GDP growth. And trough years in net investment coincided with (or followed by one year) trough years in real GDP growth. Furthermore, ten years of high net investment (1965–74) followed thirteen years (1961–73) in which real GDP growth rarely dipped below average.[6] Finally, low net investment in 1980–83 and 1990–91 followed periods during which real GDP growth fell well below average. Overall, however, Figure 16-3 reveals quite an imperfect relationship.

There are three main problems with the simple accelerator theory of equation (16.6), judging from the historical U.S. data plotted in Figure 16-3:

1. Net investment does not respond instantaneously to changes in output growth, as in equation (16.6), but rather displays noticeable lags in response. These lags can be seen clearly in several episodes.

2. The lag, however, is not of uniform length, nor does net investment respond to accelerations and decelerations in real GDP growth with uniform speed. It is as if an automobile's engine responded in a split second to some movements of the accelerator but took minutes to respond to other movements.

3. The overall level of net investment relative to real GDP (I^n/Y) does not have a consistent long-term relationship to real GDP growth $(\Delta Y/Y)$. Although average real GDP growth was slower in the 1970s than it was in the 1960s, the ratio of net investment to GDP was the same in both decades. When growth slowed further in the 1980s, the net investment ratio also fell. But even though the average GDP growth rate slowed another full percentage point in the 1990s, the ratio of net investment to GDP more than doubled.

---

[4]J. M. Clark, "Business Acceleration and the Law of Demand," *Journal of Political Economy,* vol. 25 (March 1917), pp. 217–35.

[5]To adjust for the steady growth in the size of the economy, both I^n and ΔY are divided by real GDP (Y). Thus the actual variables plotted are the ratio of real net nonresidential investment to real GDP (I^n/Y) and the percentage growth rate of real GDP $(\Delta Y/Y)$ over the previous four quarters.

[6]Average real GDP growth over the 1960–96 period plotted in Figure 16-3 is 3.1 percent.

THE UPS AND DOWNS OF NET INVESTMENT ARE NOT PERFECTLY RELATED TO CHANGES IN REAL GDP

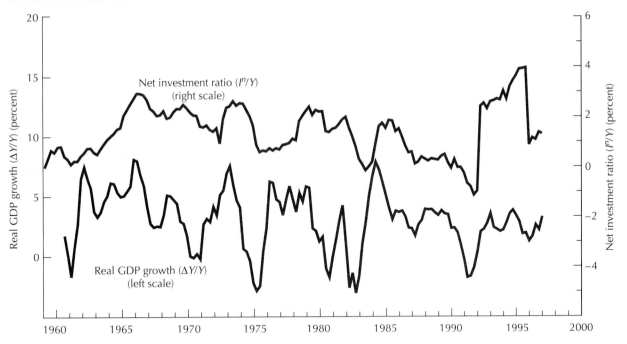

Figure 16-3 **The Relation of the Net Investment Ratio (I^n/Y) to the Growth Rate of Real GDP ($\Delta Y/Y$) in the U.S. Economy, 1960–96**

The net investment ratio does not have a perfect or simple relationship with the growth rate of real GDP. But net investment was high during 1965–74 following a long period of relatively rapid real GDP growth (1961–73). And the net investment ratio was low (1959–63, 1975–76, 1980–83, and 1990–91) following periods of relatively slow real GDP growth. The failure of the net investment ratio to recover after 1984 is puzzling, in view of relatively rapid real GDP growth in 1984–88. During the 1990s net investment, particularly purchases of information processing equipment, soared.

Period	Average	
	$\Delta Y/Y$	I^n/Y
1960s	4.4	1.6
1970s	3.2	1.6
1980s	2.8	0.9
1990s	1.8	2.0

Prominent Features of Postwar Investment Behavior

Figure 16-3 allows us to reach some general conclusions about the behavior of investment spending, beyond its relationship with the change in output. What do we learn from a visual inspection of the net investment ratio (I^n/Y), the red line in Figure 16-3? Two main facts stand out in the figure:

1. **Variability.** As we saw earlier, total GPDI is highly variable, as is the net investment ratio. The past three decades have shown that the net investment ratio sometimes shifts by about 2 percentage points of GDP within

just two years (as in 1973–75 and 1981–83). This represents a large potential shock for the economy, since 2 percentage points of GDP was $150 billion in 1996. The potential for fluctuations in investment is even greater than this, however, as indicated by the experience of the Great Depression, when the net investment ratio fell from +3.6 percent to −7.9 percent between 1929 and 1933.

2. **Persistence.**   The net investment ratio does not zigzag up and down each year but often stays relatively high or relatively low for several years in a row. The period of high net investment between 1965 and 1974 is a good example of this tendency: In every year from 1965 through 1974, the net investment ratio exceeded its 1959–96 average. The persistence of low investment in the Great Depression decade was even more pronounced: The net investment ratio was *negative for the entire decade 1931–40.*

16-5   The Flexible Accelerator

Defects of the Simple Accelerator

The **flexible accelerator** theory of investment allows for gradual adjustment of sales expectations and of the capital stock. It also allows for variation in the optimal capital-output ratio.

The simple accelerator theory of equation (16.6) depends on several restrictive and unrealistic assumptions. A more realistic version of the theory, called the **flexible accelerator,** loosens several of these assumptions.

1. The simple accelerator assumes that this period's expected output equaled last period's actual output. But the error-learning, or adaptive, hypothesis states that in general expected output is based partially on last period's actual output, and partially on last period's expected output.

2. The simple accelerator assumes that the desired capital stock (K^*) equals a constant (v^*) times expected output (Y^e). But actually the desired capital-output ratio (v^*) may vary substantially, depending on the cost of borrowing, the taxation of capital, and other factors; we will postpone until the next section a detailed consideration of the factors that change v^*.

3. The simple accelerator also assumes that firms can instantly put in place any desired amount of investment in plant and equipment needed to make actual capital this period (K) equal to desired capital (K^*). Actually, some kinds of capital take a substantial length of time to construct. Buildings sometimes take two or three years between conception and completion. Some types of electricity generating stations can take as long as eight years to complete.[7] Furthermore, investing very rapidly would be excessively costly because firms supplying capital goods might raise their prices. Also, rapid installation of new buildings and equipment might disrupt normal business activities.

Thus in the real world net investment does not always close the whole gap between desired capital and last year's capital stock; more often it closes only a fraction of it.

---

[7]At the other extreme, a shop that opens for business today in a large city could probably obtain delivery of needed equipment—cash register, computers, fax machine, and furniture—in a day or two.

Determinants of Gross Investment

To summarize, the relationship between economywide gross investment and output depends on at least four major factors.

1. *The fraction of the gap between desired capital and last period's actual capital that can be closed in a single period.* The higher this fraction, the more current investment responds to the change in last period's output.

2. *The response of expected output to last period's error in estimating actual output.* The higher this response, the more expected output and hence investment responds to any unexpected change in last period's actual output.

3. *The proportion of the capital stock that is replaced each year.* For long-lived types of capital, such as office buildings, only a small fraction of the stock is replaced each year. In contrast, because equipment depreciates more quickly, more equipment investment is required annually per dollar of equipment capital to maintain the same size equipment capital stock.

   Firms are not forced to replace old capital on a fixed schedule. If firms delay replacement investment until expected sales are strong, total investment will respond even more than the simple accelerator model suggests.[8]

4. *The desired ratio of capital to expected output (v^*). Investment responds more to changes in expected output in capital-intensive industries (those with a high v^*,* such as electric utilities, oil refining, and chemicals) than in labor-intensive industries (those with a low v^*, such as textiles, apparel, and barber shops). Thus, faster growth expected in more capital-intensive industries will spur more investment.

In the next section we investigate the determinants of the desired capital-output ratio and the policy instruments with which the government can affect the size of v^*.

16-6 The Neoclassical Theory of Investment Behavior

One of the most important contributions to the theory of investment behavior was made in the early 1960s by Dale Jorgenson of Harvard University.[9] Jorgenson's insight was to show that the user cost of capital could be derived from neoclassical microeconomic theory by examining the decision of a profit-maximizing firm. Jorgenson then demonstrated how tax policies affected how much firms invest.

---

[8]A study that confirms the procyclical behavior of replacement investment is Martin S. Feldstein and David Foot, "The Other Half of Gross Investment: Replacement and Modernization Expenditures," *The Review of Economics and Statistics,* vol. 53, no. 1 (February 1971), pp. 49–58.

[9]Dale Jorgenson, "Capital Theory and Investment Behavior," *American Economic Review,* vol. 53 (May 1963), pp. 247–57.

The User Cost of Capital

Jorgenson's theory assumes that a business firm is willing to undertake an investment project only when it expects that a profit can be made. Chapter 7 showed that an extra unit of labor will not be hired unless its marginal product—the extra output it produces—equals or exceeds its real wage. Similarly, an extra unit of capital will not be purchased unless the expected **marginal product of capital (MPK)** is at least equal to the real **user cost of capital** *(u):*

The marginal product of capital (MPK) is the extra output that a firm can produce by adding an extra unit of capital.

The user cost of capital is the cost to the firm of using a piece of capital for a specified period.

General Form	Numerical Example	
$MPK \geq u$	$MPK \geq 14$	(16.7)

Both the marginal product and the real user cost can be expressed as percentages. The marginal product of capital consists of the amount of extra output produced each year by an extra piece of plant or equipment, divided by the cost of the plant or equipment. If the purchase of an extra machine costing \$100,000 allows a firm to produce \$14,000 of extra output each year, then MPK would be 14 percent.[10]

The user cost of capital is the cost to the business firm of using a piece of capital for a period of time, expressed as a fraction of its purchase price. The user cost might be 14 percent, consisting perhaps of a 4 percent annual real interest rate and a 10 percent depreciation rate.[11]

What does equation (16.7) have to do with the profitability of a business firm? When MPK is 15 percent and user cost is only 14 percent, then the extra revenue generated by a new machine exceeds its cost, and the firm's profits are increased. On the other hand, when MPK is only 13 percent and user cost is the same 14 percent, the extra revenue is insufficient to pay the costs of the new machine, and profits go down if the machine is purchased. Only if user cost falls to 13 percent or lower will the new machine be purchased.

The effect of a reduction in user cost on the desired capital-output ratio is illustrated in Figure 16-4. The diminishing MPK means that each extra machine adds less output than the machine added before it, implying that the MPK curve slopes downward. Suppose each business initially faces a constant user cost u_0. Each business will then maximize its profits by choosing the capital-output ratio v_0^*, at which point the marginal benefit of the machine, its MPK, equals its marginal cost, u_0. Why? A smaller amount of capital, to the left of E_0, would mean giving up some of the profits indicated by the darker red area that measures the difference between the marginal product of capital and the user cost. But to purchase a larger amount of capital, to the right of E_0, would cause losses. These extra units of capital have an insufficient MPK to pay for their user cost.

---

[10]As is always true in economics, the marginal product of a single input measures the extra output produced by an extra unit of that input if the quantity of other inputs is held constant.

[11]Depreciation is part of user cost, because using a machine reduces its ability to produce and thus its value.

Figure 16-4
The Effect of a Drop in the User Cost of Capital *(u)* on the Desired Capital-Output Ratio *(v*)*

Initially the economy is at point E_0. Firms are making a profit on their capital stock indicated by the light red area in the upper left. If the user cost falls from u_0 to u_1, the desired capital-output ratio will rise to v_1^*, the economy will move from E_0 to E_1, and the darker red area of extra profit is gained.

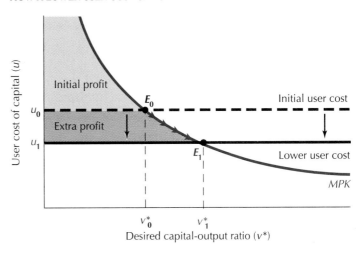

HOW A LOWER USER COST CAN SPUR INVESTMENT

Tax Incentives and Investment Behavior

The user cost of capital depends not only on the depreciation rate of capital and the real interest rate that must be paid on the funds borrowed to purchase the equipment. As derived by Jorgenson, the user cost also depends on three aspects of the tax system discussed in the next section. Thus, both monetary and fiscal policy can influence the user cost—monetary policy by changing the real interest rate, and fiscal policy by affecting real interest rates and by altering tax rates and the rules of the tax system.

We can use Figure 16-4 to illustrate the effect of a change in government tax policy designed to stimulate investment. Let us assume that the government changes tax rates or rules in order to cut the user cost. For instance, the tax rate that corporations pay on their profits might be cut in half. In effect, the tax rate reduction reduces user cost to the firm. Additional units of capital will now be purchased to bring the capital-output ratio rightward to v_1^*. Increased investment is required to raise the capital-output ratio to its new, higher desired level, v_1^*. The reduction in user cost has made available extra profits, indicated by the darker red area. Increased investment is required to raise the capital-output ratio to its new, higher desired level, v_1^*.

> *By using monetary and fiscal policy instruments, the user cost of capital can be changed. Firms can thus be induced to adopt more capital-intensive methods of production, and the opposite is true as well. Just as an increase in the wage rate can cause firms to replace marginal workers with extra machines, an increase in capital's user cost can cause firms to substitute away from elaborate machines toward more labor-intensive techniques of production.*[12]

---

[12]For instance, textile firms in the United States typically use more machines and fewer workers to produce the same products than firms in less developed countries, where the wage rate is lower and the user cost of capital is higher.

16-7   **User Cost and the Role of Monetary and Fiscal Policy**

How can government policymakers affect the user cost of capital *(u)?* The user cost of capital depends on several factors, which can be introduced in two steps. First, let us neglect the effect of taxation. In the absence of taxation a capital good that is purchased at a given real price imposes three types of cost on its user.

1. *An interest cost is involved in buying a capital good.* If funds are borrowed, interest at the nominal rate *(i)* must be paid. Alternatively, the investor loses the interest *(i)* that would have been received had the funds used to buy the capital good been used to purchase a financial asset.

2. *Physical deterioration lessens the production ability of every capital good; in addition, some capital goods become obsolete.* The **depreciation rate** indicates the annual decline in value of the capital good due to physical deterioration and obsolescence.

> The **depreciation rate** is the annual percentage decline in the value of a capital good due to physical deterioration and obsolescence.

3. *The interest and depreciation cost are adjusted by price changes for capital goods.* Rapid price increases mean that used capital goods can sometimes be resold for more than their cost when new. These price increases reduce the user cost and imply that it is a *real* interest rate that matters (the nominal interest rate minus the rate of price changes for capital goods). Conversely, declines in the prices of computers, for example, raise their user costs.

Policymakers cannot easily alter the relative price of capital goods, which depends on technical factors that influence innovations and productivity changes in capital goods industries compared to the economy as a whole. Similarly, they cannot change the rate of physical decay and economic obsolescence summarized in the depreciation rate. But the real interest rate can be influenced by policymakers. As we learned in Chapter 4, a fiscal policy stimulus raises the real interest rate and hence crowds out investment. A monetary policy stimulus, on the other hand, reduces the real interest rate and raises investment. A change in the monetary-fiscal policy mix toward easier monetary policy and tighter fiscal policy cuts the real interest rate and user cost and thus raises investment.

Taxation and Investment Behavior

So far taxation has been ignored. But fiscal policy can have a major effect on investment by altering the user cost. Three basic fiscal tools are available:

1. *Firms invest up to the point where the marginal product of the capital stock is just sufficient to cover the user cost of capital.* Imposing a tax on a firm's income effectively adds another element to user cost, the cost of taxes. The higher the firm's income tax rate is, the greater the effective user cost it faces. Thus, a higher tax rate is likely to reduce the firm's desired capital stock, and thus investment, because only with a smaller capital stock will the firm have a larger MPK.

2. *Firms can cut their corporate income tax by deducting the value of depreciation of plants and equipment.* The amount of depreciation they can

deduct depends on tax laws and how the IRS implements them. Though the government cannot change the rate of physical depreciation or obsolescence, which as we noted above enter the user cost of capital directly, it can change the accounting rules used to calculate corporate income taxes. Liberalizing the tax rules regarding depreciation, for example, effectively reduces the corporate income tax rate. Whenever the depreciation tax rules are liberalized, as occurred in 1954, 1962, 1964, and 1981, more corporate profits are protected from taxation, thus cutting the user cost of capital. The reverse happened in 1986 when the rules were tightened.

3. *During most of the period 1962–86, a substantial part of investment in the United States was eligible for an investment tax credit.* This credit often allowed business firms to deduct 10 percent of the value of their equipment investment from their corporation income tax. Naturally this reduced the effective user cost of capital for firms making profits. The investment tax credit was rescinded in 1986 but could be reinstated if the government desired to stimulate investment.

These three fiscal tools provide much more flexibility in conducting stabilization policy than would be available if the government were limited to controlling the economy by varying the level of government spending and the personal income tax rate. For instance, government spending can be restrained and the personal income tax rate raised to slow down an economy that is experiencing too much aggregate demand. At the same time, any of the investment-related fiscal instruments can be liberalized if it is believed that the economy has too little investment and too much consumption.

SELF-TEST

How may tools of fiscal policy potentially affect the user cost of capital? If the government wants to stimulate investment, how should it change these tools? Does monetary policy also have an effect on the user cost?

The Debate About the Efficacy of Tax Incentives

There was much discussion by economists of investment spending in the 1980s. Between 1982:Q4 and 1985:Q4, real fixed nonresidential investment increased by 29 percent. Then, between 1985:Q4 and 1990:Q3 (the business cycle peak), investment rose less than 3 percent. Many economists suggested investment was strong during 1982–85 because of the tax incentives for investment in the Reagan administration's tax legislation enacted in 1981.[13] Weak investment spending after 1985 is sometimes attributed to the 1986 tax reforms, which effectively raised business taxes.

A prominent advocate of the view that tax incentives have a strong effect on investment behavior is Martin Feldstein of Harvard University, who was chairman of the President's Council of Economic Advisers during 1982–84. Feldstein and a coauthor concluded that each percentage point increase in the real net after-tax return on investment raises the net investment ratio

---

[13]For a readable introduction to the behavior of investment in the early 1980s, and further references, see George A. Kahn, "Investment in Recession and Recovery: Lessons from the 1980s," *Economic Review,* Federal Reserve Bank of Kansas City (November 1985), pp. 25–39.

TOBIN'S *q*: Does It Explain Investment Better Than the Accelerator or Neoclassical Theories?

Both the accelerator theory of Sections 16-3 and 16-5, as well as the neoclassical theory of Section 16-6, define a desired level of the capital stock *(K*)*, and then assume a gradual adjustment of the actual capital stock toward the desired level. The alternative *q* theory was developed by Nobel Prize winner James Tobin (who also did pathbreaking work on the demand for money and whose picture appears in Section 13-8). Tobin's *q* theory, instead of positing a desired level of capital and a *separate* process of adjustment, merges adjustment costs directly into the firm's single calculation of the desired rate of investment at each moment of time.[a]

Tobin's theory develops an idea of Keynes's that the attractiveness of purchasing new capital equipment depends on the market value of capital in the stock market as compared with the cost of purchasing the capital. For instance, if purchasing a new Boeing 757 airplane would raise the market value of American Airlines stock by $50 million, while the cost of the plane is $40 million, then the plane should be purchased. But if the new plane would raise the market value of American Airlines stock by only $30 million, then the plane should not be purchased. To create a quantitative measure that reflects changes in market value relative to the purchase cost, Tobin defined his variable *q* as the ratio of the firm's market value on the stock and bond markets to the replacement cost of its capital stock. Investment, then, is an increasing function of the *q* ratio.

An example of an investment equation in the *q* theory would be the following relation between gross investment relative to the capital stock *(I/K)*, the *q* ratio *(q)*, and the ratio of replacement investment to the capital stock *(d)*:

$$\frac{I}{K} = j(q - 1) + d \qquad (16.8)$$

In words, this says that the *I/K* ratio is equal to *d* when Tobin's *q* ratio is unity. If $d = 0.1$ and $j = 0.2$, then *I/K* would be 0.1 when *q* equals unity; *I/K* would rise to 0.2 when *q* equals 1.5, and *I/K* would fall to zero when *q* equals 0.5. (Note that *j* in (16.8) has nothing to do with the *j* in the adaptive expectations equation.)

In practice, the most important source of movement in *q* is the change in the price of a firm's shares on the stock market. In the mid-1990s, for example, the annual changes in stock prices were sometimes 20 percent or more. Since stock prices are part of the numerator in *q*, such changes could change *q* by large amounts. As we have noted before, households' consumption spending might be affected by the stock market; higher stock prices might raise consumption by increasing households' wealth. Higher stock prices might increase the amount of investment that firms undertake. Thus, Tobin's *q* also suggests another channel through which changes in the stock market might affect aggregate demand.

Tobin's *q* theory of investment incorporates how the economic environment affects business firms' expectations of their future profitability. In addition to its theoretical appeal as a way to explain and forecast investment spending by firms, *q* has great practical appeal because it summarizes expectations about the level and riskiness of future profitability and thus makes unnecessary the exceedingly difficult job of estimating those expectations. Instead, Tobin's *q* theory states that we can simply look to the stock and bond markets for the valuation of the firm's expected future profitability, which is the numerator of *q*.

How does *q* fare in an empirical "horse race" with the accelerator and neoclassical models that we developed in Sections 16-3 and 16-6? A number of studies have tested the abilities of these three models to explain spending on fixed investment (as

well as the neoclassical model. That is one reason why we presented both the accelerator and neoclassical models in this chapter—in practice neither is a clear-cut winner. (Findings similar to those reported by Oliner, Rudebusch, and Sichel emerge from the earlier time periods examined in other studies.)

Business investment in structures has proven more difficult to explain and forecast. In general, none of the models have demonstrated any significant ability to forecast movements in construction spending by business, although again, the accelerator and neoclassical models tend to outperform the q models. An example of the shortcomings of all the models was their inability to forecast, or even account for after the fact, the enormous surge in commercial real estate construction during the 1980s. Later in this chapter we will address that experience in more detail. The large variations in business investment in structures suggests that aggregate demand for GDP may shift importantly over time. The inability to forecast those shifts suggests that it may be difficult for policymakers to anticipate and take timely action to offset them.

opposed to inventory changes) after the fact and also to forecast it.[b]

Empirical models have all been much better at explaining and forecasting business investment spending on *equipment*—so-called producers' durable equipment—than they have at explaining and forecasting investment in nonresidential *structures*. The Oliner, Rudebusch, and Sichel study, for example, shows that investment spending on producers' durable equipment can be fairly well tracked by some of the models. They find that despite the theoretical and practical appeal of the q model of investment, both the accelerator and neoclassical models explain and forecast more accurately than do models based on q, with the accelerator model performing about as

[a]Most of the references on Tobin's q theory are quite technical. For the original presentation, see James Tobin, "A General Equilibrium Approach to Monetary Theory," *Journal of Money, Credit and Banking,* vol. 1 (February 1969), pp. 15–29. More recent interpretations are Fumio Hayashi, "Tobin's Marginal and Average q: A Neoclassical Interpretation," *Econometrica,* vol. 50 (January 1982), pp. 213–24, and Andrew B. Abel, "A Stochastic Model of Investment, Marginal q, and the Market Value of the Firm," *International Economic Review,* vol. 26 (June 1985), pp. 305–22.

[b]See, for example, Stephen Oliner, Glenn Rudebusch, and Daniel Sichel, "New and Old Models of Business Investment: A Comparison of Forecasting Performance," *Journal of Money, Credit and Banking,* vol. 27 (August 1995), pp. 806–26, and the references cited there.

(I^n/Y) by 0.4 percentage points.[14] By Feldstein's calculations, the tax incentives in place in 1983–84 (as contrasted with 1978–80) raised the net investment ratio by about 0.7 percentage points.

A more recent study by Charles W. Bischoff and his coauthors at the State University of New York at Binghamton, covering the decade of the 1980s, concludes that the tax incentives of 1981, followed by their partial reversal in 1982 and in 1986, on balance canceled out. The stock of equipment capital was lifted about 1 percent between 1982 and early 1987 by the tax incentives of 1981 and the partial reversal of those incentives in 1982, as compared with the level that would have been attained had there been no tax changes in the 1980s. But this stimulus to the stock of equipment evaporated as a result of the tax reform of 1986, so that by 1989 the stock of equipment capital was almost exactly the same as if there had been no tax changes at all in the 1980s. Overall, this study attributes about 4 percent of the rapid growth of investment during 1982–85 to the initial Reagan tax incentives, and much of the slower growth in 1985–88 to the 1986 tax reform.[15]

Studies by economists suggest that changes in tax incentives probably have at least a modest effect on investment. However, such changes have numerous limitations and are not a promising instrument for an activist fiscal policy. First, changes in tax incentives are almost always subject to lengthy debate in Congress. Second, there is a substantial time lag between the passage of tax legislation and the resulting investment spending. Third, we are far from being able to estimate confidently how much investment will respond to tax incentives.

16-8   Business Confidence, Speculation, and Overbuilding

Confidence and the Flexible Accelerator

In Chapters 3 and 4 the terms *business* and *consumer confidence* were used as a convenient, shorthand way to refer to factors that could change output when government spending and the money supply were fixed at a given level. In the flexible accelerator theory of investment summarized here, the confidence of business firms may influence investment spending in three ways:

1. Investment depends on what fraction of the increase in last period's actual output is incorporated into expected output, and hence into desired capital and investment. When businesspeople lack confidence in the future, they may refuse to extrapolate a quarter or a year of increasing output, believing instead that any increase in output is temporary.

2. The user cost of capital (u) includes the borrowing costs that business firms *expect* to have to pay if they undertake an investment project. If

[14]Martin Feldstein and Joosung Jun, "The Effects of Tax Rules on Nonresidential Fixed Investment: Some Preliminary Evidence from the 1980s," in Martin S. Feldstein, ed., *The Effects of Taxation on Capital Accumulation* (University of Chicago Press, 1987), pp. 101–61.

[15]Charles W. Bischoff, Edward C. Kokkelenberg, and Ralph A. Terregrossa, "Tax Policy and Business Fixed Investment During the Reagan Era," in *The Economic Legacy of the Reagan Years: Euphoria or Chaos?*, edited by Anandi P. Sahu and Ronald L. Tracy (New York: Praeger, 1991) pp. 21–39.

businesses are pessimistic, they may underestimate how much the prices of capital goods will rise and therefore overestimate the real borrowing cost they are likely to face, making their estimate of u too high and their desired capital stock too low.

3. Perhaps most important, business firms can only guess the likely marginal product of new investment projects. It is the expected marginal product that matters. If business has recently been bad, a condition experienced by many business firms in 1930–33, or as recently as 1990–91, firms may already have more capital than they may desire. Some present capital may be underutilized, and future capital investments may appear unprofitable, with their expected marginal products being close to zero.

Investment and the Great Depression

Any event, whether political or economic, that causes a drop in business confidence can cause a sharp drop in the level of investment. In the extreme case of the Great Depression of the 1930s, a collapse in business confidence dropped the desired capital stock far below the actual inherited capital stock. Not only did businesses refuse to add to their capital stock, but they allowed net investment to become negative by refusing to replace worn-out and obsolete equipment. Gross private domestic investment plummeted more than 80 percent from 1929 to 1933. But, despite the low levels of gross investment in the 1930s, much capital remained underutilized. The overhang of too much inherited capital depressed investment for a full decade.

Cycles of Overbuilding

Periods of business overoptimism in U.S. history have led to overbuilding, underutilized capital, and extensive pessimism. This recurring sequence played out in the years surrounding 1970 and the years surrounding 1990, leaving the United States with billions of dollars worth of empty apartments, office buildings, and stores. We look at the years surrounding 1990 in more detail in Section 16-9.

Keynes placed major emphasis on the role of business confidence in determining the level of investment. In the following passage he stresses that investment decisions are based on estimates of the future yield (or marginal product) of extra capital, estimates that may be little better than a guess. Faced with identical information and uncertainty, businesspeople may go ahead with an investment project when they feel optimistic but postpone the same project when they feel pessimistic:

> The outstanding fact is the extreme precariousness of the basis of knowledge on which our estimates of prospective yield have to be made. Our knowledge of the factors which will govern the yield of an investment some years hence is usually very slight and often negligible. If we speak frankly, we have to admit that our basis of knowledge for estimating the yield ten years hence of a railway, a copper mine, a textile factory, the goodwill of a patent medicine, an Atlantic liner, a building in the City of London amounts to little and sometimes to nothing; or even five

INTERNATIONAL PERSPECTIVE

The Level and Variability of Investment Around the World

For many years, investment has been much lower in the United States than in Japan or Germany. And from the mid-1980s through the mid-1990s, the investment gap between the United States and Japan and Germany widened. The accompanying figure shows the share of each country's GDP that is devoted to gross investment (net investment plus depreciation) for the years 1983–94. If we had plotted the share of net investment, the contrast between the United States and the other countries would have been even greater.

National saving always equals national investment. A theme we have stressed repeatedly is that one reason for the low rate of domestic investment in the United States in the last quarter of the twentieth century is the low rate of U.S. national saving, which is the sum of the government surplus and private saving. Large U.S. government deficits, especially in the 1980s, meant that the government surplus was negative. U.S. private saving may also have been reduced by income tax rules and transfer payment programs that encouraged borrowing rather than saving.

Firms finance their investment spending in a number of ways. In most countries the primary source of funds for business investment in plant and equipment is retained earnings, that is, the profits that firms have not paid out in dividends but have retained inside the firms. Especially in France, Italy, and Japan, firms also rely heavily on loans from banks to finance purchases of plant and equipment.[a] Firms in Germany, the United Kingdom, and the United States are less dependent on bank loans, obtaining relatively more of the funds they use to finance investment expenditures by issuing stocks, long-term bonds, and short-term instruments like commercial paper.

In Chapter 15 we learned that consumers sometimes face liquidity constraints, which prevent them from borrowing the full amount of funds that they would be expected to be able to repay from permanent incomes. Business firms too sometimes face liquidity constraints. Young firms, like young households, may find it difficult to borrow the amount of funds justified by their longer-term prospects. And smaller firms may find that they must reduce investment when current profits or retained earnings decline, in much the same way that individuals who temporarily lose their jobs reduce consumption because they are unable to borrow the amounts justified by permanent income. Thus, for both households and firms, constraints on borrowing and therefore on spending may be more severe during recessions or when higher interest rates raise loan payments. These effects on investment have been noted particularly in Italy, the United Kingdom, and the United States. By stifling investment spending even more when the economy is weak, these borrowing constraints can exacerbate the variability of investment spending.

One way for firms to loosen these financing constraints may be to ally themselves with other firms. Firms in Korea sometimes belong to a *chaebol;* in Italy firms are sometimes linked by family connections; in Japan some firms belong to a group of firms called a *keiretsu;* businesses in Canada and in the United States may be owned by conglomerates; and some firms in Japan and in Germany have bankers on their boards of directors. Because the other firms in such alliances often are not in closely allied areas of business, the alliance is more likely to remain strong when one of its members may need financial support. Belonging to one of these business groups seems to provide some insulation from financing constraints, perhaps because the other firms in the group can either provide the funds needed for investment directly to a constrained firm, or can provide some assurance to an outside lender like a bank that the other firms will help repay a bank loan to the constrained firm.

[a]For a description and analysis of the interaction of financial markets and investment across countries, see Fabio Schiantarelli, "Financial Constraints and Investment: A Critical Review of Methodological Issues and International Evidence," in *Is Bank Lending Important for the Transmission of Monetary Policy?*, edited by Joe Peek and Eric S. Rosengren, Federal Reserve Bank of Boston, Conference Series no. 39, June 1995.

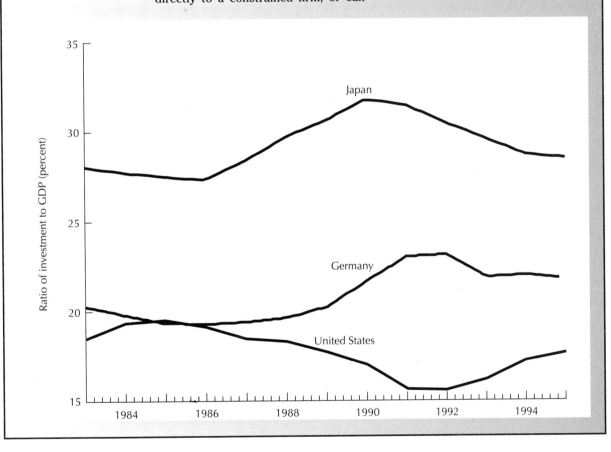

years hence. In fact, those who seriously attempt to make any such estimates are often so much in the minority that their behavior does not govern the market.[16]

Throughout this book we have treated such shifts in business confidence (as well as consumer confidence) as sources of important and unpredictable shifts in *IS,* and thus *AD,* curves.

16-9   CASE STUDY: Booms and Busts in Commercial Real Estate Construction

Figure 16-1 showed that total investment spending varies a great deal from year to year. Spending on each of the components of total investment, i.e., nonresidential construction, producers' durable equipment, residential construction, and inventory change, also varies a great deal from year to year.

Figure 16-5 plots the ratio of real spending on construction of commercial buildings to natural real GDP from 1964 through 1996. The figure depicts the extreme variability of construction spending for commercial buildings, with booms lasting several years alternating with busts. From its high level (as a share of natural real GDP) during the economywide boom of the early 1970s, real commercial real estate construction plummeted during 1974 and 1975. It then rebounded through the early 1980s, before skyrocketing during the middle of the 1980s. Then, by the late 1980s, real commercial real estate construction had fallen about 25 percent below its peak, and by the early 1990s, had fallen to less than half its peak. In the mid-1990s, real commercial real estate construction was again on the rise and neared its longer-term average level of about 1 percent of natural real GDP.

The explosion of commercial construction in the mid-1980s is attributable, in part, to the factors that the accelerator and neoclassical theories of investment point to.[17] As the economy recovered from the 1981–82 recession, there were accelerator effects on investment spending, including that for commercial real estate. At the same time, during the first half of the 1980s the user cost of structures declined as real interest rates and the effective tax rate on investment fell. Both of these declines contributed to increased investment spending.

The increase in construction, however, seems to have gone beyond what was predictable. By the mid-1980s, people began to refer to "see-through" downtowns, where from part way up an office building one could see to the horizon—right through a number of empty neighboring office buildings. From 5 percent in 1980, the average vacancy rate for office buildings in major U.S. cities rose to 20 percent in the early 1990s: The equivalent of one out of every five office buildings was a see-through. In 1990 the office vacancy rates in Dallas, in Denver, and in Houston, for example, were 25 percent. They were 23 percent in Milwaukee and Miami.

---

[16]Keynes, *General Theory,* pp. 149–50.

[17]For a more detailed discussion and a comparison of the relative performance of accelerator, neoclassical, and *q* models of construction spending, see Richard W. Kopcke, "The Determinants of Business Investment: Has Capital Spending Been Surprisingly Low?," *New England Economic Review,* January/February 1993, pp. 3–30.

CONSTRUCTION OF COMMERCIAL BUILDINGS WAS WEAK IN THE LATE 1970s,
STRONG IN THE 1980s, AND WEAK IN THE EARLY 1990s

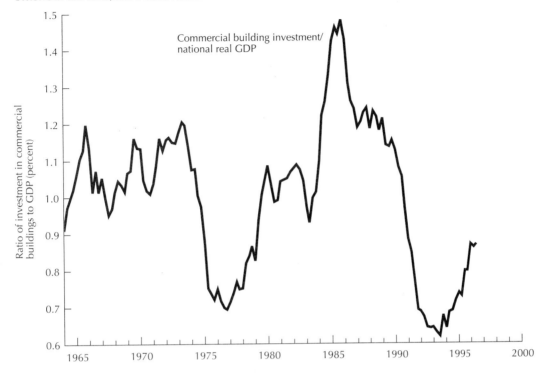

Figure 16-5   **The Ratio of Real Investment in Commercial Buildings to Natural Real GDP,
1964–96**

Construction of commercial buildings fluctuates a great deal. Periods of very strong
or very weak spending on construction of commercial buildings often last for a number of years, and spending can shift from strong to weak quite quickly and unpredictably. Construction spending dropped more than 50 percent in the second half of
the 1970s and in the first half of the 1990s; it rose sharply in the middle of both the
1980s and the 1990s.

Why were so many buildings built? Part of the answer may be that,
because office building projects take several years to complete, they are
already underway when the conditions that originally justified the projects
vanish. Another possible reason is that beginning in the early 1980s some
financial institutions, like S&Ls, were given permission to finance and even to
invest in commercial real estate, raising both the overall demand for and the
supply of it. To the extent that some of those S&Ls were already in precarious
financial condition, they may have been willing to participate in commercial
real estate construction beyond what was economically sensible.

And, partly, the 1980s boom in commercial building may be inexplicable.
Richard W. Kopcke argues that investment equations, like those based on the
accelerator or neoclassical theories, could forecast the general pattern of
spending during the 1980s on producers' durable equipment. Spending on
nonresidential structures like commercial buildings, however, greatly
exceeded what investment equations predicted. His view is that investment
spending may have been driven up by a "mania," which is an extreme version

of what we often call business "optimism." Since manic swings are by definition quite unpredictable, commercial real estate construction is likely to continue to be not only highly variable but also quite unpredictable. As such, it contributes to the instability of aggregate demand.

16-10 Investment as a Source of Instability of Output and Interest Rates

The accelerator theory resolves a favorite paradox of macroeconomics teachers. We became accustomed in Chapter 4 to associating low interest rates with high investment and high interest rates with low investment. This negative relationship between investment and interest rates has been confirmed in this chapter because a low level of the real interest rate reduces the user cost of capital, which in turn raises the desired capital stock and hence the level of gross investment.

Yet a predominant feature of business cycles in almost every nation is a positive correlation between business investment and interest rates. U.S. business investment fluctuates procyclically, reaching peaks in years of high output and troughs during recessions or soon afterward. But, since interest rates also fluctuate procyclically, years of low interest rates are usually associated with low investment, not high investment.

How can the positive correlation between investment and interest rates be explained? The accelerator theory provides the answer. Figure 16-6 repeats the *IS-LM* analysis of Chapter 4. The *LM* curve maintains an unchanged position whenever the real money supply *(M/P)* and real demand for money function are fixed. The *IS* curve fluctuates whenever there is a change in the investment purchases that business firms make at a constant real interest rate.

Causes of *IS* Shifts

We have seen that many factors can make the level of gross investment, and hence the *IS* curve, shift for a given interest rate. Among them are: (1) a change in the expected growth rate of output and thus sales, (2) a previous episode of overbuilding that makes the actual capital stock high relative to the current desired stock, (3) a shift in demand toward shorter-lived equipment, (4) a change in the relative price of capital goods, and, finally, (5) a change in fiscal incentives that alters the effective user cost of capital. A change in any of these elements shifts the level of investment that occurs at a given interest rate and, through the multiplier, shifts the *IS* curve and the level of total output.

Figure 16-6 illustrates two *IS* curves, IS_0 and IS_1. The shifts back and forth between the two *IS* curves reflect any one of the factors in the previous paragraph that cause an increase or decrease in gross investment. The positive relationship between investment and interest rates is explained in Figure 16-6 by the *IS* shifting along LM_0, which is held fixed by the fixed real money supply. That positive relationship suggests that the depressing effect of low output on investment, working through the accelerator, dominates the stimulative effect of low interest rates on investment, at least in the short run.

Figure 16-6
Effect on Output and the Interest Rate of a Shift in the Level of Investment Relative to the Interest Rate

Shifts in business confidence or in user cost (apart from those due to changes in the real interest rate) can shift the red *IS* curve back and forth between IS_0 and investment will rise and fall together. This conclusion assumes that the real money supply, which fixes the position of the *LM* curve, remains unchanged.

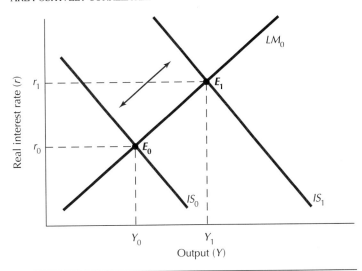

WHY THE INTEREST RATE AND INVESTMENT OFTEN ARE POSITIVELY CORRELATED

16-11   Conclusion: Investment and the Case For and Against Activism

We concluded in Chapter 15 that consumption spending on nondurable goods and services is not likely to be very volatile. Both the permanent-income and life-cycle hypotheses suggested that spending on nondurable goods and services tends to fluctuate less than disposable income. This stability bolsters the case for following a policy rule.

But this chapter tilts the balance in the opposite direction, toward the proposition of policy activists that the private economy contains sources of instability that tend to make equality of actual and natural output an infrequent coincidence rather than a frequent occurrence. The problem is epitomized by the accelerator theory of investment. Any event that causes a *permanent* increase in the desired capital stock—whether an increase in expected output or a reduction in the user cost of capital—causes only a *temporary* burst of investment spending. After the temporary burst, when net investment falls, economic instability is aggravated by the multiplier effect of Chapter 3.

Until the 1980s, the tendency for fixed investment to undergo multiyear booms and slumps formed the core of the activist case. It then became apparent, however, that net exports can be an equally important source of fluctuations in aggregate demand, as we learned in Chapters 3 and 6. The decline in net exports in the mid-1980s provided as much of a challenge for policymakers as the investment slumps of 1973–75, 1980–82, and 1990–92.

However, as we learned in Chapter 14, the opponents of activism, who advocate policy rules, still must face the tradeoff between rules for policy instruments (which are feasible but may not lead to desirable behavior by policy targets) and rules for the targets themselves (which may not be feasible). As yet, there is no consensus on whether the Fed is capable of carrying out a policy rule for a target.

The multiyear cycles in fixed investment and in net exports support the activist contention that private spending is unstable. However, this by itself does not settle the issue. Opponents counter that activist policy could still do more harm than a rules-based policy. Policymakers may not be able to forecast fluctuations in private spending far enough in advance to offset the lags in the operation of monetary policy. And substantial uncertainty exists about the multiplier effects of monetary and fiscal policy. Multiplier uncertainty, which we examined initially in Chapter 14, became even greater in the 1980s and 1990s as financial deregulation and flexible exchange rates changed the effects of monetary policy.

Thus both the proponents and opponents of activism have good cases. The activists are correct that investment and net exports can create persistent fluctuations in total aggregate demand. And the opponents of activism are correct that forecasting is highly imperfect, that stabilization policy operates with long and variable lags, and that policy multipliers are highly uncertain.

SUMMARY

1. The major source of instability in consumption spending is consumer expenditures on durables, which can exhibit large fluctuations in response to income changes. This chapter adds private investment spending as an additional source of instability, with the potential of causing major changes in GDP in response to small shocks.

2. The simple accelerator theory of investment relies on the idea that firms attempt to maintain a fixed relation between their stock of capital and their expected sales. Thus, the level of net investment—the change in the capital stock—depends on the change in expected output. The accelerator theory explains why the gross investment of most firms is relatively unstable, at first rising and then falling in response to a permanent increase in actual sales.

3. The flexible accelerator theory recognizes that net investment in the real world usually closes only a portion of any gap between the desired and actual capital stocks. Furthermore, the desired capital-output ratio may change, altering investment with a powerful accelerator effect.

4. The accelerator theory suggests that any event that causes a permanent increase in the desired capital stock, whether arising from an increase in expected output or from a reduction in the user cost of capital, causes only a temporary rise in investment spending.

5. Government policymakers can directly alter the user cost of capital. Fiscal and monetary policy can change the real interest rate component of user cost. Taxation can affect the user cost of capital through changes in the corporation income tax, depreciation deductions, and the investment tax credit. But the use of these policy instruments cannot eliminate all fluctuations in investment expenditures, because most policy measures operate only with lagged effects.

6. Spending on commercial construction has historically been quite variable, in part because the capital-output ratio for buildings is larger than that for other, shorter-lived types of physical capital. Because the lags between conception and completion of office buildings are long, booms and busts in spending for commercial real estate may last for several years. Changes in user costs and expected output also help explain this variability, but some of the fluctuations in construction still seem inexplicable and unpredictable.

7. Some firms face the same kinds of constraints on financing their spending that households face. Young and small firms seem particularly subject to constraints on how much investment they can undertake. In other countries around the world, firms sometimes are allied with other firms or with banks, which helps to reduce these constraints.

8. Shifts in the demand for investment spending tend to produce a positive correlation between investment and interest rates, even though the effect of higher interest rates, *ceteris paribus,* is to reduce investment spending. The former results from a shift of the *IS* curve; the latter from sliding along the *IS* curve.

9. The unpredictability of investment spending bolsters the case for policy activism. However, the inability to make countercyclical policy on a timely and effective basis weakens the case for activism.

CONCEPTS

accelerator hypothesis
flexible accelerator
marginal product of capital (MPK)

user cost of capital
depreciation rate

QUESTIONS AND PROBLEMS

Questions

1. Differentiate between gross investment and net investment. Can gross investment ever be negative? Can net investment ever be negative?
2. Assume that output in the economy is growing. Does the simple accelerator model predict that net investment will also grow?
3. Discuss the role of lags in the accelerator theory. How does the existence of lags change the results of the simple accelerator model?
4. In summarizing the behavior of investment spending, the net investment ratio (I^n/Y) was described as volatile and persistent. Explain what is meant by these terms.
5. Business confidence and consumer confidence are often cited as playing a key role in the investment decision. How does business confidence enter the flexible accelerator analysis?
6. A capital good purchased at a given real price imposes three types of costs on its user. What are these costs? Which of these costs are subject to manipulation by policymakers?
7. What are the three tools of fiscal policy that can be used to influence the level of investment? According to the accelerator theory, are changes in these tools

likely to lead to a permanent increase in the rate of investment?
8. What are the limitations to using tax incentives as a tool of activist fiscal policy?
9. What are the major factors that determine the relationship between gross investment and output in the economy? Briefly summarize the relationship involved.
10. According to the theory first presented in Chapter 3 and developed further in this chapter, the interest rate and investment are negatively related. Yet, both business investment and interest rates tend to fluctuate procyclically, i.e., are at their highest levels when the economy is at a high output level. Can you explain the paradox?
11. Using Tobin's q theory, explain what you would expect to happen to the construction of new houses as the prices of existing houses rise.
12. How does the existence of liquidity constraints affect the volatility of investment? Why might liquidity constraints be more binding on smaller firms than on larger ones and on U.S. firms than on firms in such countries as Germany and Japan?

Problems

1. This problem uses the example in Table 16-1 (p. 507).
   (a) The economy will reach an equilibrium when expected sales no longer increase. What will net investment be at that point? What will gross investment be?
   (b) Assume that because of a new investment tax credit, the desired capital–expected sales ratio changes to 5. What would net investment be in periods 1–5?
   (c) When the economy reaches its new equilibrium, what will be the ultimate effect of the tax credits on investment?

2. This problem also uses the data in Table 16-1.
   (a) What would expected sales have to be in periods 3 to 5 for net investment to be constant at 4.0?
   (b) What would actual sales have to be in periods 3 to 5 to achieve a constant level of net investment?
   (c) What would actual sales have to be in periods 2 to 4 to achieve a steady 20 percent increase in gross investment in each of the periods 3 to 5?
   (d) At what rate do actual sales increase in (c)?

SELF-TEST ANSWERS

p. **509** Assuming, as in this section, that replacement investment is a fixed fraction of the previous year's capital stock, replacement investment is the most stable. Net investment, which depends on the *change* in expected output, is the least stable. Gross investment, the sum of net investment and replacement investment, is inbetween. The longer-lived is capital, the smaller is the fraction of the previous year's capital stock that needs to be replaced; hence, the smaller is stable replacement investment relative to unstable net investment. Thus we would expect gross investment in office buildings to be less stable than gross investment in computers.

p. **517** The three potential tools are the corporation income tax, the value of depreciation deductions, and the investment tax credit. If the government wants to stimulate investment, it can reduce the corporation income tax rate, or raise the value of depreciation deductions (by allowing business firms to take depreciation deductions earlier), or raise the percentage rate of the investment tax credit. If there is no investment tax credit, as in the United States after 1986, the government can introduce such a credit. Monetary policy affects the user cost through its ability to change the real interest rate.

PART SEVEN

Debates at the

Macroeconomic

Frontier

CHAPTER 17

New Classical Macro Confronts New Keynesian Macro

The price of commodities in the market is formed by means of a certain struggle which takes place between the buyers and the sellers.
—Henry Thornton, 1802

17-1 Introduction: Classical and Keynesian Economics, Old and New

The development of new theories in macroeconomics and the abandonment of old theories often occur in response to major macroeconomic developments. In Chapter 7 we were introduced to the classical economists whose ideas dominated macroeconomics prior to the 1930s; they believed that the price level was flexible and would shift by the amount necessary to eliminate any inadequacies in aggregate demand. We described this approach as assuming that the economy possesses strong self-correcting properties, in the form of price flexibility, that automatically correct any tendency for real aggregate demand to be too high or too low.

In the 1930s a calamitous macroeconomic event, the Great Depression, brought a decade-long economic slump accompanied by double-digit unemployment rates. The depression discredited the old classical approach based on flexible prices and self-correction, creating among economists, journalists, policymakers, and laypeople a receptive audience for the Keynesian revolution, based on John Maynard Keynes's epochal book, *The General Theory of Employment, Interest, and Income.*[1]

However, the old Keynesian approach was not without its own problems. Only a few years after the publication of *The General Theory*, economists questioned Keynes's assumption that (as in Figure 7-11) real wages vary countercyclically, rising in recessions and falling in expansions. They pointed to data indicating that real wages do not change systematically during the business cycle. Nevertheless, the old Keynesian approach dominated macroeconomics until the late 1960s. The big event that undermined its dominance was the emergence at that time of significant inflation. The old Keynesian theory based on rigid nominal wages had little to say about the causes of inflation.

Emergence of New Classical Macroeconomics

Since the early 1970s, macroeconomics has been split between two basic explanations of business cycles. First to emerge as a challenge to the old

---

[1]The late Harry Johnson examined the reasons for the success of the Keynesian revolution and developed a parallel set of reasons for the late 1960s' monetarist "counterrevolution." See his article "The Keynesian Revolution and the Monetarist Counter-Revolution," *American Economic Review*, vol. 61 (May 1971), pp. 1–14.

Keynesian orthodoxy was the new classical approach originated by Milton Friedman, then at the University of Chicago, and more fully developed by Robert E. Lucas, Jr., also of the University of Chicago. This first approach was based on the idea that households and firms lack the full set of information needed to make their economic decisions. Later, a second strand of new classical macroeconomics emerged, based not on imperfect information but on shocks to technology and supply conditions. The second approach, the "real business cycle" model, was developed primarily by Edward Prescott of the University of Minnesota.

Common to all new classical models is the assumption of continuous equilibrium in labor and product markets. These markets "clear," in the sense that each worker and firm is acting as desired at the price and wage level that is expected to prevail during the period of employment or production. For Friedman and Lucas, business cycles emerge because workers and/or firms, while acting as desired, are doing so on the basis of incorrect information. If workers and firms had complete access to information on such macro variables as the aggregate price level and money supply, there would be no business cycles. In contrast, Prescott theorizes that business cycles emerge because a given amount of labor and capital input produces varying amounts of real GDP due to changes in the efficiency of production.

New classical macro contrasts with another recent set of theories intended in part to remedy weaknesses in the old Keynesian approach. These new theories are grouped together under the general heading of "new Keynesian" macro. Such models, examined in the last part of this chapter, accept Keynes's insight that prices and wages do not change fast enough for classical self-correction to occur. But they go beyond Keynes to examine the reasons why slow price and wage adjustment is often in the self-interest of workers and is consistent with profit maximization for firms. The implications of new Keynesian macro differ radically from those of new classical macro. For if prices and wages adjust slowly, no matter what the reasons, then markets do not always clear; workers are sometimes unable to obtain as many jobs as they want at the prevailing wages and prices, and firms are sometimes unable to sell as much as they would like to produce at those wages and prices.

17-2 Imperfect Information and the "Fooling Model"

The first theory to introduce the new classical approach was Milton Friedman's "fooling model," developed as part of his Presidential Address to the American Economic Association in 1967.[2]

Distinctive Features: Market Clearing and Imperfect Information

The first distinctive feature of Friedman's model is that (unlike some new Keynesian models) firms and workers are never required to operate off the

---

[2]Milton Friedman, "The Role of Monetary Policy," *American Economic Review,* vol. 58 (March 1968), pp. 1–17.

Milton Friedman
(1912–) Friedman, a 1976 Nobel Prize winner, is the most famous proponent of policy rules (Chapter 14) and the inventor of the permanent income hypothesis of consumption (Chapter 15).

labor demand and supply curves. Such models are often called classical, equilibrium, or market-clearing models. The second distinctive feature is that business cycles can occur only if workers *inaccurately perceive the price level,* hence the label "fooling model." This feature of the Friedman model is often called "imperfect information" and is a characteristic of many modern models of the market-clearing variety.

The fooling model is illustrated in Figure 17-1, which in the left frame copies the labor supply and demand curves of Figure 7-11 (p. 218), and in the right frame copies the short-run aggregate supply curve and one of the aggregate demand curves (AD_0) from the same figure. Friedman's treatment of the labor demand curve is identical to the Keynesian model in Figure 7-11; he assumes that the labor demand (N^d) curve depends on the actual real wage (W/P). Thus the *countercyclical* movement of the real wage occurs along the N^d line in Figure 17-1, just as in Figure 7-11. But Friedman adds one important new element. In his interpretation, the labor supply curve depends on the *expected real wage* (W/P^e), that is, the nominal wage rate (W) divided by the price level expected by workers (P^e).

Friedman's theory of the business cycle argues that an increase in aggregate demand raises the actual price level (P) and reduces the actual real wage (W/P), encouraging firms to hire more workers along their labor demand curve. For instance, in the right-hand frame of Figure 17-1 a upward shift of the aggregate demand curve from AD_0 to AD_1 shifts the economy's short-run

UNEMPLOYMENT IN THE ORIGINAL KEYNESIAN MODEL

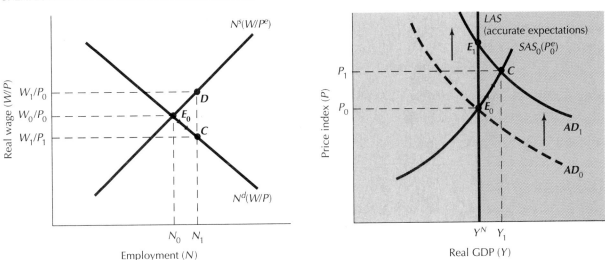

Figure 17-1   **Effects on the Price Index and Real Income of an increase in the Nominal Money Supply While the Expected Price Level Is Fixed at P_0^e**

The position of the short-run aggregate supply curve (SAS_0) in the right frame is fixed by the assumed constancy of the price level expected by workers (P_0^e). A higher nominal money supply shifts the aggregate demand curve upward from AD_0 to AD_1, and the economy moves from point E_0 to C in both the left frame and the right frame. Because the actual price level has risen from P_0 to P_1, the firms are happy to hire additional labor input at point C in the left frame, but the workers think that their real wage has increased to point D and are happy to provide more labor input for as long as W/P^e remains high.

equilibrium from point E_0 to point C, raises real GDP from Y^N to Y_1, and raises the price level from P_0 to P_1. At point C in the left frame of Figure 17-1, N_1 workers are hired as the higher price level pushes the real wage down.

Yet only the firms know that the price level has increased; the *workers do not*. They still think the expected price level is P_0^e. If the firms raise the nominal wage rate from W_0 to W_1, workers will think that the expected real wage has increased from W_0/P_0^e to W_1/P_0^e and will happily work harder, moving up their labor supply curve to point D.

To explain business cycles, the Friedman model requires that the price level *(P)* differs from the expected price level *(P^e)*. Thus, in the right-hand frame of Figure 17-1, output can differ from Y^N along the SAS_0 supply curve only if P differs from the expected price level P_0^e. What happens when the workers catch on to the fact that they have been fooled? Their expected price level will rise, and workers will demand a nominal wage increase sufficient to regain the original real wage level. As a result, the supply curve will shift up and to the left. This process will continue until output has returned to Y^N along the vertical *LAS* line at a point like E_1.

Because the level of output is always equal to natural real GDP *(Y^N)* when expectations are accurate, the vertical *LAS* line is labeled "accurate expectations" in the right-hand frame of Figure 17-1. Sooner or later any expectational errors will be corrected, so output cannot remain away from natural real GDP *(Y^N)* for long. As a result, Friedman's model is sometimes called a "natural rate" model, and in fact it is Friedman who is responsible for the terms "natural real GDP" and "natural rate of unemployment." It is common to describe a model with a vertical long-run supply curve (like *LAS* in Figure 17-1) as obeying the **natural rate hypothesis.**

A model obeys the **natural rate hypothesis** when shifts in aggregate demand have no long-run effect on real GDP.

Criticisms of the Fooling Model

How does Friedman justify the claim of his fooling model that workers will hold incorrect expectations for any significant period of time? Friedman argues that *firms have more accurate information than is available to workers.* Firms have this information advantage because they have a concentrated interest in a small number of prices of particular products and monitor them continuously. Workers, on the other hand, are interested in a wide variety of prices of the things they buy and have insufficient time to keep careful track. Thus workers do not notice immediately when the price level rises.

Three questions can be raised about Friedman's model. First, workers and their families buy many goods, particularly gasoline, food, and drug items, on at least a weekly basis and would discover almost immediately if the prices of these items had risen. Second, if expectational errors really were the source of business cycles, workers could easily discover within a month or two that the aggregate price level had risen, since the media give prominent coverage to monthly changes in the Consumer Price Index. Third, if periods of high real GDP were *always* accompanied by an increase in the aggregate price level, workers would eventually suspect that a new interval of high production and easily available job opportunities would also be accompanied by an increase in the price level.

Each of these three criticisms raises serious doubts that workers would so easily be fooled as Friedman supposes. If workers are not fooled, an increase in demand that raises the general price level would bring instant demands for nominal wage increases that exactly match the price increases. Yet equal-sized increases in W and P would leave the real wage (W/P) unchanged and would leave employment at its original level, N_0. There would be no business cycle in employment or output; so with reasonably intelligent workers the Friedman model fails as a theory of the business cycle.

17-3   The Lucas Model and the Policy Ineffectiveness Proposition

The Assumption of Rational Expectations

Rational expectations need not be correct but must make the best use of available information, avoiding errors that could have been foreseen by knowledge of history.

The **Lucas model** is based on the three assumptions of market clearing, imperfect information, and rational expectations.

Robert E. Lucas, Jr.
(1937–) Lucas, a 1995 Nobel Prize winner, is the leading developer of the new classical macroeconomics; he merged the concept of rational expectations with the assumptions of market clearing and imperfect information.

Despite its limitations, the Friedman model, with its twin assumptions of market clearing and imperfect information, appealed to many economists. Preeminent among these was Robert E. Lucas, Jr., who took Friedman's model one step further by introducing an improved treatment of the way workers form their view of the expected price level (P^e). Instead of following Friedman's rather unsatisfactory assumption that workers only gradually adapted their expectations of the price level (P^e) to the actual value of the price level, allowing themselves to be fooled for weeks or even months, Lucas introduced the theory of **rational expectations.** Thus the **Lucas model** contains three basic assumptions: market clearing, imperfect information, and rational expectations.[3]

Expectations are rational *when people make the best forecasts they can with the available data.* It is important to recognize that these forecasts do not have to be correct, and so observing forecasting errors by individuals or professional economists does not constitute evidence against rational expectations. Instead, the theory of rational expectations argues that people do not consistently make the same forecasting errors.

For instance, the errors (or fooling) of Milton Friedman's workers are not rational. If the observance of past history suggested that any increase in employment had always been accompanied by a reduction in the actual real wage to a point below the expected real wage, then workers should anticipate that such *a reduction in the real wage would always accompany offers by employers of higher employment* and the workers would refuse such job offers. Workers would not provide more employment, since in Figure 17-1 employment cannot rise above N_0 along the workers' labor supply curve (N^s), unless the actual real wage rises above the original level W_0/P_0. More generally, individuals should not make errors in the same direction week after week, especially in circumstances similar to those that have occurred before. The errors should be random, that is, independent of previous forecasting errors.

---

[3]Robert Lucas did not invent the idea of rational expectations, but rather receives credit for applying it to macroeconomics. The original idea was applied to microeconomic issues and was set forth in John Muth, "Rational Expectations and the Theory of Price Movements," *Econometrica,* vol. 29 (July 1961), pp. 315–35. Lucas's seminal contribution is contained in two articles. The more accessible of these is Robert E. Lucas, Jr., "Some International Evidence on Output-Inflation Tradeoffs," *American Economic Review,* vol. 63 (June 1973), pp. 326–34. A more technical article that motivates some of the assumed underlying microeconomic behavior is "Expectations and the Neutrality of Money," *Journal of Economic Theory,* vol. 4 (April 1972), pp. 103–24.

The Friedman-Lucas Supply Function and the "Price Surprise"

The Friedman model implies a positively sloped aggregate supply curve, as in the right-hand frame of Figure 17-1. This supply curve is drawn again in Figure 17-2 and labeled SAS_0 (P_0^e), with the term in parentheses indicating that the position of the SAS curve is shifted whenever workers change their expectations of the price level. For instance, a higher expected price level (P_1^e) would shift the SAS curve up from SAS_0 to SAS_1.

Note that we have drawn the supply curve in Figure 17-2 as a straight, positively sloped line rather than as a curved line; this allows us to use a simple equation to represent the supply curve:

$$Y = Y^N + h(P - P^e) \tag{17.1}$$

This states that real GDP (Y) is equal to natural real GDP (Y^N), plus an amount that equals a coefficient (h) times the excess of the actual price level over the expected price level. This excess of P over P^e is sometimes called the price surprise. For instance, if $P = 1.1$ and $P^e = 1.0$, while $Y^N = 4000$ and $h = 2000$, then the price surprise is 0.1 and actual real GDP will be

$$Y = 4000 + 2000 (1.1 - 1.0) = 4200$$

Although equation (17.1) or the equivalent SAS curve in Figure 17-2 is now usually called the Lucas supply function, such a function is also implied by Friedman's model. As a compromise, we describe it as the Friedman-Lucas supply function. What Lucas contributed was to take Friedman's two assumptions of market clearing and imperfect information, assumed in equation (17.1), and add the third assumption that expectations are formed rationally.

SELF-TEST | According to the Friedman-Lucas supply function, does a recession in which Y falls below Y^N require a price surprise? In which direction?

Figure 17-2
The Short-Run Aggregate Supply Curve Drawn for Two Alternative Values of the Expected Price Level

The Friedman-Lucas supply curve is fixed in position by the price expectations of workers. Real GDP can rise above Y^N in the pink region only when the actual price level (P) rises above the expected price level (P^e). An increase in the expected price level from P_0^e to P_1^e shifts the curve up from SAS_0 to SAS_1.

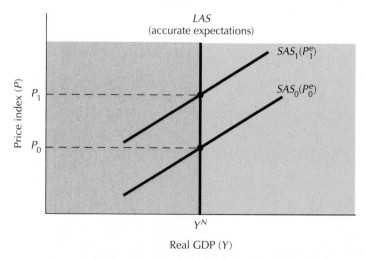

THE FRIEDMAN-LUCAS SUPPLY CURVE

Why does a positive price surprise make firms produce more output, as assumed by the Friedman-Lucas supply function? Unlike the Friedman version of the model, which emphasizes fooling workers, the Lucas version emphasizes an information barrier shared by workers and firms alike. Firms sell in competitive markets and have no control over their own prices, which rise and fall in response to demand. Lucas's firms are like small farmers who produce wheat or corn and whose sales prices are determined at the Chicago Board of Trade. For firms to produce more, the price of their product must rise relative to marginal cost, which depends on the cost of raw materials and other goods purchased from suppliers. Firms know their own price, but information barriers prevent firms from knowing about prices charged in other markets. If there is a general increase in all prices, firms will observe first only their own price, while information barriers prevent them from observing prices charged by suppliers.

Slope of the Supply Function: Local Versus Aggregate Price Shocks.   To overcome these barriers, firms use rational expectations to form the best possible estimate of the prices charged in other markets (P^e). If the price of their own product (P) rises relative to P^e, and thus relative to marginal cost, firms will anticipate higher profits and increase production. Hence Y rises above Y^N, as shown in equation (17.1). Thus the Lucas explanation of the business cycle hinges entirely on whether or not business firms believe that an increase in the price of their own product *will be experienced equally* by other firms. If firms guess that prices charged by their suppliers have risen as much as their own price, they will see no advantage to producing more now. If firms guess that prices charged by suppliers have *not* risen as much as their own price, they will produce more.

How do firms make this prediction? They apply rational expectations to their knowledge of past price behavior. If past movements in their own *prices have always been accompanied by similar movements in prices of suppliers,* then firms should expect that this will happen again. P^e will be assumed to rise in proportion to P, and output will not increase. But if the firm's price has often exhibited unique movements in response to "local conditions," for example, changes in weather altering the supply of wheat, then P may have risen without any accompanying increase in suppliers' prices. In this case firms may guess that P^e has not risen as much as P, and that this is a good time to produce.

In short, for products that in the past have experienced unique price movements in response to local conditions, firms may raise production substantially in response to a demand increase that raises the price of their own products. In contrast, for products that typically have experienced price movements that mimic those in the rest of the economy, firms will predict that their own price increase will be duplicated by increases in the costs of raw materials purchased from suppliers, and they will refuse to raise production.

A major contribution of Lucas's analysis is the conclusion that the supply response (h in equation 17.1) will be high for firms that have previously experienced unique price movements, and low for firms that have experienced price movements mimicking those in the aggregate economy. Lucas also predicted that the supply response would be high in countries like the United States, where the inflation rate has been relatively stable (making unique movements in individual prices more important). In contrast, the supply response would be small in countries like Brazil and Argentina, where the inflation rate has ranged from zero to 1000 percent per year over the past few decades, and where movements in the aggregate price level *shared by all firms* completely swamp the influence of price movements for particular products.

Lucas's key insight helps explain how countries like Brazil can have huge price movements with relatively small business cycles in real GDP. Stated another way, it explains why countries like Brazil can have a much steeper *SAS* curve than countries like the United States. Prior to Lucas, economists had assumed that the *SAS* curve in all countries would have roughly the same slope.

The Policy Ineffectiveness Proposition

The concept of rational expectations, which states that individuals use all available information in forming their expectations, leads to a startling prediction by Lucas and his followers. In a modern version of monetary impotence, Lucas argues that *anticipated monetary policy cannot change real GDP in a regular or predictable way.* Usually called the **policy ineffectiveness proposition** (PIP), Lucas's argument for monetary impotence startled the economics profession when it was developed in the early 1970s.[4]

The **policy ineffectiveness proposition** asserts that predictable changes in monetary policy cannot affect real output.

PIP can be understood in terms of equation (17.1), which states that the monetary authority (the Fed) can change output only if it can find some method of creating a price surprise. That is, the Fed must move P while not simultaneously moving P^e by the same amount. Yet if the public *knows* that an increase in the money supply raises the price level, and if the Fed's monetary stimulus is announced or can be *predicted* from the Fed's past behavior, then the public will boost the expected price level P^e along with the increase in the actual price level. Real GDP will not budge from natural real GDP (Y^N).

Thus PIP suggests that the Fed cannot announce a monetary stimulus in advance if it wants to raise real GDP. But even worse, the Fed cannot create a monetary stimulus under conditions similar to those in which it has previously created a stimulus, *because people will anticipate the stimulus and adjust P^e accordingly.* PIP seems, then, to mark the demise of a regular **feedback rule** in which monetary policy would respond to higher unemployment by stimulating the economy, or would respond to higher inflation by restrictive actions. Seeing higher unemployment or higher inflation, individuals would anticipate the Fed's response by shifting their estimate of P^e, leaving the Fed's response without any effect on real GDP.

A **feedback rule** sets stabilization policy to respond in a regular way to a macroeconomic event, like an increase in unemployment or inflation.

> **Summary:** The policy ineffectiveness proposition states only that fully anticipated changes in the money supply cannot affect real GDP. It does not deny that a money surprise (an unanticipated change in the money supply) can alter the level of real GDP. But it implies that the Fed faces a considerable problem in creating such a money surprise, since the Fed cannot respond to economic events in the same way it has in the past.

---

[4]While Lucas receives the main credit for the basic ideas underlying the Lucas model, the formal case for PIP was made by Thomas J. Sargent and Neil Wallace in "'Rational' Expectations, the Optimal Monetary Instrument, and the Optimal Money Supply Rule," *Journal of Political Economy*, vol. 83 (April 1975), pp. 241–54.

Problem: The Prompt Availability of Information

Although PIP created a revolution that dominated macroeconomic discussion in the late 1970s, by the end of the decade several weaknesses of PIP had been pointed out. The problem was not the Lucas contribution of rational expectations. Rather, the weakness was in the twin assumptions inherited from Friedman, continuous market clearing and imperfect information, which made deviations of the current actual price from the expected price the *only* source of business cycle movements in real GDP. The assumption of imperfect information implies that business cycles would be eliminated if we had accurate current information about the aggregate price level. All that is needed to eliminate the business cycle is for rational individuals to know that they could avoid departures from their own most efficient levels of activity if only they monitored published aggregate price information.

This imperfect information aspect of the Friedman and Lucas models has been widely criticized. Aggregate price information is easily available when short lags (announcements of monthly Consumer Price Index [CPI] changes) are made on the nightly television news the day they are announced. With aggregate price information easily available, why should firms or workers take any action that might move them away from labor market equilibrium, when all they have to do is wait a few days or weeks to learn the latest monthly change in the CPI?

17-4   The Real Business Cycle Model

The **real business cycle (RBC) model** explains business cycles in output and employment as being caused by technology or supply shocks.

There now appears to be general agreement that the Lucas imperfect information theory of the business cycle is unsatisfactory, since information lags are too short to be a plausible source of multiyear business cycles.[5] New Keynesian economists favor abandoning new classical economics and the assumption of continuous market clearing. Instead, they concentrate on the underlying sources of wage and price rigidity, as shown later in this chapter. Meanwhile, new classical macroeconomists have turned to an alternative theory of the business cycle, one that still assumes continuous market clearing. Their new theory is the **real business cycle (RBC) model** of economic fluctuations.

The RBC model assumes that the origins of the business cycle lie in real (or supply) shocks rather than monetary (or demand) shocks. In terms of our graphical analysis, the main source of shifts in output lies in swings in the aggregate supply curve (both long-run and short-run), not the aggregate demand curve. Contrast this with the Lucas imperfect information approach,

---

[5]For instance, Robert Barro, who made important contributions to the development of the Lucas approach and PIP, was convinced by the problems addressed in the previous section that "the upshot of these arguments is that the new classical approach does not do very well in accounting for an important role of money in business fluctuations." See Robert J. Barro, "New Classicals and Keynesians, or the Good Guys and the Bad Guys," *Schweiz. Zeitschrift für Volkswirtschaft und Statistik,* Heft 3, 1989. More recently, Robert Lucas has admitted that, "Monetary shocks just aren't that important. That's the view I've been driven to. There's no question that's a retreat in my views. See John Cassidy, "The Decline of Economics," *The New Yorker,* December 2, 1996, p. 55.

INTERNATIONAL PERSPECTIVE

Productivity Fluctuations in the United States and Japan

Productivity is simply the ratio of output to inputs and measures the efficiency with which inputs are used. Labor productivity is output per unit of labor input. As we learned in Chapter 10, a more general concept, called multifactor productivity (MFP), is output per unit of total input, including not just labor but also capital, energy, and imported materials.

Interest in the RBC model is motivated by productivity shocks that vary procyclically, that is, in the same direction as the business cycle. How important are procyclical fluctuations of MFP, that is, the ratio of output to total input? The charts on the facing page show the growth rate of output and input for the United States and Japan. Whenever output grows more rapidly than input, MFP growth is positive, as shown by the red-shaded area. Whenever output grows more slowly than input, MFP growth is negative, as shown by the gray-shaded area.

In the top frame of the figure, the data for the United States shows that in booms output growth consistently rises more than input growth (defined here as an average of growth in labor and capital input); during recessions output growth consistently falls more than input growth. As a result, MFP growth is negative in such recession periods as 1970, 1974–75, 1980, 1982, and 1991. MFP growth is most strongly positive when output itself is growing most rapidly, as in 1966, 1973, 1976, 1984, and 1992.

In the bottom frame of the figure, the

data for Japan show some striking differences. First, input growth is much smoother from year to year, with fewer cycles, particularly between 1975 and 1990. Because input growth is so remarkably stable, Japan was largely able to avoid the periodic episodes of massive layoffs that plagued the United States during recession periods. And, because input growth was so stable, Japanese MFP growth is even more strongly procyclical than in the United States.

A second difference is that output growth in Japan, while variable, fell below zero in only two years, 1974 and 1993. A third is that the pattern of MFP growth is quite different than in the United States. MFP growth (the difference between output and input growth) was positive in every year before 1992, except 1965 and 1974. But more recently, MFP growth has been negative in every year, 1992–94. This reflects the dismal performance of the Japanese economy in the 1990s, a sharp contrast to its robust output growth during the decades before 1990.

The procyclical behavior of MFP growth illustrated here is consistent with the procyclical technology shocks that drive the RBC model. However, it is also consistent with other theories, such as the idea that it is costly to hire and fire workers, with the result that firms adjust labor input only partially in response to changes in output. Other differences between Japanese and American labor markets are examined in the box on pp. 208-209.

in which unanticipated monetary shocks led to cycles in real output and employment (because information barriers prevented business firms from accurately anticipating movements in prices charged in markets other than their own). In terms of the Friedman-Lucas supply function (equation 17.1), the RBC approach is not based on price surprises, that is, deviations of P from P^e. Instead, the RBC approach states that fluctuations in Y are caused entirely by fluctuations in natural real GDP itself, Y^N.

What are these real (or supply) shocks that cause business cycles and account for the term "real" business cycle model? Shocks can include new

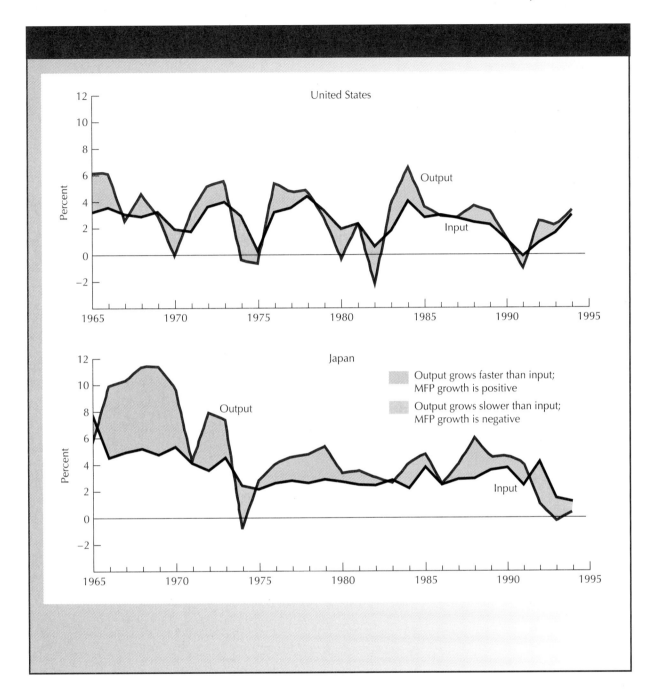

production techniques, new products, bad weather, new sources of materials, and price changes in raw materials. Recall that the Lucas model failed
to consider that information barriers are too short-lived to explain the *length*
and *persistence* of actual business cycles. In contrast, the RBC approach
assumes that these supply shocks are highly persistent, meaning that a favorable shock lasts several years, dies away smoothly, and is replaced by an
adverse shock that lasts several years. It is important to note that the RBC
theory simply *assumes* and does not explain the persistence of business
cycles that undermined the Lucas approach.

In the RBC model, the economy responds to these persistent supply shocks according to the new classical assumption of continuous equilibrium. Firms produce the amount they desire at prices and wages that respond flexibly to changing economic conditions, and hire the number of workers they want; workers obtain exactly the number of hours of work that they desire at the market-determined real wage.[6] Our aggregate supply curve diagram introduced in Chapter 7 illustrates these aspects of the RBC model.

The Labor Market in the RBC Model

The top frame of Figure 17-3 exhibits the production function *(F)*, which shows how much output can be produced by each additional worker (this is the same production function that appeared in the top left frames of Figures 7-5 and 7-6). An adverse supply shock leads to a downward shift in the production function, for instance from the normal curve F_0 to the bad shock curve F_1, implying a decline in the productivity of each worker. In the lower frame the labor demand curve, which shows the marginal product of labor, shifts down in response to the adverse supply shock from the line labeled N_0^d to the line N_1^d.

The effect of the adverse supply shock on both output and employment depends on the slope of the labor supply curve. If this slope is positive, as along the line labeled N_0^s, then a lower real wage induces workers to supply less labor (working fewer hours or leaving the labor force). Since the economy is always in equilibrium in the RBC model, the demand for labor shifts as a result of the supply shock from point *B* to point *V*. Employment falls from N_0 to N_1, while output falls from Y_0 to Y_1, seen in the upper frame.

A different slope of the labor supply curve would lead to a different conclusion. Imagine that the labor supply curve, instead of being N_0^s is a vertical line rising above N_0 through points *Z* and *B*. Then the economy's equilibrium point would be shifted downward by the adverse supply shock from *B* to *Z*. The shock would cause no change in employment, and in the upper frame there would be a much smaller decline in output, from Y_0 to Y_0'. Thus the RBC model's ability to explain why employment declines in real-world recessions requires a positive slope of the labor supply schedule, as shown by the line N_0^s.

SELF-TEST

> According to the RBC theory, why does output increase in a business expansion? What is the explanation of the theory for the increase in employment that takes place in high-employment years like 1973 and 1996–97?

---

[6]Two of the most influential papers in the development of the RBC approach are Finn E. Kydland and Edward C. Prescott, "Time to Build and Aggregate Fluctuations," *Econometrica,* vol. 50 (November 1982), pp. 1345–70, and Robert G. King and Charles I. Plosser, "Money, Credit, and Prices in a Real Business Cycle," *American Economic Review,* vol. 74 (June 1984), pp. 363–80. A sympathetic exposition is Bennett T. McCallum, "Real Business Cycle Models," in Robert J. Barro, ed., *Modern Business Cycle Theory* (Cambridge, MA, Harvard University Press, 1989), pp. 16–50. A less technical introduction is Charles I. Plosser, "Understanding Real Business Cycles," *Journal of Economic Perspectives,* vol. 3 (Summer 1989), pp. 51–77.

Figure 17-3
Effect of an Adverse Supply Shock on Output and Employment in the Real Business Cycle Model

In the top frame F_0 is the normal production function, identical to curve F_0 in Figures 7-5 and 7-6. N_0^d is the normal labor demand curve. An adverse movement in supply conditions, like bad weather for growing crops, shifts the production function down to F_1 and the labor demand curve down to N_1^d. In normal times the economy operates at point B in the upper and lower frames, and in bad times at point V. The decline in employment depends on the slope of the labor supply curve; if the labor supply curve were a vertical line instead of a positively sloped line like N_0^s, the economy would move to Z instead of V. Employment would remain fixed and output would fall only from Y_0 to Y_0'.

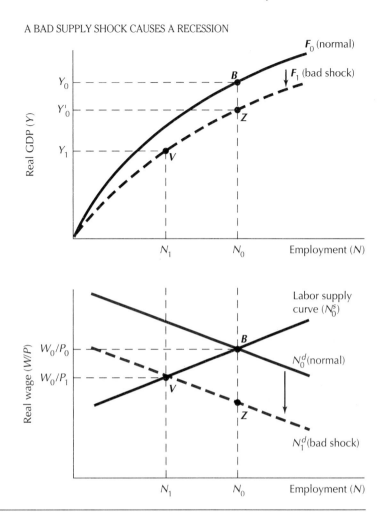

A BAD SUPPLY SHOCK CAUSES A RECESSION

Labor Supply Behavior and Intertemporal Substitution

As we have seen, it is critical for the RBC model that the labor supply curve have a positive slope, as drawn in the bottom frame of Figure 17-3. If the labor supply curve were vertical, the model would be able to explain business cycles of output (as from point B to Z in the upper frame) but would not be able to explain fluctuations of employment over the business cycle. Thus an explanation of the positive slope of the labor supply curve is an important component of RBC analysis.

The traditional microeconomic analysis of labor supply decisions stresses two conflicting effects of an increase in the real wage. A higher real wage increases the reward for work as compared to leisure (the substitution effect). But a higher real wage also raises real income and makes people want to consume more of all normal goods, including leisure, which means reducing work (the income effect). In drawing a positively sloped labor supply curve in Figure 17-3, we simply assume that the substitution effect dominates the income effect.

Intertemporal substitution occurs when workers work more in periods of high real wages and less in periods of low real wages. It also occurs when producers raise output in periods of high prices and reduce output in periods of low prices.

The RBC approach also assumes that the substitution effect is dominant, but stresses a particular dimension of substitution that takes place over time. This type of substitution is called **intertemporal substitution.** It occurs when workers reallocate the amount of working time in response to changes in the real wage. In good times, when the real wage is high, workers choose to work more. And they take more leisure in bad times, when the real wage is low.

Students face such choices during their college years. Many students want to take one summer off to go to Europe, while planning to work in the other summers. A sophomore has two summers left before graduation. Which summer should he or she choose to go to Europe? Obviously, the summer with the best opportunities to earn relatively high wages should be chosen for work, and the European trip should be taken in the summer when high-paying jobs are scarce.

Variations in the interest rate introduce another element into the choice. If the real interest rate is high enough, it would pay to work in the first summer and postpone the trip to the second summer. Even if the wages earned in the first summer are somewhat lower than they are expected to be in the second summer, the extra interest earned on the savings account containing the earnings from the first summer would make that a better choice. In short, labor supply increases in response *either* to a high real wage or a high real interest rate.

This example highlights a problem in applying the theory of intertemporal substitution to the real world—how can students predict which future summer is likely to provide the most high-paying job opportunities? If even financial experts make major mistakes in predicting interest rates, are students any more likely to be able to predict whether interest rates will be higher or lower in future summers?

How the Economy Responds to Supply Shocks

The term supply shock refers to any event that can shift the production function, changing the amount of real GDP that can be produced by a given amount of labor and capital. The RBC model posits that there are periods when productivity is temporarily high or temporarily low (the latter was assumed in drawing Figure 17-3). A period of low productivity would be one in which work effort and consumption are reduced in favor of leisure. Also, the decline in work would reduce not just consumption but also investment, so that the future capital stock would be lower.

The central element of the RBC model is that workers and firms *choose* to reduce employment and output in bad times and raise employment and output in good times. These choices are optimal, given that shocks are outside of their control. There is no room whatsoever for government stabilization policy, because government intervention would only make things worse, distorting employment and output from the optimal amounts that workers and firms have chosen.

A Broader Interpretation of the Shocks

While early versions of the RBC model focused on fluctuations in technical efficiency as the main cause of business cycles, more recent research has broadened the range of events that could cause shocks in the model. There has been special interest in studying the effects of changes in government spending and tax rates. Such changes in government policies introduce real *demand* shocks as a source of business cycles. The effects of increases in government spending in boosting output and crowding out investment are qualitatively similar to those in the *IS-LM* model. The new insight is that the quantitative impact of these changes depends on how long they last, that is, how persistent they are expected to be.

Changes in consumer tastes and preferences can also be interpreted as real demand shocks. In this broader interpretation, the RBC model does not attempt to attribute all business cycles to changes in technology or other supply factors. Both demand and supply shocks matter. The distinguishing features of the RBC approach, then, are the assumption of market-clearing equilibrium based on optimal choices of workers and firms, the lack of any role for stabilization policy, and the absence of any distinction between actual and natural (or long-run) real GDP.

17-5   New Classical Macroeconomics: Limitations and Positive Contributions

Assessment of the Real Business Cycle Model

Both the RBC model and the conventional *AD-SAS* graphical analysis of Chapter 7 agree that supply shocks can cause business cycles. Why, then, is the RBC model so controversial? The criticisms concern the unique components of the RBC analysis: the emphasis on technological shocks as the *sole* cause of business cycles, the failure to include prices or money, and the RBC interpretation of what happens in labor markets during business cycles.

Nature of Technology Shocks. Critics focus on two aspects of the RBC model's treatment of technology shocks. While it is plausible that *advances* in technology may occur at an irregular pace, causing cycles in the growth rate of output, the implication that recessions are caused by *retreats* in technology ("forgetfulness") strikes some critics as implausible. Defenders of the RBC model respond that there are several types of events that have the same effect as a decay in technology, even if people do not literally forget how to produce efficiently. These include bad harvests, oil price shocks, and government regulations that require heavy investment and extra workers to reduce air and water pollution.

Perhaps a more serious charge distinguishes between the aggregate economy and the behavior of individual industries. Unlike the *IS-LM* model of Chapter 4, the RBC model does not incorporate a multiplier effect that can magnify the impact of shocks on the economy. Therefore, to explain big recessions, the model needs big shocks. But technology is unique to particular industries. Highly distinctive technological innovations that, for instance, increase the speed of a Windows desktop computer have little impact on the productivity of coal miners. At an industry level, one would expect technological shocks (good and bad) to occur randomly, so that favorable shocks in some industries would largely cancel out adverse shocks in other industries. Any bad shock large enough to cause an economywide recession (considering that it would be partly canceled by good shocks in other industries) would be highly visible in industry data. Yet the proponents of the RBC model have as yet failed to identify any such shocks, particularly negative ones, other than the two OPEC oil price shocks.

Price and Output Changes.   Although recently there has been some attention to real demand shocks, particularly those associated with government spending, the basic RBC model is based on an alternation of good and bad supply shocks, each persisting by about as long as an average U.S. business cycle. But this leads to a troublesome implication: If business cycles occur when the aggregate supply curve shifts back and forth but the aggregate demand curve remains fixed, then prices should rise in recessions and fall in booms. The business cycle should look much like the market for wheat, with low prices and high output in years of good harvests, and with high prices and low output in years with bad harvests.

The key problem is that prices are sometimes positively related to output changes, as in the Great Depression, and sometimes negatively related to output changes, as in the supply shock episodes of the 1970s and early 1980s. This suggests that business cycles are caused both by demand and supply shocks, not just by supply shocks. The recent interest of RBC proponents in treating the effects of government policy changes as real demand shocks seems a step in the right direction.

Real Wages and Employment

As we have seen, both the RBC model and the graphical *AD-SAS* analysis can easily explain why, due to shifts in the production function, output changes in response to supply shocks. But in order to explain why employment fluctuates in the same direction as output over the business cycle, the labor supply curve must be positively sloped, as in Figure 17-3. To support this interpretation, we should observe that real wages move *procyclically,* that is, in the same direction as output. Note that this is the opposite prediction of the Friedman fooling model, which depict's the economy as operating continuously along the labor demand curve, so that the real wage rate must fluctuate *countercyclically.*

However, most of the statistical evidence shows that (with the exception of the big oil shocks of the 1970s and early 1980s) there is no systematic movement of real wages. If anything, there is a slight tendency of prices to rise more than wages in economic booms, implying countercyclical real wages. As we saw in Table 7-2, real wages actually rose during the Great Depression from 1929–33, even while the unemployment rate was rising from 3 to 25 percent. Thus it seems that the central mechanism that drives employment fluctuations in the RBC model is absent in most U.S. business cycles other than the oil shock episodes of the 1973–82 period.

Positive Contributions of New Classical Macroeconomics

Despite their limitations, both the Lucas and RBC versions of new classical theory have a strong appeal to a broad range of economists. What are the attractions of new classical theory?

Rational Expectations: Linking Micro- and Macroeconomics.   The assumption of rational expectations appeals to economists, since it requires that people do not repeat their mistakes. Instead, people make the best use of all available information to guide their economic behavior. Such an approach is much more appealing than the alternative assumption that people make repeated mistakes in the same direction, period after period. The rational expectations hypothesis also has appeal because of its grounding in microeconomics. This means that the assumption of rational expectations in macroeconomics parallels the basic microeconomic assumptions of profit maximization and utility maximization.

The Theory of Efficient Financial Markets.   Many of the ideas developed by the new classical economists have been applied successfully to markets where continuous market clearing is a reasonable assumption. This is particularly true of financial markets, including the stock market, bond market, foreign exchange market, and the markets for agricultural and crude commodities, like sugar and gold. The theory of efficient markets incorporates the assumption of rational expectations. Expectations are assumed to incorporate all available information, implying that stock prices jump the instant new information is received, and that there are no opportunities to make extraordinary profits on the stock market without access to inside information.

Greater Understanding of Economic Policy.   The idea that individuals in the private part of the economy have rational expectations has improved our understanding of economic policy. Even if long-term wage and price contracts impede the flexibility of wages and prices, as discussed later in this chapter, those who negotiate contracts attempt to do so with full information on what policymakers are likely to do. For instance, wage negotiators who suspect that the government will allow rapid inflation after a supply shock are likely to demand full cost-of-living adjustments in their contracts. In contrast, past refusal of a government to allow rapid inflation following a supply shock, as in the case of the German Bundesbank in the 1970s, will increase wage negotiators' confidence that full cost-of-living protection is not necessary.

Recall that the policy ineffectiveness proposition (PIP) developed as part of the Lucas information-barrier approach implies that fully anticipated monetary policy changes have no effect at all on output. While PIP does not appear to be valid in U.S. history, a milder and more acceptable proposition is that fully anticipated policy changes have *smaller* effects than unanticipated changes. The expansionary policies pursued in the United States in the 1960s caused the output ratio to exceed 100 percent for a few years, but not permanently. In contrast, in extreme inflationary episodes (hyperinflation), radical changes in government policy seemed to halt inflation without a major decline in output.[7]

Pervasive Effect on Economic Research.   Even if the new classical theories of the business cycle are subject to substantial skepticism, new techniques of analysis introduced by these theories have had a major influence on the way

---

[7]See Thomas J. Sargent, "The Ends of Four Big Inflations," Chapter 3 in his *Rational Expectations and Inflation* (New York: Harper & Row, 1986).

economists study variables such as consumption, investment, and the foreign exchange rate. The understanding of extreme episodes of inflation in places like Argentina and Brazil, as well as Israel, is just one contribution of techniques introduced by new classical economists. The distinction between anticipated policy changes and policy "surprises" has improved our understanding of policy changes.

Finally, the development of the RBC model has raised profound questions about the meaning of a business cycle. A simplistic view would be that natural output (Y^N) grows smoothly at the same rate forever. At the other extreme, the RBC model eliminates the distinction between Y and Y^N, instead attempting to explain why there is a business cycle in Y^N. An intermediate view is that Y and Y^N are distinct, but that the growth rate of Y^N itself may vary over the business cycle (this intermediate view is reflected in the data on Y^N listed in Appendix A). Recent research claims that a substantial fraction of the output fluctuations in quarterly data is associated with movements in long-run growth rather than purely transitory business cycles. This research aims to improve our understanding of the link between changes in long-run growth and cyclical swings and argues against a sharp dichotomy between policies to dampen cycles and those to stimulate growth.

17-6 Essential Features of the New Keynesian Economics

Common Elements of the Original and New Keynesian Approaches

The adjective *new* distinguishes modern developments in Keynesian theory from the original Keynesian model developed during the Great Depression by Keynes and his followers and reviewed in Section 7-10. The original Keynesian model combines a theory of shifts in aggregate demand (based on the *IS-LM* model of Chapter 4) with a theory of aggregate supply (based on the arbitrary assumption of a fixed nominal wage). Unlike the old and new classical models, with their assumptions of continuous equilibrium, or market clearing, the Keynesian approach does not insist that markets clear continuously. Hence the Keynesian model, either the original or the new variety, is often dubbed a **non-market-clearing model,** conveying the failure of prices to adjust rapidly enough to clear markets within a relatively short interval after a demand or supply shock. If slow price adjustment makes the return of the economy to natural output a long, drawn-out process, the economy can remain in a state of disequilibrium for years.

In a **non-market-clearing model,** workers and firms are not continuously on their respective demand and supply schedules, but rather are pushed off these schedules by the gradual adjustment of prices.

The appeal of Keynesian economics stems from the evident unhappiness of workers and firms during recessions and depressions. Workers and firms *do not act as if they were making a voluntary choice to cut production and hours worked.* A simple thought experiment is enough. Ask yourself these questions about the real world: Can each worker during every day of a recession sell all the labor desired at the going wage and price? Would every worker in a recession refuse a job offer at the going wage and price? Then ask these related questions about business firms: Can each business firm sell all the output desired at today's prices? Would each business firm turn away customers at today's prices? The history of business cycles is punctuated by recessions and depressions lasting several years, during which workers and firms could not sell all the labor and output desired at the going wages and prices. Thus, a theory of business cycles based on the failure of markets to clear, the new Keynesians believe, is more realistic than the new classical approach based on continuous market clearing.

In new classical models, business firms base their output level on news regarding their own price level, obtained from auction markets like the Chicago Board of Trade. In contrast, Keynesian non-market-clearing models turn the role of prices and output upside down. New Keynesian business firms base their choice of the price level on news regarding their own sales obtained by watching the ebb and flow of customers coming through the front door.

The New Keynesian Model

The **new Keynesian economics** explains rigidity in prices and wages as consistent with the self-interest of firms and workers, all of which are assumed to have rational expectations.

A **nominal rigidity** is a factor that inhibits the flexibility of the nominal price level due to some factor, such as menu costs and staggered contracts. Such factors make it costly for firms to change the nominal price or wage level.

A **real rigidity** is a factor that makes firms reluctant to change the real wage, the relative wage, or the relative price.

A **menu cost** is any expense associated with changing prices, including the costs of printing new menus or distributing new catalogs.

Staggered contracts are wage contracts that have different expiration dates for different groups of firms or workers.

What, then, is the difference between the original and **new Keynesian economics?** Both assume that prices adjust slowly. But unlike the original model, which assumed a fixed nominal wage, the new Keynesian approach *attempts to explain the microeconomic foundations of slow adjustment of both wages and prices.* The new Keynesian approach borrows—some would say steals—the concept of rational expectations from new classical economics. From traditional microeconomics the new Keynesian approach borrows the core assumptions that firms maximize profits and workers maximize their own well-being or utility. The achievement of new Keynesian economics is to show how firms and workers make choices that maximize business profits and worker well-being at the microeconomic level, but that have adverse social consequences at the macroeconomic level.

Two distinctions are essential to the new Keynesian model. The first is between wage setting in labor markets and price setting in product markets. Following the original Keynesian element of the rigid wage, the first wave of new Keynesian theorizing attempted to explain why wages are sticky. Yet the stickiness of wages is not sufficient to explain why there are fluctuations of real output. If profits were sufficiently flexible, prices could also be flexible, rising and falling in exact proportion to changes in nominal demand and leaving output fixed. This realization has shifted attention to the product market to uncover reasons why prices are insufficiently flexible to mimic fluctuations in nominal GDP.

The second distinction is between **nominal rigidity** and **real rigidity.** Markets will not clear if something prevents the full adjustment of nominal prices, that is, prevents movements in nominal prices *(P)* proportionate to movements in nominal demand *(X)*. The first group of new Keynesian theories explains wage or price stickiness as the result of factors that make prices costly to adjust. Included in this category are **menu costs** and overlapping **staggered contracts,** which limit the flexibility of both prices and wages. These factors are said to explain *nominal rigidity,* because they deal with barriers to the adjustment of nominal prices.

New Keynesian theories also explain *real rigidities,* the stickiness of a wage relative to another wage, of a wage relative to a price, or of a price relative to another price. Theories that explain real rigidities in labor markets include the efficiency wage model, which we will examine later in the chapter. Critics note that theories of real rigidities do not explain nominal rigidity, since nothing prevents each individual agent from indexing nominal price to nominal aggregate demand, that is, automatically changing P by the same percentage change as X, thus leaving real output (Y) unaffected. We will be particularly interested in the arguments given by new Keynesians for the absence of such full indexation, which in turn would suggest that theories of real rigidities *are* relevant to the explanation of sticky prices and wages.[8]

17-7 Why Small Nominal Rigidities Have Large Macroeconomic Effects

A basic insight of Keynesian theory, both old and new, is that decisions of individual business firms do not always serve the best interests of society. The original Keynesian model argued that stimulative fiscal policy might be needed to avoid an economic slump resulting from some combination of monetary impotence, a failure of self-correction, and fixed wages. The new Keynesian model does not place any special emphasis on fiscal policy as opposed to monetary policy. Instead, it shows how rational profit-maximizing decisions by business firms may have adverse consequences for society.

Price Setting by a Monopolistic Firm

An **auction market** is a centralized location where professional traders buy and sell a commodity or a financial security.

The new classical and new Keynesian approaches view business firm behavior from different perspectives. In the new classical model, firms are assumed to be perfectly competitive "price takers," with no control over the price. This approach may describe farmers producing goods sold on an **auction market,** like wheat or corn sold on the Chicago Board of Trade. Such farmers choose how much to produce but have no control over price. However, the assumption of perfect competition does not apply to firms in most other sectors of the economy. Imperfect competition describes a market in which the number of sellers is sufficiently small that each firm is a price setter rather than a price taker. For instance, manufacturing firms, airlines, and many other firms can choose exactly what price to set, but they have no control over the amount sold. An airline enters a price schedule into the reservations computer and then waits to see how many passengers show up on the plane.

The new Keynesian approach assumes that small menu costs will deter imperfectly competitive firms from constantly changing their prices and shows that menu costs do not have to be large to explain price stickiness. To see why, look at the left-hand frame of Figure 17-4, where we review the ele-

---

[8]The best source of accessible articles on the new Keynesian version of macroeconomics can be found in a symposium in the *Journal of Economic Perspectives,* Winter 1993, vol. 7, no. 1. David Romer provides an introduction to several of the models reviewed in this chapter; Bruce Greenwald and Joseph Stiglitz contrast the "new" and "old" Keynesians; James Tobin provides new insights on the old Keynesian model; and finally Robert G. King provides an insightful bridge between the new Keynesians and the *IS-LM* model.

HOW A MONOPOLIST SETS PRICE TO MAXIMIZE PROFITS

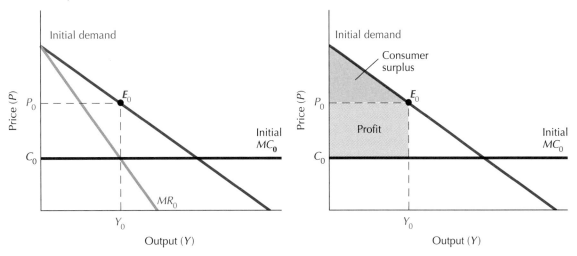

Figure 17-4 **The Price-Setting Decision of a Monopolist**

In the left frame the darker red slanted line is the initial demand curve and the red MR_0 line is the marginal revenue curve. The horizontal black line is the initial marginal cost schedule MC_0. Output is chosen where MR equals MC. Price (P_0) is shown at point E_0, the intersection of the demand curve with the quantity produced. In the right frame the gray area shows the consumer surplus, the area below the demand curve and above the price level P_0. Profit is the red rectangle, the area to the left of Y_0 between P_0 and C_0.

mentary theory of price setting by a monopolist.[9] Our diagrams are particularly simple, since they assume that marginal cost is constant along the horizontal line labeled initial MC_0. There are no fixed costs, so marginal cost and average cost are the same. The quantity produced (Y_0) is determined at the point where the marginal revenue line (MR_0) intersects the marginal cost curve. The price is determined at point E_0, where the chosen quantity Y_0 intersects the initial demand curve. The right-hand frame of Figure 17-4 shows exactly the same situation but identifies the areas that indicate the business firm's profit and the consumer surplus enjoyed by the purchasers of the product.[10]

The Firm's Response to a Decline in Demand

To understand how recessions in real output may occur, let us now examine the effects of a decline in the demand for the product. The decline is shown in the left-hand frame of Figure 17-5 by the downward shift from the dashed

---

[9]The presentation in this section is a simplified version of the first half of N. Gregory Mankiw, "Small Menu Costs and Large Business Cycles: A Macroeconomic Model of Monopoly," *Quarterly Journal of Economics,* vol. 100 (May 1985), pp. 529–37.

[10]**Review:** When the demand curve is a straight line, the marginal revenue curve is always drawn so that it lies halfway between the demand curve and the vertical axis. The demand curve shows how much each purchaser is willing to pay for the product. At the price P_0, any purchaser whose willingness to pay is greater than P_0 enjoys a consumer surplus, reflecting the fact that the price charged is less than the willingness to pay.

SMALL MENU COSTS CAN LEAD TO LARGE SOCIAL COSTS

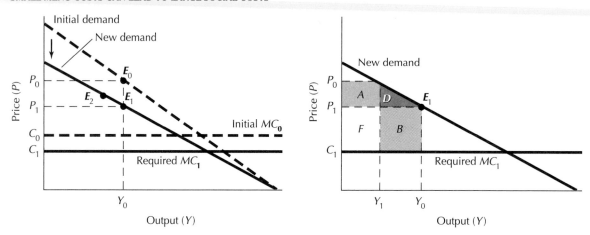

Figure 17-5   The Price-Setting Choice of a Monopolist Facing a Decline in Demand .

In the left frame a decline in demand shifts the demand curve down from the initial demand line to the new demand line. To maintain fixed output at Y_0, the price must fall from P_0 to P_1 and marginal cost must fall to required MC_1. To decide whether or not to reduce price to the profit-maximizing level P_1, the firm weighs the gain in profit (area B minus area A in the right frame) against any menu cost that may be involved in changing price. If the firm fails to cut price below P_0, the level of output falls from Y_0 to Y_1, and society loses the area D plus B, which is much larger than B minus A.

---

red initial demand curve to the solid red new demand curve. To avoid a recession, the firm must produce the same amount as before, Y_0, which intersects the new demand curve at E_1. For unchanged output to be chosen by the profit-maximizing firm at point E_1, it is necessary that marginal cost decline by the amount shown between the initial MC_0 and required MC_1 lines. The lower *black* line is called "required" because a decline in MC is needed to avoid a recession.

Will the firm avoid cutting output by reducing price from P_0 to P_1? Perhaps not, if there are menu costs, because the gain in profit by cutting price may not be sufficient to cover the menu costs. Recall from the right-hand frame of Figure 17-4 that the profit box is a rectangle lying above the MC line with its upper right corner at the equilibrium point E_0 or E_1. Comparing the two profit boxes, by lowering the price from P_0 to P_1, the firm gains the profit area marked B and loses the profit area marked A.

SELF-TEST   Why does area A measure the profit lost? Why does B measure the profit gained? Why must the area B be greater than A?

Despite the gain in profit from cutting price, the firm may choose not to cut price if the menu cost, which we can call z, is large enough. The firm cuts price if the gain in profit $(B - A)$ exceeds z, but not if z exceeds $B - A$. As drawn in Figure 17-5, the area B minus the area A is only 23 percent of the total profit that would be earned at the lower price (P_1). So a menu cost greater than 23 percent of profit would deter the firm from cutting price.

But society loses much more if the firm decides not to cut price. Output drops from Y_0 to Y_1, and society loses the consumer surplus area D and the profit area *B*. In the diagram, the area *D* + *B* is 66 percent of the total profit that would be earned at the lower price P_1. *Thus the firm's decision not to cut price can cause society to lose more than triple the amount lost by the firm.*

The Macroeconomic Externality and the Effects of Sticky Marginal Cost

A macroeconomic externality is a cost incurred by society as a result of a decision by an individual economic agent (worker or business firm).

Society's loss from the firm's profit-maximizing decision not to cut price is called a **macroeconomic externality.** The firm does not pay the costs its decision imposes on society, just as a firm causing air pollution or water pollution may not pay the costs imposed on the victims of dirty air and water. In the case of air and water pollution, society is better off if the government reduces the output of the polluting firm, for instance, by imposing a tax on smoke. Similarly, society would be better off if all firms cut price together. Their failure to do so, even though such price cuts are in society's best interest, is called a **coordination failure** because there is no guiding invisible hand to return to the firms some portion of the amount society as a whole would gain if they were to cut their price.

A coordination failure occurs when there is no private incentive for firms to act together to avoid actions that impose social costs on society.

The analysis of Figure 17-5 assumes that the marginal cost declines instantly in proportion to the decline in demand. This is required to maintain output unchanged at the profit-maximizing price. Now let us look back at the left-hand frame of Figure 17-5 and consider the case in which marginal cost does not decline at all and remains at the line labeled initial MC_0. Why might marginal cost be sticky, failing to decline at all? There are many reasons, some of them discussed later in this chapter. Among these are contracts that fix wages and contracts that fix the prices of materials purchased from suppliers. If the wage paid to labor and the price paid to all suppliers remain fixed, then the *MC* line would stay fixed as well. In this case, the profit-maximizing price is at E_2, not E_1.[11]

The most important implication is that *with sticky marginal cost, menu costs are not needed at all to explain how recessions occur.* Any factor that prevents supplying firms from cutting the price of materials, or even delays such price reductions, will tend to make marginal costs sticky, implying that E_2 is the point that maximizes profit for the firm in Figure 17-5, not point E_1.

17-8 Coordination Failures and Indexation

Our discussion of the new Keynesian model has now covered a variety of factors that may inhibit the prompt adjustment of prices in response to a change in nominal GDP, thus automatically implying a response in real GDP. Leaving aside menu costs, the full adjustment of prices to demand shock as depicted

---

[11]To simplify Figure 17-5, the marginal revenue line is not shown. To draw it in, find the point halfway along the horizontal axis between the vertical axis and the demand curve. Then draw a slanted line going up and to the left; it intersects the lower required MC_1 line directly above Y_0. Point E_2 lies directly above the intersection of this marginal revenue line and the higher initial MC_0 line.

in Figure 17-5, depends on the instantaneous response of marginal cost. Following a negative demand shock, output must fall if marginal cost declines less than marginal revenue. There are two reasons why firms may rationally expect marginal cost to move differently from marginal revenue. First, marginal revenue may move with aggregate nominal demand but marginal costs may not. This would occur if a firm believes that its costs depend on many specific factors other than the perceived level of aggregate nominal demand (for example, volatile supply conditions, price changes for imported materials, changes in cost created by exchange-rate movements). Second, with a fixed nominal aggregate demand, marginal cost would also remain fixed, while a local shift in demand (for example, a decline in beer drinking in response to drunk-driving laws) could reduce marginal revenue, providing another reason why marginal cost may move differently from marginal revenue.

The Input-Output Approach and the Absence of Full Indexation to Nominal Demand

To explain real price rigidity, the local-versus-aggregate cost distinction must apply to a world with many different firms purchasing supplies from each other. The automaker buys headlights from a firm that buys filament from a firm that buys copper from a firm that may mine copper using trucks purchased from the automaker. The input-output model emphasizes the importance of multiple buyer-supplier relations; each firm is simultaneously a buyer and a seller.[12] With only two firms, each supplying the other, firms could easily disentangle the local versus aggregate components of their costs. But with thousands of firms buying thousands of components, containing ingredients from many other firms, the typical firm has no idea of the identity of its full set of suppliers. Since the informational problem of trying to guess the effect of a demand shift on the average marginal cost of all these suppliers is probably impossible to solve, the sensible firm just "waits by the mailbox" for news of cost increases and then passes them on as price increases.

The input-output approach provides a critical contribution to understanding not just real price rigidity, but also nominal rigidity. The standard argument against the theories of real rigidity suggested above is that they are consistent with nominal flexibility achieved through indexation to nominal demand. Yet the input-output approach emphasizes how high a fraction of a firm's costs are attributable to suppliers of unknown identity, with some unknown fraction produced in foreign countries under differing aggregate demand conditions. This environment would give pause to any firm considering nominal-demand indexation of the product price, since the failure of all suppliers to adopt similar indexation could lead to bankruptcy.

There is nothing to guarantee any confidence that supplier firms will adopt any aggregate indexation formula, for no single supplier acting alone has any incentive to do so. The rewards are too small and the penalties of acting alone are too great, *for a firm's viability depends on the relation of price to cost, not price to nominal GDP.* No individual firm has an incentive to take the

---

[12]The input-output approach is developed in Robert J. Gordon, "What Is New-Keynesian Economics?" *Journal of Economic Literature,* vol. 28 (September 1990), see especially pp. 1150–52.

risk posed by nominal GDP indexation, which would take away from the firm the required essential control of the relation of price to cost.

Coordination Failures and Daylight Saving Time

The failure of marginal cost to decline instantly and fully in response to nominal demand reflects a coordination failure. Marginal cost would drop if all workers and firms cut wages and prices together by the same percentage as nominal demand. But each is afraid to act first, since they would lose out if other workers and firms failed to act also. Daylight saving time provides a simple example of government intervention in the face of a coordination failure. All firms may want to open and close earlier in the summer to allow more time in the late afternoon for recreational activities, but none does so because each store wants to keep the same hours as other stores. By simply decreeing a shift in the clock, the government solves the failure of individual stores to coordinate their actions.

17-9 Long-Term Labor Contracts as a Source of the Business Cycle

Long-term labor contracts are agreements between firms and workers that set the level of nominal wage rates for a year or more.

Long-term labor contracts are an important source of sticky marginal cost faced by business firms. Just as monopolistic firms impose social costs on society while maximizing profits, so too do firms and workers that enter into long-term labor contracts. Nevertheless, as the new Keynesian model emphasizes, there are good reasons why workers and firms desire such contracts. In this section, we study the features of long-term labor contracts and the differences between labor contracts in the United States and those in other countries, particularly Japan.

Characteristics of Labor Contracts

In the United States, with few exceptions, formal labor contracts are negotiated in the union sector, which covers about 13 percent of the labor force. Industries that are heavily unionized include much of the manufacturing sector (especially autos, electrical machinery, rubber, and steel), as well as substantial parts of the construction and transportation industries (especially airlines, railroads, and trucking). Industries that tend to be nonunion include fast food and other services, retailing, and parts of manufacturing (especially apparel and textiles).

The behavior of wage rates in the union sector of the economy is more important than this 13 percent figure would suggest, since the wage rates that are negotiated in the union sector set a pattern that is imitated (although not copied exactly) by nonunion workers. The leading role of unions in moderating the flexibility of nonunion wages is evidenced by the evolution of union and nonunion wages. Nonunion wages are only moderately more flexible than union wages over the business cycle, and they exhibit a substantial degree of stickiness. One reason that unions set a pattern for nonunion wages is that nonunionized firms (such as Delta Airlines) do not want their employees to quit and join a rival unionized firm (such as American Airlines) or to vote to become unionized, and so they tend to pay wage rates similar to those in unionized firms.

Wages negotiated under labor contracts are not completely rigid or fixed. Rather they change when a new contract is negotiated. Without labor contracts, the nominal wage rate would be free to change every day. With labor contracts, the nominal wage rate is set at the time of negotiation for the duration of the contract. Wage changes during the lifetime of the contract are allowed, but they are set in advance at the time of the negotiation.

Scheduled Wage Changes and COLAs.   There are two types of prenegotiated changes. First, there is usually a scheduled change that takes effect in each year of multiyear contracts. Second, there is sometimes a **cost-of-living agreement (COLA)** that sets in advance the change in the nominal wage that will be allowed for each percentage point of future inflation. For instance, a contract might specify that a worker will receive a 3.0 percent increase in each of the three years of a three-year contract, plus 100 percent of the inflation that occurs in each of the three years. Thus, if the actual inflation rate turned out to be 0.0 percent in a particular year, the wage increase would be 3.0 percent. Alternatively, with an actual inflation rate of 10.0 percent, the wage increase would be 13.0 percent. A COLA contract that gives workers a fixed increase, plus 100 percent of the inflation rate, is called "full COLA protection," whereas a fixed increase plus 50 percent of the inflation rate would be "half COLA protection."

COLAs are intended to help workers maintain their real wage. Without COLAs, the real wage rate is reduced by inflation. The following example shows that a sudden change of the inflation rate from zero to 10 percent would cause a sharp decline in the real wage if the worker had no COLA protection. With full COLA protection (a nominal wage change equal to 3.0 percent plus the inflation rate), the real wage change is unaffected by inflation. With half COLA protection, the nominal wage change in the example is equal to 3.0 percent plus 0.5 times the inflation rate.

	Nominal Wage Change with COLA Protection			Real Wage Change with COLA Protection		
	None	*Half*	*Full*	*None*	*Half*	*Full*
Inflation of zero	3.0	3.0	3.0	3.0	3.0	3.0
Inflation of 10 percent	3.0	8.0	13.0	−7.0	−2.0	3.0

In this example each of the figures for real wage change is equal to the corresponding figure for nominal wage change minus the assumed inflation rate.

SELF-TEST   Under what circumstances is the growth rate of the real wage rigid, showing no response at all to a change in the rate of inflation: with no COLA protection, half COLA protection, or full COLA protection?

Contract Timing.   The two main characteristics of contract timing are the duration of the contract and its expiration date in relation to other contracts. Contract duration is the length of time over which the contract applies, for instance, three years. A system in which contracts do not all expire at the same time features overlapping staggered contracts. In the United States the

---

Cost-of-living agreements (COLAs) provide for an automatic increase in the wage rate in response to an increase in the price level.

great majority (about 80 percent) of labor contracts are three years in length, whereas in Japan and in most European countries, one-year contracts are more common. And in the United States contracts are overlapping and staggered, in contrast to Japan, where the expiration date is simultaneous.

What is the significance of this difference between the United States and Japan? With one-year contracts that expire simultaneously, the Japanese can achieve a rapid adjustment of the nominal wage rate to changing macroeconomic conditions. The Japanese system makes it easier for the aggregate supply curve to shift soon after any shift in the aggregate demand curve, and to shift by the same amount, minimizing the extent and duration of cyclical unemployment caused by aggregate demand shifts. With staggered contracts, as in the United States, this rapid adjustment is impossible. Wages adjust slowly, and with a long lag, making marginal costs sticky for many business firms. Much of the economy's adjustment to shifts in aggregate demand takes the form of business cycles in output and unemployment.

17-10 "Real" Sources of Wage Stickiness

Thus far, our discussion of the new Keynesian approach has emphasized nominal rigidities, particularly the menu costs of changing nominal prices and long-term contracts for both wages and prices that are incompletely indexed. These contracts imply that a business firm's marginal cost does not respond instantly to a decline in demand. Consequently, the contracts reinforce the role of menu costs in dissuading firms from changing their prices by the full amount needed to avoid changes in output and hence recessions. Now we turn to theories that attempt to explain real rigidities, that is, the slow adjustment of wages relative to prices or to other wages. The most prominent of these is the efficiency wage theory.

The Efficiency Wage Model

This theory explains real rigidities by stressing the reasons why firms would not want to cut the wage that they pay *relative to the wage paid by other firms*. A firm believes that the productivity of its workers will increase if the firm pays a higher wage. There will be greater effort by workers, reduced shirking or goofing off on the job, lower turnover (which reduces training costs), the ability to attract higher-quality workers, and improved morale and loyalty.

The efficiency wage result is obtained in a simple model with identical, perfectly competitive firms. Each firm has a production function in which labor input is multiplied by an efficiency factor (e) that depends on the wage rate paid relative to that paid by other firms (W), as shown in the left frame of Figure 17-6. Raising W raises labor cost by making firms pay more to workers, but reduces labor cost per unit of output by making workers more efficient. As shown in the left frame, initially a 1 percent increase in W raises e by more than 1 percent, so labor cost declines, as shown in the right frame. Firms continue raising W until it reaches the equilibrium value W^*, which occurs at the point where raising W by 1 percent raises efficiency by exactly 1 percent, thus leaving labor cost per unit of efficiency unchanged. Firms will

HIGH WAGES REDUCE LABOR COSTS, UP TO A POINT

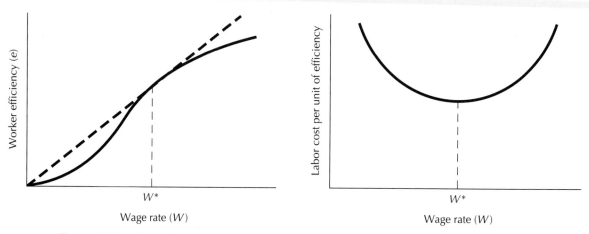

Figure 17-6   **The Relationship Between the Relative Wage Rate and Worker Efficiency**
In the left frame, worker efficiency increases faster than the relative wage up to point
W^* and more slowly thereafter. As a result, labor cost per unit of efficiency reaches a
minimum at W^*, as shown in the right frame.

refuse to raise W any further, since this would raise wage payments more than
it would boost efficiency. The value W^* is called the efficiency wage.

Because W^* is completely fixed by whatever technological and institu-
tional factors determine the e function, the firm's reaction to any change in
demand for its product is to cut employment while maintaining the wage rate
at W^*. Firms have no incentive to cut wages, since this would actually
increase their wage bill per unit of output. The efficiency wage approach
seems to explain numerous aspects of microeconomic labor market behavior,
once we allow different groups of workers to have different levels of efficiency
at any given relative wage rate. For example, the theory predicts the widely
observed phenomenon that workers line up eagerly for high-paying jobs
but firms hire only a few of them, maintaining the high wage in order to be
able to pick and choose rather than reduce the wage rate in the face of the
abundant supply of workers. The theory also predicts that less productive
workers, those whose labor cost per efficiency unit is high, will suffer higher
unemployment rates than more productive groups. The model can explain
why we do not observe work sharing in the form of fewer hours per week in
periods of low demand; such reductions in hours would raise labor cost by
cutting the wage income and hence the efficiency of the most productive
workers.

SELF-TEST   According to the efficiency wage theory, how is unemployment explained?
Assuming that the unemployed are willing to work at a lower wage rate
than existing workers, why does the firm not simply fire the existing workers and hire the unemployed in their place at a lower wage?

As a theoretical underpinning of the new Keynesian approach to wage
and price rigidity, the efficiency wage model explains why firms resist cutting

their wage rates in response to a decline in demand, and why they do not hire unemployed workers who may be willing to work for a lower wage. This approach is still subject to the same criticism as long-term wage contracts, that full wage indexation would allow firms simultaneously to maintain worker effort by paying the optimal relative wage W^* while maintaining a flexible nominal wage rate. However, for the reasons discussed in Section 17-8, firms and workers are unwilling to risk full wage indexation.

17-11 Assessment of the New Keynesian Model

The new Keynesian model introduces two improvements to the graphical short-run supply *(SAS)* analysis of Chapter 7. First, Chapter 7 simply assumed that shifts in the *SAS* curve would occur gradually. In contrast, the new Keynesian model provides the missing reasoning for wage and price adjustment to be gradual, not instantaneous. Second, Chapter 7 suffered from *asymmetry,* in assuming that firms were always on their labor demand curve but workers were forced off their labor supply curve. In contrast, the new Keynesian model allows *both* firms and workers to operate in disequilibrium.

Contrast with Other Theories. The new Keynesian model seems to solve the main dilemma of the other business cycle theories examined in Chapter 7 and the first part of this chapter, that is, how to explain observed business cycles without unrealistically assuming away output fluctuations (as does classical economics), assuming complete wage rigidity (as does the original Keynesian model), assuming unrealistic fooling of workers (the Friedman model), failing to explain persistent unemployment in the presence of easily available information on prices and the money supply (the Lucas information barrier model), or requiring procyclical real wage movements and continuous labor market equilibrium (the real business cycle model).

Workers and firms in the new Keynesian model are rational, finding it *privately advantageous* to enter into long-term agreements that may have a *macroeconomic externality,* imposing employment and output losses on other workers and firms. The other approaches fail to provide an adequate theory of the business cycle, partly because they do not distinguish between the *private interest* (for instance, signing contracts) and the *collective interest* in avoiding business cycles.

Criticisms of the New Keynesian Approach

The new Keynesian model has been criticized for suggesting *too many* reasons why wages and prices are sticky. Some of these reasons, like staggered overlapping wage and price contracts, have been criticized on the grounds that business cycles were common before the rise of labor unions in the United States in the 1930s and 1940s. To explain business cycles in eras or industries where unions are not strong, we must rely on other new Keynesian explanations that do not require written contracts. Several of these, including the input-output approach and the efficiency wage model, do not depend on the existence of organized labor unions.

Testing of the new Keynesian approach is in its infancy. There is as yet no agreement on which of the various sources of nominal and real rigidity have been most important. The degree of wage and price rigidity differs greatly across countries and in different historical eras. For instance, prices were more flexible before World War II in Japan and France than in the United Kingdom and United States. Prices are clearly more flexible in countries like Argentina and Brazil that have experienced high and variable inflation than in countries like the United States. Research that would explain why this is true has barely begun.

One reason that prices may be more flexible in some countries than in others can be linked to rational expectations. When firms and workers expect the government to pursue inflationary policies, they are more likely to insist on full cost-of-living protection and to invest time in trying to predict changes in government policy. They may also be unwilling to enter into long-term staggered contracts. In countries like West Germany, where the central bank has consistently pursued anti-inflationary policies since the early 1970s, there will be less demand for indexed contracts.

SUMMARY

1. Initially the new classical macroeconomics attempted to build a theory of the business cycle based on continuous market clearing and imperfect information. The first of these theories was Milton Friedman's "fooling model," in which workers are "fooled" into providing extra labor input because they do not have as prompt or complete information on the aggregate price level as do firms.

2. Robert Lucas added rational expectations to Friedman's assumptions of continuous market clearing and imperfect information. The central tool of the new classical model is the Friedman-Lucas supply curve, which attributes business cycles in real output to expectational errors, also called "price surprises."

3. The central implication of the Lucas model is the policy ineffectiveness proposition, which states that monetary policy cannot affect output either through an *announced* policy change or through a change that reacts to past events in a consistent and predictable way.

4. The second new classical approach is called the real business cycle (RBC) model. It explains business cycles in output as the result of slowly changing (persistent) shocks to supply conditions and technology. It explains cycles in employment as the result of intertemporal substitution by workers, who choose to work harder in periods of high real wages and enjoy more leisure in periods of low real wages.

5. The RBC model has been criticized because no one has yet identified specific technology shocks at the industry level that are large enough to explain actual recessions and depressions, except for the oil price shocks of the 1970s and 1980s. It has also been criticized for two unrealistic implications, that prices and output always move in opposite directions and that real wages vary procyclically.

6. The new Keynesian approach shares with the original Keynesian approach an explanation of business cycles based on the failure of prices to adjust sufficiently to maintain a continuous equilibrium in the labor market. The new Keynesian model differs by developing microeconomic explanations of wage and price rigidity based on rational expectations and profit-maximizing behavior.

7. Small menu costs can cause large social costs of recessions by giving profit-maximizing firms a reason not to adjust the price level to every change in demand. Sticky marginal costs imply that firms will reduce output in response to a reduction in demand, even in the absence of menu costs.

8. One source of sticky marginal costs is the role of long-term labor contracts in preventing the prompt adjustment of the nominal wage rate to changes in demand. The United States has three-year overlapping staggered labor contracts, in contrast to Japan, where labor contracts last for one year and expire simultaneously.

9. One source of real rigidity is the efficiency wage. In the efficiency wage model, firms are reluctant to cut wages for fear of reducing the efficiency of their employees and of causing their best employees to quit.

CONCEPTS

natural rate hypothesis
rational expectations
Lucas model
policy ineffectiveness proposition
feedback rule
real business cycle model
intertemporal substitution
non-market-clearing model
new Keynesian economics

nominal rigidity
real rigidity
menu costs
staggered contracts
auction market
macroeconomic externality
coordination failure
long-term labor contracts
cost-of-living agreement (COLA)

QUESTIONS AND PROBLEMS

Questions

1. According to the Friedman "fooling" model, how does the labor market clear when prices and output rise in the short run?

2. Explain how the Friedman "fooling" model predicts that an expansionary monetary policy can lead to increased output in the short run, while the Lucas model suggests that such a policy would have no effect on real output.

3. In what ways are the Friedman "fooling" model and the Keynesian model similar? In what ways do they differ?

4. In what ways are the Friedman "fooling" model and the Lucas model similar? In what ways do they differ?

5. What is meant by the term "price surprise"? What role does it play in determining the slope of the supply function in Lucas's "local" explanation of business cycles? Exposit Lucas's explanation for why the supply function in Brazil is likely to be steeper than that in the United States.

6. How does an adverse supply shock affect the production function? What is the effect of an adverse supply shock on the demand for labor?

7. What does the real business cycle model predict will happen to prices, real wages, and employment in response to an adverse supply shock? Is this prediction matched by real-world experience? What explanation(s) for the real-world behavior of prices and real wages do real business cycle theorists offer?

8. How does the real business cycle model differ from the Lucas model? Does it explain the persistence of business cycles?

9. What was the important assumption made with respect to wage rates in the original Keynesian model? How does the new Keynesian model differ in its approach to that assumption?

10. "Classical and new classical firms choose output, but new Keynesian firms choose price." Explain.

11. Explain why it is believed that greater pressure is placed on employment and output in response to shifts in aggregate demand under a situation of long-term staggered labor contracts than would be the case under shorter-term, uniform-expiration-date contracts.

12. What is a macroeconomic externality? How do long-term agreements impose a macroeconomic externality on the economy? What other sources of macroeconomic externalities are identified in this chapter?

13. In what ways are the original Keynesian model and the new Keynesian model similar? In what ways do they differ?

14. What is meant by the terms *nominal* and *real rigidities*? If nominal rigidities could be completely removed from the U.S. economy, would that solve the problem of output and employment fluctuations during business cycles?

15. Is it possible for there to be a business cycle without fluctuations in employment and output? Which, if any, school(s) of thought suggested that this would be the normal case?

16. What insights into the economy's adjustment to aggregate demand fluctuations does efficiency wage theory suggest? Is this theory consistent with new Keynesians' explanations of business cycles?

17. What are the similarities and differences between the new Keynesian model and the new classical and real business cycle models?

Problems

1. Given the following Friedman-Lucas short-run aggregate supply function:

$$Y = Y^N + h (P - P^e)$$

where $Y^N = 5000$, $P^e = 1.5$, and $h = 2500$, calculate the level of real output (Y) for:
(a) $P = 0.75$
(b) $P = 1.00$
(c) $P = 1.25$
(d) $P = 1.50$
(e) $P = 1.75$
(f) $P = 2.00$.

2. Given the Friedman-Lucas supply function in Problem 1, what would be the equilibrium real income if people accurately expected that the price level were 1.00? 1.50? 2.00?

3. Using Figures 17-4 and 17-5 as a guide, assume a price-setting monopolist firm with no fixed costs and constant marginal cost (MC_0) of $3.00 faces an original demand curve $P = 10 - .1Y$.
(a) What is the equation of the firm's marginal revenue curve MR_0 (recall that for a linear demand curve, MR is twice as steep as demand)?
(b) What quantity will the firm produce to maximize profits? What price will it set to insure that it sells all that it produces? (Hint: Recall that profit is maximized when $MC_0 = MR_0$.)
(c) At the profit-maximizing price, what is the firm's total revenue? Total cost? Profit?
(d) What is the value of consumer surplus? (Hint: Recall that the area of a triangle equals one half the area formed by its two sides.)

4. Now assume that the firm described in question 1 faces a fall in demand such that the new demand curve is $P = 8 - .08Y$.

(a) What is the equation for the firm's new marginal revenue curve (MR_1)?
(b) If the firm is to maintain its original level of output (Y_0), what must happen to its marginal cost of production? What is the "*required*" marginal cost (MC_1)? (Hint: Set Y in MR_1 equal to Y_0.)
(c) At what price on the new demand curve can the firm sell the original quantity of output?
(d) If MC remains at $3.00, and there are no *menu costs*, what output would the firm choose to produce to maximize profits? What price will it set? (Hint: Find the quantity and price associated with point E_2 in Figure 17-5.)
(e) If the firm maintains the original price, what is the maximum quantity that it can sell, given the new lower level of demand? (Hint: Find Y_1 in Figure 17-5.)
(f) Calculate the profits lost and gained if the firm chooses to reduce the price from the original price to the new lower price associated with the original quantity. (Hint: Calculate the values for area A and area B in Figure 17-5 as they apply to this problem.)
(g) What is the maximum value for *menu costs* under which we could expect this firm to maintain its original output (assuming that it could reduce its marginal costs to the required level)?
(h) If *menu costs* are greater than $22.00, and marginal costs cannot be reduced below $3.00 due to contractual input prices, would the firm seek to maximize profits by choosing the solution found in problem 2(d) above (that is, where $MC_0 = MR_1$)?

p. 538 Yes, there must be a price surprise when Y falls below Y^N in a recession. When the price level is surprisingly low, firms conclude that the current period is a bad time to produce (since they receive an unrewardingly low price for their product). Hence, they reduce production voluntarily.

p. 544 A business expansion is explained by RBC theory as the result of a favorable or beneficial supply shock, which makes factors of production unusually productive. Employment increases as workers add more hours and accept more jobs in the belief that the higher real wage, paid out by firms as a result of high productivity, makes the period an attractive one in which to expend extra work effort.

p. 554 If a price P_0 is charged, profit is the area between P_0, the new demand curve, and the "Required MC_1" line, that is, the sum of the rectangles A and F. If a price P_1 is charged, then profit is the area between P_1, the new demand curve, and the "Required MC_1" line, that is, the sum of the rectangles F and B. Since F is in common to both situations, shifting from a price of P_0 to a price of P_1 means losing the profit rectangle A and gaining the profit rectangle B. Why is B greater than A? Because E_1 is the position that maximizes profit with the new demand curve and the required MC_1 line. Thus total profits must be greater when producing at E_1 than at E_0 (given the reduction in demand), so the amount of profit gained by cutting the price from P_0 to P_1 must be positive.

p. 558 The growth rate in the real wage rate is completely unaffected by inflation when there is full COLA protection. Since this makes the growth rate in the nominal wage rate change fully in response to the change in the inflation rate, there is no change in the growth of the real wage rate, since this is defined as the growth rate of the nominal wage rate minus the inflation rate.

p. 560 The firm refuses to hire the unemployed, even at a wage lower than is being paid to current workers, because the firm does not believe that it would thereby lower its labor cost. It believes that the unemployed workers, if hired at a lower wage, will be less productive than the current workers and will be more likely to quit.

CHAPTER 18

Conclusion: Where We Stand

Experience, some people say, is like a light on a caboose, illuminating only where we aren't going. But we scrutinize the past for its elements of prologue, and consolation.

—George F. Will

We have now finished the formal task of learning macroeconomic theory. We have also seen through the Case Study text sections and International Perspective boxes that macroeconomics is a subject with close ties to the real world. Many events in U.S. history illustrate important themes in macroeconomic theory. And differences between the economic performance of the United States and other advanced nations help to clarify theory and to highlight the differences among nations which are easy to explain and those which are difficult. For instance, we learned in Chapter 12 that it is relatively easy to explain why some countries experience hyperinflation—their governments have allowed very rapid growth in the money supply; that growth in turn results from their need to finance large budget deficits. But it is relatively hard to explain why high unemployment in Europe persisted for so long in the 1980s and 1990s; the fact that it has provides an example of an unsettled issue in macroeconomics.

18-1 The Evolution of Events and Ideas

Events and ideas evolve together.[1] The Case Studies in this book show how theoretical ideas can be directly applied to the understanding of historical events. But the process also works in reverse—the outcome of historical events often challenges theorists and overturns theories, leading to the evolution of new theories. Some of the central ideas of macroeconomics, including those proposed by the old Keynesians, the monetarists, the new classicals, and the new Keynesians, can be understood as a reaction to events. In some cases the evolution of the economy helped to resolve a debate between different schools of thought. In other cases events occurred that could not be understood until new theories were formulated.

In the rest of this chapter we will review some of the events that were sufficiently important to cause a change in ideas, starting in the next section with the Great Depression. The following sections treat the post–World War II period (the postwar era) dividing it in two parts, before 1970 and after 1970, and emphasizing the performance of the domestic U.S. economy. Then we examine the effect of events in the world economy, focusing primarily on the debate between advocates of fixed and flexible exchange rates. Two final sec-

---

[1]The title of this section, and some of the analysis in this chapter, are taken from Robert J. Gordon, "Postwar Macroeconomics: The Evolution of Events and Ideas," in Martin S. Feldstein, ed., *The American Economy in Transition* (Chicago: University of Chicago Press, 1980), pp. 101–62.

tions summarize what we know, organized around the six puzzles addressed throughout this book, and what we still don't know—a remaining set of macro mysteries that are the focus of continuing debate, disagreement, and research in macroeconomics.

18-2 The Reaction of Ideas to Events, 1923–47

Perhaps the most dramatic and unexpected event in the macroeconomic history of the United States was the Great Depression of the 1930s, consisting of the Great Contraction of 1929–33, followed by a weak recovery that failed to bring the unemployment rate below 10 percent until the outbreak of World War II. In plotting the behavior of central macroeconomic variables in Figure 18-1, we begin in 1923, in order to contrast the highly volatile 1930s and 1940s with the placid 1920s.

The Economy's Behavior in the 1920s and 1930s

The four-frame format of Figure 18-1 is identical to that used subsequently to examine the postwar era. The top frame plots nominal GDP growth and M1 growth, indicating changes in the velocity of M1 by shading. The second frame plots nominal GDP growth and the inflation rate, so that the shaded areas indicate real GDP growth. The third frame plots the output ratio and the unemployment rate, and the bottom frame plots the long-term and short-term interest rates.

Prior to the Great Depression, the dominant idea in macroeconomics was the old classical approach, based on the quantity theory of money, a theory that emphasized the strong self-correcting properties of the private economy and the tendency for changes in the money supply to influence mainly the price level rather than output (Section 7-8). The placid 1923–29 period seemed consistent with the old classical approach. As shown in Figure 18-1, the inflation rate was almost zero, unemployment remained below 5 percent, and the output ratio remained near 100 percent. There were minor variations in the growth rate of nominal and real GDP and minor recessions in 1924 and 1927.

Everything changed in the 1930s. Growth in everything became negative during 1930–33, including M1, nominal and real GDP, and the price level. The output ratio fell to 65 percent, and the unemployment rate soared to 25 percent. As shown in the bottom frame, the corporate bond rate soared as increasing bankruptcies made investors shy away from purchasing corporate bonds.

The most notable facts about the Great Depression were not only its severity but its length. The unemployment rate was still above 10 percent in 1940.[2] While real GDP growth was rapid during the 1933–37 recovery, that

---

[2]There is an ongoing debate as to whether the unemployment rate in the last half of the 1930s is exaggerated, due to the counting of workers on government relief programs as unemployed rather than employed. The original critique of the official statistics is in Michael Darby, "Three and a Half Million U.S. Employees Have Been Mislaid: Or, An Explanation of Unemployment, 1934–41," *Journal of Political Economy,* vol. 84 (February 1976), pp. 1–16. A balanced assessment of the debate is contained in Robert Margo, "Interwar Unemployment in the United States: Evidence from the 1940 Census Sample," in Barry Eichengreen and T. J. Hatton, eds., *Interwar Unemployment in International Perspective* (Dordrecht, Boston, and London: Kluwer Academic Publishers, 1988), pp. 325–52.

EVERYTHING WAS VOLATILE BETWEEN THE WARS

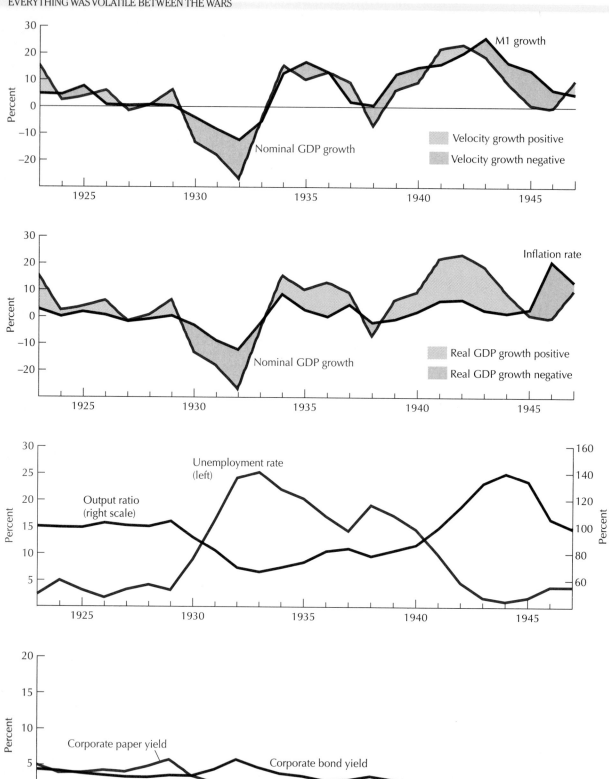

·growth was sufficient only to bring the output ratio back to 83 percent, far below the normal level of 100 percent. And despite very low short-term interest rates, a sharp setback occurred in the 1938 recession.

The Keynesian Revolution

Events cause the evolution of ideas. The Great Depression killed the old classical approach, stimulated John Maynard Keynes to develop his *General Theory,* and fostered the immediate worldwide acceptance of the Keynesian revolution (Section 7-9). Rendered obsolete was the classical idea that a decline in the money supply would mainly reduce the price level, because in 1929–33 output fell so far and recovered so slowly. Also rendered obsolete was the quantity theory idea that velocity was stable, because it depended mainly on transaction practices; in 1929–33 the economy's collapse was caused as much by a drop in velocity as a drop in the money supply.

The underpinning of the Keynesian revolution was the concept of aggregate demand. Because the price level is sticky (that is, not sufficiently flexible to respond fully and completely to each change in nominal GDP), any change in aggregate demand would cause a change in output and employment. Unlike the old classicals, with their sole emphasis on the money supply, the Keynesians stressed other factors that could cause shifts in aggregate demand, including fiscal policy and changes in business and consumer confidence.

The old Keynesian school of thought was heavily influenced by the behavior of the economy in the late 1930s, the time when Keynes's *General Theory* was being avidly discussed and absorbed at academic seminars throughout the United States. As shown in Figure 18-1, the money supply soared in 1939 and 1940, yet unemployment remained high. Short-term nominal and real interest rates were near zero, so that the economy could not be stimulated by further reductions in short-term interest rates. This led to the expression that monetary policy was like "pushing on a string," or "You can lead a horse to water but you can't make it drink." The only answer was stimulative fiscal policy, and the economy's prompt recovery in response to higher defense spending in 1941–42 reinforced the supremacy of fiscal policy for a whole generation of economists.[3]

---

[3]The stimulus of wartime government spending began long before Pearl Harbor. Exports and domestic investment began to grow soon after the European war began in September 1939, and especially after the fall of France in June 1940.

Figure 18-1   **Key Macroeconomic Variables, 1923–47**

These plots of annual data show the growth rates of nominal and real GDP, M1, and the GDP deflator. Also shown are the output ratio, the unemployment rate, the long-term interest rate, and the short-term interest rate. Notable features are the collapse of everything between 1929 and 1933, the weak 1933–37 recovery, the 1938 recession, and the takeoff of the economy as wartime spending began in 1940. Persistent unemployment and a continued low output ratio are the main features of the Great Depression.

World War II

Macroeconomists usually omit from their analyses economic events during World War II, because government regulations skewed the normal operation of the economy. Output soared and unemployment fell almost to zero, but there was no inflation, a feat made possible only because of stringent legal price controls. By 1944 government spending amounted to fully half of GDP, shifting the *IS* curve far to the right, but interest rates did not rise because the government required the Fed to "peg" the long-term government bond interest rate, printing the money to purchase any bonds that the government issued to cover its massive fiscal deficit. After the war, in 1946–47, when the price controls were lifted, inflation soared (thus reducing the real wealth of those who had patriotically purchased government bonds during the war), but interest rates remained steady, as the Fed maintained its agreement to peg long-term government bond interest rates through 1951.

> *The big event of the interwar period was the Great Depression. This event spawned a big idea, the Keynesian revolution, with its emphasis on aggregate demand, sticky prices, and fiscal policy. The behavior of the economy during World War II seemed to support the main themes of the Keynesian revolution.*

18-3 The Reaction of Ideas to Events, 1947–70

We now turn to the postwar U.S. economy, the main focus of this book. Macroeconomic behavior in the first part of the postwar period, 1947–70, is shown in Figure 18-2. Each of the four frames corresponds to Figure 18-1.

The Economy in the 1950s

The economy's performance in the 1950s looks much better in retrospect than it did at the time. The period 1950–53 was dominated by the economic effects of the Korean War, including a brief surge of inflation in 1950–51 and very low unemployment during 1951–53. Huge increases in government spending in 1950–53 and a subsequent decrease in 1953–54 caused wide swings in the *IS* curve. The 1953–54 recession was very mild and brief and, in retrospect, exhibits the potency of easy monetary policy. A small reduction in the short-term interest rate (the federal funds rate) was sufficient to let loose a torrent of spending on housing and automobiles, causing 1955 to be a

---

Figure 18-2   **Key Macroeconomic Variables, 1948–69**

The variables are the same as in Figure 18-1. Notable are the recessions of 1949, 1953–54, 1957–58, and 1960–61. Nominal and real GDP variations seem more closely related to velocity changes than changes in the money supply. Both inflation and interest rates began an uptrend after 1965.

DEMAND SHOCKS DOMINATED IN THE 1950s AND 1960s

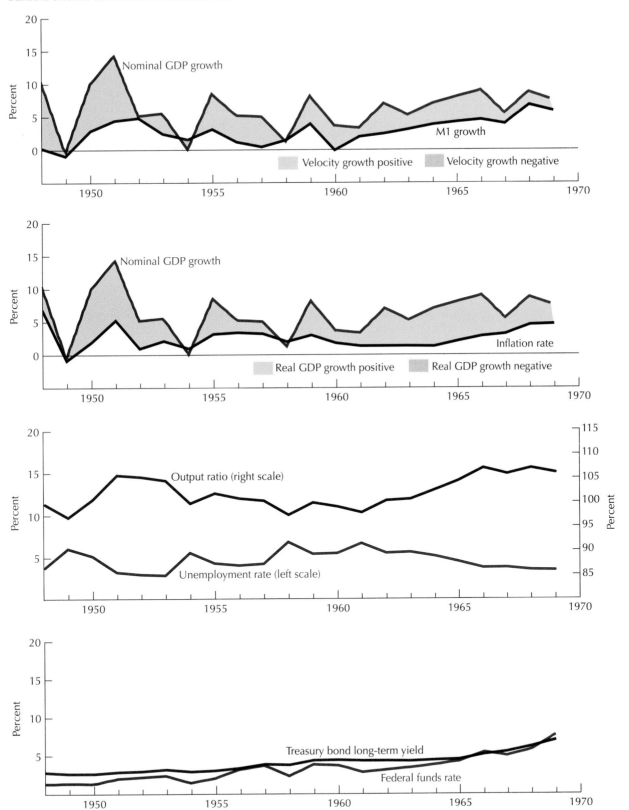

vintage year in economic annals.[4] With both the Korean War and the threat of a renewal of the Great Depression behind them, American businesses and consumers were eager to stock up on housing and durable goods to match their newly elevated estimate of their "permanent income" (Section 15-4).

The short-term Phillips curve tradeoff became evident in 1956–57, when inflation increased even though unemployment remained above Korean War levels.[5] In response, the Fed allowed interest rates to creep up, and this ultimately choked off the boom and brought on the sharp recession of 1957–58. Unemployment rose to the highest level yet seen in the postwar period. After a brief recovery, the economy promptly fell into another recession in 1960–61.

Changes in Economic Ideas Through 1960

The old Keynesian school of thought held sway throughout this period. Wide swings in nominal GDP growth were mainly accounted for by changes in velocity, not by changes in the money supply. Changes in military spending during and after the Korean War were the main source of instability. Ironically, despite the new commitment to fiscal stabilization policy brought about by the Keynesian revolution and the Employment Act of 1946, government military spending was the great destabilizer of aggregate demand.

However, leaving aside the political forces that caused the Korean War, fiscal policy managed well in this period. In 1950, tax rates were raised immediately to finance the war, helping to dampen the surge of consumer buying and moderate the 1950–51 inflation. Further, taxes were cut in early 1954, moderating the 1953–54 recession and setting the stage for the 1955 boom. The monetary policy record is mixed; money was tightened too much in early 1957, helping set off the 1957–58 recession, but at least monetary easing was prompt once the 1953–54 and 1957–58 recessions had begun.

The main shift in ideas concerned the aggregate supply curve. Unlike the 1930s or the recession of 1949, prices did not decline at all in the recessions of 1953–54 and 1957–58. Just as U.S. economists were puzzling over the seeming inflexibility of prices, in 1958 A. W. Phillips published his famous article on the Phillips curve, based on historical data for the United Kingdom (see Section 8-2).

The Economy in the 1960s

The longest economic expansion in U.S. economic history occurred between 1961 and 1969, shown in Figure 18-2 by the long period of low and stable unemployment. In its early phases the expansion responded to easy monetary policy, and then to massive fiscal stimulus in the form of income tax

---

[4]Nobel Prize winner Paul A. Samuelson of M.I.T. once announced to a graduate class that he would "flunk any student who could explain why auto sales in 1955 were so high." The auto boom was caused by the combination of attractive new models and new V-8 engines for the low-priced "Big Three" cars, by an easing of terms on installment loans, and by the normal accelerator effect that occurs in a period of rapid income growth (Section 16-3).

[5]There were price controls in effect during the Korean War, albeit milder than the draconian controls of World War II.

reductions in 1964–65 and, beginning in 1965, spending for the Vietnam War. While unemployment fell to the lowest rates since the Korean War, inflation steadily accelerated.

Stabilization policy in the 1960s went too far in stimulating the economy. The tax cuts of 1964–65 occurred when the economy had already reached its natural unemployment rate, and these cuts had a particularly potent effect, since they were accommodated by stimulative monetary policy. Although monetary policy initially did not accommodate Vietnam spending (note the spike in the short-term interest rate in 1966–67), monetary growth was allowed to accelerate in 1968. The great failure of fiscal policy was the long delay in raising taxes to finance the Vietnam War.

Intellectual Revolutions of the 1960s

Three new ideas dominated economic discussions in the 1960s: the new economics of Walter Heller, the monetarism of Milton Friedman and others, and the natural rate hypothesis, also primarily reflecting the influence of Milton Friedman.

Of these, the new economics occurred earliest and fell out of favor fastest. When President Kennedy was inaugurated in early 1961, the economy was in recession, with unemployment at almost 7 percent. Believing that monetary stimulus was a weak tool, Kennedy's chief economic advisers (including Walter Heller, Arthur Okun, and future Nobel Prize winners Robert Solow and James Tobin) insisted that a new type of fiscal activism was necessary, consisting of changes in personal income taxes.[6] To stimulate the economy they recommended a tax cut, which was implemented in early 1964 (with a second stage in 1965). To pay for the Vietnam War, they urged President Johnson in 1966 to enact an income tax surcharge.

Two events caused fiscal activism, later derided as "fiscal fine tuning," to fall out of favor. First was the legislative lag (Section 14-4), which lasted 18 months, before enactment of the 1968 tax surcharge. Second was the permanent income hypothesis (Section 15-4), which predicted that temporary tax changes would have a small multiplier. This prediction proved to be the case. By 1969–70, fiscal activism was discredited, and with it an underpinning of the old Keynesian school of thought.[7]

In retrospect, another important weakness of Heller's new economics was the failure to understand the role of the monetary-fiscal policy mix (Section 5-5). Heller's complaint that the 1959–60 full-employment budget surplus was too high would today be translated as fiscal policy being too tight. However, if accompanied by a sufficiently easy monetary policy, a tight fiscal policy is no obstacle to achieving the highest feasible level of output and employment. Ironically, a mix of tight fiscal policy and easy monetary policy, with accompanying low interest rates that encourage investment, is just the opposite pol-

---

[6]Kennedy's advisors viewed earlier attempts at fiscal stabilization as special events rather than as representative of a commitment to fiscal activism. The big tax increases of 1950–51, however successful, were viewed as a special event connected with the Korean War, and the 1954 tax cuts represented the expiration of temporary wartime tax increases, rather than a deliberate act of stabilization policy.

[7]Among the first to make this case was my colleague Robert Eisner. See his "Fiscal and Monetary Policy Reconsidered," *American Economic Review*, vol. 59 (December 1969), pp. 897–905.

icy mix from the easy-fiscal–tight-money mix of the 1980s, with its persistent budget deficits and high real interest rates (about which many of Heller's friends and supporters complained in the 1980s).

Milton Friedman's approach was the exact opposite of the new economics; he favored rules over activism and monetary policy over fiscal policy. His approach, christened "monetarism" in 1968, advocated a constant growth rate rule for the money supply and no use at all of fiscal policy for stabilization purposes. As we learned in Section 14-3, this approach reflected optimism that the private economy would remain stable and pessimism that activist policy would do more good than harm. Friedman's pessimism was reinforced by events of the 1960s, including long legislative lags for fiscal policy and the Fed's accommodative policy of 1964–65 and 1968, when aggregate demand was already growing too rapidly. Another event, the failure of the income-tax surcharge to slow the economy in the face of monetary stimulus in 1968, together with the impact of tight money in 1969 in ending the expansion, placed a final nail in the coffin of activist fiscal policy and left the stage open for the dominance of monetary policy over the following two decades.

The third new idea was the most influential and long-lasting: Milton Friedman's 1968 natural rate hypothesis, also developed concurrently by Edmund S. Phelps of Columbia University. The natural rate hypothesis took the Phillips curve (then barely ten years old) one step further by developing the distinction between the short-run and long-run Phillips curves (the *SP* and *LP* curves of Chapter 8). No longer could policy activists choose any arbitrary level for the unemployment rate; the microeconomic structure of labor markets decreed a particular natural rate of unemployment, and any attempt to push the actual unemployment rate below this natural rate would cause accelerating inflation.

Lo and behold, accelerating inflation was exactly what was occurring at the time Friedman's hypothesis was unveiled in the *American Economic Review* in early 1968. So strong was the influence of unfolding events that by 1970–71 the natural rate hypothesis had been widely accepted.

The big events of the 1947–70 period were the instability of aggregate demand, due in part to the Korean and Vietnam wars, the overstimulation of the economy after 1964 by both monetary and fiscal policy, and the ensuing acceleration of inflation. Spawned in part by these events were several new ideas, including the Phillips curve, the new economics, monetarism, and the natural rate hypothesis.

18-4   The Reaction of Ideas to Events, 1970–97

Our summary of macroeconomic events and ideas since 1970 is based on Figure 18-3, on page 576, which is arranged exactly like Figure 18-2.

Economic Behavior, 1971–82

The plot in Figure 18-3 shows that everything in the economy seemed to get worse after 1970. This deterioration in economic performance led to several of the puzzles introduced at the beginning of the book, including why unemployment, inflation, and interest rates were so high and so variable. Notable in the diagram are the twin peaks of inflation in 1974–75 and 1980–81, and the twin peaks of unemployment in 1975 and 1982. Short-term interest rates also exhibit twin peaks in 1974 and 1981. Not shown in Figure 18-3, but an additional puzzle plotted in Chapter 1 and studied in Chapter 10, is the slowdown in productivity growth that began in the early 1970s and continued into the early 1990s.

In the 1970s fiscal policy continued to be out of favor. Ironically, a relatively prompt fiscal stimulus in early 1975, with a much shorter legislative lag than in 1966–68, helped end the 1974–75 recession. Monetary policy played a passive role in 1975–79, allowing rapid M1 growth, which encouraged a further acceleration of inflation. But in October 1979, the Fed changed its policy and adopted a policy close to the monetarist rule (although based on targeting bank reserves rather than money). The Fed's shift toward a money-based target explains why interest rates were so volatile in 1979–82; basically the Fed abandoned any attempt to smooth interest rates.

Reaction of Ideas to Events

Two major ideas were developed during the 1970s, the Lucas new classical macroeconomics (Section 17-3) and the supply-shock analysis of inflation adjustment (Section 8-10). We have seen in Section 17-3 that the Lucas model combined market clearing, imperfect information, and rational expectations, and as such represented a further development of Friedman's natural rate hypothesis. The core of this approach was market clearing, which was the antithesis of Keynesian economics (based on sticky prices and the implied non-market clearing).

A macro event, namely the sharp increase in food and oil prices in 1973–75, played an important role in helping to build support for new classical macroeconomics. As is clearly visible in Figure 18-3, in the mid-1970s inflation and unemployment were positively correlated, not negatively correlated. The food-oil price shock appeared to put another nail in the coffin of the Phillips curve which assumed a negative correlation between inflation and unemployment, which Friedman had already reduced from a universal phenomenon to a short-run phenomenon. Lucas and Thomas Sargent, now of the Hoover Institution at Stanford University, declared that this positive correlation implied that not only the short-run Phillips curve but also Keynesian economics as a whole were dead: "The task which faces contemporary students of the business cycle is that of sorting through the wreckage . . . of that remarkable intellectual event called the Keynesian Revolution.[8]

The second idea of the 1970s was the integration of supply shocks into the Phillips curve analysis, as in Chapter 8. This approach combines the natural rate hypothesis (in the form of a vertical long-run Phillips curve) with a short-run analysis in which demand and supply shocks are of equal importance. A demand stimulus can cause inflation to increase and unemployment to decrease in the short run, as in 1965–69 or 1987–90. An adverse supply shock can cause both inflation and unemployment to increase at the same time, as in 1974–75 and 1980–81. The idea that demand and supply shocks

[8]Robert E. Lucas, Jr., and Thomas J. Sargent, "After Keynesian Macroeconomics," in *After the Phillips Curve: Persistence of High Inflation and High Unemployment* (Boston: Federal Reserve Bank of Boston, 1978), pp. 49–50.

SUPPLY SHOCKS DOMINATED IN THE 1970s AND 1980s

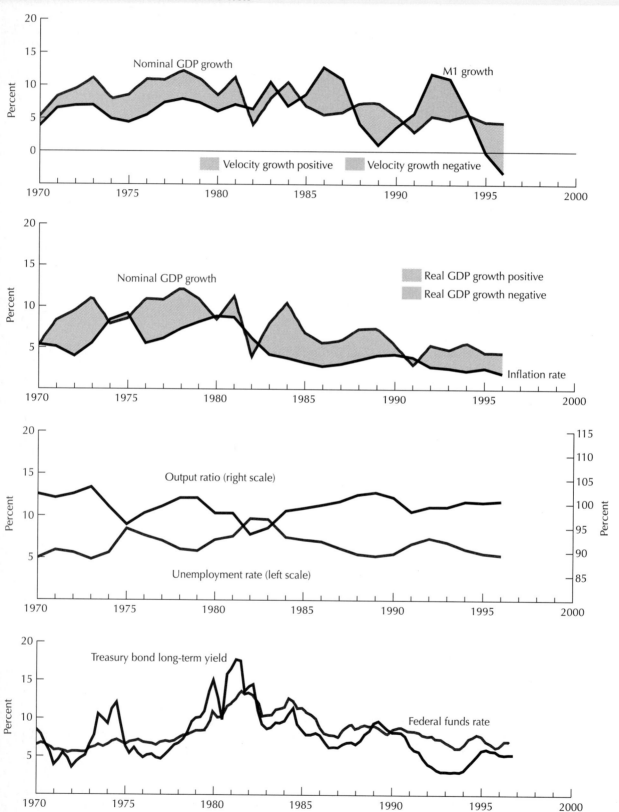

affect macroeconomic variables symmetrically helped to revive Keynesian economics. The empirical basis of new Keynesian economics has been called the "triangle model," where the triangle refers to the three features of the *SP-DG* model of Chapter 8, namely demand shocks, supply shocks, and inflation inertia (i.e., slow adjustment of inflation).

Economic Behavior, 1982–91

After a decade (1972–82) when everything seemed to get worse, everything seemed to get better for the rest of the 1980s. The unemployment rate fell from 10.5 percent in late 1982 to 5.0 percent in early 1989. The inflation rate fell from double digits in 1981 to just 3 percent in mid-1986. The long-term interest rate fell gradually from its peak (see the bottom frame in Figure 18-3).

A major theme of this book has been the displacement of fiscal policy by monetary policy as the central tool of stabilization policy. The Reagan-era tax cuts of 1981–83 led to a decade of persistent natural employment deficits. A political stalemate over the solution to the deficit problem left policymakers unable to discuss short-term fiscal policy changes and added to the skepticism about activist fiscal policy built up during the events of the late 1960s.

As we have seen, from 1979 to 1982 monetary policy attempted to target monetary growth and abandoned any attempt to stabilize interest rates, contributing to the unprecedented high level and volatility of interest rates during that period. An important legacy of high interest rates in 1979–82 was the "Volcker disinflation" (Section 8-8), which helped to return the United States from the double-digit inflation of the late 1970s and early 1980s to a more moderate inflation rate that (excluding food and energy prices) remained below 5 percent for all but a few quarters after 1984.

However in August 1982, surprised at the depth of the 1981–82 recession, the Fed abandoned its brief flirtation with monetarism. It announced that it would no longer hold short-term interest rates at high levels; short-term interest rates promptly fell and the stock market soared. For the rest of the decade of the 1980s, the Fed appeared to follow a real GDP growth rule, allowing interest rates to fall and M1 growth to soar when growth in real GDP appeared to falter (as it did in 1985–86 as a result of the strong dollar), then tightening when the economy began to overheat, as in 1988–89.[9]

---

[9]A readable and comprehensive review of changes in monetary policy in the 1980s and 1990s, with an extensive list of references to the related literature, is Marvin Goodfriend, "Monetary Policy Comes of Age: A 20th Century Odyssey," *Federal Reserve Bank of Richmond Economic Quarterly,* vol. 83/1, Winter 1997, pp. 1–22. A very contemporary assessment of monetary policy in the 1990s is Alan S. Blinder, "What Central Bankers Could Learn from Academics—and Vice Versa," *Journal of Economic Perspectives,* vol. 11/2, Spring 1997, pp. 3–19.

Figure 18-3   **Key Macroeconomic Variables: 1970–1996**
This figure duplicates the format of Figure 18-2. Evident are the positive correlation of the inflation rate in the second frame and the unemployment rate in the third frame, due largely to the supply shocks of 1973–74 and 1979–81. This diagram exhibits the puzzles of the twin peaks of inflation, unemployment, and interest rates in the mid-1970s and early 1980s. Also visible are the disinflation of the early 1980s, the relatively mild recession of 1990–91, and the "Cinderella economy" of the mid-1990s.

New Ideas of the 1980s and Early 1990s

The real business cycle (RBC) theory, that is, the second and more recent version of new classical macroeconomics (Section 17-4), was not directly a response to events. But its introduction in the early 1980s found more ready acceptance against the background of the 1973–82 period, when supply shocks seemed a more dominant source of business cycles than demand shocks. The main debate about the RBC approach, as we learned in Section 17-5, does not concern the realism of supply shocks, but rather the one-sided assumption that only supply shocks matter, while demand shocks do not (thus denying, for instance, a role for demand in the Great Depression of the 1930s) and the theoretical reliance on continuous market clearing, without allowing a role for sticky prices and non-market clearing.

As the 1990s began, two new strains emerged in macroeconomics, although they had not yet developed into a named "theory." First was the debate over the twin deficits (Chapters 6 and 11), which reflected a belief that fiscal policy now had more of an impact on long-term economic growth and on slow productivity growth than on the business cycle. In a sense, here the usual pattern of events-cause-ideas was reversed, since supply-side economics (Section 11-6) was an idea that caused an event, namely persistent budget deficits.

The second new idea of the late 1980s and early 1990s was to discredit any role for monetary aggregates (like M1) in the conduct of monetary policy by the Fed. As shown in Figure 18-3, after 1980 there was almost no connection between the growth rate of M1 and the growth rate of nominal GDP. When M1 growth exceeds that of nominal GDP, it follows that the growth rate of velocity is negative. And the top frame of Figure 18-3 shows that velocity plummeted in 1985–87 and 1991–93, but soared in 1989 and 1995–96. The wild gyrations of M1 growth did not make the economy unstable; on the contrary, the growth rate of nominal GDP was much more stable than that of M1, and this was particularly true in the years 1992–96.

Economic Behavior, 1991–97

The economic expansion of the 1990s began in March 1991, the official date for the trough of the 1990–91 recession. The expansion was unusual in at least three ways. First, the first year and a half of the expansion was very weak. Employment barely grew in the first year, leading to the label "the jobless recovery." The unemployment rate peaked at 7.7 percent in July 1992, fully 16 months after the trough of the recession. Responding to the weak growth of jobs and to high unemployment, the Federal Reserve allowed short-term interest rates to remain low long into the expansion, with the Federal funds rate remaining at 3 percent from the autumn of 1992 until early 1994.

The second unusual aspect of the expansion was the behavior of inflation. Instead of accelerating as it had in 1987–90, inflation exhibited a slight deceleration from 1993 to 1997. While many economists had previously believed that the natural rate of unemployment was 6 percent or above, no acceleration of inflation occurred when the unemployment rate declined below 6 percent in late 1994 and remained below 5.5 percent during most of 1996 and 1997.

The third unusual aspect of the expansion was the behavior of monetary policy. In early 1994 the Fed began a sustained increase in short-term interest rates that took the federal funds rate up from 3 percent at the beginning of the year to 6 percent in early 1995. This action was widely described as a pre-emptive strike, since the Fed tightened monetary policy substantially even though there was no evidence of accelerating inflation. The Fed apparently believed that the natural rate of unemployment was 6 percent or above, and it predicted that declining unemployment would set off an acceleration of inflation, as in the late 1980s. The Fed was correct that unemployment would decline but incorrect about inflation; as of late 1997 there were still no signs of an acceleration of inflation. As a result, the Fed relented on interest rates and allowed the federal funds rate to decline from 6 percent to a range of 5.25–5.5 percent during 1996–97.

New Ideas of the Mid-1990s

The economy of the mid-1990s was often described as a "dream" or "Cinderella" economy. The unemployment rate in the spring of 1997 fell below 5 percent for the first time since 1973, and inflation was 2 percent or less by some measures. How did economists explain this fortunate outcome? New research methods allowed economists to estimate *variations* in the natural rate of unemployment.[10] As we learned in Section 8-8, it appears that the natural rate of unemployment declined substantially between the mid-1980s and mid-1990s. Thus, it was possible for the Fed to allow the unemployment rate to remain near 5 percent in 1997 without the acceleration of inflation that had occurred at a similar unemployment rate back in 1988–89.

The Fed's behavior indicated that it was implicitly using the natural rate of unemployment as a target, attempting to maintain the unemployment rate reasonably close to that target. But the Fed was also using information on the inflation rate to update its estimate of the natural rate of unemployment; as long as inflation was not accelerating, the Fed deduced that the natural rate of unemployment must be close to the actual rate of unemployment currently being experienced by the economy.

An Omitted Idea

No mention has yet been made of the new Keynesian approach (Chapter 17). Almost alone among the other major macro theories covered in this book, the new Keynesians' ideas did *not* emerge as a response to an event in the economy. Rather, the development of the new Keynesian theory seems to be mainly an intellectual event. Convinced of the continuing relevance of the original Keynesian paradigm based on sticky prices and non-market clearing, while impressed by Lucas's idea of rational expectations yet unconvinced of this reliance on continuous market clearing, the new Keynesians decided that

---

[10]See Robert J. Gordon, "The Time-Varying NAIRU and Its Implications for Economic Policy," *Journal of Economic Perspectives,* vol. 11 (February 1997), pp. 11–32, and other articles on the natural rate of unemployment (or NAIRU) in the same issue.

it was time to recombine the same ingredients with a different recipe. Thus, the essential ingredient of each type of new Keynesian theory is some obstacle to instantaneous price flexibility (i.e., price stickiness), justified by an analysis based on the assumptions of profit maximization and rational expectations at the level of the individual firm.

> *The main events of the 1971–97 period were the two supply shocks of 1974–75 and 1979–81, which created twin peaks of inflation, unemployment, and interest rates. Monetary policy shifted from the accommodation of supply shocks in the 1970s, to a restrictive policy that created the Volcker disinflation of 1980–84, and finally to a policy of real GDP and unemployment targeting that helped make possible the longest peacetime U.S. economic expansion, from 1982 to 1990, and another long expansion starting in 1991. New ideas spawned by these events included the real business cycle theory, concern over the twin deficits, discrediting of monetary aggregates, and the notion of a natural rate of unemployment that varies over time. The new Keynesian theory developed during this period cannot be linked to any specific event, but rather was a natural intellectual outgrowth of preceding theories.*

18-5 Reaction of Ideas to Events in the World Economy

Between the 1930s and mid-1960s, the United States was virtually a closed economy. In 1965 nominal exports and imports were barely 5 percent of GDP. But by 1997, foreign trade had become much more important, with nominal exports and imports of about 12 percent of GDP. In most other countries trade is an even larger share of GDP.

Interactions Between the World and U.S. Economies

After the Allied victory in World War II, the United States loomed large in the world economy. Its per-person GDP was far ahead of any other nation (see p. 274). Interactions between the world and the United States primarily flowed out from the United States in the form of such aid programs as the Marshall Plan (1948–53). Interactions that flowed in toward the U.S. economy consisted primarily of political events such as the Korean War, which (as we saw in Figure 18-2) destabilized the U.S. economy during the 1950–54 period. A smaller example was the 1956 Suez crisis, which led to a short-lived boom for U.S. exports in 1956–57; the end of this boom aggravated the 1957–58 recession.

Above we described overexpansionary fiscal and monetary policies as a principal legacy of the 1960s, endowing the U.S. economy after 1970 with a higher inflation rate than would have occurred under a different policy environment. Another legacy of the 1960s was the breakdown of the fixed exchange rate Bretton Woods system (Section 6-6), as the United States exported its inflation to other countries.

International Events Spawn Ideas: The Grass Is Greener

A simple way to summarize the international economy since the late 1960s is that the "grass is greener on the other side of the fence." This refers to the widespread enthusiasm for flexible exchange rates when the fixed (Bretton Woods) exchange rate system was breaking down, then the more recent longing for a return to fixed exchange rates, once observers noted that since 1973 flexible exchange rates were much more volatile and disruptive than had been predicted.

Flexible exchange rates had been expected to enable each country to attain monetary independence and choose the particular inflation rate that it desired. However, exchange rates turned out to be highly volatile and disruptive of the real economy, most notably when the dollar appreciated by 50 percent between 1980 and 1985, and then depreciated by the same amount between 1985 and 1987. The appreciation decimated the export markets of U.S. farms and factories, creating the common mid-1980s description of the Midwest as the Rust Belt. The depreciation took a long time to revive exports, but eventually the Midwest recovered and performed better after 1990 than the coastal regions. Whichever region prospered, there was no doubt that businesses, jobs, and lives were disrupted by the volatility of exchange rates.

Since the late 1970s economists and politicians have been searching for a way to return partially or completely to fixed exchange rates. The notable example is the European Monetary System, which surprised almost everyone by achieving a convergence of inflation rates within Europe (pp. 246–247). Some European countries, however, still have much higher unemployment rates than others (Section 19-10), leading to a debate about whether a unified European currency would rob individual countries of the freedom to devalue in order to revive their economies, as the United Kingdom, Italy, and other countries chose to do in 1992. The European countries which devalued their currencies relative to the deutsche mark in 1992 enjoyed much better economic performance during 1993–96.

International economics in the United States in the 1990s was dominated by the questions of competitiveness with Japan, the huge trade surpluses of China and Japan, and the desirability of free trade, particularly with China and other East Asian countries. Questions of trade policy involve relative prices and fall within the province of microeconomics, but there is an inevitable overlap with macroeconomics. For instance, a nation with a large trade deficit faces the alternatives of devaluation and protection. But these are not the only choices, as any reader of this book already knows. Net exports, domestic investment, and national saving are linked by a definition (equation [2.5] on p. 39), and an improvement in the trade deficit can be achieved by such macroeconomic policies as reducing the government budget deficit.

The main international events affecting the U.S. economy were the transition to flexible exchange rates in the early 1970s, and the dislocations caused by the ups and downs of the dollar in the 1980s. The unexpected volatility of exchange rates and the resulting dislocation of trade patterns led to a desire by many observers to return to some version of fixed exchange rates.

INTERNATIONAL PERSPECTIVE

How Does Macroeconomics Differ in the United States and Europe?

Europe consists of a large number of economies which in the aggregate have a larger economy than the United States, but which taken individually are smaller. Four main features differentiate European from U.S. macroeconomics; these are (1) the greater emphasis on international macroeconomic issues, (2) the continuing puzzle of high European unemployment, (3) the reversed roles of monetary and fiscal policy, and (4) the greater dominance of the Keynesian school of thought.

INTERNATIONAL EMPHASIS

Since foreign trade in countries like Belgium and the Netherlands accounts for more than half of GDP, it is natural that international issues which address the interaction of different economies play a greater role in European macroeconomics, while questions of stabilization policy at the national level play a lesser role. In the 1990s European macroeconomics was dominated by debates over the desirability of moving toward a single European currency. The 1992 Maastricht Treaty set down criteria for the maximum inflation rates, and deficit–GDP and debt–GDP ratios allowed for countries to enter the European Monetary Union (EMU) in 1999. In addition, the 1989–90 collapse of the Iron Curtain and the socialist economies of eastern Europe and the former Soviet Union also provided a full agenda, e.g., how much aid to provide those nations and whether (and when) they should be allowed to join trade and monetary unions previously established by western Europeans.

UNEMPLOYMENT PUZZLE

As we learned in Section 12-12, Europeans are envious of Japan and the United States for achieving lower unemployment rates throughout the 1990s. The restrictive monetary and fiscal policies adopted by many European countries attempting to meet the Maastricht criteria for joining the EMU are a partial explanation of high European unemployment. Also, Europeans worry that they may have gone too far in regulating business through such devices as penalties for closing factories, restrictions on shop-opening hours on weeknights and weekends, legislation of high minimum wage levels, and the encouragement of strong unions. In contrast, many in the United States feel that our lack of regulations has pushed down the incomes of a large number of low-income workers, who might have done better under the European system.

REVERSED ROLES FOR MONETARY AND FISCAL POLICY

A theme of this book has been the replacement of fiscal policy by monetary policy as the U.S. government's main tool to tame the business cycle. Fiscal policy is now thought to be important mainly for discussions about foreign indebtedness and long-run economic growth. But in Europe the roles of monetary and fiscal policy are reversed. Those nations that have linked their currencies to the deutsche mark have lost their monetary independence, because their monetary policy must be entirely devoted to adjusting interest rates as necessary to maintain their currencies within the required band against the deutsche mark. This leaves fiscal policy as the only available tool for short-run stabilization. In most European nations the parliamentary form of government allows fiscal policy to act with a much shorter legislative lag than in the United States, as long as the ruling party has a relatively strong majority (thus, fiscal policy can be changed instantly in the United Kingdom but not in Italy, which has a splintered set of weak political parties). Yet even fiscal policy has been handcuffed in the recent years as nations struggle to reduce their deficits to meet the Maastricht criteria for EMU.

KEYNESIAN SLANT

As we learned in Chapter 17, the new classical macroeconomics consists both of Lucas's original version (combining market clearing, imperfect information, and rational expectations) and the real business cycle version (combining market clearing with an exclusion of demand shocks, thus relying entirely on supply shocks to explain business cycles). A notable difference in European macroeconomics in recent decades has been near-total lack of interest in new classical economics and common reliance on the Keynesian approach based on sticky prices of goods and services, while allowing for flexible prices in the auction markets for stocks, bonds, and foreign exchange. The reason for this difference is not entirely clear; perhaps the emergence of persistent European unemployment in the 1980s and 1990s prevented European macroeconomists from paying much attention to the new classicals. Perhaps the difference is political, since American new classicals tend to be more politically conservative than many Europeans. Perhaps the difference lies in the greater relevance of short-run changes in fiscal policy in Europe. Or perhaps the answer is simpler: Lucas, Prescott, and other inventors of the new classical macroeconomics live in the United States, while Keynes lived on the other side of the Atlantic!

18-6   What We Know About the Six Puzzles

The first chapter of this book introduced six macroeconomic concepts and related puzzles involving each. We have repeatedly highlighted the puzzles in the margins of the book in order to connect topics and theories with the six puzzles. We are now ready to review what we have learned.

Puzzle 1: Why Has the Unemployment Rate Been So High and So Variable?

We have learned to distinguish the high natural unemployment rate from cyclical fluctuations of actual unemployment around the natural rate. The natural unemployment rate is high (roughly 5.0–5.5 percent) in the United States, due to frictional and structural (or mismatch) unemployment, although it is much higher in some European countries. Solutions include more investment in education, training, and other programs to help people gain skills to qualify for job openings. Cyclical unemployment is caused both by demand shocks and supply shocks, and by the inability of stabilization policy to react promptly, due to lags, uncertainty, and forecasting errors.

Puzzle 2: Why Has the Inflation Rate at Times Been So High and So Variable?

In the long run inflation is equal to excess nominal GDP growth, which in turn is equal to nominal GDP growth minus the growth rate of natural real GDP. Sustained rapid growth of nominal GDP requires rapid growth of the money supply, which may result from the need to finance excessive government deficits. Short-run volatility of the inflation rate stems from the same causes as short-run fluctuations of unemployment, namely, demand and supply shocks.

Puzzle 3: Why Has Productivity Grown So Slowly?

Growth in productivity sets a limit on the feasible growth in the standard of living. If, as some suggest, this generation of college students will be the first to be less well off than their parents, the slow growth in productivity will be responsible. By calculating the growth in multifactor productivity (MFP), we have learned that we can exclude the contribution of capital input to the growth in productivity. Because MFP growth has remained slow since the early 1970s, we know that factors other than capital input are the source of the puzzle. But there is no consensus regarding which factors are the most important (see pp. 314–19).

Puzzle 4: Why Have Real Interest Rates Been So High?

We have learned to distinguish long-term and short-term interest rates, as well as nominal and real interest rates. Long-term real interest rates remained relatively high throughout the 1980s and early 1990s. Variations in nominal interest rates reflected the ups and downs of inflation (puzzle #2), while high real interest rates were believed to reflect mainly the shift toward persistent federal budget deficits, i.e., toward a mix of easy fiscal and tight monetary policy.

Puzzle 5: Why Has the Government Budget Deficit Persisted?

The persistent federal budget deficit of the 1980s and early 1990s combines an increase in the share of spending in GDP with a constant share of revenues in GDP. Successive administrations and Congress refused to levy taxes high enough to pay for growing entitlement expenditures. However, by 1996–97 the federal budget deficit finally began to shrink, as the share of spending declined while a healthy economy and higher tax rates substantially boosted the share of revenues in GDP.

Puzzle 6: Why Has the United States' Trade Dropped into Persistent Deficit?

Our basic accounting identity (equation 2.5) states that the trade deficit (negative net exports) equals the government budget deficit plus the excess of private domestic investment over private saving. For most of the 1980s and 1990s private domestic investment and private saving were roughly equal, so that the trade deficit was roughly equal to the budget deficit. The basic mechanism connecting the twin deficits is the exchange rate; real interest rates were high enough to maintain a relatively strong dollar, resulting in a persistent current account deficit and capital account surplus.

18-7 Macro Mysteries: Unsettled Issues and Debates

In their professional research papers, economists (micro and macro alike) often conclude with a section called unsettled issues or agenda for future research. This macro text also concludes by reviewing six issues where the debate is still most open and lively in macroeconomics.

How Can Productivity Growth Be Increased?

Our discussion in Chapter 10 of the productivity slowdown was inconclusive. Multifactor productivity growth in the United States has lagged behind that of most other advanced nations for more than two decades, yet no solid clue is in sight. We do not lag notably in private investment, so the most recent policy proposals have called for more public investment, particularly in infrastructure and education. Yet each of these proposals is controversial. Microeconomists claim that we do not need more roads but instead could charge higher tolls to make the use of existing roads more efficient. Critics of more spending on education note that we spend as much or more on education (per person or as a share of GDP) as most other advanced nations. These debates are spirited but take us far beyond macroeconomics.

Should We Go for Zero Inflation?

One of the fuzziest debates in macroeconomics is over the costs of inflation and the output costs of stopping inflation. Canada and New Zealand are two nations that have made a commitment to achieving zero inflation, and so far they have been successful in achieving low inflation rates, but at the cost of persistent high unemployment. Does society reap a large benefit from, say, zero inflation as compared to 2 percent inflation? Is that benefit great enough to offset the costs of high unemployment? There is as yet no consensus on these questions.

Why Did the Natural Rate of Unemployment Decline?

In 1996–97 the United States experienced a "Cinderella" economy, with sustained real income growth, the lowest unemployment rate since 1973, and relatively low inflation. Despite low unemployment, inflation did not accelerate in response, leading economists and the Fed governors to conclude that the natural rate of unemployment had fallen substantially since the late 1980s. But why did the natural rate decline? Many suggestions were offered, including weak labor unions, worker anxiety over the fear of losing jobs, competition for jobs from immigrants, and the strong dollar, and the competition of foreign workers and markets operating through imports and global competition. Recent research suggests that a surprisingly strong role in driving down the natural rate of unemployment has been played by the growing importance of computers (with prices falling by 40 or 50 percent per year, thus driving down the average rate of inflation), and the managed care revolution in American medicine that has created a rapid decline in medical care inflation.

Rules Versus Activism

Our treatment of stabilization policy in Chapter 14 focused on the ambiguity of rules. Four types of shocks (money supply, money demand, commodity demand, and commodity supply) create extensive slippage between policy instruments and such target variables as inflation and unemployment. Feasible rules involve controlling instruments like high-powered money or the federal funds rate, leaving open the possibility of wide fluctuations in target variables. But rules for target variables (e.g., a zero inflation target) may not be feasible and may require unmanageable volatility in policy instruments. The difficulty in choosing a rule, together with the temptation to use discretion in breaking away from a rule, make the conduct of stabilization policy difficult.

The Twin Deficits

Is it harmful for the United States to run persistent budget deficits? If so, is the reason the accumulation of foreign indebtedness? To some extent in recent years this issue has become secondary to the overwhelming fact of slow growth in multifactor productivity. We calculated in Chapter 6 that the buildup of foreign indebtedness by the United States had robbed us of 0.1 percentage point of productivity growth each year since 1981. For future growth in the U.S. standard of living, it appears that we could virtually forget the problems posed by the twin deficits if we could figure out a way of adding an extra 0.1 percent per year to the U.S. rate of productivity growth.

Differences Among Countries

The science of comparative macroeconomics is only beginning to address the many differences among countries. Why is productivity growth in the United States so slow? Why do individuals in Italy and Japan save so much? Why is unemployment so low in Japan and so high in France and Spain? Why do some countries like Chile and Argentina suffer from hyperinflations for a time but then enter a period of economic stability, whereas other nations cannot make the same transition, even if they implement similar policies? All these questions will remain the subject of active debate among macroeconomists for years, if not decades.

A Final Word

We have learned in this chapter about the evolution of events and ideas. Many important economic ideas respond to events, changes in economic behavior that are not compatible with previous economic theories. Virtually every theory discussed in this book has evolved in some way in response to changing macroeconomic behavior.

This book has emphasized that the United States does not stand alone. Macroeconomics makes no sense if it applies to one country but cannot explain events in other countries or differences in behavior among countries. The International Perspectives boxes in this book help to introduce readers to important differences between the United States and other advanced countries. Some differences can be explained by our theories; others cannot. A careful study of these differences reveals some that are explained by macroeconomic theory but others that require knowledge of microeconomic theory and institutions to reach a full understanding.

As we end this book, one thing is sure. While there are many things we do not understand, there are many things that we do. Any reader of this book now qualifies as an instant critic of popular and media discussions of macroeconomics. Any reader is now equipped to dissect the many misleading journalistic statements about the economy appearing almost every day, and also to recognize those statements that reflect the remaining puzzles that truly qualify as macro mysteries.

SUMMARY

1. Just as real-world events illustrate how theories work, sometimes real-world events make some theories obsolete and spur the invention of new theories. Many of the important theories discussed in this book evolved from an attempt to understand surprising events.

2. The big event of the interwar period was the Great Depression. This event spawned a big idea, the Keynesian revolution, with its emphasis on aggregate demand, sticky prices, and fiscal policy.

3. The big events of the 1947–70 period were the instability of aggregate demand, due in part to the Korean and Vietnam wars, the overstimulation of the economy after 1964 by both monetary and fiscal policy, and the ensuing acceleration of inflation. Spawned in part by these events were several new ideas, including the Phillips curve, the new economics, monetarism, and the natural rate hypothesis.

4. The main events of the 1971–97 period were the two supply shocks of 1974–75 and 1979–81, which created twin peaks of inflation, unemployment, and interest rates. Also important were the Volcker disinflation, persistent budget deficits in the 1980s and the Cinderella economy of the mid-1990s, which combined low unemployment with low inflation. New ideas spawned by these events included the real business cycle theory, concern over the twin deficits, and the suggestion that the natural rate of unemployment varies over time.

5. The main international events affecting the U.S. economy were the transition to flexible exchange rates in the early 1970s and the dislocations caused by the ups and downs of the dollar in the 1980s. The unexpected volatility of exchange rates and the resulting dislocation of trade patterns led many observers to desire a return to some version of fixed exchange rates.

6. The average level of unemployment includes frictional and structural unemployment. Cycles in unemployment, together with the volatility of inflation and interest rates, reflect the combined influence of demand shocks, supply shocks, and inflation inertia. The slowdown in productivity growth remains a mystery. Volatile interest rates reflect demand and supply shocks, as well as the Fed's policy in 1979–82 of attempting to target money and ignore interest rates. Persistent fiscal deficits reflected a political stalemate that seemed finally to be broken in 1996–97, while the foreign trade deficit was caused in part by the fiscal deficit.

7. Remaining macro mysteries still under active debate include the causes of the productivity slowdown, the costs and benefits of zero inflation, the reasons for the decline in the mid-1990s in the natural rate of unemployment, the merits of various policy rules and of activism, the sources of the twin deficits, the urgency of ending the fiscal deficit, and, finally, reasons why macroeconomic behavior differs so much among countries.

QUESTIONS

Questions

1. Explain how the period 1923–29 was consistent with the old classical approach and how the period 1930–33 was not.
2. How did the economy in the late 1930s seem to reinforce the old Keynesian school?
3. How did the behavior of the economy during World War II support the main themes of the Keynesian revolution?
4. What events caused fiscal activism to fall out of favor by the end of the 1960s?
5. What caused the twin peaks of unemployment and inflation in 1974–75 and 1980–82? What theoretical innovations developed to explain the twin peaks?
6. Why did both unemployment and inflation decline after 1982?
7. What is meant by the "Cinderella economy" of the mid-1990s? How do you explain its main features?
8. Which macroeconomic theories were responses to events and which were not?
9. What events have led to increased interest in a return to fixed exchange rates?
10. For which of the six puzzles introduced in Chapter 1 do we have a reasonably secure understanding, and for which do we not yet have a reasonably good explanation?

Appendix A
Time Series Data for the U.S. Economy: 1875–1996

Table A-1: Annual Data, 1875–1996

	Nominal GDP (X) (B $)	GDP Deflator (1992 = 100)	Real GDP (Y) (B 1992$)	Natural Real GDP (YN) (B 1992$)	Unemploy. Rate (U) (Percent)	Natural Unemploy. Rate (UN) (Percent)	Money Supply (M1) (B $)	Money Supply (M2) (B $)	Labor Productivity (Y/N) (1992=100)	Nominal Interest Rate (r) (Percent)	S&P Stock Price Index (1941-43 =100)
1875	9.3	6.9	135.2	139.5	—	—	—	2.4	11.8	4.8	—
1876	9.0	6.6	136.8	145.9	—	—	—	2.4	12.1	4.6	—
1877	9.2	6.5	141.1	152.7	—	—	—	2.3	12.3	4.6	—
1878	9.0	6.1	147.1	159.7	—	—	—	2.2	12.5	4.5	—
1879	9.8	5.9	165.1	167.1	—	—	—	2.3	12.8	4.3	—
1880	11.5	6.2	184.7	174.7	—	—	—	2.8	12.9	4.2	—
1881	11.8	6.2	191.2	182.8	—	—	—	3.4	12.9	4.0	—
1882	12.9	6.3	203.3	191.2	—	—	—	3.7	13.0	4.0	—
1883	12.7	6.1	208.4	200.0	—	—	—	3.9	13.1	4.0	—
1884	12.4	5.8	212.2	209.2	—	—	—	3.9	13.1	4.0	—
1885	12.2	5.7	213.7	214.8	—	—	—	4.0	13.2	3.9	—
1886	12.5	5.7	220.2	220.5	—	—	—	4.3	13.3	3.7	—
1887	13.1	5.7	230.1	226.3	—	—	—	4.6	13.3	3.7	—
1888	13.3	5.8	229.0	232.3	—	—	—	4.8	13.4	3.7	—
1889	14.1	5.8	243.3	238.4	—	—	—	5.0	13.5	3.6	—
1890	14.0	5.7	246.7	244.7	4.0	4.2	—	5.5	13.2	3.7	—
1891	14.4	5.7	254.7	251.2	5.4	4.2	—	5.7	13.3	3.8	—
1892	14.9	5.6	266.7	260.7	3.0	4.2	—	6.2	13.4	3.7	—
1893	14.9	5.6	266.6	270.6	11.7	4.2	—	6.0	13.6	3.8	—
1894	13.7	5.3	258.8	280.9	18.4	4.2	—	6.0	13.7	3.6	—
1895	15.1	5.2	289.1	291.5	13.7	4.2	—	6.2	14.4	3.6	—
1896	14.8	5.2	282.5	302.6	14.4	4.2	—	6.1	14.1	3.6	—
1897	15.8	5.2	305.6	314.0	14.5	4.2	—	6.5	14.8	3.5	—
1898	16.4	5.2	312.9	325.9	12.4	4.2	—	7.4	15.0	3.4	—
1899	18.6	5.3	349.2	338.3	6.5	4.2	—	8.5	15.6	3.4	—
1900	19.3	5.4	356.0	351.1	5.0	4.2	—	9.2	15.8	3.4	6.1
1901	21.8	5.5	399.5	364.3	4.0	4.2	—	10.5	16.9	3.4	7.8
1902	22.5	5.5	406.4	378.0	3.7	4.2	—	11.5	16.5	3.4	8.4
1903	23.8	5.7	418.1	392.2	3.9	4.2	—	12.2	16.5	3.6	7.2
1904	24.9	5.7	434.0	406.9	5.4	4.2	—	12.9	17.4	3.6	7.0
1905	27.2	5.7	473.7	422.2	4.3	4.3	—	14.3	18.1	3.6	9.0
1906	29.2	5.9	493.2	438.1	1.7	4.3	—	15.5	18.1	3.6	9.6
1907	30.0	6.2	485.6	454.5	2.8	4.3	—	16.2	17.5	3.7	8.1
1908	27.8	6.1	459.0	471.6	8.0	4.3	—	16.0	17.2	3.7	7.8
1909	31.1	6.1	512.6	489.3	5.1	4.3	—	17.8	18.3	3.7	9.7
1910	32.5	6.3	514.8	507.7	5.9	4.3	—	18.6	17.9	3.8	9.4
1911	33.4	6.3	531.2	524.2	6.7	4.3	—	19.7	18.1	3.8	9.2
1912	36.2	6.5	561.9	541.2	4.6	4.3	—	21.1	18.6	3.8	9.5
1913	38.0	6.5	584.0	558.8	4.3	4.3	—	22.0	19.1	3.9	8.5
1914	35.6	6.6	539.8	577.0	7.9	4.3	—	23.0	18.0	1.9	4.1
1915	37.8	6.8	559.8	595.7	8.5	4.3	12.2	24.6	18.9	4.0	8.3
1916	47.9	7.4	650.6	615.1	5.1	4.3	14.3	29.3	20.4	3.9	9.5

Continued

A1

	Nominal GDP (X) (B $)	GDP Deflator (1992 = 100)	Real GDP (Y) (B 1992$)	Natural Real GDP (YN) (B 1992$)	Unemploy. Rate (U) (Percent)	Natural Unemploy. Rate (UN) (Percent)	Money Supply (M1) (B $)	Money Supply (M2) (B $)	Labor Productiv- ity (Y/N) (1992 = 100)	Nominal Interest Rate (r) (Percent)	S&P Stock Price Index (1941-43 =100)
1917	57.3	8.8	650.4	635.1	4.6	4.3	16.7	34.2	20.0	4.1	8.5
1918	72.5	10.3	700.5	655.7	1.4	4.4	18.5	37.4	21.7	4.3	7.5
1919	80.3	11.8	680.2	677.0	1.4	4.4	21.2	43.4	21.8	4.3	9.2
1920	90.7	13.6	665.7	699.0	5.2	4.4	23.1	48.7	21.1	4.9	8.3
1921	76.2	11.9	642.3	721.7	11.7	4.4	20.9	45.9	22.6	5.1	7.2
1922	75.9	11.0	688.3	745.2	6.7	4.4	21.1	47.2	22.5	4.3	8.7
1923	89.0	11.3	784.7	769.4	2.4	4.4	22.3	51.2	23.8	4.3	8.9
1924	91.4	11.4	805.5	794.4	5.0	4.4	23.1	54.0	25.0	4.1	9.4
1925	95.1	11.6	823.6	814.8	3.2	4.4	25.0	58.8	24.7	3.8	11.6
1926	101.4	11.6	873.1	835.7	1.8	4.5	25.5	61.2	25.3	3.5	13.0
1927	100.2	11.4	878.0	857.2	3.3	4.5	25.4	62.6	25.6	3.3	15.3
1928	101.2	11.3	894.2	879.2	4.2	4.5	25.7	64.9	25.8	3.3	19.4
1929	108.1	11.4	951.7	901.8	3.2	4.5	25.9	65.2	26.9	3.5	24.7
1930	94.8	11.0	862.1	925.0	8.9	4.5	25.1	64.0	26.2	3.5	19.4
1931	79.5	10.1	788.8	948.7	16.3	4.5	23.5	59.8	26.1	4.4	12.2
1932	60.8	8.9	682.9	973.1	24.1	4.7	20.6	50.4	25.6	5.7	6.3
1933	58.2	8.7	668.6	998.1	25.2	4.7	19.4	45.1	25.3	4.7	8.2
1934	68.2	9.5	719.8	1023.8	22.0	4.7	21.3	48.2	27.7	3.8	9.4
1935	75.7	9.7	778.2	1050.1	20.3	4.7	25.2	54.7	28.4	3.5	10.2
1936	86.4	9.7	888.2	1077.0	17.0	4.7	28.7	60.9	30.1	2.9	14.4
1937	94.9	10.2	932.5	1104.7	14.3	4.8	30.1	64.0	29.8	3.0	14.4
1938	88.8	10.0	890.8	1133.1	19.1	4.8	29.7	63.7	31.1	3.5	10.8
1939	94.9	9.9	961.1	1162.2	17.2	4.8	33.3	69.0	31.9	3.0	11.6
1940	104.4	10.1	1036.6	1192.0	14.6	4.8	38.7	77.3	33.0	2.8	10.8
1941	130.5	10.7	1219.7	1222.7	9.9	4.8	45.3	87.5	35.6	2.8	9.8
1942	165.4	11.4	1448.9	1254.1	4.7	4.8	54.0	99.7	39.3	2.8	8.7
1943	200.4	11.7	1711.7	1286.3	1.9	4.9	70.4	125.8	44.7	2.7	11.5
1944	219.8	11.9	1851.7	1319.3	1.2	4.9	83.1	149.5	49.1	2.7	12.5
1945	221.9	12.2	1817.1	1353.2	1.9	4.9	96.7	177.2	50.9	2.6	15.2
1946	220.9	15.0	1471.2	1388.0	3.9	4.9	103.8	194.1	40.9	2.5	17.1
1947	244.6	17.1	1430.7	1423.6	3.9	4.9	108.9	204.4	39.0	2.6	15.2
1948	269.7	18.1	1491.0	1460.2	3.8	5.0	109.4	207.3	39.9	2.8	15.5
1949	267.8	18.1	1479.9	1508.3	6.1	5.1	108.3	206.4	41.3	2.7	15.2
1950	294.6	18.3	1611.4	1574.8	5.2	5.2	111.2	211.1	44.2	2.6	18.4
1951	339.8	19.6	1734.0	1644.2	3.3	5.3	116.2	219.0	45.3	2.9	22.3
1952	358.6	19.9	1798.7	1716.7	3.0	5.5	122.0	230.9	46.1	3.0	24.5
1953	379.7	20.2	1881.4	1790.9	2.9	5.6	125.1	239.6	47.2	3.2	24.7
1954	381.3	20.4	1868.2	1863.6	5.6	5.8	127.0	248.0	48.1	2.9	29.7
1955	415.1	20.7	2001.2	1934.3	4.4	5.9	131.0	257.2	50.1	3.1	40.5
1956	438.0	21.5	2040.2	2001.7	4.1	5.9	132.6	261.6	49.7	3.4	46.6
1957	461.1	22.2	2078.6	2059.6	4.3	5.7	133.3	268.5	50.9	3.9	44.4
1958	467.3	22.7	2057.6	2125.1	6.9	5.5	134.8	281.6	52.0	3.8	46.2
1959	507.3	23.0	2210.2	2194.2	5.5	5.4	140.0	297.8	54.2	4.4	57.4
1960	526.6	23.3	2262.9	2272.8	5.5	5.5	140.7	312.4	54.8	4.4	55.9
1961	544.8	23.5	2314.3	2350.6	6.7	5.7	145.2	335.5	56.5	4.4	66.3
1962	585.2	23.8	2454.8	2433.6	5.6	5.8	147.8	362.7	59.2	4.3	62.4
1963	617.4	24.1	2559.4	2529.4	5.7	5.9	153.3	393.3	61.2	4.3	69.9
1964	663.0	24.5	2708.4	2630.6	5.2	6.0	160.3	424.8	63.8	4.4	81.4
1965	719.1	25.0	2881.1	2746.3	4.5	6.1	167.9	459.2	65.8	4.5	88.2
1966	787.8	25.7	3069.2	2851.9	3.8	6.2	172.0	480.2	68.0	5.1	85.3
1967	833.6	26.5	3147.2	2957.6	3.8	6.3	183.3	524.8	69.2	5.5	91.9
1968	910.6	27.6	3293.9	3057.1	3.6	6.4	197.4	566.9	71.6	6.2	98.7
1969	982.2	28.9	3393.6	3173.2	3.5	6.3	203.9	587.9	71.6	7.0	97.8
1970	1035.6	30.5	3397.6	3306.1	5.0	6.4	214.4	626.6	72.7	8.0	83.2
1971	1125.4	32.1	3510.0	3452.1	5.9	6.3	228.3	710.3	75.6	7.4	98.3
1972	1237.3	33.4	3702.3	3614.3	5.6	6.2	249.2	802.3	78.2	7.2	109.2
1973	1382.7	35.3	3916.4	3759.2	4.9	6.1	262.8	855.5	80.7	7.4	107.4

Continued

1974	1496.9	38.5	3891.2	3898.4	5.6	6.1	274.3	902.5	79.4	8.6	82.9
1975	1630.6	42.1	3873.9	4029.0	8.5	6.0	287.5	1017.0	81.5	8.8	86.2
1976	1819.0	44.6	4082.9	4164.1	7.7	6.2	306.3	1152.7	84.5	8.4	102.0
1977	2026.9	47.4	4273.6	4301.7	7.1	6.4	331.3	1271.5	85.8	8.0	98.2
1978	2291.4	50.9	4503.0	4437.1	6.1	6.5	358.4	1368.0	86.9	8.7	96.0
1979	2557.5	55.2	4630.6	4565.7	5.9	6.5	382.8	1475.7	86.3	9.6	103.0
1980	2784.2	60.3	4615.0	4690.5	7.2	6.5	408.8	1601.0	86.0	11.9	118.8
1981	3115.9	66.0	4720.7	4805.3	7.6	6.5	436.5	1756.0	86.9	14.2	128.1
1982	3242.1	70.2	4620.3	4930.8	9.7	6.4	474.5	1910.9	86.3	13.8	119.7
1983	3514.5	73.2	4803.7	5071.0	9.6	6.3	521.1	2127.9	89.9	12.0	160.4
1984	3902.4	75.9	5140.1	5230.8	7.5	6.2	552.1	2312.4	91.4	12.7	160.5
1985	4180.7	78.5	5323.6	5397.1	7.2	6.1	619.8	2497.8	92.3	11.4	186.8
1986	4422.2	80.6	5487.7	5529.5	7.0	6.1	724.4	2734.6	94.7	9.0	236.3
1987	4692.3	83.1	5649.5	5650.1	6.2	6.1	749.8	2834.4	94.5	9.4	286.8
1988	5049.6	86.1	5865.2	5777.1	5.5	6.2	786.9	2997.9	95.3	9.7	265.8
1989	5438.7	89.7	6062.0	5922.9	5.3	6.2	794.2	3164.0	95.8	9.3	322.8
1990	5743.8	93.6	6136.3	6042.0	5.6	6.3	825.8	3282.2	96.3	9.3	334.6
1991	5916.7	97.3	6079.4	6158.5	6.7	6.2	897.2	3383.7	97.0	8.8	376.2
1992	6244.5	100.0	6244.4	6277.1	7.4	6.2	1024.4	3438.7	100.0	8.1	415.7
1993	6558.1	102.6	6389.6	6433.5	6.8	6.0	1128.6	3494.0	100.1	7.2	451.4
1994	6947.0	105.1	6610.7	6579.7	6.1	5.9	1148.7	3509.2	100.6	8.0	460.3
1995	7265.4	107.8	6742.1	6722.7	5.6	5.7	1124.9	3657.4	100.7	7.6	541.6
1996	7636.0	110.2	6928.4	6869.0	5.4	5.7	1076.9	3825.6	102.1	7.4	670.8

Table A-2: Quarterly Data, 1947:Q1—1997:Q2

	Nominal GDP (X) (B $)	GDP Deflator (1992 =100)	Real GDP (Y) (B 1992$)	Natural Real GDP (Y^N) (B 1992$)	Unemploy. Rate (U) (Percent)	Natural Unemploy. Rate (U^N) (Percent)	Money Supply (M1) (B $)	Money Supply (M2) (B $)	Labor Productiv- ity (Y/N) (1992=100)	Nominal Interest Rate (r) (Percent)	Real Federal Budget Surplus (B 1992$)	Trade- Weighted Exchange Rate (Mar 1973 =100)
1947:Q1	237.4	16.9	1402.5	1416.0	3.9	4.9	107.3	197.5	38.2	2.6	−84.6	—
1947:Q2	240.9	16.9	1424.6	1416.0	3.9	4.9	109.0	200.4	39.3	2.5	−76.9	—
1947:Q3	245.1	17.1	1437.5	1416.0	3.9	4.9	110.0	202.6	38.4	2.6	−55.6	—
1947:Q4	255.0	17.5	1458.1	1416.0	3.9	5.0	110.5	204.4	39.9	2.8	−82.1	—
1948:Q1	260.8	17.7	1474.3	1452.3	3.7	5.0	110.5	205.0	39.8	2.8	−72.1	—
1948:Q2	267.9	17.9	1493.9	1452.3	3.7	5.0	109.5	203.9	39.9	2.8	−55.0	—
1948:Q3	274.4	18.3	1497.0	1452.3	3.8	5.0	109.6	204.2	39.9	2.8	−29.8	—
1948:Q4	275.8	18.4	1498.9	1468.1	3.8	5.0	109.2	203.7	40.1	2.8	−16.9	—
1949:Q1	270.6	18.3	1480.1	1484.0	4.7	5.0	108.7	203.1	40.5	2.7	−2.4	—
1949:Q2	266.7	18.1	1474.1	1500.1	5.9	5.0	108.8	203.6	40.9	2.7	17.1	—
1949:Q3	268.1	18.0	1490.7	1516.4	6.7	5.1	108.5	203.2	42.0	2.6	21.3	—
1949:Q4	265.7	18.0	1474.5	1532.8	7.0	5.1	108.5	203.2	41.7	2.6	21.8	—
1950:Q1	276.0	17.9	1538.2	1549.4	6.4	5.1	109.4	204.8	43.4	2.6	25.0	—
1950:Q2	285.3	18.0	1584.5	1566.2	5.6	5.2	111.1	207.5	43.8	2.6	−40.5	—
1950:Q3	302.8	18.4	1644.1	1583.2	4.6	5.2	112.3	209.0	44.6	2.6	−84.4	—
1950:Q4	314.4	18.7	1678.6	1600.4	4.2	5.2	113.2	210.2	44.8	2.7	−87.6	—
1951:Q1	329.5	19.5	1693.1	1617.7	3.5	5.3	114.4	212.0	44.7	2.7	−89.7	—
1951:Q2	337.1	19.6	1724.0	1635.3	3.1	5.3	115.5	213.7	44.8	2.9	−41.1	—
1951:Q3	344.0	19.6	1758.2	1653.0	3.2	5.4	117.0	216.6	45.8	2.9	−5.1	—
1951:Q4	348.4	19.8	1760.6	1670.9	3.4	5.4	119.1	220.4	45.8	3.0	8.7	—
1952:Q1	351.7	19.8	1779.2	1689.0	3.1	5.4	120.7	223.6	45.8	3.0	−0.6	—
1952:Q2	352.5	19.8	1778.8	1707.3	3.0	5.5	121.6	225.8	46.1	2.9	18.9	—
1952:Q3	358.7	20.0	1790.9	1725.9	3.2	5.5	122.9	228.6	45.9	2.9	37.1	—
1952:Q4	371.4	20.1	1846.0	1744.6	2.8	5.5	124.2	231.5	46.6	3.0	18.5	—
1953:Q1	378.5	20.1	1882.6	1763.2	2.7	5.6	124.7	233.2	46.9	3.1	22.3	—
1953:Q2	382.1	20.1	1897.3	1781.7	2.6	5.6	125.5	235.4	47.1	3.3	30.4	—
1953:Q3	381.6	20.2	1887.4	1800.1	2.7	5.7	125.7	236.8	47.4	3.3	28.4	—

Continued

	Nominal GDP (X) (B $)	GDP Deflator (1992 =100)	Real GDP (Y) (B 1992$)	Natural Real GDP (Y^N) (B 1992$)	Unemploy. Rate (U) (Percent)	Natural Unemploy. Rate (U^N) (Percent)	Money Supply (M1) (B $)	Money Supply (M2) (B $)	Labor Productivity (Y/N) (1992=100)	Nominal Interest Rate (r) (Percent)	Real Federal Budget Surplus (B 1992$)	Trade-Weighted Exchange Rate (Mar 1973 =100)
1953:Q4	376.6	20.3	1858.2	1818.4	3.7	5.7	125.8	238.3	47.2	3.1	57.3	—
1954:Q1	376.4	20.3	1849.9	1836.6	5.3	5.7	126.1	240.3	47.4	3.0	49.9	—
1954:Q2	376.9	20.4	1848.5	1854.7	5.8	5.8	126.4	242.5	47.7	2.9	31.8	—
1954:Q3	381.7	20.4	1868.9	1872.6	6.0	5.8	127.6	245.8	48.5	2.9	24.7	—
1954:Q4	390.1	20.5	1905.6	1890.4	5.3	5.9	129.0	248.4	48.9	2.9	9.6	—
1955:Q1	402.9	20.6	1959.6	1908.1	4.7	5.9	130.4	251.2	49.9	3.0	−8.0	—
1955:Q2	411.3	20.6	1994.4	1925.7	4.4	5.9	131.2	252.8	50.1	3.0	−22.0	—
1955:Q3	419.8	20.8	2020.1	1943.1	4.1	5.9	131.8	254.1	50.3	3.1	−20.9	—
1955:Q4	426.4	21.0	2030.5	1960.4	4.2	6.0	132.0	255.0	50.0	3.1	−28.9	—
1956:Q1	429.0	21.2	2023.6	1977.8	4.0	5.9	132.5	255.7	49.5	3.1	−28.6	—
1956:Q2	434.7	21.3	2037.7	1995.4	4.2	6.0	132.8	257.0	49.7	3.3	−25.7	—
1956:Q3	439.6	21.6	2033.4	2010.7	4.1	5.8	132.9	258.1	49.7	3.4	−22.8	—
1956:Q4	448.5	21.7	2066.2	2022.8	4.1	5.8	133.5	259.7	50.0	3.7	−27.4	—
1957:Q1	457.2	22.0	2077.5	2036.8	3.9	5.7	133.8	261.9	50.6	3.7	−19.8	—
1957:Q2	459.0	22.2	2071.9	2051.7	4.1	5.7	133.8	263.8	50.5	3.8	−11.6	—
1957:Q3	466.4	22.3	2094.0	2067.1	4.2	5.6	133.9	265.6	51.3	4.1	−11.5	—
1957:Q4	461.6	22.3	2070.8	2083.0	4.9	5.6	133.1	266.3	51.3	4.0	5.8	—
1958:Q1	454.0	22.6	2012.6	2100.0	6.3	5.6	133.0	269.1	50.6	3.6	31.3	—
1958:Q2	458.3	22.6	2024.7	2116.4	7.4	5.5	134.4	275.7	51.6	3.6	50.0	—
1958:Q3	471.8	22.8	2072.3	2132.7	7.3	5.5	135.8	280.5	52.6	3.9	50.2	—
1958:Q4	485.2	22.9	2120.6	2151.1	6.4	5.4	137.5	283.8	53.3	4.1	41.3	—
1959:Q1	496.3	22.9	2165.0	2167.8	5.8	5.4	139.3	287.8	53.7	4.1	12.7	—
1959:Q2	509.3	22.9	2223.3	2184.6	5.1	5.4	140.5	292.1	54.4	4.4	20.5	—
1959:Q3	509.6	22.9	2221.4	2201.8	5.3	5.4	141.5	296.1	54.3	4.5	6.1	—
1959:Q4	513.8	23.0	2231.0	2222.5	5.6	5.4	140.3	297.1	54.3	4.6	5.6	—
1960:Q1	527.3	23.1	2279.2	2242.9	5.1	5.4	139.9	298.7	55.6	4.6	51.4	—
1960:Q2	526.1	23.2	2265.5	2262.9	5.2	5.5	139.6	301.1	54.7	4.5	35.7	—
1960:Q3	529.0	23.3	2268.3	2282.9	5.5	5.5	140.9	306.5	54.8	4.3	27.9	—
1960:Q4	523.9	23.4	2238.6	2302.4	6.3	5.5	140.8	310.9	54.2	4.3	12.0	—
1961:Q1	528.1	23.5	2251.7	2321.6	6.8	5.6	141.5	316.3	54.9	4.3	11.1	117.9
1961:Q2	538.9	23.5	2292.0	2341.6	7.0	5.6	142.6	322.1	56.3	4.3	4.7	117.6
1961:Q3	549.6	23.6	2332.6	2360.4	6.8	5.7	143.4	327.6	57.1	4.4	12.7	118.5
1961:Q4	562.6	23.6	2381.0	2378.8	6.2	5.7	144.7	333.3	57.8	4.4	21.2	118.6
1962:Q1	575.3	23.7	2422.6	2399.3	5.6	5.7	145.6	340.2	58.9	4.4	10.5	118.8
1962:Q2	582.8	23.8	2448.0	2420.9	5.5	5.8	146.6	347.4	58.6	4.3	10.5	119.4
1962:Q3	589.9	23.9	2471.9	2444.2	5.6	5.8	146.5	352.8	59.3	4.3	14.7	119.5
1962:Q4	592.9	23.9	2476.7	2470.1	5.5	5.8	147.3	359.9	59.8	4.3	10.9	119.3
1963:Q1	602.2	24.0	2508.7	2494.3	5.8	5.9	148.8	367.9	60.2	4.2	18.3	119.4
1963:Q2	610.9	24.1	2538.1	2518.0	5.7	5.8	150.2	375.9	60.7	4.2	27.0	119.6
1963:Q3	623.7	24.1	2586.3	2540.1	5.5	5.9	151.7	383.6	61.8	4.3	24.1	119.7
1963:Q4	632.8	24.3	2604.6	2565.0	5.6	5.9	153.2	391.0	61.9	4.3	19.3	119.6
1964:Q1	649.4	24.4	2666.7	2589.3	5.5	6.0	154.2	397.5	63.5	4.4	8.2	119.6
1964:Q2	658.4	24.4	2697.5	2614.5	5.2	6.0	155.2	404.3	63.9	4.4	−10.7	119.7
1964:Q3	669.2	24.5	2729.6	2643.9	5.0	6.0	157.8	413.5	64.3	4.4	4.1	119.6
1964:Q4	675.1	24.6	2739.7	2674.6	5.0	6.0	159.8	422.0	63.6	4.4	12.6	119.4
1965:Q1	695.6	24.8	2808.9	2704.2	4.9	6.0	161.0	430.4	64.6	4.4	31.1	119.4
1965:Q2	708.2	24.9	2846.3	2732.2	4.7	6.1	162.0	437.6	65.1	4.4	26.9	119.7
1965:Q3	725.0	25.0	2898.8	2760.9	4.4	6.1	163.9	446.1	66.1	4.5	−1.2	119.8
1965:Q4	747.7	25.2	2970.5	2787.8	4.1	6.1	166.9	455.8	67.2	4.6	−2.0	119.6
1966:Q1	770.5	25.3	3042.4	2812.9	3.9	6.1	169.7	464.6	68.2	4.8	20.9	119.7
1966:Q2	780.0	25.5	3055.5	2838.4	3.8	6.2	171.6	470.2	67.9	5.0	17.2	119.8
1966:Q3	793.6	25.8	3076.5	2865.3	3.8	6.3	171.0	472.9	67.8	5.3	5.4	119.7
1966:Q4	807.1	26.0	3102.4	2891.1	3.7	6.3	171.5	477.7	68.2	5.4	−2.3	119.9
1967:Q1	817.5	26.1	3127.2	2919.4	3.8	6.3	173.2	485.5	68.8	5.1	−34.0	119.8
1967:Q2	823.3	26.3	3129.5	2946.5	3.8	6.3	175.6	497.1	69.1	5.3	−32.7	119.7
1967:Q3	838.9	26.6	3154.2	2970.6	3.8	6.3	179.5	510.6	69.4	5.6	−28.2	119.7
1967:Q4	854.7	26.9	3178.0	2994.0	3.9	6.4	182.5	521.4	69.6	6.0	−30.5	120.6

Continued

1968:Q1	880.5	27.2	3236.2	3018.6	3.7	6.4	184.7	530.2	71.1	6.1	−23.9	122.0
1968:Q2	904.9	27.5	3292.1	3045.1	3.6	6.4	188.0	539.1	71.9	6.3	−27.6	122.1
1968:Q3	920.1	27.7	3316.1	3069.7	3.5	6.4	191.7	549.5	71.7	6.1	2.5	122.1
1968:Q4	936.8	28.1	3331.2	3095.2	3.4	6.3	195.8	562.3	71.6	6.2	7.5	122.0
1969:Q1	960.0	28.4	3381.9	3124.4	3.4	6.3	199.3	571.9	72.2	6.7	49.0	122.2
1969:Q2	974.1	28.7	3390.2	3157.0	3.4	6.3	200.9	576.9	71.6	6.9	40.0	122.3
1969:Q3	993.6	29.1	3409.7	3188.1	3.6	6.3	201.8	580.6	71.5	7.1	20.6	123.2
1969:Q4	1001.0	29.5	3392.6	3223.1	3.6	6.3	203.5	585.6	71.2	7.5	11.5	121.9
1970:Q1	1013.9	29.9	3386.5	3256.0	4.2	6.4	205.7	587.8	71.4	7.9	−7.0	121.7
1970:Q2	1029.5	30.4	3391.6	3289.9	4.8	6.4	207.1	591.7	72.4	8.1	−47.4	121.2
1970:Q3	1047.8	30.6	3423.0	3322.4	5.2	6.3	209.9	605.1	73.8	8.2	−58.5	120.7
1970:Q4	1051.3	31.0	3389.4	3356.0	5.8	6.4	213.7	621.4	73.1	7.9	−70.9	120.6
1971:Q1	1096.8	31.5	3481.4	3393.3	5.9	6.4	217.2	641.3	75.3	7.2	−67.3	120.3
1971:Q2	1117.7	31.9	3500.9	3430.2	5.9	6.4	221.8	666.0	75.6	7.5	−88.0	119.6
1971:Q3	1137.3	32.3	3523.8	3470.7	6.0	6.3	225.7	685.9	76.2	7.6	−84.0	117.5
1971:Q4	1149.8	32.5	3533.8	3514.2	5.9	6.3	227.8	704.4	75.4	7.3	−76.2	113.8
1972:Q1	1190.2	33.0	3604.7	3557.4	5.8	6.3	232.2	725.6	76.8	7.2	−47.5	109.2
1972:Q2	1224.4	33.2	3687.9	3594.0	5.7	6.3	236.1	743.8	78.2	7.3	−72.9	108.4
1972:Q3	1247.8	33.5	3726.2	3635.5	5.6	6.2	241.0	768.8	78.7	7.2	−40.9	108.9
1972:Q4	1286.8	33.9	3790.4	3670.3	5.4	6.2	246.9	794.4	79.2	7.1	−84.2	109.8
1973:Q1	1337.5	34.4	3892.2	3705.4	4.9	6.2	251.8	813.2	81.3	7.2	−38.4	104.8
1973:Q2	1369.4	34.9	3919.0	3739.6	4.9	6.2	254.8	826.6	81.0	7.3	−40.9	99.3
1973:Q3	1391.4	35.6	3907.1	3778.3	4.8	6.1	257.7	838.2	80.5	7.6	−27.2	94.3
1973:Q4	1432.3	36.3	3947.1	3813.5	4.8	6.1	260.9	849.0	79.9	7.7	−20.4	98.2
1974:Q1	1446.5	37.0	3908.1	3847.5	5.1	6.1	265.3	864.7	79.7	7.9	−31.3	104.4
1974:Q2	1482.5	37.8	3922.6	3882.3	5.2	6.1	267.7	875.1	79.7	8.4	−34.1	99.4
1974:Q3	1511.7	39.0	3880.0	3915.7	5.6	6.0	270.2	884.6	78.8	9.0	−33.4	101.7
1974:Q4	1546.8	40.1	3854.1	3948.2	6.6	6.1	273.5	898.3	79.3	9.0	−75.0	100.2
1975:Q1	1560.3	41.1	3800.9	3979.7	8.3	6.1	275.0	915.4	80.0	8.7	−126.2	95.0
1975:Q2	1597.8	41.7	3835.2	4013.8	8.9	6.0	279.1	948.9	81.4	8.9	−253.2	95.0
1975:Q3	1657.1	42.4	3907.0	4045.0	8.5	6.0	284.4	983.6	82.4	8.9	−162.4	101.1
1975:Q4	1707.3	43.2	3952.5	4077.6	8.3	6.1	286.7	1007.7	82.3	8.8	−160.7	102.9
1976:Q1	1767.3	43.7	4044.6	4113.1	7.7	6.1	290.6	1039.4	83.9	8.6	−133.7	104.0
1976:Q2	1797.9	44.2	4072.2	4150.6	7.6	6.1	295.3	1070.4	84.5	8.5	−120.9	106.6
1976:Q3	1830.4	44.8	4088.5	4181.7	7.7	6.2	298.5	1099.0	84.6	8.5	−128.0	106.3
1976:Q4	1880.3	45.6	4126.4	4210.8	7.8	6.3	304.2	1139.3	84.8	8.2	−131.0	105.7
1977:Q1	1934.4	46.3	4176.3	4247.5	7.5	6.4	311.4	1177.9	85.3	8.0	−91.8	105.3
1977:Q2	2005.1	47.1	4260.1	4284.0	7.1	6.3	316.8	1209.0	85.9	8.0	−91.4	104.5
1977:Q3	2063.2	47.7	4329.5	4321.6	6.9	6.4	322.2	1237.4	86.6	7.9	−103.5	103.2
1977:Q4	2104.7	48.6	4328.3	4353.8	6.7	6.4	329.3	1263.6	85.4	8.1	−103.2	100.4
1978:Q1	2147.7	49.4	4345.5	4384.8	6.3	6.5	335.6	1286.7	85.5	8.5	−103.4	95.9
1978:Q2	2273.7	50.4	4510.7	4418.4	6.0	6.5	343.0	1309.8	87.2	8.7	−60.7	95.2
1978:Q3	2333.9	51.3	4552.1	4453.5	6.0	6.5	349.9	1335.2	87.3	8.8	−48.2	90.6
1978:Q4	2410.2	52.4	4603.7	4492.0	5.9	6.5	356.3	1361.1	87.6	9.0	−38.8	87.8
1979:Q1	2464.5	53.5	4605.7	4520.1	5.9	6.5	360.4	1380.1	86.5	9.3	−24.3	88.1
1979:Q2	2522.3	54.6	4615.6	4544.9	5.7	6.5	369.2	1411.7	86.4	9.4	−22.3	89.8
1979:Q3	2592.8	55.8	4644.9	4578.2	5.9	6.4	378.6	1446.4	86.2	9.3	−34.0	87.0
1979:Q4	2650.4	56.9	4656.2	4619.5	6.0	6.4	382.2	1468.8	86.0	10.5	−52.0	87.4
1980:Q1	2722.3	58.2	4679.0	4646.7	6.3	6.5	388.2	1493.6	86.5	12.1	−64.1	87.4
1980:Q2	2719.4	59.5	4566.6	4677.7	7.3	6.4	384.7	1514.7	85.2	11.2	−106.0	87.8
1980:Q3	2783.4	61.0	4562.3	4706.0	7.7	6.5	399.5	1561.7	85.6	11.6	−123.8	85.4
1980:Q4	2911.8	62.6	4651.9	4731.7	7.4	6.5	410.8	1595.9	86.5	12.8	−108.8	89.0
1981:Q1	3040.2	64.2	4739.2	4763.5	7.4	6.5	414.9	1622.0	87.6	13.2	−68.3	94.5
1981:Q2	3070.3	65.4	4696.8	4792.2	7.4	6.5	424.7	1665.0	86.5	14.0	−75.0	103.1
1981:Q3	3167.7	66.6	4753.0	4820.6	7.4	6.5	427.1	1695.7	87.4	14.9	−81.3	110.0
1981:Q4	3185.5	67.9	4693.8	4844.8	8.2	6.4	433.0	1739.8	86.2	14.6	−123.9	105.4
1982:Q1	3178.6	68.9	4615.9	4879.7	8.8	6.4	442.3	1778.6	85.4	15.0	−145.4	109.9
1982:Q2	3231.6	69.7	4634.9	4915.9	9.4	6.4	446.4	1816.1	86.2	14.5	−154.9	114.0
1982:Q3	3259.1	70.7	4612.1	4948.2	9.9	6.3	452.2	1850.7	86.4	13.8	−216.1	119.8
1982:Q4	3299.1	71.4	4618.3	4979.4	10.7	6.3	471.0	1893.1	87.1	11.9	−249.2	122.2
1983:Q1	3361.0	72.1	4663.0	5017.5	10.4	6.3	483.7	1995.7	88.1	11.8	−244.7	119.4
1983:Q2	3469.2	72.8	4763.6	5051.3	10.1	6.3	498.5	2046.4	89.9	11.6	−230.0	123.0

Continued

	Nominal GDP (X) (B $)	GDP Deflator (1992 =100)	Real GDP (Y) (B 1992$)	Natural Real GDP (Y^N) (B 1992$)	Unemploy. Rate (U) (Percent)	Natural Unemploy. Rate (U^N) (Percent)	Money Supply (M1) (B $)	Money Supply (M2) (B $)	Labor Productiv- ity (Y/N) (1992=100)	Nominal Interest Rate (r) (Percent)	Real Federal Budget Surplus (B 1992$)	Trade-Weighted Exchange Rate (Mar 1973 =100)
1983:Q3	3563.3	73.5	4849.0	5086.7	9.4	6.3	510.4	2079.0	90.6	12.3	−249.7	128.7
1983:Q4	3664.6	74.2	4939.2	5128.7	8.5	6.3	519.6	2116.9	90.8	12.4	−229.3	130.2
1984:Q1	3791.1	75.0	5053.6	5166.4	7.9	6.2	527.7	2162.0	91.1	12.3	−191.6	131.6
1984:Q2	3879.7	75.6	5132.9	5208.9	7.4	6.2	536.7	2208.3	91.6	13.2	−198.6	132.8
1984:Q3	3942.2	76.2	5170.3	5250.8	7.4	6.2	542.1	2238.4	91.5	13.0	−213.4	141.7
1984:Q4	3996.7	76.8	5203.7	5297.1	7.3	6.2	547.9	2287.9	91.5	12.4	−218.2	147.2
1985:Q1	4081.2	77.6	5257.3	5338.7	7.2	6.2	562.0	2355.9	91.7	12.3	−168.5	156.5
1985:Q2	4134.8	78.3	5283.7	5379.2	7.3	6.1	576.0	2398.3	91.8	11.6	−237.0	149.1
1985:Q3	4221.4	78.8	5359.6	5418.5	7.2	6.2	596.6	2449.4	92.8	11.0	−207.7	139.2
1985:Q4	4285.3	79.5	5393.6	5451.9	7.0	6.1	613.4	2485.1	93.0	10.6	−216.1	128.2
1986:Q1	4358.2	79.8	5460.8	5482.9	7.0	6.1	626.6	2521.4	94.5	9.6	−211.9	119.5
1986:Q2	4385.6	80.2	5466.9	5513.0	7.2	6.1	651.3	2588.4	94.9	9.0	−237.3	114.2
1986:Q3	4443.3	80.8	5496.3	5545.9	7.0	6.1	679.1	2653.5	94.8	8.8	−240.1	108.3
1986:Q4	4501.7	81.5	5526.8	5576.2	6.8	6.1	708.6	2712.3	94.6	8.7	−192.1	107.0
1987:Q1	4565.7	82.1	5561.8	5607.2	6.6	6.1	731.4	2754.4	94.0	8.4	−199.9	99.9
1987:Q2	4645.1	82.7	5618.0	5634.9	6.3	6.1	744.3	2777.9	94.6	9.2	−133.0	97.0
1987:Q3	4722.6	83.3	5667.4	5664.9	6.0	6.1	745.4	2795.3	94.4	9.8	−140.5	98.7
1987:Q4	4835.9	84.1	5750.6	5693.4	5.8	6.1	753.1	2826.4	95.0	10.2	−147.8	92.3
1988:Q1	4898.2	84.7	5785.3	5725.4	5.7	6.1	758.8	2876.7	94.8	9.6	−169.8	90.0
1988:Q2	5000.4	85.6	5844.0	5759.2	5.5	6.2	773.0	2932.2	95.0	9.8	−132.5	90.4
1988:Q3	5094.5	86.7	5878.7	5792.9	5.5	6.2	783.2	2960.0	95.4	10.0	−132.4	97.6
1988:Q4	5205.3	87.4	5952.8	5830.9	5.3	6.2	785.5	2986.5	95.9	9.5	−129.5	93.0
1989:Q1	5316.8	88.5	6011.0	5869.8	5.2	6.2	784.4	3002.5	95.4	9.7	−104.0	96.0
1989:Q2	5413.2	89.4	6055.6	5909.8	5.2	6.2	776.1	3022.7	95.7	9.5	−112.1	100.4
1989:Q3	5486.9	90.1	6088.0	5941.3	5.2	6.2	779.9	3080.8	95.9	9.0	−138.4	100.5
1989:Q4	5537.8	90.9	6093.5	5970.5	5.4	6.2	789.8	3141.5	96.1	8.9	−150.2	97.3
1990:Q1	5660.6	92.0	6152.6	5999.9	5.3	6.3	798.4	3185.1	96.4	9.2	−167.5	93.1
1990:Q2	5750.8	93.2	6171.6	6029.1	5.3	6.3	807.1	3212.4	96.7	9.4	−154.6	92.7
1990:Q3	5782.2	94.1	6142.1	6055.3	5.7	6.3	816.0	3247.0	96.4	9.4	−151.5	87.4
1990:Q4	5781.7	95.1	6079.0	6083.8	6.1	6.3	822.5	3271.5	95.5	9.3	−186.8	83.0
1991:Q1	5821.9	96.3	6047.5	6112.5	6.6	6.3	833.1	3311.3	96.1	8.9	−139.8	84.6
1991:Q2	5892.5	97.0	6074.7	6142.5	6.8	6.3	850.1	3348.3	96.8	8.9	−202.8	93.0
1991:Q3	5950.2	97.7	6090.1	6175.7	6.9	6.2	866.4	3360.5	97.3	8.8	−219.0	93.3
1991:Q4	6002.1	98.3	6105.3	6203.5	7.1	6.2	887.8	3372.0	97.6	8.4	−242.9	88.1
1992:Q1	6121.8	99.1	6175.7	6230.7	7.4	6.3	924.3	3401.8	99.3	8.3	−269.8	88.2
1992:Q2	6201.2	99.8	6214.2	6255.8	7.6	6.2	950.3	3405.8	100.0	8.3	−280.2	88.0
1992:Q3	6271.7	100.2	6260.7	6291.6	7.6	6.1	975.6	3409.8	99.7	8.0	−297.0	81.8
1992:Q4	6383.1	100.9	6327.1	6330.4	7.4	6.1	1015.2	3433.8	101.1	8.0	−276.6	88.5
1993:Q1	6444.5	101.8	6327.9	6371.9	7.1	6.1	1034.8	3425.2	100.1	7.7	−273.2	93.3
1993:Q2	6509.1	102.3	6359.9	6413.1	7.1	6.0	1063.6	3441.4	99.6	7.4	−243.5	90.9
1993:Q3	6574.6	102.8	6393.5	6455.8	6.8	6.0	1094.5	3457.7	100.0	6.9	−243.7	93.7
1993:Q4	6704.2	103.5	6476.9	6493.1	6.6	6.0	1122.6	3478.8	100.8	6.8	−217.0	94.8
1994:Q1	6794.3	104.1	6524.5	6527.5	6.6	6.0	1136.7	3492.3	100.6	7.2	−200.7	95.6
1994:Q2	6911.4	104.7	6600.3	6561.7	6.2	5.9	1143.5	3500.2	100.7	7.9	−155.9	92.9
1994:Q3	6986.5	105.4	6629.5	6597.1	6.0	5.8	1150.5	3499.6	100.4	8.2	−178.0	88.8
1994:Q4	7095.7	106.1	6688.6	6632.7	5.6	5.8	1150.5	3500.8	100.8	8.6	−176.1	88.0
1995:Q1	7168.9	106.9	6703.7	6668.5	5.5	5.8	1148.6	3506.4	100.3	8.3	−179.1	86.4
1995:Q2	7209.5	107.5	6708.8	6704.5	5.6	5.7	1146.1	3539.0	100.5	7.7	−167.0	82.3
1995:Q3	7301.3	108.0	6759.2	6740.7	5.7	5.7	1143.5	3602.5	100.8	7.4	−163.4	84.1
1995:Q4	7381.9	108.6	6796.5	6777.1	5.6	5.7	1132.6	3641.4	101.2	7.0	−138.3	84.4
1996:Q1	7467.5	109.4	6826.4	6813.6	5.6	5.7	1122.7	3689.6	101.7	7.1	−140.4	86.4
1996:Q2	7607.7	109.8	6926.0	6850.4	5.4	5.7	1118.7	3730.7	102.2	7.6	−101.6	88.0
1996:Q3	7676.0	110.5	6943.8	6887.4	5.3	5.7	1100.6	3762.7	102.0	7.6	−90.0	87.1
1996:Q4	7792.9	111.1	7017.4	6924.6	5.3	5.7	1080.4	3810.1	102.4	7.2	−69.4	87.9
1997:Q1	7933.6	111.7	7101.6	6961.9	5.3	5.7	1078.5	3866.1	102.8	7.4	−49.7	93.7
1997:Q2	8034.3	112.2	7159.6	6999.5	4.9	5.7	1063.9	3901.6	103.5	7.6	−32.8	95.7

Appendix B
International Annual Time Series Data for Selected Countries: 1960–95

Table B-1 Canada, 1960–1995

	Nominal GDP (X) (B C$)	GDP Deflator (P) (1990 = 100)	Real GDP (Y) (B 1990 C$)	Labor Productivity (Y/N) (C$/Hr)	Unemploy. Rate (U) (Percent)	Money Supply (M1) (B C$)	Money Supply (M2) (B C$)	Consumer Price Index (CPI) (1990 = 100)	Long-Term Interest Rate (r) (Percent)	Labor Share (wN/X) (Percent)
1960	39.2	20.3	192.7	11.6	7.0	6.0	13.2	19.8	5.2	60.2
1961	40.6	20.4	198.8	11.9	7.1	6.7	14.4	20.0	5.1	61.0
1962	44.1	20.7	212.9	12.4	5.9	7.0	15.0	20.2	5.1	59.9
1963	47.4	21.1	224.0	12.9	5.5	7.5	16.8	20.6	5.1	59.7
1964	51.9	21.7	238.9	13.3	4.3	8.2	18.5	21.0	5.2	59.5
1965	57.2	22.4	254.7	13.8	3.6	9.4	20.4	21.5	5.2	60.3
1966	64.0	23.5	272.0	14.3	3.3	10.1	22.0	22.3	5.7	60.9
1967	68.6	24.5	280.0	14.4	3.8	16.2	25.8	23.1	5.9	62.7
1968	74.8	25.4	295.0	15.1	4.4	16.0	28.9	24.0	6.8	62.2
1969	82.4	26.5	310.8	15.6	4.4	15.3	31.1	25.1	7.6	62.7
1970	88.5	27.7	319.1	16.0	5.6	15.6	34.0	25.9	7.9	64.0
1971	96.6	28.6	337.4	16.7	6.1	17.6	37.1	26.7	7.0	64.4
1972	107.8	30.2	356.6	17.2	6.2	19.8	42.7	28.0	7.2	63.9
1973	126.4	32.9	384.1	17.7	5.5	21.5	51.5	30.1	7.6	62.6
1974	151.0	37.7	400.9	17.9	5.3	21.8	61.4	33.4	8.9	62.4
1975	170.1	41.4	411.3	18.2	6.9	26.0	70.8	37.0	9.0	65.0
1976	196.3	45.0	436.6	19.0	7.1	26.4	84.4	39.7	9.2	65.3
1977	216.1	47.8	452.2	19.7	8.0	29.1	96.2	42.9	8.7	66.5
1978	239.6	50.7	472.9	19.8	8.3	31.1	112.5	46.7	9.3	65.2
1979	274.1	55.8	491.3	19.9	7.4	31.6	132.4	51.0	10.2	64.2
1980	307.7	61.7	498.6	19.7	7.4	34.8	144.9	56.2	12.5	64.9
1981	353.5	68.4	517.0	20.1	7.5	36.9	177.5	63.2	15.2	65.7
1982	371.8	74.3	500.4	20.4	10.9	40.1	186.4	70.0	14.3	67.3
1983	402.2	77.9	516.4	21.0	11.8	44.2	184.7	74.1	11.8	65.0
1984	441.3	80.3	549.3	21.7	11.2	52.9	196.0	77.3	12.8	63.5
1985	474.3	82.5	575.3	22.0	10.4	70.3	207.4	80.4	11.0	63.7
1986	501.4	84.4	594.1	22.1	9.5	80.6	222.7	83.7	9.5	64.9
1987	546.8	88.4	618.7	22.2	8.8	85.7	242.0	87.4	10.0	64.3
1988	600.8	92.5	649.4	22.9	7.7	90.7	267.7	90.9	10.2	63.5
1989	645.1	97.1	664.8	23.3	7.5	95.9	303.7	95.5	9.9	64.1
1990	662.8	100.0	662.8	23.2	8.1	97.1	327.4	100.0	10.9	66.5
1991	669.1	102.8	650.8	22.8	10.2	101.3	343.2	105.6	9.8	67.8
1992	683.1	104.1	656.0	23.8	11.3	108.4	375.4	107.2	8.1	68.5
1993	706.0	105.2	670.9	24.6	11.2	117.4	418.8	109.2	7.2	67.3
1994	740.1	106.0	698.2	25.5	10.4	125.1	452.3	109.4	8.4	66.2
1995	768.6	107.6	714.3	25.3	9.5	137.9	480.4	111.8	8.1	65.4

Table B-2 Japan, 1960–1995

	Nominal GDP (X) (Tr Y)	GDP Deflator (P) (1990 = 100)	Real GDP (Y) (Tr 1990Y)	Labor Productivity (Y/N) (Y/Hr)	Unemploy. Rate (U) (Percent)	Money Supply (M1) (Tr Y)	Money Supply (M2) (Tr Y)	Consumer Price Index (CPI) (1990 = 100)	Long-Term Interest Rate (r) (Percent)	Labor Share (wN/X) (Percent)
1960	16.0	23.0	69.5	0.6	1.6	4.2	6.2	19.7	7.5	45.5
1961	19.3	24.8	77.9	0.6	1.4	5.2	7.4	20.8	7.3	44.7
1962	21.9	25.9	84.8	0.7	1.3	6.1	9.0	22.2	7.5	47.7
1963	25.1	27.3	92.0	0.7	1.3	7.7	11.0	23.9	7.1	48.3
1964	29.5	28.8	102.7	0.8	1.2	8.7	12.8	24.8	7.2	49.0
1965	32.9	30.2	108.7	0.9	1.2	10.3	15.1	26.5	7.2	51.4
1966	38.2	31.7	120.3	0.9	1.3	11.7	17.8	27.8	6.8	51.2
1967	44.7	33.5	133.6	1.0	1.3	13.4	20.7	28.9	6.9	49.8
1968	53.0	35.1	150.8	1.1	1.2	15.2	24.0	30.5	7.0	49.2
1969	62.2	36.7	169.6	1.3	1.1	18.3	28.1	32.1	7.0	49.4
1970	73.3	39.1	187.8	1.4	1.2	21.4	32.9	34.6	7.0	50.2
1971	80.7	41.0	196.6	1.5	1.2	27.7	39.7	36.8	7.1	54.5
1972	92.4	43.3	213.2	1.6	1.4	34.5	49.5	38.5	6.9	55.0
1973	112.5	48.9	230.3	1.7	1.3	40.3	57.9	43.0	7.1	56.0
1974	134.2	59.0	227.5	1.8	1.4	45.0	64.5	53.0	8.2	60.3
1975	148.3	63.3	234.5	1.8	1.9	49.9	75.4	59.2	8.5	63.5
1976	166.6	68.3	243.8	1.9	2.0	56.2	86.1	64.8	8.6	63.1
1977	185.6	72.9	254.5	2.0	2.0	60.8	97.2	70.1	7.5	63.5
1978	204.4	76.3	267.9	2.0	2.2	68.9	109.8	73.0	6.4	62.1
1979	221.5	78.4	282.6	2.1	2.1	71.0	122.7	75.7	8.3	61.9
1980	240.2	82.7	290.6	2.2	2.0	69.6	137.4	81.6	8.9	62.3
1981	258.0	86.0	299.8	2.2	2.2	76.5	152.7	85.6	8.4	63.5
1982	270.6	87.6	309.0	2.3	2.3	80.9	165.7	88.0	8.3	63.8
1983	281.8	89.1	316.1	2.3	2.7	80.8	182.8	89.7	7.8	64.6
1984	300.5	91.5	328.5	2.4	2.7	86.4	195.4	91.7	7.3	63.9
1985	320.4	93.4	343.0	2.5	2.6	89.0	217.8	93.5	6.5	62.6
1986	335.5	95.1	352.9	2.6	2.8	98.2	237.1	94.1	5.1	62.5
1987	349.8	95.1	367.6	2.6	2.9	103.0	269.7	94.2	5.0	61.8
1988	374.0	95.8	390.4	2.8	2.5	111.8	297.5	94.9	4.8	61.0
1989	400.0	97.7	409.2	2.9	2.3	114.5	343.2	97.0	5.2	61.5
1990	430.0	100.0	430.0	3.0	2.1	119.6	375.4	100.0	7.0	62.3
1991	459.0	102.7	447.1	3.1	2.1	131.0	376.5	103.3	6.4	63.1
1992	471.8	104.4	451.8	3.0	2.2	136.1	370.7	105.1	5.3	63.8
1993	475.4	105.1	452.4	2.9	2.5	145.6	372.6	106.4	4.3	64.9
1994	479.1	105.4	454.6	3.0	2.9	151.7	382.4	107.1	4.4	65.9
1995	481.0	104.8	458.8	3.2	3.1	171.5	377.4	107.0	3.4	66.7

Table B-3 France, 1960–1995

	Nominal GDP (X) (B Fr)	GDP Deflator (P) (1990 = 100)	Real GDP (Y) (B 1990 Fr)	Labor Productivity (Y/N) (Fr/Hr)	Unemploy. Rate (U) (Percent)	Money Supply (M1) (B Fr)	Money Supply (M2) (B Fr)	Consumer Price Index (CPI) (1990 = 100)	Long-Term Interest Rate (r) (Percent)	Labor Share (wN/X) (Percent)
1960	300.7	13.5	2226.2	40.4	1.4	94.9	105.8	14.6	5.7	48.8
1961	328.0	14.0	2348.8	42.5	1.2	109.6	124.0	14.9	5.5	50.1
1962	366.2	14.6	2505.5	45.1	1.4	129.5	147.2	15.7	5.4	50.2
1963	410.6	15.6	2639.5	47.2	1.5	148.3	167.9	16.5	5.3	51.2
1964	455.4	16.2	2811.5	49.7	1.3	160.6	184.3	17.0	5.4	51.3
1965	490.3	16.6	2945.9	52.4	1.5	175.7	204.4	17.5	6.2	51.4
1966	530.7	17.1	3099.5	56.3	1.6	189.3	226.1	17.9	6.6	51.3
1967	573.3	17.7	3244.8	59.2	2.1	198.3	255.6	18.4	6.7	51.3
1968	623.1	18.4	3383.0	63.8	2.7	214.2	285.2	19.3	7.0	52.7
1969	710.5	19.6	3619.5	65.3	2.3	209.7	299.6	20.4	8.2	52.7
1970	793.5	20.7	3826.9	68.6	2.5	232.5	344.0	21.6	8.6	54.0
1971	884.2	22.0	4012.1	72.0	2.7	259.9	407.4	22.8	8.4	54.9
1972	987.9	23.6	4190.5	75.4	2.8	299.0	484.3	24.2	8.0	55.2
1973	1129.8	25.6	4418.5	79.6	2.7	327.9	554.9	26.0	9.0	55.5
1974	1303.0	28.6	4548.0	82.0	2.9	377.7	653.8	29.5	11.0	58.1
1975	1467.9	32.5	4516.3	83.4	4.0	425.2	756.8	32.9	10.3	61.4
1976	1700.6	36.1	4711.5	86.3	4.4	457.0	850.0	36.1	10.5	61.7
1977	1917.8	39.2	4887.4	89.3	4.9	507.8	973.9	39.5	11.0	62.4
1978	2182.6	43.5	5023.0	92.9	5.2	665.9	1681.1	43.2	10.6	62.2
1979	2481.1	47.9	5174.3	96.4	5.8	751.4	1922.5	47.8	10.9	62.0
1980	2808.3	53.6	5243.1	98.1	6.2	801.2	2101.6	54.3	13.8	63.7
1981	3164.8	60.0	5276.7	101.0	7.4	899.8	2322.7	61.5	16.3	64.5
1982	3626.0	67.2	5393.6	107.4	8.0	985.0	2577.7	68.9	16.0	64.8
1983	4006.5	73.7	5436.2	109.2	8.3	1108.4	2861.1	75.4	14.4	64.8
1984	4361.9	79.2	5507.0	111.5	9.7	1219.2	3107.2	81.2	13.4	64.1
1985	4700.1	83.8	5607.5	115.5	10.2	1312.4	3318.3	85.9	11.9	63.2
1986	5069.3	88.3	5741.0	118.5	10.4	1406.8	3571.3	88.1	9.1	61.3
1987	5336.7	90.9	5870.0	120.7	10.5	1469.6	3698.0	91.0	10.2	60.7
1988	5735.1	93.7	6118.8	126.2	10.0	1530.1	3880.3	93.5	9.2	59.5
1989	6159.7	96.9	6357.3	130.9	9.4	1624.7	4075.4	96.7	9.2	58.8
1990	6509.5	100.0	6509.5	133.5	8.9	1689.6	4208.1	100.0	10.4	59.7
1991	6776.2	103.3	6560.2	134.2	9.4	1609.3	4173.8	103.2	9.5	60.3
1992	6999.5	105.6	6629.4	140.0	10.3	1607.5	4225.2	105.7	9.0	60.8
1993	7077.1	108.1	6543.9	139.7	11.7	1620.0	4386.0	107.9	7.0	61.3
1994	7389.7	110.0	6718.9	152.7	12.3	1672.5	4685.1	109.7	7.5	60.0
1995	7674.8	111.8	6861.7	157.3	11.6	1819.1	5193.2	111.6	7.7	59.8

Table B-4 Germany, 1960–1995

	Nominal GDP (X) (B DM)	GDP Deflator (P) (1990 = 100)	Real GDP (Y) (B 1990 DM)	Labor Productivity (Y/N) (DM/Hr)	Unemploy. Rate (U) (Percent)	Money Supply (M1) (B DM)	Money Supply (M2) (B DM)	Consumer Price Index (CPI) (1990 = 100)	Long-Term Interest Rate (r) (Percent)	Labor Share (wN/X) (Percent)
1960	326.2	31.7	1029.2	13.7	1.0	47.5	114.5	35.2	6.3	53.4
1961	357.5	33.2	1076.8	14.4	0.6	54.4	129.5	36.0	5.9	55.3
1962	388.8	34.5	1127.0	15.3	0.6	58.1	145.4	37.0	6.0	56.6
1963	412.1	35.6	1158.7	16.0	0.7	62.3	161.4	38.1	6.1	57.6
1964	452.8	36.6	1235.9	16.9	0.6	67.6	181.6	39.0	6.2	57.5
1965	494.8	38.0	1302.1	17.9	0.5	72.8	203.4	40.3	6.8	58.5
1966	526.1	39.3	1338.4	18.7	0.6	74.2	225.6	41.8	7.7	59.4
1967	532.7	39.9	1334.3	19.7	1.8	81.6	255.7	42.4	7.0	58.9
1968	574.7	40.8	1407.1	20.8	1.2	90.6	276.6	43.1	6.7	58.3
1969	643.3	42.5	1512.0	22.2	0.7	95.4	305.2	43.9	6.9	58.4
1970	727.7	45.8	1588.2	23.2	0.6	103.7	332.3	45.4	8.2	61.6
1971	808.0	49.4	1636.8	24.1	0.7	116.9	376.9	47.8	8.2	63.0
1972	887.0	52.0	1706.3	25.5	0.9	133.4	429.8	50.4	8.2	63.6
1973	988.5	55.3	1787.7	26.9	1.0	135.7	467.6	54.0	9.4	64.9
1974	1060.3	59.2	1791.1	27.8	2.1	150.2	501.4	57.7	10.6	67.4
1975	1106.4	62.6	1768.7	28.8	4.0	171.7	558.8	61.2	8.8	67.7
1976	1207.5	64.8	1862.9	30.1	3.9	177.3	601.0	63.8	8.2	66.6
1977	1288.1	67.2	1915.9	31.5	3.8	198.6	663.2	66.1	6.6	67.3
1978	1383.2	70.1	1973.3	32.7	3.7	227.5	731.2	67.9	6.3	66.6
1979	1496.3	72.8	2056.7	33.9	3.2	234.1	768.9	70.7	7.7	66.7
1980	1586.4	76.4	2076.8	34.3	3.2	243.4	803.9	74.5	8.6	68.9
1981	1654.2	79.6	2078.9	34.9	4.5	239.6	833.5	79.3	10.2	69.7
1982	1711.4	83.1	2059.3	35.2	6.4	256.7	890.9	83.4	9.1	69.9
1983	1798.1	85.8	2095.6	36.5	7.9	278.2	941.7	86.2	8.2	67.7
1984	1886.9	87.6	2154.5	37.7	7.9	294.8	994.5	88.2	8.1	66.7
1985	1964.8	89.4	2198.3	38.7	8.0	314.5	1074.4	90.2	7.2	66.6
1986	2074.8	92.2	2249.8	39.4	7.7	340.2	1144.4	90.1	6.3	66.1
1987	2145.1	94.0	2283.1	40.1	7.6	365.7	1212.8	90.3	6.4	66.6
1988	2258.8	95.4	2368.1	41.0	7.6	408.3	1283.0	91.4	6.6	65.7
1989	2397.2	97.7	2453.9	42.9	6.9	431.6	1348.1	94.0	7.1	64.3
1990	2614.4	100.8	2593.9	44.9	6.2	551.9	1598.7	96.5	8.7	63.9
1991	2853.6	104.7	2725.2	46.4	6.7	575.0	1700.6	100.0	8.5	63.8
1992	3075.6	110.4	2785.1	48.3	7.7	641.0	1835.7	105.1	7.8	64.4
1993	3158.1	114.7	2753.8	49.9	8.8	697.6	2048.1	109.7	6.5	64.7
1994	3320.4	117.2	2832.7	54.5	9.6	732.0	2098.6	112.7	6.9	63.3
1995	3457.4	119.7	2887.3	56.7	9.4	783.7	2195.2	114.8	6.9	62.7

Table B-5 Italy, 1960–1995

	Nominal GDP (X) (Tr L)	GDP Deflator (P) (1990 = 100)	Real GDP (Y) (Tr 1990L)	Labor Productivity (Y/N) (L/Hr)	Unemploy. Rate (U) (Percent)	Money Supply (M1) (Tr L)	Money Supply (M2) (Tr L)	Consumer Price Index (CPI) (1990 = 100)	Long-Term Interest Rate (r) (Percent)	Labor Share (wN/X) (Percent)
1960	24.78	5.85	423.8286	6.40	4.15	—	—	7.40	5.26	44.41
1961	27.55	6.01	458.6105	6.90	3.78	—	—	7.60	4.97	44.24
1962	30.96	6.36	487.0631	7.60	3.34	10.06	7.98	7.90	5.05	45.86
1963	35.46	6.89	514.3882	8.20	2.83	9.35	12.01	8.50	5.19	48.97
1964	38.82	7.34	528.773	8.50	3.18	10.88	13.18	9.00	5.74	50.22
1965	41.77	7.65	546.0581	9.20	3.96	12.56	15.14	9.40	5.39	49.19
1966	45.26	7.82	578.7381	9.80	4.32	14.02	17.35	9.70	5.49	48.43
1967	49.85	8.04	620.2836	10.30	3.96	16.20	19.43	10.00	5.59	48.54
1968	54.03	8.18	660.8781	11.00	4.20	18.72	21.74	10.20	5.61	48.56
1969	59.65	8.51	701.1789	11.80	4.19	22.14	23.29	10.40	5.80	48.39
1970	67.13	9.09	738.415	12.50	4.00	29.31	23.10	10.90	7.73	50.55
1971	73.00	9.70	752.402	13.00	4.00	35.01	26.76	11.50	7.00	53.25
1972	79.75	10.30	774.418	13.80	4.71	41.38	31.94	12.10	6.59	54.46
1973	96.60	11.71	825.08	14.80	4.69	49.51	38.64	13.40	6.92	54.41
1974	121.99	14.12	863.772	15.30	3.94	56.08	41.90	16.00	9.61	54.43
1975	138.59	16.40	845.232	14.80	4.31	64.72	57.55	18.70	10.04	58.79
1976	174.58	19.39	900.157	15.60	4.92	78.15	69.17	21.80	12.66	57.00
1977	212.71	22.97	926.17	16.00	5.26	94.91	84.33	25.60	14.71	57.18
1978	251.00	26.13	960.698	16.50	5.31	121.32	100.51	28.70	13.05	55.86
1979	307.82	30.32	1015.197	17.10	5.66	150.08	115.33	32.90	13.02	54.86
1980	385.33	36.66	1051.042	17.70	5.57	169.69	128.16	39.90	15.25	53.87
1981	461.05	43.66	1056.022	17.90	6.27	188.49	143.06	47.00	19.36	55.65
1982	542.13	51.10	1060.859	18.10	6.92	220.83	176.19	54.70	20.21	55.40
1983	631.61	58.82	1073.783	18.40	7.69	248.37	200.32	62.70	18.30	54.62
1984	722.81	65.63	1101.366	19.00	8.50	278.93	223.70	69.50	15.60	53.21
1985	810.08	71.54	1132.313	19.60	8.61	307.96	247.29	75.90	13.71	53.10
1986	898.29	77.14	1164.465	20.40	9.89	342.90	261.13	80.30	11.47	51.56
1987	982.76	81.86	1200.523	21.30	10.25	370.82	278.56	84.10	10.64	51.07
1988	1090.02	87.41	1246.966	22.10	10.45	399.46	310.45	88.40	10.90	50.57
1989	1191.96	92.91	1282.905	22.90	10.21	430.50	341.48	93.90	12.79	50.75
1990	1310.66	100.00	1310.659	23.40	9.13	462.77	387.56	100.00	13.54	52.06
1991	1427.57	107.69	1325.582	23.90	8.59	514.03	416.49	106.30	13.14	52.37
1992	1502.49	112.71	1333.072	24.85	8.84	521.03	459.92	111.70	13.71	52.58
1993	1550.30	117.65	1317.668	25.33	10.24	554.08	500.75	116.70	11.31	51.68
1994	1638.51	121.76	1345.674	26.79	11.29	575.07	498.06	121.40	10.58	49.48
1995	1770.95	127.81	1385.618	28.70	11.98	576.09	520.44	127.77	11.79	47.67

Table B-6 United Kingdom, 1960–1995

	Nominal GDP (X) (B P)	GDP Deflator (P) (1990 = 100)	Real GDP (Y) (B 1990P)	Labor Productivity (Y/N) (P/Hr)	Unemploy. Rate (U) (Percent)	Money Supply (M1) (B P)	Money Supply (M2) (B P)	Consumer Price Index (CPI) (1990 = 100)	Long-Term Interest Rate (r) (Percent)	Labor Share (wN/X) (Percent)
1960	25.86	9.82	263.33	4.00	1.47	5.90	10.42	9.88	5.86	63.72
1961	27.42	10.15	270.11	4.20	1.38	6.00	10.74	10.18	6.26	65.08
1962	28.82	10.53	273.69	4.20	1.88	5.70	10.42	10.63	5.76	65.21
1963	30.55	10.74	284.52	4.40	2.15	6.50	11.37	10.85	5.17	64.56
1964	33.39	11.17	298.86	4.50	1.51	6.80	12.00	11.23	5.70	64.04
1965	35.96	11.71	307.19	4.70	1.32	7.00	12.95	11.75	6.55	64.10
1966	38.29	12.21	313.49	4.90	1.43	7.00	13.37	12.20	6.87	64.85
1967	40.30	12.57	320.73	5.10	2.17	7.50	14.84	12.50	6.70	64.24
1968	43.67	13.09	333.51	5.30	2.25	7.80	15.91	13.10	7.51	63.57
1969	47.00	13.81	340.36	5.40	2.25	7.90	16.40	13.80	8.83	63.19
1970	51.61	14.81	348.39	5.70	2.40	8.60	17.95	14.70	8.63	64.69
1971	57.58	16.19	355.77	6.00	2.89	9.90	20.32	16.10	7.87	63.78
1972	64.48	17.50	368.36	6.30	3.06	11.30	25.99	17.20	8.37	64.59
1973	74.08	18.84	393.13	6.40	2.07	11.90	33.14	18.80	10.56	65.11
1974	83.71	21.59	387.79	6.50	2.22	13.20	37.43	21.80	14.21	69.59
1975	105.60	27.26	387.34	6.50	3.61	15.80	40.10	27.10	13.18	72.92
1976	124.99	31.56	396.03	6.80	4.84	17.60	44.74	31.60	13.61	70.32
1977	145.66	36.00	404.62	7.00	5.16	21.20	48.99	36.60	12.03	67.19
1978	168.14	40.13	419.04	7.30	4.49	24.70	56.12	39.60	12.07	66.42
1979	197.83	45.94	430.60	7.40	4.03	26.90	63.13	44.90	12.95	65.67
1980	231.23	54.60	423.54	7.40	5.34	28.00	74.79	53.00	13.91	67.80
1981	254.27	60.83	418.02	7.90	8.33	33.40	95.55	59.30	14.88	67.16
1982	278.24	65.55	424.49	8.00	9.69	37.20	106.40	64.40	13.08	64.85
1983	303.52	69.05	439.56	8.50	10.49	41.60	117.32	67.40	11.27	63.25
1984	324.84	72.10	450.55	8.40	10.67	48.00	130.81	70.70	11.27	63.17
1985	356.17	76.36	466.44	8.60	11.01	56.70	145.52	75.00	11.06	62.56
1986	383.63	78.78	486.96	8.90	11.03	69.30	178.36	77.60	10.06	62.66
1987	421.89	82.70	510.15	9.00	9.82	154.10	343.47	80.80	9.59	61.78
1988	469.76	87.71	535.56	9.60	7.78	170.70	403.05	84.70	9.67	61.83
1989	514.24	93.97	547.23	9.80	6.04	195.30	481.38	91.30	10.19	62.61
1990	549.39	100.00	549.39	10.00	5.79	214.90	533.48	100.00	11.80	65.12
1991	573.91	106.57	538.52	9.80	8.17	229.20	543.96	105.90	10.10	65.77
1992	597.01	111.45	535.66	10.23	9.86	235.71	582.81	109.80	9.06	64.34
1993	628.84	114.96	547.02	10.72	10.19	250.28	610.99	111.50	7.47	62.81
1994	665.57	117.13	568.22	11.21	9.19	267.89	646.47	114.30	8.16	61.32
1995	698.20	119.91	582.26	11.42	8.24	283.33	729.87	118.20	8.24	60.53

Appendix C
Data Sources and Methods

C-1 Annual Variables (Sources and Methods for Table A-1)

1. Nominal GDP (X):
   1875–1928: Data from Nathan S. Balke and Robert J. Gordon, "The Estimation of Prewar GNP: Methodology and New Results," *Journal of Political Economy,* vol. 97 (February 1989), pp. 38–92, Table 10. Linked in 1929 to
   1929–1996: Data from STAT-USA, U.S. Department of Commerce, "Summary National Income and Product Series, 1929–96," Table 1, published in the *Survey of Current Business,* August 1997. These data incorporate the results of the July 1997 annual revision of the NIPA series.

2. Implicit GDP Deflator (P):
   Same as Nominal GDP (X), except Table 3 for 1929–1996.

3. Real GDP (Y):
   Same as Nominal GDP (X), except Table 2A for 1929–1996.

4. Natural GDP (Y^N):
   1875–1955: Y^N is the geometric interpolation between real GDP for the benchmark years 1869, 1873, 1884, 1891, 1900, 1910, 1924, and 1949 and the value of natural real GDP in 1955 (see below).
   1955–1996: Average annual values of the natural real GDP series described in Appendix C-2.

5. Unemployment Rate (U):
   1890–1899: Lebergott's series, copied from Christina Romer, "Spurious Volatility in Historical Unemployment Data," *Journal of Political Economy,* vol. 94 (February 1986).
   1900–1946: Series B1 in Long-Term Economic Growth, 1860–1970 (Washington, D.C.: U.S. Department of Commerce, 1973).
   1947–1996: Series LFS21000000 from http://stats.bls.gov, Bureau of Labor Statistics, Department of Labor. Average of monthly values.

6. Natural Unemployment Rate (U^N):
   1890–1901: Assumed to be the same level as in 1902, 4.1 percent.
   1902–1954: U^N is the linear interpolation between the UN values of the benchmark years of 1902, 1907, 1913, 1929, and 1949 is calculated as U^N 5 B * (U/UA) where UA is the published unemployment rate that adjusts for self-employment. UA equals the number of unemployed divided by the civilian labor force net of self-employed persons. The long-run equilibrium rate for UA ("B") reflects the value of UA observed in late 1954 when the economy was operating at its natural rate of unemployment. Changes in U^N before 1954 reflect only changes in the U/UA ratio.
   1955–1996: Time-varying NAIRU for chain-weighted GDP price index–based deflator with standard deviation 5 0.2 from Robert J. Gordon, "Time-Varying NAIRU," *Journal of Economic Perspectives,* vol. 11, pp. 11–34.

7. Money Supply $(M1)$:
   1915–1946: *Historical Statistics of the United States: Colonial Times to 1970* (Washington, D.C.: U.S. Department of Commerce, 1975), series 414. Linked in 1947 to
   1947–1958: *Federal Reserve Bulletin* (Washington, D.C.: Board of Governors of the Federal Reserve System), various issues. Linked in 1959 to
   1959–1996: Data from FRED, Federal Reserve Bank of St. Louis.

8. Money Supply $(M2)$:
   1875–1907: Milton Friedman and Anna J. Schwartz, *Monetary Statistics of the United States* (New York: National Bureau of Economic Research, 1970), pp. 61–65. Linked in 1907 to
   1908–1946: *Historical Statistics,* series 415. Linked in 1947 to
   1947–1958: *Federal Reserve Bulletin* (Washington, D.C.: Board of Governors of the Federal Reserve System), various issues. Linked in 1959 to
   1959–1996: Data from FRED, Federal Reserve Bank of St. Louis.

9. Labor Productivity (Y/N):
   1875–1946: Data computed by dividing real output from item 3 above by series A173 from *Long-Term Economic Growth,* 1860–1970. Linked in 1947 to
   1947–1996: Series PRS85006093 from http://stats.bls.gov, Bureau of Labor Statistics, Department of Labor. Average of quarterly values.

10. Nominal Interest Rate (r):
    1875–1939: The yield on corporate bonds from Robert J. Gordon, ed., *The American Business*

Cycle (Chicago: University of Chicago, 1986), Appendix B.

1940–1996: Corporate bonds (Moody's Aaa) from the *1997 Economic Report of the President* (Washington, D.C.: United States Government Printing Office, 1997).

11. S&P Stock Price Index:

1875–1939: The index of all common stocks from

Gordon, *The American Business Cycle,* Appendix B. Linked in 1940 to

1940–1996: Standard and Poor's Composite Index (1941–43 = 10) from the *1997 Economic Report of the President* (Washington, D.C.: United States Government Printing Office, 1997).

C-2 Quarterly Variables (Sources and Methods for Table A-2)

1. Nominal GDP *(X):*

   1947:Q1–1996:Q4: Data from STAT-USA, U.S. Department of Commerce, Summary National Income and Product Series, 1929–96, Table 1, published in the *Survey of Current Business,* August 1997. These data incorporate the results of the July 1997 annual revision of the NIPA series.

   1997:Q1–1997:Q2: Data from STAT-USA, U.S. Department of Commerce, Gross Domestic Product, Second Quarter 1997 (Final), Table 2.

2. Implicit GDP Deflator *(P):*

   Same as Nominal GDP *(X),* except Table 3 for 1947:Q1–1996:Q4 and Table 4 for 1997:Q1–1997:Q2.

3. Real GDP *(Y):*

   Same as Nominal GDP *(X),* except Table 2A for 1947:Q1–1996:Q4.

4. Natural GDP (Y^N):

   1947:Q1–1955:Q1: Interpolated from annual series described in Appendix Table C-1, item 4.

   1955:Q1–1997:Q2: The unemployment gap *(U*gap) is defined as the difference between the actual and natural rates of unemployment. The output gap *(Y*gap) is defined as the log ratio of actual to natural real GDP. A regression was run of the old *Y*gap on a constant, the current value, and three lags of the old *U*gap, where "old" refers to the series published in the sixth edition of this textbook. The resulting coefficients were multiplied by the new *U*gap (the actual unemployment rate minus the new natural unemployment rate series described below in item 6) to derive a new *Y*gap series. A preliminary level of Y^N was calculated as the antilog of the difference between the log of actual real GDP and the new *Y*gap. The final value of Y^N was calculated as a centered twelve-quarter moving average of the preliminary level of Y^N.

5. Unemployment Rate *(U):*

   1947:Q1–1997:Q2: Series LFS21000000 from http://stats.bls.gov, Bureau of Labor Statistics, Department of Labor. Average of monthly values.

6. Natural Unemployment Rate (U^N):

   1947:Q1–1954:Q4: The quarterly values are derived by a linear interpolation between the annual val-

   ues of natural unemployment as described in section C-1.

   1955:Q1–1997:Q2: Time-Varying NAIRU for chain-weighted GDP price index–based deflator with standard deviation = 0.2 from Robert J. Gordon, "Time-Varying NAIRU," *Journal of Economic Perspectives,* vol. 11, pp. 11–34.

7. Money Supply *(M1):*

   1947:Q1–1958:Q4: *Federal Reserve Bulletin* (Washington, D.C.: Board of Governors of the Federal Reserve System), various issues. Linked in 1959 to

   1959:Q1–1997:Q2: Data from FRED, Federal Reserve Bank of St. Louis.

8. Money Supply *(M2):*

   1947:Q1–1958:Q4: *Federal Reserve Bulletin* (Washington, D.C.: Board of Governors of the Federal Reserve System), various issues. Linked in 1959 to

   1959–1996: Data from FRED, Federal Reserve Bank of St. Louis.

9. Labor Productivity *(Y/N):*

   1947:Q1–1997:Q2: Series PRS85006093 from http://stats.bls.gov, Bureau of Labor Statistics, Department of Labor.

10. Nominal Interest Rate *(r):*

    1940–1996: Corporate bonds (Moody's Aaa) from the *1997 Economic Report of the President* (Washington, D.C.: United States Government Printing Office, 1997).

11. Real Federal Budget Surplus in 1992 Dollars:

    1947:Q1–1996:Q4: Calculated by dividing the nominal federal government surplus from the U.S. Department of Commerce by the implicit price deflator.

12. Trade-Weighted Exchange Rate:

    1961:Q1–1966:Q4: Effective exchange rate (MERM) from various issues of *International Financial Statistics* (Washington, D.C.: International Monetary Fund). Linked in 1967:Q1 to

    1967:Q1–1997:Q2: Trade-weighted exchange value of U.S. dollar versus G-10 countries from FRED, Federal Reserve Bank of St. Louis.

C-3 International Variables (Sources and Methods for Table B)

1. Nominal GDP *(X):*
   Gross domestic product (expenditures) from *Organization for Economic Cooperation and Development, National Accounts, Volume I: Main Aggregates, 1960–1995,* Line 45 (Paris: OECD Publications, December 1996).
2. Implicit GDP Deflator *(P):*
   Calculated by dividing nominal GDP by real GDP.
3. Real GDP *(Y):*
   Gross domestic product (expenditures, 1990 prices) from *OECD National Accounts, Volume I: Main Aggregates, 1960–1995,* Line 56.
4. Labor Productivity *(Y/N):*
   Real output (real GDP, Y) divided by total manhours, N (the product of total employment, E, and hours worked per employee, H). Updated with annual growth rates from *OECD World Economic Outlook.*
5. Unemployment Rate *(U):*
   Unemployment rate from Xavier Bonnet, INSEE, Research Department, Paris, France.

6. Money Supply *(M1)* and Money Supply *(M2):*
   International Financial Statistics Yearbook, 1997 (Washington, D.C.: International Monetary Fund, 1997).
7. Consumer Price Index *(CPI):*
   International Financial Statistics Yearbook, 1997 (Washington, D.C.: International Monetary Fund, 1997).
8. Long-Term Interest Rate *(r):*
   Interest rate, long-term from Xavier Bonnet, INSEE, Research Department, Paris, France.
9. Labor Share *(WN/Y):*
   Calculated by dividing "compensation of employees paid by resident producers" by "national income" from *OECD National Accounts, Volume I: Main Aggregates, 1960–1995,* Lines 60 and 80.

C-4 Variables Used in Figures but Not Listed in Appendix A or B

Data and sources can be found on the textbook website http://hepg.awl.com/gordon/macro.

Glossary

Accelerator hypothesis (16-3)   Theory that the level of net investment depends on the *change* in expected output.

Accommodating policy (8-10)   Attempt by government or central bank, following a **supply shock,** to raise **nominal GDP growth** so as to maintain the original output ratio.

Actual real GDP (1-3)   The value of total output corrected for any changes in prices.

Actual real interest rate (12-3)   The nominal interest rate minus the actual inflation rate.

Adaptive expectations (8-6)   Prediction for next period's economic values based on an average of actual values during previous periods.

Adjustable-rate mortgage (13-7)   An interest rate that can change frequently in response to changes in short-term interest rates, in contrast to a fixed-rate mortgage.

Aggregate (1-8)   Total amount of an economic magnitude for the economy as a whole.

Aggregate demand curve (7-1)   The graphical schedule showing different combinations of the price level and real output at which the money and commodity markets are both in equilibrium.

Appreciation (6-3)   A rise in the value of one nation's currency relative to another nation's currency. When the dollar can buy more units of a foreign currency, say the German mark, the dollar is said to appreciate relative to that foreign currency.

Auction market (17-7)   A centralized location where professional traders buy and sell a commodity or a financial security.

Automatic stabilization (5-8)   The effect (on the government budget deficit or surplus) of the **leakage** of tax revenues when income rises or falls.

Autonomous magnitude (3-3)   An amount independent of the level of income.

Backward-looking expectations (8-6)   Predictions for next period's values based only on information on the past behavior of economic variables.

Balance of payments (6-2)   The record of a nation's international transactions, both credits (which arise from sales of exports and sales of assets) and debits (which arise from purchases of imports and purchases of assets).

Budget line (5-8)   The graphical schedule showing the **government budget surplus** or **deficit** at different levels of real income.

Business cycles (1-3)   Expansions occurring at about the same time in many economic activities, followed by similarly general recessions and recoveries that merge into the expansion phase of the next cycle.

Capital account (6-2)   The part of the balance of payments that records capital flows, which consist of purchases and sales of foreign assets by domestic residents, and purchases and sales of domestic assets by foreign residents.

Capital market instruments (13-2)   Assets, sold in financial markets, that have relatively long maturities, can experience large fluctuations in price, and often expose investors to the risk of capital loss and default.

Closed economy (1-8)   A nation that has no trade in goods, services, or financial assets with any other nation.

Cold turkey (8-7)   An approach to disinflation that implements a sudden and permanent slowdown in **nominal GDP** growth.

Comparative statics (7-1)   A technique of economic analysis in which a comparison is made between two equilibrium positions but ignoring the behavior of the economy between the two equilibrium positions—either the length of time required or the route followed during the transition between the initial and final positions.

Constant growth rate rule (CGRR) (14-3)   The rule advocating a fixed percentage growth rate for the **money supply,** in contrast to the variable growth rate recommended by policy activists.

Consumer expenditures (2-1)   Purchases of goods and services by households for their own use.

Contractionary monetary policy (4-11)   Government monetary policy that has the effect of lowering the **money supply** and raising interest rates.

Coordination failure (17-7)   Result of firms neglecting to act together, due to lack of private incentive, to avoid actions that impose social costs on society.

Cost-of-living agreements (COLAs) (17-9)   Contracts that provide for an automatic increase in the wage rate in response to an increase in the price level.

Countercyclical variable (7-7)   A variable (such as the real wage) that moves over the **business cycle** in the direction opposite to **real GDP.**

Credibility (12-5)   The extent to which households and firms believe that an announced monetary or **fiscal**

policy will actually be implemented and maintained as announced.

Cross section (15-3)   Data for numerous units (e.g., households, firms, cities, or states) observed at a single period of time.

Crowding out effect (4-12)   Reduction of one or more components of private expenditures due to an increase in government spending or a reduction of tax rates.

Current account (6-2)   The part of the balance of payments that includes **exports, imports,** investment income, and **transfer payments** to and from foreigners.

Cyclical deficit (5-8)   The amount by which the actual **government budget deficit** exceeds the **structural deficit**.

Cyclical unemployment (12-8)   The difference between the actual unemployment rate and the **natural rate of unemployment**.

Demand inflation (8-9)   A sustained increase in prices that is preceded by a permanent acceleration of **nominal GDP growth.**

Demand shocks (14-1)   Unexpected changes in business and consumer optimism, changes in **net exports,** and changes in government spending or tax rates (for example, in wartime) not related to **stabilization policy.**

Depreciation *(consumption of fixed capital)* (2-6)   The part of capital stock used up due to obsolescence and physical wear.

Depreciation (of currency) (6-3)   A decline in the value of one nation's currency relative to another nation's currency.   When the dollar can buy fewer units of a foreign currency, say the British pound, the dollar is said to depreciate relative to that foreign currency.

Depreciation rate (16-7)   The annual percentage decline in the value of a capital good due to physical deterioration and obsolescence.

Devaluation (6-6)   Under the fixed exchange rate system, a nation's reduction of the value of its money in terms of foreign money.

Discount rate (13-5)   The interest rate the Federal Reserve charges depository institutions when they borrow reserves.

Discretionary fiscal policy (5-8)   Alteration of tax rates and/or government expenditures in a deliberate attempt to influence real output and the **unemployment rate.**

Discretionary policy (14-3)   Approach that treats each macroeconomic episode as a unique event, without any attempt to respond in the same way from one episode to another.

Disinflation (8-7)   A marked deceleration in the **inflation rate.**

Disintermediation (13-7)   The withdrawal of funds from **financial intermediaries** like **thrift institutions** when market interest rates rose above the interest rate ceilings on savings and time deposit accounts.

Domestic income (2-6)   The earnings of domestic factors of production, computed as net domestic product minus indirect business taxes, which in turn are taxes levied on business taxes.

Dynamic multipliers (14-5)   The amount by which output is raised during each of several time periods after a given change in a policy instrument.

Econometric model (5-4, 14-5)   A set of equations with statistically estimated responses that can be solved to provide forecasts under alternative assumptions about policy instruments and nonpolicy exogenous variables.

Economic growth (1-15, 9-2)   Topic area of macroeconomics that studies the causes of sustained growth in **natural real GDP**.

Endogenous variables (3-1)   Variables explained by an economic theory.

Equilibrium (3-9)   A state in which there exists no pressure for change.

Equilibrium real wage rate (7-6)   The real wage rate at which the labor supply and demand curves intersect, so there is no pressure for change.

Exogenous variables (3-2)   Variables that are relevant but whose behavior economic theory does not attempt to explain and whose values are taken as given.

Expansion (1-3)   Period in the **business cycle** between the **trough** and the **peak.**

Expansionary monetary policy (4-10)   Government monetary policy that has the effect of lowering interest rates and raising GDP.

Expectations effect (7-9)   The decline in **aggregate demand** caused by the postponement of purchases when consumers expect prices to decline in the future.

Expectations-augmented Phillips curve *(SP* curve*)* (8-2)   A schedule relating the **inflation rate** to the **output ratio** (or **unemployment rate**) that shifts its position whenever there is a change in the expected rate of inflation.

Expected rate of inflation (8-2)   Rate of inflation that is expected to occur in the future.

Expected real interest rate (12-3)   The **nominal interest rate** minus the **expected rate of inflation.**

Exports (2-4)   Goods produced within one country and shipped to another.

Extinguishing policy (8-10)   Attempt by government or central bank, following a supply shock, to reduce **nominal GDP growth** so as to maintain the original **inflation rate.**

Extra convenience services (12-6)   The services provided by holding one extra dollar of money instead of bonds.

Factor inputs (9-3) The economic elements that directly produce **real GDP.**

Feedback rule (14-3, 17-3) A rule of **stabilization policy** that systematically changes a monetary variable like the money supply or interest rates in response to actual or forecasted changes in target variables like inflation or employment.

Final good (2-3) Part of final product.

Final product (2-3) All currently produced goods and services that are sold through the market but are not resold.

Financial deregulation (13-1) Change of rules for U.S. financial markets, begun in the 1970s and continuing today, that has allowed more and more types of assets to serve as money. One of the first changes was permitting banks to pay interest on checking accounts.

Financial intermediaries (13-2) Institutions, such as banks, that make loans to borrowers and obtain funds from savers, usually by accepting deposits.

Financial markets (13-2) Organized exchanges where securities and financial instruments are bought and sold.

Fiscal policy (1-7) Manipulations of government expenditures and tax rates in order to try to influence **target variables.**

Fisher effect (12-3) Prediction that a one-percentage-point increase in the expected inflation rate will raise the nominal real interest rate by one percentage point, leaving the expected real interest rate unaffected.

Fisher equation (12-3) Statement that the nominal interest rate equals the expected inflation rate plus the expected real interest rate.

Fixed exchange rate system (6-6) System in which the **foreign exchange rate** is fixed for long periods of time.

Fixed investment (2-4) All **final goods** purchased by business that are not intended for resale.

Flexible accelerator theory (16-5) Theory of investment that allows for gradual adjustment of sales expectations and of the capital stock. It also allows for variation in the optimal capital-output ratio.

Flexible exchange rate system (6-6) System in which the **foreign exchange rate** is free to change every day.

Flow magnitude (2-2) An economic magnitude that moves from one economic unit to another at a specified rate per unit of time.

Foreign exchange rate (1-6, 6-3) The amount of another nation's money that residents of a country can obtain in exchange for a unit of their own money.

Foreign exchange reserves (6-6) Government holdings of foreign money used under a fixed exchange rate system to respond to changes in the foreign demand for and supply of a particular nation's money. Such reserves are also used for intervention under a flexible exchange rate system.

Foreign trade deficit (1-1, 6-8) The excess of the nation's imports of goods and services over its exports of goods and services.

Foreign trade surplus (6-8) **Net exports.**

Forward-looking expectations (8-6, 15-1) Predictions of future behavior of an economic variable, using an economic model that specifies the interrelationship of that variable with other variables.

General equilibrium (4-9) A situation of simultaneous equilibrium in all the markets of the economy.

Government budget constraint (12-4) Limitation of government spending to the three sources available to finance that spending: tax revenue, creation of bonds, and creation of money.

Government budget deficit (1-1, 2-4) The excess of government expenditures (on goods, services, and **transfer payments**) over tax revenue.

Gross (2-6) Economic aggregate that includes capital consumption allowances.

Gross domestic product (1-3) The value of all currently produced goods and services sold on the market during a particular time interval.

Gross national product (2-4) Goods and services produced by labor and capital supplied by U.S. residents, whether the actual production takes place within the borders of the United States or in a foreign country.

High-powered money (13-4) The sum of currency held outside depository institutions and the reserves held inside them.

Hyperinflation (12-1) A very rapid inflation, sometimes defined as a rate of more than 22 percent per month or 1000 percent per year, experienced over a year or more.

Hysteresis hypothesis (12-11) Claim that the **natural rate of unemployment** follows automatically in the path of the actual **unemployment rate.**

Implicit GDP deflator (2-7) The economy's aggregate price index, defined as the ratio of **nominal GDP** to **real GDP.**

Imports (2-4) Goods consumed within one country but produced in another country.

Incomes policy (12-5) An attempt by policymakers to moderate increases in wages and other income, either by persuasion or by legal rules.

Indexed bond (12-7) A bond that pays a fixed real interest rate; its **nominal interest rate** is equal to this **real interest rate** plus the actual inflation rate.

Induced consumption (3-5) The portion of consumption spending that responds to changes in income.

Induced saving (3-7) The portion of saving that responds to changes in income.

Inflation (8-1) A sustained upward movement in the aggregate price level that is shared by most products.

Inflation differential (6-5) Foreign inflation minus domestic inflation.

Inflation rate (1-1) The percentage rate of increase in the economy's average level of prices.

Inflation tax (12-4) The revenue the government receives from inflation, the same as **seignorage** (the inflation rate times real **high-powered money**) but viewed from the perspective of households.

Infrastructure (10-5) Roads, sewers, airports, and, more broadly, education, paid for by public investment, that provide widespread benefits to consumers and raise the return on private investment.

Injections (2-4) Nonconsumption expenditures.

Interest rate (1-1) The percentage rate that is paid by borrowers to lenders.

Interest rate differential (6-9) The average U.S. interest rate minus the average foreign interest rate.

Intermediate good (2-3) A product resold by its purchaser either in its present form or in an altered form.

Intertemporal substitution (17-4) Workers work more in periods of high real wages and less in periods of low real wages. Also occurs when producers raise output in periods of high prices and reduce output in periods of low prices.

Intervention (6-6) Under the **flexible exchange rate system**, the buying or selling of a nation's money by domestic or foreign central banks in order to prevent unwanted variations in the foreign exchange rate.

Inventory investment (2-4) All changes in the stock of raw materials, parts, and finished goods held by business.

Investment (2-4) Portion of **final product** that adds to the nation's stock of income-yielding physical assets or that replaces old, worn-out physical assets.

IS curve (4-2) The schedule that identifies the combinations of income and the interest rate at which the commodity market is in equilibrium; everywhere along the *IS* curve the demand for commodities equals the supply.

Keynes effect (7-9) The stimulus to aggregate demand caused by a decline in the interest rate.

Labor force (2-9) Total of persons employed and unemployed.

Large open economy (6-9) An economy that can influence its domestic interest rate. A high domestic interest rate generates a steady stream of capital inflows that are not great enough to eliminate an interest rate differential between the domestic and foreign interest rate; a low domestic interest rate generates a steady stream of capital outflows.

Leakages (2-4) The portion of total income that flows to taxes or saving rather than into purchases of consumer goods.

Life-cycle hypothesis (LCH) (15-1) Conjecture that households base their current consumption on their total lifetime incomes and their wealth.

Liquidity constraint (15-6) Occurs when households cannot borrow as much as they wish, even though there is sufficient expected future income to repay the loans.

LM curve (4-8) The schedule that identifies the combinations of income and the interest rate at which the money market is in equilibrium; on the LM curve the demand for money equals the supply of money.

Long-run aggregate supply curve (7-7) A vertical line drawn at the natural level of **real GDP**; it shows that equilibrium in the labor market can be achieved at many different price levels but only a single level of output.

Long-run equilibrium (7-7) A situation in which labor input is the amount voluntarily supplied and demanded at the equilibrium real wage rate.

Long-term labor contracts (17-9) Agreements between firms and workers that set the level of nominal wage rates for a year or more.

Lucas model (17-3) Economic model based on the three assumptions of **market clearing**, imperfect information, and **rational expectations**.

M1 (13-3) The U.S. definition of the **money supply** that includes only currency, transactions accounts, and traveler's checks.

M2 (13-3) The U.S. definition of the **money supply** that includes M1, savings deposits, including money market deposit accounts; small time deposits; and money market mutual funds.

Macroeconomic externality (17-7) A cost incurred by society as a result of a decision by an individual economic agent (worker or business firm).

Macroeconomics (1-1) The study of the major economic totals or **aggregates**.

Marginal leakage rate (3-11) The fraction of income that is taxed or saved rather than being spent on consumption.

Marginal product of capital (MPK) (16-6) The extra output that a firm can produce by adding an extra unit of capital.

Marginal propensity to consume (3-4) The dollar change in consumption expenditures induced by a dollar change in disposable income.

Marginal propensity to save (3-6) The change in personal saving induced by a dollar change in disposable income.

Market-clearing model (7-9)   Theory that the economy is always in equilibrium, at the intersection of supply and demand curves, particularly in the labor market.

Medium of exchange (4-4)   Units used for buying and selling goods and services; a universal alternative to the barter system.

Menu cost (17-6)   Any expense associated with changing prices, including the costs of printing new menus or distributing new catalogs.

Mismatch unemployment (12-8)   **Structural unemployment;** one of the two components of the **natural rate of unemployment** (the other being turnover, or frictional unemployment); it occurs when the present location or skills of members of the labor force do not match location or skill requirements of job vacancies.

Monetarism (14-3)   A school of thought that opposes activist or discretionary monetary policy and instead favors a fixed rule for the growth rate of **high-powered money** or of the **money supply**.

Monetary impotence (7-9)   Failure of **real GDP** to respond to an increase in the real **money supply**.

Monetary policy (1-7)   Changes made in the **money supply** or interest rates or both in order to try to influence **target variables**.

Money market instruments (13-2)   Assets sold in financial markets that have short maturities, usually less than one year, small fluctuations in price, and minimal risk of default.

Money multiplier (13-4)   The ratio (M/H) of the **money supply** to **high-powered money**. There is a separate money multiplier for each definition of the **money supply** e.g., $M1/H$ and $M2/H$.

Money multiplier shock (13-5)   Any event that causes the **money multiplier** to change, such as a change in the public's demand for currency relative to deposits, or a shift between deposits having different **reserve requirements**.

Money supply (4-3)   Currency and transactions accounts, including checking accounts at banks and **thrift institutions**.

Multifactor productivity (9-5)   The growth in multifactor productivity is the growth rate of output per hour of work, minus the contribution to output of the growth in the quantity of other factors of production per hour of work, notably capital but sometimes including energy, raw materials, or other factors of production.

Multiplier (3-7)   The ratio of the change in output to the change in planned autonomous spending that causes it; also 1.0 divided by the **marginal leakage rate** (the fraction of an extra dollar of income that is not spent on consumption).

Multiplier uncertainty (14-5)   The lack of firm knowledge regarding the change in output caused by a change in a **policy instrument.**

National Income and Product Accounts (2-3)   Official U.S. government economic accounting system that keeps track of GDP and its subcomponents.

National saving (5-9, 11-1)   The sum of private saving (by both households and business firms) and government saving (the government budget surplus).

Natural employment deficit (NED) (5-8)   The government budget deficit at the **natural level of real GDP**.

Natural rate hypothesis (17-2)   The hypothesis that shifts in aggregate demand have no long-run effect on **real GDP**.

Natural rate of unemployment (1-3)   The level of the unemployment rate at which the inflation rate is constant, with no tendency to accelerate or decelerate.

Natural real GDP (1-3)   The level of **real GDP** at which the **inflation rate** is constant, with no tendency to accelerate or decelerate.

Net (2-6)   Economic aggregate excluding capital consumption allowances.

Net domestic product (2-6)   GDP minus **depreciation.**

Net exports (2-4)   **Exports** minus **imports.**

Net international investment position (6-2)   The difference between all foreign assets owned by a nation's citizens and domestic assets owned by foreign citizens.

Neutral policy (8-10)   Attempt by government or central bank, following a supply shock, to maintain **nominal GDP growth** so as to allow a decline in the **output ratio** equal to the increase of the **inflation rate.**

New Keynesian economics (17-6)   Approach that explains rigidity in prices and wages as consistent with the self-interest of firms and workers, all of which are assumed to have **rational expectations**.

Nominal (2-7)   An adjective that modifies any economic magnitude measured in current prices.

Nominal anchor (14-9)   A rule that sets a limit on the growth rate of a nominal variable, for instance, **high-powered money**, the **money supply**, the price level, or **nominal GDP**, to prevent inflation from accelerating without limit.

Nominal GDP (2-7)   The value of gross domestic product in current (actual) prices.

Nominal interest rate (1-6, 12-3)   The market interest rate actual charged by financial institutions and earned by lenders.

Nominal rigidity (7-9, 17-6)   A factor that inhibits the flexibility of the nominal price level due to some factor, such as **menu costs** and **staggered contracts.** Such factors make it costly for firms to change the nominal price or wage level.

Non-market-clearing model (7-9, 17-6)   Workers and firms are not continuously on their respective demand and supply schedules, but rather are pushed off these schedules by the gradual adjustment of prices.

Normative economics (1-7)   Recommendations for changes in economic policy to achieve an optimal or desirable state of affairs.

Open economy (1-8, 6-1)   An economy that exports (sells) goods and services to other nations, buys imports from them, and has financial flows (capital flows) to and from foreign nations.

Open market operations (13-5)   Purchases and sales of government securities made by the Federal Reserve in order to change **high-powered money**.

Parameter (3-8)   A value taken as given or known within a particular analysis.

Peak (1-3)   The highest point reached by real output in each business cycle.

Perfect capital mobility (6-9)   A condition that occurs when investors regard one nation's financial assets as a perfect substitute for foreign money (because commissions and fees are very low), and when investors respond instantaneously to an interest rate differential between domestic and foreign assets by moving sufficient assets to eliminate that differential.

Permanent income (15-4)   The average income that people expect to receive over a period of years in the future.

Permanent-income hypothesis (PIH) (15-1)   Conjecture that consumption spending depends on the long-run average (or permanent) income that people expect to receive.

Persistent unemployment (7-9)   A situation in which a high level of unemployment can last for many years, as in the United States from 1929 to 1941 and from 1980 to 1985.

Personal consumption deflator (2-8)   The price deflator for the personal consumption expenditures component of GDP.

Personal disposable income (2-6)   **Personal income** minus personal income tax payments.

Personal income (2-16)   Income received by households from all sources, including earnings and **transfer payments**.

Personal saving (2-4)   That part of **personal income** that is neither consumed nor paid out in taxes.

Pigou effect *(real balance effect)* (7-9)   The direct stimulus to aggregate demand caused by an increase in the real **money supply;** does not require a decline in the interest rate.

Policy activism (14-1)   Active use of instruments of **monetary** and **fiscal policy** to offset changes in private sector spending.

Policy credibility (14-7)   The belief by the public that the policymakers will actually carry out an announced policy.

Policy ineffectiveness proposition (17-3)   Assertion that predictable changes in monetary policy cannot affect real output.

Policy instruments (1-7, 14-2)   Elements that government policymakers can manipulate directly to influence **target variables**.

Policy mix (5-5)   The combination of **monetary** and **fiscal policy** in effect in a given situation.

Policy rule (14-1)   Requirement of a fixed path of a **policy instrument** like the short-term interest rate, of an intermediate variable like the **money supply**, or a **target variable** like **inflation** or **unemployment**. Also requirement of a specified response of a policy instrument to a given change in a **target variable**.

Positive economics (1-7)   The scientific attempt to describe and explain the behavior of the economy.

Price index (2-8)   Weighted average of prices at any given time, divided by the prices of the same goods in a base year.

Production function (9-3)   A relationship, usually written algebraically, that shows how much output can be produced by a given quantity of **factor inputs**.

Productivity (1-1)   Average output produced per employee or per hour.

Purchasing power parity (PPP) theory (6-5)   Theory that the prices of identical goods should be the same in all countries, differing only by the cost of transport and any import (or customs) duties.

Quantity theory of money (7-8)   Theory that actual output tends to grow steadily, while velocity is determined by payment practices such as the use of cash vs. checks, and that as a result a change in the **money supply** mainly affects the price level and has little or no effect on **velocity** or output.

Rate of return (4-1)   Annual earnings of an investment project divided by its total cost.

Rate of time preference (11-2)   The extra amount a consumer would be willing to pay to be able to obtain a given quantity of consumption goods now rather than a year from now.

Rational expectations (15-6)   Forecasts of future economic magnitudes based on information currently available about the past performance of the economy and future government policies.

Real balance effect *(Pigou effect)* (7-9)   The direct stimulus to aggregate demand caused by an increase in the real **money supply**; does not require a decline in the interest rate.

Real business cycle (RBC) model (17-4)   Explanation attributing **business cycles** in output and employment to **technology** or **supply shocks**.

Real consumption wage (10-2)   The nominal wage rate divided by the price deflator for personal consumption expenditures.

Real exchange rate (6-5)   The average nominal **foreign exchange rate** between a country and its trading partners, adjusted for the difference in **inflation rates** between that country and its trading partners.

Real GDP (2-7) Value of **gross domestic product** in constant prices.

Real GDP gap *(output gap)* (1-5) The difference between **actual real GDP** and **natural real GDP**.

Real interest rate (1-6) The nominal **interest rate** minus the **inflation rate.**

Real money balances (4-7) Total **money supply** divided by the price level.

Real product wage (10-2) The nominal wage rate divided by the price index for total output, such as the GDP deflator.

Real rigidity (17-6) A factor that makes firms reluctant to change the real wage, the relative wage, or the relative price.

Recession (1-3) The interval in the **business cycle** between the **peak** and the **trough.**

Redistribution effect (7-9) The decline in aggregate demand caused by the effect of falling prices in redistributing income from high-spending debtors to low-spending savers.

Regulation Q (13-7) A federal regulation that, until 1986, put ceilings on interest rates on certain types of bank deposits.

Required reserves (13-5) The reserves that Federal Reserve regulations require depository institutions to hold.

Reserve requirements (13-5) Rules, which apply only to transactions accounts, that stipulate the minimum fraction of deposits that must be held as reserves.

Residual (9-5) The amount that remains after subtracting from the rate of **real GDP** growth all of the identifiable sources of economic growth.

Revaluation (6-6) A nation's raising of the value of its money when its foreign exchange reserves become so excessive that they cause domestic inflation.

Rigid rule (14-3) A rule for policy that sets a key **policy instrument** at a fixed value as in a **constant growth rate rule** for the **money supply.**

Rigid wages (7-9) The failure of the nominal wage rate to adjust by the amount needed to maintain equilibrium in the labor market.

Sacrifice ratio (8-7) The cumulative loss of output incurred during a **disinflation** divided by the permanent reduction in the **inflation rate.**

Seignorage (12-4) The revenue the government receives from **inflation;** equal to the inflation rate times real **high-powered money**.

Self-correcting forces (7-8) The role of flexible prices in stabilizing **real GDP** under some conditions.

Short-run aggregate supply curve (7-1) Graph of the amount of output that business firms are willing to produce at different price levels.

Short-run equilibrium (7-7) The point where the aggregate demand curve crosses the **short-run aggregate supply curve**.

Short-run Phillips *(SP)* **curve** (8-2) The schedule relating **real GDP** to the **inflation rate** achievable given a fixed **expected rate of inflation.**

Small open economy (6-9) An economy with perfect capital mobility but with no power to set its domestic interest rate at a level that differs from foreign interest rates.

Solow's residual (9-5) Growth in **multifactor productivity.**

Stabilization policy (1-7) Any policy that seeks to influence the level of aggregate demand.

Staggered contracts (17-6) Wage contracts that have different expiration dates for different groups of firms or workers.

Steady state (9-3) A situation in which output and capital input grow at the same rate, implying a fixed ratio of output to capital input.

Stock (2-2) An economic magnitude in the possession of a given economic unit a particular point in time.

Store of value (4-5) A method of storing purchasing power when receipts and expenditures are not perfectly synchronized.

Structural deficit (5-8) What the government budget deficit would be if the economy were operating at **natural real GDP.**

Structuralist hypothesis (12-11) Claim that European unemployment is high because of specific impediments in the operation of the economy, including excessive real wages, high unemployment benefits, excessive government spending and regulation, high marginal tax rates, and regional imbalances.

Supply inflation (8-9) An increase in prices that stems from an increase in business costs not directly related to a prior acceleration of **nominal GDP growth.**

Supply-side economics (11-7) Theory predicting that a reduction in marginal income tax rates will create an increase in the supply of output, that is, in **natural real GDP.**

Target variables (1-7, 14-2) Economic **aggregates** whose values society cares most about—society's goals.

Thrift institutions (13-2) **Financial intermediaries** such as savings and loan institutions, mutual savings banks, and credit unions.

Time inconsistency (14-6) Policymakers' deviation from a policy after it is announced and private decisionmakers have reacted to it.

Time series (15-3) Data covering a span of time of one or more series (e.g., disposable income or consumption spending).

Transfer payments (2-6) Payments for which no goods or services are produced in return.

Transitory income (15-4) The difference between actual income and **permanent income**; it is not expected to recur.

Trough (1-3)   The lowest point reached by real output in each **business cycle.**

Turnover unemployment (frictional unemployment) (12-8)   One of the two components of the **natural rate of unemployment** (the other being **mismatch,** or **structural unemployment**), it occurs in the normal process of job search.

Unanticipated inflation (12-3)   Situation in which **actual inflation rate** (p) differs from the **expected** (or anticipated) **inflation rate** (p^e).

Unemployed (2-9)   Persons without jobs who are either on temporary layoff or have taken specific actions to look for work.

Unemployment rate (1-1, 2-9)   A percentage that expresses the ratio of the number of jobless individuals actively looking for work or on temporary layoff divided by the total employed and unemployed in the labor force.

Unintended inventory investment (3-10)   The amount business firms are forced to accumulate when planned expenditures are less than income.

Unit of account (4-6)   A way of recording receipts, expenditures, assets, and liabilities.

User cost of capital (16-6)   The cost to the firm of using a piece of capital for a specified period.

Value added (2-8)   The value of the labor and capital services that take place at a particular stage of the production process.

Wage indexation *(cost of living agreements)* (12-5)   An automatic increase in the wage rate in response to an increase in a price index.

Index

Guide to Symbols

[*Note:* For most variables, the level is indicated by an uppercase letter *(X)* while the growth rate is indicated by a lowercase letter *(x)*. Each such variable is listed only once in this list by the appropriate uppercase letter *(X)*.]

Symbol	Chapter Where Introduced	Definition
Δ	3	The change in a magnitude
a	3	Real autonomous consumption expenditure
A	3	Real autonomous expenditure
A	9	Autonomous growth factor; multifactor productivity
A	15	Assets held in life-cycle hypothesis
b	5–Appendix	Dollar change of A_p in response to a one percentage-point change in the interest rate
b	9	Elasticity of output with respect to capital input
b	13	Broker's fee in Baumol's theory of money demand
B	11	Dollar amount of government bonds outstanding
c	3	Marginal propensity to consume
c	13	Fraction of bank deposits held as currency by the public
C	2	Real personal consumption expenditures
C	13	Currency held by the public
d	9	Depreciation rate
D	11	Nominal government debt (ΔD = nominal government deficit)
D	13	Demand deposits (accounts at banks or thrift institutions that allow checks to be written)
e	6	Real foreign exchange rate
e'	6	Nominal foreign exchange rate
e	13	Fraction of deposits that banks hold as reserves
E	2	Real expenditures ($E = C + I + G + NX$)
f	5–Appendix	Dollar change of the demand for real money in response to a one percentage-point change in the interest rate
F	2	Real government transfer payments
g	8–Appendix	Slope of the short-run Phillips curve *(SP)*
G	2	Real government purchases of goods and services
h	5–Appendix	Dollar change of the demand for real money in response to a one-dollar change in real income, holding the interest rate constant
h	17	Response of output to a price surprise in the Friedman-Lucas supply function
h	2	Response of unemployment to the output ratio
H	12	High-powered money (same as the monetary base; consists of currency plus bank reserves)
i	12	Nominal or market interest rate
I	2	Real gross private investment
j	8–Appendix	Coefficient of adjustment of expectations
k	3	Spending multiplier
k_1	5–Appendix	Multiplier for autonomous spending in *IS-LM* model
k_2	5–Appendix	Multiplier for real money supply in *IS-LM* model
k	15	Marginal propensity to consume out of permanent income
K	9	Capital stock
L	4	Money demand function
L	15	Age at death in life-cycle hypothesis
M.	4	Nominal money supply